# Crystal Reports Encyclopedia Volume 1:

# Professional XI Reports

## by Brian Bischof

Crystal Reports Encyclopedia Volume 1: Professional XI Reports

Copyright © 2007 Brian Bischof

ISBN-10: 0974953601

ISBN-13: 978-0974953601

Sample reports for this book are available at www.CrystalReportsBook.com.

Bulk discounts are handled through Independent Publishers Group. 814 North Franklin Street, Chicago, IL 60610. (312) 337-0747

| Proofreaders: | Anita Bischof, John Deatrick |
| Headshot Photo: | Maria Pablo, www.MaluPhotography.com |

Dedicated to my brother Barry. As we were growing up, you were always looking out for me. Thanks for being the greatest big brother a little brother could have.

# Table of Contents

# R2 New Feature Guide

# Acknowledgements

I'm very grateful to everyone at Business Objects for all their help. Yuying Mesaros spearheaded the task to hire me as a consultant to work on internal projects. Kuhan Milroy was my "go to guy" who was always there with advice and helping me out on a daily basis. Terry Penner has a virtually unlimited wealth of knowledge about Crystal Reports and could answer any question that I (or anyone else) dreamed up. Francis Lui was the brains that came to my aid when I ran into problems with Crystal Reports .NET. Other great people that I had the chance to work with are Fred Tummonds, Oz Greenburg, Blair Wheadon, and Mandeep Jassal. And a special thanks to Robert Horne for keeping in touch since I left Business Objects and making sure I stay up to date with the latest news about Crystal Reports.

As a self-publisher, I rely upon others to help out with giving me feedback and editing the chapters. Just like my last book, my mom spent many late nights reading this entire book and finding numerous typos and grammatical errors. I don't know how she does it without going crazy, but I sure am grateful that she does. My uncle, Fr. John Deatrick, also helped out with editing many chapters. Even though he likes to say, "Even lobster gets old," I certainly hope he doesn't feel that way about this book. ☺

I was excited to see members of the book's online forum get involved with this project as well. Dell Stinnett ("Hilfy") and Lesley Murphy provided very helpful feedback for certain chapters.

Maria Pablo took a great photo for my headshot on the back cover. You can find out more about her photography at www.MaluPhotography.com.

And last, but not least, I want to say "Hi" to my great friend Vivian Wang. I had a great time exploring Vancouver with you, and I always admire your wonderful outlook on life.

# About the Author

Brian Bischof, CPA, MCSD is the author of the best selling book, "Crystal Reports .NET Programming" and "The .NET Languages: A Quick Translation Guide". He is the President of DotNet Tech, Inc.

Brian discovered a marketing niche early in his career; many software consultants were adequate working with software applications but did not understand or know the corporate language to discover a company's true needs. Contrarily, business managers knew that they wanted to improve their business processes but did not know how to communicate this information to a computer "tech". After spending years developing software and working in the accounting field as a financial auditor, Brian created a software development and training firm that provides a unique merger of business expertise and technical knowledge using Microsoft's .NET technologies.

DotNet Tech, Inc. provides expert advice, custom solutions and training in a continually fluctuating industry. Brian understands that the end product is not the software provided, but a level of commitment to its customers to support the ongoing technical changes a company experiences as it grows and develops.

You can learn more about the author and DotNet Tech, Inc. by visiting the company's website at www.DotNetTech.com.

# PREFACE

## Who This Book Is For

This book is written for users of Crystal Reports XI Professional. While most features discussed in this book can also be used with the Standard edition, I do not specify which features are not available.

This book does not cover Visual Studio .NET 2005 or Java programming. If you are an application developer using Microsoft's Visual Studio .NET 2005, you should purchase Volume 2 of this series, "Programming .NET 2005".

## Crystal Reports XI Release 2 (R2)

After Crystal Reports XI (version 11) was released, Business Objects silently updated the software to version 11.5. They refer to this update on their website as Release 2, or R2 for short. Its purpose is to make Crystal Reports compatible with the latest version of their Business Objects enterprise software and the Microsoft Visual Studio .NET 2005 developer suite (for software developers). They recommend that you only download R2 if you use one of these two software products and need it for compatibility. However, what they don't tell you is that they added some great new features to R2. Even if you don't own those other software packages, you'll get many benefits from using the R2 version Crystal Reports. And when you realize that it is also free, then why wouldn't you install it?

You can download the R2 update at this URL:

http://www.BusinessObjects.com/Products/Reporting/CrystalReports/XI_Release_2.asp

For a list of the new features and the pages they are discussed on, look at the New R2 Feature Guide found immediately after the Table of Contents.

## Technologies Used

This book is written using Windows XP and Crystal Reports XI. The specific databases mentioned in the text and tutorials are Microsoft Access and SQL Server. The book does not cover Oracle or MySql databases. The database used throughout the book is the Xtreme.mdb sample database that is installed with Crystal Reports. The default installation folder is:

C:\Program Files\Business Objects\Crystal Reports 11\Samples\en\ Databases\Xtreme.mdb

If you installed the R2 update, the version folder should be changed from "Crystal Reports 11" to "Crystal Reports 11.5".

## Advanced Tutorials

Throughout the book, tutorials are used to reinforce the concepts being taught in each chapter. At the end of most chapters is a series of advanced tutorials. The advanced tutorials are presented differently than the standard tutorials. Rather than give a detailed explanation of each step, only the necessary aspects of a step are explained. The advanced tutorials are written with the expectation that the user doing them is also advanced and familiar with the product. Thus, the trivial details that would bore an advanced user are omitted. The advanced tutorials highlight the unique aspect of the concepts being presented and details are given when necessary.

## Fonts Used

The tutorials throughout this book frequently ask you to type specific text. Rather than include the text in quotes, I use a **distinct font** to identify what should be typed in. I've seen many tutorials where people get confused as to when the quotes should be typed in or just left alone. Using a different font helps avoid that problem.

This font is also used when specifying a website address or a folder location of a file.

## Download Sample Reports

The final reports created with the tutorials can be downloaded from the book's official website at:

www.CrystalReportsBook.com

## Online Forum Community

The book's online forum is available to everyone. You can read the threads, or register to post questions and answers. Registration is free. The more you participate, the better the forum becomes! The forum is at the following URL:

www.CrystalReportsBook.com/Forum

## How to Contact Me

I can be reached via the book's online forum. There is a section called Speak with the Author where you can post messages to me that are not related to Crystal Reports problems.

# 1

# Introducing Crystal Reports

Information is power. In today's world, where we have computers that are as powerful as yesterday's supercomputers, there is a lot of information at our disposal. Being able to convert all this information into useful data is critical for many businesses. There are many products available to make this possible, and Crystal Reports is by far one of the most popular. Having been around since the mid-80's and having millions of users, Crystal Reports is probably the most easily recognized name in report writing software.

With the advance of technology and the Internet, it's possible to do business with colleagues on the other side of the world as if they were sitting next to you. This has driven business to be much more competitive and complex. Writing reports is just one small part of delivering information to business users. Business Intelligence (BI) is the gathering and analysis of data throughout an enterprise to gain a sustainable competitive advantage. In 2003, Crystal Decisions was acquired by the BI enterprise software company, Business Objects. Because of this acquisition, Crystal Reports became a part of a complete suite of tools for tracking, analyzing and managing enterprise data.

As one part of the entire BI picture, Crystal Reports gives you the ability to gather data from a variety of data sources and present it in native form, either on paper or via the computer, as well as export it to external applications such as MS Word or Excel. By giving the layman the power to pull data from all types of data sources and present it in multiple formats, Crystal Reports plays a key part in a company's BI strategy. Crystal Reports XI is the most user friendly and feature rich version of Crystal Reports to date.

# What's New in Crystal Reports XI

Crystal Reports XI is the eleventh release of this popular reporting tool. The "XI" is the Roman numeral 11 as well as an abbreviation for Xtreme Intelligence (playing on the business intelligence theme). Crystal Reports XI has exciting new functionality that goes far beyond the previous versions of Crystal Reports. In fact, until XI was released, a large percentage of users were still using version 8.5 and never upgraded. The improvements for version 9 and 10 weren't compelling enough to justify it. But with the new features in this latest release, many people have upgraded to XI and are looking forward to the enhancements. The following sections give you an overview of the new features and list which chapters have more information about them.

## Dynamic and Cascading Prompts

If you are someone who has been using Crystal Reports 8.5 and are just now upgrading to XI, I wouldn't be surprised to find out that Dynamic and Cascading Prompts are what sold you on the upgrade. Dynamic and Cascading Prompts (DCPs) are a milestone upgrade over the static prompts of previous versions.

DCPs give you two benefits. The first benefit is that the list of values is linked directly to the data source. When the underlying data changes, the list of values is updated to reflect the latest information. The second benefit is that the prompts are linked together. The value chosen in one prompt affects the list of values in the following prompt. The user only sees a list of values directly related to their previous choices.

DCPs improve the usability of parameters by ensuring that the data is always current and that the user only sees choices relevant to what they are doing. Chapter 4 covers DCPs in the advanced section.

## Dynamic Graphic Location

If you wanted to include dynamic graphics in previous versions of Crystal Reports, you either had to embed the images into binary fields within your database or write an application that programmatically loaded the images into memory and placed them on the report. There was no easy way to display images stored on the hard drive of your computer on a report. XI makes dynamic graphic locations possible. By referencing an image via a file path or URL, reports can load new images on the fly and display them on the report. Dynamic images are covered in Chapter 8.

## New Export Features

Exporting report output is a very common task -- so common, that you often find yourself exporting a report in the same way each time. Rather than requiring you to set the same options each time, Crystal Reports XI saves default values for the export options. Setting default values makes it faster to export reports and you don't have to remember which options are best.

A new RTF export format exports reports so that their final output is easier to edit. This is ideal for reports that are used for data entry forms. Previous versions of Crystal Reports allowed you to export to RTF, but the format was optimized for precise formatting. Editing the RTF wasn't very practical. You now have a choice between optimizing for editing or optimized for precise formatting. This is covered in Chapter 15.

## Parameterized Sorting

The sorting of groups and Top N/Bottom N reports now have a Formula button associated with them. Conditional formatting formulas can be used to change the sort order. By integrating this with parameters, the user gains more control over their report output. Sorting and grouping is in Chapter 3.

### Hierarchical Grouping Improvements

Hierarchical reports were very limited in how the final output looked. Columns weren't formatted very well and sometimes the report wasn't easy to read. XI gives you an improved set of formatting functionality that increases how much control you have over a report's final output. You control the indentation of report objects and the grouping sections. This is covered in Chapter 3.

### HTML Preview

A new tab in the report designer lets you view reports in their HTML format. This gives you immediate feedback about how accurately your reports will appear when viewed as a web page. HTML preview is only available when using Business Objects Enterprise or the Report Application Server. These versions of Crystal Reports are not covered in the book.

### Dependency Checker

The Dependency Checker verifies formulas and error checks a report and lists all problems found. This consists of checking the syntax of formulas, validating hyperlinks, validating database fields, and verifying subreports. This is covered in Chapter 5.

### Workbench

The Workbench makes it easy to organize multiple reports into folders. By organizing reports into specific categories you can easily find the reports you need and manage them. You can also use tools such as the Dependency Checker across all the reports in a folder. The Workbench is covered later in this chapter.

### Application Designer Improvements

Programmers have many new improvements to look forward to after installing XI. Programmers now have more control over their reports, better integration of Java functions, client-side web printing, and improved report design. Although this book doesn't include programming specific topics, this is covered in extensive detail in Volume 2 of this series, "Programming .NET 2005".[1]

 If you are a programmer who builds custom reporting applications using Visual Studio .NET 2005, you need to install Crystal Reports XI R2. Crystal Reports XI was released almost a year prior to .NET 2005 being released and they are not compatible with each other. Installing R2 updates all the .NET 2005 components.[2]

---

[1] Crystal Reports Encyclopedia Volume 2: Programming .NET 2005 will be released in January 2008.
[2] Downloading and installing R2 is covered in the book's Preface.

# Getting to know Crystal Reports

After opening Crystal Reports, you are presented with the Start Page. The start page is brand new for version XI. The goal is to make it easy to either open the most recent reports you have been working on or find out the latest news and updates about Crystal Reports. The majority of the page consists of links to online sample reports, important help topics, and the support page. In the middle of the page are links to create a new report with each report type being listed individually. The right column shows a list of the most recently used reports.

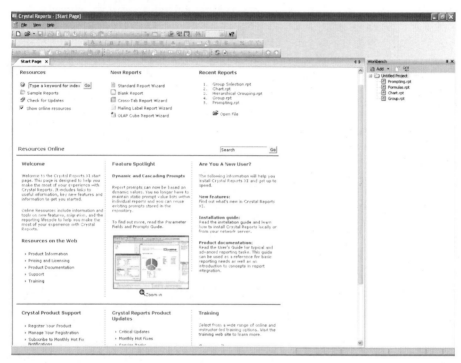

**Figure 1-1. The Start Page.**

| Tip |
| --- |

The Start Page tab is actually an HTML file called Start.html that is stored within the Crystal Reports installation directory. If you know how to build web pages using HTML, you can customize this page. You could modify the color scheme to match your company's corporate image and put your logo on it. If you are using Crystal Reports XI, the HTML files are in this folder:

C:\Program Files\Business Objects\Crystal Reports 11\en

If you are using Crystal Reports XI R2, the HTML files are in this folder:

C:\Program Files\Business Objects\Crystal Reports 11.5\
Start Page\en

An important new feature to Crystal Reports is the Workbench. The workbench is useful for managing a large number of reports. Within the workbench, you can create projects and each project has multiple reports in it. By grouping reports into different projects, it becomes easier to manage where the reports are and how they are related to each other. If you use Business Objects Enterprise, with one click of the mouse, you can publish an entire project to the enterprise software so that reports can be viewed anywhere with a Web browser.

# The Report Designer

The Report Designer lets you design reports by adding report objects, formatting the report layout, creating groups, etc. It's where you spend the majority of your time when using Crystal Reports. If you've used previous versions of Crystal Reports then you are very familiar with the designer.

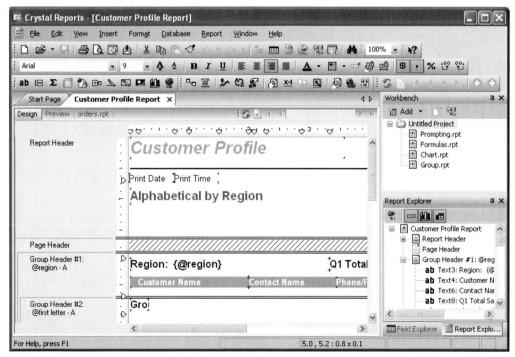

**Figure 1-2. The report design environment.**

Along the top of the screen are the different toolbars. These toolbars are Standard, Formatting, Insert, Wizards, and Navigation. By default, all of them are displayed when you open the designer the first time. You can rearrange them or disable the ones you don't normally use.

The majority of the screen consists of the report being worked on. Along the top is the tab showing the report title as well as the tabs of any other reports open. Below that tab is the Design tab. It shows each report section (Report Header, Page Header, Details, etc.) and the report objects in each section.

Along the right side of the screen are windows displaying different characteristics of the report and design environment. The top-most window is the Workbench that was discussed in the last section. Below the Workbench are the Field Explorer and the Report Explorer windows. The Field Explorer shows the different fields that can be displayed on a report. These can be database fields, formula fields, parameters, etc. The Report Explorer displays each part of the report and lists every report object in each section. For complex reports displaying many objects, this makes it easy to get an understanding of what is displayed on a report without letting the placement of the objects confuse things.

## Previewing Reports

The Report Designer also gives you the option to preview a report while working on it. Right below the tab that displays the report name are the Design tab and Preview tab. Clicking the Preview tab shows what the report looks like when it gets printed out. If the Preview tab isn't shown, you can click on the Print Preview button to display it.

In preview mode, the left side of the screen becomes a group selection tree that can jump directly to a specific group on the report. In the middle of the screen is the report as it looks when printed out.

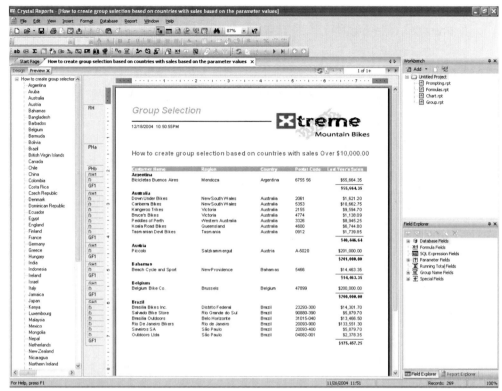

**Figure 1-3. Report preview mode.**

# Tutorial 1-1. Printing Your First Report

This lesson walks you through the steps of creating a new report. You will see how easy it is to use the Report Creation Wizard to make a simple report. When you are finished, you will have created and printed out a report that shows employee names.

1. Open Crystal Reports and make sure you are on the Start Page.

2. Click on the Standard Report Wizard link. This is the first option under the New Reports column in the middle of the page.

   After clicking on this link, the Standard Report Creation Wizard opens. This wizard walks you through the steps of creating a new report. The first step is to select the data source.

4. Double-click on the Create New Connection folder to expand it.

5. Double-click on the Access/Excel (DAO) category. This opens the Access/Excel (DAO) dialog box so that you can find the file to use as a data source.

6. Click on the button to the right of the Database Name textbox and navigate to the Xtreme.mdb database. It is located at:

C:\Program Files\Business Objects\Crystal Reports 11\Samples\en\
Databases\ xtreme.mdb.

7.  Click the OK button to select this database.

8.  Click the Finish button to close the dialog box.

9.  Expand the Tables selection to see the tables in the database.

10. Click on the Employee table name to select it.

11. Click on the Right arrow to move the Employee table to the Selected Tables list.

12. Click on the Employee Addresses table name to select it.

13. Click on the Right arrow to move the Employee Addresses table to the Selected Tables list.

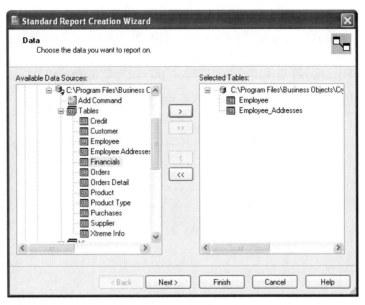

14. Click the Next button at the bottom to save the tables.

    The Link dialog appears showing you the field(s) that the two tables are joined by. In this example the Employee ID field links the Employee table to the Employee Address table. You'll learn more about linking tables in Chapter 10 on databases.

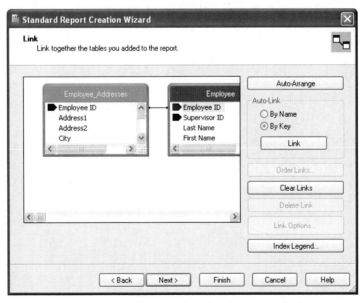

15. Click the Next button to accept the default link. The Fields dialog appears showing all the fields from each table. To add fields to the report, you would move fields from the Available Fields list to the Fields to Display list on the right.

16. Click on the following fields and then click on the Right arrow button to move them to the Fields to Display list: Employee ID, Last Name, First Name, City, and Region.

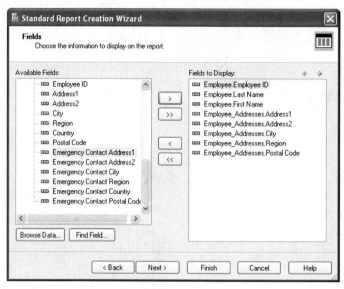

17. Click the Next button to save these fields.

The Grouping dialog appears showing the fields that were selected in the previous step. We will look at grouping and sorting records in Chapter 3. Click the Next button for now.

The Record Selection dialog determines which records from the database get displayed. We will cover this in more detail later in the book and not make any changes for this tutorial.

18. Click the Next button to move forward.

The Template dialog appears so you can choose from a list of pre-determined report formats to make your report look good. Crystal Reports comes with over a dozen different styles to choose from. As you click on each template, the preview area to the right shows an example of what the report would look like.

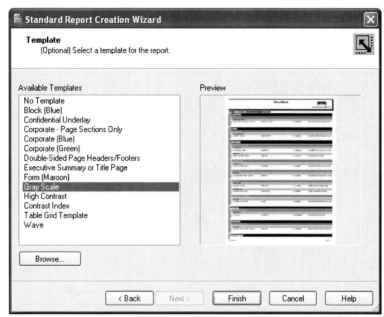

19. You can select one of the templates to automatically format your report to look a certain way. In this example, click on the No Template option to keep things simple. You can go back later and experiment with the other templates.

    Click the Finish button and Crystal Reports will create the report and preview it.

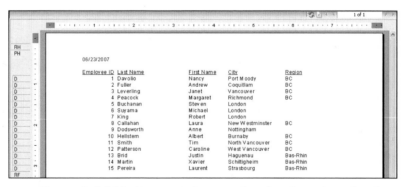

    The report lists each field in its own column and each column has a header caption.

20. Let's give the report a title so that we know what it is. On the application menu, select File > Summary Info. This opens the Document Properties dialog.

21. Enter **Employee List** as the title.

22. Click the OK button to update the report tab.

23. On the application menu select File > Print to print the report. The report will print out on your default printer.

24. Save the report as **Employee List.rpt.**

25. If you want to make more changes to the report's design, click on the Design tab above the report. This shows each section of the report and the report objects in each section. The details of modifying the report design are covered throughout the book.

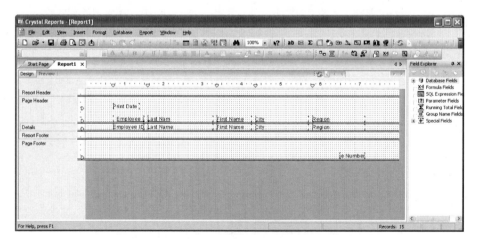

# Getting to Know the Report Designer

The Report Designer is the area where you create reporting magic. With it, you design new reports, modify existing reports, write formulas, preview reports and print them out. It gives you all the tools necessary for designing hundreds of reports. Figure 1-4 shows the designer and its various windows.

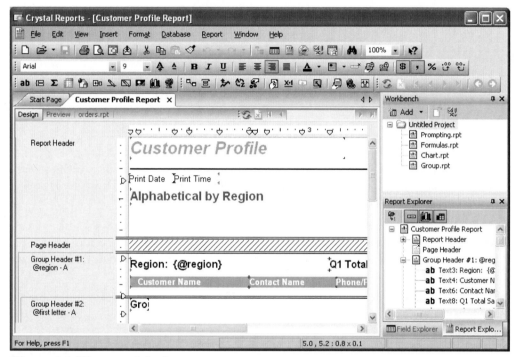

**Figure 1-4. The report designer.**

There are 7 parts of the designer that are important: the toolbars, dockable windows, the Workbench, the Report Explorer, the Field Explorer, the Design tab, and the Preview tab. Each part is explored next.

## Managing the Toolbars

The toolbars are located directly below the menu options listed along the top of the designer. The toolbars make it easy to access the different designer features by the simple click on the mouse. Most buttons either perform an action or make a change to the currently selected report object. Some of the actions are opening a new report, saving the report, adding a chart to the report, or opening a report wizard. Some of the changes that can be made to report objects are changing the font, formatting a number as currency, and aligning text to be left or right justified.

You can control which toolbars are displayed and where they are located. By default, when you first install Crystal Reports, all the toolbars are displayed. But if you're like me, I like to maximize the amount of space available on my screen and I always rearrange my toolbars and turn off the ones I don't want. To do this, right-click anywhere on one of the existing toolbars and the context-sensitive menu pops up.

**Figure 1-5. The Toolbar menu.**

The menu shows each toolbar available and there is a checkbox to the left of each toolbar currently displayed. Click on the toolbar name to toggle it on or off. This automatically updates the toolbar and closes the menu.

On the left side of each toolbar is a line of vertical dots. These are used to grab the toolbar and move it around. By moving the cursor on top of these dots, the mouse cursor changes to a navigation cursor. Hold down the mouse button and drag it around until the toolbar is in the place you want and release the mouse.

The Status Bar at the bottom of the designer is also classified as a toolbar. It shows the report object currently selected, its report coordinates, the report modification date, and the number of records to be displayed on the report. Just like the other toolbars, the Status Bar can be turned off as well. However, it can't be moved around. It has to stay at the bottom of the designer.

Any changes you make to the toolbars are saved and will be in effect the next time you open Crystal Reports.

# Dockable Windows

When you first install Crystal Reports, there are three dockable windows displayed in the Report Designer: the Workbench, the Report Explorer, and the Field Explorer. Each window is located along the right side of the designer. If you want to personalize your workspace, you can move them to another location within the designer. You can also close any windows that you don't use. Here are a few tips for working with the windows.

If you want to move a window to a new location, click on the top bar along the window and hold down the left mouse button. While holding down the mouse button move the mouse to where you want the window to move. You will see a gray outline "jump" around the screen showing you where the window will be. Once you are happy with the location, let go of the mouse and the window will be "dropped" at that location.

If you want to remove the window from the designer, click on the "X" icon in the top right corner. This closes the window. If you later decide that you want the window back (or you clicked the "X" by mistake), go to the menu and select View. Within the submenu is a list of all the windows. Click on the one you want and it will become visible again.

> ### Tip
>
> Sometime you might accidentally click on the window while moving the mouse around and "magically" reposition the window to some random place. Now it is free-floating within the designer. When this happens, it can be difficult to get it to lock back into its original position in the Report Designer. To fix this, double-click on the window's title bar and this returns the window to where it was last docked.

One feature I really like about windows is that they can be hidden but still be visible on the screen. If you look at the top of the window you'll see a thumbtack icon on the right side. This is the "Auto-Hide" icon – it makes the window visible only when you need it. Clicking on it causes the auto-hide feature to be toggled on or off. When auto-hide is on, the main portion of the toolbar is invisible and only the title bar is shown along the right side of the screen. To make the window visible, simply let the mouse hover above the title bar and it will appear again. When you take the mouse away from the window, it goes back to hiding.

## The Workbench

Do you work with so many reports that it's hard to keep track of all of them or even remember for whom or which department they were created for? The Workbench, located on the top right portion of the designer, makes it easy to organize and categorize a large number of reports. Within the Workbench, you create new projects and associate reports for each project. A project can group together reports for an internal project (e.g. Market Analysis), reports related to specific departments (e.g. Payroll Department), reports related to specific applications (e.g. SAP Accounts Receivable), etc. You can also nest projects within each other if you have different hierarchies of report classifications.

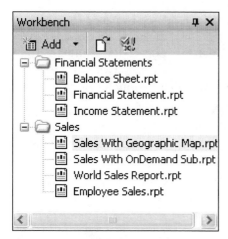

**Figure 1-6. The Workbench window showing different projects.**

The benefit of using projects is that when you are working on reports within a project you don't have to worry about the dozens of other reports stored on your computer. By keeping them displayed within the Workbench, you can quickly edit and swap between different reports. You can also perform functions across all reports in a project such as running the Dependency Checker.

Reports are added to the Workbench in two ways. The first way is to right-click anywhere on the Workbench and on the pop-up menu select Add > Add Existing Report (the report must already be saved). The second way is to drag a report from Windows Explorer and drop it onto the Workbench area. You must move the cursor onto the Project's name so that the name gets highlighted. Otherwise, it will only open the report in the designer and not add it to the project. If you later decide to delete a report from the project, it only removes it from the Workbench area and does not delete the physical report file from your computer.

 With Crystal Reports XI R2, a report doesn't have to be saved to be added to the Workbench. You can add the report you are currently working on. There is a new menu item called Add Current Report. Selecting it puts the current report in the Workbench.

Another benefit of the Workbench is that it can check for dependencies within all the reports in the project. It scans through all the report objects and verifies that all the hyperlinks and report formulas are valid. Checking for dependencies is described in more detail in Chapter 5.

## The Report Explorer

The Report Explorer shows a snapshot of every report object on the report. You can browse through all the report objects in a hierarchical tree structure and look at each section and see every object within that section. By clicking on the + or – next to the section name you can expand or collapse the section details. Figure 1-7 shows the Report Explorer with the section Group Header #4 expanded.

**Figure 1-7. The Report Explorer window.**

The Report Explorer is organized so that the report name is listed at the top of the tree and below it are the different report sections. Within each report section are the report objects placed in that section. When you click on the report object's name, the designer automatically highlights that object and repositions the designer window so that you can see where it's at. This makes it easy to locate a report object within a complex report with dozens of other report objects.

| Note |
| --- |

You can delete objects from the report using the Report Explorer, but it doesn't let you add new objects.

Since everything listed in the Report Explorer can be overwhelming for complex reports, there are buttons to filter the list down to a more reasonable size. Along the top of the window are three buttons for filtering items. The first filtering button, Show/Hide Data Fields, toggles the display of the data fields in the report. Considering that 95% of all report objects are classified as data fields, this removes most items from the list. The affect is that you only see the section names (Group Header, Details, etc.) and a few other objects within the sections (e.g. lines, subreports, and charts). The second filtering button Show/Hide Graphical Objects, toggles the display of lines, shapes, images, and charts. The third filtering button, Show/Hide Grids and Subreports, toggles the display of cross-tab objects and subreports.

An example of using the filtering buttons is to locate all the images on a report. By turning off the display of data fields and cross-tabs, you can scroll through the sections and immediately see which ones display images and what those images are.

## The Field Explorer

The Field Explorer gives you a list of all the available database fields, formulas, parameters, summary fields and special fields. The Field Explorer serves two purposes. First is that you can see and edit the different fields on the report. For example, the Database Fields category shows you which fields are part of the data source that the report uses. The Parameter Fields shows you which parameters the user will be asked to enter when the report runs. When given a report that was designed by someone else, you can scroll through this list and get a good idea of what the purpose of the report is and determine its complexity. The second purpose of the Field Explorer is for adding objects to the report. By dragging and dropping a field from the Field Explorer to the report designer, the object is added to the report. You will become very familiar with the Field Explorer because it is the primary means of building reports.

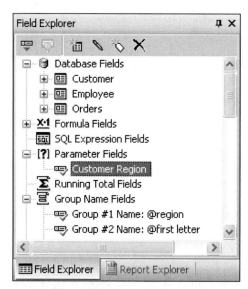

**Figure 1-8. The Field Explorer tab shows the fields that are available for printing.**

The Field Explorer also makes it easy to add Special Fields that you otherwise might forget are available (e.g. Page N of M, Current Date, Report Title, etc.). These are the last items listed in this window. Make sure you familiarize yourself with this list before building a report.

Another benefit of the Field Explorer is that it puts a check next to the fields used on the report. You can quickly see which fields have been added to the report and which ones are unused. You might find it interesting to know that it puts a check next to a field that isn't directly used on the report, but is being used in a report formula. For example, say you create a formula that uses the Customer ID field. Once you place the formula onto the report, a check appears next to the Customer ID field.

Personally, I would like to be able to click on a field and have it show me where the field is located on the report. This would be similar to how Report Explorer navigates to selected objects, but with the Field Explorer I don't have to know which section an object is located in prior to selecting it. Maybe we'll see that in a future version?

Have you ever worked on a report that someone else designed and you aren't familiar with the fields in the database or the data they contain? The Field Explorer can query the database and show the data stored in each field. Right-click on the database field you want to examine and select Browse Data. A window pops up that tells you the field's data type and lets you scroll through the data stored in that field. If you just want to see the data type of a field, right-click on the field and select Show Field Type.

My favorite part of the Field Explorer is that you can have it automatically list the data type of every field next to its name. I find it difficult to remember the data type of fields and this feature eliminates that problem. Right-click on the Database Fields category and select the Show Field Type option.

Along the top of the Field Explorer window are shortcut buttons for common tasks. These buttons are enabled or disabled depending upon whether they are compatible with the object currently selected. The first button, Insert To Report, drops the report object onto the report. This is an alternative to dragging and dropping the object onto the report. The second button, Browse, is enabled when a database field is selected. It lets you browse the field data as mentioned previously. The remaining buttons are used for creating and editing formulas and parameters. The buttons let you add a new object, edit an existing object, or delete it altogether.

## The Design Tab

If creating reports were an art, the Design tab would be your canvas. It's where you place the report objects, change colors or fonts, and set the layout of the report. The details of using the Design tab to create reports are the covered throughout this whole book. For now we will just look at the basics.

Along the left side of the designer is a gray area that lists each section name.[3] A basic report always has the sections Report Header, Page Header, Details, Page Footer, and Report Footer. Later in the book, you'll see how to work with sections to create advanced reports.

Along the left and top border of the designer are rulers that are used for positioning objects on the report. The default units that the ruler displays are controlled by the regional

---

[3] This gray area has no official name that I know of. So it will be referred to as 'gray area' on the left. ☺

settings of your operating system.[4] For example, if the regional setting is 'English (United Kingdom)' then the ruler is in centimeters. Most people won't need to worry about changing this setting unless you are a working on reports to be used in different countries.

Notice the little triangles along the top ruler? These are markers for guidelines. By attaching report objects to a guideline, you can reposition the guideline and all the attached objects move with it. This lets you place multiple objects along the same column and if you need to move the column then all the objects will stay lined up. Guidelines are discussed in more detail in the next chapter.

The center of the designer shows the report sections and the objects within each section. As you move the cursor around the design area you'll notice that the outline of each object is highlighted as the mouse passes over it. For a complex report with many overlapping objects, it clearly identifies the boundary of each object.

## The Preview Tab

The Preview tab shows you what the report looks like when sent to the printer. This makes it easy to see if what you built in the designer meets your expectations. The Preview tab uses actual data so that you have an accurate presentation.

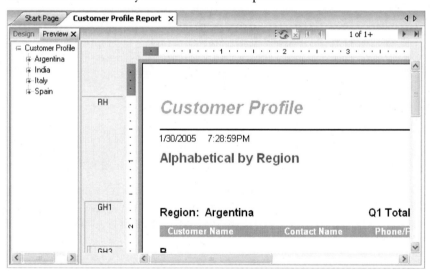

Figure 1-9. Previewing a report with the Preview tab.

The leftmost portion of the preview tab is the Group Tree window. This shows you all the groups in the report. Click the + sign next to the group name to expand the sub-groups or see the detailed records.

---

[4] To change the Regional settings, open the Control Panel and select Regional and Language Settings option.

The top-right portion shows the navigation toolbar. By clicking on the arrows, you can navigate to the next page, the previous page or even jump to the first or last page in the report. There is also a button to refresh the report data, as well as stop querying the database for new data (this is useful when a report is taking too long to load and you want to cancel it).

An interesting aspect of the Preview tab is that it lets you make changes to the report as if you were still in the designer. It only allows for simple changes, but you can make changes nonetheless. For example, you can move an object around the report and immediately see the effects on all the pages. You can also change the formatting of each object. Making changes while previewing the report is much faster than switching back and forth between design and preview modes.

Since the Preview tab allows changes to be made, it has a few aspects in common with the Report Designer. Along the left side of the preview window are the section names. It identifies which section each report object is in. This is helpful for complex reports that have nested groups, as well as sections that are conditionally hidden. Being able to determine which section a report object is displayed in lets you see whether groups are displaying the proper data or to see if sections are being hidden at the appropriate time.

Along the top and left edges of the Report Preview is the ruler. Since you can move objects around the report in preview mode, it makes sense to see their exact location on the ruler. This is especially useful for reports used with pre-printed forms where proper placement is critical.

| Tip |
| --- |

One problem I've always had with the Preview tab is that it shows the report within the designer. Unlike other programs (e.g. MS Word), Crystal Reports doesn't use the full screen and the report is still surrounded by the various toolbars, windows, etc. This makes it difficult to review densely formatted reports because you have to shrink it down to get it to fit within the preview area. Luckily, as I was finishing this book, Business Objects announced the beta release of a new .RPT viewer program as a free download. "Crystal Reports Viewer" previews a report using the full area on your computer screen and makes it much easier to read large reports. See their website for more information on when it will be ready.[5]

---

[5] When an official URL is announced, I'll post it on www.CrystalReportsBook.com.

# Understanding the Report Wizards

The report wizards make it easy to create most types of reports. By selecting your data source and clicking on a few buttons, you can quickly create new reports.

Depending upon your needs, creating reports can be a simple or complicated process. For example, it is very easy to print mailing labels from an address database or print a form letter to a list of subscribers. On the other hand, it can be very complicated to write a report that uses multiple sub-reports which are based off of user entered parameters. Fortunately, the report wizards that come with Crystal Reports make it easy to quickly produce a variety of reports. The wizards are useful for writing complex reports because they give you a way to quickly make a professional looking report that you can build upon with more complexity for your specific needs.

Since wizards are designed to be easy to use, you might be wondering why this chapter needs to explain them. The problem with wizards is that although they are supposed to be simple to use, a tool that is too simple is generally not very useful. As a result, many of today's applications use wizards that are designed to achieve many tasks and sometimes require explanation to clarify their advanced functionality. Such is the case with Crystal Reports.

Each wizard consists of a multi-tabbed dialog box. Many of the tabs on each wizard are used elsewhere within the main functionality of Crystal Reports. This chapter summarizes each tab and the details are covered in later chapters, where applicable.

## Using the Wizard's Dialog Boxes

Each report wizard uses a combination of different dialog boxes to question you about how to build your report. Each wizard presents a slightly different combination of these dialog boxes. This section describes how to use each dialog box and explains any aspects of it that may not be obvious. The report wizard dialogs are called Data, Links, Fields, Grouping, Summaries, Group Sorting, Chart, Record Selection, Template, Drill and Mailing Labels.

## *The Data Dialog Box*

The Data dialog box is the first one presented. It's where you select the database and tables that store your data. The database can be a standard data source such as SQL Server or a non-standard data source such as an Excel spreadsheet.

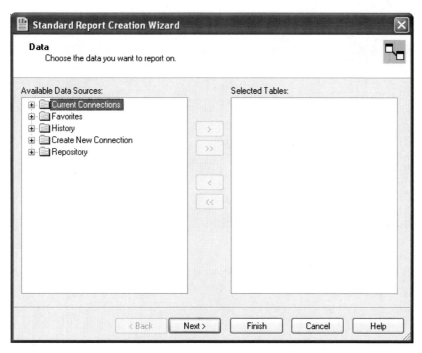

Figure 1-10. The Data dialog of the report wizards.

## The Links Dialog Box

Reports that use two or more tables need to have the tables linked so that data can be pulled from all of them. The Links dialog box sets the fields for creating relationships between the tables. Crystal Reports does its best to attempts to automatically link the tables together. If the links are not what you need, you can always delete them and add your own

Figure 1-11. The Links dialog of the report wizards.

## The Fields Dialog Box

After selecting which tables you want to use for your report, the Fields dialog box allows you to select which fields will be shown. Adding and deleting fields is done in the standard manner of dragging and dropping them between windows or selecting a field and clicking on the appropriate arrow button.

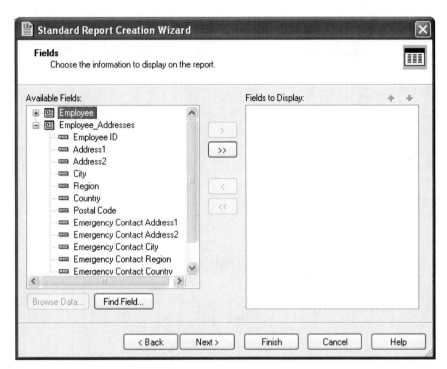

**Figure 1-12. The Fields dialog of the report wizards.**

After you add all the necessary fields to your report, you are free to reorder them by using the arrow buttons above the window. Select the field to move and click the up or down arrow to reposition it. The order that the fields are listed in is the order in which the report wizard places them on the report.

## The Grouping Dialog Box

Some reports have so much data that they can be a little hard to understand. When reports are dozens or even hundreds of pages long, you need to organize the information in a way that makes it easier to absorb the data in smaller pieces. You do this by creating groups within the report. Some examples are grouping on months of the year or the names of the different branch offices for a company.

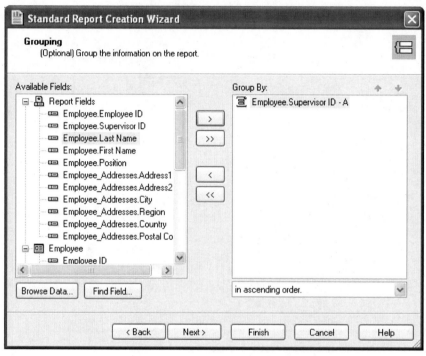

Figure 1-13. The Grouping dialog of the report wizards.

### The Summaries Dialog Box

It is very common for reports to calculate sub-totals and other summary calculations on the numeric fields. The Summaries dialog box, shown in Figure 1-14, is where you define the summary calculations for the different fields. The left list box shows all the available fields. The right list box shows the fields that will have summary functions calculated for them.

**Figure 1-14. The Summaries dialog of the report wizards.**

You have to be careful because the report wizard automatically places all numeric fields in the Summarized Fields list. Many numeric fields hold non-quantitative data and you don't want to perform any summary calculations on them. For example, in the figure above you wouldn't want to sum the Supervisor ID field. Be sure to review this default list created by the report wizard and delete all unwanted summary calculations.

## *The Group Sorting Dialog Box*

When adding a group to a report, you probably assume that every record within the group
will be displayed. In most circumstances, this is the case. However, you can tell Crystal
Reports to only display a certain number of records based upon their rank. For example,
you could have a top salesperson report, where you show the top 10 salespeople in your
office. You could also have another report that shows the 10 worst salespeople. The Group
Sorting dialog box does this by sorting the groups based on a summary field

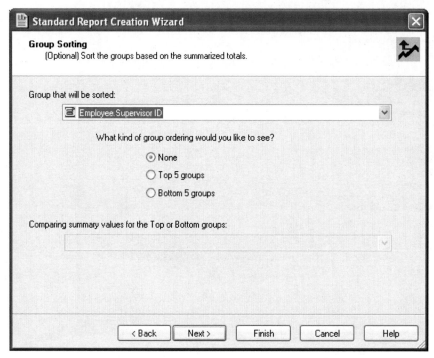

Figure 1-15. The Group Sorting dialog from the report wizards.

## The Chart Dialog Box

This dialog box adds a chart to your report. You can also set a variety of options for what type of chart to display and how to display it.

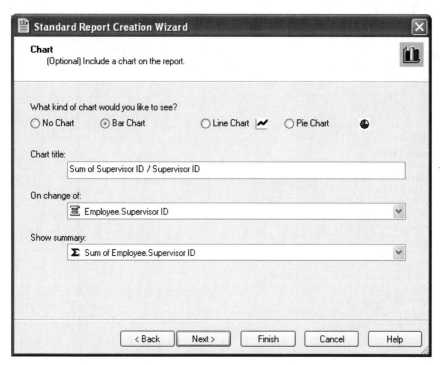

Figure 1-16. The Chart dialog from the report wizards.

## *The Record Selection Dialog Box*

Some reports need to only show a sub-set of all the data that is in a table. For example, a financial report may only show the corporate data for a single quarter or a range of quarters. To filter out certain data so that you limit how much information is shown on a report, use the Record Selection dialog shown in Figure 1-17.

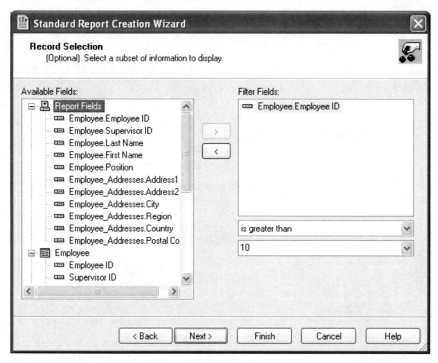

Figure 1-17. The Record Selection dialog from the report wizards.

### The Template Dialog Box

After specifying the report details, use the Template dialog box to format everything so that the report has a professional look to it. This dialog, shown in Figure 1-18, lists over a dozen different pre-determined templates that can be applied to your report. These templates make it easy for you to take some raw data and spice it up enough to make everyone think you worked really hard to create the report!

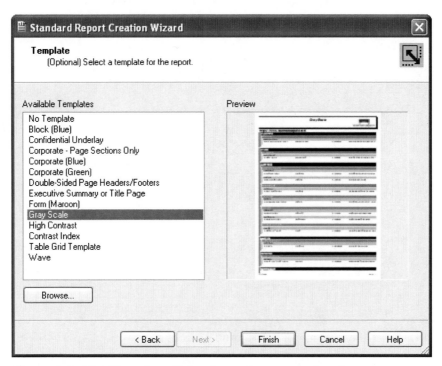

Figure 1-18. The Template dialog from the report wizards.

## The Label Dialog Box

The Label dialog box is used when you select the Mailing Labels report wizard. After selecting the database tables and fields to display, you select the label size. You can choose from a list of the standard Avery labels or choose a User Defined Label.

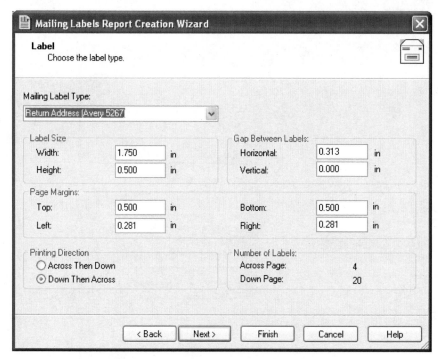

**Figure 1-19. Mailing Labels dialog of the Report Wizard**

In the middle of the dialog box are the various settings of how the labels are sized and the gaps between each label. At the bottom, you select whether you want the labels to go across the page or down the page in a column. The bottom right corner gives you a general idea of whether you entered the parameters properly by calculating how many labels are printed per page. Creating mailing labels is discussed in Chapter 8.

## The Cross-Tab and Customize Style Dialog Boxes

The Cross-Tab and Customize Style dialogs are only available when using the Cross-Tab Wizard. They let you modify the cross-tab data for what appears in the rows and columns. Modifying these tabs is very involved and is explained in detail in Chapter 13.

## The Drill Dialog Box

The Drill dialog is only available when using the Drill-Down Wizard. When creating drill-down reports, you allow the user to see a summarized view of their data. If they want to examine the data in more detail, they can expand a record to see more detail relating to the summarized information. The summarized fields are listed on this tab. When you click on the field's name, it will toggle back and forth between "Show" and "Hide". This will alternate the default of whether it gets displayed or not.

# Two-Pass Report Processing Model

It's quite possible that one of the most important parts of learning how to use Crystal Reports is understanding how Crystal Reports reads data and processes formulas while building a report. This is called the two-pass report processing model and it is the reason why you can and can't do certain things in a report. While it is certainly possible to create basic reports without understanding the internal workings of Crystal Reports, it won't be long before you find that some subtotals don't seem to be calculating correctly and that certain formulas aren't available when you want them. This is due to the order in which report objects are processed. Throughout this book, I will warn you when these situations can cause you problems and I refer back to this section for more information. Understanding the two-pass report processing model will help you make proper design decisions and avoid problems later.

Crystal Reports processes reports in two passes. The first pass creates the primary data to be printed. During the second pass, Crystal Reports processes grouping data and formulas that can only be calculated while the report is printing. Figure 1-20 shows the two-pass report processing model diagram found in the Crystal Reports documentation. Along the left side of the diagram is the pass number. To the right are the actual processes performed during each pass.

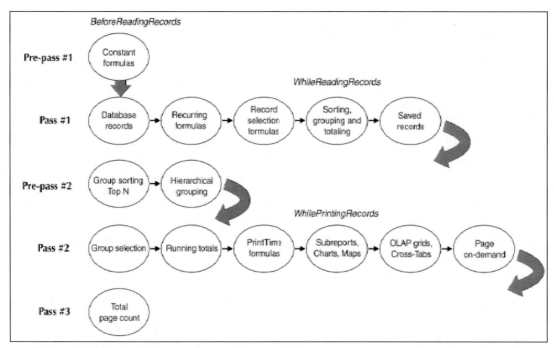

**Figure 1-20. Two-pass report processing model**

The first thing you might notice is that it looks like a lot more is going on here than just two passes. This is because the diagram also shows "pre-passes" that get the data ready for the pass. There is also a third pass shown, but this is only used when the report prints a total page count at the bottom of each page. Without getting caught up in the semantics, there are two primary passes performed for the majority of reports.

The first pass reads individual records one at a time from the database and calculates any formulas that use them. This pass will only calculate the formulas that are based on raw data within a record or that perform simple calculations. As each record is read and the formulas are calculated, the results are stored in a temporary file to be used during the second pass.

After the first pass is finished, Crystal Reports performs a second pass where it evaluates all summary functions on the data and selects the data to be displayed for groups. This wasn't possible during the first pass because all the data had not been read yet. During the second pass, all the raw data has been read into the temporary file and it can be evaluated and summarized as a whole.

The key to getting the most out of this diagram is to look at the relationships between each step and see where a process appears within the hierarchy. The steps are processed from top to bottom and from left to right. For example, in pass #1 the first step is to read the database records. After that, it will calculate formulas and the record selection formula. You certainly can't calculate the formulas prior to reading the data.

A rule of thumb is that formulas should only reference formulas from a previous pass. For example, a formula that is calculated in pass #1 can't reference a formula calculated in pass #2. The formulas calculated in pass #2 generally involve using more than one record and the formula's value hasn't been calculated yet in pass #1. Formulas that reference a formula in the same pass can cause unpredictable results as well.

For example, if you have Formula A and Formula B and they are both calculated in pass #1 you can't be certain which one gets calculated first. If Formula B makes reference to Formula A, the calculation might be wrong because it's possible that Formula A doesn't have a value yet. Luckily, there are ways to fix this so that your formulas are accurate. We talk about this more in the chapters on formulas.

Many times, Figure 1-20 is used to explain why you can't do something rather than explain why you can do it. For example, you can't chart the value of a summary formula. This is because summary formulas and charts are both processed in pass #2. Since they are on the same level, the summary formula hasn't been calculated yet.

Let's define exactly what types of formulas and data are processed during each pass. This makes it easier to categorize your own formulas and determine how they can be used in a report. In many parts of this book, you'll find that certain types of formulas aren't allowed with certain report objects. You can refer back to this section to quickly identify which formulas are being referred to.

## *Pre-pass #1*

Pre-pass #1 calculates formulas that don't reference any database fields. This usually involves simple math or assigning constants to a variable. For example, the next two formulas are both calculated in pre-pass #1.

```
TaxRate := .05;
Pi := 3.14;
```

## *Pass #1*

Pass #1 reads in data from the database one record at a time. After each record is read, the record selection formula evaluates whether the data should be printed or if it should be filtered out. Formulas that only reference database fields from the current record are calculated next. The last step is to perform sorting, grouping and build cross-tabs. When finished, all the data is saved to a temporary table for use in pass #2.

In summary, the primary steps that happen during pass #1 are:

- Read the data from the database.
- Filter records using the record selection formula.
- Calculate formulas that use database fields.
- Sort and group data.

## Pass #2

Pass #2 has steps that involve more complex data processing. The data is grouped, running totals are calculated, charts and maps are built, and complex formulas are calculated. As a general rule, the steps in pass #2 are performed while the report is printing data. All the data used during this pass is read from the temporary table created in pass #1 and the database isn't read anymore.

The key aspect of pass #2 is understanding which formulas get processed during this stage. The list of formula types that get calculated in pass #2 is extensive. Formulas that have the following characteristics are processed in pass #2:

- Using the WhilePrintingRecords function. This forces a formula to be calculated while the report is printing the individual records.

- Using summary functions such as Sum, Count, Average, etc.

- Using Print State functions such as Previous, Next, TotalPageCount, etc.

- Using shared variables with subreports.

### Tip

An easy way to determine whether a formula is calculated in pass #1 or pass #2 is to let Crystal Reports tell you. First, make sure the formula is being used somewhere on the report (if not, temporarily add it to the Details section until you are finished with this tip). Right-click on the formula and examine the pop-up menu. If you see the Insert menu option (for summary formulas), the formula is a first pass formula. If Crystal Reports doesn't list the Insert option on the pop-up menu, it is a second pass formula. Summary calculations can't be performed on second pass formulas, and therefore, Crystal Reports removes that option from the pop-up menu.

## Pass #3

In pass #3, Crystal Reports only calculates the total number of pages in the report. If your report doesn't print the total number of pages on each page (e.g. "Page 1 of 20"), this pass isn't run. For optimal report performance, you don't want to print the total number of pages in the report because Crystal Reports has to internally generate the entire report prior to printing the first page. If you do need to print this on your report, it's best to leave it off while you are designing the report so that testing of the report goes faster. Put it on the report once you feel that the report is finished.

# 2

## Learning the Report Designer

Many people like to spend their weekends fiddling around their home doing small projects to keep their place fixed up. But before starting any new project, you have to make sure you are familiar with the tools you are going to use on the project. For example, if you just got a new electric saw, then you better read the instruction manual for how it works or who knows what will happen! You need to first spend a little time figuring out how to control the saw and understand how everything works.

The same applies to Crystal Reports. Even though you are anxious to start dropping charts onto a report and creating cross-tabs, you first need to become familiar with the different parts of the report and how the pieces work together. This chapter gives you a solid understanding of the fundamentals for using the report designer before you embark on the more adventurous aspects of creating reports.

You will first see how to set the designer's properties and how to setup the report's basic structure. Secondly, you learn how to add and manipulate report objects within the designer. By getting comfortable with how to use the different features of the Report Designer, you will be ready to create more complex reports in the remaining chapters of the book.

## Setting Designer Defaults

When working with reports, there are certain aspects that you want to be the same for every report. These are called the default settings (or default properties) because when you open the report they are set by default. For example, you can set the report to automatically force report objects to snap to the grid so that it's easier to line up objects next to each other. Crystal Reports lets you set these default properties of the report designer so that they are the same for every report you work on.

The primary areas of the Report Designer that you can control are the design area and the formatting properties of certain fields. To change these defaults, select the menu items File > Options. It shows the Options dialog box in Figure 2-1.

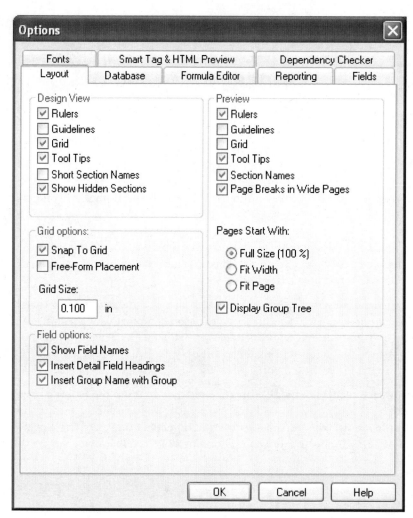

**Figure 2-1. Report designer Options dialog box.**

The Options dialog box might look a little overwhelming at first glance. There are eight different tabs to choose from and each tab has many options listed on it. To make it easier to understand, we are only going to look at the options that affect the Report Designer. We'll look at the other options later in the book for the sections that they apply to. Table 2-1 shows a description of each tab.

**Table 2-1. Option dialog box tab descriptions.**

| Tab Name | Description |
|---|---|
| Layout | Sets the defaults for the report designer and the report preview. |
| Database | Changes how the report interfaces with the database and sets advanced optimization properties. This is discussed in Chapter 10. |
| Formula Editor | Sets the default programming language and code formatting properties. This is discussed in Chapter 5. |
| Reporting | Specifies how report data is treated. For example, it determines how to handle Null values, whether to save report data with the report, etc. This is discussed in various areas throughout the book. |
| Fields | Set the default formatting of each type of data. For example, you can have strings formatted differently than numbers. This is discussed in this chapter. |
| Fonts | Similar to the Fields tab, the Fonts tab sets the default formatting for different types of data. For example, you can specify a default format for summary fields that is different than the format of group name fields. |
| Smart Tag & HTML Preview | Sets up the properties used by Office XP smart tags and previewing reports in HTML format. This applies to Business Objects Enterprise and is not discussed in this book. |
| Dependency Checker | Determines which aspects of a report the dependency checker should analyze. This is discussed in Chapter 5. |

# Setting the Layout Options

The Layout tab (see Figure 2-1) specifies the default properties for both the report designer and the report preview. For example, it sets how the designer looks, changes the preview window, and displays field information. The options within the Layout tab are divided into four different categories based upon their functionality. The four categories are: Design View, Grid Options, Preview Options, and Field Options.

## Design View Options

The Design View options determine what is shown on the designer. Each option has a checkbox next to it that either turns it on or off. The first option shows or hides the rulers along the top and side of the designer. As a general rule, the rulers make it easy to position and size objects on the report. For reports that are used built to be used with a paper based form, the rulers make it possible to place the report objects so that they have exact placement on the form.

The second option turns guidelines on or off. Guidelines are dashed lines that extend from the edge of a report object to the ruler. They show exactly where a report object appears at all times. Although these lines don't appear on the report, you can make them visible in the designer so that you can see which objects are associated with each guideline. Guidelines are discussed in more detail later in this chapter.

The third option turns the grid on or off. The grid is a series of equally spaced dots that make it easier to position objects on the report. The fourth option displays tool tips as the mouse hovers over report objects. The tool tips give short descriptions of each object or tell you the database field being displayed. The fifth option determines whether the section names should be shortened. For example, rather than show "Report Header a" the section name would show "RHa". The benefit is that shorter names give you more room for working on the report.

The last option in the Design View area toggles hidden sections. When this option is checked, the hidden sections appear as grayed out. They are only grayed out because it can be helpful to see how the sections are designed. When the report runs, they aren't visible.

## Grid Options

The purpose of the grid is to make it easy to keep report objects lined up with each other. By making report objects snap to the grid points, you know that the objects will have a professional appearance. Of course, there are times when you need to make minute adjustments to the location of a report object and in this case the grid becomes a hindrance.

The first option, Snap To Grid, forces report objects to be placed on a grid point when they are added to the report or moved around a report. The second option, Free Form Placement allows objects to be placed anywhere in the section without snapping to the grid. The last item specifies the distance between grid points. You can make it smaller if you need more granularity over object placement.

## Preview Options

The Preview tab has functionalities similar to the Design tab. It can display rulers, tool tips, guidelines, etc. It also allows you to make changes to the report while you are previewing it. This gives you the ability to immediately see how a change affects the final report output.

Since the Preview tab serves two purposes, previewing the report and modifying the report layout, you get to decide what modification tools to use. The Preview options on the Layout tab has settings to show or hide the same things as the Design View section: rulers, guidelines, tool tips, etc. Each of these has a checkbox that shows or hides each tool.

The unique options for the Preview tab are as follows: the option Page Breaks in Wide Pages indicates where the edge of a page is. You can also set the default zoom level to be Full Size, Fit Width, or Fit Page. The last option sets whether the group tree should be displayed. The group tree summarizes the group names in a tree format and lets you navigate to the group details.

### Field Options

The primary purpose of a report is to display data from database fields. How these fields are displayed in the Design tab can be customized. By default, each field shows the field name. This makes it easy to see what data is going to be displayed to the user. But sometimes you want to get a feel for how the data will appear. When the option Show Field Names is unchecked, the Design tab replaces the field names with symbolic characters. For example, text fields are replaced with "XXXX" and numbers are replaced with "555,555". See Figure 2-2 for an example.

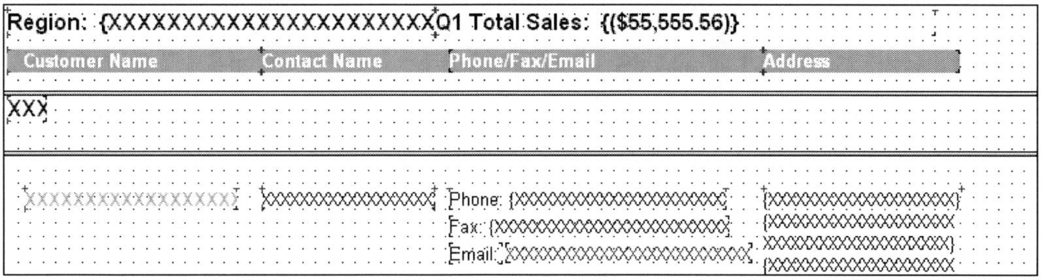

**Figure 2-2. The Design tab showing symbolic characters.**

When adding fields to a report, it is assumed that most fields have a header (or caption) displayed above them so that the user knows what the data represents. A bunch of numbers on a page typically doesn't make a lot of sense to the reader unless you identify what they are. To make it easier on you, when you add a field to the Detail section, the header text is automatically inserted in the page header section. If you want to turn this feature off, uncheck the option Insert Detail Field Headings. A similar feature is available for groups. When you add a field to the group section, a header text field is added to the Group header section. To turn this feature off, uncheck the option Insert Group Name With Group.

> **Note**
>
> Any changes you make within the Options dialog box will apply to every report. To make changes specific to only the current report, do so within the Report Options dialog box which is described later.

## Setting the Default Format Options

After adding fields to a report, you frequently have to format each one to the proper font, alignment, format, etc. If you need to format report objects a particular way for multiple reports, you can set the default properties that are applied to each field. This saves you work because their default formatting is applied when the report object is added to the report.

The Options dialog box has two tabs that set formatting properties. The first is the Fields tab shown in Figure 2-3.

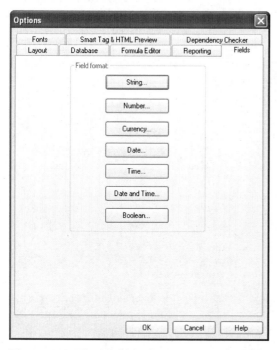

**Figure 2-3. The Fields tab sets the default formatting properties.**

The Fields tab controls the default formatting based upon field type. For example, the formatting for a String field is different than the formatting of a Boolean field. By clicking on the button for each type of field, the Format Editor dialog box appears. This dialog box has more tabs for setting properties such as Can Grow, Alignment, CSS Class, Border styles, etc. Set the properties that you want to be the default and then click the OK button. The next time that you add that field type to your report, the formatting properties will already be set.

Not all formatting options apply to each type of field. For example, the String object doesn't need to specify the default date format. Thus, the date related formatting options are only shown for Date fields. Setting the default properties for some objects is more useful than for other objects. For example, the String object lets you set properties such as Suppress, Can Grow, Text Rotation, and the line styles of the border. Each of these properties is really only used in unique circumstances and therefore isn't something that generally gets set as a default property. On the other hand, the way you format a Date object is usually the same throughout all your reports. For example, a company might have a policy that all dates show the month using three letters and the year is four digits. This isn't going to change so it's a good idea to set it as the default. The same applies to how numbers and Boolean values are displayed.

The second formatting related tab within the Options dialog box is the Fonts tab. It sets the default font style depending upon what the field represents. You can set the font for Summary fields, Group Name fields, Field Titles, etc. For example, it's very common for a summary field to have different font properties than the group name field. Setting the default font properties saves you time when designing reports and apply consistent formatting rules to different parts of the report.

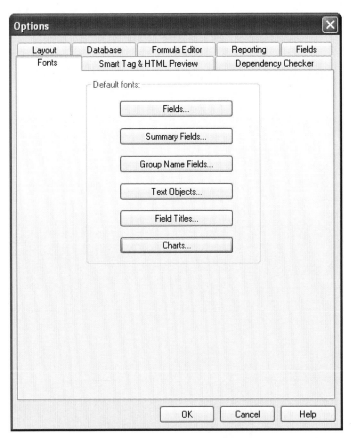

**Figure 2-4. The Fonts tab formats different field objects.**

| Note |
| --- |

The default formatting settings are only applied to an object when it is initially dropped onto the report. If you later change the default formatting, these changes are not applied to objects already on the report. To apply the default

settings to an existing object, you have to delete the object and then add it back
to the report.

# Setting Report Options

After setting the options for customizing the report design experience, the next step is
customizing the settings for an individual report. There are different options that affect a
report's behavior and how it is printed. These options are based upon how the report is to
be used.

## Page and Printer Options

The first aspect of a report that needs to be decided is the page size and orientation. These
properties are set with the Page Setup dialog box. Click on the menu options File > Page
Setup.

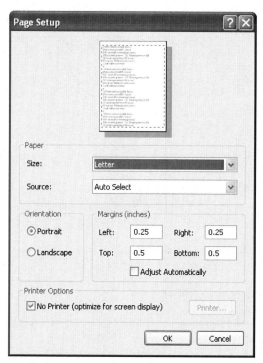

**Figure 2-5. Page Setup properties.**

The Page Setup dialog box is pretty self-explanatory. In fact, it's similar to the Printer Page
dialog box you see in most Windows applications. The first two options set the paper size
(Letter, A4, etc.) and the printer's paper bin. The options after that set the paper
orientation (portrait, landscape) and the margins.

The last option is the most interesting of them all: No Printer. Even though you assume most reports will be sent to a printer, there are times when it's beneficial to not specify a default printer. Let's look at how this works.

We first need to talk about printer drivers. Although you might assume that each report will look the same no matter which printer it is printed on, this isn't the case. Each printer has a software driver associated with it that determines how something gets printed. There are very small differences between each type of printer and that can change the output just slightly. Although this probably seems insignificant right now, when you are creating reports that require each object to be in a precise location on the paper (e.g. forms based reports), even a small variation can have a big impact. Another time this is important is when a report tries to print so much data on a single page that you try to squeeze everything down to fit. You shrink the report so that when it prints on your printer everything is sized perfectly. But then you distribute the report to the rest of the company and people start complaining that the digits of some numbers are getting chopped off. When you investigate the problem you find that they have a different type of printer than you do and the fonts are slightly different than your printer. This wastes all the time you spent sizing everything perfectly. In some circumstances you will find that the person has the same printer as you do, but they haven't downloaded the latest printer drivers like you did and this messes things up as well. So you can see how print drivers can have a big impact on a report's output.

There are two options for using the No Printer setting. When it is checked, the report is optimized to be displayed on the screen. When the No Printer option is not checked, the report uses your computer's default printer driver to display the report preview.[6] This gives a more accurate representation of how it will look when printed on your specific printer. If there is a specific network printer that everyone in the office uses, click the Printer button and select that printer from that list. This optimizes the report to be printed on the office printer. If you want to use a type of printer that your users have but you don't have access to, you need to at least install the printer driver so that Crystal Reports can use it for the report preview. Although you won't personally print on that type of printer, Crystal Reports will format the report just for that printer driver.

Please note that all this worrying about printer drivers is overkill if your reports are printing fine. This is only a concern when precise placement of report objects is required and people are complaining that their reports don't look quite right. Then you can go back to these printer settings and test whether changing them improves the output or not.

### Tip

If your users all have different types of printers then it is sometimes best to choose the No Printer option. By telling Crystal to not format the report according to one particular type of printer then you aren't locking the report

---

[6] Your computer's default printer is set through the Windows Control Panel.

into a specific printer driver. Setting the No Printer option keeps the formatting generic enough so that the report prints fine on all types of printers. This can be your best bet for solving those tough printer problems.

## Summary Info

Each report has summary information associated with it. This makes it easy to determine who designed the report and what its purpose is. The Document Properties dialog box is where you enter this information. Open it by selecting the menu options File > Summary Info.

**Figure 2-6. The Document Properties dialog box sets the summary info.**

The fields you can enter information for are: Author, Keywords, Comments, Title and Subject. Entering good descriptions into the Comments and Subject fields makes it easier for someone else to look at the report and quickly see what the report does. Entering your contact information into the Author field makes it easy for them to locate you for more information.

One interesting benefit of entering summary info is that it is displayed in the Open File dialog box. This makes it easy to find out about a report and see a preview of it before opening it. Considering that report file names sometimes use cryptic abbreviations, this makes it easier to determine which report to open. Enabling this feature of the Open File dialog box is discussed later in the chapter.

The Save Preview Picture checkbox sets whether or not to save a snapshot of the first page of the report with the report file. If a preview picture is saved, you will see a snapshot of the report when opening a file.

## Miscellaneous Report Options

The last location for setting report options is the Report Options dialog box. It lets you set a variety of different options such as database optimization settings, using report alerts, the handling of grouping data, etc. I hesitate to mention this dialog box at this point in the book because all these options are advanced settings and aren't appropriate for an introductory chapter. They are all discussed within the appropriate chapters later in the book. However, just so that you see what I'm talking about, you can get to the Report Options dialog box by selecting the menu options File >Report Options. It is shown in Figure 2-7.

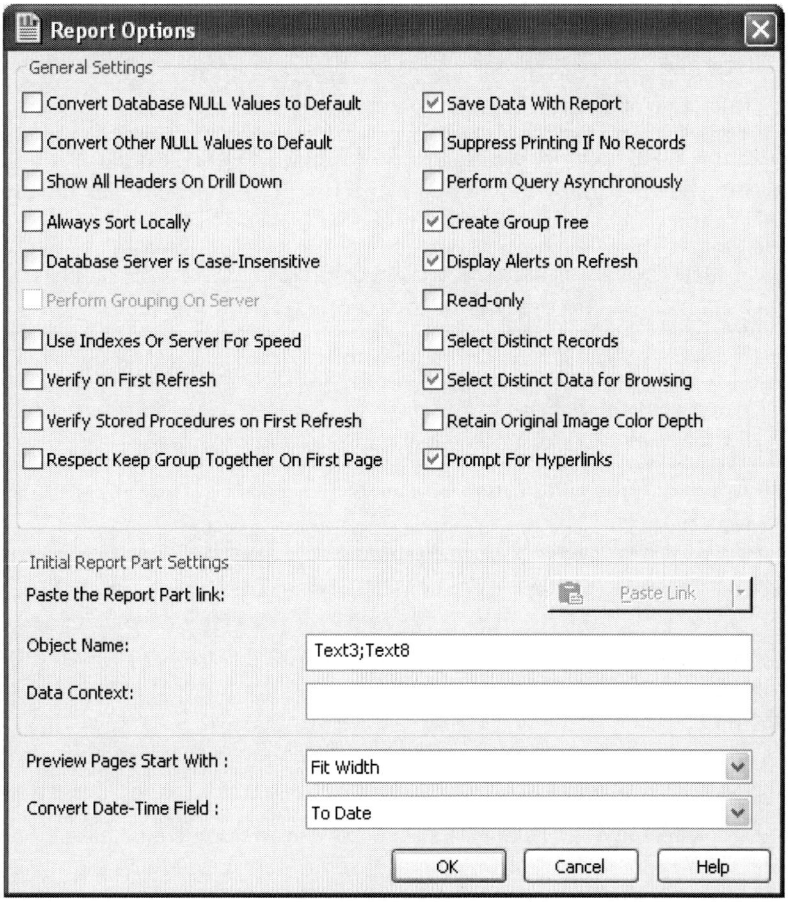

**Figure 2-7. The Report Options dialog box.**

# Designing Reports

The best way to become familiar with how to design reports is to start with the basics. Once you understand how the designer and the individual report objects work, you'll be ready to move on to advanced topics of report design (and finally start doing something fun!)

The default view of the Design tab is divided into five sections: Report Header, Page Header, Details, Report Footer, and Page Footer. Each section determines where its related data appears on the report. Table 2-2 gives you a summary of each section.

**Table 2-2. The five report sections.**

| Section Name | Description |
| --- | --- |
| Report Header | Appears at the top of the first page of the report. It only appears once on a report. |
| Page Header | Appears at the top of the page. It is repeated on each page. For the first page of a report it appears after the Report Header. |
| Group Header | Shown when before the first record in new group is printed. Although not shown initially shown in a blank report, it appears when you add a grouping field to the report. This is covered in Chapter 3. |
| Details | A Detail row is printed for every record selected from the database. It usually makes up the bulk of the report content. |
| Group Footer | Shown after the last record in a group is printed. |
| Page Footer | Appears at the bottom of the page. It is repeated on each page. For the last page of a report, it appears before the Report Footer. |
| Report Footer | Appears at the end of the last page of the report. It only appears once on a report. |

If you think of a report as a book, the Report Header is like the Title Page or the Preface. It appears at the very beginning of the report and can be used to display a corporate logo, the report title, the date and time the report was printed, or even an introductory paragraph explaining the purpose of the report. The Report Header is also useful for displaying summary information to the user. For example, by showing some carefully thought out charts, the user can get an overview of the data that is shown within the report.

Continuing with the book analogy, the Page Header typically shows non-data information on each page. Some examples are the page number and field headers. For reports that have many columns of data, it's important to display the column headers in the Page Header.

This keeps the user from having to flip back to the first report page to see what each number represents.

The Details section of the report is where the true content of the report appears. This is the primary section for displaying the database fields and it gets repeated for each record.

The Page Footer, like the Page Header, usually displays non-data fields. This could be the page number, report author or the print date. Sometimes it is used to print summaries of the data on that page.

The Report Footer typically displays summary information for all the data in the report. This includes a grand total for the numeric columns as well as displaying summary calculations such as the total number of records printed.

Although I listed general suggestions for what is shown in each section, this is not a hard and fast rule. For example, I said that the Page Header usually shows non-data information. But that doesn't mean that you can't put database fields and formulas in the Page Header. A report that prints invoices will use the Page Header to show the customer's name and address as well as the P.O. Number. The Page Footer shows the invoice total, any applicable discounts, and the payment terms. Proper use of graphics in each section helps highlight different parts of a report and gives it a touch of class. Remember that the key to designing professional reports is to be creative with object placement, but not over do it.[7]

# Adding Report Objects

The majority of your time spent designing reports is spent working with the report objects. Crystal Reports gives you many types of objects for designing reports. Learning how each works is critical to being a proficient report writer. This section covers most of the available report objects (the more complex ones have their own chapter).

There are two classifications of objects that can be added to a report: report objects and field objects. Report objects are the building blocks of a report. They let you display data from a database, draw graphics and show charts for more complex printing. By understanding the purpose of each report object and how to best use it, you can create reports that display complex information in an easy to read format.

Field objects are shown in the Field Explorer window and they can be dragged and dropped onto the report. For this chapter, we'll keep it simple and focus on report objects. The different field objects are covered in separate chapters because they are much more complex than the typical report objects.

---

[7] Do you remember when the Internet first became popular and everyone was learning HTML for the first time? You frequently saw web pages that displayed every color imaginable, used too many types of fonts, and displayed awful graphics. This proves that just because you have a lot of options, it may not be best to use them all at the same time. Fortunately, website design has improved dramatically since the early days.

The easiest way to add a report object to the report is using the Insert toolbar (shown in Figure 2-8). The toolbar has an icon for each type of object that can be dropped onto the report. Click on the object to insert and, depending upon the type of object it is, the mouse changes so that you can place it on the report.

**Figure 2-8. The Insert toolbar**

The second method of adding an object to a report is using the Insert menu. Click on the Insert menu at the top of the program and it lists all of the objects that can be added. It works the same as the toolbar: click on the object to insert and move the mouse to where the object should be placed.

**Figure 2-9. The Insert menu option.**

A third method is to right-click on a report and the pop-up menu gives you a few insert options. However, this menu only lets you insert text objects, a cross-tab or a chart. Its uses are limited and I personally find myself relying on the Insert toolbar most of the time.

There are a lot of different objects that can be used on a report and there are many ways to use them. Most people learn best by example, so let's create a report that uses all the objects and shows the different ways they can be used. What we're going to do is create a report "sandbox." I call it a sandbox because we're just going to play around with the different objects and see what happens. It's like being a kid, where you just want to throw all your toys in it and get messy. We're not going to worry about making things look pretty right now. We just want to see how everything works.[8]

The first thing to do is create the "sandbox" that we'll be working in. We'll create a blank report that uses the Employee table as its data source. For right now, we won't even add any fields to the report. We just want them to be available when we need them.

1. Go to the Crystal Reports Start Page and click on the Blank Report option under the New Reports heading. This opens the Database Expert dialog box.

2. In the Database Expert dialog box, open the Create New Connection category and select the Access/Excel (DAO) option. This opens the Access/Excel (DAO) dialog box.

3. Click on the button to the right of the Database Name input box and navigate to the Xtreme.mdb database. The default installation folder is

   C:\Program Files\Business Objects\Crystal Reports 11\Samples\en \Databases\Xtreme.mdb.

4. Click the Finish button to save the database connection.

5. Open the Tables category and double-click the Employee table. This adds the Employee table to the Selected Tables list on the right.

6. Click the OK button to accept the changes.

7. Click the menu options File > Save As and enter the filename **Sandbox.rpt**. Click the Save button.

You now have a blank report that uses the Employee table as its data source. If you look in the Field Explorer window and click on the Database Fields category, you should see the Employee table listed. Let's play!

## The Text Object

The text object is used to display text, database fields, and special report fields. Each text object can display one of these or a combination of all three. After adding a text object to the report, you have to enter the text to display. If you want to go back and edit the text, double-click on it.

## Tutorial 2-1. Formatting Text Objects

This tutorial demonstrates various formatting properties of the text object. Over the next few pages, you'll add text objects to the Sandbox.rpt report and see how different formatting options affect the output.

---

[8] Don't worry, after this chapter we'll go back to being "professional" and getting some serious work done. ☺

1.  Add a text object to the report by right-clicking anywhere on the report and selecting Insert Text Object. You can also click on the menu option Insert > Text Object. This changes the mouse to a crosshair.

2.  Move the mouse to where you want the top left corner of the text object to be. I'm going to place my text object in the Report Header section, but you can add yours wherever you like.

3.  Click on the mouse button and hold it down to expand the text object to the size you want it. Let go of the mouse to finish. This places the cursor in the text object so you can type something.

4.  Type whatever you like in the text object. In my report I entered "This is a text object." Remember, we are just playing around here so don't stress out over what you put in the text object. Hopefully you are more creative than I am!

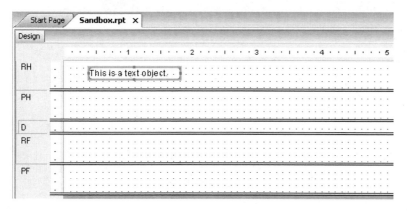

## Using Fonts and Borders

This text object isn't very exciting, so let's spruce it up a bit! The most obvious thing you can do with text is change the font. Right-click on the text object and select Format Text. This opens the Format Editor. There are five formatting tabs here, but we'll just look at the Font tab for now. The other tabs are discussed soon.

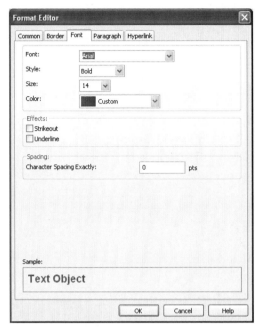

**Figure 2-10. Font properties on the Format Editor dialog box.**

The Font tab is pretty simple to understand. The top section lets you change the font, the style (regular, bold, italic), the font size and the color. The other sections let you set effects like strikeout and underline. You can also set the spacing between each character. I'm going to make my text a little more interesting.

1. Right-click on the text object with the mouse and select Format Field. This opens the Format Editor dialog box.

2. Click on the Font tab.

3. Set the font to Comic Sans MS, the size to 30 and enable strikeout. At the bottom of this dialog box is a preview of the changes.

4. Feel free to experiment making any more changes you wish. Click the OK button when you are finished and want to see it on the report.

 The Color property has a color scale to specify a custom color. A new feature of Crystal Reports XI R2 is that it automatically saves any custom colors you create. When you open a new report, it shows all custom colors created on previous reports.

The Border tab of the Format Editor adds a border around the text object, changes the border style (single, double, dashed, dotted), and sets the color. It also adds effects like a drop shadow or a background color.

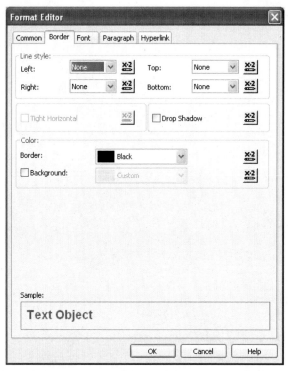

**Figure 2-11. Border properties on the Format Editor dialog box.**

Let's create a new text object and format it to be inverse.

1.  Create another text object (displaying any text you want) and open the Format Editor dialog box using the steps shown earlier.

2.  Click the Border tab.

3.  Click the Background option to select it and change the background color to Blue. Since the background is blue and the text is black, it will be difficult to read.

3.  Go to the Font tab and set the color of the text to White. Also set the style to Bold so that it stands out more. Click the OK button to save your changes. If you click on the Preview button your report might look similar to mine.

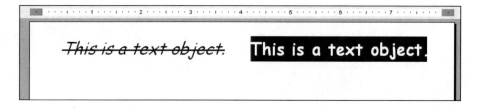

| Tip |
| --- |

Financial reports use border formatting to give emphasis to certain types of numbers. The most common being sub-totals and grand totals. Sub-totals frequently display a single line below the number. Grand totals will have a single line above the number and a double-line below the number to make it stand out more.

Even though it's easy to open the Format Editor dialog box to change the font and borders, it's much easier to use the Formatting toolbar. Look at the top of the screen and it should be the second toolbar below the menu items (assuming you haven't moved your toolbars around).

The first few items set the font and the font size. The next few buttons change the style. After that you can change the alignment, color, borders, etc. Just highlight the text you want to format and click on the button. Although not every formatting option is on this toolbar, the most common ones are there.

## Rotating Text

Crystal Reports has another trick up its sleeve. Text can be rotated vertically. You can rotate it either 90 or 270 degrees. Go to the Format Editor again and on the Common tab you'll see the Text Rotation property in the middle. It's set to zero by default (horizontal).

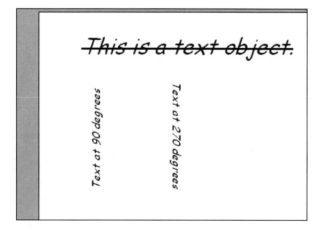

## Formatting Paragraphs

The text objects we've created so far only display one line of text. But some formatting options are designed to display text in paragraph format. But first you have to make the text object large enough to display multiple lines. Select the text object and drag its corners to make the text object taller. The Paragraph tab from the Format Editor dialog box is shown in Figure 2-12.

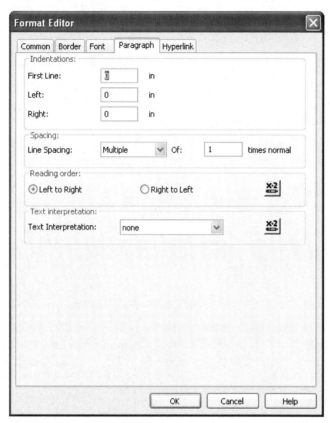

**Figure 2-12. Paragraph properties on the Format Editor dialog box.**

The top portion has the paragraph indentation properties for the first line and left and right margins. It offsets the first line from the remaining text. The other options control the line spacing and the alignment.

If you have to print a lot of text in one area, some parts of the text might need to be formatted differently than the rest. For example, you might want to underline individual words to signify importance. Rather than format a bunch of text objects and line them up side by side, Crystal Reports supports RTF (Rich Text Format) output. This means that a single text object can have multiple formats applied to different parts of the text. To do so, type in all the text as you normally would. Then go back and highlight just the text that needs special formatting. Click the appropriate button on the Format toolbar and it gets applied to the highlighted text. Let's try another example.

# Tutorial 2-2. Applying Multiple Formatting Properties

1. Add a new text object anywhere on the report and make it tall enough to show a few lines of text. But don't make it too long.

2. Enter some text to fill up the text object. Notice how the cursor automatically moves to the next line when it gets to the edge of the box.

3. Right-click on the text object and select Format Text. Click on the Paragraph tab.

   We want the first line to be indented and the margins to be offset from the border of the text object.

4. Enter 0.25 for the First Line property. Enter 0.05 for both the Left and Right properties.

5. Click the OK button. Notice how much nicer it looks.

6. Let's change some of the formatting within the text. Double-click inside the text object to put it in edit mode. Highlight one of the words and make it bold. Highlight another word and make it underlined. Your paragraph might look similar to mine.

> This is the start of a new paragraph. Sometimes when I'm <u>bored</u> I just sit at the keyboard and type in meaningless sentences for **hours** and **hours**. *Zzzzzz*

The benefit of learning how to format text objects is that the same formatting options are available for many of the objects on a report. For example, the next section discusses the field object and it can be formatted just like text objects.

If you want to change the formatting within strings, see the section Manipulating Strings in Chapter 6.

## *Field Objects*

The typical field object displays data from a table or a formula. Some other fields in the Field Explorer are formulas, parameters, and special fields. Special fields are discussed later in this chapter and the other fields types are discussed in their appropriate chapters.

The previous tutorials demonstrated how to use different formatting properties within a single text object. Another interesting aspect of the text object is that you can embed field objects within text objects. The benefit is that the spacing between fields is automatically adjusted and extra space is eliminated. Let's look at an example of an employee's address where the city, state and zip code are placed next to each other using text objects. Figure 2-13 shows the address fields adjacent to each other in the Details section. Figure 2-14 shows what they look like in Preview mode.

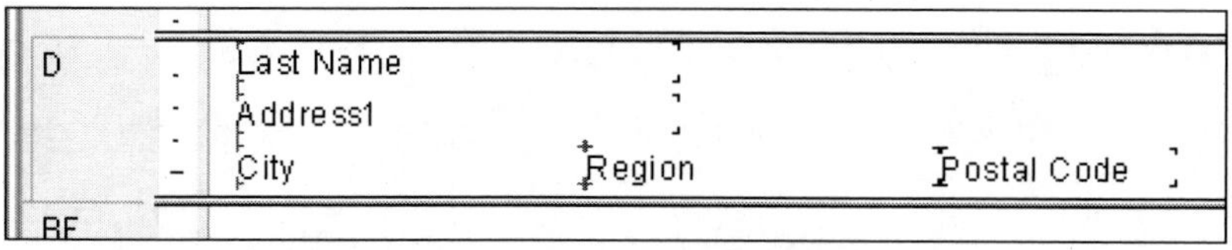

| | | |
|---|---|---|
| D | Last Name | |
| | Address1 | |
| | City | Region          Postal Code |

**Figure 2-13. Addresses in the designer.**

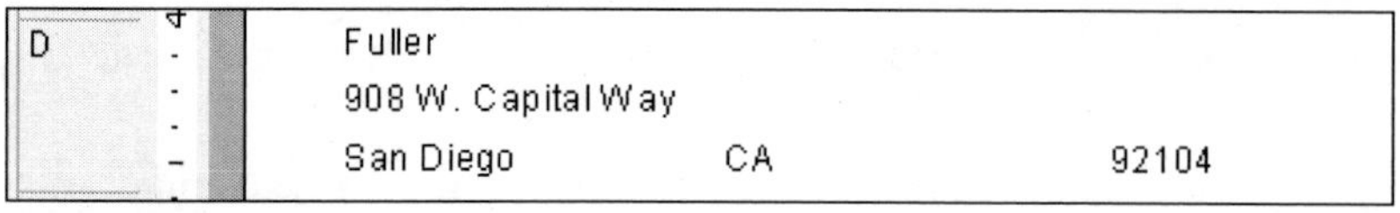

| | |
|---|---|
| D | Fuller |
| | 908 W. Capital Way |
| | San Diego          CA          92104 |

**Figure 2-14. Addresses in preview mode.**

Notice in the first figure that when the fields are placed next to each other in the Details section that each field has to be large enough to accommodate the maximum amount of characters. If the field is too small then part of the data will be cut off. As you can see in the second figure, using text objects results in the address fields being spaced too far apart.

The way to solve this problem is to embed the fields in a text object. Text objects are flexible because not only can you type text in them, but you can put fields into a text object as well.[9] This squeezes all the fields together so that they are adjacent to each other with no extra space between them. You can also type regular text between the fields and they all fit accordingly. This is useful when writing form letters where there are large paragraphs of standard text and you want to insert a field into certain sections (e.g. the person's name or something they purchased from you). And lastly, we saw in the previous tutorial that the fields within a text object can each have their own formatting.

When you drag the database field into the text object, the mouse changes to a blinking cursor to show you where the field will be inserted. Look at the next figure to see how a single text object uses all three address fields and inserts a comma after the city. The figure after that shows how much better it looks in Preview mode.

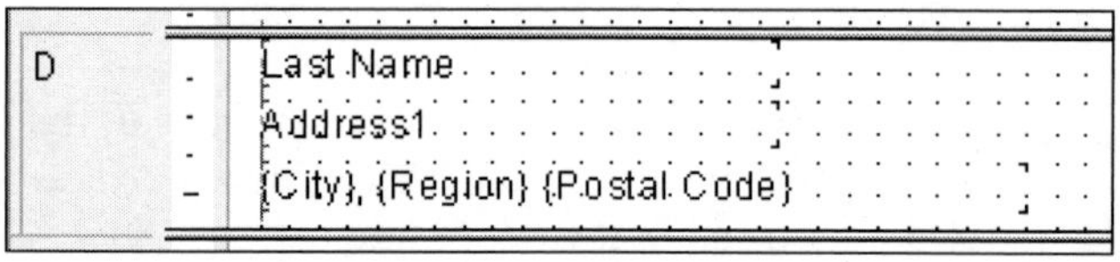

| | |
|---|---|
| D | Last Name. . . . . . . . . . . . . . . |
| | Address1. . . . . . . . . . . . . . . |
| | {City}, {Region} {Postal Code} . . . . . . . |

**Figure 2-15. Embedded fields in the text object.**

---

[9] This includes any of the fields listed in the Field Explorer window.

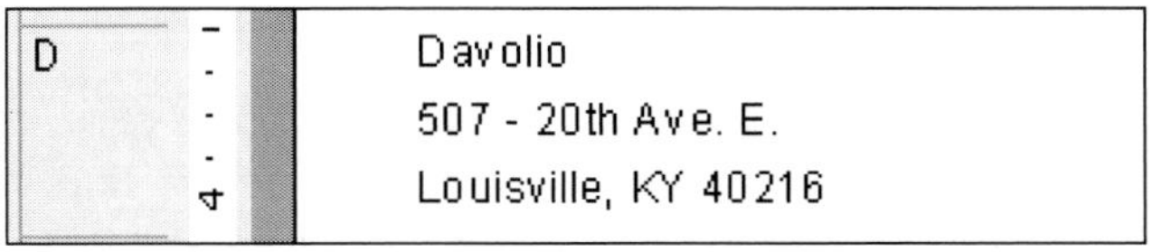

```
D          -            Davolio
           :            507 - 20th Ave. E.
           ·
           :            Louisville, KY 40216
           ₄
```

**Figure 2-16. Embedded fields in preview mode.**

| Tip |
| --- |

A bit of caution should be exercised when embedding database fields into text objects. If this is very large report and the text object is printed repeatedly, this can slow down performance. Instead of embedding fields into the text object, create a formula that concatenates the fields together and returns a single string.[10] This decreases report processing time. The only drawback to using a formula for concatenating fields is that you can't use the Format toolbar to apply special formatting to individual parts of the string. The entire string is uses the same formatting properties. Luckily, in Chapter 6 you'll learn a trick that uses HTML to fix this problem.

## Fields that Can Grow

When working with database fields, it's common to show fields that display a large amount of data. For example, an inventory table can have a Description field that stores a lot of data. Depending upon the inventory item, some descriptions will be short and other will be long. When you add the Description field to the report, you want to make it tall enough to display multiple lines of information, but this will leave a lot of empty space when the descriptions are short. The way to solve this problem is to make the field only one line tall and enable the Can Grow option. The Can Grow option lets the field expand to as many lines as necessary so that the full field is displayed. The Can Grow option is located on the Common tab of the Format Editor.

| Note |
| --- |

Fields can only grow taller. They won't grow wider.

The next two figures illustrate printing a person's first and last name as well as some notes about the person. The first figure shows the fields in the Design window. Notice that the Notes field is only one line tall. Although you can't see it here, the Can Grow option has been enabled for the Notes field. The second figure shows the preview of the report. Notice that the Notes field changes size based upon how much data it has to display.

---

[10] Concatenating strings is covered in Chapter 6.

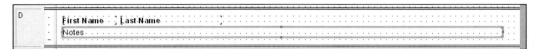

**Figure 2-17. A Can Grow text object in design mode.**

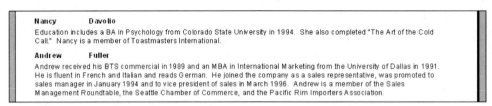

**Figure 2-18. The text object displaying multiple lines of text.**

Sometimes there can be so much data in a field that displaying it causes the report to look unusual and could even span over multiple pages. As a precaution to make sure the field doesn't grow too large, there is a property to set the maximum number of lines. It is also on the Common tab of the Format Editor dialog box and is located next to the Can Grow checkbox. By default, the number of lines is set to zero which effectively disables the option and there is no limit. If you want to set a limit, override the zero with the maximum number of lines. The field height will not exceed the number specified.

One thing to be aware of, is that if another field is located below a field that has the Can Grow option enabled, it's possible that the top field will expand over the field below it and overwrite it. There are two ways to prevent this. The first way is to make sure that no fields are close enough to the Can Grow field that they might be overwritten. This isn't a very practical solution because it requires leaving a lot of blank space between the fields. The second option is to put the Can Grow field at the bottom of the section, so as the field grows the section enlarges to compensate for the extra lines needed. The data in one section won't overwrite the data in the next section. If it isn't practical to put the Can Grow field at the bottom of the section, insert another section below the current section and put the extra fields in the second section. This trick is discussed in Chapter 8.

One final feature of the text object is that you can import an external text file into it. Double-click on the text object to go into edit mode. Then right-click on it and select Insert from File. This opens the File Open dialog box that lets you select the text file. The file's content gets inserted into the text object at the cursor location.

## Special Formatting

There are two types of data that have their own formatting built-in: Rich Text Format (RTF) and HTML. Crystal Reports supports displaying both types of data. The rule is that the object must be a string or memo field or formula. If these conditions are met, when you go to the Format Editor and look at the Paragraph tab, a new item is listed: Text Interpretation. This is a drop-down box that lets you select if the field should be displayed as an RTF field or as HTML. If you select either one of these items then Crystal Reports will convert the text to match the expected output.

## Formatting Strings

The tutorials earlier in the chapter showed you different ways to format a text object. But it didn't discuss every formatting option available. The Format Editor has many more options for modifying the way string based report objects appear. The different formatting options are available for textbox objects as well as formulas, report fields, and special fields.

The first tab of the Format Editor dialog box is the Common tab (see Figure 2-19).

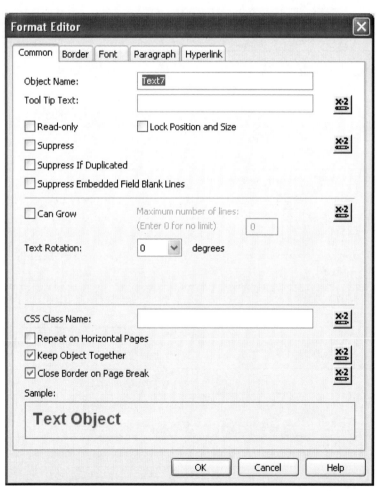

**Figure 2-19. The Common tab of the Format Editor dialog box.**

If you look to the right of many of the properties, there is a button next to it. This is the Formula button. It lets you apply custom formatting to the object using formulas. This is discussed in more detail in Chapter 5.

The properties shown on this tab are common to most of the report objects available. These properties are described in Table 2-3.

**Table 2-3. Properties of the Common Tab**

| Property | Description |
| --- | --- |
| Tool Tip Text | Use the formula editor to set a string that is displayed when the mouse hovers above the field. |
| Read-only | Prevent the object from having any additional formatting changes made to it. |
| Lock Position and Size | Prevent the object from being moved or resized. |
| Suppress | Hide the object. |
| Suppress If Duplicated | Hide the object if it had the same value in the prior record. |
| Suppress Embedded Field Blank Lines | Suppress fields with no data so that a blank line doesn't appear. |
| Can Grow | Allow the field to expand if the object isn't big enough to hold the data. The field will only expand vertically and result in the height increasing. The width does not expand. |
| Text Rotation | Rotate the text to a specified angle. A value of 0 is the default and the text displays horizontally. A value of 90 rotates it vertically upward. A value of 270 rotates it vertically downward. |
| CSS Class Name | If you use a CSS file to format report objects, enter the CSS class name that should be applied to the object.[11] |
| Repeat on Horizontal Pages | Repeats an object when a cross-tab expands horizontally across multiple pages. |
| Keep Object Together | Do not let the object cross over into another page. |
| Close Border on Page Breaks | If a field has a border, and the field extends to another page, then this will close the border on the first page. |

---

[11] CSS files are used for formatting HTML web pages. The specifics of creating a CSS file is not within the scope of this book. You can find reference books at your local bookstore in the Internet section.

# Adding Hyperlinks

Crystal Reports lets you assign fields to be hyperlinks to other sources of information. The most common example is a hyperlink to an external website. But, you can also link to an email address or a file. Clicking on the Hyperlink tab of the Format Editor, shown in Figure 2-20, lets you makes these settings.

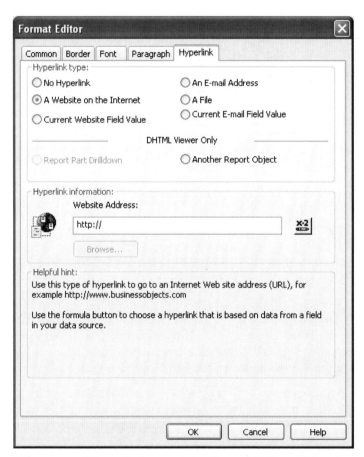

**Figure 2-20. Hyperlink tab of the Format Editor dialog box.**

The top section of the Hyperlink tab is where you set the hyperlink type. After specifying the link type, the Hyperlink Information section in the middle changes according to the link type. It lets you enter a website's URL, a file name[12] or an email address. If the link information is based upon the underlying data, click the Formula button to create a formula which returns the appropriate link information. For example, an international sales report could have a link to a website that shows the current monetary exchange rate

---

[12] This can be the name of a data file or an executable program.

for each currency. The formula can create a dynamic link based upon the country being printed. As another example, you can have a hyperlink on the company name that links to the corporate headquarter's location on the MapQuest.com site.

Many databases store company website URLs and employee email addresses within the table. When this is the case, you can select one of the two options, Current Website Field Value or Current E-mail Field Value. This tells Crystal Reports that the field's current value is also the link information.

If the hyperlink opens a file, you have the option to give the user a confirmation prompt before opening it. This lets them change their mind if they decide that the file might take too long to open. The setting that lets the user confirm whether they want to open the file or not is found by selecting the menu items File > Report Options. The setting is called Prompt For Hyperlinks. It is selected by default. Uncheck it if you want the file to open with no user confirmation.

When you are previewing the report and you want to click on the field to open the hyperlink, the report might act a little funny. As you move the mouse around and it passes over a field with a hyperlink, the icon turns into a hand with an extended finger. This lets you know that you can click on the field to jump to the hyperlink.

Link
http://www.google.com
http://www.yahoo.com

After you view the hyperlink and go back to the report, you can't click on that same field to open a different hyperlink. After the first click, Crystal Reports thinks you are trying to edit the object instead of open the hyperlink. What you have to do is right-click on the field and choose Go To Hyperlink on the pop-up menu.

The problem is that Crystal Reports doesn't let you jump to a hyperlink for objects that are already selected. After you click on it the first time, you can't do it again unless you click somewhere else on the report. This can also be observed by going to the Design tab and selecting a field that has a hyperlink. Then, click on the Preview tab and try to click on that field to go to the hyperlink. It won't let you do it because it was already selected the first time from the Design tab. Fortunately, this isn't a major cause for concern. It's just an interesting behavior that might cause you confusion if you aren't aware of it.

**Tip**

You can go directly to the Hyperlink tab for the currently selected report object by selecting the menu options Format > Hyperlink or by clicking on the Hyperlink button.

# Formatting Numbers

Numbers are very similar to regular text objects in that they display characters on the report. The difference being that they can only display numeric characters. Thus, while they have similar formatting features (fonts, borders, etc.), they also have their own unique formatting settings (currency, number of significant digits, etc.).

The Number tab of the Format Editor, shown in Figure 2-21, displays the most common ways of formatting numbers in the Style list.

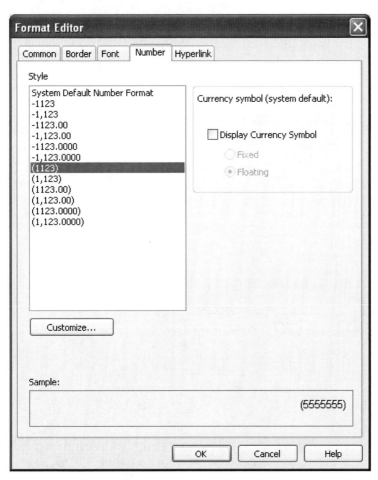

**Figure 2-21. Formatting number with the Number tab.**

To format a number, look in the Style list and find the format you want and click on it. To the right of the Style list is the Display Currency Symbol option. Check it to format the number as currency. You can make the currency symbol fixed (it always stays along the outermost edge of the field) or floating (it stays directly next to the numbers).

At the bottom of the Numbers tab is the Customize button. Click this button when you need more precise formatting than what is available in the Styles list. Clicking on the Customize button opens the Custom Style dialog box shown in Figure 2-22.

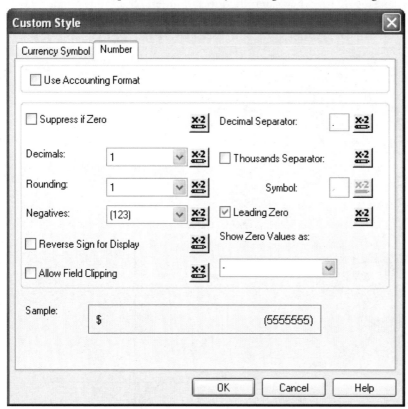

**Figure 2-22. Custom Style dialog box for formatting numbers.**

The Custom Style dialog box initially opens at the Number tab. It has a lot of information on it, but it is pretty simple nonetheless. You can set how many decimals to display, what the decimal separate should be, whether it should be suppressed when zero, etc. As you make changes to the number format, a preview of what the number looks like is shown at the bottom.

An important setting is the Allow Field Clipping checkbox. This tells Crystal Reports to chop off the leftmost digits if the number is too big to be displayed within the size of the report object. Unfortunately, this is a very dangerous setting because you can lose significant digits and not realize it. For example, the number "599,000" could be displayed as "9,000". When Allow Field Clipping setting is unchecked and the number is too big to fit on the report, Crystal Reports displays "######" instead. This alerts you to the fact that you need to resize the report object so that it is large enough to display the full number.

The Custom Style dialog box also has a Currency Symbol tab. It is simple to use as well. It lets you set the character to use for the currency symbol, specify where it is located and set whether it is fixed or floating.

## The Line Object

The line object does exactly what you expect. It draws a line. There isn't a whole lot you can do with it except change the color, the width and its style (single line, dashed line, etc.) It does have one interesting feature that solves a common problem with line objects. There are times when the detail section has a field that can grow down the report and make the section longer than expected. Since a line has a certain length, when the text object grows the line stays the same size. If you want the line to grow and be unbroken across each row, set the property ExtendToBottomOfSection to True. This ensures that no matter how tall the section grows, the end point will extend to the bottom of the section. If it is a horizontal line, this always moves it to the bottom of the section.

### Note

The line object can only display horizontal and vertical lines. It can't print lines at an angle.

## The Box Object

Like the line object, the box object isn't too exciting. You can change its color, width and style. One nice feature about it is that you can change its properties to round the edges. Depending on how you set the properties, you can make it elliptical or even turn it into a circle. The properties that affect this are CornerEllipseHeight and CornerEllipseWidth. Rather than modify these directly, it is much easier to use the Format dialog box. The second tab is the Rounding tab. It has a picture of what the box looks like and below it is a slider. As you move the slider from the left to the right, it increases the curvature of the edges. When the slider is at the far right, the box is a circle. Once you click OK, the dialog box automatically sets the corner ellipse properties for you.

## The Picture Object

The picture object is used for displaying the following image file formats: BMP, JPG, TIFF, and PNG. It doesn't display GIF files. The formatting options are similar to the other controls in that it has the tabs Common and Border with similar functionality. The Picture tab, shown in Figure 2-23, lets you resize, scale and crop the image. If at any point you feel that you resized or scaled it improperly and you want to restore it back to its original size, click the Reset button located in the middle of the dialog box.

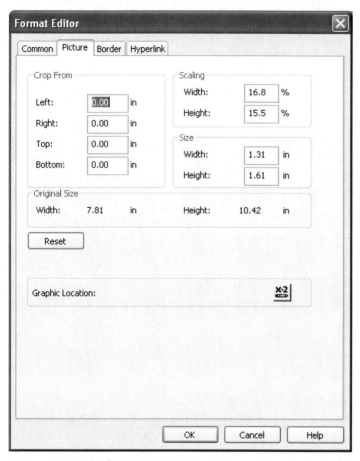

**Figure 2-23. The Picture tab of the Picture object's dialog box.**

Dynamic graphics are discussed in Chapter 8, Advanced Formatting Techniques.

## Printing Wingding Fonts

Don't think that printing graphics involves just displaying JPG and BMP files. You can also get some interesting results using the non-standard fonts. One font in particular that is very useful is the Wingdings font. You can add special symbols such as checkboxes, arrows, folder, etc. For example, open the Windows Character Map application and select the Wingdings font from the dropdown list. You'll see the characters in Figure 2-24.

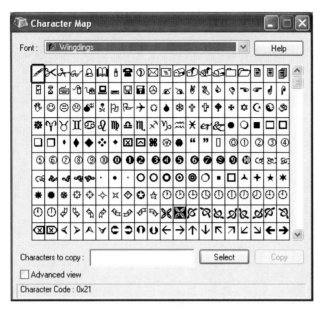

Figure 2-24. A sample of the Wingdings characters

## Tutorial 2-3. Using Wingdings Font to Display a Book Icon.

Let's walk through a tutorial of how to add a picture of a book to the report.

1. Open the Character Map application on Windows XP by selecting Start > All Programs > Accessories > System Tools > Character Map.

2. Choose the font Wingdings.

   Look at the first row and find the picture of a book. It should be the sixth picture on the left.

3. Double-Click on the book picture (that makes it appear at the bottom) and click the Copy button. It has been saved to the Clipboard's memory.

4. Go into the Crystal Reports' designer and add a new text object. This puts you in edit mode.

5. Press Crtl-V to paste the picture into the text box. You should see the picture of the book in the text object.

In Chapter 5 we'll walk through a tutorial that uses formulas to display checkboxes.

## The Chart Object

The Chart object lets you add a chart to your report. There are a variety of options to choose from so that you can customize it however you need. There is so much to cover with this object that it was given a separate chapter. See Chapter 12 for more information.

# The Special Field Object

The special field object is used for printing report-related information. For example, it can print the current page number or the total number of pages. Since there isn't a way for you to calculate this information yourself, this field was created as a catch-all for all the miscellaneous types of report information that you need. Table 2-4 lists the available fields and what they mean. These fields are treated the same as a database field object. They can be added to the report by themselves, or included in a textbox object. They also have all the same formatting options that were described in the Formatting Strings section.

**Table 2-4. Special fields described.**

| Special Field | Description |
| --- | --- |
| Data Date | The date when the report was last refreshed. |
| Data Time | The time when the report was last refreshed. |
| File Author | The file author that is stored with the report. |
| File Creation Date | The date when the report was created. |
| File Path and Name | The report's file name. |
| Group Number | The current group number. |
| Group Selection | The group selection formula. |
| Modification Date | The date the report was last modified. |
| Modification Time | The time the report was last modified. |
| Page N of M | Prints "Page X of Y". |
| Page Number | The current page number. |
| Print Date | The date the report was printed. |
| Print Time | The time the report was printed. |
| Record Number | The current record number. |
| Record Selection | The record selection formula. |
| Report Comments | The report comments that are stored with the report. |
| Report Title | The report title. |
| Total Page Count | The total number of pages. |

## The OLE Object

The OLE object lets you embed objects inside of your report. Some examples are embedding Word documents or Excel spreadsheets.

# Moving and Sizing Report Objects

Even though we all wish our reports were perfect the first time through, this is rarely the case. After adding objects to the designer, you frequently need to reposition objects and change their size. An earlier section of this chapter showed you how to add report objects to the designer. This section shows you how to manage objects within the report designer.

If you have an existing control that you want to reuse so that you don't have to redo its formatting, you can click on it and copy and paste it. This creates a copy that is attached to your pointer and will move around as you move your mouse. When you have it positioned properly, click the mouse button to drop it there. You can also select multiple objects for copy and paste.

Selecting multiple objects is done by holding down the control or shift key and clicking on the individual controls. You can also draw a temporary window on the report and any controls that are included in the window get selected. Do this by holding down the mouse button and moving the mouse to enlarge the box. Let go of the mouse when the box is large enough and any object that is fully or partially within the box gets selected.

There is a strange behavior to be aware of when selecting multiple objects using the window technique. You can't draw a window if another object is already selected. You have to first click on an empty portion of the report designer to unselect the current object and then you can draw the box. For example, assume that you selected a text object and then you decided that you really wanted to select multiple text objects instead. After clicking the first text object, you click elsewhere on the report and attempt to draw a window. Unfortunately, nothing happens. It only results in the textbox getting unselected. You need to click the mouse a second time to start drawing the window.

| Tip |
| --- |

Certain objects can be more difficult to select than others. For example, some reports have so many objects in a section that the objects overlap or they are not currently visible in the designer. Other objects like the line object are simply hard to click on because they are so small. You can select all the objects in a section by right-clicking in gray area to the left of the section and choosing Select All Objects. This highlights every object in the section, including the ones you can barely see. This also makes it easy to move all the objects from one section to another section. A second way of highlighting a small object is to click on it in the Report Explorer window. This automatically selects it in the

Design tab. You can also hold down the shift key in the Report Explorer window to select multiple objects.

Resizing a control is done by first clicking on it to highlight it. This creates little dark squares in the corners of the object and in the middle sections. These are sizing handles that can be clicked on and dragged around. Position the mouse over one of the sizing handles and click the mouse button to drag the handle to the new position. Let go of the mouse button to release the handles when you are finished.

When resizing multiple objects, the sizing handles only appear on the last object selected. As you resize the last control, its new size dynamically changes as you move your mouse. The other controls will not change until you release the mouse button. At that point they all "snap" into their new shape.

There are times when you have a lot of different sized objects on the report and you need them all to be the same size. This often happens after using the report wizard to create the first draft of a report and it puts the objects on the report for you. You have to go back and adjust their position and size to make the report look they way you want it to. You can have Crystal Reports adjust the size and position of all the objects to be consistent with each other. Do this by selecting all the objects and then right-clicking on the main one and select the Size menu option. From there you can choose Same Width, Same Height, or Same Size. The objects will be resized to match the object that you right-clicked on.

When moving objects around the report, it can be helpful to display the grid lines. This makes it easier to line up objects with each other. Turning the grid lines feature on or off is controlled by changing the designer properties. Right click on the report and select Designer > Default Settings.

An alternative for doing precise adjustments to an object is to use the keyboard instead of the mouse. Due to the design of a mouse ball, it can sometimes be hard to move the mouse a very small distance without it jumping around a bit.[13] Instead of using the mouse, use the keyboard to change an object. By pressing down the Control key and hitting the arrow buttons, the object moves in the direction of the arrow. Pressing down the Shift key and hitting the arrow buttons adjusts the right side and bottom edge of the object. You can make the object larger or smaller in all directions.

When placing objects that should all line up either horizontally or vertically, it can be difficult to make sure they all line up along the exact same axis. Crystal Reports allows very precise placement of objects and this means that objects can easily be one or two pixels off. You have to tweak them with your mouse to make sure they line up exactly. The Snap To Grid option makes this much easier because it makes sure that as long as you come close to lining one object next to the other, they will both land on the same grid marker.

---

[13] This only applies if the Snap To Gridlines option is disabled because otherwise the mouse can move easily between gridlines.

If you are working on a report with multiple sections, lining up columns can be trickier even with the help of the grid points. It gets harder to judge the exact location and width of different objects if they are in different sections of the page. Crystal Reports gives you a few different ways to help make sure that the appropriate objects are lined up correctly. They are the alignment markers and the functions on the alignment menu.

Alignment markers are temporary transparent lines that extend both horizontally and vertically from the edges of the object to the page perimeter. They make it easy to see which objects have the same alignment. They only appear when you click on the object and hold down the mouse. Once you release the mouse, the lines disappear. You can even move the object around and the lines stay visible until you release the mouse. This is probably best understood with a picture. See Figure 2-25.

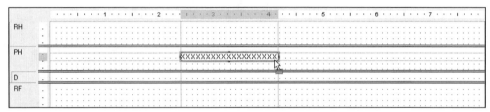

**Figure 2-25. Alignment markers make it easy to align objects.**

The object in Figure 2-25 has the border emphasized and each border has thinner lines extending past it in every direction. This makes it easy to see exactly where the object is along the ruler markers, but you can also see which objects have the same alignment. It becomes easy to add an object to the Page Header section and position it so that it is in exact alignment with an object in the Page Footer.

Even though the alignment markers are helpful when adding new objects to the report, they are only really useful for working with single objects. Sometimes you have a report with multiple objects along the same column and you need a quick way to get them all aligned. The Alignment menu options give you many options for multiple aligning objects. You can select multiple objects and set them to all line up along their right edge, their left edge, the top border and many other ways.

To align multiple objects, select the group of objects that need to be aligned. Once the objects are selected, right-click above one of the objects and select the menu option Align. This presents a sub-menu of the different ways to align the objects. There are eight ways in total and each is self-explanatory.

A key part to remember is that the "anchor" object is the object that the mouse was hovering over when you did the right-click. What this means is that when you tell the program to align all the objects along the Top for example, the program needs to know which object should be used to define where the top is. The "anchor" object is the object that you right-clicked on after they were all selected. If you make the mistake of right-clicking on an area of the report where there isn't an object, the grouping is reset and you have to start all over again. So be careful where you right-click!

## Moving objects with Guidelines

The previous section discussed how to add objects so that they lined up with existing objects. But it didn't cover how to move multiple objects so that they stay lined up. This is where Guidelines are used.

Guidelines create an anchor for attaching multiple objects. The benefit is that anytime you move the guideline, all the objects attached to it move also. If you have a multi-column report with many columns and you have to insert a new column, it can be difficult to move all objects over to make room for the new column. But if you anchor all the objects in a column to a guideline, you can move the guideline and all the objects move with it. You can move entire rows and columns of fields, trouble-free, without losing alignment.

Guidelines are inserted into a report by clicking on either of the rulers. A small red colored marker appears (similar to the letter T turned on its side), to represent where the guideline is. You can see in Figure 2-26 that there is an example of a guideline on each ruler. If you added guidelines to your report and they aren't visible, select the menu option File > Options > Layout Tab to check that the Guidelines option is enabled.

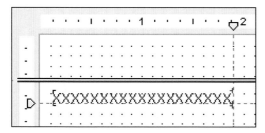

**Figure 2-26. Guidelines on the ruler.**

Once a guideline has been added, you can attach objects to it. Drag an object so that one of the edges lines up with the guideline. This automatically attaches the object. Objects can also be attached at the center points. A small red marker appears in the corners of the object along the edge that is attached. This makes it easy to see which objects are attached to which guidelines. Do this for all the objects in a row or column that need to stay aligned while being moved around.

Text objects behave a little differently than other report objects. Most report objects attach along the border of the object. But a single-line text object attaches to the guideline along the base of the text, not the bottom edge of the object. This guarantees that all the text on a line lines up correctly even when the fonts are different. A multi-line text object can either use the bottom edge of the object or the base of the first line of text.

### Best Of The Forum

**Question:** At the bottom of a page I have multi-line text objects that can grow. I want to align them so that the bottom of each text object is aligned with each other. Right now when they grow they move down the page and the bottoms are at different places. How do I align the bottoms?

**Answer:** You are effectively trying to change the Can Grow option so that it "grows upward" on the page instead of growing down the length of the page. This is not possible.

Be careful when moving guidelines to make sure that your mouse stays within the ruler's region. Personally, I have a very bad habit of accidentally moving my mouse out of the ruler region and this makes the guideline disappear. Hence, if you deliberately want to remove a guideline then click on it and drag it off the ruler. If you did this by mistake, press Ctrl-Z to undo the action and the guideline appears back on the ruler.

One thing to be aware of is that even though you can move a guideline and it takes the objects with it, it doesn't work the other way around. You can't move an object that is attached to a guideline and expect the guideline to move with the object. Instead, the object becomes unattached from the guideline and moves around independently. It is no longer anchored to the guideline.

# 3
## Sorting and Grouping

After learning the basics of creating simple reports, you will quickly find yourself developing reports that are more involved then just listing sequential records one by one. For reports that consist of dozens, if not hundreds, of pages, providing a meaningful format that groups the data into logical units goes a long way towards making reports easier to read. Crystal Reports makes this possible by giving you the ability to sort and group data. Grouping reports also gives you the ability to create drill-down reports. This chapter starts out by showing you the simple task of sorting records and then builds on that knowledge by creating groups and customizing them.

## Sorting Records

Being able to sort records in either ascending or descending order is a fundamental reporting skill. Sorting makes it easy for a user to quickly find a particular piece of data buried within a large report. For example, when you use the phone book to look up a phone number, it would take a long time to find a name if they weren't listed in alphabetical order. The same applies for the reports you create. Figure 3-1 shows a report sorted by Order ID.

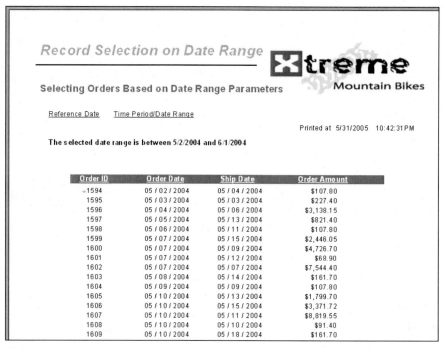

**Figure 3-1. Sorting by Order ID.**

Controlling a report's sort order is done with the Record Sort Expert dialog box. To open this dialog box, either click on the Record Sort Expert button shown in Figure 3-2 or select the menu items Report > Record Sort Expert.

**Figure 3-2. Record Sort Expert button.**

The Record Sort Expert dialog box gives you all the options necessary for selecting the fields to sort and choosing their sort order. It is shown in Figure 3-3.

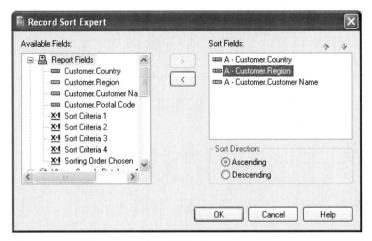

**Figure 3-3. The sort order dialog box.**

On the left side of the dialog box are the available fields. The fields are categorized by which fields and formulas are currently being used on the report (since that is most likely your first choice) and after that are all the available fields in the database.

Reports can be sorted on a single field or on multiple fields. Sorting on multiple fields is only useful when the first sort field has duplicate values in it. To resolve which duplicate should be listed first, the value in the second field is used to resolve the conflict. An example of this type of report is an employee report that sorts by name. The first sort field is the last name. When there are duplicate last names (e.g. Smith), the second sort field, which is the first name, is used to resolve the sort order. When sorting on multiple fields, you have to specify which field gets first priority.

To select a field for sorting, either drag and drop it onto the Sort Fields window on the right or click on the arrow buttons to move it over. The order in which you add the fields determines which one gets priority in the sort order. The first field listed becomes the primary sort field. The next field is the secondary field, and so on. When there are duplicate values in one of the fields, then the next field on the list is used to resolve the conflict. This continues for all the sort fields whenever there are duplicates. If a field has a duplicate value without another field after it, then the one that gets listed first isn't always predictable.

If you find that the fields are not listed in the order you want, you can use the arrows in the top right corner. Click on the field and then click the up or down arrow to change the field's placement in the list.

The bottom of the dialog box is where you establish whether the field is sorted in ascending or descending order. There are two radio buttons that set the sort order and only one can be selected at a time. Since multiple fields can be shown in the Sort Fields list and there is only one place to set the sort order, both radio buttons apply to the currently selected field. To set the sort order of a field, first click on the field you want and then click on the sort order.

Let's look at the example sort order shown in Figure 3-4. The primary sort field is Country. The secondary field is Region and this is followed by the Customer Name.

**Multiple Field Sort**

5/31/2005   10:29:23PM

**Xtreme** Mountain Bikes

**How to do a multiple field sort based on a parameter**

**Sort Order chosen: Country, Region, Postal Code, Customer Name**

| Country | Region | Customer Name | Postal Code |
|---------|--------|---------------|-------------|
| Argentina | Mendoza | Bicicletas Buenos Aires | 6755 56 |
| Aruba | St. George | Aruba Sport | 655456 |
| Australia | New South Wales | Canberra Bikes | 5353 |
| Australia | New South Wales | Down Under Bikes | 2061 |
| Australia | Queensland | Koala Road Bikes | 4600 |
| Australia | Tasmania | Tasmanian Devil Bikes | 0912 |
| Australia | Victoria | Bruce's Bikes | 4774 |
| Australia | Victoria | Kangeroo Trikes | 2155 |
| Australia | Western Australia | Peddles of Perth | 3326 |
| Austria | Salzkammergut | Piccolo | A-5020 |
| Bahamas | New Providence | Beach Cycle and Sport | 5466 |
| Bangladesh | Dhaka | Dhaka Bike Store | 346457 |
| Barbados | Bridgetown | Barbados Sports, Ltd. | 4532 |
| Belgium | Brussels | Belgium Bike Co. | 47899 |
| Bermuda | Pembroke Parish | Royal Cycle | 46557 |
| Bolivia | La Paz | Bicicletas de Montaña La Paz | 4542 |
| Brazil | Belo Horizonte | Brasilia Outdoors | 31015-040 |
| Brazil | Distrito Federal | Brasilia Bikes Inc. | 23293-300 |
| Brazil | Rio de Janeiro | Rio De Janeiro Bikers | 20093-900 |
| Brazil | Rio Grande do Sul | Salvado Bike Store | 90880-390 |
| Brazil | São Paulo | Outdoors Ltda | 04082-001 |
| Brazil | São Paulo | Saveiros SA | 20093-400 |
| British Virgin Islands | Tortola | Paradise Sports | F3R 6T9 |

**Figure 3-4. Sorting records on Country, Region and then Customer Name.**

The report first lists all the countries that start with the letter "A". The country Australia has duplicate values, so the report performs a secondary sort on the Region field. The region New South Wales is duplicated so the final sort order is by Customer Name.

If you later determine that you need to change the sorting order, modify it using the same steps mentioned earlier.

# Grouping Records

When a report has a lot of pages, it is sometimes hard to quickly get a general idea of what the report is telling you. Sorting the data helps you find a specific record, but it doesn't help give you a high-level summary of what the data means. Grouping records lets you summarize data so that the reader gets a quick overview of the report.

Creating groups is one step beyond basic sorting. Groups lets you create categories to visually organize the records. They summarize the data based on critical fields and perform summing operations on the data within each group. If you need to see more information you can explore the detail records that make up the group.

Sorting records is more simplistic than grouping records because sorting simply changes the order that data is listed. It doesn't have any impact on how the report is structured. Grouping is more complex because it creates new sections in the report structure and organizes the data based on the new sections. For every group added to a report there are two sections created: the Group Header and the Group Footer.

The Group Header and Group Footer sections are the dividers between the detail data that is printed within each group. They let you show group specific report fields, formula fields and summary fields to the report. You can also format the fields differently so that they stand out from the detail records. For example, it's common to make fields in the header to be a different font (possibly bold) and in the footer it's common to show sub-totals. The footer is also beneficial because the reader can understand the data by looking at the sub-totals without having to read every line. If you don't need to display the group header or footer, they can be hidden.

## Adding and Customizing Groups

Just like sort fields, multiple fields can also be used for creating groups. Each field is given its own group header and footer. An example of grouping on one field is a sales report that groups the sales people by their territory. If there are a lot of sales people within each territory, then you could add additional groups such as product category and sales manager. Each group added to the report categorizes the data to make it easier to quickly find what you are looking for.

To add a new group to the report, select the menu items Report > Group Expert. This displays the dialog box shown in Figure 3-5.

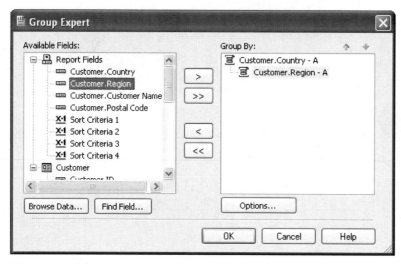

Figure 3-5. The Group Expert dialog box.

You can also show this dialog box by clicking on the Group Expert button on the Experts toolbar.

Figure 3-6. The Group Expert button.

The Group Expert has a lot in common with the Record Sort Expert. The left side shows the fields that are available for grouping and the right side shows the fields that have been selected. Move fields between the two sides by dragging and dropping them or by clicking on the arrow buttons.

The Group Expert has some new features that weren't included in the Record Sort Expert. It lets you preview the current data in a field as well as search for field names within the available fields list. Clicking the Browse Data button at the bottom of the dialog box opens a new dialog box that shows the data for the currently selected field. Scroll through this list to verify that this is the data that you want to group on.

| Tip |
| --- |
| If you have a Memo field in your report, you might notice that it isn't included in the list of available fields for grouping. That's because Crystal Reports doesn't allow creating a group on a Memo field. The same rule applies for sorting records – not allowed for Memo fields. As a workaround, create a formula based on the Memo field and then you can sort and group on the formula field. The formula can return the full Memo field unchanged or it can |

parse part of it if you just want to work with a portion of the data. Although the formula returns the exact same data as the original Memo field, Crystal Reports now lets you sort and group on it.

The Find Field button lets you search for a field in the list of available fields. This is useful for data sources that have many fields and you can't quite remember the name of the field you want. By clicking the Find Field button you can type in part of a field name and it will find the field that matches what you entered.

**Note**

The Find Field button doesn't have a Find Next feature. Once it finds the first field that matches your text, clicking on the Find Field button won't search any further. It just stays on the same field. To make it search the rest of the list, you have to manually click on the following field before clicking the Find Field button again.

## Tutorial 3-1. Creating a grouping report

To practice working with groups, let's modify the Employee List report created in Chapter 1. That report listed each employee on a separate line. We are going to modify the report so that it first groups by the region and then by the city.

1. Open the Employee List report you created in Tutorial 1-1.
2. Select the menu items Report > Group Expert. This opens the Group Expert dialog box.
3. In the Available Fields list click on the Employee_Addresses.Region field and drag it to the Group By list.
4. Click on the Employee_Addresses.City field and drag it to the Group By list.
5. Click the OK button. The dialog box closes and the two groups have been added to the report.
6. In the report designer, move the report object Group #2 Name a little to the right so that it is offset from Group #1 (the Region).
7. Click the OK button to save your changes. Your report's design should look similar to Figure 3-7. The report preview is in Figure 3-8.

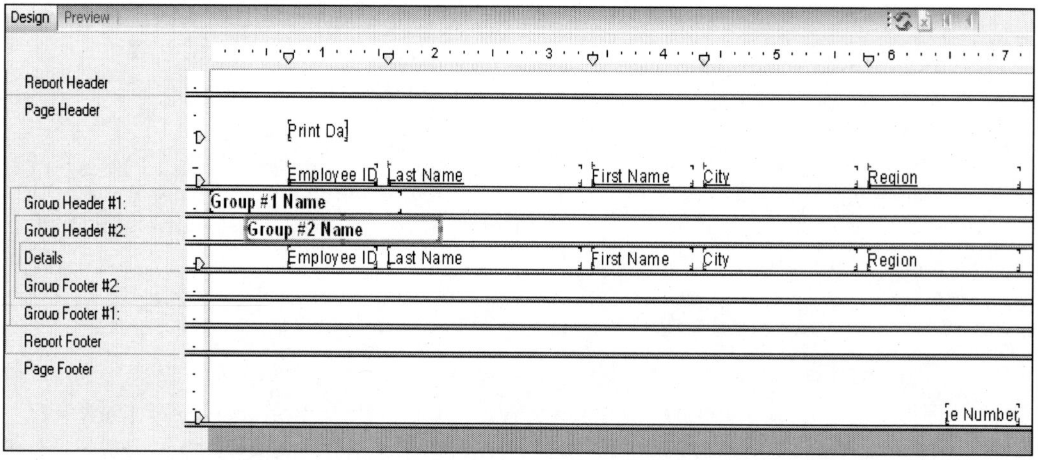


**Figure 3-7. Employee List with groupings.**

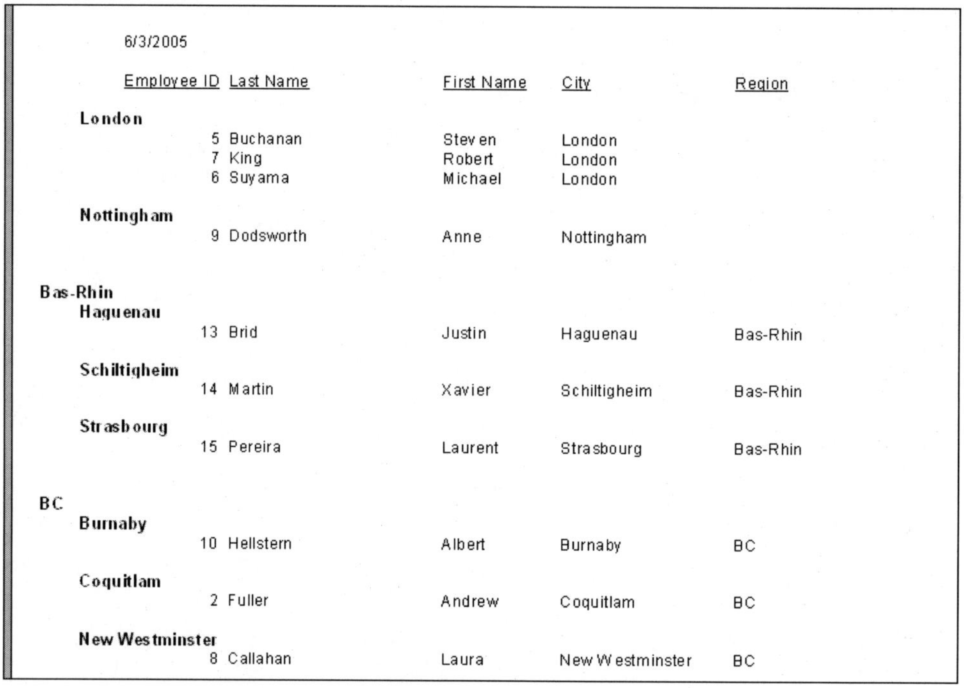

6/3/2005

| | | Employee ID | Last Name | First Name | City | Region |
|---|---|---|---|---|---|---|
| | **London** | | | | | |
| | | 5 | Buchanan | Steven | London | |
| | | 7 | King | Robert | London | |
| | | 6 | Suyama | Michael | London | |
| | **Nottingham** | | | | | |
| | | 9 | Dodsworth | Anne | Nottingham | |
| **Bas-Rhin** | | | | | | |
| | **Haguenau** | | | | | |
| | | 13 | Brid | Justin | Haguenau | Bas-Rhin |
| | **Schiltigheim** | | | | | |
| | | 14 | Martin | Xavier | Schiltigheim | Bas-Rhin |
| | **Strasbourg** | | | | | |
| | | 15 | Pereira | Laurent | Strasbourg | Bas-Rhin |
| **BC** | | | | | | |
| | **Burnaby** | | | | | |
| | | 10 | Hellstern | Albert | Burnaby | BC |
| | **Coquitlam** | | | | | |
| | | 2 | Fuller | Andrew | Coquitlam | BC |
| | **New Westminster** | | | | | |
| | | 8 | Callahan | Laura | New Westminster | BC |

**Figure 3-8. Employee List preview.**

One unusual aspect about this report is that the first few records don't have any data in the Region field and all you see are the two cities listed (London and Nottingham). It would be nice to classify these records so that they are separate from the records that have data in the Region field. Soon we'll look at options for customizing the grouping format as well as fixing problems such as this.

# Navigating Groups

Adding groups to a printed report makes it easier to flip through the report and get a quick overview of the report's information. But the Preview tab makes it even easier to work with groups. To the left of the preview window is the Group Tree window which lets you navigate to each group as well as the sub-groups.

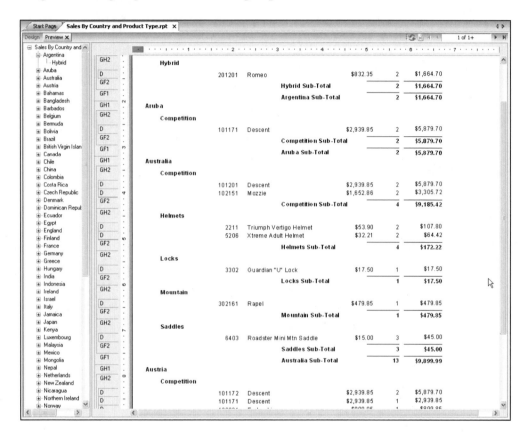

The Group Tree is toggled on and off by selecting View > Group Tree or by clicking on the Toggle Group Tree button on the Standard toolbar.

**Figure 3-9. The Toggle Group Tree button.**

**Tip**

If the Toggle Group Tree button is disabled, or you don't have the View > Group Tree menu options, this is because grouping is turned off. Select the menu options File > Report Options and check the Create Group Tree setting. Of course, if you want to disable grouping for a report, then uncheck this setting. The Preview tab has to be closed before the change takes effect.

If you don't want the group tree displayed in the report preview, select File > Report Options and un-check the Create Group Tree setting. The Preview tab has to be closed before this takes affect.

By default, only the top-most groups are shown. When you click on the group name, the report immediately jumps to the page that has that group on it. If there are sub-groups, then a plus sign is shown next to the group name. Click on the plus sign to expand the group and list the sub-groups below it. You can also double-click on the group name to expand it. Clicking on the sub-groups jumps to the page in the report where the sub-group is located.

When you move the cursor over a group header in the report and it becomes a magnifying glass, you can double-click on the group heading and it opens the group in its own tab. This lets you review the group data separately from the rest of the report.

**Best Of The Forum**

**Question:** I want to format the data in my Group Tree a certain way, but it doesn't appear to have any formatting properties that I can modify. Is this possible?

**Answer:** The Group Tree doesn't let you set the formatting properties directly. The way it formats data is determined by the settings in the Fields tab of the Options dialog box.[14] The Fields tab has a button that sets the default formatting properties for each data type. These properties are used by the Group Tree when previewing a report. This is of primary importance when you are grouping on numbers or dates and they aren't appearing the way you want them to.

You should also know that if you want to change the formatting in the Group Tree, you can't just change the default formatting specified on the Fields tab. It won't update the Group Tree. The Group Tree uses the formatting specified at

---

[14] To open the Options dialog box, select the menu items File > Options. Then click on the Fields tab to set the formatting properties.

the moment the group was created. If you want to change the current formatting of the Group Tree to use the new default settings, you have to change the group to a different field and then change it back. This forces a 'reset' of the Group Tree and tells Crystal Reports to apply the new default formatting.

# Formatting Groups

The default layout for groups is that they print one after the other. When the group footer is printed, the subsequent group's header is printed right after it. Some reporting requirements require changing this default behavior. For example, an invoicing report is designed so that it is grouped by client and each client gets their own invoice. For this report, you will put the client information in the group header section and force the group header to be printed at the top of a new page. The summary values appear in the group footer. The group footer is set to always print at the bottom of the page.

The formatting options for groups are in the Section Expert dialog box. The Section Expert is discussed in detail in Chapter 8, but for now we are going to look at the options that are used with grouping.

To get to the Section Expert dialog box, right-click on the group section and select Section Expert. This opens the Section Expert dialog box which lists all the sections along the left side and the section properties are listed to the right. The properties of interest here are Print at Bottom of Page, New Page Before, New Page After, Reset Page Number After, and Keep Together.

## Print at Bottom of Page

This forces a section to always print at the bottom of the page even if the detail records stop printing in the middle of the page. This is commonly set for the Group Footer section. It is useful for reports that print summary information (sub-totals, disclaimers, logos, etc.). It is also useful for form letters where the bottom of the page must have exact placement.

## New Page Before / New Page After

These two properties are used to force the groups onto individual pages. This is so that you can split the reports apart and distribute them independently. For example, a report grouped on Employee ID can be broken apart and each employee can be given their own report without seeing any information about the other employees.

You can either set the New Page Before property for the Group Header or set the New Page After property for the Group Footer. Both give you the same results of splitting the groups onto separate pages. The only problem is that sometimes these options cause a blank page to be printed either at the beginning of the report or at the end of the report. I address this more fully in the Advanced Tutorials section because it requires writing formulas.

### Reset Page Number After

This sets the page number back to 1 after the Group has been printed and is usually associated with the Group Header. It ensures that the page number for each group starts at 1. Just like the New Page Before property, this is useful for reports that are separated and distributed to different parties.

### Keep Together

The Keep Together property forces a section to stay on the same page. For example, if the group header has the Keep Together property enabled and the entire header can't fit on the page, then it will be started at the top of the next page. The important thing to note is that this only applies to an individual section and it won't take other sections into account.

The Keep Together property may cause a little confusion because there is another property which has similar characteristics and also has a similar name. It is the Keep Group Together property. Let's look at what each property does and how they differ.

The Keep Group Together property looks at the entire group (its header, details and footer) and tries to keep them on the same page. If the entire group can't fit on the remainder of the current page, then the group is started at the top of the next page. This is clearly different than the Keep Together property because that property only applies to a single section while the Keep Group Together property looks at multiple sections.

It's important to note that the Keep Group Together property is in a totally different dialog box than the Keep Together property. The Keep Group Together property is in the Change Group Options dialog box (select Report > Group Expert > Options).

There are some rules associated with the Keep Group Together property. If a group starts in the middle of a page and it can't be fully printed by the end of the page, then it starts printing at the top of the following page. If a group requires more than a full page to print, then it will start printing at the top of the following page and continue onto the next page. The Group Header will not be printed on the additional pages unless the property Repeat Group Header on Each Page is set (also in the Change Group Options dialog box). If a group is small enough to fit on the remainder of the page without being broken apart, it will do so. If you wish to always start a group on a new page, use the New Page After property on the Group Footer section.

There is a setting on the Report > Options dialog box called Respect Keep Group Together On First Page. This is there to fix some backward compatibility issues with previous versions of Crystal Reports. Basically, it forces every group start on a new page. Even the first page of the report will only show the report header because the first group will print at the top of the next page. This option is best left unchecked unless you have older reports that need it.

# Advanced Grouping Options

The majority of the time that you add a group to a report you just need something simple that displays the group name and sorts it in ascending order. This is the default behavior when you add a group to the report and nothing additional is required. But there are times when you need to customize the group, such as changing the sorting order, overriding the group name field, and setting how the group headers are displayed. Making changes like these, and more, are available within the Change Group Options dialog box.

On the Group Expert dialog box there is an Options button located at the bottom right corner. Clicking on the Options button opens the Change Group Options dialog box where you set the advanced grouping features.

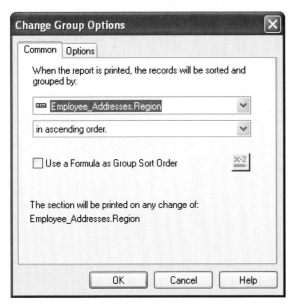

**Figure 3-10. The Change Group Options dialog box.**

The Change Group Options dialog box has two tabs: Common and Options. The Common tab sets the grouping field and the sorting order. The Options tab customizes the group name and how the group is displayed.

Clicking on the Options button lets you modify the grouping properties of the field currently selected on the Common tab. Make sure you have the proper grouping field selected before clicking the Options button.

## *Selecting the Grouping Field*

The top dropdown on the Common tab selects the field the group is based on. Most likely you will leave this as is, but if you need to change the field that a group is based on, then this is the place to do it. You can choose from a current field on the report, any fields in the current data source, or a formula field.

If the grouping field is a Date or Time data type, you have more options for how to group the records. A new dropdown list appears that lets you group on the specific part of the date or time (e.g. per week, month, quarter, hour, etc.)

### Sorting In a Specified Order

The second dropdown list at the top selects the sorting order of how the groups are listed. With one exception, the sorting options are what you would expect and don't need any explanation. You can choose a sort order that is Ascending, Descending, Original Order (no sorting) or Specified Order. The first three options are straightforward, but the Specified Order option requires more explanation.

Specified order means that you specify the exact order to display every value in that field. You manually go through each possible value and specify the order in which it appears on the report. If you leave any values out, then they all get consolidated into a single group that appears at the end of the report.

Once you select the Specified Order option, two new tabs appear in the dialog box: Specified Order and Others.

Figure 3-11. The Specified Order tab of the Insert Group dialog box.

The Specified Order tab is where you build the list of how the values are to be sorted. At the top is a dropdown list that shows all the possible values for the group field. Under the dropdown list is another list that shows the named groups and their order.

There are two ways of adding items to the list: adding individual items or adding named groups (a sub-group). Adding individual items is the easiest method because you simply select a value from the dropdown list and it gets added to the bottom list. The order that you add them to the list is the order that they appear on the report. If you want to rearrange where an item appears in the list, select the item to move and click on either the up or down arrows located to the right of the list.

If you have a lot of possible values, adding them all to the list could be very time consuming. For example, a sales report grouped by region would have a lot of values if it were for an international company. To make this a little easier, there is a faster way of adding items to the list.

The second way of adding items is by creating Named Groups that specify a range of values. It may be easier to think of this as a sub-group. Specifying a named group is done by specifying a lower and upper bounds for the range or building a formula using Boolean logic. Any value that falls within this range is included in the named group. This is obviously a faster way of adding the items because one sub-group can consist of many values. Named groups also give you a lot of flexibility because the formulas can be quite complex.

### Caution

Be careful that you don't add an individual item that could also fall within the classification of a named group. If this happens, the data will appear in both the named group and listed separately. This effectively doubles the data and gives incorrect summaries. Always check that the formula used in a named group doesn't accidentally include individual items already listed.

To create a Named Group, click on the New button located below the list. This brings up the dialog box called Define Named Group. You can see in Figure 3-12 that this is a fairly simple dialog box.

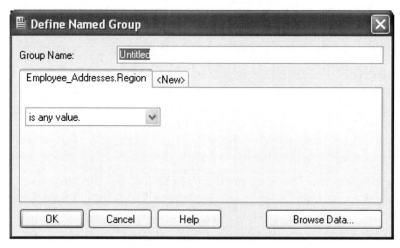

**Figure 3-12. The Define Named Group dialog box.**

Assign a name to the group in the top input box. This name is what will be displayed on the report in the group header. In the left dropdown list you specify how to filter the range of values. The dropdown list shows numerous ways to select a range of values. A few of these are: Is Equal To, Is Not One Of, and Is Between. When you select one of these operators, the proper input controls automatically appear to the right of the dropdown list. The input controls change depending upon the information needed to complete the filter. There are so many different variations of filtering options and their associated input controls, that they won't be explained here. They are all very intuitive and you shouldn't have any problem entering the proper data.

Within a named group, you have the option of using more than one filter. By clicking on the <New> tab, you are shown the same filtering options as on the first tab. But now you can make new selections and the resulting values are also associated with the current named group. These filters are linked together using an OR operand. Thus, any of conditions can be true and the record will be included in the named group.

The last tab in the Change Group Options dialog box is the Others tab. It lets you decide what to do with the records that aren't otherwise specified. Since it is possible that some reports won't need to specify how every value is grouped, this tab accumulates all the remaining values that didn't get included on the Specified Order tab. You have the option of discarding these records, accumulating them in a separate tab, or leaving them as their own group.

As an example of when to use the Others tab, consider a company that has five primary products that generate over 90% of its sales and the remaining products produce an insignificant amount of revenue. In a sales report, the five primary products will be listed separately and the miscellaneous products would be put into the Others group.

The Others group is also useful for reports that group on fields where the data is dynamic and new values are added after the report is created. If the new values don't fall within the current named groups, they get lumped in with the group called Others. To build on the previous sales report example, any new products that are added to the company's product line after the report was created will be accounted for in the Others group. Once the product becomes more popular and its sales become significant then it can be added as a separate group item.

You have different ways of how to handle items that are not included in the Specified Order tab. The Others tab of the Change Group Options dialog box lets you set how to handle these items.

**Figure 3-13. The Others tab of the Change Group Options dialog box.**

There are three options for handling how the Others group data is handled. The first option is to discard the data. This is useful when the data is frivolous and you don't want it appearing on the report. The second option puts all the values into a single group. The default value of this group is "Others" but you can type in a different name that is more appropriate. The third option is to leave the remaining fields in their own groups. They get displayed within the report as they normally would. This is useful when there are a lot of values that get their own group and it would be very time consuming to list each one in that box. Setting this property includes them in the report without you having to list them.

When grouping values into the Others group (or whatever name you give it) it is always shown at the end of the report as the last group.

## Customizing the Group Name

In most circumstances, the Group Name field displayed on the report is the field's current value. For example, if you are grouping by country, then the group name shown on the report is the current country name. If you don't want to display the current value as the group name, you have the option of customizing the name instead. For example, consider a report group that lists how many products were sold for each day of the month and it's grouped by the Inventory Number field. If the report is intended for users who recognize a product's name, but not the inventory number, then displaying the inventory number in the group header isn't a very good idea. It's better to show the product's name as the group name instead of the inventory number. The Options tab of the Change Group Options dialog box allows you to override the Group Name field with another field.

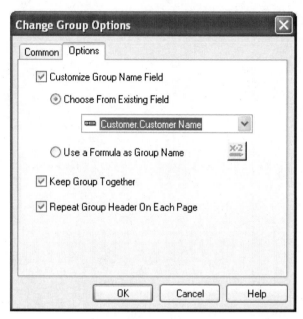

**Figure 3-14. The Options tab of the Change Group Options dialog box.**

The first checkbox, Customize Group Name Field, modifies the Group Name field. Click the option button Choose From Existing Field to use another field as the group name. Then select the field from the dropdown list below it. When the Group Name is displayed, the value from the field in the dropdown list is displayed instead.

There are times when the group name you want to display isn't a field in the table. It could be a custom formatting field where you join multiple fields together or where you parse text out of a field. To make the group name display a formula instead, click the option button Use a Formula as Group Name and then click the formula button. Formulas are covered in detail in Chapter 5.

## Keeping the Group Together

The second and third checkboxes on the Options tab control whether the report should try to keep the entire group on the same page. These properties were mentioned earlier in the Keep Together discussion within the Formatting Groups section. Setting the Keep Group

Together checkbox is important if you want to prevent having only a few records of a group appearing at the bottom of a page. When this option is on, the entire group is analyzed before it is printed. If it can't fit on the rest of the page, then the remainder of the page is left blank and the group is started at the top of the next page.

The third checkbox, Repeat Group Header on Each Page, forces the group header to print at the top of every page. This is important for groups that can span multiple pages. Most of the time the group header displays information that makes it easier to understand the meaning of the groups detail records (like the group name and column headers). By default, if a group extends to a second page then its header is not printed at the top of the second page. If you feel that repeating the group header at the top of every page makes your report easier to read, then you should click this checkbox.

## Sorting the Group Data

After creating the groups and running a test report, you may notice that although your groups are fine, the detail rows within the group are out of order. They might appear to be printed randomly or their natural sort order isn't how you want it sorted. For example, in Figure 3-15 the detail records are sorted naturally by Employee ID but you want them sorted by Last Name.

| Employee ID | Last Name | First Name | City | Region |
|---|---|---|---|---|
| 5 | Buchanan | Steven | London | |
| 6 | Suyama | Michael | London | |
| 7 | King | Robert | London | |
| 9 | Dodsworth | Anne | Nottingham | |
| **Bas-Rhin** | | | | |
| 13 | Brid | Justin | Haguenau | Bas-Rhin |
| 14 | Martin | Xavier | Schiltigheim | Bas-Rhin |
| 15 | Pereira | Laurent | Strasbourg | Bas-Rhin |
| **BC** | | | | |
| 1 | Davolio | Nancy | Port Moody | BC |
| 2 | Fuller | Andrew | Coquitlam | BC |
| 3 | Leverling | Janet | Vancouver | BC |
| 4 | Peacock | Margaret | Richmond | BC |
| 8 | Callahan | Laura | New Westminster | BC |
| 10 | Hellstern | Albert | Burnaby | BC |
| 11 | Smith | Tim | North Vancouver | BC |
| 12 | Patterson | Caroline | West Vancouver | BC |

**Figure 3-15. Detail records that aren't sorted on the right field.**

Sorting the detail records is done separately from sorting the grouping records. Telling the report how to group data doesn't mean that it knows which fields to use for sorting the detail records within the group. If no sort fields are used, then the records appear in their natural order. Sorting the records within the group is the same as adding a Sort Field for a report which was discussed earlier in the chapter. Just open the Record Sort Expert and add the sort field to the Sort Fields list.

It's important to understand the differences between fields that are sorted within a group and fields that are sorted within a detail section. The Record Sort Expert is strictly used for sorting detail records. It has no control over how the groups are sorted. That said, even though it doesn't control the group fields, it still shows them in the Sort Fields list. For example, Figure 3-16 shows a report that is grouped by Region and City and the detail records are sorted by Last Name.

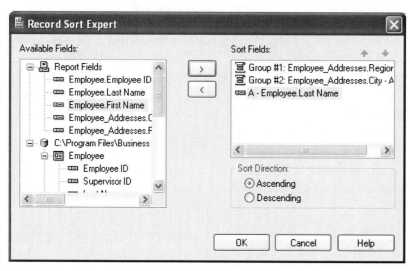

**Figure 3-16. Record Sort Expert showing groups.**

Notice that the first two sort fields are the two grouping fields. After that, it shows the Last Name field. If you click on one of the two grouping fields, all the buttons become disabled because you're not allowed to change the grouping within this dialog box. If you want to change the group fields, you have to go back to the Group Expert to do so. The reason the group fields are shown here is because Crystal Reports wants to remind you that the group fields always take precedence for sorting and the detail records always come last.

## Reordering the Groups

Sometimes you might create a report with multiple groups and then decide that groups should be rearranged. For example, a report that sorts first by state and then by product could be changed to sort by product first and then state. There are two ways to reorder the group fields. The first is to go into the Group Expert and use the arrows above the Group By list. Click on the field that you want to change and then click on the appropriate arrow to either move it up the list or down the list. The second way to reorder the group fields is by clicking on the Group Header on left side of the report and dragging it to the new position. This changes the mouse cursor to a hand and highlights the group that will be changed. This is illustrated in Figure 3-17.

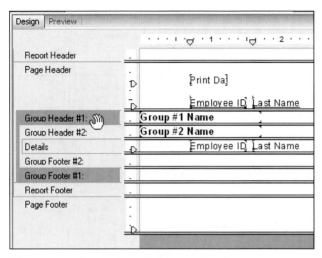

**Figure 3-17. Dragging the group header to a new position.**

# Tutorial 3-2. Grouping by a Specified Order

Crystal Reports has an excellent sample report that demonstrates how to create a grouping report using the specified order option. The report Group By Intervals.rpt is a sales report that shows total sales from the prior year for each customer. Each customer is broken down into three categories based on their sales volume: Less than $10,000, $10,000 to $25,000, and Greater than $25,000. Within each category the records are sorted by the Customer Name field. We're going to see how this report works by creating the same report from scratch.

1. On the Start Page click Standard Report Wizard to create a new report.

2. In the Data dialog box, select the Xtreme.mdb database as the data source. Do this by clicking on Create New Connection > Access/Excel > Make New Connection.

3. For the Database Name property, navigate to the Xtreme.mdb database that is installed in the Crystal Reports sample folders. Click the Finish button once you've selected it.

4. Open the Tables category and double-click the Customer table to add it to the Selected Tables list on the right. Click the Next button.

5. In the Available Fields list, select the fields Customer Name, Region, Country, Postal Code, and Last Year's Sales. Click the Next button to go to the Grouping dialog box.

6. In the Grouping dialog box, select Last Year's Sales as the grouping field. The Grouping dialog box doesn't let you set any of the advanced options, so we will have to wait till later before setting the specified order options.

7. Click the Next button to go to the Summaries dialog box. Crystal Reports saw that the field Last Year's Sales was numeric and automatically created a summary field for it. This isn't necessary for this example so you can delete it.

8.  Click the Finish button to skip the rest of the Wizard's dialog boxes and go to the report designer. Your report preview should look similar to the following.

| Last Year's Sales | Customer Name | Region | Country | Postal Code |
|---|---|---|---|---|
| **$27.00** | | | | |
| $27.00 | Phil's Bikes | CT | USA | 05667 |
| $27.00 | Caledonia Cycle | LA | USA | 70121 |
| **$27.00** | | | | |
| **$33.90** | | | | |
| $33.90 | Barry's Bikes | DE | USA | 19850 |
| **$33.90** | | | | |

The report is grouped by last year's sales and consequently there is a group for almost every record in the database. This isn't very practical, so let's clean it up by consolidating the values into three categories.

9.  Open the Group Expert dialog box by clicking on the Group Expert button or selecting the menu items Report > Group Expert. The field Last Year's Sales is listed in the grouping fields on the right.

10. Click the Options button to open the Change Group Options dialog box. On the sorting property (the second dropdown list), select the In Specified Order option. This displays the Specified Order tab.

11. Click the New button to create the first group. This opens the Define Named Group dialog box.

12. Enter a name of **Under $10,000**. In the criteria dropdown list select Is Less Than. For the Value property enter **10,000**. Click the OK button to save it.

13. **Under $10,000** is now listed on the Specified Order tab. Click the New button to enter the second group.

14. Enter a name of **$10,000 to $25,000**. In the criteria dropdown list select Is Between. For the two Value properties enter **10,000** and **25,000**. Click the OK button to save it.

15. For the final group, click the New button again and enter the name **Over $25,000**. For the criteria, select Is Greater Than and enter a value of **25,000**. Click the OK button to save it.

16. At this point, you've created the three groups that will categorize the records. In some reports you would now go to the Others tab to tell Crystal Reports what to do with the records that didn't fall into one of the groups. But in this example, all the records will be included in one of the three groups. Click the OK button to save your changes on the Specified Order tab.

17. As another option, you might want to list the customers with the most sales first. If so, you can re-order the groups on the Specified Order tab by selecting the group and clicking on the arrow keys to move it up or down in the list. For this example, we'll just leave it as is.

As we learned earlier in the chapter, specifying the order of the groups doesn't change how the records within the group are sorted. We want the detail records to be sorted by Customer Name.

18. Open the Records Sort Expert dialog box by selecting the menu items Report > Record Sort Expert.

19. Double click the Customer Name field to add it to the Sort Fields list. Click the OK button to save it.

20. You've made all the changes necessary. Save it as **Specified Order Tutorial.rpt** and then preview it. If you page through it, you'll see that each group is in the order that you added them to the Specified Order tab and that the detail records are sorted by customer name. Your report should look similar to the following.

| Under $10,000 | | | | |
|---|---|---|---|---|
| $8,819.55 | 7 Bikes For 7 Brothers | NV | USA | 89102 |
| $2,409.46 | Against The Wind Bikes | NY | USA | 14817 |
| $5,879.70 | AIC Childrens | Hong Kong SAR | China | 439433 |
| $3,239.85 | Aruba Sport | St. George | Aruba | 655456 |
| $5,179.98 | Auvergne Bicross | Auvergne | France | 03200 |
| $4,443.80 | Barbados Sports, Ltd. | Bridgetown | Barbados | 4532 |
| $33.90 | Barry's Bikes | DE | USA | 19850 |
| $2,944.00 | Beach Trails and Wheels | Waikato | New Zealand | |

# Displaying Top N Reports

An alternative to standard grouping is to create reports that show the first or last set of records in a certain group. For example, rather than showing all the sales people for the company, you could show the top 5 sales people that have the best sales for the month. Or you can do the opposite and show the 5 sales people with the lowest sales for the month. The first report shows who deserves a bonus and the second report shows who should be talked to about improving their performance. This type of report is called a Top N report.

Generating a Top N report has two requirements. The first is that your report must have at least one group in it. The second requirement is that the group must have a summary field in it (a sub-total, average, etc). The summary field is required because a Top N report uses the summary value to determine the ranking position of each group.

To create a Top N report, select the menu items Report > Group Sort Expert. You can also click on the Group Sort Expert button on the toolbar. If it is grayed out, that means that the report either doesn't have at least one group section or it doesn't have a summary field within that group. Correct this and it won't be grayed out any more.

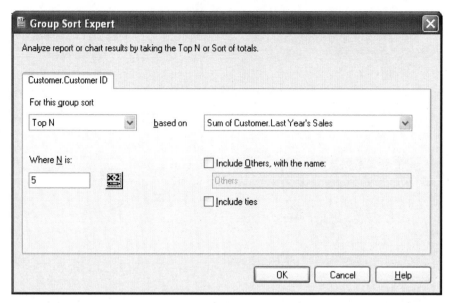

**Figure 3-18. The Group Sort Expert dialog box.**

Figure 3-18 shows the Group Sort Expert dialog box. For each group that has a summary field in it, there will be a tab along the top with the group field listed. The tabs give you the option to create different Top N selections for each group. In this figure there is only one tab for Customer ID. So either this is the only group on the report or this is the only group that has a summary field in it.

When the Group Sort Expert dialog box opens, the first property has a setting of All. This is because the group defaults to displaying all values. By clicking on this dropdown list, you can choose from Top N, Bottom N, Top Percentage, or Bottom Percentage. This bases the calculation on either a certain quantity or a percentage of the total records. It lets you select which field to base the comparison on (this must be a summary field), how many groups to show and whether all the non-selected groups should be lumped into a final group called Others (or another name that you specify). If you want to select the number of groups based on the percentage of the total groups, then select that in the dropdown list and N will now represent a percentage.

One item of interest is the Include Ties checkbox. Select this option if you there is a chance that two or more groups will be tied for the same place. If this is checked, then both groups will be displayed. If this box is not checked, then only one of the groups will be displayed and the other won't be shown. It is not possible to determine ahead of time which group will be the one that gets displayed.

## Grouping on Summary Values

The Group Sort Expert dialog box actually has a dual purpose. In the previous section, I quickly skimmed over the fact that the dropdown list defaults to the value All so that all groups are displayed. But this setting is also useful for creating new ways of sorting your groups.

Normally, a group is sorted based on the Group Name field (as specified in the Change Group Options dialog box). However, the Change Group Options dialog box doesn't give you the ability to sort groups based upon a summary value. For example, you might want to sort your customers based upon the total current year's sales. The Group Sort Expert lets you do this by selecting a sort type of All and then choosing the summary value to sort on. Effectively, you are no longer sorting on a text field and instead sorting on a numeric field (the summary value).

The summary value to sort on is selected using the right-most dropdown list. Each summary field you select gets added to the list below it. You can change whether the field is sorted in ascending or descending order by clicking on it in the list and then selecting the sort order. By using summary fields to sort your groups, you get a lot more flexibility with how the groups get displayed.

| Tip |
| --- |

If you decide to sort a group on a summary value rather than the group field, you should show the summary value in the group header. Otherwise, someone reading the report will see that the values in the group field aren't sorted by the group name and think that there is no organization to the report. By making it clear that the summary value is the sort field, the reader will understand the significance of why certain groups appear first in the report.

# Displaying Hierarchical Reports

A hierarchical report shows the relationship between records in the same table using a tree format. An example is an Organization Chart that uses the personnel table to display a list of its employees and their supervisors. Each employee has a record in the personnel table. But each employee also has a supervisor that they report to and that supervisor is in the same personnel table. Thus, there is a relationship between the employee and their supervisor and both entities come from the same personnel table. This is ideal for using a hierarchical report to show the relationship between employees and their supervisors.

There are three requirements for using hierarchical reports.

1. A record has two fields that represent the same data. In the Org Chart example the Employee ID is the key field for the record. Within the record is the Supervisor ID field and it points to a different record within the same table.
2. The report must be grouped on the child field (e.g. the Employee ID).
3. The parent and child fields must be the same data type.

Trying to figure out how to make an Organizational Chart using records that point back to themselves can get a little complicated. Rather than do the work yourself, let Crystal Reports do it for you. Open the Hierarchical Options dialog box by selecting Report > Hierarchical Grouping Options.

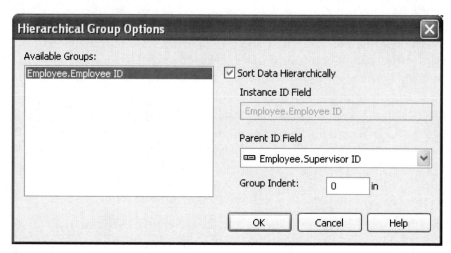

**Figure 3-19. The Hierarchical Group Options dialog box.**

This dialog box shows a list of all the groups within the report. The Available Groups list shows the current groups in your report. You can only create a hierarchical report using one of these existing groups. To use it for hierarchical grouping, click on the group that uses the child field (e.g. Employee ID) and check the Sort Data Hierarchically checkbox. In the Parent ID dropdown list below the checkbox, select the field that will be the parent field (e.g. Supervisor ID). This establishes the relationship between the two fields and Crystal Reports automatically groups the records so that the parent records are shown before the child records.

The last option in the dialog box is the Group Indent value. This sets the indentation level between a parent record and its child record. The default value is 0.25 inches.

You need to be careful when formatting a hierarchical report for the first time. As mentioned earlier, the default format for printing is a tree-view format. As you can see in Figure 3-20, the parent records start on the left-most side of the report and the child records are indented at each level.

**Hierarchical Grouping**

**X**treme
**Mountain Bikes**

**How to group records with a hierarchical structure**

12/11/2005    3:15:07PM

| Name | Position | Salary | Total |
|------|----------|--------|-------|
| Andrew Fuller | Vice President, Sales | $90,000.00 | $668,000.00 |
| Steven Buchanan | Sales Manager | $50,000.00 | $305,000.00 |
| Nancy Davolio | Sales Representative | $40,000.00 | $40,000.00 |
| Janet Leverling | Sales Representative | $33,000.00 | $33,000.00 |
| Margaret Peacock | Sales Representative | $35,000.00 | $35,000.00 |
| Michael Suyama | Sales Representative | $30,000.00 | $30,000.00 |
| Robert King | Sales Representative | $37,000.00 | $37,000.00 |
| Laura Callahan | Inside Sales Coordinator | $45,000.00 | $45,000.00 |
| Anne Dodsworth | Sales Representative | $35,000.00 | $35,000.00 |
| Albert Hellstern | Business Manager | $60,000.00 | $103,000.00 |
| Tim Smith | Mail Clerk | $18,000.00 | $18,000.00 |
| Caroline Patterson | Receptionist | $25,000.00 | $25,000.00 |

**Figure 3-20. The Hierarchical Grouping report with indenting.**

Shifting the columns to the right is fine when there are only a few columns. But when a report has many columns, then there isn't room for shifting and the data can be pushed into the adjacent column. If this causes a problem, you can either make the Group Indent value small or just set it to zero. Setting it to zero ensures that the data in each column is lined up exactly with the column header above. This looks the same as a typical report, as you can see in the next figure.

**Hierarchical Grouping**

**X**treme
**Mountain Bikes**

**How to group records with a hierarchical structure**

12/11/2005    3:16:30PM

| Name | Position | Salary | Total |
|------|----------|--------|-------|
| Andrew Fuller | Vice President, Sales | $90,000.00 | $668,000.00 |
| Steven Buchanan | Sales Manager | $50,000.00 | $305,000.00 |
| Nancy Davolio | Sales Representative | $40,000.00 | $40,000.00 |
| Janet Leverling | Sales Representative | $33,000.00 | $33,000.00 |
| Margaret Peacock | Sales Representative | $35,000.00 | $35,000.00 |
| Michael Suyama | Sales Representative | $30,000.00 | $30,000.00 |
| Robert King | Sales Representative | $37,000.00 | $37,000.00 |
| Laura Callahan | Inside Sales Coordinator | $45,000.00 | $45,000.00 |
| Anne Dodsworth | Sales Representative | $35,000.00 | $35,000.00 |
| Albert Hellstern | Business Manager | $60,000.00 | $103,000.00 |
| Tim Smith | Mail Clerk | $18,000.00 | $18,000.00 |
| Caroline Patterson | Receptionist | $25,000.00 | $25,000.00 |

**Figure 3-21. The Hierarchical Grouping report with indentation set to 0.**

Another option is to only indent the description fields and not indent the numeric values. This requires using advanced functions and the process for doing can be found in the Advanced Tutorials at the end of this chapter.

# Drilling Down on Data

The purpose of creating groups is to organize a lot of data in a report so that the reader can quickly find their data by scanning through the different groups. This lets the reader skip over the data that doesn't relate to them and instead focus on what is important. But there is more to it than that.

You can use groups to make the report's data dynamic and allow the user to drill down into the details of each group. Crystal Reports lets you double-click on a group header and open the detail information in a new window. This is called drilling down on data. It lets you see just the data for that group without worrying about the rest of the data on the report. For example, Figure 3-22 shows a report grouped by country.

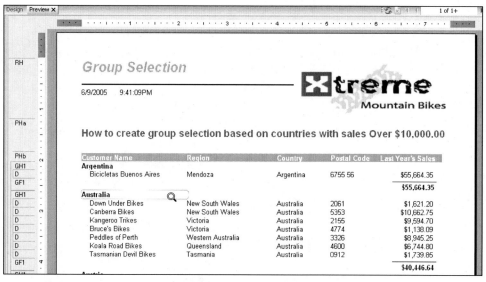

**Figure 3-22. Grouping by country.**

Notice how the cursor is positioned on the Australia group header and it is a magnifying glass. The magnifying glass means that you can double click on the group header and it will open a new tab with only its detail information shown. Figure 3-23 shows what happens when you double-click on the group.

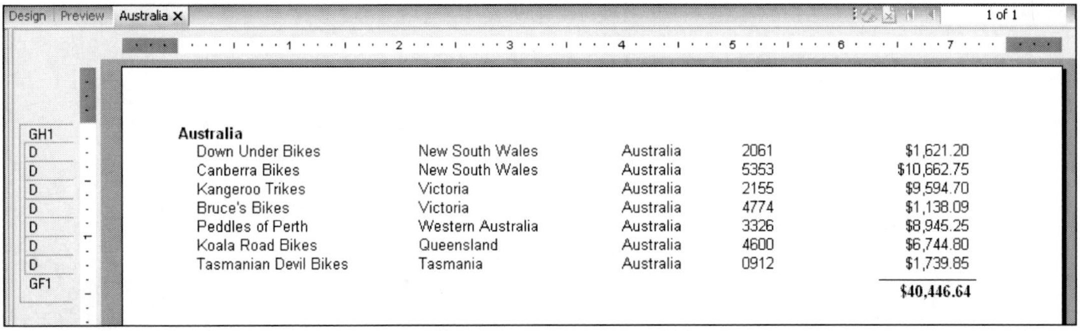

**Figure 3-23. Drilling down into the Australia group.**

Notice that a new tab was created for Australia. Since it has its own tab, you can switch back and forth between the main report and the group data. This tab also brings up another aspect of drilling down on data: it can only be done on the computer. Since it requires double-clicking on the group header, then this isn't something that can be done with a paper based printout. However, you can print just the data in the drill down tab. This way, you don't have to print out the whole report if you just want to see the data for a particular group.

One drawback to drilling down on data is that only the data is displayed and no column headers are displayed (see Figure 3-23 above). Thus, if you were to print this out and give it to someone, then they would have to already know what each column represents. Otherwise, they won't know how to read the numbers on the page. One way to get fix this is to move the column headers from the Report Header section (which isn't shown in the tab) to the Group Header section so that they get displayed with the drill down data.

Another feature of drill down reports is that the detail sections can be turned off. This lets the user only see the summary data when reading the report. If there is a section that they want to see the details of, then they can double-click on the group header and the detail records are shown on their own tab. This gives you the benefit of creating a report that presents an overview of all the data with the option of only seeing more details when necessary. Figure 3-24 shows the same report modified so that the details are hidden.

**Figure 3-24. Group details hidden.**

In this report, only the group header and Last Year's Sales subtotals are shown. The detail records are not visible. To see the detail records, double-click on the group header just like before and they will be displayed in a separate tab.

The group details can also be suppressed so that they can't be viewed by anyone. This is beneficial when you want to distribute a report that has classified information in it but you don't want to recreate the report from scratch just to hide the data. For example, you can give a manager a travel expense report that shows the total expenses and how much was charged by each employee. You can also give this same report to others in the department to see the totals but hide the detail amounts.

Hiding and suppressing data can be done in two different ways. The easiest way is to use the pop-up menu by right-clicking the section in the gray area on the left side of the report designer. The pop-up menu has the items for toggling the Hide and Suppress properties of the section. Click on the menu item to either enable or disable the property. The other way to set the properties is to select the Section Expert menu item from the pop-up menu and modify it via the dialog box.

## Tutorial 3-3. Hiding and Suppressing Details

This tutorial walks you through the process of toggling the detail data on and off so that it can be drilled down into.

1.  Open the report Group Selection.rpt. This is one of the example reports installed with Crystal Reports. It is located in the Feature Examples folder.

2.  Right-click on the Details title along the left sidebar and select the Section Expert menu item. When it opens, make sure that the Details section is highlighted on the left side of the dialog.

3. Under the Common tab, click on the Hide checkbox (this checks it).

4. Click Ok.

   Preview the report and you'll see that the detail section is hidden. If you double-click on one of the group headers, then it will open a new tab and show the detail records.

5. Go back to Design view.

6. Open the Section Expert again (see Step 2) and uncheck the Hide option.

7. Click on the Suppress checkbox so that it becomes checked.

8. Click Ok.

9. Preview the report and it looks the same as it did when the Hide option was checked. The difference is that if you double-click on the group header nothing happens. Since the details are suppressed, you are not allowed to view them.

# Summarizing Data

A major benefit to grouping data is that it lets you put summary data within the group footer and header. This is beneficial because when there are a lot of detail records, you don't want the reader to have to get out a calculator to calculate sub-totals and averages of columns. You want the report to do this automatically.

Crystal Reports gives you a multitude of functions for adding summary calculations to a report. Table 3-1 shows a complete list of the summary functions available.

**Table 3-1. Summary functions for groups.**

| Function | Description |
| --- | --- |
| Average | Calculate the average value. (2) |
| Correlation | Calculate the correlation of two fields. (1) (2) |
| Count | Count the number of detail records. Fields with Null values are not included in the calculation. (3) |
| Covariance | Calculate the measure of the linear relation between paired variables. (1) |
| DisctinctCount | Calculate the number of unique values for that field. |
| Maximimum | Find the maximum value of all the fields. |
| Median | Return the middle value if all the fields were sorted. (1) |
| Minimum | Find the minimum value of all the fields. |
| Mode | Returns the value with the most duplicates. |
| Nth Largest | Finds the largest value of all the fields with a ranking of N. For example, if N were 6, it returns the sixth largest value. |

| Nth Most Frequent | Finds the Nth ranking field with the most duplicate values. For example, if N were 6, it returns the value with the 6th most duplicates. |
|---|---|
| Nth Smallest | Finds the smallest value of all the fields with a ranking of N. For example, if N were 6, it returns the sixth smallest value. |
| Pth Percentile | Returns the value for the specified percentile of the field. (2) |
| Pop Standard Deviation | Calculates how much a field deviates from the mean value. (1) (2) |
| Pop Variance | Find the population variance of a set of values in a report. (1) |
| Sample Standard Deviation | Returns the sample standard deviation for the field. (1) (2) |
| Sample Variance | Returns the sample variance for the field. (1) (2) |
| Sum | Returns the total of all the detail fields.(2) |
| Weighted Average | Returns the weighted average of all the detail fields. (2) |

Chart Notes:

(1) See a statistics book for detailed calculation information.

(2) Can only be used for numeric data.

(3) Null values can be included if you set them to return their default values. To do this, select the menu options File > Report Options. Then check the box for converting Null field values to their default.

**Note**

Summary fields can be put in both the Group Header and Group Footer sections. It might seem strange that a summary field can be in the Group Header section since it is printed before the detail records are printed. But if you recall from Chapter 1, Crystal Reports uses a two-pass process to build the data printed on a report. The summary fields are calculated in the first pass and are already known before any of the records are printed. That's why summary calculations can appear prior to printing the actual data.

To create a summary value for a group field, right-click on the field that you want to summarize and select Insert. The pop-up menu gives you the option of inserting a summary or a running total[15].

| Tip |
| --- |

If the Insert option is missing from the pop-up menu, then the report object you clicked on is a second-pass formula and it can't be summarized on. Please see Chapter 1 for more information about how the two-pass reporting process works.

Inserting a summary brings up the dialog box in Figure 3-25. The top dropdown list shows the field you had selected. Below that is a dropdown list that selects the summary function to perform. The third dropdown list tells where the field should go. If you put it in the report footer, it is a grand total. If you put it within an existing group, it is a sub-total. If there are no groups based upon the field you want to associate this summary field with, then click the Insert Group button and after you close the dialog box a new group will be created. Ideally, this won't be necessary because you will plan out your report so that it already has all the necessary groups created.

**Figure 3-25. The Insert Summary dialog box (Crystal Reports XI R2)**

---

[15] Running Totals are covered later in this chapter.

By default, sub-totals are automatically placed in the group footer. You can move this field to the group header if you want to keep all the summary information in the same section and printed before the detail rows.

> **R2** New to Crystal Reports XI R2 is the ability to add a summary field to all groups simultaneously. If you look in Figure 3-24, in the middle of the dialog box is the checkbox called Add To All Group Levels. This option is only available with the R2 edition. If you have multiple groups in a report, checking this box saves you the time of having to open and re-open this dialog box to insert a summary field into every group footer section.

To change the summary function after it has been created, right-click on the summary field and select Edit Summary. This brings up a dialog box with a dropdown list of all the available summary functions. Select the one you want to change it to and click on the OK button.

### Note

If you move a summary field into a new group, it takes the new group as its parent and calculates the summary value for that group.

If you were really paying close attention earlier, you might have noticed that none of the summary functions in Table 3-1 calculate the percentage of a number. For example, if you want to show the percent sales that a sales person had in relation to the entire department, there is no way to do it. Of course, you could always do this calculation yourself using a custom formula, but you might think that with all the advanced functionality that Crystal Reports gives you that it would be a standard function. Well, it turns out that it is available. At the bottom of the Insert Summary dialog box is an option to show the summary as a percentage of another total.

Percentages are always calculated based on a total from an outside group. In other words, the percentage is calculated using an interior group value compared to a value outside of that group. For example, if you want to calculate the percentage of a value in a group, then this percentage will be based on the grand total amount because the grand total is outside of the group level. If you want to calculate the percentage of a value in sub-group, then it will either be based on the parent group or the grand total. You can't calculate the percentage of a grand total value because it is already at the outer-most level and there is no outer number to calculate the percentage from.

# Tutorial 3-4. Creating Summary Fields

This tutorial walks you through the process of creating summary fields that are displayed in the Group Footer. You will build a sales report that lists the number of purchases they had, their total sales and their average sales.

1. Go to the Start Page and click on Standard Report Wizard.

2. When asked for the data source, choose the Xtreme.mdb database like you did in the previous tutorials.

3. Select the Customer table and Orders table and click the Next button. When the Link dialog box appears, it shows that the two tables are related by the Customer ID. This is what you want so click the Next button.

4. From the Customer table, choose the fields Customer ID and Customer Name. From the Orders table, choose the field Order Amount. Click the Next button.

5. For the grouping field, choose the Customer ID field and click the Next button.

6. The Summaries dialog box appears and you see that it has already pre-selected two summary fields: Customer ID and Order Amount. It makes sense to summarize the Order Amount, but not the Customer ID. Unfortunately, Crystal Reports obviously has no idea what the meaning of each field is so it automatically creates a summary for every numeric field being printed. You have to remove the fields you don't want. Click on the Customer Id summary and click on the left arrow button to remove it from the list.

7. Click the Finish button and the report is generated automatically. Your report should look similar to the one below.

```
6/1 7/200

Customer ID  Customer Name              Order Amount

1
                  1  City Cyclists           $119.43
                  1  City Cyclists         $1,515.35
                  1  City Cyclists         $4,078.95
                  1  City Cyclists         $6,682.98
                  1  City Cyclists            $46.50
                  1  City Cyclists            $41.90
                  1  City Cyclists           $659.70
                  1  City Cyclists            $27.00
                  1  City Cyclists         $3,884.25
                  1  City Cyclists         $2,939.85
                  1  City Cyclists           $764.85
                  1  City Cyclists            $70.50
                  1  City Cyclists            $62.33
                  1  City Cyclists         $2,294.55
                  1  City Cyclists            $42.00
                  1  City Cyclists           $931.05
                  1  City Cyclists           $122.65
                  1  City Cyclists         $3,520.30
                  1  City Cyclists           $185.20
                  1  City Cyclists           $764.85
                  1  City Cyclists            $63.90
                  1  City Cyclists            $68.00
                  1  City Cyclists            $75.80
                  1  City Cyclists         $2,378.35
                  1  City Cyclists           $136.47
                  1  City Cyclists         $5,549.40

    1                          $37,026.11
```

This is a decent first attempt at a report, but it needs some obvious corrections before we go any further. The first problem is that the sub-total for the Order Amount doesn't line up with the Order Amount column. It is too far to the left. The second problem is that the Company Number and Company Name are repeated on each detail line when it really only needs to be shown in the group header. Let's make those corrections now.

8. Click on the Design tab so that you can modify the report.

9. Look in the Group Footer and find the summary field for Order Amount. Move it to the right so that it is aligned with the Order Amount column (this would be a good time to practice using the Align feature). Also make the field width smaller because it doesn't need to be that big.

10. Delete the Customer Number field from the Details section so it doesn't get repeated.

11. Move the Customer Name field by clicking on it and dragging it from the Details section, up to the Group Header section.

12. Since the Customer Name field is now in the Group Header, it needs to match the formatting of the Customer Number field already in the group header. Right-click on the Customer Number field and select the Format Painter menu item. Move the cursor onto the Customer Name field and the cursor will become a paint brush. Click on the field and it gets the same formatting as the Customer Number field. Now they both match.

13. Preview the report and it should look much nicer.

```
6/17/2005

                      Customer Name          Order Amount

     1                City Cyclists
                                                  $119.43
                                                $1,515.35
                                                $4,078.95
                                                $6,682.98
                                                   $46.50
                                                   $41.90
                                                  $659.70
                                                   $27.00
                                                $3,884.25
                                                $2,939.85
                                                  $764.85
                                                   $70.50
                                                   $62.33
                                                $2,294.55
                                                   $42.00
                                                  $931.05
                                                  $122.65
                                                $3,520.30
                                                  $185.20
                                                  $764.85
                                                   $63.90
                                                   $68.00
                                                   $75.80
                                                $2,378.35
                                                  $136.47
                                                $5,549.40

     1                                         $37,026.11
```

Next we'll add the summary fields to show how many purchases each customer made as well as their average sales amount.

14. Click on the Design tab so you can make changes to the report.

15. On the menu, select Insert > Summary (or click the Insert Summary button). The Insert Summary dialog box appears so you can choose the field to summarize.

16. Select the field Order Amount. For the type of summary, choose Count. For the summary location, choose Group #1. This creates a summary field that counts how many times the Order Amount field appears in the group. Consequently showing you how many purchases were made.

17. Click the OK button and the summary field is automatically added to the Group Footer section. Move it next to the existing Order Amount summary field.

18. Add another summary field by selecting the menu items Insert > Summary.

19. Select the field Order Amount. For the type of summary, choose Average. For the summary location, choose Group #1. This creates a summary field that calculates the average order amount for all the orders placed by each customer.

20. Click the OK button and the summary field is automatically added to the Group Footer section. Move it next to the previous summary field.

21. The report is now finished and it includes three summary fields: the total sales (created by the report wizard), the number of sales and the average sales (both created by you). It is shown in the next figure.

```
┌─────────────────────────────────────────────────────────┐
│  6/17/2005                                                │
│                                                           │
│                   Customer Name          Order Amount     │
│                                                           │
│  1                City Cyclists                           │
│  ─────────────    ─────────────────────────────           │
│                                           $119.43         │
│                                         $1,515.35         │
│                                         $4,078.95         │
│                                         $6,682.98         │
│                                            $46.50         │
│                                            $41.90         │
│                                           $659.70         │
│                                            $27.00         │
│                                         $3,884.25         │
│                                         $2,939.85         │
│                                           $764.85         │
│                                            $70.50         │
│                                            $62.33         │
│                                         $2,294.55         │
│                                            $42.00         │
│                                           $931.05         │
│                                           $122.65         │
│                                         $3,520.30         │
│                                           $185.20         │
│                                           $764.85         │
│                                            $63.90         │
│                                            $68.00         │
│                                            $75.80         │
│                                         $2,378.35         │
│                                           $136.47         │
│                                         $5,549.40         │
│                                         ───────────        │
│  1              26     $1,424.08        $37,026.11        │
└─────────────────────────────────────────────────────────┘
```

Of course, if you were preparing this report for your company, you would want to spruce it up by creating column headers for the new summary fields and changing the formatting to make it fit the corporate image.

| Tip |
| --- |

If you want to customize the formatting of common fields based upon which group is currently being printed, you can use the GroupNumber function with conditional formatting to do so. The GroupNumber function returns the current group number being printed (1, 2, 3, etc.). Conditional formatting is covered later in the book.

# Running Totals

Running totals are like an advanced version of summary fields. They give you more ways of summing data and give you more flexibility for determining which data to summarize. The primary difference is that summary fields are calculated by group and running totals can be calculated many ways (by group, record by record, etc.)

Running totals are built-in fields that accumulate the total of another field. It is so common to summarize numerical data that Crystal Reports has this functionality built-in. Otherwise, you would have to create formulas for summing these values and zeroing them out when appropriate.

A running total takes a field on a report, performs a calculation on it, and adds the result to a report-wide variable that keeps track of the total amount so far. There are various calculations that can be used with running totals so that they can be customized to your exact needs. You can also set the interval for when to perform the calculation. For example, you can do it on every field or whenever the field changes values.

Calling the field a running total is deceiving because the calculation doesn't have to calculate a running total. There are over a dozen different calculations available. It could calculate the average of all the numbers printed so far, or it can print the largest of all the numbers. The simplest calculation, and the default, is the Sum operation. It sums a value as it is printed.

To add a running total field to your report, right click on the numeric field that you want to track and select the menu item Insert > Running Total. This presents you with the dialog box in Figure 3-26.

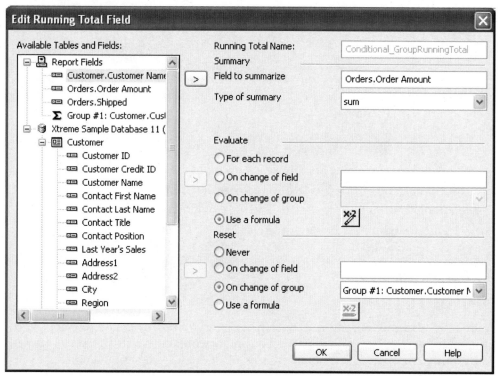

Figure 3-26. The Edit Running Total dialog box.

When this dialog box opens, a default field name is already filled in for you. You should immediately change the name to something descriptive. The dialog box has three areas where you can set the field's properties. They are the Summary area, Evaluate area, and Reset area. They control how and when the running total is calculated. Each area is described next.

It should be immediately obvious that this dialog box is much more advanced than the simplistic Insert Summary dialog box you worked with in the previous section. A few things that stand out are that in the middle of the dialog box is an evaluate area which sets when the running total should be calculated (for each record, on change of group, etc.) and at the bottom is a reset area that determines when the running total gets set back to zero. These options alone make it obvious that you can do a lot more with running totals than you can with summary fields.

## The Summary Area

The Summary area is very simplistic and is similar to the Insert Summary dialog box discussed in the last section because. It lets you set the field to base the running total on and which summary calculation to perform (sum, average, count, etc.).

## The Evaluate Area

The Evaluate area determines when the field's value gets added to the running total calculation. You can have a value get recalculated every time a detail record is printed, or if it is based on a group level field, then you can calculate it for every new group. You could also calculate it only when the summary field changes value. There are four options for when to evaluate the field and they each have a different purpose. They are described next.

### For Each Record

Evaluating the running total field as each record is printed is the most common way of using running total fields. As each row is printed, the selected field's value is used to update the running total field. You can use this option when you want to show the current running total in the Details section beside the field's current value. Even if you don't show the running total field in the Details section, you should use this option when every row in the report is going to be included in the running total.

### On Change of Field

This option only includes the field's value in the calculation when the field's value changes from one record to the next. If the current record has the same value as the previous record, then it won't be counted. Evaluating the running total when a field changes is useful when there is repeated data in a field and you only want to count each value once. This frequently happens when the data source links two tables in a parent-child relationship. When this is the case, the fields from the parent table are repeated each time that the fields from the child table are listed. If you are summarizing a value from the parent table, then the totals will be wrong because they will be incremented each time a child record is printed. To correct this problem, select the On Change of Field option and select a field from the parent table. This ensures that the running total is only evaluated once for each record in the parent table.

When using this option, the way to select the field isn't completely intuitive. There is a text box to the right of the option, but it won't let you type anything into it. Instead, you have to select the field from the field list on the left and click on the arrow button beside the option. Once you click on the arrow button, the field name is entered into the text box. If you want to change the field, you have to use the arrow button again. Although you can click on the text box and move the cursor around with the arrow keys, no typing is allowed.

When selecting the field from the parent table, it's best to choose the primary key from the parent table.[16] If you aren't careful, you might think that you can choose any field in the parent table to determine when to evaluate the running total. But this isn't always true because some records in the parent table will have the same value over consecutive records. For example, if the parent table is the Employee table, you might select the Employee Name field. But it is very common for some employees to have the same name and selecting this field will result in the second employee's data not being evaluated. Thus, in this example, you should use the Employee ID field or the Social Security Number so that uniqueness is guaranteed.

## On Change of Group

This option is pretty self explanatory. The running total field is evaluated whenever the group changes. It is only calculated one time for each group in the report. This is similar to the On Change of Field option except that this option can only be used when the report has groups. When selecting this option, the dropdown list only shows you the available group names.

## Use a Formula

Evaluating the running total field based on a formula lets you create more advanced running total calculations. There are times when the other options are too simplistic to give you the running total result you need. You could have a running total which is only calculated when a field is a certain value or is within a range of values. For example, this can be used to create multiple running totals and each one only summarizes data for a particular country. One field could just summarize data when the country is USA and another field could do so only when the country is Canada. Another example is a running total field that only summarizes data for values that exceed a certain limit. For example, a sales report that prints sales details could print a grand total of all the deals that exceeded a million dollars.

---

[16] Primary key fields always have a unique value throughout the entire table. There are no duplicates.

## The Reset Area

Just as important as setting when to evaluate the running total is determining when to reset its value back to zero. If you are tracking the running total for individual groups, then you want it to reset every time the group changes. There are also times when you don't want the value to get reset at all. If you want a running total to accumulate throughout the life of the report so that the last record shows the grand total, then you don't want to reset the value.

The Reset area gives you the option to never reset the running total, reset it when a field's value changes, reset it when the group changes or by using a formula. Clicking the formula button brings up the Formula Editor dialog box so that you can write more advanced formulas for determining when the running total is reset. Just like the Evaluate area, using the formula gives you the ability to reset the value using additional functionality not provided in the other options.

## Placing the Running Total Field

You might recall from earlier in the chapter that when printing a summary on a group, you can put that field in either the group footer or group header and it still prints the same result. The location of a summary field doesn't affect its value. This isn't true for running totals because they are calculated while printing records. Thus, they are only accurate to the point that they get printed. Where you place the running total is very important. If you put a running total in the group header, then it shows the calculation as of the first record in the group. Since the other records haven't been printed yet, they aren't calculated. An example report showing this behavior is shown in Figure 3-27.

6/14/2002 3:17:33PM

MOUNTAIN BIKE INC

How to maintain running totals for a group

| Customer Name | Order ID | Order Amount | RunningTotal |
|---|---|---|---|
| **Tienda de Bicicletas El Pardo** | | | **5,219.55** |
| Tienda de Bicicletas El Pardo | 1323 | 5,219.55 | 5,219.55 |
| Tienda de Bicicletas El Pardo | 1332 | 5,219.55 | 10,439.10 |
| | | | 10,439.10 |
| **Mad Mountain Bikes** | | | **8,897.31** |
| Mad Mountain Bikes | 1339 | 8,897.31 | 8,897.31 |
| | | | 8,897.31 |
| **Bikes, Bikes, and More Bikes** | | | **8,819.55** |
| Bikes, Bikes, and More Bikes | 1317 | 8,819.55 | 8,819.55 |
| | | | 8,819.55 |
| **Piccolo** | | | **5,895.20** |
| Piccolo | 1348 | 5,895.20 | 5,895.20 |
| | | | 5,895.20 |
| **Whistler Rentals** | | | **16.50** |
| Whistler Rentals | 1330 | 16.50 | 16.50 |
| Whistler Rentals | 1319 | 5,219.55 | 5,236.05 |
| | | | 5,236.05 |

**Figure 3-27. The results of a running total field with a grouping report.**

The report in figure 3-27 shows a running total column and there are three identical running total fields. The running total field calculates the sum of each order amount, and it is reset when a group changes. There is a copy of it in the header, the detail, and the footer. You can see that the field in the detail section changes for every record and that the footer matches the value of the last record printed. But the header record doesn't match the footer value. Instead, it is equal to the first record printed in the group.

## Best Of The Forum

**Question:** I currently have a running total field displayed in the page footer. I want to carry that same value forward to the next page in the header section. Unfortunately, it doesn't work because the header section often shows a different total than what was in the previous page footer.

**Answer:** This is because the running total field always includes the current record being printed. When it appears in the page header of the following page, it is also adding the first record that is getting printed on that page. Even though the first record on that page hasn't printed yet, it still gets included in the running total balance. That's why the two values are different. To fix this, you have to create a manual running total formula and place it in the details section.[17] This synchronizes the running total balance with the actual printing of the detail data. To get the balance to appear in the report footer and header sections, the formula has to use a shared variable and create a second formula which simply prints the value of that shared variable. Put this second formula in the report header and footer.

# Running Totals Compared to Summary Fields

Running totals are interesting because they have similar functionality to summary fields, and they can also be duplicated with formula fields. This can cause some confusion as to when you should use a running total, a summary field, or a custom formula field. Each of these options has unique characteristics that you need to be familiar with to make the best choice.

Summary fields are an easy way to summarize data outside of the Details section. For example, you can put subtotals in the Group Footer and put a grand total in the Report Footer. But you can't put a summary field in the Details section.

Running Totals have more flexibility because they can be evaluated at different times. They can summarize data in the Details section, across groups, or only when a field's value changes. They can even use a formula to summarize on specific records only.

Both summary fields and running totals have a limitation that if the report group suppresses data, then the calculations will include the records that don't get printed. It will show an incorrect value. If you recall from Chapter 1's coverage of the two-pass report process, even though a record is suppressed, the data was still read into memory during Pass 1 of the reporting process and its summaries formulas were calculated. The grouping is done in pass #2 and this is after the formulas have been calculated.

To get around this limitation, you can create a running total field that evaluates based on a formula. This formula uses the same logic as the conditional formatting formula for the Suppress property of the Details section. By doing this, the running total is calculated as the records are being printed and the data matches the report grouping. For example, assume the report only wants to show records where the Region field is equal to "West". The Suppress property for the Details section would have the following conditional formula:

{Customer.Region} <> "West";

Any records where the Region isn't "West" are suppressed. To make the running total field calculate properly you have to modify it so that it only gets evaluated for the records that are displayed. In the Evaluate area, you would set the option Use a Formula and enter the following formula:

---

[17] Manual running totals using formula fields are discussed later in this chapter.

{Customer.Region} = "West";

Thus, if the Region is "West" then the value is included in the running total field. As an example of this, the report in Figure 3-28 is the same report as the last example, but it suppresses some of the records from printing. The grand total field in the Order Amount column is a summary field that was added by right-clicking on the Order Amount field and selecting Insert Grand Total. This doesn't have any special logic associated with it and it will include values that aren't printed. The grand total in the right-most column is a running total field that also sums the order amount. But this running total field is evaluated using a formula that matches the suppress formula. It is only evaluated for records that get printed.

**MOUNTAIN BIKE INC**

## How to maintain running totals for a group

| Customer Name | Order ID | Order Amount | RunningTotal |
|---|---|---|---|
| Tienda de Bicicletas El Pardo | | | 5,219.55 |
| Tienda de Bicicletas El Pardo | 1323 | 5,219.55 | 5,219.55 |
| Tienda de Bicicletas El Pardo | 1332 | 5,219.55 | 10,439.10 |
| | | | 10,439.10 |
| Mad Mountain Bikes | | | 8,897.31 |
| Mad Mountain Bikes | 1339 | 8,897.31 | 8,897.31 |
| | | | 8,897.31 |
| Bikes, Bikes, and More Bikes | | | 8,819.55 |
| Bikes, Bikes, and More Bikes | 1317 | 8,819.55 | 8,819.55 |
| | | | 8,819.55 |
| Piccolo | | | 5,895.20 |
| Piccolo | 1348 | 5,895.20 | 5,895.20 |
| | | | 5,895.20 |
| Whistler Rentals | | | 16.50 |
| Whistler Rentals | 1330 | 16.50 | 16.50 |
| Whistler Rentals | 1319 | 5,219.55 | 5,236.05 |
| | | | 5,236.05 |
| | | 89,615.16 | 39,287.21 |

Figure 3-28. Summary field incorrectly calculates the grand total.

You can see that the grand total that is calculated with the summary field is much larger than the running total that uses a formula. The summary field is including records that aren't printed on the report.

# Using Formulas instead of Running Totals

Running totals have two limitations. The first is that you are limited in the types of calculations you can do (Sum, Avg, etc.). The second limitation is that running totals are restricted to using only first pass data. For example, the formulas can't use summary functions, the NextValue() or PreviousValue() functions or shared variables. They also can't use the WhilePrintingRecords keyword. If you want to calculate the running total of this type of formula, you have to do so using another formula. This is often called a Manual Running Total because you are writing the formulas that implement it. Let's look at manual running totals in more detail.

A formula can perform the same functionality as a summary field and running total. The difference being that you have to do the work of writing the code and debugging it to make sure it works properly. Formulas give you the benefit of being in complete control and you can use advanced functionality not provided with the Edit Running Total Field dialog box. You have to balance how much work you want to do with how much control you need over the calculations.

> ### Tip
>
> You might be surprised to learn that using formulas is actually more efficient than using a running total object. In performance tests on reports, replacing a running total field with a manual running total formula resulted in faster page views. If you have a large report that uses running total fields and the performance is slow, you should try replacing them with manual running totals.

When using a formula to calculate a running total, you need to create up to three formulas to do the job. The first formula, the summary formula, replaces the functionality of the Summary area and the Evaluate area. It performs the running total calculation. It has to have a global variable that tracks the current value of the running total so that this can be shared with the other two formulas. If the formula doesn't reference any database fields, it should also use the WhilePrintingRecords keyword so that it gets calculated while the report runs.

Once you write the formula and save it, you have to put it on the report so that it gets calculated. If the formula isn't used on the report, then Crystal Reports ignores it. Where you put it on the report determines when it is evaluated. If you want it evaluated for every record, then put it in the Details section. If you want it evaluated once per group, then put it in the Group Header section.

The second formula, the reset formula, resets the total back to zero. Just like the first formula, where you put it determines when it sets the running total back to zero. If you want it reset for every group, then put it in the Group Footer. If you want it reset for every page, then put it in the Page Footer. Since the reset formula always has the same value (zero), you don't want the user to see this formula on the report. You should open the Format Editor dialog box and check the Suppress property.

For running totals that accumulate their value for every record in the report and don't need to be reset, then the reset formula isn't necessary.

**Best Of The Forum**

**Question:** How do I sum the values of a column for each page?

**Answer:** Create a manual running total but put the reset formula in the page footer. This sets the running total to zero at the start of each new page.

After creating the summary formula and reset formula and placing them on the report, you have replaced the functionality of the running total field and you are finished. However, there are times when you will also need a third formula. Let's look at when a third formula is necessary and what it does.

In most circumstances, you will put the summary formula in the Details section so that the user sees the running total for every record on the report. But what if you want the running total to only be displayed in the group footer or page footer? In this case, you will still keep the summary field in the Details section, but you will suppress it so that the user doesn't see it. By suppressing the field, it still gets calculated but it won't be shown to the user. Since the summary formula is suppressed, you need to create a third formula to display the running total value in another report section. This third formula's purpose is simply to print the value on the report. You could put it in the group header or report header if you wish.

# Tutorial 3-5. Using a Formula for the Running Total

Using a formula to replace the running total field probably sounds like a lot of work. But you'll see that it's really quite simple once you do it a couple times. This tutorial uses a formula to print the line number on every row, and for each page it gets reset back to zero. This is similar to the RowNumber function in Crystal Reports except that the RowNumber function is cumulative over the entire report and never gets reset back to zero.

1.  Open the Crystal Reports sample report, Group By Intervals.rpt. Save it as RunningTotalFormula.rpt.

2.  We want to put the line number in the left most column of the page, but there isn't room because the Customer Name is left justified. So move the Customer Name field and its header one quarter inch to the right.

3.  Let's create the summary formula which tracks the line number. In the Field Explorer window, right-click on the Formula Fields category and select New. Name the formula LineNumber. Click the OK button to open the Formula Workshop.

4.  Enter the following formula:

```
WhilePrintingRecords;
Global NumberVar LineNumber;
LineNumber := LineNumber + 1;
```

This formula creates a global variable, LineNumber, and increments it by one each time it is called. Since this formula doesn't use any database fields, it has to have the WhilePrintingRecords keyword to force it to be calculated while the report runs.

5. Click the Save and Close button to save the formula and return to the designer.

6. Drag the LineNumber formula onto the report in the Details section. Put it directly to the left of the Customer Name field and resize it so that it fits.

7. By default, the LineNumber field will display two decimal places. You need to format this field so that it displays as an integer. Right-click on the field and select Format Field. On the Number tab select the format "-1123". Click the OK button to save the change.

8. Now we need to create the reset formula so that the line number gets reset back to zero for every page. Create another new formula and name it LineNumberReset.

9. In the Formula Workshop dialog box, enter the following formula:

```
WhilePrintingRecords;
Global NumberVar LineNumber;
LineNumber := 0;
```

10. This formula resets the LineNumber variable back to zero. Click the OK button to save the formula and return to the designer.

11. Drag the LineNumberReset formula onto the Page Footer section.

12. Since you don't want the user to see a zero in the page footer, it should be suppressed. Right-click on the field and select Format Field.

13. In the Format Editor dialog box, click on the Common tab and check the Suppress property. Click the OK button to close the dialog box.

12. Preview the report and you should see a line number on every row and the line number gets reset for every page printed. It should look similar to the following figure.

*Group Data in Intervals*

11/12/2005  12:03:28AM

## How to group data in intervals

| Customer Name | Region | Country | Postal Cod |
|---|---|---|---|
| **Less than $10,000** | | | |
| 1  7 Bikes For 7 Brothers | NV | USA | 89102 |
| 2  Against The Wind Bikes | NY | USA | 14817 |
| 3  AIC Childrens | Hong Kong SAR | China | 439433 |
| 4  Aruba Sport | St. George | Aruba | 655456 |
| 5  Auvergne Bicross | Auvergne | France | 03200 |
| 6  Barbados Sports, Ltd. | Bridgetown | Barbados | 4532 |
| 7  Barry's Bikes | DE | USA | 19850 |
| 8  Beach Trails and Wheels | Waikato | New Zealand | |
| 9  Benny - The Spokes Person | AL | USA | 35861 |
| 10  Berg auf Trails GmBH. | Nordrhein-Westfalen | Germany | D-40608 |
| 11  Berlin Biking GmBH. | Bayern | Germany | D-80042 |
| 12  Bicicletas  de Montaña Cancun | Quintana Roo | Mexico | 02994 |

# Advanced Tutorials

As you learned throughout this chapter, Crystal Reports gives you many options for grouping report data and customizing the output. It will probably take some practice before you become familiar with the different ways each option can be used. As you learn more about each option, you'll discover new ways of creating advanced reports that use these features to the fullest. The following advanced tutorials present you with common challenges that many people on the internet report having trouble with. By walking through these tutorials you'll become more experienced with the grouping and sorting features of Crystal Reports. When the time comes where you need to create a similar report for your own project, you'll already know how to design it.

The first challenge you might encounter is with creating dynamic groups within a report. There are times when two reports are identical except for how they group data. Rather than create two different reports, it would be much easier to use the same report and just switch out the group fields.

Another example of dynamic grouping is letting the user choose the field that they want to group on. It would be much nicer to prompt the user with a parameter and then use that parameter for selecting which group to display.

In the next figure we see a report that has two groups. It groups by Country and then groups by Product Type. This report shows how many products were sold within each country.

| Corporate Product Sales | | | | | |
|---|---|---|---|---|---|
| | Product ID | Product Name | Unit Price | Quantity | Sale Amount |
| **Argentina** | | | | | |
| **Hybrid** | | | | | |
| | 201201 | Romeo | $832.35 | 2 | $1,664.70 |
| | | | Sub-Totals | 2 | $1,664.70 |
| **Aruba** | | | | | |
| **Competition** | | | | | |
| | 101171 | Descent | $2,939.85 | 2 | $5,879.70 |
| | | | Sub-Totals | 2 | $5,879.70 |
| **Australia** | | | | | |
| **Competition** | | | | | |
| | 101201 | Descent | $2,939.85 | 2 | $5,879.70 |
| | 102151 | Mozzie | $1,652.86 | 2 | $3,305.72 |
| | | | Sub-Totals | 4 | $9,185.42 |
| **Mountain** | | | | | |
| | 302161 | Rapel | $479.85 | 1 | $479.85 |
| | | | Sub-Totals | 1 | $479.85 |
| **Helmets** | | | | | |
| | 5206 | Xtreme Adult Helmet | $32.21 | 2 | $64.42 |
| | 2211 | Triumph Vertigo Helmet | $53.90 | 2 | $107.80 |
| | | | Sub-Totals | 4 | $172.22 |
| **Locks** | | | | | |
| | 3302 | Guardian "U" Lock | $17.50 | 1 | $17.50 |
| | | | Sub-Totals | 1 | $17.50 |
| **Saddles** | | | | | |
| | 6403 | Roadster Mini Mtn Saddle | $15.00 | 3 | $45.00 |
| | | | Sub-Totals | 3 | $45.00 |
| **Austria** | | | | | |
| **Competition** | | | | | |
| | 103221 | Endorphin | $899.85 | 1 | $899.85 |
| | 101172 | Descent | $2,939.85 | 2 | $5,879.70 |
| | 101201 | Descent | $2,939.85 | 2 | $5,879.70 |

If you want to change this report to only show sales by Product Type, you can suppress the Country group. This is easy enough to do by right-clicking on the group name and selecting Suppress. But even so, the report still looks very similar to the original report.

| | Product ID | Product Name | Unit Price | Quantity | Sale Amount |
|---|---|---|---|---|---|
| **Corporate Product Sales** | | | | | |
| **Hybrid** | | | | | |
| | 201201 | Romeo | $832.35 | 2 | $1,664.70 |
| | | | Sub-Totals | 2 | $1,664.70 |
| **Competition** | | | | | |
| | 101171 | Descent | $2,939.85 | 2 | $5,879.70 |
| | | | Sub-Totals | 2 | $5,879.70 |
| **Competition** | | | | | |
| | 101201 | Descent | $2,939.85 | 2 | $5,879.70 |
| | 102151 | Mozzie | $1,652.86 | 2 | $3,305.72 |
| | | | Sub-Totals | 4 | $9,185.42 |
| **Mountain** | | | | | |
| | 302161 | Rapel | $479.85 | 1 | $479.85 |
| | | | Sub-Totals | 1 | $479.85 |
| **Helmets** | | | | | |
| | 5206 | Xtreme Adult Helmet | $32.21 | 2 | $64.42 |
| | 2211 | Triumph Vertigo Helmet | $53.90 | 2 | $107.80 |
| | | | Sub-Totals | 4 | $172.22 |
| **Locks** | | | | | |
| | 3302 | Guardian "U" Lock | $17.50 | 1 | $17.50 |
| | | | Sub-Totals | 1 | $17.50 |
| **Saddles** | | | | | |
| | 6403 | Roadster Mini Mtn Saddle | $15.00 | 3 | $45.00 |
| | | | Sub-Totals | 3 | $45.00 |
| **Competition** | | | | | |
| | 103221 | Endorphin | $899.85 | 1 | $899.85 |
| | 101172 | Descent | $2,939.85 | 2 | $5,879.70 |
| | 101201 | Descent | $2,939.85 | 2 | $5,879.70 |
| | 101171 | Descent | $2,939.85 | 1 | $2,939.85 |
| | 103201 | Endorphin | $899.85 | 2 | $1,799.70 |
| | 101152 | Descent | $2,939.85 | 2 | $5,879.70 |
| | | | Sub-Totals | 10 | $23,278.50 |

You can see that the Competition product type heading is duplicated because in the original report it was spread across multiple countries. It is still spread across multiple countries, but now the group headings aren't visible. If this were truly a report that only grouped on Product Type, each product type would be consolidated into its own group. There would only be one Group Header for each Product Type. We need to fix this report so that it can be used to either show both groups or just the Product Type grouping.

The typical method of creating a group is to use a database field as the grouping field. But this locks you into a single group field and doesn't give you any flexibility. An alternative which gives you more options is to create a formula that points to the database field and base the group on that formula. Doing this lets you change the formula field and the group automatically changes as well.

# Tutorial 3-6. Sales By Country and Product Type.rpt

Before getting into the tutorials, we first need to build the base report that is used for tutorial 3-7 and 3-8. This will be used for demonstrating how to modify an existing report so that it can handle dynamic groups.

1. On the Start Page click Standard Report Wizard to create a new report.

2. In the Data dialog box, select the Xtreme.mdb database as the data source. Do this by clicking on Create New Connection > Access/Excel > Make New Connection.

3. For the Database Name property, navigate to the Xtreme.mdb database that is installed in the Crystal Reports sample folders. Click the Finish button once you've selected it.

4. Open the Tables category and double-click the following tables to add them to the Selected Tables list at the right: Customer, Orders, Orders Detail, Product, Product_Type.

5. Click the Next button twice to go to the Fields dialog.

6. In the Available Fields list, select the following fields: Customer.Country, Product.Product ID, Product.Product Name, Product Type.Product Type Name, Orders_Detail.Unit Price, and Orders_Detail.Quantity.

7. Click the Next button to go to the Grouping dialog box.

8. Select the following fields to group on: Customer.Country and Product_Type.Product Type Name. Click the Next button.

9. On the Summaries dialog, remove all fields from the Summarized Fields list.

10. Click the Finish button and go into design mode.

11. Right-click on the Formula Fields category in the Field Explorer window and select New.

12. Enter the formula name **SalesAmount**.

13. In the Formula Workshop dialog box, enter the following formula:

    {Orders_Detail.Quantity} * {Orders_Detail.Unit Price}

14. Click the Save and Close button to save the formula.

15. We need to put the SalesAmount formula on the report, but there isn't any room. Move the Unit Price and Quanity fields to the left.

16. Drag and drop the SalesAmount formula onto the far right side of the report.

    Now we need to add the summary fields for both the Quantity and SalesAmount fields.

17. Right-click on the Quantity field and select Insert > Summary. On the Insert Summary dialog box, set the summary location to be Grand Total and click the OK button.

18. Repeat the previous step to insert summaries for Group #1 and Group #2.

19. Right-click on the SalesAmount formula field and select Insert > Summary. On the Insert Summary dialog box, set the summary location to be Grand Total and click the OK button.

20. Repeat the previous step to insert summaries for Group #1 and Group #2.

    At this point you've created the report with two grouping fields and there are summaries for the Quantity and SalesAmount fields. Your report should similar to the following figure.

| Country | Product Type Name | Product ID | Product Name | Unit Price | Quantity | SalesAmount |
|---------|-------------------|-----------|--------------|-----------|----------|-------------|
| Austria | Competition | 103,201 | Endorphin | $899.85 | 2 | $1,799.70 |
| | **Competition** | | | | **10.00** | **$23,278.50** |
| | | | | | | |
| | **Gloves** | | | | | |
| Austria | Gloves | 1,104 | Active Outdoors ( | $14.50 | 2 | $29.00 |
| Austria | Gloves | 1,109 | Active Outdoors L | $16.50 | 1 | $16.50 |
| Austria | Gloves | 1,110 | Active Outdoors L | $16.50 | 1 | $16.50 |
| Austria | Gloves | 1,106 | Active Outdoors L | $16.50 | 2 | $33.00 |
| Austria | Gloves | 4,104 | InFlux Lycra Glov | $15.50 | 1 | $15.50 |
| | **Gloves** | | | | **7.00** | **$110.50** |
| | | | | | | |
| | **Helmets** | | | | | |
| Austria | Helmets | 2,215 | Triumph Vertigo F | $53.90 | 1 | $53.90 |
| Austria | Helmets | 5,204 | Xtreme Adult Hel | $33.90 | 2 | $67.80 |
| Austria | Helmets | 2,212 | Triumph Vertigo F | $53.90 | 2 | $107.80 |
| Austria | Helmets | 2,201 | Triumph Pro Helr | $41.90 | 3 | $125.70 |
| Austria | Helmets | 5,205 | Xtreme Adult Hel | $30.51 | 2 | $61.02 |
| | **Helmets** | | | | **10.00** | **$416.22** |

21. It isn't the most beautiful report, but it will do for this tutorial. Save the report as **Sales By Country and Product Type.rpt**.

This report is now ready to be used as the starting point for the next two tutorials. So make sure to remember where you saved it so that you can re-load it when necessary.

## Best Of The Forum

**Question:** I have a report that usually prints two groups. But, I want to give the user the option to add a new grouping field when they run the report. Can I dynamically add a group to the report?

**Answer:** No, you can't add new groups to a report while it is being printed. You can only hide existing groups. For example, if you have a report that needs to show between one to three groups, you need to create the report

using the maximum number of groups (three in this example) and then hide
the ones that aren't needed.

# Tutorial 3-7. Dynamic Grouping Fields

In this tutorial we will base the groups on formulas. We will fix the previous report so that
it shows either both groups or only one group. This gives the user the ability to choose
how the type of report they want to see. There are three changes that need to be made.
The first change is creating a parameter that prompts the user for the type of report to
print. The second change is basing the two groups on a formula rather than a database
field. The third change disables certain report objects (group header and footer, summary
fields, etc.) so that only the appropriate ones are displayed when the report displays just
one group.

| Caution |
|---|

Although formulas can give you advanced grouping options, be careful if you
have a report that is hundreds of pages long and you want better performance.
Using formulas as the grouping/sorting fields will incur a slight performance
hit. Normally, this isn't a problem. But for large scale reports that take a long
time to run, this could be a factor.

1. Rename the previous report so that we can re-use it again after this tutorial. Select File
   > Save As and enter the name Sales – Multiple Groups.rpt.
2. Create a parameter to prompt the user for the type of report they want to print. Call
   the parameter Report Type. The prompt has two possible values: Country or Product.
   A screen shot of the parameters appears below.

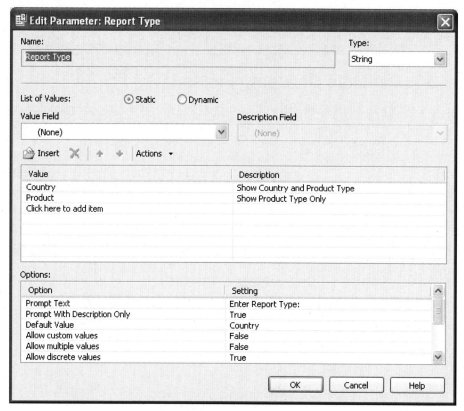

This report has two groups that are both based on a database field. We need to create two new formulas that will be used for grouping instead. The first formula will return either the Country field or the Product Type Name field.

3.   Create a new formula and name it **MainGroup**. Type in the following code:

```
if {?Report Type}="Country" then
    {Customer.Country}
else
    {Product_Type.Product Type Name};
```

This formula looks at the parameter value and if it is equal to "Country" then the formula returns the Country field. If not, then we know that the report should only group on the Product Type Name field.

## Caution

When using a formula to return the value to group on, each possible value must be the same data type. For example, you can't have an If statement where the success portion returns a string data type and the failure portion returns a number data type.

4. Create a second formula and name it **SubGroup**. Type in the following code:

```
if {?Report Type}="Product" then
    ""
else
    {Product_Type.Product Type Name}
```

This formula is for the secondary group field, which is optional. If the user only wants to group by product type, then this formula doesn't need to return a value at all. Thus, it's assigned an empty string as the grouping value. If the user chooses to sort by Country, then both fields will be grouped on and the Product Type Name field becomes the secondary group.

5. Now that the formulas have been created, modify the groups to replace the current fields with the new formulas. Right-click on Group Header #1 and select Change Group. In the drop-down list, select the Main Group formula. This sets the group to be based on that formula instead of the Country field.

6. Repeat the previous step to change Group Header #2 so that it uses the SubGroup formula.

7. Preview the report (selecting the Country parameter value) to see what it looks like. It should look identical to the original report because you've only added the logic to duplicate the existing fields. No formatting changes have been made yet.

8. Preview the report again and select the Product Type parameter value. There are two problems immediately noticeable.

| | | | | | | |
|---|---|---|---|---|---|---|
| **Hybrid** | | | | | | |
| | 1013 | 202161 | Wheeler | $539.85 | 2 | $1,079.70 |
| | 1039 | 202221 | Wheeler | $485.87 | 1 | $485.87 |
| | 1046 | 202201 | Wheeler | $539.85 | 3 | $1,619.55 |
| | 1051 | 202181 | Wheeler | $539.85 | 1 | $539.85 |
| | 1052 | 201161 | Romeo | $832.35 | 2 | $1,664.70 |
| | 1063 | 201221 | Romeo | $832.35 | 3 | $2,497.05 |
| | | | Sub-Total | | 12 | $7,886.72 |
| | | | Hybrid Sub-Totals | | 12 | $7,886.72 |

See how there is too much space between the group header and the first detail record? There are also two sub-total rows instead of one. Even though Group 2 doesn't have any data, the header and footers are still being printed.[18] Printing an empty group

---

[18] Technically, Group 2 does have data because it is using the empty string as its grouping value. But for our purposes, we are using the empty string to simulate no data to group on.

creates unnecessary space on the report. The next step is to suppress these sections when only grouping on the Product Type field.

9.  Let's first disable the Group #2 Header when the report is only grouping on the Product Type. Right-click on the Group #2 Header section and select Section Expert.

10. On the Section Expert dialog box, look for the Suppress property and click on the Formula Workshop button to the right. Enter the following formula:

```
if {?Report Type}="Product" then
    True
else
    False;
```

This formula checks to see which type of report is being printed by analyzing the {?Report Type} parameter. If the parameter value is "Product" then this is the Product Type only report and the group header should be suppressed. Otherwise False is returned and the group header is displayed.

11. Repeat the last two steps, but this time do it for the Suppress property of the Group #2 Footer. Make sure to enter the same formula exactly.

12. Preview the report and select the Product Type only report. It should look much better now because the header doesn't have extra white space below it and there is only one sub-total.

| Kids | | | | | | |
|---|---|---|---|---|---|---|
| | 1004 | 402002 | Micro Nicros | $274.35 | 3 | $823.05 |
| | 1010 | 401001 | Mini Nicros | $253.67 | 3 | $761.01 |
| | 1016 | 401002 | Mini Nicros | $281.85 | 2 | $563.70 |
| | 1032 | 401002 | Mini Nicros | $281.85 | 2 | $563.70 |
| | 1036 | 402002 | Micro Nicros | $274.35 | 1 | $274.35 |
| | 1040 | 401001 | Mini Nicros | $281.85 | 2 | $563.70 |
| | 1057 | 402001 | Micro Nicros | $274.35 | 2 | $548.70 |
| | 1058 | 401002 | Mini Nicros | $281.85 | 3 | $845.55 |
| | | | Kids Sub-Totals | | 18 | $4,943.76 |
| Locks | | | | | | |
| | 1013 | 3305 | Guardian Mini Lock | $20.81 | 3 | $62.43 |
| | 1045 | 5302 | Xtreme Rhino Lock | $9.98 | 3 | $29.94 |
| | 1054 | 3301 | Guardian Chain Lock | $4.50 | 2 | $9.00 |
| | 1062 | 3305 | Guardian Mini Lock | $21.90 | 3 | $65.70 |
| | | | Locks Sub-Totals | | 11 | $167.07 |

This tutorial showed that creating groups with dynamic fields can be done by creating a parameter to prompt the user for the report type and then using this parameter in formulas to dynamically change the formatting of the underlying report objects.

| Tip |
|---|

Using a formula as the grouping field gives you a wide variety of ways to customize groups. Formulas can do complex calculations that aren't possible when referencing simple database fields. For example, you can parse text out of an existing field to group on a sub-string. Formulas can examine the values of other fields and create a new value based upon a calculation. For example, a shipping report could calculate the area of a package and group it as Small, Medium or Large. There are an unlimited number of ways to use formulas to create custom groups.

# Tutorial 3-8. Dynamic Group Sorting

When creating a group, you have to specify the order to sort the data in (the default is ascending order). To make a report more flexible, you can let the user choose how to sort the report. For example, a person who wants to see the most recent sales activity would sort the report in descending order by date. But someone performing an audit would want to sort the date in ascending order so that they can see historical data first. Crystal Reports allows dynamic sorting by letting you specify a formula for the group sorting order.

| Note |
|---|

Dynamic sorting is only allowed on group fields. Crystal Reports doesn't allow modifying the sort order of detail records. How unfortunate!

1. Open the report Sales by Country and Product Type.rpt that you created in Tutorial 3-6.

2. Rename it to **Sales with Custom Sorting.rpt.**

3. Create a new parameter called Product Type Sort Order. This parameter prompts the user to sort the Product Type group in either ascending or descending order. The following screen shot shows how to set the parameter settings.

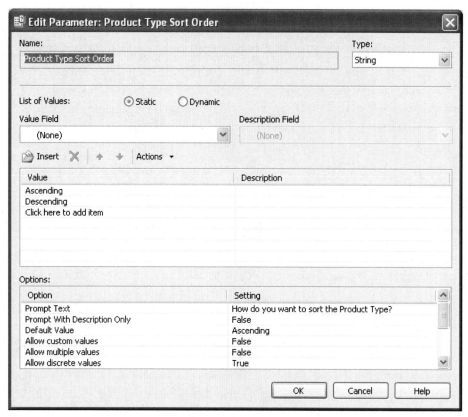

4.  Now we want to modify the group sorting so that it uses a formula to determine the sorting order. Select Report > Group Expert to open the dialog box.

5.  Select the Product Type Name field on the right and click the Options button. This opens the Change Group Options dialog box.

6.  Click the checkbox Use a Formula as Group Sort Order. This enables the Formula button.

7.  Click on the Formula button and enter the following formula:

```
If {?Product Type Sort Order} = "Ascending"
    crAscendingOrder
Else
    crDescendingOrder;
```

This formula checks the value of the parameter and sets the sort order accordingly. Notice how the sort order uses the constants crAscendingOrder or crDescendingOrder. These are predefined constants by Crystal Reports.

8.  Preview the report and select the different parameter values. You'll see that the Product Type sort order changes based upon the parameter value.

This tutorial demonstrated how to integrate parameters and formulas together to customize group sorting. Certain problems that arise with the basic grouping features are overcome with advanced programming techniques.

## Tutorial 3-8. Group Headers that Repeat

When grouping data, it is common to repeat the group header section at the top of each group. This can include printing the group name and column headers. While this is very helpful, there are times when this makes things tricky because you don't always want the group header fields printed every time. For example, consider a report that has a group header which displays the group name at the top of the page and right below it are the column headers. The report has a requirement where the group name should be printed at the beginning of each group but not on successive pages. However, the column headers should always be printed on every page.

This requirement creates a problem because part of the header (the group name) should only be printed once per group and the other part (the column headers) should be printed at the top of each page. Both of them belong in a Group Header section, but they have different behaviors. The solution is to break the header into two sections and format each section differently.

Crystal Reports gives you the ability to find out when a group is repeated on a page. You can use the function InRepeatedGroupHeader to disable certain fields so that they only get printed once for each group.

| Function | Description |
| --- | --- |
| InRepeatedGroupHeader | Call this function within the group header section. It returns false the first time a group header is printed. It returns true for the second and later time that the group header is printed. Note: For the group header to be printed at the top of each page, you have to have the option Repeat Group Header on Each Page enabled. |

1. Open an existing report that has uses a group header with multiple fields in it. You can use the report in Tutorial 3-6 if you wish, but you'll first need to move the column headings from the Report Header into the Group Header.
2. To make the group header repeat on each page, select Report > Group Expert. This opens the Group Expert dialog box.
3. Click on the group field in the list on the right and click the Options button. This opens the Change Group Options dialog box.
4. Select the Options tab.
5. Click the checkbox Repeat Group Header on Each Page. This forces the repeated header to appear at the top of each successive page.

6. Since you only want part of the header to appear at the top of each page, you need to add a second group header section. Right-click on the Group Header. On the pop-up menu select Insert Section Below. This creates a second group header section directly below the existing one.

7. Move the column headers into the new section. You can do this by selecting them and dragging them into the new section, or by cutting and pasting them there. Leave the other text objects in the top group header section. At this point the group header looks the same, but the fields are split into two different sections.

8. Right-click on the group header and select Section Expert. This opens the Section Expert dialog box.

9. Click on the group header for Section A and click on the Formula button for the Suppress property.

10. Enter the following formula:

   InRepeatedGroupHeader

   This function returns True when the group header is about to be printed on a second page. By returning True, it turns on the Suppress property so that the group name doesn't get printed after the first page. Since this formula is only used in Section A, it doesn't affect Section B. The column headers in Section B will be printed on every page.

11. Click the Ok buttons until all the dialog boxes close and you return to the report designer.

12. Save and preview the report. Notice that the group name only gets printed once per group and the column header gets printed at the top of each page.

13. You can also use the InRepeatedGroupHeader function to add a "Cont." string to subsequent group headings. This tells the user that the group started on a previous page. Set the Suppress property of the text object to use the following formula:

   Not InRepeatedGroupHeader;

   Since the Boolean Not operator prefixes the function, this causes the "Cont." to be suppressed the first time the group header is printed and to be displayed on the successive pages.

## Tutorial 3-9. Formatting Hierarchical Groups

Hierarchical groups (discussed earlier in this chapter) give you the option to customize the indentation level of each child record. This shows a tree-view structure illustrating the relationship between the parent and child records. You can also have them line up directly below each other when there is a limited amount of space on the report. Personally, I don't think either option is ideal. When indentation is turned on, you have to be sure that the column headers are positioned in a way that makes the data legible even when as it is shifted across the page. In addition to that, when numbers in the same column aren't right-justified with each other, they are difficult to read. The option to turn off indentation altogether isn't very practical either because it forgoes using a tree-view structure that makes it easy to quickly understand the relationship between the parent and the child records. So which one should you choose? Both!

Formulas can be used so that you can combine both types of indentation to create professional looking hierarchical reports. What you need to do is indent the text-only fields and right-align up the numeric fields. The reason for indenting the text fields is that they are generally wider and can accommodate the extra space needed for the text to shift from left to right. It also makes it possible to see the parent-child relationship between them. Indentation is turned off just for the numeric columns because people find it easier to read and compare values when the numbers are perfectly lined up with each other.

Crystal Reports lets you customize the indentation of each field using a combination of the functions HierarchyLevel() and GroupLevel(). This lets you indent the text fields but not indent the numeric fields.

| Function | Description |
| --- | --- |
| HierarchyLevel(grouplevel function) | Returns the hierarchy level of the current group member. This only works for groups that are sorted hierarchically. |
| GroupingLevel(field) | Return the group level for the field being printed. Pass it the field that you have a hierarchical grouping on. |

Let's see the steps to make this work.

1. Using a report with hierarchical grouping, open the Hierarchical Group Options dialog box by clicking Report > Hierarchical Grouping Options.

2. Set the Group Indent value to 0. This turns off indentation for all columns. The report now looks like a typical columnar report.

3. Right-click on a text field and select Object Size and Position. This dialog box lets you set the size of the object as well as its coordinates.

4. The X coordinate property controls setting the indentation level so that is the one we want to modify. Click on the Formula Workshop button associated with the X coordinate.

5. Enter the following formula:

(HierarchyLevel (GroupingLevel ({Employee.Employee ID})) - 1)*1440/4

This formula calculates the hierarchy level by getting the current grouping level of the current record using the Employee ID field. It multiples it by 1440 (the number of twips per inch) and divides by 4 (to get a quarter of an inch). Each time a child record is displayed, it is offset by ¼ of an inch from the parent record above it.

6. Enter the same formula for all text fields that you want to indent.

7. When finished entering the formula for all text fields, preview the report and you should see that the text fields are being indented and the numeric fields are aligned with each other. This creates a report which makes it easy to see how the parent and child records are related and still have numeric columns that can be quickly compared and analyzed.

*Hierarchical Grouping*

**Xtreme**
Mountain Bi

**How to group records with a hierarchical structure**

6/7/2005    10:39:35PM

| Name | Position | Salary | Total |
|------|----------|--------|-------|
| **Andrew Fuller** | Vice President, Sales | $90,000.00 | $668,000.00 |
| **Steven Buchanan** | Sales Manager | $50,000.00 | $305,000.00 |
| **Nancy Davolio** | Sales Representative | $40,000.00 | $40,000.00 |
| **Janet Leverling** | Sales Representative | $33,000.00 | $33,000.00 |
| **Margaret Peacock** | Sales Representative | $35,000.00 | $35,000.00 |
| **Michael Suyama** | Sales Representative | $30,000.00 | $30,000.00 |
| **Robert King** | Sales Representative | $37,000.00 | $37,000.00 |
| **Laura Callahan** | Inside Sales Coordinator | $45,000.00 | $45,000.00 |
| **Anne Dodsworth** | Sales Representative | $35,000.00 | $35,000.00 |
| **Albert Hellstern** | Business Manager | $60,000.00 | $103,000.00 |
| **Tim Smith** | Mail Clerk | $18,000.00 | $18,000.00 |
| **Caroline Patterson** | Receptionist | $25,000.00 | $25,000.00 |
| **Justin Brid** | Marketing Director | $75,000.00 | $170,000.00 |
| **Xavier Martin** | Marketing Associate | $50,000.00 | $50,000.00 |
| **Laurent Pereira** | Advertising Specialist | $45,000.00 | $45,000.00 |

 Step 4 and 5 show you how to use conditional formatting to change the indentation level of a report object using conditional formatting. With Crystal Reports XI R2, you can use the same dialog box to change the width of the report object based upon the data being printed. As you can see in the Figure 3-29, a Formula button was added for the Width property.

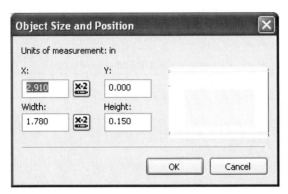

**Formula 3-29. Conditional formatting for object widths (Crystal Reports XI R2).**

# Tutorial 3-10. Breaking Reports Apart by Group

As discussed earlier in the chapter, the properties New Page Before and New Page After are used to cause page breaks between groups. This lets you break apart the report and distribute the individual pages. Unfortunately, setting these properties causes a blank page to be printed either at the beginning or at the end of the report. For example, if you choose to enable the New Page Before property for the Group Header, then it always prints a new page before the first group record is printed. This causes a blank page to print as the first page. If instead, you set the New Page After for the Group Footer section then you will get a blank page at the end of the report.

One way to fix this is to have an introductory page in the Report Header or a report summary page in the Report Footer. This ensures that something relevant always prints before the first group or after the last group and you don't have blank pages appearing. But sometimes, adding these extraneous pages to the beginning or ending of a report isn't acceptable. You need a way to disable these blank pages from being printed at all. This is done with a simple formula. The formula you use is dependent upon whether you want to use New Page Before or use New Page After. The one you choose doesn't matter and it's more of a personal preference. Just make sure you match up the property with the correct formula.

### *Option 1: Setting New Page Before for the Group Header*

1. Open the Section Expert and select the Group Header.
2. Find the New Page Before property and click on the Formula Workshop button.
3. Enter the following formula.

   Not OnFirstRecord

   This disables the New Page Before property for the first record in the first group and prevents a blank page from printing.

### Option 2: Setting New Page After for the Group Footer

1. Open the Section Expert and select the Group Footer.
2. Find the New Page After property and click on the Formula Workshop button.
3. Enter the following formula.

Not OnLastRecord

This disables the New Page After property for the last record in the last group and prevents a blank page from printing.

# 4

# Selecting Records and Using Parameters

The previous chapter showed you how to make reports easier to read by sorting and grouping the data. This made it possible to break down large amounts of data into smaller and easier to understand sections. Another way to make it easier to understand reports is by filtering out unnecessary data prior to printing the report. Filtering data lets you customize the report to the user's preferences so that only information specific 2to their current needs is shown.

Filtering data consists of two levels. The first level uses the Select Expert to specify which data to print on the report and which data should be filtered out. But the Select Expert by itself only creates a static selection formula. It doesn't take into account the user's preferences. So the second level builds upon the Select Expert by creating parameters that query the user for the specific data they need. These preferences are used within the selection formula so that the report is customized to the user's needs.

This chapter first shows you how to filter data using the Select Expert and then shows you how to create advance filters using parameters. Parameters are covered in great detail because they are also used within report formulas and for custom formatting. The effective use of parameters within record selection formulas and custom formatting lets you create dynamic reports that are tailored to each specific user.

## Selecting Records

Prior to this chapter, the sample reports have selected records from a table without regard to selecting specific data. It was assumed that you wanted to display every record in the table. While this is true some of the time, it is more the exception than the rule. You frequently need to filter data so that only a subset of records gets printed.

Here are a few examples of reports that select data for a specific purpose:

- A sales report shows the sales figures for a specific region or sales person. Another shows data for a specific month and groups it by sales person.

- A user is prompted to enter their User ID and Password and a payroll report uses their security level to determine what salary information should be printed.

- An Inventory Alert report shows products whose inventories are below the required minimum level. The purchasing department uses this report to order products that are at risk of going out of stock.

Crystal Reports makes selecting records easy. It provides a Select Expert that lets you pick one or more fields and set a selection formula for each field. Each record in the database is evaluated with the selection formula and this determines whether it appears on the report or not. The Select Expert dialog box is similar to other Crystal Report experts and is easy to learn.

# Using the Select Expert

To open the Select Expert, select the menu items Report > Select Expert. The other method is to click on the Select Expert button on the Toolbar.

If this is the first time the Select Expert has been run for the report, it shows the Choose Field dialog box. This is where you chose the field to filter on. As you can see in Figure 4-1, it simply lists all the fields available. The fields already used on the report are shown first and they are followed by every available field from the report's data source. A field from either of these groups can be selected.

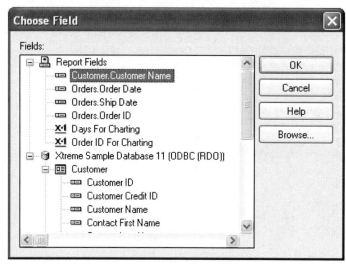

**Figure 4-1. The Choose Field dialog box.**

Once you select a field from this dialog box and click the OK button, the dialog box is not shown again. Instead, you are always taken to the Select Expert dialog box shown in Figure 4-2.

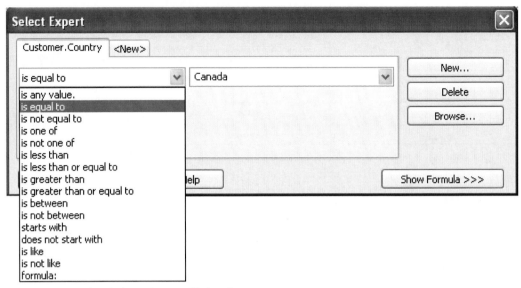

**Figure 4-2. The Select Expert dialog box.**

There are two tabs in the Select Expert dialog box. The first is titled with the field that was just selected in the Choose Field dialog box. The second tab is titled <New>. The first tab with the field name has a dropdown list for selecting the filter criteria. This is set to Is Any Value. By default, reports don't have any filters turned on and every record gets selected. Click the dropdown list to view available filtering options and select the one you want. The dialog box in Figure 4-2 shows all the options in this dropdown list. This list is the textual equivalent of the basic comparison operators. They are described in detail in Table 4-1.

**Table 4-1. Comparison operators for filtering data.**

| Criteria | Description |
| --- | --- |
| Is Any Value | Every record is selected. This is the same as not specifying a record selection formula. |
| Is Equal To | The field must exactly match a specified value. |
| Is Not Equal To | All records where the field does not match the specified value are selected. |
| Is One Of | Lets you build a list of acceptable values. As long as the field's value matches any one of the values in the list then the record is selected. |
| Is Not One Of | The opposite of Is One Of. The record is selected if the field's value doesn't match any of the values in the list. |

| | |
|---|---|
| Is Less Than | The value must be less than the value specified. |
| Is Less Than or Equal To | The value must be equal to or less than the value specified. |
| Is Greater Than | The value must be greater than the value specified. |
| Is Greater Than or Equal To | The value must be equal to or greater than the value specified. |
| Is Between | You specify a range of values and the field's value must be within this range. It can also be equal to the endpoints of the range. For example, if the start and end points are 100 and 200, then the following values would be acceptable: 100, 101, 199, 200. |
| Is Not Between | The value must be outside the range. For example, if the start and end points are 100 and 200, then the following values would be acceptable: 1, 99, 201, 202. |
| Starts With | Selects string fields that start with one or more characters. For example, a value of "B" would match the names "Brian" and "Barry". |
| Does Not Start With | Selects string fields that do not start with the characters specified. For example, a value of "B" would match the names "Lynn" and "Karen" because they do not start with the letter "B". |
| Is Like | Let's you use wildcards for specifying the matching criteria. Using wildcards is discussed more later in the chapter. |
| Is Not Like | The opposite of Is Like. |
| Is True | This criterion is only available for Boolean fields. It selects fields that are equal to True. |
| Is False | This criterion is only available for Boolean fields. It selects fields that are equal to False. |
| Formula: | Lets you type in the formula directly. Useful when the formula is too complex for the available criteria. |

Selecting a DateTime field gives you two additional options listed with the comparison operators. These options let you select dates based on sophisticated date ranges. For example, you can select fields that fall within the last 7 days or select fields that are in the first quarter of the calendar year.[19] See Figure 4-3 for a list of the available functions.

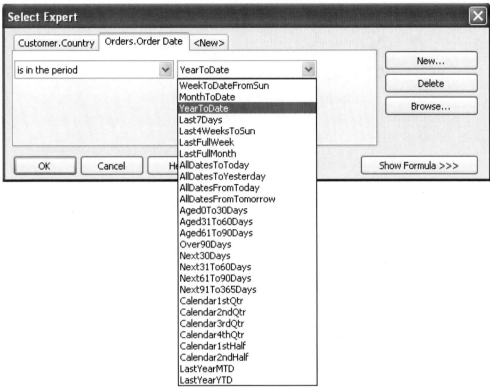

**Figure 4-3. Available date range functions.**

After selecting a comparison method, the right side of the dialog box changes so that you can enter the value to compare the field to. With the majority of the comparisons, only a single dropdown list is shown. For example, comparisons such as Is Equal To or Is Greater Than compare the field to a single value.

There are exceptions to the rule of only having a single dropdown list. The Is Between and Is Not Between comparisons give you two dropdown lists. This lets you create a range of values by entering the beginning and ending values. The Is Between comparison is inclusive. As mentioned in Table 4-1, if the range is from 100 to 200 then the numbers that would be included in this range start at 100 and go up to, and including, 200. The Is Not Between comparison is exclusive. The valid numbers would be any number less than 100 or greater than 200.

---

[19] Using date ranges that involve fiscal years, the don't start on January 1st of the year requires you to build your own formulas.

A very helpful feature for setting the filter is that all the current values for the field are listed in the dropdown list. Crystal Reports queries the database and populates the list with the current data for that field. Clicking on the arrow lets you see what those values are. In fact, the first time you click on the arrow you will probably notice a short delay while Crystal Reports opens the database and reads the records. You can either select one of these values from the list or type in a new value that isn't in the list.

### Caution

If a report uses data from a data source on an external server, make sure you have an active connection to it. Otherwise, Crystal Reports temporarily freezes up while it attempts to connect to the server and wait for a response.

The comparisons Is One Of and Is Not One Of also let you enter more than just a single value to compare to. These criteria let you build a list of items where the field should either be in the list or not in the list. As you select items from the dropdown list, they are added to the list below it. This dialog box is shown in Figure 4-4.

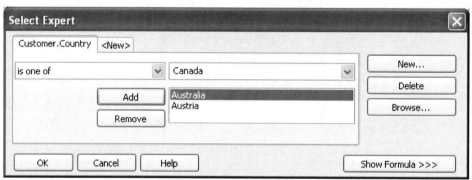

**Figure 4-4. Building a list of items.**

You can also manually type in values and add them to the list by clicking on the Add button. If you add an item by mistake, delete it from the list by clicking the Remove button.

You are not limited to selecting records based on a single field. The <New> tab lets you select additional fields for record selection. Clicking on this tab shows the same Choose Field dialog box that you saw in Figure 4-1. After selecting a field, you are brought back to this tab and that field is now in the tab header. The rest of the selection process is the same as what was just discussed. You can add as many fields as you want.

When you have more than one field in the Select Expert, Crystal Reports examines each field separately to see if it matches the criteria specified. After making each comparison, it only selects a record if it matches every condition. This is referred to as a Boolean And comparison. If there are four fields listed in the Select Expert, and a record only matches three of them, then it isn't selected.

| Tip |
| --- |
| If you have a report that needs faster performance and it uses multiple fields in the Select Expert, you might get better performance by rearranging the order of the fields. When there are multiple fields in the selection formula, the performance is affected by which fields have an index and how much data each one filters out. Although this is far from an exact science, for large reports you should try experimenting with the field order and see if you get significant improvements. |

If a record selection formula doesn't return any records, the report still prints any non-data type of information like the report header, report header, footers, etc. If you want to prevent the report from printing at all and only show a blank page, turn on the setting called Suppress Printing If No Records. This is found by selecting the menu options File > Report Options.

The Report Options dialog box also has a setting called Select Distinct Records. When checked, it tells the database not to return any duplicate records. If every field in a record matches every field in a record that has already been printed, it is skipped.[20]

# Filtering with Wildcards

The comparisons Is Like and Is Not Like have two characteristics which require more explanation. The first characteristic is that they let you build a custom list of allowable criteria. This is similar to the comparisons Is One Of and Is Not One Of described previously. As long as a field's value matches any one of the values in the list, the record is printed.

The second unique characteristic is that you can use wildcard characters to create a search string. Wildcards let you create a group of matching data without being limited by a beginning and ending range. The strings are selected if they fit the pattern's search criteria.

Search filters use two wildcard characters: ? and *. The ? allows any character to be in that position in the string. For example, let's say that you want to print a report with all employees with the first name of Brian. You know that Brian is commonly spelled with a "y" as well as with an "i" and you want to find both spellings. The filter "Br?an" would match both spellings. The ? in the third position tells Crystal Reports that you don't care which letter is used there as long as the rest of the string matches exactly.

Another example of using the ? wildcard is to generate a report showing records where there is a typo in the social security number. Sometimes, people mistakenly skip a number when typing in the SSN or they forget to include the dashes. Using a criteria of Is Not

---

[20] If you are familiar with the Transact SQL language, Crystal Reports changes the SELECT statement to SELECT DISTINCT.

Like and setting the filter to ???-??-???? tells Crystal Reports which characters should have a number in them and which ones can only be the dash. By using the Is Not Like comparison, the report lists the records that have a typo in them because they don't match the filter.

The second wildcard character is the *. It matches any number of characters in the string. This is best used when you want to find values that start a certain prefix. For example, if you want to find all the names that start with the letter C then you would use a filter string of C*.

# Introducing the Formula Editor

The Select Expert is a very helpful tool for selecting one or more fields using the basic comparison operators. This is probably adequate for many of the reports you write, but what about the reports where you need to build more complex filtering criteria? For those reports, there is the Formula Editor. Using the Formula Editor and writing formulas is described in complete detail in the next few chapters, but here is a summary of how to use it.

The Formula Editor lets you use the built-in programming language (either Crystal syntax or Basic syntax) to create sophisticated selection formulas. There is a large library of functions to choose from for building a selection formula.

> **Caution**
>
> When opening the Formula Editor from within the Select Expert, you are only given the option of using Crystal syntax as the programming language. As you will see in Chapter 5, Crystal Reports usually gives you the option of using Basic syntax, which is very similar to the Microsoft programming language Visual Basic. Unfortunately, the Formula Editor requires using Crystal syntax.

There are two ways to enter a custom formula. The first way is to click the Show Formula button. This shows the existing formula built using the fields already selected. You can change this formula directly so that it matches the selection criteria you need. If you can't remember the different built-in functions well enough to type them in directly, click on the Formula Editor button. This brings up the Formula Editor dialog box and you can use it as a reference tool to build the formula. The second way to enter a formula is to click on the comparison list dropdown list and at the very bottom is an item called formula:. Clicking on this item changes the right side to a multi-line text box that lets you type a formula from scratch.

# Selecting Records for Grouping

The Select Expert is used for selecting records based upon the value of one or more fields in each record. Thus, each record is looked at individually to determine whether it should be used in the report or not. Crystal Reports also lets you filter data based upon group values. In this case, records are not selected based upon their individual values but are selected according to whether the group they belong to is selected.

Selecting records based on grouping data is slightly different than what you've seen so far. When selecting records based on data at the grouping level, you have to use summary functions. For example, consider a report that prints the individual product sales and groups the data by customer. In the group footer, it prints the total sales for each customer. To show all the customers that have a minimum purchase level you have to use the Sum() function in the select expert. Otherwise, it will use the individual purchase records to perform the comparison and the results won't be accurate.

It's easy to create a filter based on grouping data. When selecting the field to filter on, look in the Choose Field dialog box at the end of the list of the report fields. The grouping fields are listed last and they are identified by their group number and the summary function. Choose one of these as the field to group on.

It's helpful to realize how filtering on grouping data is different than filtering on database fields. As mentioned in Chapter 1, Crystal Reports uses a two-pass system of processing data. In the first pass the individual records are processed and summarized. This is where the non-grouping selection formulas are used to filter out the raw data. It is in the second pass that all the summary calculations have been performed and their totals are known. This is where the selection formulas based on summary data are used to filter out groups of records.

# Tutorial 4-1. Selecting Records

Let's put what we learned about selecting records to use. In this tutorial, we set a filter on two fields: Country and Last Year's Sales. For Country, we want to select a specific set of countries to print (Canada, England, and USA). For the Last Years Sales field, we only want to see records with a sales amount over $25,000.

1. Open the Crystal Reports sample report Group.rpt. This report demonstrates grouping data on the Country and Customer Name fields. It shows the previous year's sales by customer and their percentage of the total sales.

2. Save the report as **Select Expert Tutorial.rpt.**

3. Click the menu items Report > Select Expert.

4. The Choose Field dialog box opens for you to select the field to filter on. Select the Customer.Country field.

5. The Select Expert dialog box opens with the Customer.Country tab shown. For the comparison type, select Is One Of from the dropdown list.

6. In the second dropdown list, select each of the following values: Canada, England and USA. This selects all records that are from one of those three countries.

7. Create a second filter field by clicking on the <New> tab and select the field Customer.Last Year's Sales. Click the Ok button to go back to the Select Expert dialog box.

8. For this field, we want all sales that are greater than $25,000. For the condition criteria, select Is Greater Than or Equal To. In the second dropdown list type in $25,000.

9. To make sure you've entered both conditions properly, click on the Show Formula button in the bottom right hand corner. Compare your formula to the following:

```
{Customer.Country} in ["USA", "England", "Canada"] and
{Customer.Last Year's Sales} >= $25000.00
```

10. Make any necessary corrections to your formula if there is a mistake.

11. Preview the report and it should look like the following. Notice that each sales amount is greater than $25,000.

## Grouping Data

9/29/2005   11:22:36PM

**Xtreme**
**Mountain Bikes**

### How to group data

| Customer Name | Region | Last Year's Sales | Percentage of Total Sales |
|---|---|---|---|
| **Canada** | | **$146,105.93** | 5.45% |
| Biking's It Industries | BC | $30,348.92 | |
| Crazy Wheels | BC | $38,280.53 | |
| Cycles and Sports | BC | $38,199.10 | |
| Pedal Pusher Bikes Inc. | BC | $39,277.38 | |
| **England** | | **$536,330.00** | 20.00% |
| BBS Pty | Greater London | $500,000.00 | |
| Tom's Bikes | Nottinghamshire | $36,330.00 | |
| **USA** | | **$1,998,564.20** | 74.55% |
| Alley Cat Cycles | MA | $298,356.22 | |
| Backpedal Cycle Shop | PA | $25,162.05 | |
| Bike Shop from Mars | CA | $25,873.25 | |
| Bikes, Bikes, and More Bikes | IA | $25,379.10 | |
| Blazing Saddles | WI | $42,709.86 | |
| C-Gate Cycle Shoppe | VA | $29,618.11 | |
| Changing Gears | CA | $26,705.65 | |
| Corporate Cycle | IA | $27,081.31 | |
| Cyclopath | RI | $38,492.56 | |
| Extreme Cycling | FL | $69,819.10 | |
| Feel Great Bikes Inc. | MN | $40,944.47 | |
| Hooked on Helmets | MN | $52,963.82 | |
| Mad Mountain Bikes | ID | $35,009.22 | |
| Making Tracks | MA | $32,249.55 | |
| Mountain Madmen Bicycles | NJ | $28,190.52 | |
| Off the Mountain Biking | CA | $25,000.00 | |

## Tutorial 4-2. Selecting Records by Grouping Data

Let's modify the previous report so that it shows the details for all countries that had last year total sales greater than $100,000. This requires deleting the two previous fields from the record selection and summing the total of last year's sales.

1. Open the report from the previous example, Select Expert Tutorial.rpt. Save it as Grouping Tutorial.rpt.

2. Select the menu items Report > Select Expert. This opens the Select Expert showing the two fields added in the previous example.

3. Click on the Delete button twice to remove the two existing fields.

4. Click on the <New> tab to open the Choose Field dialog box.

5. In this example, we don't want to simply select the field Customer.Last Years Sales because this field is at the record source level. We want to filter the records based on the total of Last Year's Sales for the entire Country group. This is listed near the end of the field list as "Group #1: Customer.Country – A: Sum of Customer.Last Years Sales". Select this field and click on the OK button.

6. For the comparison, select Is Greater Than and enter a value of $100,000.

7. Click on the Show Formula button to see the formula's text. Notice that the radio button Group Selection is selected. Crystal Reports recognized that your record selection formula is using a summary field and consequently flagged it as a group selection formula. This is automatic and you don't have to worry about doing it manually.

8. Click the OK button to save the changes. Preview the report and you'll see that the detail records don't have to have a value of more than $100,000, but the country total does. Quite a few countries had sales over $100,000 and the report is seven pages long.

# Filtering with Parameters

The first part of this chapter showed how filtering data lets you customize a report to fit a specific user's needs. The only drawback to this approach is that you have to know in advance what that user's needs are when you are designing the report. And if different users have different needs, then you either have to save a separate copy of the report for each variation or the have each user customize the report themselves. Neither of these options is a very practical approach. A much better solution is to create a filter that uses parameters to prompt the user for their input prior to printing the report. This lets you create one report that satisfies many users.

In their most basic form, report parameters are simply a means of asking the user questions about what they want printed. When the user opens the report, he or she is prompted with a question and the answer is used within the report (e.g. for filtering data). Some examples of typical questions are, "What sales district do you want to report on?" and "What is the minimum sales amount you want to see?" Questions such as these let the user take a report that was designed to be used by multiple people and only view the data that he or she is interested in. The biggest benefit is that you don't need to save a separate copy of the report for each user. New parameter values can be entered each time the report is viewed. Figure 4-5 shows a parameter prompting the user for a report date and the print range.

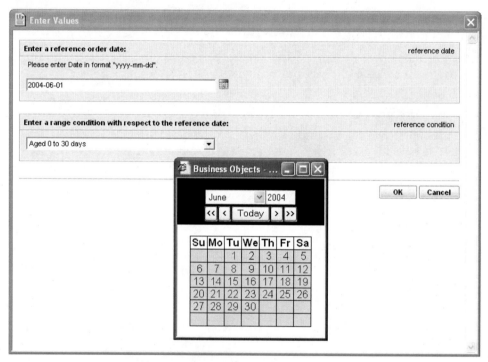

**Figure 4-5. Parameter prompt dialog box.**

In this example, the user is being prompted to enter two parameters. The first being an Order Date and the second is a date range. You can see a calendar displayed on the screen as well. Crystal Reports lets the user enter dates by typing them in directly or picking the date from this calendar control.

## Best Of The Forum

**Question:** I would like to change the prompting dialog box to match our corporate color scheme. Is it possible to modify the prompting window?

**Answer:** Yes, you can modify how this window is formatted. Crystal Reports uses a CSS file for formatting the objects displayed. The advanced tutorial at the end of this chapter shows you the details of modifying the prompting window.

Parameters are used for many purposes. As I mentioned already, the single biggest purpose is filtering data based upon a user's needs. But there are many other uses for parameters. They are also used to customize the report format. For example, a sales report can highlight in red all sales persons whose quarterly sales fall below a certain level. A standard report can be customized to hide report objects that aren't relevant to the user. Requiring a user to enter their User ID lets you hide or show sensitive information. And in the Chapter 3 Advanced Tutorials, you saw how to use parameters to perform dynamic grouping and sorting. Creative use of parameters gives you a multitude of ways to make a report respond to a user's needs.

# Creating Parameters

When creating a report that uses parameters, you have many jobs to do. You have to determine how the parameter will prompt the user to enter a value, determine the types of values that can be entered, decide if there are default values, and use the parameter within the report. The remaining portion of this chapter walks you through all the steps of creating parameters and using them in your reports.

---

### Note

New to Crystal Reports XI is the ability for parameters to present the user a list of live data values to choose from. In previous versions of Crystal Reports the user could only choose from a static list of values that you created in advance. The values weren't able to reflect recent changes to the database. Crystal Reports XI now gives you this powerful new feature that connects the list of values to the data source. This is discussed in more detail later in the chapter.

---

Creating a new parameter is controlled via the Create New Parameter dialog box. This is accessible via the Field Explorer window. Right-click on the Parameter Fields category in the Field Explorer window and select New.

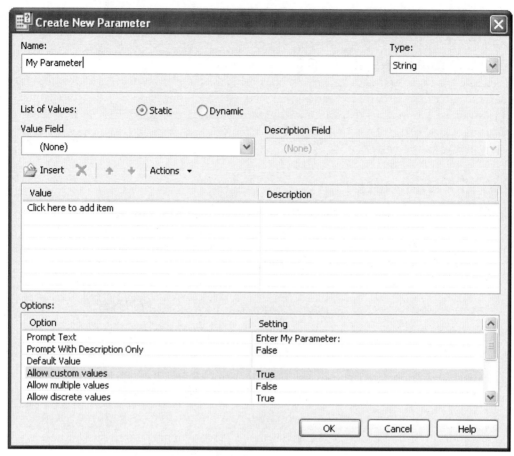

**Figure 4-6. Create New Parameters dialog box.**

This dialog box has a multitude of properties that can be set and it's going to take some time to discuss them all. So let's start at the top and work our way down.

The top of the dialog box lets you enter the parameter's name and data type. The parameter name is how you identify the parameter within the report (e.g. how you would reference it in a formula). It should be something that makes sense to you as the report designer. Although it will be shown to the user, it won't be in a prominent position and you shouldn't worry about how it looks to the user. Look at Figure 4-5 and you'll see that the name is shown in the top right corner of each parameter prompt. It isn't very obvious and most users might not even notice it.

The problem a lot of people have when they first start creating reports is that they give parameters generic names that don't specifically state their purpose. For example, if a parameter is used to filter purchases by date range, then you might give it the name PrintDates. This seems like a good idea at first, but when you come back to make changes to the report in six months you won't have any recollection about which dates this parameter is referring to. Is it the date the product was ordered or the date it was sold or the date it was shipped? You can't tell by looking at the parameter name. You have to edit the record selection to find out which field it is being compared to. A much better idea would be to call it something like PurchaseDateRange. If you have to edit the report at a later date, you'll immediately know what the parameter refers to. You want to keep the parameter names short, but also meaningful.

## Choosing the Data Type

After entering the parameter's name, you have to select its data type from the dropdown list in the top right corner of the dialog box. A parameter stores information inside the computer's memory as one of five possible data types: Boolean (True/False), String (text entries), Number, Currency (monetary values) and Date/Time. Selecting the right data type is critical because each data type has benefits and limitations.[21]

Determining the proper data type is usually not very difficult because the data type is defined by how the parameter is going to be used in the report. For example, if you are asking the user a Yes/No question then the data type is Boolean. If you are asking the user to enter their User ID for security purposes, then the parameter is a String data type. Another example is a parameter used in the calculation of a sales commission. It must be a Number data type. Although the user could type in the same numbers using a String data type, you wouldn't be able to use it in any calculations.

| Tip |
| --- |

Most reports use parameters to compare their value to a database field. This is commonly done for the purpose of filtering data. The rule of thumb to follow is that the parameter's data type must be the same as the field it is being compared with.

## Creating a List of Values

When the user is presented with a parameter prompt, rather than make them type in a value for the parameter, you can give them a list of possible values to choose from. This is called a List of Values. It is a predefined list of default values that the user can choose from. For example, rather than having them type in the State, you can show them a list of all possible states and let them pick the one they want.

A list of values is helpful for two reasons. The first benefit is that the user doesn't have to know the options ahead of time. It's not hard to remember the name of a state, but it might be difficult to remember the names of every product your company sells. The second benefit of using a list of values is that it prevents data entry errors. For example,

---

[21] Each of these data types are explained in more detail in Chapter 7.

someone might not remember the exact abbreviation for each state and they could type in the wrong value. Choosing from a list of values ensures that the value is entered exactly as expected. Figure 4-7 shows a parameter that prompts the user to select the Country to print and letting them choose from a list of all available countries on the report.

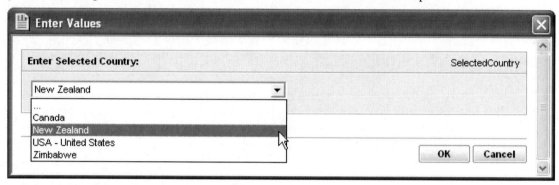

**Figure 4-7. Prompting with a list of possible states.**

The middle section of the Create New Parameter dialog box is where you define the list of values. The first option sets whether the list is static or dynamic. A static list is a predefined list of values that are the same every time the report is run. For example, if you create a report that lists employees by department, you would type in the name of every department into the static list and this is what the user could choose from. The problem with using a static list is that the only way to update the list is to modify the report definition and add or delete values. The list can easily become out of date if you are too busy to maintain it. If copies of the report were distributed throughout the organization, then you may not even know who actively uses it anymore.

New to Crystal Reports XI is the option to make a list dynamic. This is called Dynamic Cascading Prompts (DCPs). The prompts are directly linked to the database and the list never goes out of date. As soon as the data in the database changes, the report recognizes this and presents the user with a list of values that reflects any changes. One problem with DCPs is that they incur more overhead because every time the report is run it has to query the database to get the latest list of values. Thus, although DCPs ensure that the data is always up to date, there are times when it isn't the most efficient solution.

Learning how to create DCPs is a much more advanced topic than building a static list of values. In fact, it builds upon the learning concepts for creating a static list. Consequently, this chapter first covers the steps of creating parameters based upon a static list of values. The end of the chapter builds upon this knowledge and shows how to take the same concepts and use them to create DCPs.

There are three ways to create a static list of values: type each entry manually, pick values from the database, and import values from a text file. The next three sections show you the details of doing each method.

## Manually Entering a List of Values

The easiest method of populating the list of values is to manually type each entry. By clicking the Insert button on the Create Parameters window, the cursor is moved to the first available line in the list so you can type in the value. Alternatively, you can also click directly on the next empty line. After entering a value, hit the Enter key to save the value in the list. Repeat this to add as many items as necessary. Every item listed in the Value column appears to the user as one of the default values that they can choose from for that parameter.

Sometimes the items in the Value column are codes or abbreviations for data and the user may not understand what these codes mean. For example, a financial report parameter that specifies a range of revenue account codes might need the value to be formatted in a certain way. But the user has no idea what "50xxx" means. It would be better if they could choose the item "Revenue Accounts" from the list and behind the scenes let the computer take care of the fact that it is really "50xxx". You can do this with the Description column. The Description column, located next to the Values column, gives you the option of showing descriptions of the values to the user. For values that are somewhat cryptic (e.g. inventory codes), this makes it easy for the user to understand what they are selecting.

Entering a description is optional. If all the values in the list are clear enough, you don't have to enter a description at all. If some of the values are cryptic, but not all, then you can enter a description just for the ones that need it. And lastly, there can be a description for every value, if necessary.

There are two ways to display the description to the user. It can either be shown next to its value or instead of it. For example, look at the next two figures and compare how the value United States is displayed in each one.

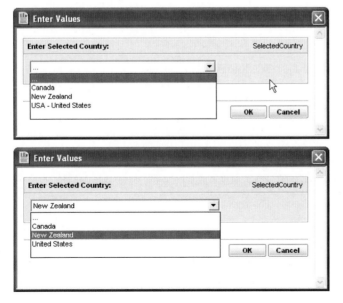

The first figure shows the value, "USA" listed with its description "United States". But in the second figure you see the description listed by itself. Only showing the description is useful when showing the value could be confusing. The property for doing this is the second item in the Options box below, Prompt with Description Only. Set it to True to only display the description field (this is described in more detail later).

If you want to sort the list of values, simply click on the column header. It automatically reorders the list so that all the items are sorted in ascending order. Clicking on the header again toggles the sort direction to be descending. If you want to sort by description instead of the actual values, click on the description column header.

## Using a Table to Populate the List of Values

The drawback to populating tables manually is that you have to type in each entry yourself. If the list of values is going to be large then this could take a lot of effort. In addition, you have to be careful that you spell everything exactly and that there are no typographical errors. An easier way to enter values is to import the values from a database table. This saves you time by not having to do any typing and you don't have to worry about making mistakes.

Populating a list of values from a database is done by selecting the database field that has the data you need and then selecting which entries to use. On the dialog box, look below the option where you select either Static or Dynamic and there are two dropdown lists labeled Value Field. Click on the dropdown list to see a list of all the tables and fields in the report's data source. Find the table which has the data you need and then select the field to pull that data from.

If you are using a database field to populate the list of values, then the Description column can also be populated with a database field. Click on the Description Field dropdown list to do so. Then the Description Field dropdown list automatically becomes enabled. By default, this dropdown list is disabled until you select a field for populating the Values column. The reason for this is that if you aren't going to use a database field for populating the Values column then you can't do it for the Description column either.

### Note

When selecting the field for the Description column, make sure that it is a field that is in the same table as the field selected for the Values column. For example, if the Values column uses the ProductID field from the Product table, then the Description column, ProductName, should come from the Product table as well. If you select a field for the description that is in a different table, Crystal Reports will try to find a relationship between the two tables and guess the correct record for the description. This educated guess may or may not be what you expected.

## Choosing the Proper Fields

Before deciding which fields to use in the list of values and its description, you should consider the database structure first. For the purpose of importing values, you need to figure out whether the field you want to display has a primary table or not (it may not exist). A primary table lists every possible value for a field and has a single field that is a unique identifier for each row (called the Primary Key). If you aren't familiar with the database, then you should consult the database administrator for help.

If you have a basic familiarity with databases, then you can probably identity the primary table yourself. One way to determine if a table is the primary table is that there is exactly one record for each value you want to display (i.e. there are no duplicate records). You can usually tell this if there are related fields that store its name, description, etc. For example, a Product table would list each Product ID (the primary key) as well as listing its name, price, and possibly size or weight.

A table that isn't the primary table usually lists a field as a secondary field within another table and the values are duplicated. For example, consider a Customer table which is the primary table for customer data. It lists exactly one record per customer. Within the Customer table are fields such as the Address and Country. Both the Address and Country fields are secondary fields within the table. They give additional information about the Customer record but aren't the primary information. Consequently, the values in the secondary fields can be repeated multiple times within the table. For example, many customers are going to have a Country field with values such as USA, Canada, Australia, etc.

Depending upon the data that you are displaying, there isn't always a primary table in the database. For example, the data source for a sales report that lets a user filter by Country probably doesn't have a Country table available. Instead, you have to use the Country field from another table. If you aren't working with the primary table, then there can be a problem for you when you import the data. The table might not have a complete list of values. If the table doesn't have much data in it yet, then it is very likely that it won't be an exhaustive list. If this is the case, after you import the data from the table, you will have to add the missing values manually. That is why it is best to first determine if the database has a primary table for your data because this will make sure that you load every possible value at once.

| Note |
|------|

You don't have to worry about importing duplicate data into the list. Before importing data from a table, Crystal Reports examines the table and generates a unique list of values. This ensures that each value is only imported once.

Just telling Crystal Reports the field to populate the list of values isn't enough to get the values there. There are two ways of importing the values. You can either add them one at a time or add the entire list at once. Of course, adding the entire list is most efficient if there are a lot of values. But if you only need a subset of all the possible values, then you can pick and choose which ones to import on an individual basis.

To import every value into the list, click on the Actions button and select Append All Database Values. This scans through the entire table and adds each value to the list. If you selected a field for the Description column, then the descriptions get imported as well.

If you don't need to import every single value, you can import them individually. This is more work, but it's a practical solution if you only need a few of the values. To select values individually, click on the row that says Click Here to Add Item. This displays a dropdown arrow on the right side of the column. Click on the arrow to see a list of all the values in the table. Select the one you want and it gets added to the list. Repeat this procedure for every item to be added to the list.

### Tip

If you need to import a lot of the values from the table, but not every one, a better idea is to import the entire list and then delete the ones you don't need. Depending upon how big the list is, this can be much faster than selecting the values on an individual basis.

A word of caution when using a database to add individual items to the list of values: when adding individual items, the Description column doesn't get filled in for you. Even if you have a field specified for the Description column, nothing gets inserted. Only the Values column gets populated. You have to type entries in the Description column manually. Hopefully, this problem will be corrected in a future maintenance release.

### Caution

Building a static list using a database field doesn't create a live connection to the database. If the values in the database field change, then this will not be reflected in the list of values. You will have to go back and add the entries yourself. This is where dynamic prompts are beneficial and this is covered later in the chapter.

The final method of populating the list of values is by importing them from a text file. If you have a text file that lists each value and its description, this can save you a lot of typing. This can be useful if you are importing values from a third-party application and it has the option to export data. It can also be useful to manually create a list of values in a report and export that list to a text file. Then you can reuse it in other reports by importing it. The format of the text file is that the Value is listed first and the Description should be separated with the TAB key. Each Value/Description pair should be on its own line.

### Editing the List of Values

After you populate the values and descriptions that the user chooses from, you need to know how to revise the list and keep it updated. After importing or entering the values, you might notice that they are listed in no particular order. The first thing you might want to do is sort the list in either ascending or descending order. There are two arrow buttons shown directly to the left of the Actions button. Clicking on the first arrow sorts the values in descending order and clicking on the second arrow sorts in ascending order. If you need to delete an item, click the delete button located directly to the right of the Insert button (it looks like an X).

If you make a mistake during the process of adding values, you can clear the entire list by clicking on the Actions button and selecting Clear.

## Tutorial 4-3. Creating Parameters

Let's do a tutorial illustrating what we've learned so far about creating parameters. We'll create a parameter that lets the user specify which country to print. We'll populate the list by importing all the records from the database. Secondly, we want to practice creating a record selection formula that is more complicated than what can be created using the Select Expert. We will give the user the option of printing just the specified country or printing all countries by selecting "ALL" from the drop-down list.

The sample report we are going to start with is the Group.rpt file that was used in the earlier tutorials. It shows last year's sales by Country and Customer Name. Tutorial 4-1 was similar except that it hard-coded the country names into the selection formula. This tutorial improves upon that idea by letting the user select the country from a drop-down list.

Lastly, we are going to use the Select Expert to create a record selection formula that uses these two parameters to perform the filtering of the data. We are going to modify it so that the user can enter only one of the two parameters and the report will filter on just the field they want.

1. Open the Crystal Reports sample report Group.rpt. This report shows the last year's sales for each customer and it is grouped by the Country field.

2. Save it as **Basic Parameter Tutorial.rpt**.

3. Right-click on the Parameter Fields list in the Field Explorer and select New. This opens the Create New Parameter dialog box.

4. Enter the parameter name "Selected Country" and leave it as a String data type.

   We want to give users the ability to either select a specific country to print or print all countries. The standard way of doing this is to make the word "ALL" the first entry in the list of values and after that show the full list of countries.

5. In the Value list box, click on the first row and enter **ALL**.

6.  The database has a huge number of countries to choose from and we aren't about to type them all in manually. It's much better to import them directly from the database. Click on the Value Field dropdown list and select the Country field.

7.  Click the Actions button and select Append All Database Values. This imports every value from the database and automatically populates the list of values.

8.  Click the OK button to save the parameter.

9.  Now that the parameter has been created, it's time to build the selection formula. Click on the menu items Report > Select Expert.

10. Select the field Customer.Country and click OK.

11. Select the comparison Is Equal To and select the parameter {?Selected Country}.

    If we kept the selection formula as it is, then the user would only be able to select a single country. The selection formula doesn't have the functionality to let the user print all countries. We need to modify it so that the user can select "ALL" from the list of values and print all the countries.

12. Click on the Show Formula button and look at the current selection formula prior to our changes.

    {Customer.Country} = {?Selected Country}

13. Change it to the following:

    {?Selected Country} = "ALL" OR {Customer.Country} = {?Selected Country}

    This formula checks to see if the user selected "ALL" and if so it returns true. If the user didn't select "ALL" then the second part of the formula checks whether the current record is the country that was selected. If so, then the record is printed. Otherwise it is skipped.

14. Click the OK button to save the selection formula.

15. Preview the report and play around with it for a minute. You'll see that you can filter just by Country or view all countries in the database.

## Setting Parameter Options

At the bottom of the Edit Parameters dialog box is an Options area that lists the available options that can be set for a parameter. It has options that let you do more with parameters than just display a list of default values for the user to pick from. Some of the advanced features are the ability to enter single or multiple values, set a range of valid entries, and control data entry using an edit mask. Each of the options on the Edit Parameters dialog box is listed below with a description of how to use it.

### Prompt Text

The prompt text is the question that prompts the user to enter a value. You can type in any text that describes to the user what type of information they need to enter. It can also be helpful if you tell the user how the parameter is going to be used. For example, rather than just saying, "Enter the country", the prompt could say, "Enter the country you want to print the sales for". This tells the user what data is needed and why.

## Prompt with Description Only

We already talked about this option in an earlier section. It gives you the option of showing the value and its description or of just showing the description. Only showing the description is useful when the value wouldn't make sense to the user (e.g. a cryptic Inventory ID).

| Note |
| --- |

Even though you have the option of showing the description to the user instead of the actual value, behind the scenes Crystal Reports is storing the value field in the parameter. The user will never see this, but you need to make sure that any formulas you write with that parameter are done so with the expectation of using the value field. The description is strictly used for display purposes and nothing else.

## Default Value

Even though some parameters have a large list of values to choose from, there are times when one value is used the majority of the time. When this is the case, you can have Crystal Reports display a default value. Rather than typing in the value, the user can just click the OK button. Of course, if the user doesn't want to use the default value, he can override it with a new value.

## Allow Custom Values

So far, everything we discussed in reference to the list of values assumes that the user always wants to pick a value from the list that you created. But this isn't always the case. For example, the list of values might be out of date and you haven't had time to add the new entries. Thus, the user needs to enter a value not in the list. You could also have a list of values that just show the user the most commonly used values, but it doesn't show every single value because there are too many to view. In this case, the user can enter a new value if the value he needs isn't in the list.

When the Allow Custom Values option is set to True, the user is presented with a second text area directly below the dropdown list. The text area allows you to enter a new value for the parameter. This is illustrated in Figure 4-8.

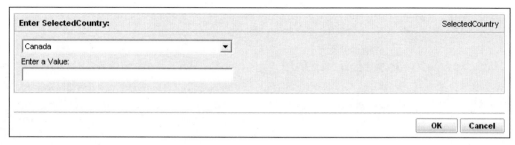

**Figure 4-8. Letting the user enter a custom value.**

Since there are two input areas now, you might be confused about which one Crystal Reports will use. Crystal Reports always uses the value in the text box. If the user enters a custom value, it is entered in the text box at the bottom and Crystal Reports knows to use it. If the user picks an item from the drop-down list, then when they select that item Crystal Reports will automatically enter it in the bottom text box as well. This ensures that the text box has the correct value even when the user picks an item from the drop-down list.

## Min/Max Length

When a parameter's data type is String, you can set the minimum and maximum number of characters that the user can enter. Crystal Reports will only accept a parameter if its length falls within the specified range. This helps enforce data integrity. For example, if a parameter filters on the state abbreviation (e.g. KY, CA, etc.), then the Min Length is 2 and the Max Length is also 2.

When setting restrictions on the length, you aren't required to enter a value for both the Min Length and Max Length properties. You can set just one of the properties or neither. For example, most passwords have a minimum length requirement but no limit on the maximum number of characters you can enter.

The Min Length and Max Length properties are not available for Numbers, Dates or Boolean data types. However, both Numbers and Dates do let you specify a minimum and maximum range of values (described next).

## Min/Max Value

Numbers and dates can have valid ranges assigned to them. You can specify what the minimum and maximum values are. This prevents the user from entering a parameter value that is outside the acceptable range.

For dates, the range properties are called Start and End. Although they are named differently than the number properties, they mean the same thing.

## Edit Mask

Some string parameters have a format where special characters appear within the string at particular locations. For example, a phone number has the format of (999) 999-9999. No matter what the phone number is, it has to be formatted the same every time. Crystal Reports gives you the ability to specify an edit mask for string parameters that forces the user to enter a string in a very precise way. If there are special characters such as a dash or colon, it forces the user to type in the field exactly and it guarantees that the data they entered is formatted properly.

Creating edit masks can be a little confusing if this is the first time you've ever used them. Each edit mask consists of a bunch of characters and each character has a rule that specifies what the user can and can't type in that position. But edit masks aren't hard to use once you understand the rules. You just have to practice a few times to get the hang of them. Let's start by looking at a few examples and then we'll look at what the rules are.

Social Security Number: 000-00-0000

This edit mask requires the user to enter a social security number in the precise format. The "0" in the edit mask says that the user must enter a digit from 0-9. The first three characters will be numbers. The dash is a literal character that can't be replaced with another character. Thus, this edit mask requires the user to enter a certain quantity of numbers with dashes in between.

Phone Number: (000)000-0000

This phone number edit mask is similar to the social security edit mask. The only difference being that it uses two parentheses. These are also literal characters and must be typed in exactly.

State Abbreviation: >AA

A state abbreviation is always two characters long. This edit mask uses the A character to force the user to enter a letter. What makes this edit mask interesting is that is also uses the greater-than sign at the beginning. This requires all letters to be entered as upper-case. This is useful when doing text searches that are case-sensitive.

| Note |
| --- |

One thing to be aware of is that by using an edit mask you are indirectly specifying what the Min Length and Max Length properties are. Since the edit mask specifies how many characters must be typed in, the user can enter no more and no less. Thus, when using an edit mask, it isn't necessary to also specify the Min Length and Max Length properties because this is already implied.

**Table 4-2. Edit mask characters and the rules for usage.**

| Character | Edit Mask Rule |
| --- | --- |
| A | Must enter an alphanumeric character. |
| A | Allows entering an alphanumeric character, but it's optional. |
| 0 | Must enter a number from 0-9. |
| 9 | Must enter a number from 0-9 or a space. |
| # | Must enter a number from 0-9 or a space or the plus or minus sign. |
| L | Must enter a letter from A-Z. |
| ? | Allows entering a letter from A-Z, but it's optional |
| & | Must enter a letter from A-Z or a space. |
| C | Allows entering a letter from A-Z or a space, but it's optional. |
| , . : ; - / | Special characters that must be entered exactly by the user. |
| < | Any characters following the less-than sign must be lowercase. |
| > | Any characters following the less-than sign must be uppercase. |
| \ | This makes any character a special character that must be entered exactly. |
| Password | All characters are shown as an asterisk so that the data can't be read by someone nearby. |

**NOTE**

When the user enters a parameter value that doesn't match the edit mask, the error messages aren't always very helpful. First of all, if there are multiple errors in the value, the user is only told about them one at a time. After she corrects one error and clicks the OK button, she is then presented with the next error message. It would be helpful if a bullet-point list of all the errors were shown at once. Secondly, the dialog box always displays the edit mask to the user so that they know what type of data entry is expected. This is certainly helpful for the person who designed the report, but most users are not going to have any idea what all these funny characters mean. For some users, seeing the edit mask can do more harm than good. The best way to keep this from hindering your reports is by using preventive medicine. Within the prompt text, you should indicate to the user what the edit mask rules are so that the user knows in advance the proper way to enter the data. For example, if you want them to enter a two digit state abbreviation and have each letter upper case, then just say so. Make the prompt text say something like, "What state do you want to filter on? Please enter the two letter abbreviation using uppercase letters (e.g. KY)."

## *Multiple, Discrete and Range Values*

A parameter has the flexibility to store a single value, a range of values, or a combination of the two. This gives you a lot to think about when deciding which is appropriate for each parameter. Since these three options can be used in conjunction with each other, it's best to get an overall understanding of them at the same time.

Discrete parameters are good when you need to store a single value. An example is when you want to print a report based on a Company ID. Another example is storing a Boolean value that determines when a report feature is to be displayed or hidden.

Range values give you more flexibility by allowing you to set a start and end point of acceptable values. Any value that falls within this range is included. This is useful when you want to print multiple values and these values have a definite starting point and ending point. Range values are frequently used when filtering dates because you can set the beginning and ending dates and all dates in between get included.

Parameters let you go one step further by combining both discrete values and range values into the same parameter. These are called multi-value parameters. A multi-value parameter is a list of different values (i.e. an array of values[22]). This gives the user the ability to create a list of acceptable values that can be discrete values, range values, or a combination of the two. This can result in a complex list of acceptable values. For example, consider financial reports which are often based on account codes. Each type of account category (assets, liabilities, etc.) is represented by a starting and ending range. An auditor that is investigating fraudulent information could print out certain related accounts by entering multiple account codes such as 10000-11000, 50000-51000, and the individual accounts 05928 and 05970. The multi-value parameter lets all the accounts be printed on the same report for easier analysis. If the report didn't use a multi-value parameter, then each of these accounts and account ranges would have to be printed on a separate report and pieced together. Table 4-3 shows a summary of the different type parameter options.

---

[22] If you aren't familiar with the concept of arrays, they are discussed in detail in Chapter 7.

**Table 4-3. Options for parameter fields**

| Option | Description |
| --- | --- |
| Discrete value(s) | The user must enter a single value. |
| Range value(s) | The user enters two the start and end points of a range. The range will include the values entered. For example, if you entered a range of 1,000 and 1,999 then it would include all numbers from 1,000 up to and including 1,999. The numbers 999 and 2,000 would not be included. |
| Allow multiple values | Allows a parameter to accept discrete and range values and store them as a series. |

Now that you understand the different data types and options available for parameters, let's look at how to create parameters in a report.

# Using Boolean Parameters

Boolean parameters are unique from the other parameter types because they can only hold one of two values and they can be grouped together. With other types of parameters, you can list many possible choices in its list of values. But Boolean parameters don't let you decide the list of values.

Although the possible values are always True and False, you aren't required to display True and False to the user. You can present the user with a better prompt by changing the Description of each parameter. For example, a report that optionally formats low inventory items in red could have two prompts which say: "Highlight low inventory items" for True and, "Don't show inventory alerts" for False. Changing the description makes it easier for the user to understand what the report is asking for. The following figure shows a parameter that displays Yes and No rather than True and False.

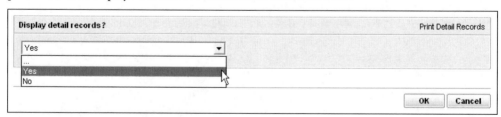

**Figure 4-9. Entering a Boolean parameter value.**

## *Grouping Boolean Parameters*

Boolean parameters have an optional property called Boolean Group #. This property lets you associate different Boolean parameters within a group. By grouping Boolean parameters together into different categories you get more options for how the parameters are displayed to the user and how they work together.

There are two ways to specify a Boolean group: Non-Exclusive and Exclusive. The non-exclusive group says that all or none of the parameters can be set to True. By definition, since this is a non-exclusive grouping, then there are no limits to how many parameters can be set to True. For example, a report can have certain features enabled or disabled and the user selects which options she wants to see. The user can select no options, one option, or multiple options. No parameter excludes the other parameters from being selected.

Since the user can specify one or all of the parameters within the group to be True, this really isn't any different than just creating individual Boolean parameters. But there are a couple of benefits to using non-exclusive Boolean groups over individual parameters. The first is that by grouping the parameters into a single area, it makes it clear to the user that all the parameters are logically related to each. The second benefit is that there is only one prompt for all the parameters. If they weren't included in the same group, then you would be multiple prompts with very redundant information Putting related Boolean parameters into the same group makes it easier for the user to understand what she is selecting. The next figure shows an example of a parameter that lets the user choose which sensitive fields should be hidden so that people reading the printed report don't see this information.

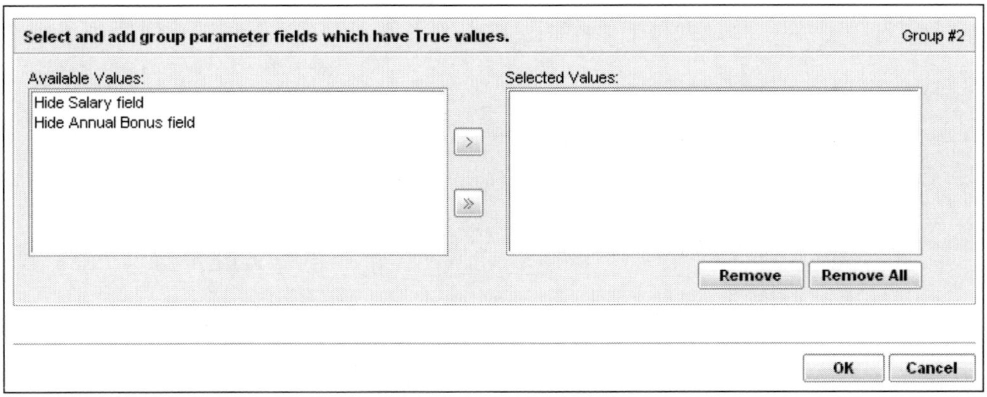

**Figure 4-10. Entering a Boolean parameter that uses a group number.**

Setting the grouping properties of a Boolean parameter is done in the Options dialog box. When a parameter's data type is set to Boolean, two new properties appear at the end of the Options list: Boolean Group # and Exclusive Group. If you want the parameter to be in a group, then enter a group number in the option Boolean Group #. The group number is an arbitrary number that you make up and you have to make sure you keep it consistent so that the proper parameters are put into the right group. If you want the group to be a Non-Exclusive group, then enter the value False in the Exclusive Group option. Enter True to make it an Exclusive group (discussed next).

An exclusive group only allows one parameter within the group to be set to True. All the other parameters must be false. The parameter names are displayed in a dropdown list and only one item can be chosen within the dropdown list. For example, a sales report could group the data based on a single field and the user gets to choose which field that is. You could prompt the user to specify whether the report should be grouped by Sales Manager, Sales Person, or Region. Thus, this is an exclusive group. The next figure shows an example of an exclusive group that prompts the user for the field to group by. The dropdown list shows all three parameters and the user can only select one of them.

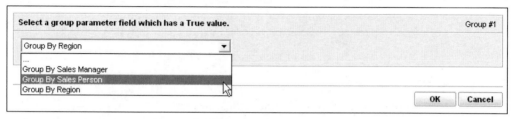

**Figure 4-11. Entering a Boolean parameter that is in an exclusive group.**

### Caution

Looking at the above figure, you should notice a few unusual aspects of it that differ from the typical parameter prompts we've seen so far. First, notice that in the top right corner it shows the group number. This is normally where the parameter name is displayed. Personally, I don't think many users care about the parameter number in which this group belongs. Secondly, notice that the prompt text is very generic. This is because every parameter group always shows the same prompt text. Even if you specify the prompt text in the Options area, this is ignored by Crystal Reports and it never gets displayed. Lastly, notice that the values in the dropdown list are actually the parameter's names. If you enter a description in the list of values, it gets ignored. Since both the prompt text and the description properties are ignored for Boolean groups, you have to make sure you name the Boolean parameter in such a way that it will make sense to the user when it is shown in the dropdown list.

## Managing the Parameter List

After adding a parameter to the report, you often need to modify it. This could be renaming it or changing its options. As you might expect, Crystal Reports lets you perform the typical maintenance tasks with parameters. You can modify them, delete them, rename them and reorder them.

All the tasks for working with parameters are in the pop-up menu that appears when you right-click on a parameter in the Field Explorer window. To edit a parameter, select the Edit option from the pop-up menu and it opens the Edit Parameter dialog box that you've been working with in this chapter. Make the necessary changes and click the OK button to save it.

To delete a parameter select the Delete option from the pop-up menu. Prior to deleting a parameter, make sure that there isn't a checkmark next to its name indicating that the report is using it. If there is a checkmark, Crystal Reports gives you an error that it is still being used and it can't be deleted. Make sure no formulas are using the parameter prior to deleting it.

### Best Of The Forum

**Question:** I have a large report and sometimes I can't determine where the parameter is being used. Do I have to search through every formula to find which one is using a parameter field?

**Answer:** If you can't find the parameter in the list of formulas, also check the record selection formula or the subreport links (if it has a subreport). It might be hiding in one of these places. There is a "trick" to make Crystal Reports tell you every formula that is using the parameter. Simply edit the parameter and change its data type. When you run the report Crystal Reports will tell you that there is a data type error and show you the formula using that parameter. Remove the parameter from the formula(s) and you will be able to delete the parameter field from the report.

If you wish to rename the parameter, you have to select the Rename option. Interestingly enough, if you try to rename the parameter within the Edit Parameter dialog box it won't let you do it. The dialog box has the parameter name as a read-only property that you can't change. You are only allowed to rename the parameter using the pop-up menu.

### Note

When you rename a parameter field, Crystal Reports automatically finds all references to the parameter and updates them to use the new name.

When a user opens a report with parameters, the parameters are listed within the same dialog box. You may not have given much thought to the order that the parameters are listed in, but they are listed in the order that you created them. In fact, if you look at the Parameter Fields list in the Field Explorer window, you'll see that their order in the Parameters Fields list is how they appear to the user. You can reorder the parameters so that the more important parameters are listed first. Right-click anywhere on the Parameter Fields list and select the option Set Parameter Order. The Parameter Order dialog box appears and shows you a list of every parameter in the report.

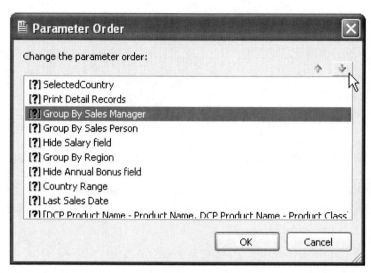

**Figure 4-12. Change the parameter order with the Parameter Order dialog box.**

To change the parameter order, click on the parameter you wish to move and then click on the up and down arrows located in the top right corner. Click OK to save your changes and you'll see that the Parameter Fields list is updated to reflect the new order.

## Tutorial 4-4. Creating Multi-Value Parameters

The benefit to setting parameter options is that they give the user a more robust user interface for selecting parameter values. Let's modify the report we created in the previous tutorial so that rather than just selecting a single Customer to print, the user can select multiple customers.

1. Open the report Basic Parameter Tutorial.rpt from Tutorial 4-3. Save it as **Multi-Value Parameter Tutorial.rpt**.

2. Look in the Parameter Fields list and find the Selected Customer parameter. Right-click on it and select Edit.

3. For the optional properties, set the Allow Multiple Values option to True. This lets the user select the customers they want to print by either adding or creating a list of valid customers.

4. Click the OK button to save your changes. This immediately opens the Enter Values dialog box so that you can enter a new value for the parameter.

5. Refresh the report multiple times and select a different number of customers each time. They will all appear on the report.

   Notice that even though we changed the parameter to be multi-value, the selection formula stayed the same. When Crystal Reports compares a single field to an array of values, you can still use the = operator to do the comparison. Crystal Reports automatically scans through the array looking for a value that matches. This is discussed more in the next section.

# Using Parameters

After you've created the necessary parameters, you need to know how to use them within your report. After doing all this work, you don't want it to go to waste! There are three primary ways of using parameters: filtering records, displaying them directly on the report, and using them in conditional formatting. We'll discuss the first two methods here, but the discussion of conditional formatting will wait till Chapter 5.

At the beginning of the chapter, we learned how to filter records by setting criteria for a database field to meet in order for a record to be displayed. The discussion was confined to the examples where you hardcode within the selection formula the text/number/date that the field is compared to. The problem with this approach is that the report uses the same filter every time it is run. There isn't any room for flexibility based on the user's needs. This is where parameters come in. By using parameters within a record selection formula, the filter changes each time a user runs the report because the user can enter a new value for each parameter and this is immediately reflected in the selection formula.

## Selecting Records with Parameters

Using a parameter within a record selection formula involves the same process that was discussed in the first half of the chapter. You follow the steps to set which field to filter on and set the filtering condition (equal to a value, within a range, etc.). The difference is how you set the value to filter with. You now choose a parameter field. Parameters are listed with a ? in front of it. The next figure shows using a parameter to filter the Country field.

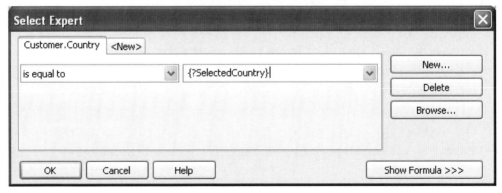

**Figure 4-13. Setting a filter that uses a parameter.**

Filtering on range and multi-value parameters has a few idiosyncrasies that you need to be aware of. As you know, these types of parameters are more complex due to the fact that they store more than just a simple value.

Range parameters consist of a start value and end value. The only conditions you can use with range parameters are Is Equal To and Is Not Equal To. This is the equivalent of testing whether a value falls within the range (Is Equal To) or if it falls outside the range (Is Not Equal To).23 Multi-value parameters consist of multiple discrete values or multiple range values. Just like range parameters, the only conditions you can use are the Is Equal To and Is Not Equal To conditions. Using the Is Equal To comparison looks at each of the individual values within the parameter and determines if it is equal to any one of those values. It only needs to match one value for the record to match the condition. Consequently, the Is Not Equal To condition is a match if the value isn't any of the parameter values.

## Best Of The Forum

**Question:** Rather than use a List of Values for my parameter, I want to let users type in their own list and separate each value with a comma. How would I write the record selection formula to handle this?

**Answer:** I think this is a great question because most people are used to writing down items in this format and Crystal Reports doesn't have a way that lets them do this. Of course, the reason is that anytime you ask people to type in values manually, there is a huge likelihood for error. Nonetheless, I can see where this is practical for small amounts of data or when the user is very familiar with the data being selected.

The difficulty with creating the record selection formula is that Crystal Reports is designed to compare individual fields to singular pieces of data; not compare a field to a string of multiple data items. But, there are two ways to get around this. The first is to use the InStr()function to see if the field's value is part of the string. I don't like this because you can get incorrect results when a small string matches part of a larger string. A better way is to use the Split() function to break the string into an array of strings. This lets Crystal Reports do one-to-one comparisons with each element of the array. For example, say that you have a parameter which lets the user enter a list of two character state abbreviations. I would create the following record selection formula:

```
{Customer.State} IN Split({?State Parameter},",");
```

This function breaks the list of states into an array. The IN operator checks if the Customer.State field matches any of the items in the array. This function

---

[23] It might make more sense to you to think of it as In Between or Is Not Between since this is what the comparison is actually doing behind the scenes.

works well with string data, but not if you try to use it with a number or date field. It will give you an error. This is because the Split() function always returns an array of strings. This isn't compatible with non-string data. To fix this, use the CStr() function to convert the field to a String. Also, make sure to format it properly or else Crystal Reports can add in extra digits that won't match your parameter list (e.g. the number "2" could be returned as "2.00"). Strings have to be exactly the same for a match to be successful. An example record selection formula for a list of numbers is as follows:

```
CStr({Customer.Customer ID}, "#") IN Split({?Customer Parameter},",");
```

## Printing Parameters

The second method of using parameters is displaying their value on a report. There are various reasons for displaying parameters on a report. A very common reporting requirement is that when filtering data, it is helpful to print the filter criteria so that anyone reading the report knows that only a subset of all the available data was printed. For example, if a report prints records within a certain date, then you could show the date range within the report header. You can also use a parameter strictly for the purpose of displaying it on the report. For example, printing an invoice could use a parameter to let the user enter a note at the bottom of the invoice to alert the reader of new shipping requirements or tell them about an upcoming price increase.

The way you print the parameter on the report is dependent on the type of parameter it is. Printing a discrete parameter on a report is simple because a parameter is treated the same as any other field. Simply drag and drop it from the Field Explorer onto the report and it will be printed. Printing range and multi-value parameters is more complex because they are represented internally by more than one value. You have to use formulas to tell the report how to display the data. Each parameter type requires a different formula for displaying its information.[24] The rest of this section looks at each parameter type and shows you how to print its value on the report.

Range parameters have a start value and end value. Crystal Reports has two functions for working with range parameters: Minimum() and Maximum(). When you pass a range parameter to these two functions, they return the beginning and ending values respectively. Here is an example of using these functions in a formula:

```
"This report covers the dates from " & Minimum({?DateRange}) & " to " &
Maximum({?DateRange})
```

---

[24] If some of these formulas aren't completely understandable yet, you might want to come back to this section after reading Chapter 5.

This formula concatenates the functions Minimum() and Maximum() within a string telling the user the selected date range.

If the parameter is a String data type and can have multiple values, you can use the Join() function to combine them into a single string with a separator. The following code uses the {?Names} parameter to create a comma separated list of user names. Note that the Join() function only works if the parameter is a string data type, not numbers or dates.

```
Join({?Names}, ",");
```

If you have a more complex parameter that can include multiple values or a range, then more complex programming logic is required. This is because each element in the parameter can have different printing requirements. To print a multi-value parameter, you need to loop through each item in the array and print it out. I built a sample formula for displaying all the multi-value parameter values and separate each one with a comma. This Crystal syntax formula prints the output in a very basic format and you will probably want to modify it to make it specific to your needs.

```
NumberVar Index;
StringVar Output;
StringVar LowerValue; StringVar UpperValue;
for Index := 1 to UBound({?Country Range}) Do
(
    //Add a comma to separate values
    If Output <> "" Then
        Output := Output & ", ";
    LowerValue := "";
    UpperValue := "";
    //Get the upper and lower values
    If HasLowerBound ({?Country Range}[Index]) Then
        LowerValue := Minimum({?Country Range}[Index]);
    If HasUpperBound ({?Country Range}[Index]) Then
        UpperValue := Maximum({?Country Range}[Index]);
    //Discrete values have the same upper and lower bound
    If LowerValue = UpperValue Then
        Output := Output & LowerValue
    Else
    //Print the range values
        (If LowerValue <> "" Then
            Output := Output + " From " & LowerValue;
        If UpperValue <> "" Then
            Output := Output + " To " & UpperValue;)
);
//Clean up the Output string
Output := "The valid values are: " & Output;
```

The formula starts out by declaring the necessary variables. Then it uses a For Loop to cycle through each item in the array. Within the For Loop, it builds the Output string. The first task is to check if the Output string has a value from a previous iteration of the loop and if so append a comma to the end.

The LowerValue and UpperValue variables are populated based upon whether the parameter value has an upper and lower bound. It uses the HasLowerBound() and HasUpperBound() functions to determine this.

Lastly, it concatenates the values to the Output string. If the lower and upper bound values are the same, then this is a discrete parameter value. If they are different, then it is a range parameter value and we want to display the minimum and maximum values.

The For Loop performs this logic for all values in the parameter. An example of the final output is:

The valid values are: Argentena To Australia, Canada

### Creating Formulas with Parameters

The third method of using parameters is within formulas. You've already seen examples of this throughout the chapter by modifying the records selection formulas. This can also be used with formulas for conditional formatting or for performing calculations.

# Entering Parameters

Creating parameters and using them within a report's selection filter and its formulas is just one aspect of parameters. The second aspect is when the user runs the report and enters the data into the parameter fields. Although this is a pretty simple process, it helps to review it to make sure you are familiar with each aspect of it.

When a report opens the first time, it presents you with the Enter Values dialog box. This dialog box lists all the parameters used in the report.[25] Each parameter is listed in the order that they appear in the Field Explorer window and each parameter is enclosed within its own grey box. Within each box is the prompt text that tells the user what to enter and an input area for entering the values. At the bottom of the dialog box are the OK and Cancel buttons for accepting or canceling the input. An example is shown in Figure 4-14.

---

[25] If you created a parameter but it isn't being used in the report yet, then you won't be prompted to enter a value for it. Only parameters that affect report output are prompted for a value.

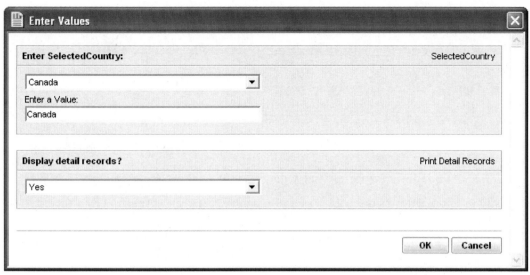

**Figure 4-14. The Enter Values dialog box for entering parameters.**

### Note

If you don't see the OK and Cancel buttons or you notice that some of the parameters are missing from the dialog box, it is because there are too many parameters to display within the dialog box's default size. You have to scroll down to the bottom of the dialog box to see the remaining parameters as well as the buttons.

When you refresh the report data by pressing the F5 key or clicking the Refresh Data button on the toolbar, you are asked whether you want to use the existing parameter values or enter new values. If you select the option to enter new values, then the Enter Values dialog box is presented again and you can override the existing parameter values. If you select the option to keep the existing values, then the report opens without prompting you for the parameters.

Crystal Reports presents different prompts for each data type and option. This creates numerous possible combinations for entering values. Fortunately, they are presented in such a way that it's pretty obvious how to use each one. We'll cover the basics here so that you are familiar with them.

The most basic type of parameter prompt is for the single value parameter type. It simply presents you with an input box for entering the value. If the data type is Boolean, then you are shown a dropdown list that lets you choose True or False.

If the data type is Date, you have to enter the date in the format of "yyyy-mm-dd". There is a button listed next to the input box that you can click on to display a pop-up calendar (see Figure 4-5 at the beginning of the chapter). The calendar is useful if you need to enter a date at a particular time (the last Friday of the month) and you need to see an overview of the entire month to figure out which date it is. Clicking on a day in the calendar automatically causes the pop-up window to close and it fills in the date for you.

### Best Of The Forum

**Question:** Is there a way to override the default input format for dates? I want to let the user enter a date in the format of MM/DD/YYYY but Crystal Reports doesn't let me.

**Answer:** There are two ways to change the default input format for dates. The first way is to change your browser locale settings. Crystal Reports uses the current locale for setting the date format.[26] If you want to manually set the date format, there is a trick you can use. Change the parameter to a String data type and set the edit mask to "00/00/0000" (or the local date format you use). This requires the user to enter the date in the proper format. To filter on the parameter value use the Date() function to convert the string to a date. The drawback to using this technique is that since the parameter is now a string data type, there isn't a pop-up calendar for selecting the date.

The next parameter type that affects how the user is prompted is a parameter with default values. This was already discussed in detail in an earlier section. To summarize, a parameter with default values presents you with a dropdown list showing all the possible default values. Click on the one you wish to use. When using default values, you can set the option that allows the user to enter a custom value. When this is selected, an input box is shown below the dropdown list and the user can enter a value not shown in the default value list. This was shown in Figure 4-14 as the Selected Country parameter.

Entering range parameters presents you with more options than the simplistic discrete parameter does. Range parameters let you select a start range and end range. In addition to that, you can specify whether these values should be inclusive or exclusive. You can also specify if there should be no start or end range at all. Figure 4-15 shows an example of entering a range parameter and the options that can be selected.

---

[26] Unfortunately, as of the time I'm writing this, this feature doesn't actually work. I talked to my contact at Business Objects and he said that this would be fixed in a service pack to be released near the end of 2007. So if you are reading this chapter in 2008 or later then you should be able to go to http://support.BusinessObjects.com and download the fix.

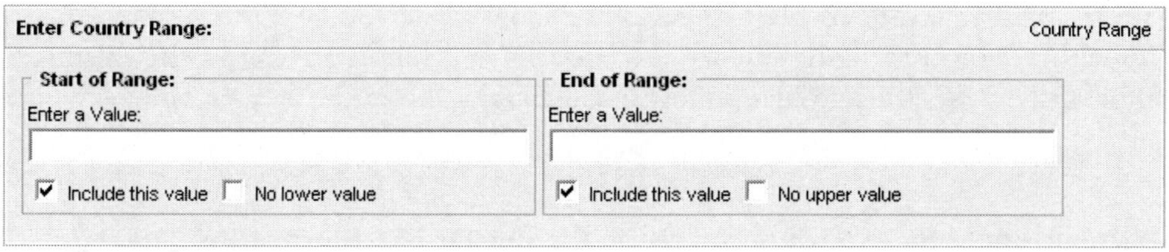

**Figure 4-15. Range parameter dialog box.**

Entering the start and end values is done via the two input boxes located adjacent to each other. Below each input box are the two options that specify how the value should be used. The first option is Include This Value and it is checked by default. It specifies that the value you entered should be included as part of the range. For example, let's say that you are entering values for a date range parameter. If you enter the values 10/1/2005 and 10/31/2005, then by default the range is inclusive and the first valid date is 10/1/2005 and the last valid date is 10/31/2005. However, if you uncheck the Include This Value option then the date you entered won't be included in the range. If you did this for the start range, then the first valid date would be 10/2/2005 because 10/1/2005 would be excluded. If you did this for the end of range, then the last valid date would be 10/30/2005.

Excluding one of the range values is useful when the beginning or end of a range is always changing. For example, let's say that you want to print the entire month of February but you can't remember when there is a leap year. In this case, you would enter an ending range of 03/01/2005 and uncheck the Include This Value option. That way you know that the valid date range will always go to the day before the first day of March, but not include March 1st. This lets Crystal Reports determine what the last day of the month is and whether February is in a leap year or not. Another example is printing an employee directory of everyone with a last name that starts with the letter B. You would enter the start range of "B" and an end range of "C". For the end range, you would uncheck the Include This Value option. This will include every possible last name that starts with the letter "B" without you having to actually know what the last one is.

The second option is No Lower Value/No Upper Value. This means that you don't want to specify a value for the start or end of the range. By checking the option No Lower Value, there is no minimum value in the range. For example, if you have a date range with No Lower Value checked and an end range of 10/31/2005 then the report will print every record with a date prior to, and including, 10/31/2005. It doesn't matter if the first date in the table is from last year or ten years ago, it's going to be included. The option No Upper Value means that there is no maximum value. Any date greater than the start range is treated as a valid date.

Of course, all these range related options can be combined to let you select any possible date range you need. The one thing to be aware of is that when you select one of the options No Lower Value or No Upper Value, then you can't enter a value for that part of the range. This makes sense because if you specify that there is "No Lower Value" then why would you try to specify a lower value? You wouldn't, and consequently Crystal Reports disables the input box.

The last parameter type to consider is the multi-value parameter. This parameter lets you build a list of acceptable values. It is also the most complex because it lets you combine both discrete and range parameters within this list of acceptable values. Figure 4-16 shows an example of a parameter that lets you specify a list of countries to print. This list can consist of a range of values or the names of individual countries.

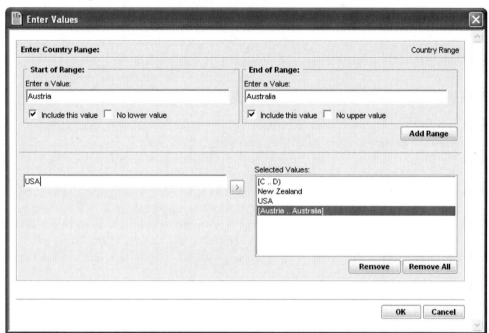

**Figure 4-16. Enter multiple values for the Country parameter.**

The top of the dialog box is where you enter the range values. Enter the start and end values and click the Add Range button. It gets added to the list in the bottom right corner. You can see in the figure that it lists both the start and end range with "..." between them showing that it is a range value. The input box below the range values lets you enter discrete values. Click the arrow button to add it to the list to the right. If you accidentally add an incorrect item to the list, you can select it and click on the Remove button. You can also remove all the items in the list and start over from scratch by clicking on the Remove All button.

As of this edition of Crystal Reports, all prompts are displayed as simple input boxes or lists. You can't use prompts such as check boxes or radio buttons. Hopefully, this will be a feature we see in a future edition!

**Best Of The Forum**

**Question:** Is it possible to use a formula field to set the default value of a parameter?

**Answer:** The normal behavior of parameters is that the user has to enter a value for each one. But you can get around this by making the report a subreport of a blank report and in the blank report create a formula which is linked to the parameter field. By linking the formula in the main report to the parameter in the subreport, you are giving the parameter a default value. When you link the formula in the main report to the existing parameter in the subreport, ignore the default parameter that Crystal Reports shows by default and select your own parameter instead. See Chapter 9 for more information.

# Dynamic Cascading Prompts

Crystal Reports XI gives you a wonderful new feature for working with parameters: Dynamic Cascading Prompts, commonly referred to as DCPs. This gives parameters the ability to be dynamic because they are linked directly to the database. They can also be cascading because the value in one parameter is used to filter the list of values in the next parameter. This collection of related prompts is defined as a "Prompt Group".

Up to now, when discussing how to create a list of values for prompts for the user to choose from, this chapter has focused on building a static list of values. This was done by either manually typing in the default values or selecting them from a live database connection. The drawback to both of these methods is that the list of values can only be guaranteed to be accurate as of the date you create the report. For example, if a list of values lets the user choose from a list of current customers and your company is always adding new customers, then the list of values will quickly be out of date. You, as the report designer, will have to continuously update the list of values to reflect the new customers.

DCPs solve this problem by letting you create a list of values that is linked directly to the data source. The default values presented to the user are always accurate and you never have to revise the report to make sure they stay current.

The way that cascading prompts work together is that when you select a value from the first prompt, Crystal Reports queries the database for all the records that have that value in them and uses this result to populate the next prompt list. This is repeated for each prompt in the group until you get to the last prompt. At which point, the last prompt in the list should be fairly small depending upon how much filtering was done prior to it.

As an example, assume the first prompt is Country and the second prompt is Region. If you select USA for the country, then the second prompt group displays a list of all the regions where the records have the value USA in the Country field. Now, let's assume that the first prompt is a multi-value prompt and you select USA and Canada as the two values. The second prompt will list all the regions where the records have a country equal to USA or Canada. Thus, when using a multi-value prompt, then the next prompt will list all records that match at least one of the selected values.

### Caution

When using DCPs, you have to make sure that everyone who opens the report will have an active link on the network. If they can't connect to the database then they can't enter parameters.

The beauty of DCPs is that they give you the ability to link prompts together so that each successive parameter's list of values is determined by the selection in the previous parameter. The value chosen for one parameter is used to filter the data in the next parameter. Thus, each prompt's selection "cascades" down to the next prompt.

DCPs are used when the list of values is so large that it would be overwhelming for the user to select from. For example, if the user needs to specify which city to filter on, then this list would be enormous if you are selecting from every possible city in the country. However, you can use cascading prompts to ask the user to first select which state they want and then only select the cities within that state. Cascading prompts effectively let you take a large list of values and significantly decrease its size by asking the user preliminary questions to filter out the non-necessary values. Cascading prompts also give your reports a performance boost because there is less load on the database server as the list of values gets filtered down with each parameter.

The benefits of dynamic cascading prompts are as follows:

- Reduces report maintenance because the list of values is always current.

- Simplifies the user interface because the list of values is more manageable.

- Report file size is smaller because the list of values isn't stored internally.

- Users make better decisions because they get an exact view of their information.

- Improves report performance by querying the database for smaller resultsets.

Dynamic cascading prompts also have limitations. They are as follows:

- Crystal Reports Standard edition can't create DCPs. This version can use them to prompt the user properly, but you as the report designer can't use it to create DCPs in a report.

- Cascading prompts must be dynamic. Static prompts can't be used.[27]

---

[27] There is actually a work-around for this limitation. See the Advanced Tutorials for the solution.

Since dynamic prompts are connected to the database, the database server will be queried every time the parameters are refreshed. If a list of values is small and doesn't change frequently, you might be better off creating static parameters so that there isn't unnecessary usage of the database server.

DCPs are backwards compatible with Crystal Reports 10, but only partially. Crystal Reports 10 can open an XI report that has DCPs, but it won't be able to display the list of values to the user. The user can manually enter parameter values and the report will use them. But the dynamic connection to the database won't be enabled.

## Creating Dynamic and Cascading Prompts

Creating a parameter that uses DCPs involves entering options in the same Create New Parameters dialog box that you learned about when we were discussing static parameters. The difference being that instead of choosing the Static option you will now choose the Dynamic option. When you do so, the dialog box changes to reflect the new options.

Creating a parameter that uses DCPs has the same steps that you've already practiced earlier in the chapter. Create a new parameter by right-clicking on the Parameter Fields category in the Field Explorer and select New Parameter. Enter the parameter name and for the List of Values option select Dynamic. With DCPs you don't specify the parameter's data type. This is because the data type is determined by the field you choose from the database.

By selecting the Dynamic option, the dialog box immediately changes to reflect the new requirements for inputting DCPs. The data type option is disabled, a new Prompt Group Text input box is displayed, and the area for entering default values changes so that you can select a data source and pick the fields to display.

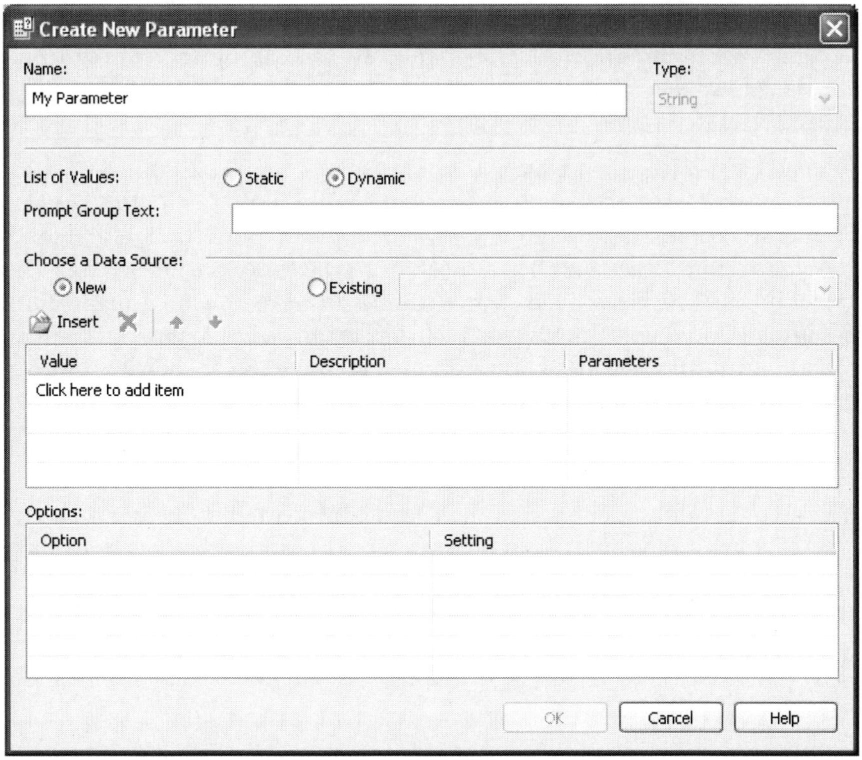

**Figure 4-17. Creating a new parameter using DCPs.**

The Prompt Group Text input box displays the overall question that the user is presented with when he is going to enter the parameter data. If this is a cascading prompt, it's important to enter a question that clearly conveys to the user that he will be selecting from multiple lists before getting to the final one.

The option Choose a Data Source specifies which fields are the data source for the list of values. They display the data for the user to choose from. Keep the default option of New selected and click on the Insert button. It displays a list of the fields in the report's data source. You have to select a field that is in a table already referenced by the report.

| Tip |
|---|

If the table you need isn't being used by the report, you can go back and add it to the report. Click on the Cancel button, modify the report's data source to include the necessary table, and then create the DCP again. The new table appears in the list of available data sources.

When selecting which field to display, it's important to choose the proper table. As we discussed earlier in the chapter, some tables have a complete list of all the available values and some tables only show the values that have been selected as part of another record.

This second list is most often incomplete. For example, the Customer table will list every customer your company has. But the Invoice table will only show customers with a current invoice on file. The Customer table will be complete, whereas the Invoice table will probably be missing values.

The table you choose has a big impact on the prompts. For example, if you select the Customer table, then the user will be able to see and choose from a complete list of customers. But this list could be quite large and it will take longer for the user to find the customer they want to print. Selecting the Invoice table makes it easier for the user to choose a customer because the list will have fewer entries. However, the user might still want to see the customers with no current invoices so that he can print a report that shows the user had no activity for the month. This can be just as important as showing which users do have activity. If you would have shown only the list of customers with current invoices, then this wouldn't be possible. This shows that there can be a tradeoff between speed and thoroughness.

Another possible point of confusion is that if you select the Invoice table, then some users might get confused when seeing that a certain customer isn't in the list. They might wonder if the customer is no longer working with the company or if it's a new customer, then they might question whether the report has all the current data. So you have to consider the goals of your user before deciding which table will populate the list of values. Again, a properly phrased Prompt Group Text can help prevent any possible confusion from your users.

After selecting a field for populating the list of values, you can also select a field for showing a description within the list of values. Displaying a description is useful for fields whose values wouldn't make sense to the layman. For example, rather than displaying a cryptic Inventory ID, you could display the Inventory Name as the description and the user immediately knows which inventory item to choose.

The last column is the Parameters column. This is used for creating a parameter that references the user's selection. Since there are DCPs involving multiple prompts, each one can be assigned its own parameter. This parameter can be referenced anywhere within the report. The last prompt is required to have a parameter associated with it, but not the prompts leading up to it.

The primary purpose of DCPs is to use the selection from one prompt as the filtering criteria for the next prompt. The final prompt will have a significantly simpler list of values for the user to choose from than if DCPs were not used. This implies that the only prompt that would be used on the report is the last prompt. Thus, only the last prompt needs to have a parameter field associated with it so that the report can be filtered on it. However, this isn't always the case. There are times when the report will need to reference every value that the user selected within this prompt group. For example, if the DCPs use the following order of fields: Country -> Region -> City, then it's very likely that in addition to filtering on the City selection, the report will print out the Country and

Region the user selected as well. To achieve this, you need to have a parameter associated with each prompt level.

By clicking on the third column, the text within the cell changes to [?] My Parameter and a parameter is automatically created to store the value that the user selected with this prompt. If you decide later not to use a parameter then you can click on the cell again and the parameter is removed.

There are times when you want a parameter to be actively linked to the data source, but you don't need to use multiple prompts. To do this, create a DCP that only has a single prompt. It doesn't have the cascading property associated with it. This is a big improvement over the static prompts that you created earlier in the chapter.

### Note

The last prompt in the group must always be associated with a parameter. If you forget to click on the third column to create a parameter for the final prompt, then Crystal Reports will do it for you when you click the OK button to save the parameter. This makes sense for two reasons. The first being that if you didn't want to assign a parameter to any of the prompts, then there would be no reason to create DCPs in the first place. The second reason is that since the ultimate goal of DCPs is to create an optimized list of values for the last prompt, then this is obviously the prompt you will want to use in the report.

After entering all the prompts for the parameter, you can set the options in the grid at the bottom of the dialog box. These options are the same as what was already discussed for static parameters. They let you set whether it stores discrete or multi-value parameters, allows range values, etc. What makes these options unique is that each prompt gets its own set of options. If you remember from the discussion of static parameters, the options normally apply to the current parameter. Since DCPs create a prompt group within a single parameter, this is almost like having multiple prompts. Thus, each prompt gets its own set of options. For example, the first prompt could be a discrete value and the second prompt could be restricted to a multi-value.

By combining a combination of parameter options with each prompt group, Crystal Reports lets you create sophisticated prompt groups. But you need to understand how these features work together and what the limitations are. The first thing to be aware of is that not every option is available for each prompt. The final prompt always gets access to all the options. But the prompts leading up to it must be discrete values. They can't use range values. However, you are allowed to have multiple values associated with each prompt. In summary, all prompts prior to the final prompt can set all the options except for allowing range values. The final prompt is allowed to use range values. Figure 4-18 shows a prompt group using the fields Region and City.

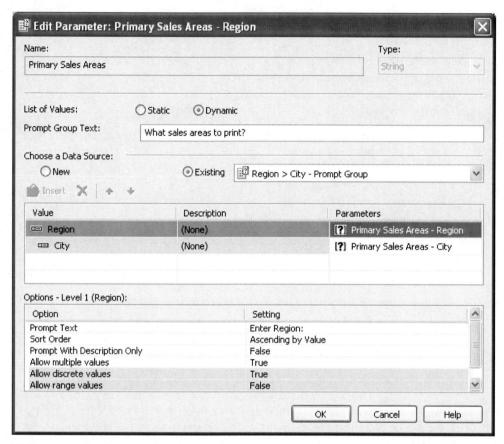

**Figure 4-18. Setting options for the first prompt in a prompt group.**

There is a strange behavior with DCPs that isn't applicable to static parameters. After you click the OK button and save the DCP, you can't go back and edit the fields associated with each prompt. You are literally locked into using those fields with that prompt group. If you wish to change the fields associated with the value or description, you can't do it. Instead, you have to click on the New option and rebuild the list of prompts from scratch.

## Best Of The Forum

**Question:** My field has over 200 unique values in it, but the DCP is only showing 30 of them. Is there a limit to how many records a DCP displays to the user?

**Answer:** Yes, there is a limit to how many records are displayed in a DCP. To conserve resources, Crystal Reports reads a maximum of 1,000 records from the database. If there are a lot of duplicates in the table, then considerably fewer records are displayed. To get around this behavior, you need to add a

Windows registry entry that tells Crystal Reports to override the internal default value of 1,000 records.[28]

On your computer, select the Windows menu options Start > Run. Enter RegEdit. Create the following registry key:

HKEY_LOCAL_MACHINE\SOFTWARE\Business Objects\Suite 11.0\Crystal Reports\ DatabaseOptions\LOV.

If you are using XI R2, then change the 11.0 to 11.5. Add a string value called MaxRowsetRecords and give it a new value for the maximum number of records to read. I suggest you make it very large so that no data is missed.[29]

# Tutorial 4-5. Creating DCPs

The previous tutorials in this chapter have focused on different ways to modify the Group.rpt sample report and customize it with parameters. This tutorial is no different. It builds on the other tutorials by showing you how to use DCPs to create the same parameters and demonstrates how it makes them more user friendly.

The previous tutorials created a parameter for the fields Country and Customer ID. They used the database tables to build a static list of values that the user chose from. The downside to doing it this way is that the list of customers to pick from was quite large. Even though the user could only choose to print the customers from either the USA or Canada, they still had to scroll through every customer in the database even if that customer was located in a different country.

We're going to modify the report requirements to illustrate the usage of DCPs. The report will now let the user print the report for one or more customers and the user will narrow down the list of customers to pick from by first picking the Country. Once they pick the Country, then only the customers located in that country will be displayed.

1.  Open the Crystal Reports sample report Group.rpt. Save it as Tutorial DCPs.rpt.
2.  Right-click on the Parameter Fields list and select New.
3.  Enter the parameter name Customers to print.
4.  Select the Dynamic option.
5.  For the Prompt Group Text type in Select the customers to print.
6.  Click on the Insert button and select the Country field. Leave the Description and Parameters column alone because they aren't needed.

---

[28] Adding a Windows registry can be confusing and dangerous if you aren't familiar with how it works. I suggest calling an IT support person if you haven't done this before.

[29] Entering a value of 0 will not give you unlimited records. You have to enter an actual limit.

7.  We want to let the user enter customers from more than one country. In the Options, set the option Allow Multiple Values to True.

8.  For the second field select Customer ID and for the description field select Customer Name. Click on the Parameters column so that a parameter is created for this field.

9.  We want to let the user print multiple customers as well. In the Options box, set the option Allow Multiple Values to True.

10. At this point, two prompts have been created and the final prompt saves the Customer ID field to the parameter. Click the OK button to save the parameter.

11. Now we want to set the record selection formula so that it filters on the Customer Id parameter. Select the menu items Report > Select Expert.

12. When the Choose Field dialog box opens, select the Customer.Customer ID field and click the OK button.

13. For the selection criteria choose Is Equal To.

14. For the field to match to, choose the parameter {?Customers – Customer ID}.

15. Click the OK button to save your changes. The Enter Values parameter will automatically open. It should look similar to the following figure.

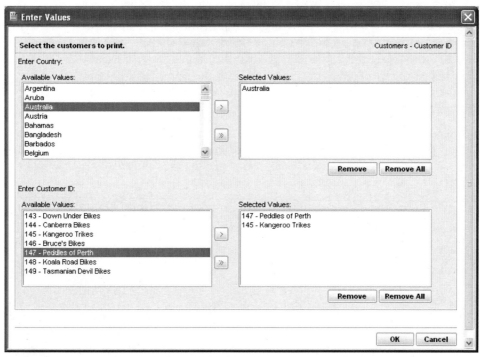

The first prompt lets you select multiple countries. As you choose each country, the Customer list changes to reflect which customers are in that country. Choose as many customers as you wish to print and click the OK button. Your report is updated to reflect the customers you picked.

# Advanced Tutorials

## Tutorial 4-6. Selecting Records Using the 'Or' Operator

If you recall from the discussion about using the Select Expert dialog box with multiple fields, Crystal Reports builds the selection formula for you automatically. When there is more than one field used, each field's selection criteria must be met for the record to be selected. For example, if the first criteria is Country='USA' and the second criteria is Last Years Sales>25,000, then a record has to meet both conditions for it to be printed. If the Country field is 'USA' but Last Year's Sales were only 10,000, then it won't be printed.

There will be times when your report needs to display records that meet ANY of the conditions. If only one of the two conditions is met, then the record should still be printed. To do this, you have to use the OR operator to join the conditions.

For example, let's take the formula from Tutorial 4-1. When you clicked on the Show Formula button, it displayed the formula

```
{Customer.Country} in ["Canada", "England", "USA"] And
{Customer.Last Year's Sales} >= $25000.00
```

Notice the And operator at the end of the first line of code. This requires both conditions to be met. To fix it so that only one of the two conditions need to be met, manually change the And to Or and save the formula. Now when you preview the report, there will be a lot more pages. There will be a lot more records that only need to match one of the criteria, rather than both.

The benefit to using the Show Formula button is that you can create very complex formulas for performing record selection. You can have formulas that use a combination of And and Or operators as well as using custom functions you created yourself.

Be aware that once you enter a custom formula, you can't use the Select Expert prompts for modifying the record selection anymore. Since your custom formula is too complex to be represented by the Select Expert, the prompts are disabled.

## Tutorial 4-7. Mixing Static and Dynamic Parameters

In the discussion about DCPs, I said that Crystal Reports doesn't allow you to mix static and dynamic parameters. If you want to use DCPs, then every prompt within the prompt group must be dynamic (i.e. pull its data from the data source). The problem with this is that if you want to customize the list of values presented to the user, then you are limited to using the data already in the data source. There are times when this isn't going to work for you. For example, when I originally wrote Tutorial 4-5 I wanted to show how to replace static parameters with DCPs. But I ran into a problem – in the earlier tutorials I only let the user pick from the countries Canada and USA. I had to change the report requirements around a little bit because using DCPs required me to show the user every country in the data source. Ideally, I would have been able to use a static list of values for the country and then followed up with a dynamic list of customers based on the country that the user selects. But Crystal Reports doesn't let you mix static and dynamic parameters and I had to modify the tutorial accordingly. Fortunately, there is a way to get around this rule by simulating static parameters using Command objects.

Command objects are discussed in more detail in Chapter 11, but for now you need to understand that a Command object is a custom SQL statement that you write manually. By getting creative with SQL statements, we can filter out certain data we don't want from the list of values before it is shown to the user. Very cool!

There are two criteria for using a Command object with DCPs.

- All levels for the entire DCP must be derived from a single Command object. Each field in the DCP must come from this one Command object.

- The Command object must not be linked to the other tables in the report. It has to be completely independent of the report data.

To create a Command object, select the menu items Database > Database Expert. Find the database and click Add Command. This opens a text area where you can type in your SQL statement. After you type in the SQL statement, click the OK button to save it. You can now reference the Command object from your DCPs and use it as the source for the list of values.[30]

The one thing to be careful of is that after creating the Command object, Crystal Reports will try to link it to an existing table in the data source. If this happens, delete the link. To use the Command object with DCPs, you want it to be completely separate from the other tables. The second thing that will happen is that Crystal Reports will give you a couple of warning messages that it doesn't recommend using tables that aren't linked to the other report tables. Just ignore these messages and click OK a couple times to make them go away.[31]

To solve the problem I had in Tutorial 4-5, where I just wanted to list the countries Canada and USA, I'll create a SQL statement that selects the same customer data from the report but this time it will pre-filter all countries except Canada and USA.

Select Country, [Customer Id], [Customer Name] FROM Customer WHERE Country IN ("Canada', 'USA')

In this SQL statement, I selected the three fields to be used by the DCP prompts. I use the WHERE clause to specify that I only want data with the countries Canada and USA.

---

[30] If you aren't familiar with creating and using Command objects, then come back to this tutorial after you've had a chance to read Chapter 11.

[31] In previous versions of Crystal Reports, having unlinked tables wasn't allowed at all. It's nice that this is now acceptable because there are obviously times like this where you need them.

When I create the DCP, I only use these three fields for the prompts and the report works just like I want it to.

> **Caution**
>
> You have to be careful when using Command objects so that you don't accidentally select a field from the report's data source instead of from the Command object. The reason this is easy to do is because the Command object will have some of the same fields used in the report and the Command object is always listed last. Thus, it is easy to mistakenly pick a field from the report's data source, since those fields are shown first. DCPs do not support mixing fields from the live data source along with fields from the Command object. If you find that the list of values in your DCP is missing data or it looks unusual, then go back and make sure that all the DCP fields are coming from the Command object.

## Tutorial 4-8. Adding "ALL" to the List of Values

When using the Select Expert for filtering report records, it forces the user to either enter a single value to filter on or pick from a list of values. The problem with this is that sometimes the user will want to print every record in the data source but they can't because the selection formula doesn't account for this. You need some way to let the user specify that they want to print all the records when the need arises.

You can use Command objects with DCPs to create a list of values that has the word "All" at the beginning of each list. This lets the user choose the "All" value when they want to print every record or they can pick any other value to filter the list by that value. The Crystal Reports sample report, "Prompting.rpt" shows us exactly how this is done. Let's examine it to see the details.

Open the report "Prompting.rpt" found in the Crystal Reports Samples folder. After it opens, click on the Refresh Report button and select the option to prompt for parameters. You'll see that each prompt has the value "All" as the first item in the list. As you select different values for each prompt, you'll see that each successive prompt still lists "All" as the first item in the list of values.

Let's look behind the scenes to see how the report was built. First, click on Database > Database Expert to view the data source. Find the Command object GeographyPrompt and right-click it to select View Command. It uses the following SQL statement:

```
SELECT Country, Region, City FROM Customer
UNION
SELECT Country, Region, '...All' FROM Customer
UNION
```

```
SELECT Country, '...All', '...All' FROM Customer
UNION
SELECT '...All', '...All', '...All' FROM Customer
```

The first SELECT statement in the SQL statement selects a complete list of every value for Country, Region and City. The second SELECT statement selects a complete list of every value for Country and Region but for the City, it substitutes the word "All" in each record. This makes it possible for the user to see the word "All" in the list of values no matter which combination of Country and Region was selected. The third SQL statement does the same for every possible Country value. The last SQL statement uses "All" for each field so that the user can pick "All" for every prompt in the DCP.

It's important to use the UNION keyword between each SQL statement. This keyword lets you combine multiple SELECT statements into a single resultset. Crystal Reports thinks it is reading from a single table when in reality it is multiple tables combined into one.

Notice that each "All" value is preface with "…" Since the list of values is sorted alphabetically, you don't know where the All option will appear in the list. By prefacing it with "…", you ensure that it always appears as the first item on the list.

After creating the Command object that builds the list of values for each prompt, you need to create a record selection formula that selects every record when the user selects the "All" value. Click on the menu items Report > Selection Formulas > Record. This opens the Formula Workshop dialog box. The selection formula is as follows:

```
if {?Country} = '...All' then
  {Orders.Employee ID}={?Employee}
else if {?Region} = '...All' then
  {Orders.Employee ID}={?Employee} and
  {Customer.Country} = {?Country}
else if {?City} = '...All' then
  {Orders.Employee ID}={?Employee} and
  {Customer.Country} = {?Country} and
  {Customer.Region} = {?Region}
else
  {Orders.Employee ID}={?Employee} and
  {Customer.Country} = {?Country} and
  {Customer.Region} = {?Region} and
  {Customer.City} = {?City}
```

This selection formula looks at each parameter value and determines if it is equal to "All". Depending upon which parameter this applies to, it sets the other fields to match their respective parameter field. It does this in a tree-like manner where it starts at the least restrictive level and works its way down through the more restrictive levels. This results in the report only filtering on the fields that do not have the value "All" selected for them.

# Tutorial 4-9. Customizing the Enter Values Parameter Interface

In an effort to make Crystal Reports accessible for all people regardless of disability or impairment, the Enter Values dialog box is fully customizable. This enables you to make it easier for all your users to enter parameter values for a report. You can increase the size of the text, change the background color, and make a plethora of other modifications. But just because this was done for the purpose of making your reports accessible, that doesn't mean you can't use it to make them look better. In fact, you can customize the Enter Values dialog box so that it matches your corporate identity.

The Enter Values dialog box is designed using HTML and CSS (Cascading Style Sheets). If you are familiar with website design, then you know that CSS files let you centralize the look and feel of your website within a single text file. Each web page references the same CSS file so that they have a consistent format with a minimal amount of work. That same logic is used with the Enter Values dialog box.[32]

Crystal Report uses the file "promptengine_default.css" as the template for displaying the Enter Values dialog box. That file is located in the following directory (assuming you performed a default installation):

C:\Program Files\Common Files\Business Objects\3.0\crystalreportviewers11\prompting\css\

This file is a basic text file that can be opened with any text editor or your favorite CSS editing program. Here is an excerpt of a few lines of sample code from that file.

```
.pePromptMessage
{
    color: black;
    font-family: Arial, verdana;
    font-weight: bold;
    font-size: 8pt;
}

.pePromptTextBox
{
    font-size: 8pt;
    background-color: #FFFFFF;
    font-family: Arial, verdana;
    width: 300px;
}
```

This book doesn't teach you how to program with CSS, but the basic idea of this code snippet is that it defines how to display the prompt message and the prompt text box. It

---

[32] If you aren't familiar with how to work with CSS files, there are plenty of books on the market that will teach you how to program them.

defines the font color, font size, and font style. If you modify this text file and save it, you'll immediately see the changes next time you enter parameters in a report. Let's walk through the steps for making some simple changes to this file and see what the effects are.

The changes you make to the CSS file are not report specific. Since the CSS file is external to the report files, the changes you make to the Enter Values dialog box will be visible on every report. If you open the report on a different computer, the Enter Values dialog box will default back to normal because the modified CSS file was only stored on your computer. If you want other users to have the changes applied on their computer, then you have to copy the new CSS file over the one on their computer.

1. To modify the CSS file, open the Windows Explorer and navigate to the folder:

   C:\Program Files\Common Files\Business Objects\3.0\crystalreportviewers11\ prompting\css\

2. Right-click on the file "promptengine_default.css" and select Copy.

3. Right-click anywhere in that window and select Paste. This makes a backup copy of your CSS file. You MUST make a back-up copy because what we are doing is only for training purposes and you will want the original file restored after we are finished.

4. Click on the Start menu and select All Programs > Accessories > Notepad. Click File > Open and navigate to the CSS file and open it.

5. Scroll through the file and look at the different options you have for changing the format of the Enter Values dialog box. Some of it may appear cryptic, but it shouldn't be too hard to figure out because they are named very descriptively.

6. Let's make a couple of changes and see what the results are. Find the style .pePromptElementText near the middle of the file. Double the font-size property from 8 to 16.

7. Find the style .pePromptRuler and change its height property from 1px to 20px.

8. Did you really create a backup copy of this file in Step 3 like I suggested? If you did, then save this file. If not, this is your last chance to make a backup copy before overwriting it!

9. After saving the changes, open any report with parameters and refresh its data. You'll see something similar to the following screen shot.

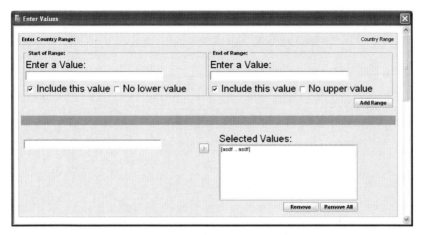

Notice how the prompt text is twice as large as the rest of the text? That is because we doubled the font size. And the gray bar separating parameters (the ruler) is huge compared to the thin line it used to be. Of course, I used these specific changes because they are easy to illustrate in the book, but they aren't very practical. If you wish to modify the Enter Values dialog box for your own reports, then you should get a book on CSS to make sure you have a basic understanding of what you are doing. It isn't very hard to change the fonts and color scheme to give it your own personal touch or make it match your corporate image.

| Tip |
| --- |

If you are making a lot of changes to the CSS file and going back and forth to see how the changes affect the dialog box, press the F5 key in the dialog box. It automatically refreshes the interface to reflect the latest changes saved to the CSS file. This is much easier than refreshing the report data and reopening the Enter Values dialog box each time to see the changes.

After playing around with these changes, you'll want to go back to the folder and delete this new CSS file and replace it with the backup copy you made earlier.

# 5

# Using the Formula Workshop

Crystal Reports comes with a powerful set of tools that let you build sophisticated formulas in your reports. You can perform tasks such as conditional formatting, specialized calculations, selecting records and report alerts. Formulas give you advanced functionality that is often only limited by your experience or imagination. The next three chapters are a thorough training manual for creating and programming formulas.

| Note |
| --- |
| If you don't have any past experience writing computer programs, the next few chapters could get a little overwhelming. To make it easier, this chapter focuses on learning how to use the Formula Workshop (where you write the formulas). The following two chapters focus on the logic and syntax of writing formulas. Crystal Reports has so much functionality built in it, you can do a lot with only a little knowledge. But if you want to get the most out of Crystal Reports formulas, then you should look into taking a programming course at night. It can take some training and a lot of practice to really get the hang of how to write more complex formulas. Although the next three chapters give you a lot of material to learn from, they are more of a reference guide than an introductory course for how to learn to program from scratch. |

It's my opinion that there are three levels of understanding how to program formulas. The first level consists of indirectly creating formulas by responding to prompts within the report expert dialog boxes. This doesn't require any knowledge of formulas except for understanding what the prompts mean. The second level goes a little deeper by using the Formula Workshop to create formulas that simply call one of the built-in report functions and return a value. This consists of using conditional formatting to make reports dynamic, using parameters so that a report changes based upon a user's needs, and dynamically manipulating the grouping and sorting of a report. The third level involves using sophisticated programming constructs with Crystal syntax and/or Basic syntax. This gives you very advanced formulas for creating professional reports. Being adept at the third level requires a solid understanding of programming logic.

Of the three levels mentioned above, the first level is covered throughout the book wherever report experts are used. This chapter and the next focuses on level two by showing you how and when to use the Formula Workshop and how to work with the built-in report functions. The third chapter is a programming tutorial and syntax reference for writing formulas with Basic syntax.

Before getting into how to use the Formula Workshop editor, let's start out with a quick tutorial that illustrates conditional formatting. This will give you a high level understanding of how this functionality is used to improve your reports. We won't get into the details of how each feature works right now. That will be covered later in the chapter.

# Turtorial 5-1. Creating "Green Bar" Reports

Let's create a "Green Bar" report that simulates the paper style that was used to be common in business reports printed on wide paper. Every other line was shaded in a light green color. This made it easy for the reader to scan across a long line of data and not lose track of which row they were reading. We'll use conditional formatting to simulate the green bar paper.

1.  Open the Crystal Reports sample report, Group By Intervals.rpt. Save it as **Green Bar.rpt.**

2.  This report has many rows within each group and the readability could be improved by shading every other row.

## How to group data in intervals

| Customer Name | Region | Country | Postal Code | Last Year's Sales |
|---|---|---|---|---|
| Nairobi Sports Center | Nairobi | Kenya | 646411 | $6,923.70 |
| New Trails | Canterbury | New Zealand | | $1,716.20 |
| Newpeople Biking Ltd. | Hong Kong SAR | China | 863356 | $7,981.41 |
| Nogoya Paths | Hiroshima Ken | Japan | 106-4553 | $8,819.55 |
| Off Road Bikes | SD | USA | 52115 | $140.90 |
| Offroad Bike Verleih | Berlin | Germany | D-14059 | $1,623.15 |
| On The Edge Cyclery | RI | USA | 02896 | $9,751.45 |
| One Track Mind | ME | USA | 04401 | $46.50 |
| Orléans VTT | Champagne-Ardenne | France | 10000 | $6,655.90 |
| Outdoors Ltda | São Paulo | Brazil | 04082-001 | $2,378.35 |
| Oympic Bikes | NC | USA | 27701 | $1,036.20 |
| Paradise Sports | Tortola | British Virgin Islands | F3R 6T9 | $1,529.70 |
| Pedals Inc. | WI | USA | 53795 | $5,000.00 |
| Peddles of Perth | Western Australia | Australia | 3326 | $8,945.25 |
| Phil's Bikes | CT | USA | 05667 | $27.00 |
| Picadilly Cycle | Greater London | England | SW19 4UE | $5,321.25 |
| Ride Down A Mountain | KS | USA | 64152 | $1,570.08 |
| Royal Cycle | Pembroke Parish | Bermuda | 46557 | $3,493.65 |
| Salvado Bike Store | Rio Grande do Sul | Brazil | 90880-390 | $5,879.70 |
| Sanstone Cycle | Singapore | Singapore | 311435 | $3,300.00 |
| Saveiros SA | São Paulo | Brazil | 20093-400 | $5,879.70 |

3.  In design mode, right-click on the gray area to the left of the Details section and select Section Expert from the pop-up menu. This opens the Section Expert dialog box.

4.  On the right side of the dialog box, click on the Color tab.

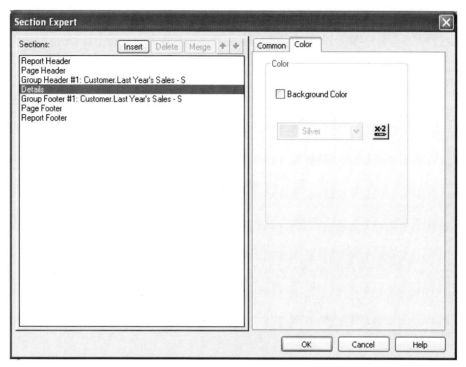

5.  The color tab only lets you choose the background color. You can either click on the checkbox and select a background color or click on the Formula button to apply conditional formatting. We want the background color to change dynamically, so click on the Formula button.

    The Formula Workshop dialog box opens with the cursor in the text editing area. We want the formula to assign crSilver to the background color of every even row on the report.

6.  Type in the following formula:

```
If (RecordNumber Mod 2 = 0) Then
    crSilver
Else
    DefaultAttribute;
```

    The calculation divides the current row number by two and gets the remainder. If the remainder is zero, then the current row number is an even number and crSilver is assigned to its background color. If the remainder is not zero, then this is an odd row and we assign the DefaultAttribute to the background color (this is the same as telling it not to modify the original color).

7.  Click the Save and Close button in the top left corner to save the changes.

8.  Click the OK button of the Section Expert to save your changes.

9.  Preview the report and you'll see that every other row now has silver shading.

How to group data in intervals

| Customer Name | Region | Country | Postal Code | Last Year's Sales |
|---|---|---|---|---|
| **Less than $10,000** | | | | |
| 7 Bikes For 7 Brothers | NV | USA | 89102 | $8,819.55 |
| Against The Wind Bikes | NY | USA | 14817 | $2,409.46 |
| AIC Childrens | Hong Kong SAR | China | 439433 | $5,879.70 |
| Aruba Sport | St. George | Aruba | 655456 | $3,239.85 |
| Auvergne Bicross | Auvergne | France | 03200 | $5,179.98 |
| Barbados Sports, Ltd. | Bridgetown | Barbados | 4532 | $4,443.80 |
| Barry's Bikes | DE | USA | 19850 | $33.90 |
| Beach Trails and Wheels | Wakato | New Zealand | | $2,944.00 |
| Benny - The Spokes Person | AL | USA | 35861 | $6,091.96 |
| Berg auf Trails GmBH. | Nordrhein-Westfalen | Germany | D-40608 | $2,939.29 |
| Berlin Biking GmBH. | Bayern | Germany | D-80042 | $2,989.35 |
| Bicicletas de Montaña Cancun | Quintana Roo | Mexico | 02994 | $1,551.18 |
| Bicicletas de Montaña La Paz | La Paz | Bolivia | 4542 | $6,269.25 |
| Bicycle Races | AZ | USA | 85234 | $659.70 |
| Bicyclette Bourges Nord | Centre | France | 18000 | $2,099.25 |
| Bicyclette du Nord | Nord Pas-de-Calais | France | 62000 | $8,819.55 |
| Bike-A-Holics Anonymous | OH | USA | 43005 | $4,500.00 |
| Bikefest | AR | USA | 72206 | $5,879.70 |

This tutorial showed you how to use the Formula Workshop to create a conditional formatting formula. You'll learn the details of using the Formula Workshop in the next section.

# Adding and Editing Formulas

Formulas are used by many parts of a report. You can create formulas from scratch and display their results directly on the page. You can attach reports to different properties of a report object so that the property can be conditionally turned on or off. Crystal Reports also filters report data using the record selection formula. But the method that you will probably use most frequently is the within Field Explorer window in design mode (see Figure 5-1).

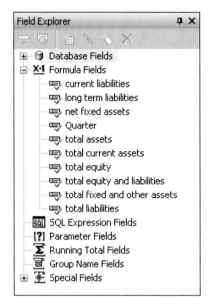

**Figure 5-1. Field Explorer window.**

Within the Field Explorer is the Formula Fields category. By clicking on the plus sign next to it you can see all the formula fields in the report. To add a new formula, right-click on the category name and select the New menu option. Enter a formula name and click the OK button to open the Formula Workshop dialog box (discussed in the next section).

To edit an existing formula, right-click on the formula name and select Edit. If you with to delete the formula, right-click on it and select Delete. However, don't delete a formula that has a checkmark on it because it is being used on the report. Delete it from the report prior to deleting it from the Field Explorer Window.

Crystal Reports XI R2 has some great new features for working with formulas in a report. To edit a formula, simply double-click on it. This automatically opens it in the Formula Workshop. I think it's great that they added this feature because I've seen it in other programs and always wished we had it in Crystal Reports. This also works for editing SQL Expressions, Running Totals, and Parameters.

If you need to create a new formula that is similar to an existing formula, right-click on the existing formula and select Duplicate Formula. This makes a copy of the formula for you.

Sometimes it can be difficult to figure out which formulas are using a field. In a complex report, there can be too many formulas to

figure out which ones use a certain field. With Crystal Reports XI
R2, you can right-click on any field and select Find In Formula and
it opens the Formula Workshop dialog box. At the bottom is a
search result list of all the formulas that use that field. Double-click
each formula to edit it.

# Writing Formulas with the Formula Workshop

Formulas are referenced in different ways depending upon which part of the report is using
them. But they all share the same editor. The Formula Workshop is the command center
for entering and editing formulas. Getting a solid understanding of how to use the
Formula Workshop is essential before getting into the details of writing formulas. The
Formula Workshop is shown in Figure 5-2.

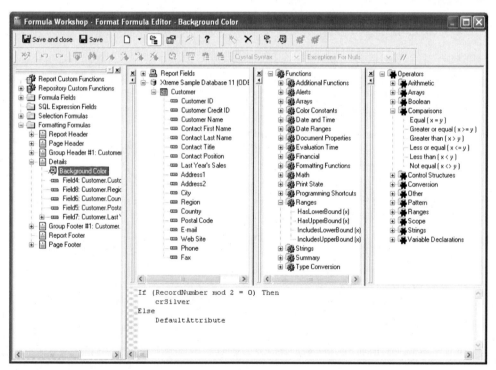

Figure 5-2. The Formula Workshop window.

The Formula Workshop consists of five separate windows. The left window along the side
is the Workshop Tree. It shows every formula being used in the report and is categorized
by the type of formula. The three windows along the top present the library of fields and
functions used for writing formulas. Within these three windows is every available database

field, built-in function, and operator. The bottom window is the Definition area where you write and edit formulas. It is like a fancy Notepad editor where you enter text and it highlights different keywords.

# Using the Toolbars

Before getting into the details of what each window does and how to use it, let's first explore the toolbars and the buttons on each toolbar. Each group of buttons has a different way of assisting you with writing formulas.

## *Displaying Windows*

These buttons make minor modifications to the windows within the Formula Workshop. The first button toggles the categories and items to be either sorted or unsorted. Sorting the categories makes it easier to find an item in the tree. Clicking the button a second time returns them to their natural order.

The last three buttons hide one of the three other windows. The three windows that they hide are the Report Fields window, Functions window, and the Report Operators window. Clicking the button a second time displays the window again.

There are some other buttons that work with the windows, but they are scattered in different locations around the toolbars. The Workshop Tree button toggles the display of the Workshop Tree window along the left side. It is located above the other three buttons.

The Show Formatting Formulas button toggles the display of formatted report objects within the Workshop Tree. This makes it easy to see which report objects have conditional formatting. For example, when you initially open the Formula Workshop and look in the Workshop Tree, under the Formatting Formulas category is a list of every report section. Clicking on each section expands that category and shows every report object in that section. The objects that have conditional formatting can be expanded one more level to see those formulas.

Of course, not every report object has conditional formatting formulas associated with it. When you click the Show Formatting button, the report objects that don't have any conditional formatting formulas are hidden. This makes it easy for you to look at the report sections and quickly see how much conditional formatting has been used and look at the details. If this is a report you haven't worked on in a while (or a report that someone else created), then this button helps you quickly understand what is happening behind the scenes.

The Use Expert/Editor button opens the Formula Expert.

When clicking this button, all the windows except the Workshop Tree are removed and the Formula Expert appears in their place. It helps you create formulas based on a custom function. The Formula Expert is discussed in more detail in Chapter 6.

### Creating New Formulas

The New button creates a new formula. When you click on it, it shows you a list of the different types of formulas and you click on the type you want to create.

**Figure 5-3. Menu items for the New Formula button.**

If you've been working on an existing formula and haven't saved it yet, you are asked if you want to save it before continuing.

### Editing Code

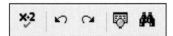

These five buttons assist you with writing formulas. The first button checks the syntax of the formula. If it finds an error in the formula, it prompts you with a message box telling you if there is a syntax error or not. You can check the syntax after you are finished writing the formula or you can do it after each line. Checking the syntax after each line lets you find a problem and correct it before going forward. This is good when you are just learning how to write formulas and you aren't confident of what you are doing yet. It's also useful if you are writing a complex formula and you want to double check that you didn't make a typo.

The next two buttons are the Undo and Redo buttons. You are probably familiar with these from other programs such as Microsoft Word or Excel. The Undo button removes the last change you made. The Redo button puts that change back if you decide that you shouldn't have clicked the Undo button. It's like an Undo-The-Undo button. ☺

The last two buttons help you find information. The magnifying glass browses data of a field. This is the same as the Browse Data button we saw with the report experts. It is only available when a field in the Report Fields window is selected.

The last button is the Find button. As you might expect, it finds the specified text within the formula and highlights it. But that is just one part of its functionality. What is a really nice feature is that it not only searches your formula, but it searches the text within any of the windows. Look at Figure 5-4 to see what the Find dialog box looks like.

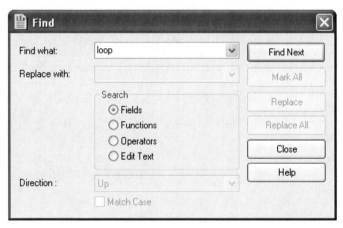

**Figure 5-4. The Find dialog box gives you advanced search functionality.**

Notice in the center of the dialog box that it has radio buttons that specify where to search for the text. It finds text in Fields, Functions, Operators, and Edit Text (the Definition area). If you've ever tried to find a function name in the Functions tree, it can be confusing to figure out which category the function is listed under. The Find dialog box finds it for you. And if you only know part of the name, then it does partial text finds as well.

The Find feature also replaces existing text with new text. But this is only enabled for the Edit Text option (you aren't about to start renaming Crystal functions!) If you want to rename a formula name that is referenced within another formula, remember from before that you don't have to do this with Crystal Reports. When you rename the formula within the Field Explorer window, Crystal Reports automatically searches throughout the entire report and updates all formula references to use the new name.

Crystal Reports has an auto-complete feature that saves you time typing. When you are typing in a function name you can press CTRL + Spacebar and the rest of the function name will be typed for you. If there is more than one function name that start with the letters you typed in then a drop-down list will appear with all the function names listed in it. This is helpful if you can remember part of a function name but you aren't sure of what the full name is. Just type in the part you know and press CTRL + Spacebar.

 If you are using Crystal Reports XI R2, the auto-complete feature is more advanced. Upon typing the open bracket for a field name, it automatically displays a list of all fields in the data source. You can use the down arrow to find the one you want or continue typing. This also works for formulas, parameters and SQL Expressions.

## *Working with Programming Code*

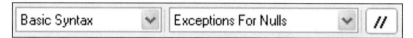

These three buttons assist you with programming specific tasks. The first button tells Crystal Reports whether you are programming with Crystal syntax or Basic syntax. We'll discuss programming languages in more detail in the next two chapters. For now you just need to know that this button lets you choose the language you want to program with.

Record selection formulas must be written in Crystal Syntax. Crystal Reports tries to convert every record selection formula into an SQL expression so that it can make the database do the work of filtering the data. It can only do this if the formula is written in Crystal syntax. Thus, switching to Basic syntax is not option in the Formula Workshop when writing record selection formulas.

### Tip

Most people always program in the same language. By default, Crystal Reports is set to use Crystal syntax as the programming language. If you prefer to program with Basic syntax then you should change the default programming language. To do this, select the menu items File > Options > Formula Editor. Near the bottom of the dialog box is a dropdown list that lets you choose the default language. Click on it and select Basic syntax.

The Exceptions for Nulls button determines how to handle null values in your data. Normally, when a field in a formula has a Null value, the formula generates an error or returns an invalid result. To get around this you should test for Nulls within your code. But another option is to set this button to Default Values For Nulls. This tells Crystal Reports to replace Null values with the default value for each field type (e.g. Numbers are

0, Strings are the empty string, etc.). This keeps your code cleaner because you don't have to write extra error checking.

The last button is the Comment/Uncomment button. It's pretty slick because it lets you comment out a bunch of code with the click of a button. If you have a section of code that you want to temporarily remove because it is causing errors, use the mouse to highlight the lines of code and then click on this button. Crystal Reports automatically makes each line a comment by inserting the comment character at the beginning of the line. If you later want to use the code again, highlight the same lines and click the button again. It removes the comment character so that the lines become active again.

## *Setting Bookmarks in Large Formulas*

Although it is common for formulas to only have a few lines of code, there are certainly times when you need to write a very complex formula that consists of dozens of lines of code. Of course, a formula this complex will require quite a bit of debugging to make sure it works. When this happens, it is common to be working on one part of the formula and you need to review another part of the formula. For example, you are working with variables derived from multiple calculations and you need to look back at the details of what each calculation does. It can be confusing to scroll back and forth between different parts of the formula without losing track of where you are. Bookmarks make it easy to review different sections of code without losing your place.

Bookmarks let you mark a line of code as important and move to another part of the formula. You can jump back to the bookmark whenever you want. By using two bookmarks, you can toggle back and forth between the two locations with ease. This is a lot easier than scrolling back and forth. The buttons that work with bookmarks are as follows.

The first button sets the bookmark. Clicking it sets the bookmark at the cursor's current location. The next two buttons jump to either the following bookmark or the previous bookmark. The last button deletes the bookmark. This only works when the cursor is on a line that has an existing bookmark.

### Saving Data

After finishing all your hard work, you'll want to save it. There are two buttons for saving the formula.

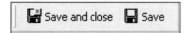

The first button saves the formula and closes the Formula Workshop window. The second button only saves it but doesn't close the Formula Workshop window. This lets you continue working on the formula. The interesting aspect of both of these buttons is that they do more than just save the formula. Prior to saving, they also check the syntax of the formula and alert you to any errors found. You should fix any errors prior to saving the formula. At the end of the chapter we'll look at the options for debugging report errors.

## Understanding the Formula Workshop Windows

The Formula Workshop lists all available fields, formulas and operators. It makes it possible to almost write your formulas without doing any typing. Just double-click the appropriate functions and report fields and let the formula be built for you. Personally, I don't find this very practical on a regular basis. Scrolling through a hierarchy of syntax trees isn't nearly as efficient as just typing it in. However, it is very useful to have these trees available when you can't remember something. It also shows you all the arguments a function requires. These windows are almost like having a mini-help file available. Each window is explained in more detail next.

As mentioned earlier, there are four primary windows that make it easier for you to write formulas. They are shown here again for review.

### Workshop Tree Window

The first window, the Workshop Tree, shows you the existing formulas. Rather than having to remember the names of all the database fields and function names, each is listed in one of these windows. When you double-click any of the items, that item appears in the Definition area at the bottom. You can also drag and drop the item into the code window.

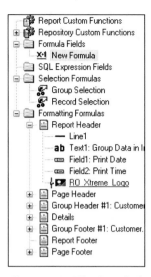

**Figure 5-5. The Workshop Tree window.**

The Workshop Tree lists every formula stored in the report. It breaks them down by the following categories:

Report Custom Functions are functions that you create and can be shared among all formulas in the report. Custom functions store common functionality that needs to be used in different places throughout the report. This is discussed in more detail in Chapter 6.

Repository Custom Functions are custom functions stored in Crystal Reports Server. They are shared among different reports within the enterprise.

Formula Fields perform calculations and implement conditional formatting. They are the focus of this chapter.

SQL Expression Fields are used directly with your database server. The formula only calls functions that are compatible with the database. This is discussed in more detail in Chapter 11.

Selection Formulas were discussed in Chapter 4. They determine which data is shown on the report and which data gets filtered out.

Formatting Formulas list the report sections and objects and show the conditional formulas associated with them. It lists each section of the report as a category and by expanding the category you see every report object in that section. If an object has conditional formatting applied to one of its properties then you'll see that listed as well. If you recall from Tutorial 5-1, we added conditional formatting to the Background Color property of the Details section.

## *Report Fields Window*

Located to the right of the Workshop Tree window is the Report Fields window. It lists every field used in the report as well as every field available from the report's data source.

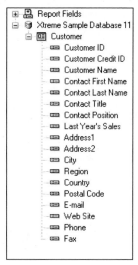

**Figure 5-6. The Report Fields window.**

The first category listed is the Report Fields category. By expanding it, you'll see each field currently used in the report. This makes it easy to quickly find and reference a report field in another formula. The second category shows the report's data source. Expand it to see every field available in the tables. This lets you reference a field in your formula even if the field isn't being used on the report.

## *Formula Functions Window*

The Formula Functions window shows all the functions available.

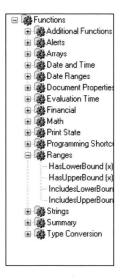

**Figure 5-7. The Formula Functions window.**

At first, this tree is a nice crutch to lean on as you learn the Crystal Reports programming language. As you get better at writing formulas you will quickly learn the language and not rely on the Function Tree.

## Report Operators Window

The Report Operators window shows all the available operators that can be used in a function.

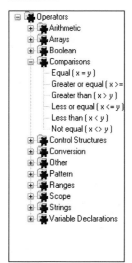

**Figure 5-8. The Report Operators window.**

Just like the other windows, the Report Operators window shows them grouped by category. Some of these categories are Arithmetic, Boolean, Comparisons, etc. It is similar to the Function Tree in that it is a nice crutch when you are new to writing formulas, but you may outgrow it with enough practice.

# Creating Formulas

The two most common reasons for using the Formula Workshop are for performing calculations and using conditional formatting. Both of these tasks involve different steps for creating the formula and working with it. The steps for doing each are described next.

## Creating Calculations

A report gets the majority of its data from a data source. The data source could be a table in a database, an XML data feed or a proprietary data source. Since databases are designed to only store the necessary information, they don't have extraneous information that can be derived by other means (e.g. calculations). It is more efficient to perform calculations on an as-needed basis than save the results within the database. It's your job as the report designer to create the formulas that perform the calculations needed on a report.

To add a new formula in the Report Designer, go to the Field Explorer window and right-click on the Formula Fields category. Select New from the pop-up menu. This opens the Formula Workshop window where you type in the formula in the Definition area. When you are satisfied with the formula, click the Save and Close button. If there are no errors in the formula, the Formula Workshop closes and the Report Designer is shown again. The formula you just created is listed under the Formula Fields category.

Formulas are displayed on the report by dragging and dropping it from the Field Explorer window onto the report. When looking at a report, you can tell the difference between database fields and formulas because formula fields are prefixed with a @. To edit an existing formula field on the report, right click on it within the report designer and select Edit.

## Using Conditional Formatting

Reports by their very nature are static. Although the printed data changes and the calculation results are different every time, the report format stays the same. For example, if the first field in a column has a font of Arial and is black, every field in that column is also going to have a font of Arial and be black. After all, if the fields in a column each had a different font, it would be very hard to read and people would question the abilities of the report designer. But wouldn't it be nice to use visual cues to highlight important data? For example, you could change the color of an inventory quantity to red when it is below the minimum level. The reader immediately knows that the item needs to be reordered. There might even be a special note to the side of the report stating whom to notify. In this circumstance, making a report dynamic increases its usefulness to the reader without adding clutter.

Crystal Reports gives you the ability to write formulas that dynamically modify the properties and behavior of fields and sections on a report. This is done by attaching a conditional formatting formula with an object's property. For example, you can show or hide a section by using a formula that returns either True or False in the Suppress property. You could also use a formula that returns a special message at the bottom of each page.

Modifying the formatting of a report object is done by right-clicking on it and selecting Format Field from the pop-up menu. This opens the Format Editor dialog box which lets you modify each property. Next to each property is a Formula button. It looks like a horizontal pencil with a blue "X-2" above it.

**Figure 5-9. The Formula button.**

Clicking on this button opens the Formula Workshop dialog box. Just like we discussed earlier, type your formula in the Definition area. Click the Save and Close button when you are finished.

After saving the formula, you are returned to the Format Editor dialog box to make more changes. You'll notice that the Formula button looks different now. Since it has a conditional formula associated with it, it has red letters and the pencil is at a 45 degree angle.

**Figure 5-10. Conditional formatting has been applied.**

This new button makes it easy to look at the Format Editor dialog box and immediately know which properties have conditional formatting associated with them. This is important when you are trying to fix formatting problems because conditional formatting often overrides the default property value and you need to know when something is going on behind the scenes.

# Using the Highlighting Expert

The Highlighting Expert is a simplified version of the Formula Workshop. If you're having a tough time learning how to use the Formula Workshop, you can use the Highlighting Expert until you get more experience with formulas. However, it has limitations on what you can modify. It only lets you modify the font and border properties. Figure 5-11 shows you what the Highlighting Expert looks like.

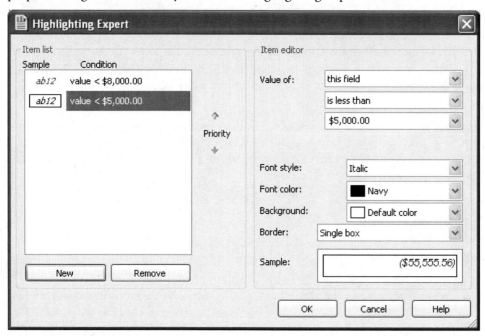

**Figure 5-11. The Highlighting Expert dialog box.**

To open the Highlighting Expert, right-click on the field you want to format and select Highlighting Expert. The left side of the dialog box is the Item List. It lists the formatting rules you created. The left column, Sample, shows an example of what the formatting changes will look like when applied. The right column, Condition, shows the formula. As you add new formulas, they get added to this list.

The right side is the Item Editor where you create new formatting rules. This is similar to the Select Expert in that you choose the field you want to base the condition on, select the value and the type of condition to compare it to (Is Less Than, Is Greater Than, etc.). One thing you will notice is that the list of comparisons is significantly smaller than the ones listed in the Select Expert. This is because you can only use discrete values. The Highlighting Expert doesn't let you build conditions using range values or a list of values.

The bottom portion of the Item Editor is where you select the formatting that is applied if the condition is met. You can set the font style, color, border, etc. The Sample box at the bottom also shows you an example of what the formatting looks like.

An interesting aspect of the Highlighting Expert is that the formulas in the Item List are cumulative. If a field matches more than one condition, both formatting rules are applied to it. For example, let's say that one rule changes the border and the other rule changes the font color. If the data in a field matches both conditions then it will have both its border and font changed. In some circumstances, the two rules might conflict with each other. For example, they both might set the font to be a different color. Crystal Reports resolves rule conflicts by starting at the bottom of the list and works its way up. Rules at the top of list always override the rules below.

---

### Caution

I don't recommend using the Highlighting Expert. Yes, it is an easy way to do conditional formatting, but it has some drawbacks. The first drawback, as mentioned earlier, is that you are limited to only changing the font and border of an object. But there are two much larger problems. The formatting changes made in the Highlighting Expert are stored behind the scenes in hidden formulas. They aren't listed in the Formula Workshop. The Formula Workshop is the "Command Center" for doing all conditional formatting and not having a formula listed there makes it easily forgotten. The other problem is that the formulas created by the Highlighting Expert override the formulas in the Formula Workshop. So not only are these formulas hidden, but they take precedence over the other formulas that you can see.

Consider the following scenario: One of your co-workers left their job and you are now in charge of maintaining their reports. You add some conditional formatting formulas to modify the sales field. When you run the report most of the rows look as expected, but some of them don't have the correct formatting. You go back to debug your formula, but you get frustrated when it appears that your changes don't have any affect. Then it occurs to you: Check the Highlighting Expert! Sure enough, the person who built the report had some rules hidden in the Highlighting Expert and that is overriding your changes. You delete these rules and add them back using the Formula Workshop so that you don't get surprised again. Everything looks fine now. Unfortunately, you have no idea how many other places the Highlighting Expert was used and the only way to figure this out is to right-click on every report object and open the Highlighting Expert. Sigh…

I recommend taking the extra time to learn how to use the Formula Workshop so you save yourself (and possibly others) from headaches.

# Error Checking Reports

This chapter gave you an introduction to using the Formula Workshop and the next chapter dives deeper into writing programming code. But before you jump in the water head first, you need to be aware of the debugging tools available to you. No matter how good your intentions are of writing the best formulas, things will occasionally go wrong. This section addresses understanding error messages, validating a report for errors, and fixing errors found while a report is running.

## Understanding Error Messages

If you have any experience with writing programs or macros, then you know that computers have a strict set of rules that must be followed when you are telling them what to do. If you make a mistake, even something that seems as insignificant as a missing comma, the computer can't run the program. This is called a syntax error. When a syntax error is found in Crystal Reports, a message box appears informing you of the problem. This message can be as useful as "A string is required here" and you know that you need to replace the number or date value with a String value. Sometimes the error messages are very generic and don't really give you any idea of what the problem really is. In these cases you have to get creative and try to figure out what is wrong.

Finding an error in your program is never any fun. Sometimes they are easy to fix and other times it can be quite frustrating. The Crystal Reports help file has two good sections for helping you resolve error messages. Go to the help file and click on the Search tab. Type in the following phrase, "Error Messages and Formula Compiler Warnings" and click the List Topics button. The first title found is the one you want to read. It lists all the error messages and tells you what causes them. It also gives you hints on how to fix them. The second help section is found by clicking on the Index tab and typing in "Error Messages, Described". It lists each error message on its own page and you click through each page to find the error message you want to read. This is harder to use when you want to find a specific error because you don't know which page it is on. But when you do find it, it is more helpful because there is a lot more detailed information to read.

If you find a syntax error in your formula, you are not required to correct it right away. You can save it as is, and come back later to fix it. This is helpful when you are too busy to figure out what went wrong or you need to find someone to ask for help. Just don't forget to come back and fix it or else your report won't run properly.

## Validating Reports with the Dependency Checker

Not only can you have syntax error in formulas, but there are many types of problems that can occur in a report. Function names can be typed wrong, links can be broken, and database fields can change. In a complex report it can be very difficult to verify the correctness of everything that might be wrong. Luckily, Crystal Reports makes this easy for you.

Crystal Reports has a new feature called the Dependency Checker which searches through a report and finds everything wrong. It looks at many different aspects of a report and creates a list of everything it finds that needs fixing. Table 5-2 lists the different parts of a report that get evaluated.

**Table 5-2. The Dependency Checker features.**

| Part Checked | Description |
|---|---|
| Formulas, Functions and SQL Expressions | Compiles the formulas and functions in a report and checks for errors. Looks for syntax errors as well as missing functions. |
| Hyperlinks | Verifies that the hyperlinks are valid. |
| Database | Verifies that the database connection exists and that the fields the report references are in the tables. |
| Subreports | Checks that any external subreports are located in the proper location. If the subreport has been moved, an error is reported. |

The Dependency Checker is run by selecting the menu options Report > Check Dependencies. This opens the Dependency Checker window which lists the errors found and their location.

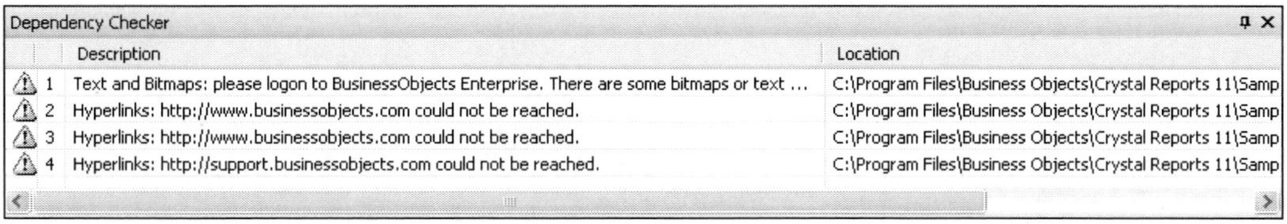

| Dependency Checker | 🔲 ✕ |
|---|---|
| Description | Location |
| ⚠ 1  Text and Bitmaps: please logon to BusinessObjects Enterprise. There are some bitmaps or text ... | C:\Program Files\Business Objects\Crystal Reports 11\Samp |
| ⚠ 2  Hyperlinks: http://www.businessobjects.com could not be reached. | C:\Program Files\Business Objects\Crystal Reports 11\Samp |
| ⚠ 3  Hyperlinks: http://www.businessobjects.com could not be reached. | C:\Program Files\Business Objects\Crystal Reports 11\Samp |
| ⚠ 4  Hyperlinks: http://support.businessobjects.com could not be reached. | C:\Program Files\Business Objects\Crystal Reports 11\Samp |

**Figure 5-12. The Dependency Checker window**

Each error in the Dependency Checker is listed along the left and its location is listed to the right. You can go directly to the object causing the error by double-clicking on the error message or selecting it and pressing the Enter key. Not all errors need to be fixed. Icons that are a yellow caution sign should be looked at but will not prevent the report from running. For example, a link may be broken on your computer because your network link is disconnected, but it will work fine when the report is run in a production environment. Icons with a red stop sign and an X in the middle are critical errors. You should fix them prior to finalizing the report.

If no errors are found in the report, a green checkmark is displayed.

## Setting Which Options to Check

The Dependency Checker doesn't have to run every type of test on a report. You can disable certain tests from being called by the Dependency Checker. This is done with the

Option dialog box on the Dependency Checker tab. Select the menu options File > Options.

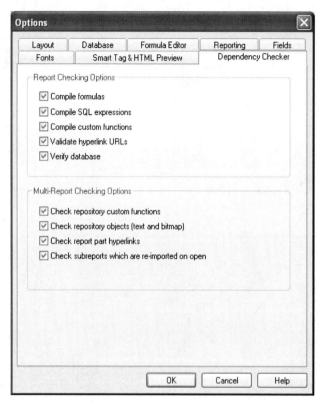

**Figure 5-13. The Dependency Checker options.**

The options tab is broken into two groups. The first group lists the categories of error checking that are done within the current report. For example, if you know that your computer doesn't have an active link to the current database, then you can turn off the Verify Database option. The changes you make here are saved with the current report and don't affect other reports.

The second group lists categories related to validating across multiple reports. This applies to users who have the Crystal Reports Server or Business Objects Enterprise.

## Checking Run-Time Errors with the Call Stack

Run-time errors occur while a report is being generated. These errors are not caught while you are designing the report because they are syntactically correct. They are usually triggered by data that the report is processing. For example, here is a syntax error that would be caught immediately by the Formula Workshop editor while you are designing the report because you aren't allowed to divide by zero.

Formula = {Customer.AnnualSales} / 0

Here is a formula that won't cause a syntax error but could generate a runtime error depending on the data.

Formula = {Customer.AnnualSales}/MonthsOfSales}

This formula is correct as long as the MonthsOfSales field is non-zero. But when the value is zero Crystal Reports triggers an error. When that happens, the Call Stack is displayed within the Formula Workshop dialog box. The Call Stack is displayed in the top left corner and it shows the formula name that triggered the error, as well as the data being used in the formula.

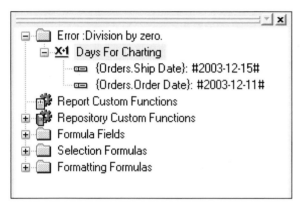

**Figure 5-14. The Call Stack.**

At the top is the current error and it is followed by the formula causing the error. Under the formula name are the variables and fields that are being used and their current values. By examining this information along with seeing the formula, you should be able to figure out what is causing the problem and devise a method to correct it.

# Programming with Crystal Syntax

The Formula Workshop in Crystal Reports gives you the ability to write very powerful formulas. In addition to writing your own formulas, Crystal Reports has dozens of built-in functions that decrease the amount of work you have to do. After all, why re-invent the wheel when you don't have to? This chapter lists and explains the different functions that come with Crystal syntax. The functions are grouped by category so you can quickly find the ones you want. The categories are: String Functions, Converting Data Types, Formatting Values for Output, Math Functions, Generating Random Numbers, and Date and Time Functions. If you prefer to have an alphabetical list, then reference the Index at the back of the book to see the page number of the one you are looking for.

| **Note** |
| --- |

Crystal syntax is the first programming language that came with Crystal Reports. It is also the default language in the Formula Workshop dialog box.[33] Basic syntax was added to Crystal Reports at some point later in its evolution because people needed a language that was easier to use. If you are familiar with programming languages, then you might notice that Crystal syntax has a lot of similarities to the C programming language. Unfortunately, the C language is a difficult language to learn and not exactly the easiest one to get started with. With the huge popularity of the Microsoft Office suite of products (Word, Excel, and Access), many people are already familiar with how to program macros using VBA (Visual Basic for Applications). It's also very common for universities to teach VBA in their basic business courses. There was a need for Crystal Reports to have a second programming language that was easier for people to learn, and making it similar to Microsoft's VBA would be even better. Hence, Basic syntax was added to Crystal Reports.

This chapter and the next use Crystal syntax for all the code listings. Since this is the default programming language, it is the one most people learn first. For

---

[33] As mentioned in the previous chapter, to change the default programming language, from the menu bar choose File > Options > Formula Editor. Near the bottom of the dialog box is the dropdown list where you can set the default language to be Basic syntax.

those of you who want to learn Basic syntax, Appendix A is a Basic syntax programming reference that can be used in conjunction with these two chapters.

The Formula Workshop makes it easy to use the built-in functions. It gives you a Formula Functions window which lists every available function in Crystal Reports. Each category in the tree is a function category. Clicking on the plus sign next to a category expands it and shows all the functions in that category. As a refresher, the Formula Functions window is shown again here.

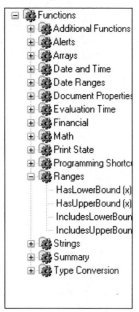

**Figure 6-1. Formula Functions window.**

Not only is the function listed for you, but if it needs you to pass any additional information to it, this is listed as well. For example, if you want to select a certain number of characters from the left-most portion of a string, you would use the Left() function. In the Formula Functions window it is shown as Left(str, Length). This tells you that the first argument is the string you want to parse and the second argument is how many characters you want to copy.

While most of the functions give you helpful argument information, some are not as helpful as others. For example, the CStr() function converts any data type to a string and it can take up to four arguments. But when you look at this function in the Formula Functions window, it only says CStr(x, y, z, w, q). This is pretty cryptic and to figure out what each argument means you'll have to either consult the help file or look for the reference in this chapter. When you see the function you want to use, double-click on it and it gets added to the Definition area at the bottom.

# String Functions

The ability to modify and concatenate strings is a powerful feature of many programming languages, and Crystal syntax doesn't disappoint. This section breaks out the different categories of string functions and summarizes how they work. The categories are: Analyzing a String, and Manipulating Strings.

Throughout this section, many of the functions listed use one or both of the arguments called compare and start. Rather than repetitively list their descriptions throughout the chapter, they are explained here for your reference.

The compare argument determines when string comparisons are supposed to be case sensitive. If compare is 0, the search is case-sensitive. If it is 1, the search is not case-sensitive. Case sensitivity means that even if two strings consist of the exact same letters, they will be treated as different strings if one is upper-case and the other is lower-case. For example, "Joe" would not be the same as "joe". If the comparison is not case-sensitive, then "Joe" would be the same as "joe". The compare argument is optional. If it is left out, the comparison defaults to 0 (case sensitive).

The start argument tells the function to process characters starting at a specified position.[34] Any characters that are prior to that position are ignored. This argument is optional. If it is left out, then the function is performed for the entire string.

## Analyzing a String

Strings are used to store a variety of data displayed in a report. They can come from a variety of sources such as database tables, user input or even XML. Most of the time, you will want to output the string directly to the report. But there are times when the information you want is stored as part of a larger string and you need to extract that data. To do this, it is necessary to analyze and parse a string's contents. Crystal syntax gives you many functions for doing this. Table 6-1 shows the functions for analyzing a string's contents. Table 6-3 shows the functions for extracting sub-strings from a string.

**Table 6-1. String Analysis Functions**

| Function Name | Description |
| --- | --- |
| AscW(str) | Returns the ASCII value of a character. |
| ChrW(val) | Returns the character equivalent of an ASCII value. |
| Len(str) | Gets the number of characters in the string. |
| IsNumeric(str) | Tells if the string can be properly converted to a number. |

---

[34] The first character of a string is at position 1.

| InStr(start, str1, str2, compare) | Determines if str2 is a sub-string of str1. The start and compare arguments are both optional. |
|---|---|
| InStrRev(start, str1, str2, compare) | Same as InStr() except that it starts at the end of the string and searches towards the beginning. |
| StrCmp(str1, str2, compare) | Compares two strings to each other. The compare argument is optional. |
| Val(str) | Returns the numeric equivalent of the string. |

The StrCmp() function returns a value based upon how the two strings compare to each other. Table 6-2 summarizes what these results mean. Just like the Instr() functions, you can pass a compare argument to set case sensitivity.

**Table 6-2. StrCmp(str1, str2) Return Values**

| Return Value | Description |
|---|---|
| -1 | str1 < str2 |
| 0 | str1 = str2 |
| 1 | str1 > str2 |

**Table 6-3. String Parsing Functions**

| Function Name | Description |
|---|---|
| Trim(str) | Trim the spaces from both sides of a string. |
| LTrim(str) | Trim the spaces from the left side of a string. |
| RTrim(str) | Trim the spaces from the right side of a string. |
| Mid(str, start, length) | Return a given number of characters starting at a specified position. The **start** and **length** arguments are optional. |
| Left(str, length) | Return a given number of characters starting with the leftmost character. |
| Right(str, length) | Return a given number of characters starting with the rightmost character. |

The Trim() function deletes all extraneous spaces from either side of the string, depending on which function you call. Trimming space from a string is useful for fields that involve data entry. This is because users will accidentally hit the space bar either before or after entering a value. Since a space is effectively invisible to the user, they will not realize that they did this. When you use this field in comparisons with other text, Crystal Reports will say that the two fields are different because they have different lengths (even though they look identical). You must use the Trim() function to get rid of any extraneous space before and after the field when doing the comparison.

> **Tip**
>
> Sometimes when my reports are not coming out right and I'm doing text comparisons, I like to test if there are extraneous spaces by concatenating the letter "x" before and after the field. For example, I would use the following formula:
>
> "x" & {Customer.CustomerName} & "x"
>
> Then I would scan the report to see if there are any spaces between each "x" and the field. This lets me quickly see if spaces might be causing problems.

The Mid(), Left(), and Right() functions return a partial string where the number of characters returned is based on the length argument. If you don't pass a length argument to the Mid() function, it returns all characters starting with the first one you specified.

## Manipulating Strings

It is common for a string to be modified before it is displayed on a report. This can consist of reformatting the string or even joining the different elements of an array into a single string. Table 6-4 shows the functions for manipulating strings. Descriptions of each function are listed next to its name. The functions Filter(), Split(), and Picture() are more complex and are explained in more detail after the table.

**Table 6-4. String Manipulation Functions**

| Function Name | Description |
| --- | --- |
| &, + | Concatenate (combine) two strings into a single string. |
| Filter(str, find, include, compare) | Search an array of strings for a sub-string and return an array matching the criteria. |
| Replace(str, find, replace, start, count, compare) | Find a string and replace it with another string. The arguments **start**, **count** and **compare** are all optional. |
| StrReverse(str) | Reverse the order of all characters in the string. |
| ReplicateString(str, copies) | Returns multiple copies of a string. |

| Space(val) | Returns the specified number of spaces as a single string. |
|---|---|
| Join(list, delimiter) | Join an array of strings into one string and separate them with the specified delimiter. |
| Split(str, delimiter, count, compare) | Split a single string into an array of strings based upon the specified delimiter. The arguments **count** and **compare** are optional. |
| Picture(str, template) | Formats the characters in a string onto a template. |

The & or + is used between two string variables (or fields) to combine them into a single string. An example is:

```
{Customer.LastName} & ", " & {Customer.FirstName};
```

Although you can use + to concatenate strings, it is recommended that you use & because it is most commonly recognized as the standard operator for concatenating strings. Using + can be confused with arithmetic functions.

If you want to use the quote literal in a string ("), this can be a little challenging at first. Since the quote represents the beginning and end of a string literal, then when you try to insert it in the middle of a string it gets Crystal Reports confused and thinks you are trying to end the string twice. There are two ways to put the quote into a string literal. The first is to repeat it twice in the string and Crystal Reports will translate this into a string literal. Here is an example:

```
// Display "Ben Hur"
"""Ben Hur"""
```

The first quote tells Crystal Reports that you are starting a string literal. Then it sees two quotes in a row and replaces them with a single quote in the string. The effect is that there is a quote at the beginning and end of the string. The next example is a little less confusing because it puts the quote in the middle of the string.

```
// Display The quote (") can be confusing
"The quote("") can be confusing"
```

An easier way to insert the quote into a string is to use the ChrW(39) function. This returns the quote literal and it is much easier to read.

```
// Display "Ben Hur"
Chrw(34) & "Ben Hur" & Chrw(34)
```

The Filter() function searches an array of strings for a matching sub-string. It returns an array of all the strings that have that sub-string in them. The first argument is the string array and the second argument is the sub-string to search for. Essentially, this function calls the InStr() function for every string in the array. If the InStr() finds a match, the string is added to the result array.

The Filter() function has an optional include argument that tells the function to return an array of strings that don't match the sub-string. Essentially, this would be the same as saying that it returns all strings where the InStr() function returns a zero. Pass the include argument the value False to get an array of the strings that don't have the sub-string in them. If you don't pass a value for this argument, then the default value of True is used. The next listing demonstrates using the Filter() function with different arguments.

```
//Demonstrate the Filter() function
StringVar Array StringArrayVar;
StringVar Array ResultArrayVar;
StringArrayVar := MakeArray("abcd", "bcde", "cdef");
//This will return an array with two elements: "abcd", "bcde"
ResultArrayVar := Filter(StringArrayVar, "bc");
//This will return an array with one element: "cdef"
//This is because it is the only element that doesn't have the sub-string
ResultArrayVar := Filter(StringArrayVar, "bc", False);
```

The Replace() function searches for a sub-string within another string, and if it finds it, then it replaces it with the new string. It uses an additional optional argument called count. The count argument lets you limit how many string replacements are done. If you pass a number for this argument, then the number of replacements done cannot exceed that value. If you don't pass a value for this argument, then all the sub-strings are replaced.

```
//Change the addresses so that they use abbreviations
StringVar Streets;
Streets := "123 Main Street, 456 Cherry Avenue, 999 Brook Street";
Streets := Replace(Streets, "Street", "St.");
Streets := Replace(Streets, "Avenue", "Ave.");
//Streets is now "123 Main St., 456 Cherry Ave., 999 Brook St. "
Streets;
```

The Split() and Join() functions work together nicely. The Split() function takes a string and splits it into a string array. The string is separated based upon a character you pass to the function. This is typically a comma, but it can be anything you need it to be. Splitting the string apart makes it is easy to work on the individual strings. After you are done making any necessary changes to the individual strings, you can combine them back into one string using the Join() function. How convenient!

The next example demonstrates combining the functionality of the Split() and Join() functions. A string with the names of customers is available and each name is separated with a comma. We want to only select strings where the names have a prefix of "Mr." This is done by splitting the names into an array of strings. Then the Filter() function is used to return an array with only the strings that match our criteria. This array is combined back into a comma-delimited string using the Join() function.

```
//Demonstrate the Split() and Join() functions by finding the names prefixed with "Mr."
StringVar Names;
StringVar Array NamesArrayVar;
Names := "Mr. Jones, Sir Alfred, Ms. Bee, Mr. Smith";
NamesArrayVar := Split(Names, ",");
//Get the names that only use Mr.
NamesArrayVar := Filter(NamesArrayVar, "Mr. ");
//RJoin the array back into a comma-delimited string
Names := Join(NamesArrayVar, ",");
//Names is now "Mr. Jones, Mr. Smith"
Names;
```

The Picture() function maps a string onto a template. The first argument is the source string and the second argument is the template.

The template consists of a series of "x"s with other characters around it. Each character in the source string gets mapped onto each of the "x"s in the template. The source string can use any character and it will get mapped. If the source string has more characters than can fit in the template, then all remaining characters are added to the end. If the template has any non-"x" characters, then they stay as they are.

```
//Demonstrate mapping a string with non-alphanumeric characters
Picture("ab&[{1234", "xxx..xx..x.. ")
//The result is "ab&..[{..1..234"
```

This example illustrates that all characters in the source string were mapped onto the "x"s. It also shows that since the source string has nine characters and the template has six "x"s, then the extra three characters are added to the end.

## Best Of The Forum

**Question:** When I use a text object to mix text with database fields, Crystal Reports lets me apply different formatting properties to each field. But, when I put a string formula on the report, the entire string has to use the same formatting. Is there a way to apply different formatting to parts of a string?

**Answer:** Yes, you can do this by including HTML formatting tags within the string. For example, the following formula puts bold emphasis on the address field:

"Hello " & {Customer.Name} & ". Are you still located at <B>" & {Customer.Address} & "</B>?";

After adding the formula to the report, right-click on it and select Format Field. Go to the Paragraph tab and set the Text Interpretation property to HTML.

Using HTML formatting within a string formula gives you great flexibility for modifying its output.

# Converting Data Types

Crystal syntax is a type safe language that requires all constants and variables in the same formula to be of the same data type. It also requires you to pass constants and variables as arguments using the exact data type that the formula expects. Even though the data types in Crystal syntax are fairly simple, you still have to make sure that they are compatible. Fortunately, this shouldn't cause problems because there are functions to convert between the different data types. Table 6-5 lists these conversion functions.

**Table 6-5. Conversion Functions**

| Conversion Function | Description |
|---|---|
| CBool(number), CBool(currency) | Convert to Boolean. |
| CCur(number), CCur(string) | Convert to Currency. |
| CDbl(currency), CDbl(string), CDbl(boolean) | Convert to Number. Equivalent to ToNumber(). See the section "Formatting Values for Output". |
| CStr() | Convert to String. Equivalent to ToText(). |
| CDate(string), CDate(year, month, day), CDate(DateTime) | Convert to Date. |
| CTime(string), CTime(hour, min, sec), CDate(DateTime) | Convert to Time. |
| CDateTime(string), CDateTime(date), CDateTime(date, time), CDateTime(year, month, day) | Convert to DateTime. |
| CDateTime(year, month, day, hour, min, sec) | Convert to DateTime. |
| ToNumber(string), ToNumber(Boolean) | Convert to a Number. |
| ToText() | Convert to String. Same as CStr(). |
| IsDate(string), IsTIme(), IsDateTime() | Test a string for being a valid date/time. |

| ToWords(number), | Convert a number to its word equivalent. |
| ToWords(number, decimals) | |

Most of the above functions are very simple. Pass the function a field/variable of one data type and it returns the equivalent in the other data type. The CBool() function takes a number or currency value and converts it to Boolean True or False. Any non-zero value is converted to True and zero is converted to False. When it is displayed on a report, it prints the words "True" or "False".

The CCur() function takes a number or string and converts it to the Currency data type. When converting a string, it can have formatting characters in it ("$", ",", etc.) and it will still be converted properly.

The CDbl() and ToNumber() functions are equivalent. Pass each a value and it gets converted to a number.

The CDate(), CTime() and CDateTime() are all similar. Pass them a string and it gets converted to the proper data type. The string parser for this function is very sophisticated. It lets you pass strings as diverse as "Jan 19, 1991", "5/26/1998" and "2002, Feb 04". You can also pass numbers as individual arguments for representing the different parts of a date and time. See Table 6-5 for the various argument options.

When converting a string to a date or number, you run the risk of raising an error if the string isn't in the expected format. You can avoid this by testing the string's validity before converting it. The IsDate() and IsNumber() functions do this for you. They return True if the string can be properly converted. If not, they return False. For example, here is a function that converts a string to a date, but only if it is a valid date.

```
If IsDate({Invoice.ExpirationDate}) Then
    CDate({Invoice.ExpirationDate});
```

The ToWords() function takes a number and converts it to its equivalent in words. This is similar to writing a dollar amount on a check and then spelling out the full amount in words. It prints the decimal portion as "##/100". You can set the number of decimals it displays by passing a number to the second argument, which is optional. Notice in the second example how it only displays one decimal place and it rounds it up to the next higher number.

```
//Demonstrate the ToWords() formula
ToWords(123.45);  //Result is "one hundred twenty-three 45 / 100"
ToWords(123.45,1);       //Result is "one hundred twenty-three and 5 / 100"
```

| Tip |
| --- |

The conversion functions format the value based upon the settings in the Fields tab of the Option dialog box.[35] When you place the formula on the report, it looks at the current default settings and uses these to format the formula object. For example, if you create a formula that uses the CCur() function, it is displayed on the report using the current formatting specified in the Fields tab for Currency. This rule applies to all the conversion functions that have settings on the Fields tab. If you later change the default formatting settings in the Options dialog box, it does not go back and reset report objects that are already on the report. The new settings are only applied to new report objects.

# Formatting Values for Output

When formatting output to be displayed in a report, the output is usually a combination of different data types. For example, there will be a standard text message that also displays the current value for a field. But this can cause problems because Crystal syntax is a type safe language. It doesn't allow you to concatenate text with non-string data. To build an output string with a combination of data types, you have to convert everything to a string using the CStr() function. This method works with all data types. Since the CStr() function is designed primarily for outputting data on a report, it also lets you specify how to format the data.

The CStr() function is passed the value to format as the first argument and a formatting string as the second argument. The formatting string is used as a template that describes how the value should look after it gets converted. Table 6-6 shows the different formatting characters that can be used. Table 6-7 shows examples of how different values will look after being formatted.

**Table 6-6. CStr() Formatting Characters**

| Format | Description |
| --- | --- |
| # | Use with formatting numbers. Each instance of it allocates space for a single digit. If the number isn't very large, the remaining part is filled with spaces. If the number is too large, the integer part is still fully displayed. Unused digits after the decimal are zero filled. |

---

[35] To open the Options dialog box, select the menu items File > Options. Then click on the Fields tab to set the formatting properties.

| 0 | Use with formatting numbers. If the number isn't large enough, it is padded with zeros. If the number is too large, the integer part will still be fully displayed. Unused digits after the decimal are zero filled. |
|---|---|
| , | Use with formatting numbers to designate the thousand separators. |
| . | Use with formatting numbers to designate the decimal separator. |
| d, M | Day and month as a number (without a leading zero). |
| dd, MM, yy | Day, month and year as a two digit number (with a leading zero when necessary). |
| ddd, MMM | Day and month as a three letter abbreviation. |
| dddd, MMMM, yyyy | Day, month and year fully spelled out. |
| h, m, s | Time portions (12 hour) as a number without a leading zero. |
| hh, mm, ss | Time portions (12 hour) as a two digit number (with a leading zero when necessary). |
| H, HH | Show hours using a 24 hour clock (military time). |
| T | Single character representation of AM/PM. |
| TT | Two character representation of AM/PM. |

**Table 6-7. CStr() Example Output**

| # | CStr() | Output |
|---|--------|--------|
| 1 | CStr(1234, 2) | 1,234.00 |
| 2 | CStr(1234.567, 2) | 1,234.57 |
| 3 | CStr(1234.567, "#") | 1234 |
| 4 | CStr(1234.567, "0") | 1234 |
| 5 | CStr(1234, "0.##") | 1234.00 |
| 6 | CStr(1234, "0.00") | 1234.00 |
| 7 | CStr(1234.567, "#.##") | 1234.57 |
| 8 | CStr(1234.567, "0.00") | 1234.57 |
| 9 | CStr(1234.567, "#####") | 1234 |
| 10 | CStr(1234.567, "00000") | 01234 |
| 11 | CStr(#1/2/2003 04:05:06 am#, "d/M/yy H/m/s t") | 2/1/03 4: 5: 6 A |
| 12 | CStr(#1/2/2003 04:05:06 pm#, "dd/MM/yyyy HH/mm/ss tt") | 01/02/2003 16:05:06 AM |
| 13 | CStr(#1/2/2003 04:05:06 am#, "dd/MM/yyyy hh/mm/ss tt") | 01/02/2003 04:05:06 AM |
| 14 | CStr(#3:20 PM#, "HH:mm") | 15:20 |

Examples 1 and 2 are easy. The first argument is the number to format and the second argument is the number of decimals to display. If the number to format doesn't have any decimals, then they are zero filled. Notice that in these examples as well as all the others, Crystal Reports rounds the decimals portion up.

With one exception, examples 3 through 10 are easy as well. The exception is that unlike the first two examples, the second argument is the format string. Using this format string lets you be very specific about how to format the number.

Stop for a moment and look at examples 1 and 5. Do you notice one thing different between them? The difference is that the output in example 5 doesn't have a thousands separator. In both example 1 and example 5, no thousands separator is specified, but example 1 has it by default. This isn't the case when you use a format string. The documentation says that the format string needs to use an optional argument to specify the thousands separator. But example 14 shows that Crystal syntax has a bug that keeps this from working.

Examples 5 and 6 show that if there aren't enough decimals then both the "#" and the "0" will zero fill their positions.

Examples 9 and 10 show that if there aren't enough digits to fill the whole number, then the "#" fills it with a space and the "0" fills it with a zero.

For examples 11 thru 14, be careful with capitalization. The compiler is case sensitive when formatting date strings. When entering a format string, refer back to Table 6-6 so that you get it right.

# Math Functions

**Table 6-8. Math Functions**

| Function Name | Description |
| --- | --- |
| Abs(number) | Return the absolute value. |
| Ceiling(number, multiple) | Rounds up to the nearest multiple you specify. |
| Truncate(number, decimals) | Return a number with a specified number of significant digits. |
| Int(number), numerator \ denominator | Return the integer portion of a fractional number. |
| Pi | 3.14... |
| Remainder(numerator, denominator), | Return the remainder of dividing the numerator by the denominator. |
| numerator Mod denominator | Return the remainder of dividing the numerator by the denominator (same as the Remainder function). |
| Round(number, decimals), RoundUp(number, decimals) | Round up a number with a specified number of significant digits. |
| Sgn(number) | Return a number's sign. |
| Sqr(number), Exp(number), Log(number) | The standard arithmetic functions. |
| Cos(number), Sin(number), Tan(number), Atn(number) | The standard scientific functions. |

Most of these functions perform basic mathematical functionality. There are only a couple of interesting points to notice. Working with whole numbers and decimals is done numerous ways. The Fix() and Round() functions take a fractional number and truncate it to a specified number of digits. The Round() function will round up to the nearest decimal. The number of decimals to display is optional and the default is zero. The Int() function is similar to the Round() function except that it only returns the whole number and will round down to the nearest whole number. Table 6-9 shows how the three functions will return a different number depending upon the decimal portion and whether the number is positive or negative.

**Table 6-9. Examples of Truncating Decimals**

| Function | 1.9 | -1.9 |
| --- | --- | --- |
| Fix() | 1 | -1 |
| Round() | 2 | -2 |
| Int() | 1 | -2 |

If you want to get the whole number and you have the numerator and denominator available. You can use the \ operator to perform integer division. This does the division and only returns the integer portion of the result. The Mod operator and Remainder() function return the remainder after doing the division.

```
'Demonstrate the integer division and the Mod operator
10 \ 3;            //Returns 3
10 mod 3; //Returns 1
Remainder(10, 3); //Returns 1
```

# Generating Random Numbers

Generating random numbers is a very common task for programmers. But if you aren't familiar with it, the way they work isn't very intuitive. This section gives you an overview of what random numbers are and how to use them.

Crystal Reports uses the function Rnd() to return a random number. The purpose of the Rnd() function is to generate numbers that are mostly non-repeating and without a pattern. The numbers are fractional and range between 0 and 1. Some examples are 0.39, 0.77, 0.5, etc. (of course these change each time).

Random numbers are used within a formula by multiplying them against the maximum value in the range of numbers you need. For example, if you need a random number between 0 and 100 then you would multiply the random number by 100. If you need a random number between 0 and 500 then you would multiply it by the number 500. To make things a little more interesting, if you need a number between 25 and 100, then you would multiply it by 75 and add 25. The following code lists some examples for you to use as a reference.

**Table 6-10. Sample formulas for generating random numbers.**

| Desired Values | Formula |
|---|---|
| Integer Between 0 and 1000 | Formula = Int(Rnd()*1000) |
| Integer Between 0 and 25 | Formula = Int(Rnd()*25) |
| Fractional number between 50 and 75 | Formula = Rnd()*25 + 50 |

The computer generates random numbers by using a complex algorithm and usually uses the system clock as a starting point. This is called the "seed value'. The problem with random numbers is that since they are calculated using an algorithm, then the numbers aren't truly random. If the algorithm is passed the same seed value each time, then the algorithm generates the same sequence of numbers. That is why it's a good idea to use the system clock as the seed value because the time is always changing.

There are times when you don't want to generate completely random numbers. If you are testing the calculations of a report that uses random numbers, it can be helpful to have the same set of random numbers generated each time. This lets you compare the results after all iterations. You can reproduce the same results each time for predictability purposes. Crystal Reports also lets you pass your own seed value to repeat the same random number sequence each time. Again, this helps when creating and testing your report output.

The Rnd() function takes a single argument which tells Crystal Reports what seed value to use when calculating random numbers. The possible argument values are shown in Table 6-11.

**Table 6-11. Argument values for the Rnd() function.**

| Argument Value | Purpose |
|---|---|
| Any negative number (-1, -500, etc.) | Use this negative number as the seed value for producing the list of random numbers. By using the same negative number it will produce the same list of random numbers. |
| Any number greater than zero | Generate the next random number using the system clock as the seed value. |
| 0 | Return the same random number as the last time the Rnd() function was called. |

By passing different arguments to the Rnd() function you control how random numbers are created and whether the system clock is used as the seed value or not.

# Date and Time Functions

Crystal Reports gives you a plethora of date and time related functions to utilize. You can also combine different functions together to create very powerful date calculations. There are a lot of new concepts to learn.

**Table 6-12. Date and Time Functions**

| Function Name | Description |
|---|---|
| CurrentDate, CurrentTime, CurrentDateTime, PrintDate, PrintTime | Returns the current date and/or time based on the Windows. |
| DataDate, DataTime | The date and time that the report data was last refreshed. |
| DateSerial(year, month, day), DateTime(hour, minute, second) | Returns a date or time. |
| DateAdd(interval, number, date) | Increases the date by a certain interval. |
| DateDiff(interval, startdate, enddate, firstdayofweek) | Find the difference between two dates. |
| DatePart(interval, date, firstdayofweek, firstweekofyear) | Return a number representing the current interval of a date. |
| Day(date) | Return the day component as a number. |
| Hour(time), Second(time), Minute(time) | Return the time related components. |
| Month(date) | Return the month component as a number. |
| MonthName(date, abbreviate) | Return the full month name. When the second argument is True, it returns the 3-letter abbreviation. |
| Time(time), Time(hour, min, sec), TimeValue(time) | Return a Time data type given a string ("11:59:00 PM") or numeric representation of time (). |
| Timer | The number of seconds since midnight. |
| DayOfWeek(date, firstdayofweek) | Return a number representing the day of the week. |
| WeekdayName(weekday, abbreviate, firstdayofweek) | Return the full week name. Return the 3-letter abbreviation if the second argument is True. |
| Year(date) | Return the year component as a number. |

**Table 6-13. Interval Strings for DateAdd(), DateDiff() and DatePart()**

| String | Description |
|--------|-------------|
| yyyy | Year |
| Q | Quarter |
| M | Month (1 through 12) |
| ww | Week of the year (1 through 53) |
| W | Day of the week (1 through 7) |
| Y | Day of year (1 through 366) |
| D | Day part of the date (1 through 31) |
| H | Hour |
| N | Minute |
| S | Second |

## Printing the Current Date and Time

There are five functions which return a report's date and time. The functions CurrentDate, CurrentTime, CurrentDateTime, PrintDate, and PrintTime all return the date or time that the report was printed. Although the functions Currentxxx and Printxxx have different names, they are synonymous with each other.

If you wish to back date a report, you can override the print date and time so that it doesn't use the Windows clock. Go to the menu options Report > Set Print Date and Time. In this dialog box there is the option to use the Windows system date/time (the default selection) or you can set a specific date and time.

The functions DataDate and DataTime return the date and time that the report data was last refreshed. If a report has the Save Data With Report option turned on, this will tell you how current the data is.

## DateAdd(interval, number, date)

For adding and subtracting dates and times, the easiest function to use is the DateAdd() function. Using the DateAdd() function requires passing a string representing the type of interval to modify, the number of units to add or subtract, and the date to modify. There are a number of different strings that designate the interval to modify. These interval strings are listed in Table 6-13. There is no such thing as a DateSubtract() function. To subtract a date interval, pass a negative number of units. The DateAdd() function returns a

DateTime value and this may need to be converted to either a Date or a Time depending on how you intend to use the result.

The q interval is for adding financial quarters. Using one q interval unit is the same as using three m intervals (for months). The benefit of using the q interval is that many financial reports are printed on a quarterly basis. After the user is prompted for how many quarters they wish to print, you can take their input and use it to calculate a final date. Although you could use the month interval and multiply their input by 3, having a shortcut is nice and it helps make your code self-documenting.

Rather than using the DateAdd() function to add and subtract days, it is just as acceptable to directly add a number to the Date variable. Since the date is stored as a number, adding another number to it increases the date by that number of days. The following examples both produce the same result.

```
DateAdd("d", 10, #1/1/2002#);    //Returns 1/11/2002
#1/1/2002# + 10;                 //Returns 1/11/2002
```

The benefit to using the DateAdd() function is that it takes into account how many days are in each month and it checks for valid dates. As an example, say that you want to find out the last day of the next month. To do this with the addition operator, you need to know how many days are in the next month. You also need to track which years are leap years. Using the DateAdd() function is much easier because if you add one month to the current date, it will check that this returns a valid date. If there aren't enough days in the month then it will return the last valid day of the month. The same applies to using the quarter interval. The function adds three months to the current date and makes sure that this is a valid date. If not, it returns the last valid date of the quarter.

# DateDiff(interval, startdate, enddate, firstdayofweek)

The DateDiff() function returns the difference between two dates or times. It can return the difference in different intervals. These intervals can be days, months, years or any of the intervals listed in Table 6-13.

Be careful when using the DateDiff() function for calculating an interval other than the number of days. When performing a difference calculation, it counts any interval less than a single unit as zero. For example, if you want to find out how many months have elapsed between two dates, and the two dates are the Jan 1 and Jan 31, then the result is 0. This is because the interval is only a partial month and doesn't constitute a full month. The fact that the dates are 30 days apart is irrelevant. If you change this example so that rather than use the last day of the month, you use the first day of the next month, then the result is 1. Even though the two examples had final dates that only differed by one day, the result is different. This applies to all the intervals including dates and times.

There is an optional argument that lets you specify the first day of the week. This is only used by the DateDiff() function when the interval is ww. This counts the number of times a particular day of the week appears within a date range. To pass this argument to the function, prefix the day by cr For example, Friday is crFriday. The start date does not get counted when doing the calculation, but the end date does. Thus, if you pass the function a start date that falls on a Friday, and the argument is crFriday, then the result will not include this date.

```
//Demonstrate counting the number of paydays
DateVar StartDate;
NumberVar NumberOfFridays;
StartDate := DateSerial(Year(CurrentDate), 1,1);   //First day of year
NumberOfFridays := DateDiff("ww", {Payroll.Last Pay Date}, StartDate, crFriday);
//If the first date was a Friday, add it back
If DayOfWeek(StartDate) = 6 Then
    NumberOfFridays = NumberOfFridays + 1;
NumberOfFridays \ 2;   //Paid on every other Friday
```

The DateDiff() function treats the w and ww intervals differently than the DateAdd() and DatePart() functions. In both the DateAdd() and DatePart() functions, the w interval represents a single weekday and the ww interval represents a seven day period. However, the DateDiff() function treats the w interval as the number of weeks between two dates and the ww interval counts the number of times a certain weekday appears. Thus, the ww interval counts the number of times a seven-day period occurs and the w interval counts the number of times a single day occurs. These two functions treat the intervals in opposite ways.

## DatePart(interval, date, firstdayofweek, firstweekofyear)

The DatePart() function returns a number representing the part of the date that you specify using the interval argument. These intervals were listed in Table 6-11. Pass the interval as the first argument and the date as the second argument.

```
//Get the current quarter
DatePart("q", CurrentDate);   //Returns a number 1 – 4
```

Use interval "w" to display the weekday and it returns a number from 1 to 7. By default, Sunday is represented by a 1. The optional third argument designates which day of the week is considered the first day of the week. It effectively shifts the numeric representation so that the day you passed is treated as the first day. If you passed this argument crTuesday, then Tuesday is represented by a 1 and Sunday becomes 6.

Use "ww" to display which week of the year a particular date falls in. It returns a number from 1 to 53. By default, the first week is the week that has January 1st in it. Use the optional fourth argument to designate a different way of determining the first week of the year. There are two other methods to do this. The first method specifies that the first week is the one with at least four days in it. The second method specifies the first week as the first one to have seven full days in it. Table 6-14 lists the different constants that are used to specify the first week of the year argument.

**Table 6-14. First Week of the Year Constants**

| Constant | Description |
|---|---|
| crFirstJan1 | The week that has January 1st. |
| crFirstFourDays | The first week that has at least four days in it. |
| crFirstFullWeek | The first week that has seven days in it. |

What happens if you specify the first week to be the first one with seven full days, and you pass it a date of 2/1/2002 that only has five days in the week? Does DatePart() return a 0? No, it returns 53 to let you know that the date falls before the first official week of the year.

Since the third and fourth arguments are both optional, if you want to specify the fourth argument, then you are also required to specify the third argument (the first day of the week). Although by default this is crSunday, you must still pass it to the function in order to be able to use the fourth argument. In this circumstance, the third argument is ignored and the DatePart() function always assumes Sunday to be the first day of the week.

# MonthName(date, firstdayofweek)

# WeekDayName(weekday, abbreviate, firstdayofweek)

# DayOfWeek(date, firstdayofweek)

Just like the DatePart() function, these functions are given a date value and they return part of the date. The difference is that these functions are more specialized than the DatePart() function.

The MonthName() function is passed a number representing the month and it returns the name of the month fully spelled out. There is an optional second argument that lets you specify whether it should be abbreviated to three letters or not. Pass True to the second argument to get the abbreviated name. By default, this is False and it returns the full name.

The WeekDayName() function is passed a number representing the day of the week and it returns the name of the day fully spelled out. Just like MonthName(), you can pass True to the optional second argument to get the 3 letter abbreviation.

The DayOfWeek () function is passed a date and it returns a number.

Both the WeekDayName() and DayOfWeek() functions use a number to represent the day of the week. By default, this number is a 1 for Sunday and a 7 for Saturday. As discussed for the DatePart() function, you can shift this number by specifying a different first day of the week. If you passed crMonday to the function, then Sunday is represented by a 7. You pass this as the third argument for the WeekDayName() function and as the second argument for the DayOfWeek() function.

```
//Demonstrate using the first day of the week argument
WeekDayName(2, True, crMonday);    //Returns "Tue" for Tuesday
DayOfWeek(#1/6/2002#, crMonday);        //Returns 7 b/c it is a Sunday
```

# DateSerial( ) and TimeSerial( )

The DateSerial() and TimeSerial() functions can be used to create a date or time by passing the parts of the value as separate arguments to the function. The DateSerial() arguments are the year, month and day. The DateTime() arguments are the hour, minute, and seconds.

In the simplest form, these functions create a date or time using three arguments. But these functions are also very powerful for adding and subtracting values to a Date and Time. They are different from the DateAdd() function in that they perform the calculations using a cumulative process. They start by calculating a partial date (or time) value and then build upon it and modify it each step of the way. It starts by calculating the year, then it calculates the month and finally the day. This is easiest to understand by looking at a simple example first and then a more complex example. All of the examples use the following statements to declare and initialize the variable MyDate.

This code snippet shows the variable declaration that is used for the remaining examples.

```
//Declare the variable for use in the examples
DateVar MyDate;
MyDate := CDate("2/4/2006");
```

This next code snippet gets the current year and month from the current date and passes them to the DateSerial() function. It passes the value 1 as the day argument to force it to return the first day of the current month.

```
DateSerial(Year(MyDate), Month(MyDate), 1);    'Returns 2/1/2006
```

The next function calculates the last day of the prior month by using each argument to create the next part of the date in sequence and then modifying the result according to the arithmetic.

```
Formula = DateSerial(Year(MyDate), Month(MyDate), 1 - 1)        'Returns 1/31/2006
```

How it calculates the result is best shown using the steps listed here.

1.  Calculate the year. This returns a date with the year of 2006

2.  Calculate the month. This returns a date of 02/2006.

3. Calculate the day. The first part of the argument is 1 and this returns a date of 02/01/2006.

4. The subtract operator tells it to subtract one day from the date as it has been calculated to this point. Thus, it subtracts one day from 02/01/2006 to give a date of 1/31/2006.

The next example is the most complex, but uses the same rules as the last example. It calculates the last day of the current month.

```
DateSerial(Year(MyDate), Month(MyDate) + 1, 1 - 1);      //Returns 2/28/2006
```

1. Calculate the year. This returns a date with the year of 2006.

2. Calculate the month. This returns a date of 02/2006

3. The addition operator tells it to add one month. This returns a date of 03/2006.

4. Calculate the day. The first part of the argument is 1 and this returns a date of 03/01/2006.

5. The subtract operator tells it to subtract one day from the date as it has been calculated to this point. Thus, it subtracts one day from 03/01/2006 to give a date of 2/28/2006.

You can see from the three previous examples that using a cumulative approach to calculating the date is very powerful. It's almost like using a single function to write a simplified macro.

## Timer

The Timer function returns the number of seconds that have elapsed since midnight. This can be used for doing performance evaluations of how long it takes a report to run. Unfortunately, it is only significant to the nearest second. So it is only useful for analyzing reports that have lengthy run times. The following code demonstrates timing how long it takes a report to run.

In the Report Header put the following formula:

```
BeforeReadingRecords;
Global NumberVar StartTime;
StartTime := Timer;
""; //Need to at least return an empty string even though it isn't used
```

In the report Footer put the following formula:

```
WhilePrintingRecords;
Global NumberVar StartTime;
Timer – StartTime;
//This returns the number of seconds it took to run the report
```

# Other Functions

Although this chapter and the last two have listed many useful functions, Crystal Reports still has many more to choose from. You've seen all the primary ones and I'm going to leave the remaining ones for you to explore on your own.

# Building Custom Functions

This chapter has shown you a multitude of functions built into Crystal Reports. But these functions were designed to be utilized by a wide variety of people and they can't possibly do everything you need them to do. Because of this, Crystal Reports gives you the ability to create your own custom functions that are designed for your specific needs. Just like the Crystal Reports' functions, your custom functions can be used within any formula on your report.

If you write a lot of formulas for your reports, you might notice that some of the logic is repeated in different formulas. For example, if your company has offices in multiple countries, performing currency conversions in a formula is very common. You have to re-type this logic into each formula. To make matters worse, if the logic ever changes then you have to go back and fix it in every formula that used it. This can become a maintenance headache. By taking this common logic out of the formulas and putting it into a custom function, you centralize the code into a single location. The custom function can now be referenced by other formulas in the report and making changes to it is done in a single place. When the function is updated, all the formulas that reference will have new results.

Before getting into the steps for creating a custom function, let's make sure we thoroughly understand how they work. This will make it easier to see how to best utilize them as well as understand what their limitations are.

## How Custom Functions Work

To understand how custom functions work, you first have to understand their purpose. Custom functions allow you to share and reuse formula logic. Putting common logic into a single function makes it easier to maintain this code and makes it possible to simplify formulas that use the function.

Sharing program logic is a huge benefit because this isn't possible with formulas. Throughout this whole chapter we've discussed how to use the Formula Workshop to build formulas, but these formulas are all independent of each other. They can't talk to each other or have one call the other. A custom function's sole purpose is to help other formulas do their job.

Since we were working with formulas in the previous chapter, let's look at their characteristics and see how functions are different. Formulas are listed in the Field Explorer under the Formula Fields category. They are displayed on a report by dragging and dropping them onto a report. Custom functions can't be used on their own (i.e. dragged and dropped onto a report). They have to be called from a formula. Since they can't be displayed directly on a report, you won't find them listed in the Field Explorer window. They are only listed within the Formula Workshop window under the Custom Functions category.

Formulas work with report data to produce their return value. As the report data changes, their results change. Custom functions are stateless. This means that they don't have access to any report data and they have to have all external data passed directly to them via their arguments.

Formulas can't directly pass data to another formula. If you want to share data, you have to use Global variables that are available to all formulas. Custom functions define a set of arguments that are used to get data from a formula. A formula talks directly to a custom function by passing data to these arguments.

Formulas are not allowed to return an array or a range type variable. Custom functions are allowed to do this.

Due to the differences between formulas and custom functions, limitations are imposed on custom functions.

- You can't use report fields and database fields. This would violate the rules of being stateless.

- You can't use global variables or shared variables (unless passed as an argument). However, you can create local variables and use them within the custom function.

- You can't use recursion (a function calling itself repeatedly).

- You can't use Evaluation Time, Print State or Document Properties functions.

- You can't use the functions: Rnd(), CurrentFieldValue(), DefaultAttribute(), and GridRowColumnValue().

Now that you have an understanding of how custom functions work and what their limitations are, let's see how to create them.

# Creating Custom Functions

There are two ways to create a custom function. The first is to use an existing function as the basis and have Crystal Reports analyze it and build a new function from it. This is referred to as extracting the formula. The second is to create it from scratch on your own. You do this when you don't have an existing formula to work with. Formula extraction is the easier of the two methods because you let Crystal Reports do most of the work.

# Understanding the Formula Extractor

The easiest way to create a new function is to use an existing formula as the template. Crystal Reports gives you the option of specifying an existing formula and having it extract the code from it and use it to create a new custom function. This has two benefits. The first benefit being that Crystal Reports does the work for you. But the second benefit is that it also error checks the existing formula to make sure it is compatible with custom functions. As mentioned earlier, functions have a set of rules that they must follow and Crystal Reports won't let you create a new function that doesn't follow these rules. If it finds that a formula can't be converted, it lists the reasons why so that you can learn from it and make changes if necessary.

The job of the formula extractor is to convert a formula into a generic format so that it can be used as a custom function. It does this by copying the majority of the programming code and scanning the formula for any report fields or database fields that need to be replaced. Since these fields aren't allowed in custom functions, it creates an argument for each one and replaces the field name with an argument name. To see how this works, let's look at a simple formula that calculates the number of days between two fields. Here is the original formula:

```
//This formula calculates the number of days it takes to ship
//an order from the original order date (includes the order date).
{Orders.Ship Date} - {Orders.Order Date} + 1;
```

The first two lines are a comment telling you the formula's purpose. The third line calculates how many days it took to ship the product after the order was placed. It adds 1 to the difference so that the date of ordering is counted as one full day. This prevents it from saying that an order was shipped in zero days. The problem with this formula is that it only works with the fields Ship Date and Order Date. If you later wanted to perform the same calculation on two different fields, then you would have to repeat this logic in another formula.

Let's use the formula extractor to convert this to a custom function that can be called from any formula. The results of running the formula extractor are as follows:

```
Function  (dateVar v1, dateVar v2)
//This formula calculates the number of days it takes to ship
//an order from the original order date (includes the order date).
v1 - v2 + 1;
```

The first line uses the Function keyword to declare that this is a custom function. The function's arguments are listed within matching parentheses. They are called v1 and v2 by default (we'll see how to change this to a more significant name in the next section). The original formula had two report fields, Ship Date and Order Date. This corresponds exactly to how many arguments were created in the custom function.

The next two lines of code are just a copy of the comments and don't have any significance except to show that the function extractor will copy everything from the original formula. The last line calculates the difference between the two dates, but this time using the argument names instead of the field names. You can see how the formula extractor copied the original formula almost verbatim. The only differences being that it declared arguments for each field and replaced the field names with the argument names.

Before leaving this example, there is one more question we haven't answered yet: What happens to the original formula? Since the formula's logic is now inside the new custom function, shouldn't the formula be updated to call the new function? Yes, it should. And what's even better is that the formula extractor will do it for you. Here is the revised formula so that it calls the custom function:

DateDifference ({Orders.Ship Date}, {Orders.Order Date});

It simply calls the new function and passes the two date fields to it. The formula is greatly simplified and anytime the custom function gets modified, the changes are reflected directly in this formula.

Creating custom functions is frequently done later in the report development process. For example, you might create a report formula and display it in the report. Then a little later, as you are writing another formula, you realize that some of its logic is similar to an existing formula. Rather than redo the logic, you decide to create a custom function using the formula extractor to convert the original formula. This saves you the work of having to rewrite the entire formula from scratch.

## Using the Formula Extractor

The formula extractor is found within the Formula Workshop. When you create a new custom function you are given the option to use the editor to type it in directly or use the formula extractor. If you click the button Use Formula Extractor, it opens the Formula Extractor dialog box shown in Figure 6-2.

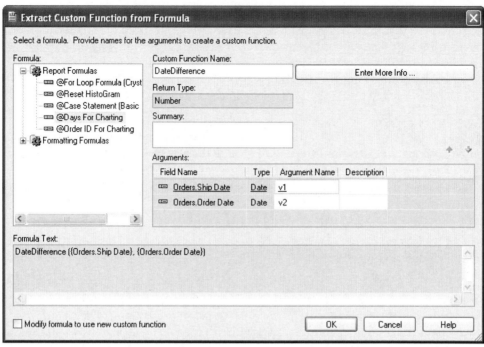

**Figure 6-2. The Formula Extractor dialog box.**

The Formula window on the left displays the report formulas and formatting formulas. You can select a formula from either list. To select a formula for conversion, you only have to single-click it. The right side of the dialog box automatically changes to show you the internal workings of that formula.[36] At the top is the custom function name and below it is the data type that will be returned. You can change the name if you like, but you can't change the data type because the formula controls that. Under the Return Type is a summary text box. Type in a description of what the custom function does.

The Arguments window lists each argument that the formula extractor will create. It shows you the field name that it is derived from, the data type, the argument name, and the description. Both the field name and the data type are fixed. You can't change them because they are derived from the original formula. The Argument Name and the Description can and should be changed. By default, the formula extractor names each argument as v1, v2, v3, etc. This is a meaningless name and should be changed to a name that is more descriptive. The Description is where you can type in a more thorough description of the argument.

At the bottom of the dialog box is the Formula Text window. This tells you how the original formula should be changed so that it calls the custom function. Notice that it also

---

[36] If the formula can't be converted to a custom function, then right side changes to a text area that shows a list of the problems encountered.

tells you which fields need to be passed to the function and the order that they are passed. In this example, the Ship Date field maps to v1 and the Order Date field maps to v2.

A nice feature is the checkbox below the Formula Text window. By selecting it, the Formula Extractor automatically modifies the formula so that it uses this text that calls the custom function.

When you click the OK button, the new custom function is automatically created and added to the Formula Workshop in two different places. The first place it's listed is the Report Custom Functions list. This lets you come back to edit the function at a later time. The second place it's listed is in the Report Functions window with all the other Crystal Report functions. It is shown under the Custom Functions category. This lets you reference it when you are writing report formulas.

If you selected the Modify Formula checkbox, the original formula that this custom function was derived from is modified so that it calls the new custom function and passes the proper fields as arguments.

## Custom Function Properties

At the top right corner of the Formula Extractor dialog box is the Enter More Info button. Clicking on it opens the Custom Function Properties dialog box shown in Figure 6-3. This lets you set additional properties for the custom function.

**Figure 6-3. The Custom Function Properties dialog box.**

This dialog box lets you set various properties about the custom function. The Summary area is the same summary that you typed in the Formula Extractor dialog box. But now it's bigger so that you can type in more information.

The second input box is the Category option. It lets you group custom functions together in a more logical fashion. By default, all the custom functions are listed in the Report Custom Functions category. But if the report uses numerous custom functions, then it is helpful to create function categories and group each function within the appropriate category. That makes it easier to find a function when you want to use it. If you need to create sub-categories, use the forward slash between each category name. For example, entering a category name of Financial/Accounts Receivable creates the category Accounts Receivable under the Financial category.

The other properties only affect how the custom function works with the Formula Expert. The Formula Expert is discussed in detail in the next section, but it basically makes it easy to create a new formula that calls a custom function.

The property Display in Experts determines whether the function is listed as an available function when the user runs the Formula Expert. If you uncheck this property, then the custom function is not available in the Formula Expert dialog box. Note that the custom function will always be listed in the Report Functions window so that you can reference it when writing formulas manually.

The Help Text button lets you write help information about the function. This help information is only displayed when using the Formula Expert dialog box.

The Arguments window at the bottom of the Formula Extractor dialog box is similar to what you've already seen. It shows each argument name, the data type and the description (which you can change). The difference is that there is a new column for entering default values. These default values are listed in the Formula Expert dialog box. They can be selected as one of the arguments that get passed to the function. By clicking on the Default Values box, it opens a dialog box which lets you build a list of default values.

When you are finished changing the additional function properties, click the OK button to save them and return to the Formula Extractor dialog box.

# Tutorial 6-1. Using the Formula Extractor

Let's practice converting a formula using the formula extractor. As an added bonus, we're going to convert a formula that breaks some of the rules of custom functions and see how to handle it. The formula we're going to convert displays the histogram chart on the Crystal Reports sample report Formulas.rpt.

```
WhilePrintingRecords;
NumberVar i;
NumberVar delimit;
StringVar HistoGram;
if {Orders.Ship Date} - {Orders.Order Date} >= 254 then
    delimit := 0
else
    delimit := {Orders.Ship Date} - {Orders.Order Date};
for i := 0 to delimit  do
    HistoGram := HistoGram + "6";
HistoGram
```

1. Open the Crystal Reports sample report Formulas.rpt. This is found in the Crystal Reports samples directory. Save the report as **Custom Histogram Function.rpt**.

2. Preview the report and look at the Histogram column. It displays a string with hourglass icons. Each icon represents how many days it took to ship a product after it was ordered. The formula that creates this string is called For Loop Formula and was written with Crystal syntax.

3. Open the Formula Workshop dialog box by clicking on the Formula Workshop button.

4. Create a new custom function by right-clicking on the Report Custom Functions category and selecting New. Enter the name **HistogramChart**.

5.  Click the Use Extractor button. The dialog box immediately opens and tells you that the formula can't be converted because it contains the function WhilePrintingRecords and it uses global variables. Let's see if we can get around this.

6.  Click the Cancel button so you return to the Formula Workshop dialog box. Find the For Loop Formula and edit it. Since the function WhilePrintingRecords can't be called, comment it out. We will add it back into the original formula after it gets converted. The new code should look like this:

```
//WhilePrintingRecords
```

7.  The second error is that the formula uses global variables. The variable declarations don't define a scope, but Crystal syntax says that if a scope isn't specified then the default scope is Global. If you look at the formula you'll see that the variables are really only used locally and declaring them as global isn't necessary. To fix this, add the Local keyword at the beginning of the variable declarations.[37]

```
Local NumberVar i;
Local NumberVar delimit;
Local StringVar HistoGram;
```

8.  Save your changes.

9.  Try to run the formula extractor again (see steps 3-5). This time there are no errors listed and the Formula Extractor dialog box opens.

10. Change the argument names from v1 and v2 to ShipDate and OrderDate respectively.

11. At the bottom of the dialog box is the Modify Formula checkbox. Click on it so that For Loop Formula gets automatically updated to call this function.

12. Click the OK button to save your changes. At this point the HistogramChart custom function gets created and the For Loop Formula gets updated.

13. We are almost finished except for one thing. In Step 6, you commented out the WhilePrintingRecords function because it isn't allowed in a custom function. But we still need to call it from the report formula. So let's edit the formula and add this function back.

14. You should still be in the Formula Workshop dialog box, so click on the For Loop Formula to edit it. The dialog box probably doesn't look like what you are used to. This is because the formula was modified with the formula extractor. Click on the Use Wizard button[38] to return the screen to normal.

15. The formula's code is shown in the Definition area. It has one line that calls the HistorgramChart() function and passes the two date fields as arguments. We originally

---

[37] In this example, we got lucky that the global variables could be converted to local variables. When global variables really need to be global, then you can add them to the custom function's argument list. Within the calling formula declare them as global and pass them as arguments to the function.

[38] The Use Wizard button looks like a magic wand and it's located to the left of the Help button.

commented out the WhilePrintingRecords function, so let's add it back as the first line of the formula so that it gets called for every detail record.

16. At this point, you've added the custom function and modified the original formula. Click the Save and Close button to close the Formula Workshop and save your changes.

17. Preview the report and you should see that the Histogram column still displays a list of hourglasses representing how many days it took to ship a product. Even though the report looks the same, you've made a lot of changes behind the scenes. The HistogramChart() can now be called elsewhere in the report if you need to display it.

This tutorial walked you through the steps of converting a fairly complex formula into a custom function. You also learned that even though the formula extractor might initially tell you that a formula can't be converted, you can temporarily modify the formula to convert it and then go back and correct it later.

# Writing Functions Manually

Without a doubt, using the formula extractor makes creating functions easy. But it only works if you have existing functions already written. For those times when a formula doesn't already exist, you have to write the custom function from scratch. Luckily, if you are adept at writing formulas, then writing custom functions is not much different.

Writing functions manually has two additional requirements compared to writing formulas. The first is that you have to declare the function and the second is that you have to create the argument list. Declaring the function is pretty simple. In Basic syntax, use the Function keyword followed by the function name. Crystal syntax is the same except that it doesn't require specifying the function name. Luckily for us, when you create a new function, Crystal Reports gives you a head start by creating a code template with the basic syntax already typed in.

Here is the code template for Crystal syntax:

```
Function()
```

All you need is the Function keyword and nothing else. You can write the programming logic just as you do with formulas.

Here is the code template using Basic syntax:

```
Function DaysToShip()
    DaysToShip=
End Function
```

Basic syntax uses the Function keyword to start the code block and the End Function keyword to finish it. It also gives you the code to return the value back to the calling formula.

## Declaring Function Arguments

Arguments are how you pass external data from a formula to the function. The arguments for a custom function are listed on the same line as the function declaration and they have two rules. The first is that they must be enclosed in a set of matching parentheses and the second is that multiple arguments are separated with commas.

In Crystal syntax the function declaration would look like this:

```
Function(DateTime BeginDate, DateTime EndDate)
```

In Basic syntax the function declaration would look like this:

```
Function DaysToShip(BeginDate As DateTime, EndDate As DateTime)
```

Function arguments have a unique feature that variables don't have: they can be declared as optional. This means that when a formula calls a function, it doesn't have to pass a value for every argument. When an optional argument isn't passed a value, it uses a default value instead. This ensures that every argument has a value even though it may not have come from the formula that called it.

To declare an argument as optional, use the Optional keyword before the argument declaration and specify the default value after the declaration.

In Basic syntax, declaring optional arguments looks like this:

```
Function ShowName(LastName As String, Optional FirstName As String="")
```

In Crystal syntax, optional arguments look like this:

```
Function (StringVar LastName, Optional StringVar FirstName :="")
```

After making the function declaration and defining the arguments, the final step is typing in the custom function's code. As I mentioned before, this is no different than writing a formula. However, there is one exception for Basic syntax. When returning a value from a function, you have to assign the return value to the function's name. For example, the following code listing assigns the result to the function name DaysToShip.

```
Function DaysToShip(BeginDate As DateTime, EndDate As DateTime)
    DaysToShip=EndDate – BeginDate + 1
End Function
```

# Using the Formula Expert

The previous section made references to the Formula Expert dialog box, but unfortunately, you probably didn't completely understand what it was because it had not been discussed yet. The Formula Expert is a tool that makes it easier for you to use the custom functions you've written. It lets you select a custom function and populate the arguments without writing any code. When you select the custom function to use, it lists every argument within the function. You fill in a value for each argument and save it. Behind the scenes, it is creating the call to the function for you. Effectively, you created a formula without writing a single line of code. It was all done by pointing and clicking the mouse.

At first, this sounds like a pretty good way to write formulas in your report. After all, not writing any code is much easier than learning Basic syntax or Crystal syntax. Unfortunately, there is a caveat. The Formula Expert is very limited in what it can do. It is so limited that you may find that you rarely use it. Here are the limitations of the Formula Expert:

- It is only compatible with custom formulas that you already created.

- It can only reference a single custom function.

- You can't add any additional logic around the custom function.

What I find ironic about the Formula Expert is that it is designed to be easy for someone who doesn't know how to write formulas. But if you are smart enough to write a custom function, then it goes without saying that don't need the Formula Expert to help you call the custom function from a formula. The exception is someone who is working on a report created by someone else or if there are functions in the Business Objects Enterprise Repository that you need to use.

To use the Formula Expert, create a new formula as you normally would by clicking on the Formula Fields list and selecting New. After entering the formula name, the Formula Workshop dialog box appears. Along the top of the toolbar is the Use Expert button.

**Figure 6-4. The Use Expert button.**

When you click on this button, the entire Formula Workshop dialog box changes. The three report tree windows along the top and the Definition area disappear. They are replaced by a Custom Function window, a Summary window, and the Function Arguments area.

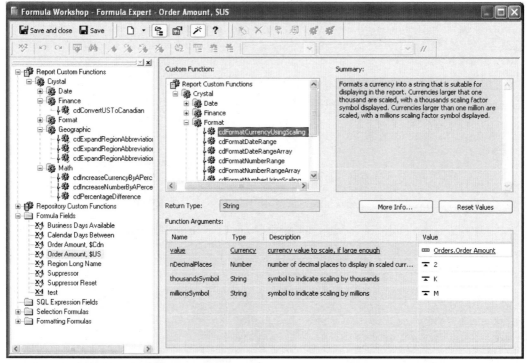

**Figure 6-5. The Formula Expert dialog box.**

When you click on one of the custom functions, its summary is displayed to the right and its arguments are displayed at the bottom. Figure 6-5 shows what the dialog box looks like after selecting the custom function cdFormatCurrencyUsingScaling (found in the Crystal Reports sample report Formulas.rpt).

After selecting the custom function to use, the only step left is specifying the data to pass to the function's arguments. The list of arguments is at the bottom of the dialog box in the Function Arguments area. This area lists the argument name, its data type, and a description. The last column is the Value column. This is where you tell Crystal Reports what data you want to pass to the argument. This can be an existing report field, a constant that you type in, or any field in the report's data source. In Figure 6-5, four arguments are shown.

One interesting thing about the Formula Expert is that if you click the Formula Expert button again, the dialog box switches back to the normal Formula Expert dialog box that you are familiar with. If you look in the Definition area you'll see the actual formula you just created using the Formula Expert. For example, the formula that was created in Figure 6-5 is this:

cdFormatCurrencyUsingScaling ({Orders.Order Amount}, 2, "K", "M")

You can see that the end result is a one line formula that calls the custom function cdFormatCurrencyUsingScaling and populates its four arguments. It's really quite simple.

### Caution

The Formula Expert button can be clicked on when you are editing any formula. It toggles the view back and forth between the normal Formula Workshop dialog box and the Formula Expert dialog box. But you need to be careful if you are editing a formula that wasn't created with the Formula Expert. Switching to Formula Expert mode could erase all your changes. Since the Formula Expert has the limitation of only being able to work with a single custom function, if you are editing a formula that is more advanced, then the Formula Expert won't know how to handle it. So it just erases all your work and you have to start from scratch. Luckily, before doing this, it gives you a warning message and lets you cancel it.

Overall, my feelings about the Formula Expert are similar to my feelings about the Highlighting Expert: it's a nice crutch for the very beginning report writer, but you'll quickly outgrow it.

# Writing Formulas

Formulas are used in Crystal Reports for enhancing report functionality as it prints. For example, Tutorial 5-1 showed how to use a formula to have the rows on the report alternate colors. Another example is suppressing a row by comparing a field against its current value.

Crystal Reports gives you the option to program formulas in either Crystal syntax or Basic syntax. The default programming language is Crystal syntax and that is what this chapter focuses on. Basic syntax is covered in Appendix B.

This chapter gives an overview of programming Crystal syntax and focuses on areas that are not as intuitive and that require more explanation. When I say, "intuitive", I mean this from the standpoint of someone already familiar with how to program. If you have never programmed before, then this chapter might be a bit intimidating at first time. I try to give enough examples so that you can see how each concept is used in practice, but if you really want to create detailed formulas then you might be best off reading a book dedicated to teaching you how to write programs.

# Formula Fundamentals

To learn how to program with Crystal syntax, you want to start with the fundamental tasks that might seem pretty mundane. There are certain aspects that you need to know even if you only plan on writing some very simple formulas. By understanding the basic structure of a formula, you can build on this knowledge to create more complex logic. This section covers the fundamentals of writing formulas.

## Case Sensitivity

When a language is case sensitive, it considers identical words to be different when the letters use a different case. Crystal syntax is not case sensitive. For example, the variable FirstName is the same as the variable firstname. Although these two variables are syntactically equivalent and can be used interchangeably, it is recommended that you keep the case consistent so that your program is easier to read.

## Writing Comments

Comments let you add notes to your code so that it is easier to understand. You can explain why you did something or add clarity to the purpose of the formula. It is common to write a formula and think that its functionality is so obvious that there is no reason to write comments. But six months later you have to modify the report and when you look at the formula you have no idea why you wrote it the way you did. Adding comments ensures that at a future date you'll understand why you did something. If someone else comes along later to review your report, then they will be thankful for the comments.

Crystal syntax uses // to designate a comment. It can be at the beginning of a line or in the middle. Anything after it is ignored.

//This is a comment

## Line Terminator

When a formula has more than one line of code, you need some way to mark the end of the line. In some programming languages each programming statement has to be on a new line. Crystal syntax allows more than one statement on the same line. A semi-colon is used as the separator between statements. Even if each statement is on a new line, you still need to put the semi-colon at the end.

If the whole formula only has one line of code, no semicolon is needed (but you can put it there if you wish).

X := 5;  // This is a single line
Y := 3; Z := "This puts multiple statements on one line";

## Returning a Value

Formulas are generally used to calculate a value that gets displayed on a report. This could be someone's average salary or concatenating a first name and last name into a single string value. Consequently, Crystal Reports requires every formula to return a value.

| Note |
| --- |

If a formula doesn't specifically return a value, then Crystal Reports assigns the Null value to it and defines it as a string data type. There are times when this can actually be useful. For example, if you need to link to a subreport using a field with a null value then you can create an empty formula and link it to the subreport.

Crystal Reports uses the value of the last line executed in a formula as the return value. Any value on the last line will be returned. Here are a few examples. This formula returns the number 5.

```
//Return a single number
5;
```

The next formula assigns the result of a calculation to a variable. That result is returned by the formula.

```
NumberVar AnnualSalary;
AnnualSalary := {Employee.MonthlySalary} * 12;
```

In the next example, the last line executed is what returns the value. The If-Then statement has two exit points and the one chosen is dependent upon the condition.

```
If {Employee.Bonus} > 0 Then
    True
Else
    False;
```

When you have a statement that can return multiple values, make sure that each one is of the same data type. Crystal Reports will check all the values and give you an error if they don't match up.

# Referencing Report Fields

Writing formulas requires referencing all types of data from your report and the tables that the report uses. The types of data that can be referenced consist of running totals, functions, formulas, and table fields. The syntax for referencing a field is to put curly brackets around it. In addition to that, each type of field has a special character which designates its type. Some examples follow.

Formulas are referenced by putting @ in front of their name.

```
{@Formula}
```

Parameters are referenced with a ? in front of the name.

```
{?Parameter}
```

Running total fields are referenced by putting # in front of the name.

```
{#RunningTotal}
```

Table fields are referenced by separating the table name and the field name with a period between the two. Spaces are allowed.

{Customer.First Name}

Group fields use the field name with the GroupName() formula.

GroupName({Table.GroupField})

Summary fields pass the field name and the group field as parameters to the summary function.

Sum({Table.FieldName}, {Table.GroupName})

# Simple Data Types

Crystal syntax supports the standard data types that we expect in a language: number, Boolean, currency, string, date and time.

**Table 7-1. Data Type Default Values**

| Crystal Data Type | Basic Data Type | Default Value |
|---|---|---|
| NumberVar | Number | 0 |
| CurrencyVar | Currency | $0 |
| BooleanVar | Boolean | False |
| StringVar | String | "" |
| DateVar | Date | Date(0,0,0) – The Null Date value 00/00/00 |
| TimeVar | Time | No default value. Null. |
| DateTimeVar | DateTime | No default value. Null. |

Notice that rather than have a large number of numeric data types such as integer, double, etc., there is simply a single data type called NumberVar. There is no need to worry about whether the number is fractional or what its largest possible value is. One data type handles all situations.

The CurrencyVar data type is treated the same as a NumberVar data type with a few exceptions:

Currency can only have two decimal places. If assigned a number with more than two decimal places, it rounds up to the nearest penny.

Currency automatically gets formatted as a monetary value. This eliminates the overhead of having to format the variable whenever it gets printed.

Since Currency is a different data type, it must be converted to a number to be used in mathematical assignments using non-currency variables. See the section "Converting Data Types" for more information.

Strings use the double quote, ", to specify a string literal. A character is represented by a string of length one. Referencing a position within a string is Base 1. Thus, if you want to refer to the first character in a string, you would use an index of 1. The maximum length of a string constant is 65,534 characters. Information on using the built-in string functions is in Chapter 6.

```
//Demonstrate assigning a string constant to a variable
Local StringVar Title;
Title := "This is a string";
```

Dates are a little unusual in that there are three different data types available. The DateVar type can only store a date and the TimeVar type can only store a time. It's preferable to use these data types if you don't need both values stored in a variable. If you do need both types in the same variable, use the DateTimeVar type. To assign a constant to a DateTimeVar , use the Date() function. You can use a variety of formats to pass the date to the function.

```
//Show different ways of assigning a date to a variable
Local DateVar MyBirthday;
MyBirthday := Date(#5/23/1968#);
MyBirthday := Date(1968, 5, 23);
MyBirthday := Date("May 23, 1968");
```

# Null Values

The Null value isn't a data type, but a type of data. It is a non-value used to mark when a field doesn't have a specific value stored in it. For example, if you are filling out a data entry form, there might be certain personal questions that you skip because you aren't comfortable answering them. When the program saves your answers to the database, it might put a null value in the questions you skipped to mark that you didn't answer them. Unfortunately, databases are meant to have data in them and using the null value can wreak havoc on your reports and formulas. If there is a chance that you are reporting from a database that has null values in it, you need to account for that so that your report runs smoothly.

In most cases you want to convert nulls to their default values. The default value is determined by the data type of the field being used. These values are shown in Table 7-1. There are two settings that control this and they are both found by selecting File > Report Options.[39] The first option, Convert Database NULL Values to Default, converts nulls

---

[39] If you want to changes the settings for all reports, and not just the current report, select the menu items File > Options and click on the Reporting tab.

when reading data from the database. The second option, Convert Other NULL Values to Default, applies to non-database null values (such as formulas). Check both of these options to keep null values from impacting your report.

There are times when you don't want to convert nulls to their default values because you want to know whether the data field is empty or if no value was saved at all. In this circumstance you have to be careful when using conditional statements that involve fields with null values. Crystal Reports will stop the evaluation and return no results. You need to test for this using the IsNull() function and handle the results correctly.

The IsNull() function returns true when the field is null and returns false for any other value. The following example tests whether the ID field is null or not. If so, it returns the dummy value of 9999.

```
If IsNull({Sales.PersonID}) Then
    9999
Else
    {Sales.PersonID};
```

If you want to use the IsNull() function in conjunction with another test, you have to perform the IsNull() test first. Otherwise, the report could error out. The next example tests whether a valid ID was entered.

```
If IsNull({Sales.PersonID}) OR {Sales.PersonID}=0 Then
    "This ID is not valid"
Else
    "The ID is valid";
```

In this example, if a field has a null value, the IsNull() function returns true and the test for zero doesn't need to be evaluated. But if the test for zero was performed first, the test would fail immediately when the null value was encountered.

Many times, a report will want to look ahead one record and see what a field's upcoming value is. Again, you need to test for null values. This is done with the NextIsNull() function.

```
If NextIsNull({SalesOrders.ShipDate} Then
    "This is the last order shipped.";
```

The PreviousIsNull() function performs the same test as the NextIsNull() function. But it looks at the previous record.

## Declaring Variables

Variables store a piece of data so that it can be used again within the formula. For example, if a calculation is performed multiple times in a formula, then you can store the result in a variable and reference that variable wherever it's needed. This makes the formula easier to read and it improves performance because you don't have to repeat the calculation.

Variables are also used to pass data between other formulas and even to sub-reports. For example, by declaring a variable as Global it can be used by other formulas. If you couldn't share variables, then you would have to duplicate the same calculation in different report sections.

When a variable is declared, it is automatically assigned a default value. For example, a NumberVar variable is assigned the value 0. See Table 7-1 in the previous section for a list of the default values for each data type.

To use a variable in a formula, you first have to declare it. Declaring a variable follows the format of specifying the scope followed by the data type and the variable name.

```
scope datatype variable;
```

```
//Declare a date variable
Global DateVar StartDate;
//You can also assign an initial value within the declaration
Local NumberVar X := 23;
```

A variable's scope determines which formulas have access to that variable. You can set the scope so that a variable can only be used within the formula it's declared in, or you can make it available to the rest of the report. There are three operators that are used to declare scope:

1. Local (Dim for Basic syntax): The variable can only be seen within the current formula. The variable is private to that formula and can't be used anywhere else in the report. This is the default scope if you don't specify it. Dim is the default scope for Basic syntax.

2. Global: The variable can be seen within any formula inside the same report. Sub-reports do not have access to the variable. Global is the default scope for Crystal syntax.

3. Shared: Similar to Global, but the variable can also be seen within sub-reports.

### Caution

In Crystal syntax, if you do not declare a scope then it defaults to Global, not Local. You should be aware of this since this is the exact opposite of how Basic syntax handles the scope when it isn't declared.

If you want to specify the variable's default value, you can do so in the variable declaration statement. For example, the next example declares the variable PI as a global number and assigns a value of 3.14 to it. Now any formula in the report (or sub-report) can reference it.

```
Global NumberVar PI := 3.14;
```

Local variables and global variables also differ in how they get initialized. Local variables are always reset back to their default value every time the formula is called. Thus, the result of any calculations made to a variable are cleared when the formula exits and it doesn't have any affect the next time the formula is executed. But global variables keep their value the entire time the report is running. Once you declare a variable and assign a value to it, that variable retains its value for the life of the report. Any future calls to that same formula will not initialize the global variable back to its default value. If you need to have a global variable reset back to its default value every time the formula is called, you need to write this initialization code at the beginning of the formula.

Crystal Reports doesn't reset global variables because of two reasons. The first is that a global variable is designed to be shared with other functions. If Crystal Reports reset it when exiting the formula, then the other formulas that reference it would only see the default value (zero, an empty string, etc.). This defeats the purpose of sharing variables. Another reason is the way formulas and report sections work together. Formulas are usually added to a report section that is printed multiple times. If a global variable lost its value every time a new record was processed, then you wouldn't be able to track what happened when the last record was processed. Making it easy for variables to retain their values while different records are processed is one reason why Crystal Reports is so powerful.

All variables must be declared in the formula that uses them. This might seem obvious because we already learned that if you don't declare a variable then Crystal Reports won't know its scope or what data type it's supposed to be. But if a variable has a scope of Global or Shared, then you might think that another formula has already declared it so there is no need to repeat this information. Any formula should be able to reference it anywhere in the report. But this isn't the case. You still have to declare variables in each formula that uses it. For example, if you declare a variable as Global, Crystal Reports will search the other formulas for another global variable with the same name. If it finds one, then it will have them share the same value.

If you don't re-declare the variable, Crystal Reports gives an error stating that the variable doesn't exist.

## Using Global Constants

One item that is very important, but I rarely see addressed, is the different ways to create global constants. A global constant is a variable that has a fixed value for the entire duration of the report. It stores a common number/string/date that can be shared among all the formulas. For example, Crystal Reports gives you the constant crPI which stores the value PI as 3.1415... Your reports might need to create a fixed value that can be shared among all formulas. For example, you could store the state sales tax rate or the current monetary exchange rate between two currencies. There are different methods of storing global constants, and as you might expect, each has its own benefits and drawbacks.

The first way to store a constant is by using parameter fields. When the report opens, the user is prompted to type in a value and that value is used throughout the report. Since the user is only prompted to enter a new value when the report opens, the value stays the same while the report runs. The only problem with this approach is that if the user doesn't know what the value should be, then this might prevent them from getting accurate report output. For example, it may not be a good idea to prompt the user for the number of sales offices within the company unless that is common knowledge. You need to make sure that what you are asking the user for is something that they are familiar with. Another consideration for parameters is that since the user gets prompted to enter it every time they refresh the report, it should be used for data that changes frequently.

The second way to store a constant is within a field in the database table. I've worked on many applications where we use a table strictly for the purpose of saving setup values that the application needs to run. These fields can save options such as the company address and contact information (it seems like companies are always merging with another company). You can create an Options table that uses one field for each option needed. It has one row of data that stores the current value for each field. Referencing a value in your report formulas is a simple matter of referencing a field from this table just as you would a normal data field.

Storing constants in a database has two concerns. The first is that there needs to be a way to change the values when necessary. You'll probably need a programmer to write a user interface to the Options table. This method is best used for values that don't change very often.

The third method of storing constants is putting them in a formula field. The purpose of a formula is to perform a calculation and return a value. But who says you always need to perform a complex calculation? You can have the formula that just always returns the same value. For example, the following formula returns a sales tax rate of 7.75%.

```
//California sales tax is currently 7.75%
Formula := 0.0775;
```

This is nice and simple and it does the job. Using a formula saves you the trouble of creating an additional table in the database. One thing to be aware of is that since this value is stored within the report, you should only use this method for values that rarely change. Updating the report and redistributing it can be a hassle if you have to do it frequently.

Another limitation to using formulas is that they can only be shared within a single report. If another report needs the same value then you have to copy that formula to the additional report. When the time comes to change the value, then you'll have to remember which report uses it and modify each report individually. Storing constants in a database table doesn't have this drawback because its data is in a central location. Making the change in the database table guarantees that each report is automatically updated.

Table 7-2 gives you a summary of each method for storing global constants as well as some guidelines to follow when doing so.

**Table 7-2 Methods and guidelines for storing constants.**

| Method | Usage Guidelines |
| --- | --- |
| Parameters | The value changes frequently. |
| | The user knows the value. |
| Database | The value changes somewhat frequently. |
| | There is an interface for modifying the data. |
| | The value is shared among multiple reports. |
| Functions | The value rarely changes. |
| | The user doesn't know what the value should be. |
| | The value is only needed in the current report. |

# Variable Assignment

After creating a variable, you need to assign a value to it. This can be a simple constant, a data field, or the result of a more complex calculation. The key thing to remember is that the data types on both sides of the assignment must be the same. For example, you can't assign a string to a DateTime variable. Crystal Reports gives you an error when it sees this. You either have to reconsider the validity of what you are attempting to do, or use a type conversion function to make the two compatible.

Crystal syntax uses := to assign a value to a variable.

```
X := 5;
Y := "Mr. " & {Customer.Last Name};
```

# Array Data Types

Arrays provide a means of storing a collection of data in a single variable and accessing each element of the array using an index. Think of it as storing data in a list and you can reference each item in the list using its position in the list. The first element is referenced using 1 as the index. The maximum size of an array is 1,000 elements (items).

Declaring an array is as simple as putting the Array keyword after the data type.

```
Local NumberVar Array X;
```

After declaring the array, you need to create it. You have three options before using it. You can create a new array using the MakeArray() function, assign an existing array to it, or redimension it using the ReDim keyword. Each of these options are shown in the code sample below.

```
 //Declare an array
Local NumberVar Array X;
Local NumberVar Array Y;
//Create an array with three elements using the MakeArray() function
X := MakeArray(5, 10, 22);
//Rediminsion the array to have 20 elements
Redim X[20];
//Copy an array from one variable to another variable
Y := X;
```

The ReDim statement changes the number of elements in the array and resets their values. If you don't want to lose the current, then also use the Preserve keyword.

```
Redim Preserve X[25];      //Redim an array and preserve existing values
```

If you want to reference a specific element within the array, Crystal syntax uses square brackets.

```
//Assign the number 5 into the second element of the array
X[2] = 5;
```

Assigning values to an array is done in different ways. If you know what the values of an array are during the development process, you can initialize the array with these values using the MakeArray() function. Pass the MakeArray() function all the elements as a comma delimited list and it returns an array that is fully populated with these elements. When using the MakeArray() function you don't have to specify the array size. Crystal Reports figures that out for you.

As expected, if you want to simply assign a value to an individual element in the array, then the index must be within the array's bounds. But if you are assigning an entire array to another array variable and they are different sizes, you do not have to redimension the target array. The target array gets overwritten and it will be replaced with the existing array.

```
//Demonstrate initializing an array and then overwriting it
StringVar Array MonthsInSeason;
MonthsInSeason := MakeArray("May", "June", "July");
If LongWinter = True Then
   MonthsInSeason = MakeArray("June", "July", "August");
```

If you don't know the array values during the development process, you will probably assign the initial values to the array by looping through it. A common way of doing this is using a For Next loop where the range of the loop is the lower and upper bounds of the array. Another common method of assigning values to each element is to do so as the report is looping through its detail records. For each pass through the detail section, you increase the array's size by one using ReDim Preserve and then you assign the field to the new array element.

```
//Sample code within the detail section to record customer sales as each record is printed
NumberVar RecordCounter;
NumberVar Array SalesDetail;
RecordCounter := UBound(SalesDetail) + 1;
Redim Preserve SalesDetail[RecordCounter];
SalesDetail[RecordCounter]::= {Customer.Sales};
```

Once the array is populated, you can test to see if a certain value already exists in the array by using the In operator. Using the In operator saves you the trouble of looping through the entire array searching for a particular value. If the value already exists, the In operator returns True.

Crystal syntax has many predefined functions for summarizing the values in an array. These functions range from summing the total of all the values in the array to getting the maximum value in the array. Table 7-3 lists the array functions.

**Table 7-3. Array Summary Functions**

| Array Function | Description |
|---|---|
| Average(array) | Calculate the average of all numbers in the array. |
| Count(array) | Count how many items are in the array. |
| DistinctCount(array) | Count how many unique item there are (no duplicates). |
| Maximum(array) | Return the maximum number in the array. |
| Minimum(array) | Return the minimum number in the array. |
| PopulationStdDev(array) | Return the Population Standard Deviation calculation. |
| PopulationVariance(array) | Return the PopulationVariance calculation. |
| StdDev(array) | Return the Standard Deviation calculation. |
| UBound(array) | Returns the largest available subscript. |
| Variance(array) | Return the Variance calculation. |

Although the functions in Table 7-3 are designed to only work with arrays, you can still use them with individual fields. Improvise by creating an array on the fly and passing the function this new array. This is done by creating a new array with the MakeArray() function and passing it the fields to work with.

```
//Sample code for getting the maximum value of three fields
NumberVar MaxSales1stQtr;
```

MaxSales1stQtr := Maximum(MakeArray({Sales.Jan}, {Sales.Feb}, {Sales.Mar}));

There are two special functions that only work with arrays of strings. The Join() function concatenates all the elements into a single string. By default it separates each element with a comma. You can override that by passing another delimiter as the second parameter. The corollary function is the Split() function. It takes a delimited string and splits it apart into an array of strings. Just like the Join() function, you can specify a specific delimiter by passing it as the second parameter.

```
//Demonstrate creating a delimited string from an array and then splitting it back up.
StringVar Array OrigArray;
StringVar Array SplitArray;
StringVar JoinedString;
//Populate the array elements
OrigArray := ["One", "Two", "Three"];
//Combine the elements in the array into a single string seperated with "|"
JoinedString := Join(OrigArray, "|");
//Now split the string apart and put it in a new array
SplitArray := Split(JoinedString, "|");
```

## Range Data Types

The Range data type is a very useful data type that allows you to store multiple values within a single variable. It is used to store a range within one variable and perform tests to see if another variable falls within that range. However, you can't just store any values in this variable. It must be a group of values with a definite starting and ending point. All values in between are included. Of course, it should go without saying that the starting point and end point must be of the same data type.

To declare a variable as a Range data type, declare it as one of the standard data types and put the Range keyword after the data type. The data types that are allowed to have a related Range data type are NumberVar, CurrencyVar, StringVar, DateTimeVar, DateVar, and TimeVar.

```
Scope datatype Range var;
```

Defining a range uses a variety of different operators. These operators specify the beginning and end of the range. The most basic operator is the To operator. It is placed between the start and end values. Using the To operator means that you want the start and end values to be included as valid members of the range.

```
//Demonstrate creating a range of all the days in a year.
DateVar Range DaysInYear;
DaysInYear := Date(#1/1/2002#) To Date(#12/31/2002#);
```

A variation of the To operator is to use it with the underscore character. Placing the underscore on one side of the To operator states that you want all values leading up to that constant to be included, but you don't want the constant specified to be included. The underscore can be placed on either side, or both sides.

The following example demonstrates creating a range with all the days in a month. We only want to do so using the first day of the month in our range. The date 2/1/2002 won't be included in our range. Instead, the last day of the month just prior to it will be included.

```
DateVar Range ExemptionPeriod;
ExemptionPeriod:= Date(#1/1/2002#) To_ Date(#2/1/2002#);
```

By placing the underscore on the right side of the To, then the end date won't be included in the range. The range of valid dates for this formula is from 1/1/2002 thru (and including) 1/31/2002.

When you want to find out if a field or variable is included within a specified range, use the In operator.

```
If {Employee.HireDate} IN ExemptionPeriod Then
    True
Else
    False;
```

Crystal syntax has many predefined date range constants that can be used in your report. These are commonly used to filter out records that have dates that don't fall within the specified range. Table 7-3 lists the predefined date ranges and specifies which dates are considered to be included. Many of these constants use today's date to determine one of the end points of the range. You can tell the report to use a date other than the system date by setting the PrintDate property. This is done by selecting the menu options Report > Set Print Date and Time. Be warned that the PrintDate is saved with the report and will be the same even if you print the report in the future.

**Table 7-4. Predefined Date Range Constants**

| Name | Description |
| --- | --- |
| AllDatesToToday | Includes all days prior to, and including today. |
| AllDatesToYesterday | Includes all days prior to today. Today is excluded. |
| AllDatesFromToday | Includes every day in the future, including today. |
| AllDatesFromTomorrow | Includes every day in the future. Today is excluded. |
| Aged0To30Days, Aged31To60Days, Aged61To90Days | Groups dates in 4 blocks of 30 days prior to today. Today's date is included in the Aged0To30Days range. |
| Calendar1stQtr, | Groups dates in blocks of 3 months each. The first date is Jan 1 |

| Calendar2ndQtr, Calendar3rdQtr, Calendar4thQtr | of the current year. |
|---|---|
| Calendar1stHalf, Calendar2ndHalf | Start: Jan 1 of the current year thru June 30. End: July 1 of the current year thru December 31. |
| Last7Days | Start: The six days prior to today. End: Today. |
| Last4WeeksToSun | Start: The first Monday of the four weeks prior to last Sunday. End: Last Sunday. Note: Does not include the days after the last Sunday thru today. |
| LastFullWeek | Start: The Sunday of the last full week. End: The Saturday of the last full week. Note: Does not include the days after Saturday thru today. |
| LastFullMonth | Start: The first day of last month. End: The last day of last month. |
| MonthToDate | Start: The first day of this month. End: Today. |
| Next30Days, Next31To60Days, Next61To90Days, Next91To365Days | Groups dates in 4 blocks of 30 days after today. Today's date is included in the Next30Days range. |
| Over90Days | Includes all days that are older than 90 days from the report date. |
| WeekToDateFromSun | Start: Last Sunday. End: Today. |
| YearToDate | Start: Jan 1 of the current year. End: Today. |

# Conditional Structures

Conditional structures provide you with a way of testing one or more variables to see if they meet a certain condition. This could be testing if they are equal to a certain value or are within a range of values. If the test succeeds, then a code block is executed. If the test fails, then a different code block is executed. Since there are many different times where you will want to do this, Crystal syntax provides you with a lot of options to match your circumstance. Each has its own benefits and drawbacks that you need to consider when deciding which to use. The conditional structures are the If statement and the Select Case statement.

The If statement tests a condition and performs one action if the condition is true and another action if it's false. The code after the Then keyword is executed if the test succeeds. The code after the Else keyword is executed if the test returns false. Crystal syntax also supports the Else If statement.

Crystal syntax does not have an End If statement. It considers the entire If block a single statement. Put the line terminator after the Else block to terminate it. The Else If keyword is actually two words.

If there is more than one statement within a code block, enclose the statements within parentheses and use the semicolon to terminate each statement. If you don't put parentheses about all the statements in the code block, Crystal Reports terminates the If statement after the first statement.

```
If condition1 Then
    ...code...
Else If condition2 Then
    (
    ...code...;
    ...code...;
    )
Else
    ...code;
```

Here are some actual examples using Crystal syntax.

```
//Test if a field is greater than a number
If {Employee.HoursWorked} > 40 Then
    True
Else
    False;
//Use parentheses to perform multiple statements for each result
Global BooleanVar PayOvertime;
Global BooleanVar PayDoubleTime;
Global NumberVar PayRate;
If {Employee.HoursWorked} > 50 Then
(
    PayDoubleTime := True;
    PayRate := {Employee.PayRate} * 2.0;
)
```

```
Else If {Employee.HoursWorked} > 40 Then
(
    PayOvertime := True;
    PayRate := {Employee.PayRate} * 1.5;
)
Else
(
    PayOvertime := False;
    PayRate := {Employee.PayRate};
)
```

When you have to compare a single value to multiple conditions, this can result in a lot of If statements nested within each other. Rather than next If statements, you can replace the entire If structure with a single Select Case statement. The Select Case statement lets you test a field against multiple conditions and execute a block of code when a condition matches. Each condition has a separate code block associated with it.

In Crystal syntax, the Select Case statement is built by first typing the keyword Select followed by the variable name you want to test. After that, you list each case block. A case block consists of the keyword Case followed by the condition to test and terminated with a colon. The next series of lines are the lines to execute if the condition matches. You can list multiple conditions for a single Case statement by separating each condition with a comma. If none of the Case statements are true, then the code in the Default block is executed. Finish a Case block with two semicolons. The following code block is a template for how to fill in a Select statement.

```
Select var
    Case condition1:
        ...code...
    Case condition1, condition2:
        ...code...
    Default:
        ...code...
```

Demonstrate assigning a fiscal year starting in July.

```
Select Month({Journal.TransactionDate})
    Case 7, 8, 9:
        1
    Case 10, 11, 12:
        2
    Case 1, 2, 3:
        3
    Case 4, 5, 6:
        4;;
```

The next example demonstrates testing a value across a range of values

```
//Demonstrate calculating a volume price discount
NumberVar UnitsSold := 2000;
NumberVar Price := 5;
Select UnitsSold
Case (1 To_ 1000):
   Price
Case (1000 To_ 5000):
   Price * .95
Case Is >= 5000:
   Price * .90;;
```

Note that the last line uses the Is operator in the condition. This is used when you want to use one of the comparison operators (>, <. >=, etc.)

# Conditional Functions

Conditional functions let you evaluate different conditions and return a value based upon the result. These are very similar to the conditional structures If Then and Select because both allow you to evaluate different conditions and perform some action. Conditional functions are different in that they evaluate all the conditions and return a value using only one line of code. Conditional structures like the If Then and Select Case statement need multiple lines of code to evaluate a condition and return a value.

Conditional functions have another benefit in that since they return a value, they can be used within another function! This gives you the ability to create a function that performs its operations using a number that changes depending upon certain conditions.

Let's use an example to try to help illustrate it. Say you have an If statement that evaluates a condition and returns the result. This number is later used in another calculation. To make this work, there would have to be a function just for the If statement and this function would be called elsewhere in the report. You can replace this code with a single IIF() function (discussed next) that evaluates those conditions within the function and returns the value for use in the function. Everything is cleanly written with one line of code. An example that demonstrates how this works is within the discussion of the IIF() function.

Although conditional functions sound pretty good, they do have a drawback. If you get carried away with their use, your code will be harder to read and maintain. For example, an IIF() function is good at replacing a single IF statement. But if you want to replace a nested If statement, you will have to write nested IIF() functions. Although this will compile and run, it can be pretty hard for you or another person to read and understand. Use caution when deciding what is appropriate for the task at hand.

Being able to test conditions and return a result within a single function is very powerful. This section describes three conditional functions: IIF(), Choose(), and Switch().

# The IIF() Function

The IIF() function is a shortcut for the standard If statement. Its purpose is to put both the True and False actions on the same line. It consists of three parameters. The first parameter is the test condition. If the test condition is True, the function returns whatever is in the second parameter. If the test condition is False, then the function returns whatever is in the third parameter. This function can return any data type except for an array.

Although the IIF() function is convenient because you can condense a multi-line If statement into one line, there are two restrictions. The first is that the second and third parameters can only be a constant, a variable or a function. You can't put a statement or code block within these parameters. The second restriction is that both parameters must be the same data type.

The syntax for the IIF() function is as follows:

```
var := IIF(condition, true_result, false_result);
```

I frequently use the IIF() function when concatenating strings together and one of the strings is optional. Since it is a function, I make it return a string. The following example creates a person's full name. If the middle initial wasn't entered into the database then we want to make sure we don't insert a "." inappropriately.

```
//Demonstrate using the IIF() function to create a user's full name
StringVar FullName;
FullName := {Person.FirstName} & " " & IIF({Person.MI}<>"", {Person.MI} & ". ", "") &
{Person.LastName);
```

This IIF() function tests whether the middle name exists, and if it does, it adds it to the string with the proper formatting.

For purposes of comparing conditional functions with conditional structures, the following example is the same except that it uses an If Then statement.

```
//Demonstrate using the If Then statement to create a user's full name
StringVar FullName;
StringVar MI;
If {Person.MI}<>"" Then
    MI := {Person.MI} & ". "
Else
    MI := "";
FullName := {Person.FirstName} & " " & MI & " " & {Person.LastName};
```

This example shows that using the If Then statement requires more coding. However, it does have the benefit of being easier to understand. It's a matter of personal preference as far as which one you choose to use. Personally, I always choose the IIF() function because it is an easy function to read and quick to type in. However, if the IIF() function were complex, then using it might decrease the readability of your code.

---
**Caution**
---

Do not use the IIF() function to check for Divide By Zero errors. For example, the following code will cause an error:

```
IIF({Emp.NumberSales}<>0, {Emp.TotalSales}/{Emp.NumberSales}, 0);
```

The IIF() function executes every argument before returning a result. In this example, even if the number of sales is zero, the function will still attempt to divide the total sales by the number of sales and give you an error. You should use the standard If-Then statement when trying to handle any possible errors that could occur in a formula.

# The Choose() Function

The Choose() function returns a value chosen from a list of values. The value returned is determined by an index that is passed to the function. This function is like a shortcut for the If Then statement and the Case statement. You can use it when the range of possible values is relatively small and sequential.

The Choose() function works by passing it an index number as the first parameter and a list of return values after it. The index number is used to determine which value is returned. The first position in the list of return values is indexed at 1. For example, if the index number is 3 and there are five values in the list, then the third item would be returned. This function can return any data type except for an array. As expected, each item in the list must be of the same data type.

If the index is a value that is greater than the number of items passed, then the last item in the list is returned. For example, if there are five items in the list and the index number is 10 instead, then the fifth item would be returned because it is last in the list.

The syntax for the Choose() function is as follows:

```
Var := Choose(index, value1, value2, value3, ...);
```

An example of displaying a person's place in a race using text is as follows. The range of possible values is 1 to the number of participants. This function will only consider the first three positions. Everyone ranked after that is given a generic classification.

```
StringVar Position;
Position := Choose({Race.Position}, "First Place", "Second Place", "Third Place", "Sorry, you
were not one of the top three finishers.");
```

## The Switch() Function

The Switch() function is a slight variation of the Choose() function. The Switch() function uses pairs of test conditions and return values. The first parameter is an expression to test and the second parameter is a result value that is returned if the expression is true. This is repeated with every two parameters being in one group.

The syntax for the Switch() function is as follows:

```
Var := Switch(condition1, result1, condition2, result2, ....);
```

This function can return any data type except for an array. The data types of each result must be the same.

What makes this unique from the If Then and Select statements is that every parameter is evaluated before a result is returned from the function. Even if the first parameter is true, all the remaining parameters are still evaluated. This can have good or bad consequences depending upon your needs. The result can be bad because there could be a performance issue if you are passing it time-intensive functions. It could also result in an error being raised if every condition wasn't meant to be evaluated (e.g. divide by zero errors).

Executing every line can be good if you want to force various functions to be called prior to returning a value. For example, it can perform a list of financial functions prior to returning a value.

# Looping Structures

Looping structures let you execute a block of code multiple times. The number of times this code block is executed depends upon the type of loop used and what happens within the code block. The looping structures covered are: For Next, While, and a variety of Do loops.

## For Next Loop

The For Next loop has the syntax of using the For statement followed by a variable and the start and ending range. You have to decide in advance how many times the code block gets executed.

The default loop increment is 1. Use the Step keyword to define a new increment. Terminate the For block using the Next statement. Putting the variable name after the Next statement is optional. You can prematurely exit the loop by using the Exit For statement.

Crystal syntax uses := to assign the loop range and it has the Do keyword at the end of the line. Rather than terminating the loop with the Next keyword, it requires parentheses to surround the code block.

```
For var := start To end Step increment Do
(
    ...code...
    If condition Then
       Exit For
    End If
)
```

The next example uses a loop to summarize all the salary balances that were stored in a global array (which was populated elsewhere in the report).

```
//Demonstrate looping to calculate total salaries
NumberVar TotalSalary;
NumberVar ArrayIndex;
Global NumberVar Array Salaries;
For ArrayIndex:=1 to UBound(Salaries) Do
(
    TotalSalary := TotalSalary + Salaries[ArrayIndex];
);
```

# While and Do Loops

The While and Do loops all have the standard syntax. The While keyword is used to continue looping as long as the condition evaluates to True. The While block is terminated with a Wend statement. The Do loops are terminated with a Loop statement. The Until keyword is used to continue looping when a condition evaluates to False. You can exit a Do loop with an Exit Do statement.

Crystal syntax uses parentheses to define the code block.

Code template for While...Do:

```
While true_condition Do
(
    ...code...
)
```

Code template for Do...While:

```
Do
(
    ...code...
) While true_condition
```

The next example takes an array of names (populated elsewhere in the program) and uses a While loop to combine the names into a single string.

```
//Combine all names from an array into a single string
```

```
Global StringVar Names;
StringVar NameList;
NumberVar Counter := 1;
While Names[Counter] <> "" Do
(
    NameList := NameList & Names[Counter] & " ";
    Counter := Counter + 1;
);
//Return the name list
NameList;
```

# Conditional Expressions

When performing actions based upon how a condition evaluates, there are numerous ways to build the condition. For example, when writing an If statement, you can compare a field to a constant using a variety of relational operators and you can join multiple conditions using Boolean operators. This section shows you all the ways you can evaluate fields and variables to see whether they match a certain value or a range of values.

You can test against a single constant or variable using the standard relational operators: <, >, <=, >=, =, <>.

You can compare multiple expressions using the Boolean operators And, Or, Not. The And operator takes two expressions and states that both expressions must be true for the condition to return True. The Or operator takes two expressions and states that only one of the two expressions need to be true for it to return True. The Not operator only uses one expression and makes it the opposite. If the expression is true then it returns False. If the expression is false then it returns True.

The Not operator should always use parentheses around the conditional expression. This makes it clear to Crystal Reports what expression should be negated. This applies even if you are only negating a single expression. For example, the next two lines of code have completely different results.

```
//Reverse the result of the two comparisons
Not (A>B And C>D)
//Reverse the result of only the first comparison
Not (A>B) And C>D
```

A few operators that might be new to you are Xor, Eqv and Imp. Eqv is for logical equivalence. It determines when the two expressions are the same. It returns True when both are true or both are false. If they are not the same, it returns False. The syntax is as follows:

```
exp1 Eqv exp2
```

Xor is for logical exclusion. It determines when the two expressions are different. It returns True if one is true and the other false. If both expressions are the same (either both are true or both are false), then it returns False. The syntax is as follows:

exp1 Xor exp2

Imp is for logical implication. If the first expression is true, it implies that the second expression will also be true. If the second expression is also true, Imp returns True. If the second expression is false, Imp returns False because it didn't meet what was implied. On the other hand, if the first expression is false, nothing is implied and the result will be always be True. Thus, there is only one instance where Imp ever returns False: when the first expression is true and the second expression is false. All other circumstances return True. The syntax is as follows:

exp1 Imp exp2

The Is operator is used with the Select statement when you want to use the relational operators (e.g. >, <, etc.). An example demonstrating this was already shown in the discussion on the Select statement.

The In operator is used for testing if a field or variable exists as an element in an array or if it falls within a range of values. For more information, see the previous sections Array Data Types and Range Data Types.

# Evaluation Time Defaults

Chapter 1 discussed the Two-Pass Report Processing model. Knowing how this model works is especially important when writing formulas. The type of formula determines when it is processed. Where you place a formula on a report and the functionality within that formula also affects when the formula is evaluated and whether it returns the expected value or not. A formula can be placed on any section of your report, but you should plan this in advance so that you can guarantee the proper results. To determine where to place a formula, you need to know the rules that Crystal Reports uses to evaluate functions. The following list shows the rules that are applied.

- A formula that only references variables (it doesn't use database fields or group/summary fields) is evaluated before any records are read. It is only evaluated one time and its value is saved for the duration of the report.

- Formulas using database fields are evaluated while records are being read. It is re-evaluated every time a new record is read from the data source.

- Formulas using group fields, summary fields, or page related fields (e.g. the page number) are evaluated after the records are read and while the report is being printed.

- When there are multiple formulas within a section, you can't determine which formula will be called first. This is because formulas within the same section are not evaluated in any particular order. The exception to this rule is in the next bullet point.

- Crystal Reports does evaluate formulas based upon the order that they were added to the section. As you add formulas to the section, Crystal Reports adds each formula to an 'internal list' and processes each formula based upon its order in the list. The problem with putting this into practical use is that you have no way of knowing which formula was added first. Unless you have a photographic memory of when you added every formula to every section, it's impossible to use this rule on a regular basis. If you only have two formulas in a section then you could use this rule, but anything more than that and you start leaving a lot to chance.

There are times when the default rules listed above will not give you the results you desire. For example, there may be a situation where you have four formulas in the same section and two formulas rely upon one other to be called first. According to the default rules listed above, you know that it is difficult to determine which one will be called first. You need some way to force one formula to be called before the other. Fortunately, Crystal Reports lets you override the default rules to fit your particular situation. There are four keywords that let you set when a formula will be evaluated: BeforePrintingRecords, WhileReadingRecords, WhilePrintingRecords, and EvaluateAfter. The keyword is added to the beginning of a formula to force it to be evaluated at a time that is different than its default behavior. These keywords are listed in Table 7-5.

**Table 7-5. Evaluation Time Keywords**

| Evaluation Time | Description |
| --- | --- |
| BeforeReadingRecords | Evaluate the formula before any database records are read. |
| WhileReadingRecords | Evaluate the formula while reading the database records. |
| WhilePrintingRecords | Evaluate the formula while printing the database records. |
| EvaluateAfter(formula) | Evaluate after another function has been evaluated. |

If a formula isn't returning the expected results and you debugged the logic enough to feel confident about it, there is a good chance it's because of when the formula is being evaluated. If you are trying to debug a formula, then you have to take many things into consideration: does the formula only use variables; should the formula be put in a different section; is the formula being evaluated while reading records or while printing records; does the report use a grouping section that may be affecting the order of evaluation? This is a lot to think about.

You can cut down on the amount of time spent debugging formulas if you start out by following some general guidelines. The remainder of this section gives guidelines and examples to consider when writing your formulas. If you're having problems getting a formula to work, then you should come back to this section as a refresher and see if any of these guidelines would help you.

Place formulas that reset variables to their default value in the Report Header, Page Header or Group Header section. This ensures that they are called before the formulas in the detail section are evaluated. For example, if you have a variable that prints the row number on a page and you want the first row on each page to be 1, then reset the variable in the Page Header. If a variable sums data within a single group, reset the variable in the Group Header section so that it gets reset with each new group printed.

Be careful when using formulas that only have variables in them without any database fields. They only get calculated one time prior to reading the records. If the formula is cumulative in nature, you need to force the evaluation time to be WhileReadingRecords. If the report uses groups, then you should use the WhilePrintingRecords keyword.

The keyword BeforeReadingRecords can't be used with formulas that have database fields or grouping/summary fields in them.

When you place multiple formulas within the same section, you can't assume the order that they are executed in. If you need one formula to be evaluated before another formula (its result is used in other formulas) then put the EvaluateAfter keyword in the dependent formula. The following example shows how this is used. This formula relies upon the formula ParseName to take the {Customer.Name} field and parse the first name and last name out of it. The values are put into the global variables FirstName and LastName. This example formula returns the LastName variable so that it can be displayed on the report. The @ParseName formula isn't shown here.

```
EvaluateAfter({@ParseName});
Global StringVar LastName;
LastName;
```

Summary calculations are performed while printing records. They can only do calculations on formulas that were evaluated beforehand (i.e. while reading records). Thus, a formula that uses WhilePrintingRecords can't have summary functions performed on it.

Of course, these guidelines won't be able to prevent every problem from happening, but they are here to help give you a start in the right direction.

To illustrate the importance of using the proper keyword in a formula, let's look at an example that shows you each stage of writing a formula and how the output is affected by the evaluation time keyword.

The example report is a customer report that uses the Xtreme.mdb database. The report has the first column as the row number. The row number is tracked using a variable called

RowNumber and it is placed in the Details Section. You would assume that it will be called every time a detail row is printed. The formula is as follows:

```
Global NumberVar RowNumber;
RowNumber := RowNumber + 1;
```

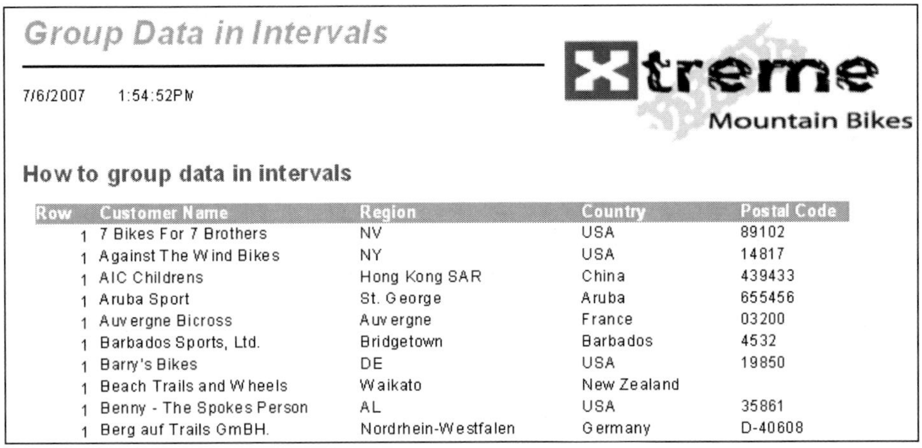

**Group Data in Intervals**

7/6/2007    1:54:52PM

**Mountain Bikes**

**How to group data in intervals**

| Row | Customer Name | Region | Country | Postal Code |
|-----|---------------|--------|---------|-------------|
| 1 | 7 Bikes For 7 Brothers | NV | USA | 89102 |
| 1 | Against The Wind Bikes | NY | USA | 14817 |
| 1 | AIC Childrens | Hong Kong SAR | China | 439433 |
| 1 | Aruba Sport | St. George | Aruba | 655456 |
| 1 | Auvergne Bicross | Auvergne | France | 03200 |
| 1 | Barbados Sports, Ltd. | Bridgetown | Barbados | 4532 |
| 1 | Barry's Bikes | DE | USA | 19850 |
| 1 | Beach Trails and Wheels | Waikato | New Zealand | |
| 1 | Benny - The Spokes Person | AL | USA | 35861 |
| 1 | Berg auf Trails GmBH. | Nordrhein-Westfalen | Germany | D-40608 |

**Figure 7-1. Row Number example output with same row number.**

Notice that all the row numbers are 1. This is because the default rule states that if a formula only has variables in it, then it is evaluated before any records are read. Even though this formula is placed in the detail section, it only gets evaluated once and the value never changes.

To fix this problem, use the keyword WhileReadingRecords in the formula.

```
WhileReadingRecords;
Global NumberVar RowNumber;
RowNumber := RowNumber + 1;
```

Figure 7-2 shows that the row number is now accurate because the formula is evaluated every time a record is read.

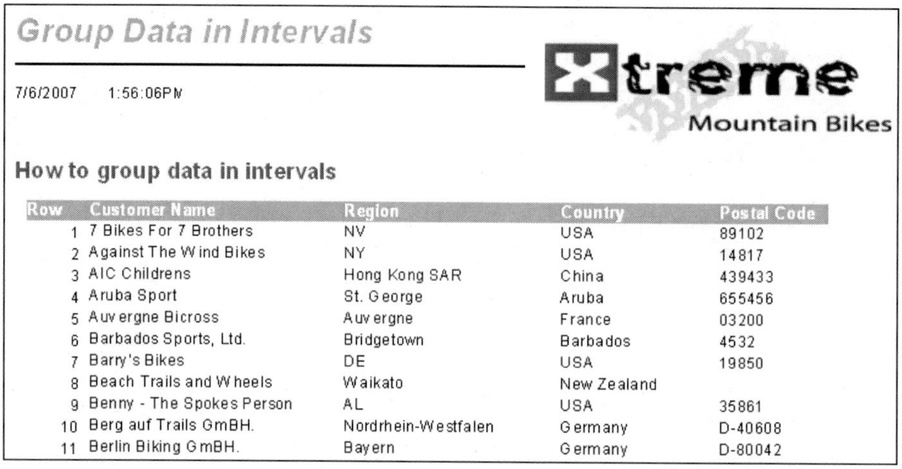

**Figure 7-2. Row Number example output with correct row numbers.**

Let's modify the example so that the report uses a grouping section based on the country name.

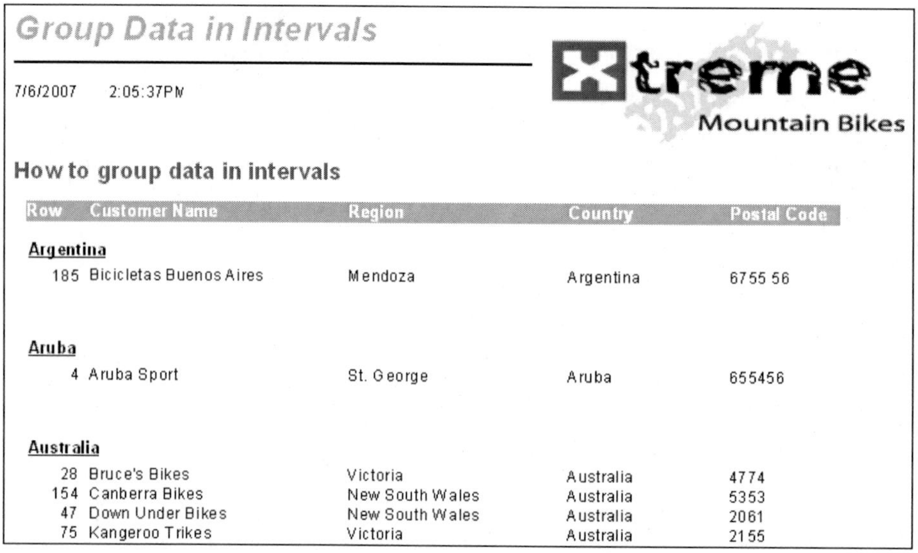

**Figure 7-3. Row Number example output with grouping.**

Figure 7-3 shows that the report now groups by country and uses a group header. Unfortunately, this change has introduced a bug in the report because the row numbers are now out of order. This is because the row number is being calculated while the records are being read. After being read, the rows get sorted based upon their group and the row numbers get reordered during this process. To fix this, change the formula so that the row number is being evaluated while the records are being printed and not when being read.

```
WhilePrintingRecords;
Global NumberVar RowNumber;
RowNumber := RowNumber + 1;
```

Figure 7-4 shows that the row number is now accurate.

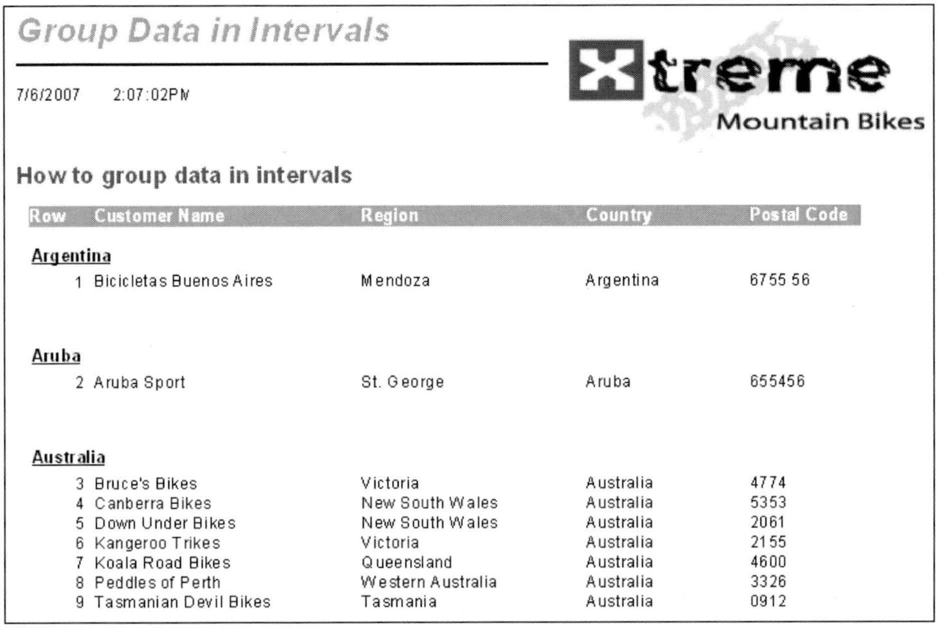

Group Data in Intervals

7/6/2007 2:07:02PM

Xtreme Mountain Bikes

How to group data in intervals

| Row | Customer Name | Region | Country | Postal Code |
|---|---|---|---|---|
| **Argentina** | | | | |
| 1 | Bicicletas Buenos Aires | Mendoza | Argentina | 6755 56 |
| **Aruba** | | | | |
| 2 | Aruba Sport | St. George | Aruba | 655456 |
| **Australia** | | | | |
| 3 | Bruce's Bikes | Victoria | Australia | 4774 |
| 4 | Canberra Bikes | New South Wales | Australia | 5353 |
| 5 | Down Under Bikes | New South Wales | Australia | 2061 |
| 6 | Kangeroo Trikes | Victoria | Australia | 2155 |
| 7 | Koala Road Bikes | Queensland | Australia | 4600 |
| 8 | Peddles of Perth | Western Australia | Australia | 3326 |
| 9 | Tasmanian Devil Bikes | Tasmania | Australia | 0912 |

**Figure 7-4. Row numbers are correct with grouping.**

This series of examples illustrates that putting an Evaluation Time keyword at the beginning of a formula has a drastic effect on the formula's value.

# Advanced Tutorials

When using conditional formatting to customize report output, the typical report property uses one of the simple data types to store its value. Many properties use the Boolean constants True or False to turn them on or off. For example, properties such as Suppress, Italic, and Keep Object Together uses True to enable the property and False to disable the property. But there are certain properties that use pre-defined constants to set their values. You have to be aware of when to use these pre-defined constants so that your formulas return the correct data. Otherwise the Formula Workshop returns an error when you try to save it.

As an example of using the proper data type, Figure 7-5 shows the Section Editor dialog box. All the properties displayed here use checkboxes. These properties are either checked or unchecked, and formulas that are associated with these properties have to return True or

False. As expected, returning True is the same as a checked box, and returning False is the same as an unchecked box.

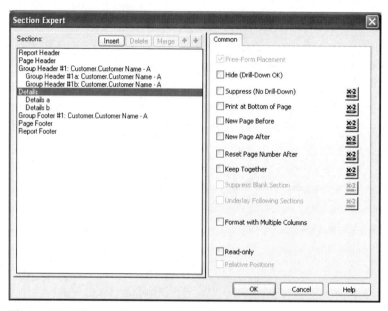

**Figure 7-5. The section expert window.**

As a more varied example, Figure 7-6 shows the Border tab of the Format Editor dialog box. This dialog box not only uses checkboxes, but it uses some new values you haven't seen yet: line styles and colors.

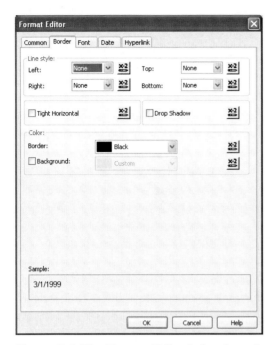

**Figure 7-6. The Format Editor's border tab.**

The values for the line style and color are Crystal Reports predefined constants. The line style property can have values such as crDashedLine, crNoLine, etc. The color property can have values such as crAqua, crYellow, crRed, etc.

There are two ways to determine the predefined constants used with a property. The first and easiest way is when you open the Formula Workshop, it lists all the predefined constants as comments in the code. The following code excerpt is what you see when modifying the Line Style property of the border. It shows you every possible predefined constant that the formula can return.

```
// This conditional formatting formula must return
//one of the following Line Style Constants:
// crSingleLine
// crDoubleLine
// crDashedLine
// crDottedLine
// crNoLine
```

A second way of determining the predefined constants for a certain property is to look in the Function Tree. When you open the Formula Editor, the predefined constants for the current property are listed. This list is dynamic and won't show constants for other properties. For example, if you are modifying a line style property, the Function Tree will show the different line styles, but won't list any colors. This is illustrated in Figure 7-7.

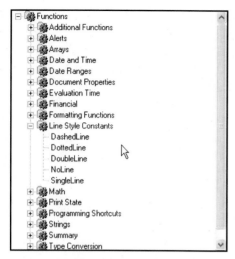

**Figure 7-7. The Function Tree for line styles.**

If you are modifying a color property, it will show the available colors, but no line styles. This is illustrated in Figure 7-8.

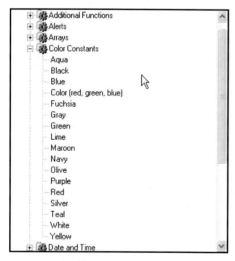

**Figure 7-8. The Function Tree for colors.**

### Note

If the Function Tree doesn't list the Color Constants or if the Formula Workshop doesn't have any constants listed, then use True and False to turn the property on or off.

## Using the Default Attribute and Current Field Value

The value assigned to a property in design mode is called the property's default attribute. When assigning a formula to that property, the default value is overridden by what is in the formula. There are many times when a formula is only used to specify what happens in a unique circumstance (e.g. an inventory item being out of stock) and you don't want the formula to override the default value each time. You want the default property value to be left unchanged. To use the current property value without overriding it, return the DefaultAttribute keyword.

For example, let's set the Inventory On Hand field to be red if its value is less than the minimum quantity. Otherwise, use the default attribute to leave it the color specified in the Format Editor. You can use a formula like the following:

```
If {Inventory.OnHand} < {InventoryItems.MinimumQty} Then
    crRed
Else
    DefaultAttribute;
```

## Tutorial 7-1. Printing Checkboxes

Displaying checkboxes on a report presents a new challenge. Checkboxes represent when a Boolean value is either true or false. But Crystal Reports doesn't have a way to print checkboxes. There are other ways to display a Boolean constant. For example, you can display the words Yes/No or True/False by right-clicking on the field and selecting Format field. The dialog box displays a drop-down box that lets you select how you want the data to be displayed (Yes/No, True/False, etc.).

Displaying Boolean values as a checkbox requires a little more creativity. You have to trick Crystal Reports into printing checkboxes by switching to the Wingdings font. There are a variety of interesting characters in the Wingdings font. But five of them can be used for displaying checkboxes. Figure 7-9 shows some of the Wingdings characters available.

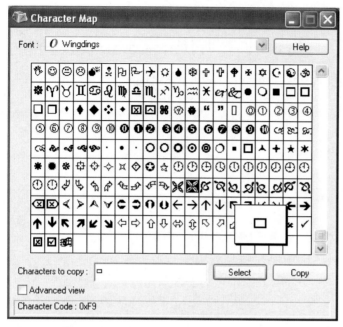

**Figure 7-9. Wingdings control characters.**

In the last two rows are the checkboxes. There are four types to choose from as well as an empty checkbox. To use these characters in your report you have to create a formula that uses the ASCII code for the checkbox you want to display and return the appropriate character. The only problem with this idea is that it is very difficult to determine the correct ASCII code. In previous versions of MS Windows, you could open the Character Map and it showed you the ASCII code at the bottom. You could easily type this number into your formulas. But with Windows XP, they stopped showing the ASCII code and now they only show the Hexadecimal equivalent. I don't know why Microsoft implemented this "feature" because it's very difficult to convert the hexadecimal number to a decimal. So rather than make you figure out the math, I'm going to give you a cheat-sheet to use for your reports. Table 7-6 shows each checkbox and its ASCII equivalent.

**Table 7-6. The Wingdings checkboxes and their ASCII equivalents.**

| Checkbox | ASCII Value |
| --- | --- |
| ☐ | 168 |
| ✘ | 251 |
| ✓ | 252 |

| | |
|---|---|
| ☒ | 253 |
| ☑ | 254 |

To display a checkbox on the report, create a new formula field and insert the following formula.

```
If {Table.Field} = True Then
   //Display the checkbox of your choice here
   Chr(254)
Else
   //Display empty checkbox
   Chr(168);
```

This formula tests a field to see if it is True. If so, it returns the control character 254 (a checked box). If it is false, it returns the control character 168 (an empty checkbox). Save the formula and close the Formula Workshop.

Drag this formula from the Field Explorer onto the report. Finally, change the font to be Wingdings by right-clicking on the field and selecting Format Field. Click on the Font tab and use the dropdown list to select the Wingdings font. Save the report and preview it to see the checkbox displayed.

I recommend using a font that is two point sizes larger than the font size of the rest of the report text. The Wingdings font is slightly smaller than regular text and increasing its size makes it easier to see. You should experiment with the font size to see what suits your tastes.

| Note |
|---|

The Wingdings font has many unusual characters. You can use them in your report to print interesting graphics. For example, you can print a telephone graphic in the header of the phone number column and an envelope in the email column. You could print a time bomb on a row that requires immediate attention. Getting creative with the Wingdings font lets you have a little fun with a report and still keep a professional image.

# Advanced Formatting Techniques

Once you've mastered the basics of creating reports, it's time to learn some of the finer points of report design. Crystal Reports gives you numerous formatting options for printing report sections for specialized purposes. For example, you can create specialized reports such as labels or multi-column reports. You also have the option of creating multiple sections within a report and format each section individually. This one feature gives you an almost unlimited number of ways to make a report fit different scenarios and customize it for individual users. The first part of this chapter covers how to format Sections to create professional reports for any circumstance. You are given lots of creative examples of how to use Sections in real world reports.

Crystal Reports also makes your life easier by using report templates to quickly format a report in a certain way. You can use existing reports as the template for new reports. This creates consistency among all your reports without requiring any work on your part. You can also create report templates that are designed solely for the purpose of being used as a template and are never printed as a separate report.

Report alerts make it easy to highlight records that trigger special circumstances. The user is immediately alerted when data falls outside of acceptable ranges. By combining conditional formatting with report alerts, you can make a report that gives the user the option of viewing the alert records in a separate tab or having the detail data reflect which records should be reviewed.

# Sections

Sections are used to determine where report objects appear on a report. Each section has a different purpose and different rules that determine when and where it should appear on a report. Certain sections only appear at the beginning or end of a report and other sections are only used when grouping data. We already discussed each type of section in Chapter 2, but here is a quick refresher. The Report Header/Footer sections appear on the first and last pages respectively. The Page Header/Footer sections appear at the top and bottom of a page respectively. The Group Header/Footer appears at the beginning and end of a group. The Details section appears once for every record displayed on the report.

Although each section follows certain rules, there are many options available for customizing a section so that the report comes out just right. We'll look at the different formatting options available as well as how to add sub-sections to a report for greater customization. Let's start by looking at the basic formatting options available for each section.

# Formatting Sections

Report sections have many formatting options. You can hide a section, force it to print at the bottom of the page, force a page break afterwards and many other options. Creative use of these formatting options gives you control over how the report looks.

The Section Expert dialog box controls the formatting of each section. As shown in Figure 8-1, it lists each section on the left-hand side and the formatting properties on the right-hand side.

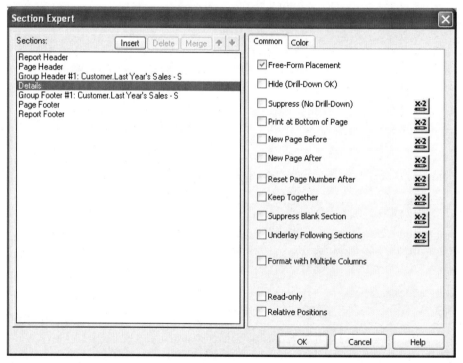

Figure 8-1. The Section Expert dialog box.

The section expert is accessed three different ways. The first way is to select the menu items Report > Section Expert. The second way is to right-click anywhere on the report and select Section Expert from the pop-up menu. The final way is by clicking the Section Expert button on the Expert Tools toolbar. The Section Expert button is shown in Figure 8-2.

**Figure 8-2. Section Expert button.**

The Section Expert, shown in Figure 8-1, lists every section in the report and the formatting options available. The formatting options are represented by checkboxes because they are either enabled or disabled. Beside each option is a Formula Workshop button that uses conditional formatting to set the property value based upon a formula. This gives you flexibility for setting when a formatting option is turned on because the formula can use data from the record currently being printed. Every time a section is printed, the formula is evaluated and its result determines whether the formatting option should be applied. This was described in more detail in Chapter 5.

When selecting the section from the list on the left, the formatting options on the right change depending upon which section was selected. The applicable properties are enabled and the other properties are grayed out. The list of formatting options doesn't change (for the most part), but you are prevented from choosing the ones that don't apply. Table 8-1 lists the different formatting options for sections.

**Table 8-1. The formatting options for sections.**

| Formatting Option | Description |
| --- | --- |
| Free-Form Placement | Allows you to place report objects anywhere in the section without being confined to the positioning of the grid lines. |
| Hide (Drill-Down OK) | Doesn't show the section, but allows the user to drill-down into the data. |
| Suppress (No Drill-Down) | Doesn't show the section. Drill-down is not allowed. |
| Print at Bottom of Page | Force the section to always print at the bottom of the page. |
| New Page Before | Force a page break before the section prints. |
| New Page After | Force a page break after the section prints. |
| Reset Page Number After | Reset the page number counter back to 1 after the section prints. |
| Keep Together | Keep the section together on the same page. |
| Suppress Blank Section | If there is no data in the section, do not print it. |
| Underlay Following Sections | Print the current section on top of the following sections. Proper alignment is critical so that objects don't overlap each other. |

| | |
|---|---|
| Format With Multiple Columns | Creates mailing labels and newspaper column style reports. This is only listed for the Details section. |
| Read-Only | Locks the positioning and formatting of all report objects in that section. You can't move the objects or modify their properties. |
| Relative Positions | Sets objects within a section to keep their horizontal position relative to a grid object. If the grid object grows to the right, the other objects will shift accordingly. Primarily used with Cross-Tab reports. |
| Reserve Minimum Page Footer | Maximizes the amount of space available for printing report details by minimizing the amount of space reserved for the Page Footer. |

## Hiding and Suppressing Sections

Hiding a section is used for drilling-down on detail records. This presents the user with a much smaller report because the groups only show summary information. They can look at the detail information by double clicking on the group header. This creates a new tab in the viewer with the detail information being displayed inside.

Suppressing a section is similar to hiding a section, except that suppressing the section doesn't let you drill-down into the data. Of course, this leads to the question that if you don't want the user to see the information then why did you add the section? Suppressing sections is usually used in conjunction with conditional formatting. The Formula Workshop is used to turn this option on or off depending upon other data that the report has access to. For example, if this is sensitive data, then you would only let administrators see the detail information. All other users would have the detail section suppressed and they would only be able to see the summary information. This effectively lets you use the same report for different users and different purposes.

## Printing Sections at the Bottom of a Page

Printing sections at the bottom of the page is useful when printing reports that are one page long and have summary data listed at the bottom. An example is an invoice where the bottom of the page prints the total amount due. Invoices also print the aging schedule of past due balances at the bottom of the page. Another example is a form letter that requires authorized signatures of certain parties. Printing sections at the bottom of the page is done by adding a group to the report and checking the Print at Bottom of Page option for the Group Footer.

| Note |
| --- |

Although the Details section has the Print at Bottom of Page option available, it has no effect. The detail records always print one after the other from top to bottom.

## Forcing a Page Break

It is very common to want groups to appear by themselves. Data in each group is listed separately from the other groups. Forcing page breaks makes data from each group appear on their own pages. The group is used to identify where one report ends and the next one starts. An example is a report that has to be broken apart and distributed to multiple people.

Page breaks can be forced to occur either before or after a section. Unfortunately, each option has the problem of always printing an extra blank page. If you force a page break before a group header, then the first page of the report is blank. If you force a page break after the group footer, then the last page is blank. The way around this is to use one of two built-in functions in the conditional formula: OnFirstRecord or OnLastRecord. By doing a Boolean Not in the formula, it temporarily turns page breaks off for the section. For example, if you wanted to force a page break after the group footer, use the following formula in the New Page After format option:

Not OnLastRecord

This formula returns True for every record leading up to the last record. Thus, there is always a page break after the group footer. Once the last record is printed, this formula returns False and the option to force a page break is turned off. The last page will not have a page break printed after it.

## Resetting the Page Number

Resetting a page number back to Page 1 makes the page appear as if it is the first page in the report. This is good to use in combination with forcing a page break after a section. For example, for the Group Footer, set the both of the properties New Page After and Reset Page Number After to True. When you distribute the pages of the report to different people, each person will have a report that starts on page 1. They won't know that the pages they received were part of a much larger report that was broken apart.

## Keeping Sections Together

Since it is common to print a lot of data in a section and since it is very hard to control exactly where a section is printed on a page, sections are commonly split across pages. A report can start printing a section at the bottom of the page but not have enough room to print all of it and print the remaining portion of the section on the next page. If it is important that all the information within a section be printed together, check the Keep

Together option. Before the section is printed, it is analyzed to see whether it fits on the page. If it doesn't fit, a page break is forced and the section starts printing at the top of the next page.

When using this formatting option with groups, the report tries to fit the entire group (including the header and footer) onto the page. If the group is larger than one page, a page break is forced and the group gets printed on the next page.

### Suppressing Blank Sections

Printing sections that don't have any data leaves blank rows in the report. This makes a report look unprofessional because of the gaps that seem to randomly occur. To fix this, set the option Suppress Blank Section to skip over sections that don't have any data. This option is used most frequently in conjunction with creating multiple report sections. This is covered in more detail later in the book, "Adding Multiple Sections".

### Underlaying the Following Sections

When formatting a section so that it underlay the following sections, the following sections print on top of it. This has the effect of superimposing one or more sections on top of another section.

Underlaying sections is useful when working with images or charts and the related information is printed beside the image. This concept might be tough to grasp at first, so let's look at two examples. Figure 8-3 shows an employee report with the employee's picture on the left and the employee detail listed next to it. It doesn't use the Underlay Following Sections option.

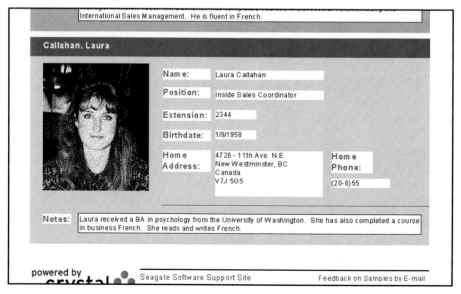

**Figure 8-3. Employee Profile report with photo.**

In Figure 8-3, the data listed next to the employee picture is from the Employee table. It shows the different fields from a single employee record. There is a one-to-one relationship between the employee photo and the employee data.

This example is limited in that the photo can only be printed next to the data within a single employee record. If you wanted to print a photo with multiple detail records next to it, this approach won't work. The next example shows how to fix this problem by underlaying sections.

Figure 8-4 shows the design of an inventory report which lists how many products are on-hand for each inventory item. These items are grouped together by category and a generic picture of each category is displayed.

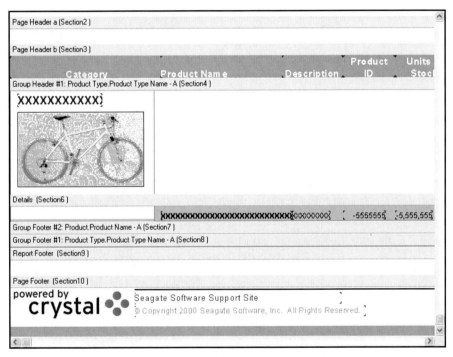

**Figure 8-4. The Inventory report with pictures for each category.**

To create this report, put the photo in the group header section and place it along the left edge of the section. Put the detail fields in the detail section and make sure that all the fields are to the right of the picture. Lastly, turn on the Underlay Following Section format option for the group header.

| Category | Product Name | Description | Product ID | Units Stoc |
|---|---|---|---|---|
| Saddles | Roadster Jr BMX Saddle | youth | 6401 | 75 |
| | Roadster Micro Mtn Saddle | youth | 6402 | 124 |
| | Roadster Mini Mtn Saddle | youth | 6403 | 165 |
| | Vesper Comfort ATB Saddle | mens | 7401 | 41 |
| | Vesper Comfort Ladies Saddle | ladies | 7402 | 69 |
| | Vesper Gelflex ATB Saddle | mens | 7403 | 88 |
| | Vesper Gelflex Ladies Saddle | ladies | 7404 | 97 |

**Figure 8-5. Inventory report using Underlay Following Sections.**

This causes all the group's detail records to be printed on top of the group header. Since the image and the records aren't on the same part of the page, this gives the effect of printing multiple detail records beside a single image.

## Printing a Watermark

Using the underlay feature is useful when you want to print a watermark image on each page. Put the image in the page header and set the Underlay Following Section option on. Everything after the header is printed on top of the watermark image. Be sure to test the image to make certain it isn't too dark. A faint image works best as a watermark because it allows the report text to be easily read.

## Formatting with Multiple Columns/Mailing Labels

The default layout of a report is designed so that each detail record uses the entire width of the page and each row is printed one after the other. Sections aren't designed to only use a partial page width. However, if you want to print mailing labels or a multi-column report, then you need to use sections that are small enough that they can be repeated across the page. Setting the Format With Multiple Columns option does just that.

The Format with Multiple Columns option is only available for the Details section. When selecting this option, a Layout tab appears in the dialog box. This tab lets you set the column width and spacing so that your information is put into multiple columns. You can also set whether the records go down the page first and then to the next column, or go across the page first before going down to the next row. Figure 8-6 shows the options on the Layout tab.

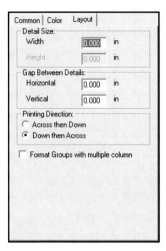

**Figure 8-6. The Layout tab of the Section Editor.**

The only problem with using the Layout tab is that it takes a little experimentation to get the formatting right. Precision is a necessity when printing labels and making a mailing list could take some work. You are much better off using the Mailing Label Report Wizard to create mailing labels. As Figure 8-7 shows, using the Mailing Label Report Wizard lets you pick from a list of standard Avery numbers for the label format.

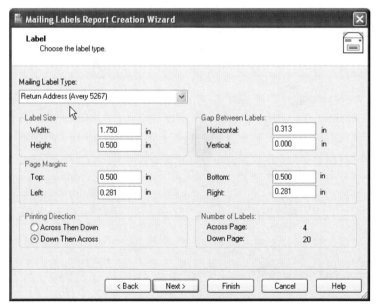

**Figure 8-7. The Mailing Labels Report Creation Wizard.**

Most labels fit into one of the standard Avery formats and unless you are using a custom designed label, you can let Crystal Reports do all the work. This makes it easy to create mailing labels that are printer perfect the first time!

Notice in Figure 8-7 that nowhere on this dialog box is there a property that sets how many columns a report has. This is because Crystal Reports calculates how many columns there are by adding up the label width and label gap to see how many labels will fit. It puts as many labels as possible onto the page. As you adjust the label size, the Number Of Labels section in the bottom right-hand corner changes to tell you how many labels are on each page.

### Caution

After you create a report using the Mailing Label Report Creation Wizard, you cannot go back to the wizard to change the label size. The Mailing Label Report Creation Wizard is only available when creating a new report. Modifying the label format requires using the Layout tab of the Section Expert.

## Adding Multiple Sections

Throughout this book, when different parts of a report were discussed, they were referred to by their section name. For example, when adding an object to be displayed in the header of a group, the portion of the report would be called the Group Header section. But what you weren't told is that each section is actually contained in an Area. Areas let you build more complex reports. Simple reports don't require working with Areas so they weren't mentioned. But in this section, you'll see that Areas are actually a container for one or more sections and you'll see how to use them to create advanced report formatting.

By default, when you create a new report, each area is composed of a single section. There is an area for the Report Header, Page Header, Details section, etc. Every section is contained inside a single area. This initially gives you a one-to-one relationship between areas and sections.

Crystal Reports lets you create dynamic reports by adding multiple sections within an area and format each section independently of the other. This changes the relationship between areas and sections to a one-to-many relationship. One area can have multiple sections within it. You have the option of displaying all the sections or you can use conditional formatting to set which sections are visible and which ones are suppressed.

### Note

An area can have more sections added to it, but the sections must be of the same type. For example, the Details area can have two Detail sections in it, but it can't have a Group Footer section in it.

An example of multiple sections is shown in Figure 8-8.

| Group Header #1: @ViewDate () - D (Section6 ) |
| Details a (Section3 ) |
| 3/1/1999 XXXXXXXXX XXXXXXXXXXXXXXXXXXXXXXXXXXXX XXXXXXXXXXXXXXXXXXXXX 5,5 |
| Details b (Section8 ) |
| Group Footer #1: @ViewDate () - D (Section7 ) |

**Figure 8-8. Multiple detail sections.**

In this example, there are two sections between the group header and footer: Details a and Details b[40]. Each section is part of the Details area. The benefit of having two sections within the same area is that it gives you a lot of flexibility for formatting the report. Creative use of multiple sections solves many reporting problems.

Before seeing how to work with multiple sections, you first have to understand the rules. The first rule is that multiple sections are printed consecutively. The first section (labeled with the 'a') prints first. The 'b' section is printed second, and so on. The second rule is that you can change the formatting of any section and it doesn't affect the formatting of the other sections. A section can be suppressed or have its background color changed and this has no effect on the other sections within that area.

Multiple sections can be inserted, deleted and merged with other sections. When you right-click on a section header, you get the menu shown in Figure 8-9.

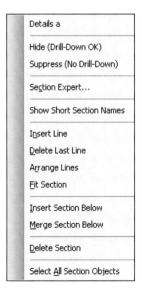

**Figure 8-9. Menu for managing sections.**

---

[40] Adding additional sections automatically gets the next letter of the alphabet assigned to it.

When selecting Insert Section Below, it inserts a new section below the section that was clicked on. Select Merge Section Below to combine the current section with the one below it. Crystal Reports merges the two by taking all the objects in the lowest section and copying them to the section above it. All the new objects go underneath the existing objects. Select Delete Section to delete a section from the report.

If a section has too much white space underneath the report objects, make the space tighter by placing your cursor at the top of the section below it and dragging it higher. An easier, and more accurate, way of doing this is to select the Fit Section menu option. Crystal Reports adjusts the section height to fit the exact space needed for the report objects. No extra space is allocated.

Selecting Move Section brings up the Section Expert again. This dialog box displays all the report sections on the left-hand side. Now that you have multiple sections, you can use the arrow keys shown at the top to move the sections up or down. This changes the order that they are printed in.

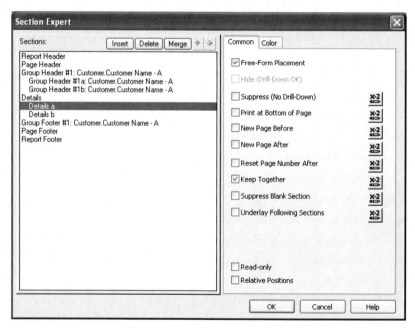

**Figure 8-10. The Section Expert with multiple sections.**

When looking at the menu options along the top of this dialog box, you see that it also has the options to Insert, Delete and Merge sections. If you are working in the designer, you can also go to this dialog box by right-clicking on a section header and selecting Format Section.

The key to making multiple sections work is to tie their properties with conditional formatting formulas. As discussed in Chapter 5, conditional formatting is used to turn formatting options on and off using built-in functions with other data in the report. The best way to understand this is to see examples. The following tutorials present common uses of conditional formatting with multiple sections that you can use in your own reports.

## Tutorial 8-1. Eliminating blank address lines.

A common problem with printing addresses is that not every line is always used. Every address has a line allocated for the street address, but some addresses need a second line for other miscellaneous information. This could be an "Attention:" comment or the suite number. If an address doesn't use this second line, it appears as a blank line and messes up the formatting of the address. An example of these labels is shown in Figure 8-11.

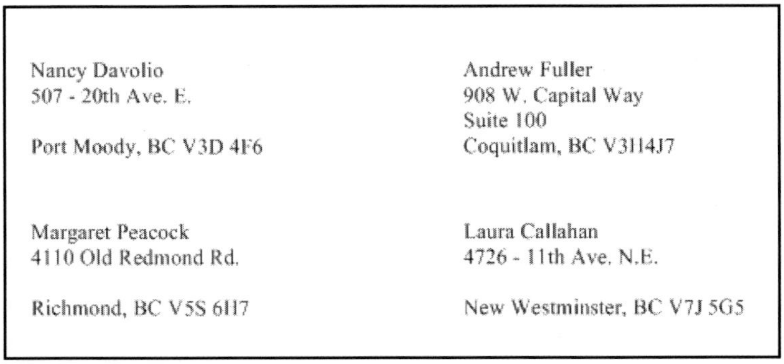

```
Nancy Davolio              Andrew Fuller
507 - 20th Ave. E.         908 W. Capital Way
                           Suite 100
Port Moody, BC V3D 4F6     Coquitlam, BC V3I14J7


Margaret Peacock           Laura Callahan
4110 Old Redmond Rd.       4726 - 11th Ave. N.E.

Richmond, BC V5S 6I17      New Westminster, BC V7J 5G5
```

**Figure 8-11. Address labels with blank lines.**

To fix this problem, create three sections. The first section has the addressee's name and street. The second section only has the optional second address line. The third section has the rest of the address fields.

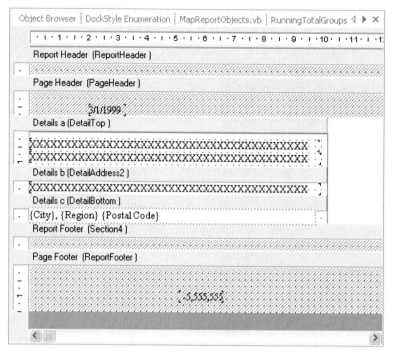

**Figure 8-12. Address labels in design mode.**

To make the second section only appear when there is data in the second address line, set the formatting option Suppress Blank Section. If the second address line doesn't have any information, then the section isn't printed and the blank line is eliminated. The printed labels are shown in Figure 8-13.

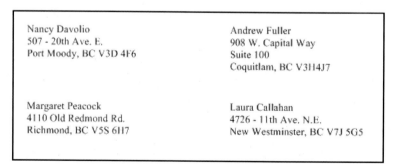

**Figure 8-13. Address labels that suppress blank sections.**

# Tutorial 8-2. Adding optional sections.

If you can use sections to suppress blank lines, it makes sense that you can use sections to do the opposite: add optional information. For example, a report can print a section just for unique circumstances. An employee report could print a special note if an employee's birthday falls within the current month. Invoices can print reminders to late customers that they need to pay or else penalties will be incurred. A recipe listing can print additional notes for favorite recipes. Each of these examples benefits from using multiple sections because if the section doesn't have any data to print, additional room isn't allocated on the report.

You might be wondering what the benefit of an optional section is. If you want to add report objects below other report objects, why don't you just do it in the same section and hide them when they aren't used? The reason why you want to use an additional section is so there isn't any wasted space when the information isn't needed. If you were to hide the individual objects in the same section, they will still take up space on the report and leave an obvious gap. By adding an additional section and only showing it when necessary, the report keeps a consistent look.

1. To add an optional section, right-click on the section it should go below and select Insert Section Below.

2. Add the optional report objects to the new section and format them appropriately.

3. Right-click on the section and select Section Expert. This opens the Section Expert dialog box.

4. Click on the Formula Workshop button and enter a formula for the Suppress option. It should return False for the condition that should show the section and return True for the condition that should suppress it. An example in Basic syntax is below.

```
if {Orders.Order Amount} > (Customer.Credit Limit} then
    false
else
    true;
```

This formula is from an invoice that warns the customer when they are over their credit limit. If the Order Amount is greater than the Credit Limit, then it returns False. Thus, the section is not suppressed and the customer sees the warning. Otherwise it returns True to suppress the section.

# Tutorial 8-3. Suppressing sections for a repeated field.

Individual report objects have a Suppress If Duplicated property which suppresses the object if its data is the same as the previous record. This prevents the report from duplicating the same information multiple times. But sections don't have this property because Crystal Reports would have to analyze every field within the report section to make this decision. But you can write your own formula to do this and only base it on the fields that are important.

Crystal Reports gives you two formulas for comparing the current record to an adjacent record. In the Function Window under the Print State category, it lists the functions PreviousValue() and NextValue(). The PreviousValue() function compares the current record's value to the previous record's value. The NextValue() function does just the opposite by comparing it to the following record's value. It returns True if the values match. You can use these functions to suppress an entire section if certain fields don't change from one record to the next.

The following code is the conditional formatting for the Suppress property of the Details section. It tests if the Orders.CustomerId field is the same as the previous record, and if so, the section is suppressed.

```
If {Orders.Customer Id} = PreviousValue({Orders.Customer Id}) then
    True
Else
    False;
```

**Best Of The Forum**

**Question:** Is it possible to use a function such as NextValue (NextValue (field))? This would let me print out the value of the next two or three records.

**Answer:** No, you can't nest multiple NextValue() functions inside each other. You can only get the value of one record at a time.

## Tutorial 8-4. Swapping sections with each other.

Another practical application of using multiple sections is having the same information in each section but formatting them differently. Conditional formatting lets you toggle each section so that only one section is printed at any given time and the other sections are hidden. To implement this, set each section to print using the opposite logic of the other section. For example, a company could have one client that generates a large percentage of revenue. That client asked that their invoices get formatted in a particular way. Although the data is the same as all the other invoices being printed, the format is customized for this one client.

To solve this problem, create duplicate sections for each part of the invoice. In the Suppress formatting option set the formula to only display the special sections for that customer. The other sections will have the opposite logic so that they get printed when it isn't that customer.

Another example is when printing multi-national reports that are grouped by country. Countries have data that is unique and isn't filled in for the other countries. People reading the report would get distracted if there were a lot of blank fields allocated for data that doesn't apply to the current country. To fix this, create a different section for each country and only put the fields in the section that are applicable to that country.

The following code listings demonstrate displaying a section based upon the country. The first section should be shown every time the country is "USA". The second section only gets shown when the country is "CA".

For the first section, go to the Section Editor and click the Formula Workshop button for the Suppress section. It would have the following formula:

```
If {Customer.Country} ="USA" Then
    False
Else
    True;
```

In this formula, if the country is "USA" then the formula returns False so that the section is shown. Otherwise it returns True to suppress the section. For the second section, we want to use similar logic but return opposite Boolean values.

```
If {Customer.Country}="CA" Then
    False
Else
    True;
```

One last example of using multiple sections is for alternating the type of chart displayed. Many formatting properties of a chart can use conditional formatting formulas, but some properties, like the type of chart (Line, Bar, etc.) can't be changed dynamically. Instead, you can use multiple sections to display different types of charts that couldn't be changed just by using conditional formatting. To do this, create multiple sections and put a different type of chart in each section. The charts show the same data, they just do so using a different chart type. Then use conditional formatting with the Suppress property to show the appropriate chart at the right time.

## Designing with Report Templates

Report templates make it easy to create reports that all have common formatting. This can save you a considerable amount of time because you don't have to format the objects on a report individually. The template formats all the objects at one time.

Report templates work by examining how the report objects in a template are formatted and applying those same formatting rules to an existing report. The formatting properties of the existing report are overridden by the template and the report takes on the appearance of the template. Report templates make it easy to give your reports a consistent look and feel.

You've already seen how Crystal Reports makes it easy to create reports that use consistent formatting. The Options dialog box has a Fields tab and Font tab that sets the default formatting of each type of report object. For example, you can set Field objects to be Arial with a size 10 and you can set String objects to have a thin border. Every string object added to the reports takes on that formatting. But this has its limitations because report formatting is a much more granular process. Strings can be formatted one way in a group header, and have a totally different formatting in the details sections The Options dialog box is too generic to take this into account. It gives you a good start and saves you a little time, but there is still work to be done to make the report look polished. Another limitation with the Options dialog box is that it doesn't take into account the positioning of objects on a page and more global aspects of a report, like having a corporate logo at the top and formatting page numbers a certain way at the bottom of a page. Templates make up for the short-comings of the Options dialog box.

You've already had a brief introduction to templates when using the Report Wizard. The final step of the Report Wizard lets you select the report template for applying default formatting. Crystal Reports installs a set of default report templates to give you a head start on formatting your reports.

You aren't limited to using the report templates that are installed with Crystal Reports. You can use an existing report as a template or you can create custom templates as well. Creating custom templates lets you specify graphics and color schemes that display the logo and match the corporate image. We'll talk more about custom templates in a later section.

## Applying Report Templates

Crystal Reports makes it easy to apply a report template. Select the menu items Report > Template Expert. This opens the Template Expert dialog box. It shows a list of the available templates along the left side and on the right side is a preview of the currently selected template.

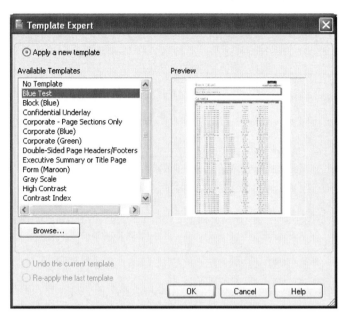

**Figure 8-14. The Template Expert dialog box.**

Crystal Reports gives you over a dozen pre-built templates to work with. You can use any of them for your own reports. If there isn't a template that you like but you have an existing report that you've used in the past, then you can use it as a template also. The Browse button on the bottom left-hand corner lets you select an existing report as a template file.

After clicking the Browse button and finding the report you want to use as a template, it appears in the Available Templates list. When you click on it in the list, you'll see a thumbnail of it in the Preview window to the right. Unfortunately, the new report template doesn't stay in the Template Expert after you close it. You'll have to click the Browse button each time you want to use that report as a template. If you want it to appear in the list of available templates permanently, copy it to the folder:

C:\Program Files\Business Objects\Crystal Reports 11\Templates\en

As you might imagine, for Crystal Reports to properly map a template onto a target report, it has to do a lot of analysis of every report object. After clicking the OK button to apply the template, the report is temporarily hidden while Crystal Reports processes it. Objects that don't exist in the target report will be added. This includes charts, graphics and special fields. If the target report has extra fields in the Details section that don't map directly to the template, then new sections are created on the report and the additional objects are placed in these sections. No objects are deleted. Once Crystal Reports finishes processing the template, you will see the report again with the template applied.

If applying a template doesn't give you the results you expected, you can undo it and return the report back to the way it was. The radio button at the bottom of the Template

Expert dialog box lets you undo the template changes and restore the original report format. If you later decide that you do want the template, then the other radio button lets you re-apply the template.

The caveat to using the Undo option is that you have to do this immediately after applying the template. If you start making changes to the report and later click the Undo button, it will lose your changes. The Undo button restores the report back to the way it was before you applied the template.

One interesting feature of templates is that they are cumulative. You can apply more than one template to a report and each template builds on the one before it. If you are going to use multiple templates then be aware that the Undo button only goes one level deep. In other words, you can only click the Undo button once. All previous templates are permanent. So make sure you save a copy of the report if you are experimenting with templates.

### Note

Templates can only be applied at design time. They cannot be applied while a report is running. For example, let's say that you have a customer who wants their invoices formatted a certain way that does not use your company's standard invoice format. You might think that you could use conditional formatting to apply a different template just for that customer. But this won't work. Instead, you'll have to do what we discussed earlier and use conditional formatting to modify the individual report objects during runtime. Or use multiple sections and enable the section that applies to that customer.

## Creating Custom Report Templates

Being able to use existing reports as a template is a nice feature. But you can take this one step further by creating report templates from scratch. Custom templates are more flexible because the fields can be formatted to account for any data type.

Creating a report template is very similar to creating any other report. The difference being that you want to do so in such a way that is generic so that it can be used with a variety of other reports. Crystal Reports has a new report object used just for custom templates: the Template Field Object. It is a generic object which isn't associated with a specific data type. This object can be used to map any type of field and apply the applicable formatting. Add it to your report by selecting the menu items Insert > Template Field Object. Drop the template object on the report and repeat as necessary for all the possible fields. Format the fields using the Format Editor dialog box.

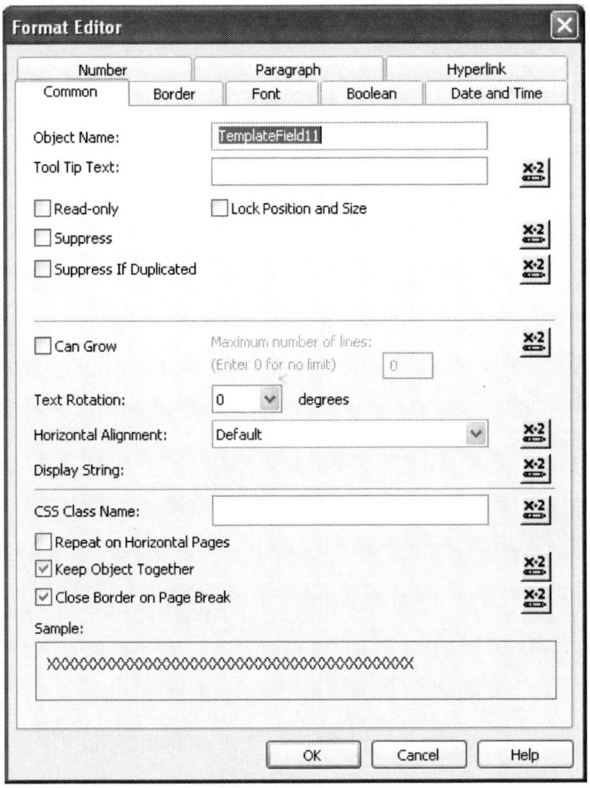

**Figure 8-15. The Format Editor dialog box for template field objects.**

The Format Editor has a tab for every data type available. This lets you set the formatting properties for every type of report object. When the object is mapped onto a field in the target report, only the applicable formatting properties get applied.

When you preview a custom template, the template objects don't display any data because they aren't associated with a field in a database. They are blank by default. If you want to have the field display default data on the report in preview mode, you can use the Formula Workshop to set a value to display in the template object.

When you add a new template object to the report, Crystal Reports automatically creates a new formula for that template object. The formula's only purpose is to assign a value that gets displayed in preview mode. The formula is as follows:

```
//Crystal Report Template Field
WhileReadingRecords;
Space(10);
```

By changing the function Space(10) to a string, the text object will be visible on the report in preview mode.

Using the menu Insert > Template Field Object to add template objects isn't the most efficient way to create a template. Every time you do this a new formula is added to the report. This quickly results in numerous formulas to manage. If you want each one to display a non-empty string, you have to modify each formula to display dummy text. Rather than do that, you are better off adding a single template object, modifying its formula, and then copying and pasting this object throughout the report. This means that you will only have one formula to manage. It's also very likely that many of the fields in each section will have similar formatting. By copying and pasting the template object throughout a section, you only have to modify the formatting of the first object and the rest will be an exact match. This is a big time saver.

Once you are finished creating the template, you should go to the Document Properties dialog box[41] and enter the Title of the report. The title is what gets displayed in the Template Expert dialog box. If you want a preview of the report to be shown as well, you must select the option "Save Preview" and preview the report prior to saving it.

# Dynamic Graphics

A long overdue feature of Crystal Reports is the ability to print images using a file location or a web address. Previous versions required that the graphic files be stored within the database. In many cases, this caused problems because the files were stored on the computer's hard drive. Moving the files into the database either wasn't practical or simply not possible. Crystal Reports XI now lets you print graphics using a fully qualified filename, a network share or a URL address.

The Graphic object has a new property called Graphic Location that is located on the Picture tab of the Format Editor dialog box. It uses conditional formatting to specify a string field which points to the graphic location on your computer or the Internet. The Graphic Location property is the last one shown.

---

[41] Choose the menu item File > Summary Info.

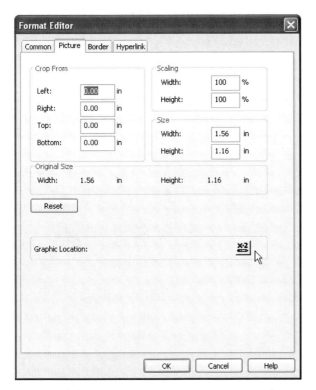

**Figure 8-16. Graphic Location property on the Format Editor dialog box.**

Click the Formula button to enter field with the graphic location and save your changes. Once you print the report or click the Preview tab, Crystal Reports queries the database and displays the dynamic graphic files.

You should be aware that when you add the graphic object, you have to select a local file stored on your computer. This is the default graphic and it is normally ignored once the report runs. If, for whatever reason, Crystal Reports can't find any of the dynamic graphic files, then it displays the default graphic instead. So, try to use an appropriate graphic file just in case an unexpected problem occurs.

# Tutorial 8-5. Printing Graphics from the Internet

1. Open any existing report that you wish to experiment with.
2. Select the menu options Insert > Picture.

    The Open dialog box appears so that you can select a picture to display on this report. You need to find a select any graphic file stored on your computer. The actual file doesn't matter because it will only be displayed on the Design tab. It won't be used when the report prints.

3.  Find a graphic file and click the Open button. Place the graphic in the Report Header section (or whichever section you want to display it at).

4.  Right-click the graphic and select Format Graphic. This opens the Format Editor dialog box.

5.  Click on the Picture tab.

6.  Click the Formula button for the Graphic location. This opens the Formula Workshop.

7.  For the formula, enter the database field that stores the graphic location. For this example, I'll just enter a URL that points to a picture from the book's website. You can either enter this URL for testing purposes (since it is a string, be sure to include the quotes), or enter a field from your database.

    "http://www.crystalreportsbook.com/forum/avatars/animal_butterfly_neg.jpg"

8.  Click the Save and Close button to close the Formula Workshop.

9.  Click the OK button to close the Format Editor.

    Preview the report and you should see the new graphic file in the report. If you entered a database field that points to a dynamic location, then the graphic should change on every page.

# Report Alerts

Report alerts prompt the user when certain report data falls within an unacceptable range. For example, report alerts are used to warn the user when inventory quantities fall below a certain level, when sales levels don't meet a monthly quota, or when customer credit limits have been exceeded. The user has the option of opening a separate tab within the viewer and just seeing the records that triggered the report alert.

Crystal Reports already has an acceptable substitute for report alerts: conditional formatting. With conditional formatting you combine formulas with object properties so that the user can easily see when data is not within an acceptable range. For example, a low inventory quantity can be changed to red and made bold or the top sales person's name can be shown on a reverse background. There are countless ways to highlight a record so that a user knows that it should be looked at in more detail.

But report alerts have two benefits over conditional formatting. When opening a report, report alerts immediately prompt the user with a message that they should look at certain records. In addition to that, they can open a separate tab that only shows the records that triggered the alert. With conditional formatting it isn't immediately obvious to the user that certain records meet the condition and it's harder to find those records because they could be buried in the middle of the report.

# Viewing Alerts

When the user opens a report which has records that trigger an alert, they are presented with the Report Alerts dialog box, shown in Figure 8-l7.

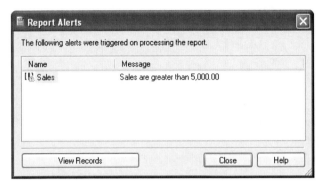

**Figure 8-17. Prompting the user that there are report alerts.**

The Report Alerts dialog lists each report alert that was triggered and gives a message describing what it is. The user has the option to view the records that triggered the alert or to close the dialog box and just view the report in its entirety. If the user clicks the View Records button, a new tab opens showing the records that caused the alert.

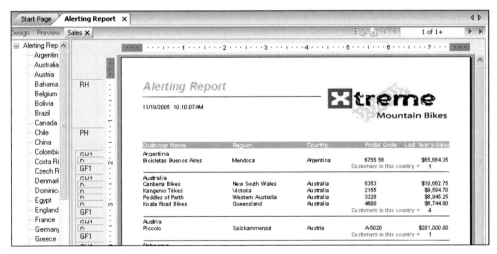

**Figure 8-18. Viewing report alert records.**

Since the report alert tab only shows the records that triggered the alert, this is similar to creating a report and using a record selection filter that only shows the bad data. The difference being that with report alerts you have the option of viewing the whole report or just those specific records. When using a record selection formula, you can only view the records that meet the criteria. But don't think that record selection formulas and report alerts are mutually exclusive. It is perfectly acceptable to have a report that uses a record selection formula and also have report alerts to notify the user of special circumstances.

If you close the alert tab and want to see the alerts again, you can either refresh the report or select the menu items Report > Alerts > Triggered Alerts.

# Creating Alerts

Adding and modifying report alerts is a very easy process. To create a new report alert, select the menu items Report > Create > Create or Modify Alerts. This opens the Create Alerts dialog box in Figure 8-19.

**Figure 8-19. Managing alerts with the Create Alerts dialog box.**

The left side of the dialog box lists the existing report alerts. On the right side are three buttons: New, Edit and Delete. As you might expect, these buttons let you create a new alert, edit an existing alert or delete an alert. When you click the New button, the Create Alert dialog box opens and prompts you for alert name and the alert criteria.

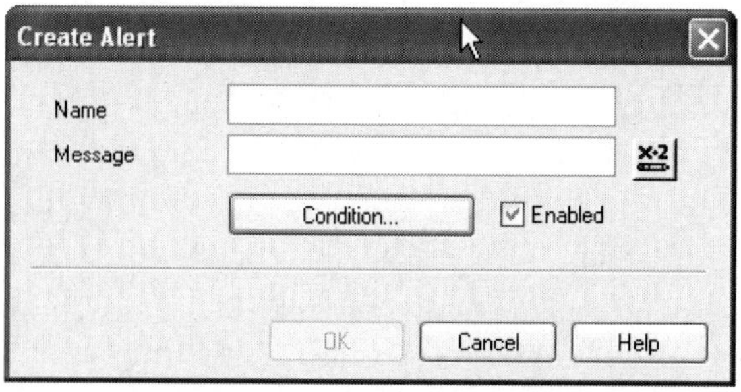

**Figure 8-20. Entering a new alert with the Create Alert dialog box.**

This dialog box has two input boxes. The first input box is for the alert name. The alert name is shown on the preview tab when the user views the alert report. The second input box is for the message. As you saw in Figure 8-16, the message is what the user is prompted with when they are told that certain records are triggering the alert. This message doesn't have to be static, as we'll soon see in one of the tutorials; the Formula Workshop button to the right can be used to customize the message for the user.

The Condition button lets you enter a formula that triggers the report alert. Click on it to open the Formula Workshop dialog box and enter the alert formula. The formula has to return either a Boolean True or False. If a record causes the formula to return True, then it triggers an alert and appears in the alert report.

The Enabled check box toggles whether the alert is in affect. If it is unchecked, then the alert is temporarily disabled until you check the box again.

Click the OK button when you are finished and want to save the alerts.

## Using Alerts in Formulas

Crystal Reports gives you functions that let you work with alerts. You can find out if alerts are enabled, which records trigger the alert, and what the alert message is. The alert functions are listed in Table 8-2.

**Table 8-2. Report alert functions.**

| Function | Description |
| --- | --- |
| IsAlertEnabled("AlertName") | Returns True if the Enable Alert checkbox is checked. Otherwise returns False. |
| IsAlertTriggered("AlertName") | Returns True if the current record meets the condition in the report alert. |
| AlertMessage("AlertName") | Returns the message associated with the report alert. |

Since a report can have more than one alert, each alert function is passed the alert name that you are inquiring about. This is a string value enclosed in quotes. By combining these alert functions with conditional formatting, you can add special formatting to the report rows that triggered the alert. This benefits the user because if they are looking at the full report then they will still know which records meet the alert condition. For example, by associating the following formula with the font color of the sales amount, records that trigger an alert are shown in red.

```
If IsAlertEnabled("Sales") and IsAlertTriggered("Sales") Then
  crRed
Else
```

DefaultAttribute;

The first line tests whether the alert is enabled and whether the current record triggered it. If both of these conditions are true, then the font color crRed is returned. If either one of these conditions isn't met, the font color stays the same. This is because either the alert isn't turned on or the record didn't trigger it. Either way, you want the font to remain unchanged.

In one respect, these alert functions in Table 8-2 aren't completely necessary because you could have just used the same logic from the report alert in the conditional formatting formula. This would give you the same results because the conditional formatting would still modify the report object when necessary. The benefit of using the alert functions is that you aren't duplicating the same logic in two different places. If you need to go back to modify the report alert, then the conditional formatting will still work properly. If you had retyped the same logic in both places, then updating the report alert would mean that you have to remember to update the conditional formatting logic also. If you forget to do both, then the report formatting won't be correct.

| Tip |
| --- |

As a general rule, you always want to share formula logic whenever possible because not doing so makes it easier to make mistakes.

## Tutorial 8-6. Creating a New Report Alert

Let's see how easy it is to create report alerts by walking through a simple tutorial. This example uses a report that prints sales by product and also shows which country the purchase was made in. Management has been worried that sales within South Africa have come to a halt over the past few months and they want the report to alert the user whenever there are new sales within South Africa.

1. Open the Crystal Reports example report Group By Intervals. Save it as **Report Alert Tutorial.rpt.**

2. Select the menu options Report > Alerts > Create or Modify Alerts. This opens the Create Alerts dialog box.

3. Enter an alert name of South African Sales. Enter an alert message of Sales within South Africa.

4. Click the Condition button to open the Formula Workshop. Enter the following Crystal syntax formula:

   {Customer.Country} = "South Africa"

5. Save the formula and close the Create Alerts dialog box.

6. Refresh the report and you will be prompted that there is a report alert. Click the View Records button and you will see a tab of all the sales made within South Africa.

# Tutorial 8-7. Using Parameters with Report Alerts

Crystal Reports comes with an excellent example of a report that not only uses report alerts, but combines it with report parameters. The sample report, Alerting.rpt, prompts the user for a sales amount that they want to be alerted to. The user enters an amount and if any records have a sales amount greater than that amount, then the report alert is triggered and the records are shown to the user. In addition to that, the report alert message uses that parameter to customize the alert message so that the dollar amount is also shown within the message. This example links together parameters with report alerts with the alert message. We'll walk through it to see how it works.

1. Open the Crystal Reports sample report Alerting.rpt.

2. Look in the Field Explorer and find the parameter Amount of Sales. Right-click on it and select Edit.

3. Examine the parameter to see that it is a static parameter which asks the user to enter a specific dollar for sales amount. When done reviewing this parameter, close the Edit Parameter dialog box.

4. Examine the existing report alert by selecting Report > Alerts > Create or Modify Alerts. The Create Alerts dialog box opens and it has the Sales alert listed. Click on the Edit button to open the Create Alert dialog box.

5. Notice that the Message input box is empty. That is because the message is created using conditional formatting. Click on the Formula Workshop button and you'll see the following formula:

"Sales are greater than " + ToText({?Amount of Sales})

6. This formula uses the parameter Amount of Sales and appends it to the end of the text, "Sales are greater than". This makes the message dynamic so that it always displays what the user entered as the parameter value when the report was refreshed. Of course, you wouldn't want to hard-code a value here because the sales amount is always changing.

7. Close the Formula Workshop when you are finished reviewing the formula. Click on the Condition button to open the Formula Workshop again and this time it displays the following Condition formula:

{Customer.Last Year's Sales}> {?Amount of Sales}

This formula triggers an alert whenever the dollar value of last year's sales is greater than the parameter value entered by the user. Again, the parameter is used within the alert so that it is derived from the user's choice.

8. Close the Create Alert dialog box. Refresh the report and select the option to prompt for parameter values. Enter a dollar value and look to see if any records generate a report alert. If so, you'll see that the alert message states the dollar value you entered as the parameter.

This example showed you how effective it is to link the parameters with report alerts to create a dynamic report. You could also add conditional formatting that uses the alert functions to make the records which caused the alert to stand out.

# Incorporating Subreports

Have you ever worked on a report and wanted a way to show multiple reports one right after the other? For example, if you wanted to print a corporation's annual report, you would first print the Balance Sheet, then the Income Statement and finally the Statement of Cash Flows. Each of these reports is different, but you want them all to appear together. Or have you wanted to print information from two different tables even though they weren't related to each other? For example, you could have printed out monthly invoices for each customer and put your company information in the header of the invoice. Even though the company information isn't directly related to the sales data, you still want to show it on the report. In both of these circumstances, and many more, subreports are used to solve these problems that standard reports can't handle.

A limitation of the standard report is that only a single view of the data source can be displayed. This means that you can only print data that comes from a single table (or a group of related tables). You can't print data that comes from two unrelated tables. You would have to create a separate report to print each data source. Rather than create separate reports to present additional views of the data sources, you can combine the multiple reports into a single report. This gives the impression to the reader that it is all one big report. These multiple reports are referred to as subreports because they are included within a main report.

From a functional and design standpoint, a subreport is virtually identical to a standard report. It has the same layout as a standard report and it uses the same report objects. The subreport differs from a standard report in that it is an object on a report. Thus, it is part of another report. There are also a few rules and restrictions associated with subreports, but we'll cover those later.

# When are Subreports Necessary?

If you aren't familiar with subreports, it can be a little confusing at first to determine when they are needed. I said in the introduction that a subreport is useful for printing data from multiple groups of tables, but we already know that a regular report can print from a group of tables. So what makes subreports different?

As a general rule, subreports are needed when you want to print out more than one set of unlinked detail records. For example, consider an employee payroll report that shows a list of an employee's paychecks for the year. In this report, you would only need a single report because there is only one set of detail records to print. But let's change the report requirements so that you also want to show a salary history for each employee. The salary history pulls data from a different table than the payroll history and there is also more than one salary record for most employees. Thus, this report now needs to show two types of lists for each employee. To make this work you would add a subreport that just shows the employee salary history. By adding a subreport, you have now delegated the two lists to be on their own report. The payroll history is printed by the main report, and the salary history is printed by the subreport.

If you are familiar with database technology, another way to think of this in "geek speak" is that subreports are necessary when you have tables with multiple one-to-many relationships. "One-to-Many" refers to having a main table (the parent table) where each individual record can have multiple matching records in a secondary table (the child table). For example, a Customer table and an Address table can have a one-to-many relationship. The parent table, Customer, has one record for each customer. The child table, Address, has multiple records for each customer because a customer can have multiple offices and shipping locations. This is also referred to as a parent-child relationship and the Customer ID field would be the linking field.

# Types of Subreports

There are two types of subreports available: Unlinked and Linked. The type defines the relationship between the report and the subreport as well as whether their data sources are related to each other.

Unlinked subreports have no relationship to the main report. The data sources used on each report are completely unrelated to each other. As each data source is printed, its contents have no effect on how the other data source is printed. In the chapter introduction, an invoice was given as an example of an unlinked subreport. An invoice prints billable items for a client during the month. The invoice header lists the address and contact information for the company (or its local division). The table containing the corporate address is in no way related to the table containing the client's sales data, but the report has to pull information from each table to print the invoice. To create this invoice, you would build a normal report showing the sales detail in the body of the report and in the page header you would add an unlinked subreport which prints the corporate contact information.

Linked subreports have a direct relationship with the main report. Data from the main report is passed to the subreport and this is used to filter what the subreport prints. For example, you could use a linked subreport in an invoice. In the page footer, you can add a linked subreport which shows any credits issued to the customer during that time period. The subreport shows the correct credit charges because it filters the data using the Client ID field from the main report.

# Adding a Subreport

Adding a subreport to a main report involves two steps: adding the report and setting the linking field. When adding the report you can choose to add an existing report or create a new report from scratch. If you create a new report from scratch, you will go through the Report Wizard to set its data source and specify the fields to print. After adding the subreport, you have the option of setting it to be an on-demand subreport. The on-demand subreport is displayed as a clickable link on the report and doesn't open until the user clicks on the link.

The second step of adding a subreport is setting the linking field. You have three options for linking reports. You can link them by a data field, a formula, or even leave it unlinked. Each one of these options gives you different benefits. Let's look at the details of adding the subreport next.

| Note |
| :---: |
| Subreports can only be one level deep. A subreport object can only be added to a main report and it can't be added to another subreport. If you are editing an existing subreport, then the menu options Insert > Subreport are disabled. |

To add a subreport to an existing report, select the menu options Insert > Subreport. You can also use the Insert Subreport button shown in Figure 9-1.

**Figure 9-1. Insert Subreport Button**

This opens the Insert Subreport dialog box, shown in Figure 9-2.

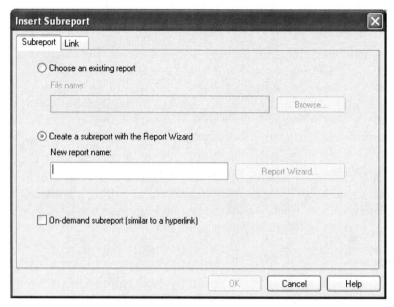

**Figure 9-2. The Insert Subreport dialog box.**

The top portion of this dialog box lets you choose the method for adding the subreport. The first way of adding a subreport is to select an existing report. Click the top radio button to enable the Browse button. Clicking the Browse button lets you find the report on your local computer or on the network. After selecting the report and clicking OK, the full filename and path is entered onto the dialog box.

The second way of adding a subreport is creating a report from scratch. When selecting this option, the Report Wizard button stays disabled until you enter a new report name. Once you enter a report name and click the Report Wizard button, the Report Expert dialog box opens and walks you through the steps for creating a new report.

| Note |
| --- |

When importing an existing report as a subreport, the subreport becomes a copy of the original report. When you make changes to the subreport, the original report is not modified. The subreport is saved within the same .rpt file as the main report.

Browsing for an existing report is fairly trivial and creating a new report using the Report Wizard has been covered earlier in the book, so there is no point in rehashing those details here. Let's move forward to the second step of adding a subreport: setting the linking field. Click on the Links tab (shown in Figure 9-3) to set how the reports are linked. Leave it alone if this is an unlinked report.

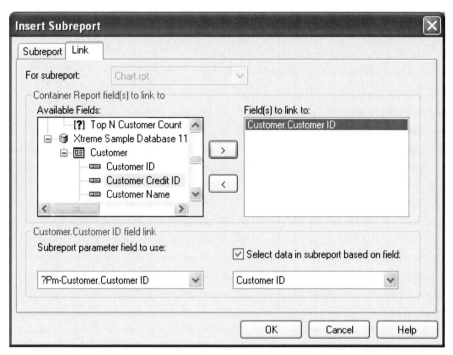

**Figure 9-3. The Link tab of the Insert Subreport dialog box.**

This dialog box is where you set the properties that determine how the subreport is linked to the main report. The Link tab has a list on the left side that shows the available report fields, formulas and data fields. These fields are from the parent report that holds the subreport. Select one or more of the fields and click the right arrow button to move it to the Fields To Link To list on the right. You can also double-click a field to add it to this list. The fields in this list are the ones that are passed to the subreport.

Once a field is added to the Fields To Link To list, the bottom section of the dialog box changes to show that a new parameter will be added to the subreport for that field. This parameter is automatically created by Crystal Reports for you. It's shown on the bottom left corner of the dialog box and starts with "?Pm-".

The bottom right side of the dialog box is where you tell Crystal Reports how to interact with this new parameter. The checkbox tells Crystal Reports whether or not you want this to be a linked subreport. If it is a linked subreport, the dropdown list below the checkbox tells it which field to link to. Crystal Reports tries to guess which field in the subreport should be linked with the parameter. It basically does this by looking to see if the subreport has a field with the same name as the field in the master table. If not, it will also try to match up data types. Be sure to check the field that it picked because it may not be the one you want.

## Best Of The Forum

**Question:** I clicked on the drop-down box to select the subreport field to link to, and the field I want to use isn't listed. Why don't I see all subreport fields in this list?

**Answer:** Crystal Reports only shows fields that have the same data type as the field in the main report that it is being linked to. For example, if the field in the main report is a string, the list of subreport fields will only show strings as well. Be careful with date fields because the data type Date is not the same as the DateTime data type.

By default, the subreport is linked and the option Select Data In Subreport Based on Field is checked. If you uncheck this option, then the subreport becomes an unlinked report and the dropdown list below it becomes disabled.

When you click the OK button to save your changes, the dialog box disappears and you are taken back to the main report in design mode. However, there is now the outline of a rectangle attached to the mouse cursor. This rectangle represents the new subreport. Move your mouse around on the report to position the rectangle where you want the subreport to be. Once it is positioned correctly, click the mouse button to release it and drop the subreport at that location. If you didn't place it exactly right, you can always click on it again and drag it to a new position.

## Caution

If the subreport spans more than a single page, then you can't place it in the Page Header section. Page headers aren't allowed to span more than one page and a large subreport will break this rule. If you do so, Crystal Reports will give you the error message, "The page size is not large enough to format the contents of an object."

Crystal Reports automatically modifies the subreport so that the information from the main report can be passed to the subreport and select the data. It does this by creating a new parameter field (using the name specified in the dialog box) and modifying the record selection formula. If you look at the subreport, you can see how these changes take affect. Figure 9-4 shows a subreport that has the new parameter field in it.

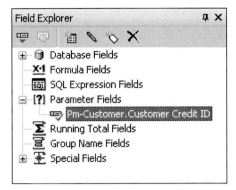

**Figure 9-4. The new parameter field created in the subreport.**

The subreport parameter field works differently than how you expect parameters to work. For subreports, you are not prompted to enter a value for the parameter. Instead, Crystal Reports automatically fills in the parameter for you with the value of the data field from the main report. This is done for you behind the scenes.

The second step that Crystal Reports does when you create a linked subreport is to modify the subreport record selection formula. The selection of the subreport is modified so that the subreport field is equal to the new parameter field. Figure 9-5 shows the Select Expert dialog box of the subreport.

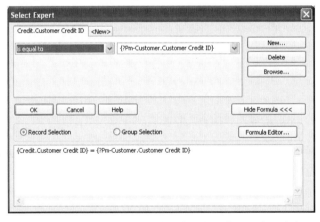

**Figure 9-5. The new record selection formula of the subreport.**

You can see from these two figures that there is nothing magical about linked subreports. Crystal Reports creates a parameter to hold the main report's value and the record selection formula ensures that the subreport's data gets filtered.

The record selection formula isn't restricted to filtering data based on this one field. You can add more selection criteria to further filter the data. For example, you could also add date range filters, product categories, etc.

# Editing the Subreport

Once the subreport object has been added to the main report, you will probably need to
edit it. Depending upon the types of changes you want to make to the subreport, there are
different ways of editing it.

To edit the content of the subreport, go to the main report and either double-click on the
subreport object or right-click on it and select Edit Subreport. This opens the subreport in
its own same design tab. The subreport is treated the same as any other report. You can
add new report objects, modify existing ones, or delete report objects.

You can also modify other aspects of the subreport. When viewing the main report in
design mode, right-click on the subreport object and there are two menu options called
Format Subreport and Change Subreport Links. The Format Subreport menu item opens
the standard format dialog box where you set properties such as Suppress, Keep Object
Together, etc. The formatting options on the Border and Font tabs are for on-demand
subreports. They control how they are displayed on the main report. This is discussed in
the next section.

The Change Subreport Links item on the pop-up menu opens the Subreport Links dialog
box. This lets you change the fields that are used to link the main report to the subreport.

```
WhileReadingRecords;
"";
```

Create a new group on this formula (it must be Group #1 so that it surrounds the rest of the report). In the new group header section, add the column headers or whatever report objects belong in the page header. Make sure it is set to print on every page. When you run the report, the group header will appear on every page of the subreport and it will look like it is a page header.

# Tutorial 9-1. Building the Customer Sales Report

Before we practice using subreports, let's first build the main report. This is going to be the foundation for all the tutorials throughout this chapter. It is a sales report which shows the detail sales record for each customer.

1. First, create a new report using the Standard Report Wizard and select the Xtreme.mdb database.

2. Select the tables Customer and Orders. Click the Next button twice to get to the Fields tab.

3. Select the following fields from the Customer table: Customer ID, Customer Name.

4. Select the following fields from the Orders table: Order Num, Order Date, Ship Date, Order Amount. Click the Next button.

5. For the groups, select the field Customers.Customer ID. Click the Next button.

6. For the Summaries tab, there will be three summaries already selected (Crystal Reports automatically summarizes all numeric fields), but we only want one of them. Keep the Order Amount summary and delete the summaries for Customer ID and Order ID.

7. Click the Next button four times to skip forward to the template tab. Select the template called Block (Blue).

8. Click the Finish button to save your changes and preview the report. It should look similar to the following:

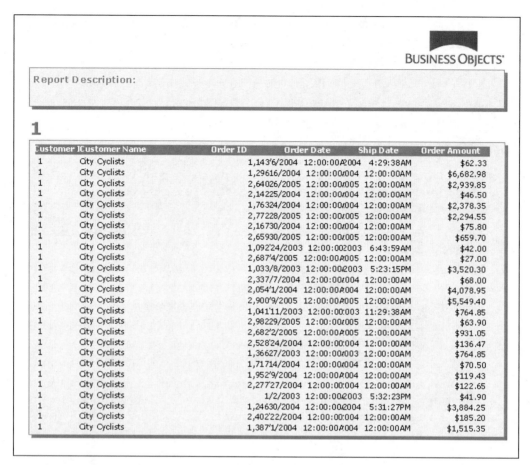

9. This report is a good first attempt, but let's clean it up a bit before we move on to adding the subreport. Click on the Design tab to start making changes.

10. Click on the Business Objects logo in the top right corner and delete it.

11. Double-click on the Report Description textbox. Replace the text with "Customer Sales Report".

12. In the Details section, click on the Customer ID field and delete it. It's already displayed in the group header so we don't need to repeat it on every row.

13. We don't want the customer name repeated on every row either, so we'll put it in the group header. Enlarge Group Header #1b and move the Customer Name field from the Details section into the group header.

14. Format the Order ID so that it doesn't have commas in it. Right-click on it and select Format Field. On the Number tab, set the Style to be -1123.

15. For both of the date fields, right-click on them and select Format Field. On the Number tab, set the date format to '03/01/1999'.

16. Save the report **as Customer Sales.rpt** and preview it. It should look similar to the following:

**Customer Sales Report**

**1**

| Customer Name | Order ID | Order Date | Ship Date | Order Amount |
|---|---|---|---|---|
| City Cyclists | | | | |
| | 1143 | 01/06/2004 | 01/08/2004 | $62.33 |
| | 1296 | 02/16/2004 | 02/16/2004 | $6,682.98 |
| | 2640 | 01/26/2005 | 01/26/2005 | $2,939.85 |
| | 2142 | 09/25/2004 | 10/06/2004 | $46.50 |
| | 1763 | 06/24/2004 | 06/30/2004 | $2,378.35 |
| | 2772 | 02/28/2005 | 03/05/2005 | $2,294.55 |
| | 2167 | 09/30/2004 | 09/30/2004 | $75.80 |
| | 2659 | 01/30/2005 | 02/01/2005 | $659.70 |
| | 1092 | 12/24/2003 | 12/26/2003 | $42.00 |
| | 2687 | 02/04/2005 | 02/10/2005 | $27.00 |
| | 1033 | 12/08/2003 | 12/20/2003 | $3,520.30 |
| | 2337 | 11/07/2004 | 11/13/2004 | $68.00 |
| | 2054 | 09/01/2004 | 09/02/2004 | $4,078.95 |
| | 2900 | 04/09/2005 | 04/16/2005 | $5,549.40 |
| | 1041 | 12/11/2003 | 12/13/2003 | $764.85 |
| | 2982 | 04/29/2005 | 05/02/2005 | $63.90 |
| | 2682 | 02/02/2005 | 02/04/2005 | $931.05 |
| | 2528 | 12/24/2004 | 12/24/2004 | $136.47 |
| | 1366 | 02/27/2003 | 02/28/2003 | $764.85 |
| | 1717 | 06/14/2004 | 06/15/2004 | $70.50 |
| | 1952 | 08/09/2004 | 08/09/2004 | $119.43 |
| | 2277 | 10/27/2004 | 10/31/2004 | $122.65 |
| | 1 | 12/02/2003 | 12/10/2003 | $41.90 |
| | 1246 | 01/30/2004 | 01/30/2004 | $3,884.25 |
| | 2402 | 11/22/2004 | 11/23/2004 | $185.20 |
| | 1387 | 03/01/2004 | 03/01/2004 | $1,515.35 |

# Linking Techniques

To determine whether your subreports are going to be linked or unlinked, you first need to understand the different techniques available for linking reports together. That enables you to make an intelligent choice about which type of subreport to use. Even though unlinked subreports aren't officially related to each other, there are still ways that they can pass information to each other as well.

Table 9-1 is a summary of the different linking options between a main report and a subreport. This is for linked as well as unlinked subreports. A more thorough description of each of these options and related examples are listed in the following sections.

**Table 9-1. Subreport linking options**

| Linking Option | Description |
|---|---|
| Linked with a data field | A field from the main report is passed to the subreport |

| | and this is used for filtering records. If the field is from a PC database (e.g. MS Access), then it must be indexed. |
|---|---|
| Linked with a formula field | A formula's value from the main report is passed to the subreport and this is used to filter records. This is a way to trick Crystal Reports into linking with non-indexed fields in PC databases (e.g. MS Access, Excel). |
| Unlinked | The subreport is not connected to the main report. There is no data passed between the main report and the subreport. The subreport uses a data source that is independent of the parent report. This is used for combining unrelated reports into a single report. |
| Unlinked using a formula field | A formula's value from the main report is passed to the subreport, but it doesn't affect record selection. It can be used for displaying non-critical data on the subreport. |
| Unlinked using global variables | Multiple variables are used to pass data back and forth between the parent report and the subreport. This lets the parent report keep track of what the subreport is printing or possibly display subreport totals. |

# Linked Subreports

Linked subreports require the main report to pass information to the subreport so that the subreport can filter its data. There are two ways that the reports can be linked to each other. You can use a field from the data source or use a formula for custom linking. Let's look at the details of the different linking methods and practice with some tutorials.

## Linking with a Data Field

Linking subreports with a data field lets you filter the data in the subreport based upon a data field that comes from the main report. This is useful when you are printing data derived from tables that have a parent-child relationship (as discussed earlier).

An example of linking with a data field is shown in Figure 9-6. This report shows the sales detail for each customer. Below the detail records is a list of all the credits that have been issued to the customer. Since there are two listings of detail records, the second list must be printed as a subreport. In this example, the subreport is linked via the Customer ID and it was added to the main report's Group Footer section.

## Customer Sales

| ID | Customer Name | Order | Order Date | Ship Date | Amount |
|----|---------------|-------|------------|-----------|--------|
| 1 | City Cyclists | | | | |
| | | 1,143 | 06-Jan-1997 | 08-Jan-1997 | $62.33 |
| | | 1,246 | 30-Jan-1997 | 30-Jan-1997 | $3,884.25 |
| | | 1,296 | 16-Feb-1997 | 16-Feb-1997 | $6,682.98 |
| | | 1,387 | 01-Mar-1997 | 01-Mar-1997 | $1,515.35 |
| | | 1,717 | 14-Jun-1997 | 15-Jun-1997 | $70.50 |
| | | 1,763 | 24-Jun-1997 | 30-Jun-1997 | $2,378.35 |
| | | | | | **$14,593.76** |

Credits Issued For City Cyclists

| Credit Authorization Number | Amount |
|-----------------------------|--------|
| CR1608 | ($1,792.91) |
| CR5241 | ($951.33) |
| CR6321 | ($1,484.68) |
| CR6592 | ($1,237.54) |
| CR6798 | ($727.56) |

| ID | Customer Name | Order | Order Date | Ship Date | Amount |
|----|---------------|-------|------------|-----------|--------|
| 2 | Pathfinders | | | | |
| | | 1,145 | 06-Jan-1997 | 17-Jan-1997 | $27.00 |
| | | 1,171 | 14-Jan-1997 | 14-Jan-1997 | $479.85 |
| | | 1,233 | 27-Jan-1997 | 29-Jan-1997 | $139.48 |
| | | 1,254 | 03-Feb-1997 | 04-Feb-1997 | $2,497.05 |
| | | 1,256 | 04-Feb-1997 | 04-Feb-1997 | $70.50 |
| | | 1,288 | 12-Feb-1997 | 12-Feb-1997 | $8,819.55 |

**Figure 9-6. Linked subreport in the Details section.**

There are two requirements for linking with a data field. The first is that the two fields must be of the same data type. The second requirement is that if this is a PC database, then both fields must have an index already set up in the database.

To create a linked subreport, go to the Link tab of the Insert Subreport dialog box. Select the data field from the Available Fields list on the left and add it to the Fields To Link To list on the right. Once the data field is added, the linking frame at the bottom appears and shows you the parameter field name and the field in the subreport's data field to link to. The parameter name is automatically filled in for you.

The checkbox on the right tells the subreport that the main report's data field is being linked to a field in the subreport. Leave this checked. Below the checkbox is a dropdown list showing the fields in the subreport. Select the one that is used to filter the data in the subreport. It must be of the same data type as the field from the main report. Click the OK button to save your changes and preview the subreport.

# Tutorial 9-2. Linking the Subreport with a Data Field

Let's start working with subreports by creating a subreport that links to the main report using a data field. We are going to take the Customer Sales Report we created in the previous tutorial and list the customer credits on it. We'll link the two reports together using the Customer Credit ID field which is found in both tables.

1.  Open the report you just created, 'Customer Sales.rpt' and save it as **Customer Credits.rpt**.

    The group footer was created using two sections. The lower edge of the gray box is in section A and section B is empty. We want to fit the subreport within the gray box, so we're going to put it in section A.

2.  Go into design mode and look at the gray box surrounding the group sections and details section. Right now, it stops in section Group Footer #1a. Click on it and drag it so that it extends into the next section below, Group Footer #1b. This frees up space in Group Footer #1a so we can insert the subreport.

3.  Make Group Footer #1a larger (about double its current size) so you can place the subreport object into it.

4.  Create a new subreport by selecting the menu options Insert > Subreport. This opens the Insert Subreport dialog box.

5.  The default option is to create a new report using the Report Wizard. That is what we want. Enter a report name of **Customer Credits** and click the Report Wizard button.

6.  When the report wizard opens, select the Xtreme.mdb database.

7.  Select the Credit table and put it in the Selected Tables list on the right. Click the Next button.

8.  For the fields to display, select Credit Authorization Number and Amount.

9.  Click the Finish button to save your report settings and return to the Insert Subreport dialog box.

10. Click on the Link tab so that we can set the linking field.

11. The Customer table and Credit table are linked together by the field Customer Credit ID. Find it in the Available Fields list on the left and double-click it to put it in the list Fields To Link To.

    At the bottom, you will see that Crystal Reports has created a link between the reports. On the left side is a parameter that will be used internally by Crystal Reports to pass the field data to the subreport. On the right side is the Customer Credit ID field in the Credit table. Since the tables in both the master report and subreport both have the same field name, Crystal Reports was able to accurately pick the linking field. However, many times this won't be the case and you will have to click the dropdown list and choose the linking field manually. For this example, everything is fine as it is. The dialog box should look like the following figure.

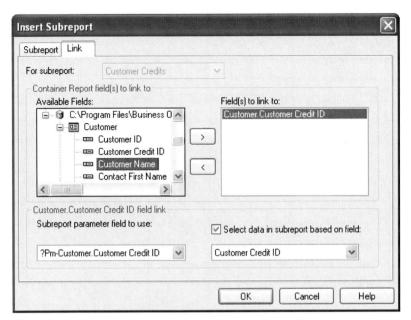

12. Click the OK button to save your changes and close the dialog box.

    When you return to design mode of the main report, an outline of the subreport object is shown as a rectangle. Use the mouse to position the subreport within Group Footer #1a. Click the mouse button to release it.

    When you preview the report, you should see the credits for each customer listed below the sales detail. Since we linked the subreport on the field Customer Credit ID, each customer has only their credits listed. Let's clean up the report just a little before we are finished.

13. Go back into design mode and resize the subreport object. Shorten the width of the subreport by dragging the right side closer to the left. Then move the subreport object to the right so that it is centered on the report.

14. Double-click on the subreport object. This opens the subreport in design mode on its own tab.

15. Click on the Report Date object in the Report Header section and delete it. The subreport doesn't need to show the report date.

16. Now that we deleted the report data, there is too much empty space in the report header. Select the column headers and move them to the top of the report header section. Then resize the report header section to make it smaller. Also, resize the Report Footer to make it a lot smaller (there isn't anything being displayed in it).

17. Save the report (make sure you renamed it in Step 1) so that you don't lose your changes. Preview the report and it should look similar to the following figure.

Customer Sales Report

3

| Customer Name | Order ID | Order Date | Ship Date | Order Amount |
|---|---|---|---|---|
| Bike-A-Holics Anonymous | | | | |
| | 1357 | 02/26/2004 | 02/26/2004 | $1,664.70 |
| | 2060 | 09/01/2004 | 09/01/2004 | $87.80 |
| | 1538 | 04/18/2004 | 04/18/2004 | $872.65 |
| | 1907 | 07/27/2004 | 07/28/2004 | $134.70 |
| | 1509 | 04/10/2004 | 04/10/2004 | $67.80 |
| | 2162 | 09/28/2004 | 09/30/2004 | $1,019.70 |
| | 2751 | 02/23/2005 | 02/23/2005 | $1,664.70 |
| | 1553 | 04/21/2004 | 04/21/2004 | $976.20 |
| | 1466 | 03/29/2004 | 03/30/2004 | $33.90 |
| | 2187 | 10/05/2004 | 10/07/2004 | $45.00 |
| | 1331 | 02/22/2003 | 02/27/2003 | $178.20 |
| | 1964 | 08/12/2004 | 08/13/2004 | $1,721.25 |
| | 1096 | 12/27/2003 | 01/05/2004 | $47.63 |
| | 1097 | 12/27/2003 | 01/03/2004 | $1,439.55 |
| | 2750 | 02/22/2005 | 02/22/2005 | $1,664.70 |
| | 1457 | 03/28/2004 | 03/31/2004 | $659.70 |
| | 2112 | 09/16/2004 | 09/24/2004 | $5,545.42 |
| | 1294 | 02/15/2004 | 02/15/2004 | $5,879.70 |
| | 2568 | 01/04/2005 | 01/10/2005 | $959.70 |

| Credit Authorization Number | Amount |
|---|---|
| CR2149 | ($1,005.58) |
| CR2160 | ($1,670.54) |
| CR4103 | ($2,457.20) |
| CR4331 | ($1,435.78) |

# Linking with a Formula Field

Linking records in a subreport can also be done using a formula field. This gives you more creativity for how it is linked to the main report. There are many reasons for wanting to link with a formula field rather than a data field.

When using a formula to link to a subreport, you aren't restricted to using indexed fields. Linking with formulas lets you use any field in the table to link the two reports together. As long as the data in both tables match, you're good to go.

It is a common task to have to link tables from two different programs together when the data isn't compatible. Using formulas to parse or join multiple data fields and using the results to link to a subreport is perfect for this. This situation can happen when the programs were developed by different teams in the same company or when one company acquires another company and they have to consolidate their data. Formulas give you the flexibility to massage the data from one table into a format compatible with the data in another table. This can consist of converting the field to a different data type, concatenating multiple fields together or parsing a field to extract out the extraneous characters.

Telling Crystal Reports to link on a formula involves the same steps as linking on a data field, the key difference is that you have to make sure that the formula is already created prior to creating the subreport. When you create the subreport and click on the linking tab, the formula is shown in the Available Fields list on the left. Simply double-click on it to add it to the Fields to Link To list on the right.

Unlike other dialog boxes in Crystal Reports, the Link tab doesn't have a Formula button to create a new formula at that moment. That is why if you want to link your subreport using a formula, then you have to create it before the subreport. Otherwise, you have to close this dialog box, go back to the main report to create the formula, and then edit the subreport again to link on the formula. A little pre-planning makes your life easier!

Once the formula field has been added, the frame at the bottom of the dialog box appears and it works the same as adding a data field: the parameter name is automatically filled in and you pick a subreport field from the dropdown list to link to.

Here are some examples of useful formulas for linking subreports.

## Linking on multiple fields

Formulas are often used for linking concatenated string fields together. It is common to have tables with similar information, but a slightly different structure.

For example, the part number for an inventory item is usually broken up into different groups of numbers and each group has a different meaning. The groups could be category, product grade, and item number. One table could list the inventory number as a single field with each group separated by dashes (e.g. 999-99-9999) and another table could list the number across three different fields (one field for each group). Normally, it isn't possible to link these two tables together because you can't link one field to three different fields. However, you can use a formula to combine the three fields so that they match the format of the field in the other table. For example, we can create a formula that combines the three fields together and link the formula to the other table.

{Inventory.Category} & '-' & {Inventory.Grade} & '-' & {Inventory.Item}

## Linking on a non-indexed field

As we just mentioned, formulas can be used to link on non-indexed fields. This is a very simple process. Simply create a new formula and set it equal to the non-indexed field. Then use that formula as the linking field. In the example below, the field Customer Credit ID is not indexed, but you can link to it using a formula field.

{Customer.Customer Credit ID}

This formula simply repeats the name of the field in it. It's very simple, but that is all that is needed when the field isn't indexed.

## Linking on a partial string

There are times when a field has too much information in it. You only need part of the string for linking to another table. Consider the previous inventory example where the table has all three groups of the inventory number in one field. The middle portion of the string is the product grade and you want to link to a subreport which summarizes the sales for all products with that specific grade. You can't link to the whole inventory number because it has the other grouping data in it as well. Instead, you have to pull out just the product grade portion and use that to link to the subreport.

Mid({Inventory.Inventory ID},5,2)

In this formula, the Inventory ID field stores the product grade as the middle portion of the Inventory ID. So the formula uses the Mid() function to extract the two middle characters from the string, starting at position five. Now the formula can be used to link to a subreport which summarizes data on product grade.

A very common report type is a directory listing. This report groups everything by the first letter of the person's name (or product name). So the first group is on the letter A and the second group is on the letter B, etc. When you put a subreport in the group header or footer, you want the subreport to also print by the same letter. The formula for doing this is easy enough. Use the Left() function to parse out the first letter of the product name.

Left({Inventory.Product Name},1)

What is good about this example is that the formula for grouping the data in the main report is also the same formula for linking to the subreport. The main report groups all its data on the first letter of the product name and so does the subreport. You don't have to create an extra formula for linking to the subreport. Use the same one that you used for creating the groups.

## Linking with Memo Fields

Crystal Reports doesn't let you use a memo field to link reports together. Memo fields aren't displayed in the Subreport Links dialog box. However, you can use a formula field instead. Create a formula and make it equal to the memo field. Now when you go to link to the subreport you'll see the new formula in the Available Fields list.

## Converting data types

A common problem with databases is that they can be developed over a long period of time and worked on by different people. This creates a situation where the same fields can have different data types in different tables. Ideally, there would be clear specifications on the data type that each field has. But unfortunately this doesn't happen often enough.

For example, a company could originally have their inventory IDs being a combination of strings and numbers. But at a later point in time, they decide to buy new inventory management software and it only uses numbers. It's easy enough to convert the original inventory IDs to numbers, but the problem comes when you try to build a report with the new tables and include a subreport that uses historical data from the archived tables. You can't link the tables together because the original table uses a string data type and the new inventory package uses a numeric data type. To fix this problem, you have to convert the field from the new inventory system into a string so that it can link to the subreport that uses the original data.

CStr({InventorySystem.InventoryID, 0})

This formula uses the CStr() function to convert the number to a string. It also specifies that we want zero decimal places so that it returns a whole number.

# Linking to Subreport Parameters

If the subreport has parameter fields in it, when the user refreshes the report they are prompted to enter values for the subreport parameters. If you don't want the user to be prompted to enter a parameter value, you can link a field from the main report to the subreport parameter. This automatically populates the subreport parameter field with a value from the main report without prompting the user.

To link a field from the main report to a subreport parameter, right-click on the subreport in design mode and select Change Subreport Links. This opens the Subreport Links dialog box previously shown in Figure 9-4. In the Available Fields list, double-click the field from the main report that holds the value you want to pass to the subreport parameter. This adds the field to the Fields To Link To list on the right.

When you move a field to the Fields To Link To list, Crystal Reports' default behavior is to automatically create a matching parameter in the subreport which is passed the value from the main report. If you look in the bottom left hand corner of the dialog box you'll see that there is a parameter name with a prefix of "?Pm-…" However, in this circumstance you don't need Crystal Reports to create a new parameter for you because the subreport already has a parameter that you want to link the data to. Instead of letting Crystal Reports create a new parameter, click on the dropdown list and select the existing parameter from the list. This links the field on the main report to the existing subreport parameter.

| Tip |
|---|

If you don't see the subreport parameter in the dropdown list, then there is a data type mismatch between the chosen field in the main report and the parameter. Cancel your changes and go back to make sure that both the main report field and the subreport parameter have the same data type. If not, create a formula in the main report which converts the field to the proper data type and use this formula to link to the subreport parameter.

After selecting the existing subreport parameter to link to, the option to the right, Select Data In Subreport Based On Field, becomes disabled. This option is no longer necessary since you are passing the data to an existing parameter.

Save your changes and refresh the report data. The subreport will get its data from the main report and you will no longer be prompted to enter a parameter value.

# Linking to a Stored Procedure with Parameters

I recently saw two very similar questions about stored procedures posted to the book's online forum. I thought they were excellent questions and that many people would benefit from all the details.

Both questions said that they had a main report and a subreport that were linked to a SQL database. The data sources were stored procedures and each had an input parameter associated with it. When they ran the report, they were prompted with two parameters instead of one. They wanted to only enter one parameter and have it passed to the stored procedure for both the main report and the subreport. However, they couldn't figure out how to get rid of the second parameter prompt for the subreport.

The key to fixing this problem is to understand what the previous section said about how to pass data to a subreport parameter. In the previous section, the parameter was created by the report designer (presumably you) and we learned how to pass a data field from the main report to it. This told Crystal Reports not to prompt the user for the subreport's parameter. The questions on the forum are very similar, but with a couple of differences.

The first difference being that in this case Crystal Reports created the subreport parameter automatically when you selected the stored procedure as the data source. The second difference is that instead of eliminating the parameter prompts altogether, you want to keep one parameter prompt and have its value shared between both reports.

You first have to understand that whenever you create a report whose data source is a stored procedure with an input parameter, Crystal Reports automatically creates a parameter with a similar name and the same data type.[42] When you run the report, you are prompted to enter a value for the parameter and that value gets passed to the stored procedure. In the previous section, we saw how to link a data field from the main report to the subreport parameter and this keeps the user from getting prompted to enter the parameter value. The same applies here except that we want be prompted for the first parameter only, and have its value passed to the subreport.

The key to making Crystal Reports pass the same data to both the main report and subreport is to link the two parameters together on the Subreport Links dialog box. Instead of double-clicking a data field in the Available Fields list, you want to double-click the parameter field from the main report's stored procedure. After that, at the bottom of the

---

[42] This is discussed in great detail in the Database Connectivity chapter.

dialog box, select the parameter field for the subreport's stored procedure. For example, Figure 9-7 shows a Subreport Links dialog box which links the two reports based on the @Customer ID parameter from each report.

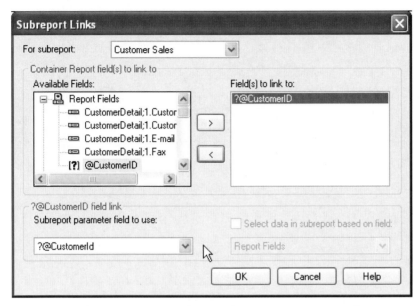

**Figure 9-7. Linking two stored procedure parameters together.**

When you preview the report, you are prompted to enter a value for the main report's parameter. Crystal Reports takes this value and passes it to the stored procedure for the main report. Crystal Reports also sees that the main report's parameter is the linking field for the subreport and passes the same value to the subreport's parameter field. Since this value gets passed to stored procedure for the subreport and there is no need to prompt you a second time.

# Unlinked Subreports

An unlinked subreport is used when you want to combine two or more reports onto one report and these reports don't have any common data for creating a relationship between them. The unlinked subreport is completely independent of the main report and the main report's data doesn't affect the subreport.

Figure 9-8 shows an example of an unlinked subreport. It is a customer sales report that shows the prior year sales amount for each customer.

## Customer Sales Detail By Country

### Summary of Sales by Country

| Country | Sales |
|---|---|
| Australia | $40,446.64 |
| Austria | $201,000.00 |
| Bahamas | $14,463.35 |
| Bangladesh | $4,683.50 |
| Barbados | $4,443.80 |
| Belgium | $200,000.00 |

|  | ID | Customer Name | Last Year's Sales |
|---|---|---|---|
| **Australia** | 149 | Tasmanian Devil Bikes | $1,739.85 |
|  | 148 | Koala Road Bikes | $6,744.80 |
|  | 147 | Peddles of Perth | $8,945.25 |
|  | 146 | Bruce's Bikes | $1,138.09 |
|  | 145 | Kangeroo Trikes | $9,594.70 |
|  | 144 | Canberra Bikes | $10,662.75 |
|  | 143 | Down Under Bikes | $1,621.20 |
|  |  |  | $40,446.64 |
| **Austria** | 66 | Piccolo | $201,000.00 |
|  |  |  | $201,000.00 |
| **Bahamas** | 156 | Beach Cycle and Sport | $14,463.35 |
|  |  |  | $14,463.35 |

Figure 9-8. Unlinked subreport being used in the report header.

This report is grouped by country and within each group it shows the customers from that country and what their sales were last year. At the top of the report, it shows a summary of the prior year sales for each country. This lets you analyze how each country compares to the other before looking at detail records for each customer. This is implemented by creating the summary report separately and adding it as a subreport in the main report's header section. Since there isn't a field that can be linked between the summary report and the customer detail report, these two reports are unlinked.

To create an unlinked subreport, do not set any properties on the Link tab. Since the subreport is completely independent of the main report, no fields should be listed on the Link tab.

Let's consider an example of an unlinked subreport that at first may appear to be a linked report. This example is a form letter that has a variable number of standard attachments printed at the end of it. This could be a legal document where each client needs to have signature pages attached to the end of it.

Within the Report Footer are multiple sections. Within each section is one subreport that represents a standard attachment. The report has conditional formatting to suppress the section if a field in the main report doesn't meet a certain value. In this case, the person receiving the form letter would have Boolean fields that are set to True for each attachment that should be included. If the proper field isn't True, then the section is suppressed and the attachment isn't printed. Although this may appear to be a linked subreport because data in the main report determines whether to print the subreport, it isn't. It is an unlinked subreport because there is no data that is being passed to the subreport. The Boolean field in the main report determines which sections get suppressed or printed. But this is all done at the main report level and not at the subreport level. The Boolean field never gets passed to the subreport and its value doesn't affect the content of what is printed.

# Tutorial 9-3. Unlinked Company Header

Let's create an unlinked subreport that displays the company address in the report header. You might be tempted to think that it is easier to just type in the company address manually rather than going through the effort of adding a subreport. But there are benefits to using a subreport here. The first benefit is if the company changes location then you can simply update the database with the new address and the report gets updated automatically. If you do this for multiple reports, then every report will be updated as well. It's also useful to pull the company address out of a database when there are multiple divisions within the company. Each division can share the same reports without having to make any changes to the report header.

Let's modify the report from Tutorial 9-2 and add a subreport which lists the company information.

1.  Open the report Customer Credits.rpt' that you created in the last tutorial. Save it as **Company Header.rpt** so that you have a new copy to work with.

    The subreport is going to go into the report header section, but right now that section is suppressed. We want to make it visible and then create the subreport and place it in the report header.

2.  Go into design mode and select the menu items Report > Section Expert. Click on the Report Header section and uncheck the Suppress option. Click the OK button to close the dialog box.

3.  Select the menu options Insert > Subreport. This opens the Insert Subreport dialog box.

4.  On the Subreport tab, enter a report name of **Company Header**.

5.  Click the Report Wizard button to build the report.

6.  When the Report Wizard opens, select the table Xtreme.mdb.

7.  Double-click the table Xtreme Info to move it into the Selected Tables list on the right.

8.  Click the Next button to go to the Fields section.

9.  Select the fields Xtreme Name, Address, and Logo Color.

10. Click the Finish button to close the wizard.

    You are now back at the Insert Subreport dialog box. Normally, you would click on the Links tab and set the fields that link the report together. But since this is an unlinked report, we are going to skip the Links tab altogether.

11. Click the OK button to close the Insert Subreport dialog box.

12. You are returned to design mode of the main report so that you can place the subreport object. Move it to the Report Header and click the mouse button to place it there.

    The initial design of the subreport that Crystal Reports created isn't even close to what we want. So we have a lot of cleanup to do. The goal being to have the address on the left side and having the company logo on the right side.

13. Double-click on the Company Header subreport object to open it in design mode. We want to delete everything on the report except what is in the Details section.

14. Delete all objects in the Report Header section. Then resize it so that it doesn't use any space.

15. Resize both report footers so that they don't use any space either.

16. We want to put the company logo on the right side of the report. Drag the field Logo Color from the Field Explorer window into the Details section and place it along the right side. Crystal Reports will automatically resize the Details section to make it large enough to fit the company logo image. Delete the field heading that Crystal Reports automatically added when you dropped the logo onto the report.

17. We want the company name and address to be listed on the left side of the report with the fields going down the left edge, but they are locked onto the guideline on the left side of the report. Right-click on the guideline and select Remove all Horizontal Guidelines. This releases the fields from the guidelines.

18. Move the field Xtreme Name to the top left of the Details section. Place the Address field directly below it.

    The one thing missing from the report is the city and state info. We want these fields to be shown adjacent to each other so we are going to add a text object and insert the fields into the text object. This automatically concatenates the fields next to each other.

19. Select the menu items Insert > Text Object. Use the cursor to draw the text object below the Address field.

20. Drag the following fields onto the text object: City, Province and Postal Code. They should be adjacent to each other.

21. To ensure proper punctuation, insert a comma between the City and Province fields. Insert a space between the Province and Postal Code fields.

    We are now finished formatting the Company Header subreport. You've done a lot of steps, so review the following figure to check your subreport for accuracy.

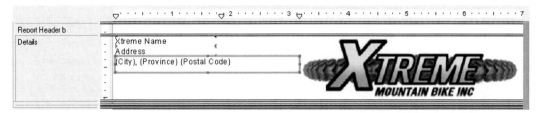

22. Preview the main report and you'll see the Company Header subreport displayed at the top of the first page. It should look similar to the following figure. If the report looks good, save the report to keep your changes.

Xtreme Mountain Bikes, Inc
2001 Meridian Way
Vancouver, BC V6G 3G6

Customer Sales Report

**1**

| Customer Name | Order ID | Order Date | Ship Date | Order Amount |
|---|---|---|---|---|
| City Cyclists | | | | |
| | 1143 | 01/06/2004 | 01/08/2004 | $62.33 |
| | 1296 | 02/16/2004 | 02/16/2004 | $6,682.98 |
| | 2640 | 01/26/2005 | 01/26/2005 | $2,939.85 |
| | 2142 | 09/25/2004 | 10/06/2004 | $46.50 |
| | 1763 | 06/24/2004 | 06/30/2004 | $2,378.35 |
| | 2772 | 02/28/2005 | 03/05/2005 | $2,294.55 |
| | 2167 | 09/30/2004 | 09/30/2004 | $75.80 |
| | 2659 | 01/30/2005 | 02/01/2005 | $659.70 |
| | 1092 | 12/24/2003 | 12/26/2003 | $42.00 |
| | 2687 | 02/04/2005 | 02/10/2005 | $27.00 |
| | 1033 | 12/08/2003 | 12/20/2003 | $3,520.30 |
| | 2337 | 11/07/2004 | 11/13/2004 | $68.00 |
| | 2054 | 09/01/2004 | 09/02/2004 | $4,078.95 |
| | 2900 | 04/09/2005 | 04/16/2005 | $5,549.40 |
| | 1041 | 12/11/2003 | 12/13/2003 | $764.85 |
| | 2982 | 04/29/2005 | 05/02/2005 | $63.90 |
| | 2682 | 02/02/2005 | 02/04/2005 | $931.05 |
| | 2528 | 12/24/2004 | 12/24/2004 | $136.47 |
| | 1366 | 02/27/2003 | 02/28/2003 | $764.85 |
| | 1717 | 06/14/2004 | 06/15/2004 | $70.50 |
| | 1952 | 08/09/2004 | 08/09/2004 | $119.43 |
| | 2277 | 10/27/2004 | 10/31/2004 | $122.65 |
| | 1 | 12/02/2003 | 12/10/2003 | $41.90 |

# Tutorial 9-4. Re-using Subreports

The subreport that you just created, Company Header, is completely independent of the detail data printed within the report. Since the company header is an unlinked subreport, it would be smart to re-use it on other reports. However, we know that subreports are saved within the definition of the main report. So we need to save it independently of the main report.

1.  Open the report 'Company Header.rpt' and go into design mode.

2.  Double-click on the Company Header subreport to open it in design mode.

3.  Select the menu option File > Save Subreport As. Enter the filename **Company Header Subreport.rpt** and click the Save button to save it.

4.  To use this subreport within other main reports, when the Insert Subreport dialog box is open, select the option Choose Existing Report and click the Browse button and find the subreport file to insert it into the main report.

# Unlinked with a Formula

Formulas are used with unlinked subreports so that information can be passed to the subreport without filtering any data. The benefit of using a formula is that although the subreport isn't linked, you can still pass information from the main report to the subreport. This information can be displayed on the report or used in the subreport's formulas.

To create an unlinked formula field, go to the Link tab and select the formula from the main report's list of available fields. Once the formula has been selected, the frame at the bottom of the dialog box appears and the parameter name is already filled in. Since this is an unlinked report, click on the checkbox labeled, "Select data in subreport based on field", to deselect it. This causes the linking field dropdown list to become disabled and no linking field will be specified. The parameter field in the bottom left corner of the dialog box still gets created, but it doesn't get linked to a specific field in the subreport.

When the subreport runs, it can reference the parameter that is created by this dialog box to get the formula's value from the main report.

# Unlinked with Shared Variables

Shared variables can be used to pass data between the main report and the subreport. This lets you perform calculations, track subtotals and create strings in one report and pass this data to the other report. The difference between using a parameter field and a shared variable is that shared variables can be used to pass data in both directions. When using parameter fields, data can only be passed from the main report to the subreport.

Since the subreport is not linked to the main report and no formulas are being passed to the subreport, then you shouldn't set any properties on the Link tab. The difference is that both reports have to have a formula that declares and uses the shared variable.

## Tutorial 9-5. Using Shared Variables

To illustrate how to use shared variables, let's modify the example report shown earlier that lists the customer sales and credits issued to the customer. That report showed the detail sales entries and credit items, but doesn't tie the two together. We want to modify this report so that it subtracts the credits from the total sales amount to give you the net sales figure. The subreport will pass the total credits to a shared variable and this shared variable will be used on the main report to calculate the net sales.

1.  Open the report 'Customer Credits.prt' and save it as **Customer Net Sales.rpt**.

    The first thing we want to do on both reports is show the subtotals. Not only is it important to see the total sales and credits for each customer, but showing them on the report will make it easy for us to verify that the net sales amount is accurate.

2.  In design mode on the main report, right-click on the Order Amount field and select Insert > Summary.

3.  On the Insert Summary dialog box, look for the Summary Location property near the middle and change it to Group #1. This puts the subtotal in the group footer so that you can see it for each customer. Click the OK button to save your changes.

4.  Double-click on the Customer Credits subreport so that it opens in design mode.

5.  Right-click on the Amount field and select Insert > Summary.

6.  On the Insert Summary dialog box, keep the default settings and click the OK button to save changes. This inserts a total of all the credits in the report footer.

    Since the sales amount is on the main report and the credits are listed on the subreport, a shared variable is needed so that the two reports can share their data. We have to create a formula on both the main report and the subreport that declares the same shared variable.

7.  On the subreport, create a new formula called Net Credits. Enter the following code for the formula.

    ```
    Shared CurrencyVar TotalCredits;
    TotalCredits := Sum({Credit.Amount});
    ```

    This formula assigns the total credits to the shared variable TotalCredits. However, Crystal Reports won't calculate the formula's value unless it is placed somewhere on the report. We already have the total listed on the report and the formula is just duplicating this information. So, we are going to put it on the report and then suppress it. This tells Crystal Reports to calculate the formula's value, but not show it on the report.

8.  Save the formula and return to design mode of the subreport.

9. Drag and drop the formula onto the report in the report footer.

10. Right-click on the formula and select Format Field. Go to the Common tab and click the Suppress property. Click the OK button to save your changes. The formula will no longer be visible, but it will still get calculated.

11. Click on the design tab of the main report.

12. Add a new formula to the main report called **Net Sales**. Enter the following code for the formula.

```
Shared CurrencyVar TotalCredits;
CurrencyVar NetSales;
NetSales := Sum ({Orders.Order Amount},
{Customer.Customer ID}) + TotalCredits;
```

This formula is adding the total credits shared variable to the total sales figure. Since the TotalCredits value is negative, it will be subtracted.

13. Save and close the formula to return to the design view of the main report.

14. Drag and drop the formula into the section Group Footer #1b.

15. Unfortunately, there isn't enough room in the group footer to fit the formula within the gray box. Click on the bottom edge of the box to make it larger.

16. Let's add a description of the net sales formula so that the reader knows what is being calculated. Select the menu options Insert > Text Object. Enter the text **Net Sales**.

17. Click on both the text object and the formula and make them bold. This will make it easier for the reader to see the amount.

    The bottom portion of the report in design view should look similar to the following figure.

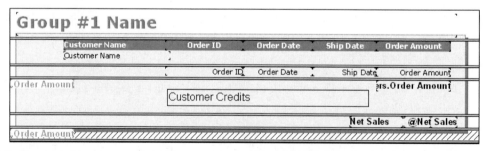

18. Preview the report and the bottom portion should look like this.

| | | | |
|---|---|---|---|
| 1246 | 01/30/2004 | 01/30/2004 | $3,884.25 |
| 2402 | 11/22/2004 | 11/23/2004 | $185.20 |
| 1387 | 03/01/2004 | 03/01/2004 | $1,515.35 |
| | | | **$37,026.11** |

| Credit Authorization Number | Amount |
|---|---|
| CR1608 | ($1,792.91) |
| CR5241 | ($951.33) |
| CR6321 | ($1,484.68) |
| CR6592 | ($1,237.54) |
| CR6798 | ($727.56) |
| | **($6,194.02)** |

**Net Sales** $30,832.09

The Net Sales subtotal at the bottom uses the shared variable to combine the total sales less the net credits.

# Tutorial 9-6. Using Subreports for Hidden Calculations

You learned in Chapter 1 that Crystal Reports uses a 2 pass processing model to generate reports. This can cause problems if you want to share data between two objects that are both processed in pass 2. An alternative around this problem is to use a subreport for performing one of the calculations and pass the value to the main report using a shared variable. Although the subreport is basically repeating a calculation that already appears on the main report, by using a subreport you get around the limitation of not being able to share data within the second pass of the report processing model.

You can also use subreports to perform calculations that don't appear on the main report at all. You can use them to process supporting data that needs to be used on the main report in other calculations, but that data doesn't need to be shown. For example, someone once put a crosstab object in a subreport and then pulled the monthly subtotals out of the crosstab object and displayed them in the main report.

In both of these scenarios, you need the subreport to process data but you don't want the subreport to be shown on the main report. The problem you will encounter is that if you add the subreport to the main report and then suppress it, its formulas won't be calculated. The main report will have a zero value for the shared variables. The subreport object has to be shown on the main report to perform its calculations. Some people make the subreport really small so that it is almost hidden. This works pretty well, but it's not the best solution.

There is a way to trick Crystal Reports into hiding the subreport but still perform its calculations. The key is that even though you can't suppress the subreport object, you can suppress the sections within the subreport. Suppressing the sections will still call the subreport formulas and the shared variables will return a value. But, the subreport won't have any output. Follow these steps on your own report to carry out this trick.

1.  Create the subreport and build the formula as you normally would. Test it to make sure it works.

2.  Click on every section in the subreport and choose the Suppress option. If you preview the report now, you should see a blank area where the subreport object is located, but there won't be any data in it. This tells Crystal Reports to calculate the formulas in the subreport but not display them.

3.  On the main report, move the subreport in its own section. If you have to create a new section just for the subreport then that is fine. You want the subreport to be the only object in that section.

4.  The next step is to tell Crystal Reports not to show the subreport if its sections are all suppressed. On the main report, right-click on the subreport object and select Format Subreport. This opens the Format Editor dialog box.

5.  Click on the Subreport tab. Then click on the option Suppress Blank Subreport.

6.  Click the OK button to save your changes and close the Format Editor dialog box.

7.  On the main report right-click on the grey area to the left of the section that holds the subreport and select Section Expert.

8.  Select the option Suppress Blank Section and click the OK button.

When you run the report the section holding the subreport will be suppressed and the shared variables will still be calculated correctly.

## Troubleshooting Shared Variables

Shared variables are a great way to pass data between the subreport and the main report. But you have to be careful because using them requires following certain rules. If you forget the rules, you'll often find that either your calculations do not come out as expected or the report will print a zero where you expect a number to be.

The first two rules actually work together. The first rule is that variables are calculated in the order that they are printed on the report. The typical printing order is to start by printing the page header, followed by any group headers, followed by the detail records, etc. The formulas included in each section are not calculated until that section prints. So, formulas in the group header are printed before formulas in the details section.

The second rule is that within a particular section, the formulas in the main report are calculated before printing the subreport. Even if a formula is displayed after the subreport, if they are in the same section, then the main report formula is calculated prior to the subreport running. If the formula in the main report uses a shared variable from the subreport, then the shared variable will not have the correct value because it hasn't been calculated in the subreport yet. This is the source of many problems because when looking at the report you see that the subreport is shown first and you assume that its formula is passing the correct value to the formula in the main report. You can easily forget that the subreport is called last.

The best way to design reports that use subreports with shared variables is to have a separate section for each subreport. Don't put any fields from the main report in this section. This forces each section to finish printing and calculating its formulas prior to moving to the next section. This prevents any potential confusion that arises from having a subreport's formulas calculating after the main report's formulas.

The third rule of subreport formulas is that they don't get reset by themselves. Another common assumption is that each time a subreport is printed that all its variables are reset back to zero. This isn't the case for shared variables because their values stay alive for the entire life of the main report. If the subreport doesn't have any records to print, then the shared variable keeps the same value from the last time the subreport printed. The main report will start printing incorrect totals because its formula is basing its calculation on a value from the previous subreport. To correct this, you have to reset the variable to zero at the top of the report. This is usually done in the report header, but sometimes in the group header. And don't forget to use the WhilePrintingRecords function to force it to call the formula each time.

Let's go through two tutorials that show how these rules are used and what can happen when they are ignored.

## Tutorial 9-7. Putting Subreports in Separate Sections

In this tutorial, we will examine the first two rules mentioned above and demonstrate why each subreport should be put in its own section.

1. Open the report 'Customer Net Sales.rpt'.

   The first rule we want to test is whether formulas in the subreport get calculated after the formulas in the main report. If you recall, I recommended that subreports always be put in their own sections to prevent this from happening. In this report, the subreport is already in a different section than the Net Sales formula (that is why the totals work properly). Let's experiment and see what would have happened if we didn't follow that rule.

2. In design mode, find the Net Sales formula and move it from Group Footer #1b into the bottom of the section right above it, Group Footer #1a. Notice that this is the same section the subreport is in (and will probably cause problems). Preview the report to see what the result is.

Now that the Net Sales formula is in the same section as the subreport, it has the same value as the total sales figure. This is because the shared value in the subreport hasn't been calculated yet and it is zero. Thus, the credits aren't being subtracted from the total sales. This proves that the main report's formula has to be in a separate section to be calculated properly.

Another interesting consequence of not following this rule is that the following Net Sales calculations will use the previous Net Credits value. Since the subreport wasn't calculated yet in that section, the current value of the TotalCredits shared variable will be what was calculated for the previous customer. This makes all the Net Credits amounts to appear to be one-off.

3.  Don't save the changes to this report. Since the data is bad, simply close the report without saving.

## Tutorial 9-8. Resetting Subreport Variables

One thing you might not have noticed in the previous report is that there is actually a problem with it. The subreport doesn't reset the shared variable back to zero. If there is a customer without any credits, the net sales figure would be wrong because it will still be using the total credits from the previous customer. If you open the report and go to page 8 (the first customer without any credits), you'll see that the net sales figure is, in fact, completely wrong.

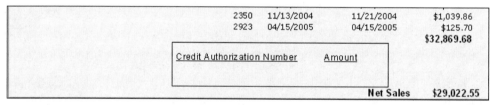

The net sales amount should be the same as the total sales because there aren't any credits to subtract from it. Instead, the net sales are off by $3,847.13. If you go back to page 7 to the previous customer, you'll see that their credit sub-total is exactly $3,847.13. Since the subreport didn't have any data, it didn't calculate a new value for the TotalCredits shared variable. The previous customer's amount got carried forward to the next customer. Let's fix this right away so that all customers have the correct totals.

1.  Open the report '11 Customer Net Sales.rpt'.

2.  Double-click on the Customer Credits subreport to open it in design mode.

3.  Add a new formula and call it Reset Credits. Enter the following code:

```
WhilePrintingRecords;
Shared CurrencyVar TotalCredits;
TotalCredits := 0;
```

This formula declares the shared variable and sets it to zero. It also uses the function WhilePrintingRecords to force it to be called each time the subreport prints.

4.  Save and close the formula.

5. Drag and drop the Reset Credits formula into the report header.

6. Since the formula is always zero, we don't want it to be visible on the subreport. Right-click on it and select Format Field. Go to the Common tab and click on the Suppress property to select it. Click the OK button to save your changes.

7. Preview the report and go to page 8 again. This time the net sales amount should be equal to the total sales amount because the credits from the previous customer did not get carried forward.

8. Save this report as **Customer Net Sales Corrected.rpt**.

## Hiding Empty Subreports

Another problem that you'll eventually encounter with subreports is when they don't have any data but they still print. You'll see the column headers but no detail records. In fact, you can see this in the previous tutorial. The column headers for the credit report are there, but no data is displayed. This makes for an unprofessional looking report. Correcting this requires making two changes.

The first change is suppressing the subreport when it is blank. You do this by going to the Format Editor dialog box and setting the property Suppress Blank Subreport. But just suppressing the subreport will still leave a large empty section on the report. The second change is modifying the section on the main report that holds the subreport so that it is also suppressed when the subreport is empty. Do this by going into the Section Expert and setting the property Suppress Blank Section. Since we are suppressing the entire section of the main report when the subreport has no data, this is another reason why you should put subreports in their own section.

## Tutorial 9-9. Hiding Empty Subreports

1. Open the report 'Customer Net Sales Corrected.rpt'.

2. We want to suppress the subreport when it doesn't have any data, so right-click on it and select Format Subreport. This opens the Format Editor dialog box.

3. Click on the Subreport tab and select the property Suppress Blank Subreport. If the subreport doesn't have any data, then all the report objects will be suppressed.

4. Click the OK button to save your changes.

   Now we want to modify the main report so that the section holding the subreport is suppressed as well. Unfortunately, section #1a also has the subtotal for the total sales in it. We need to put the subreport in a new section all by itself.

5. On the left side of the designer, right-click Group Footer #1a and select Insert Section Below. This creates new section #1b and renames the previous section #1b as #1c.

6. Drag the subreport down into Group Footer #1b. Now the subreport is in its own section with no crossover from fields in the main report.

7. Right-click the Group Footer #1b name and select Section Expert. This opens the Section Expert dialog box.

8. Click the option Suppress Blank Section property for Group Footer #1b. Click the OK button to save your changes. This will suppress the section when the subreport is empty.

9. Preview the report and skip to page 8. You'll see that the Customer Credits subreport is completely gone because this customer has no credit records. This is a nice improvement.

| | | | |
|---|---|---|---|
| 2550 | 12/30/2004 | 01/03/2005 | $789.15 |
| 2350 | 11/13/2004 | 11/21/2004 | $1,039.86 |
| 2923 | 04/15/2005 | 04/15/2005 | $125.70 |
| | | | $32,869.68 |
| | | Net Sales | $32,869.68 |

10. Save the report as Customer Net Sales Empty Subreport.rpt.

# Using On-Demand Subreports

By default, subreports are run at the same time as the main report. When you view or print the main report, the subreport information is printed as well. This may result in a performance decrease because the subreport could require just as much time, if not more, to process as the main report. If performance becomes a problem, a solution is to declare the subreport so that it isn't bound to the main report. This is called an on-demand subreport.

An on-demand subreport doesn't print at the same time as the main report. Instead, a hyperlink that describes the subreport is shown where the subreport should appear.[43] When the user clicks on the hyperlink the subreport is processed and shown to the user. The on-demand subreport is shown on a separate tab in the viewer.

> **Caution**
>
> On-demand subreports are for reports meant to be viewed on a computer. If you send the report directly to the printer, only the placeholders are printed and not the subreport. This doesn't give the reader the detail information they are looking for and will probably be confusing.

To define a subreport as being an on-demand subreport, use the Subreport tab of the Insert Subreport dialog box. At the bottom of the dialog box is an On-Demand Subreport checkbox. It is unchecked by default. Click on it to make the subreport an on-demand subreport.

---

[43] A placeholder can be displayed instead of the hyperlink.

By default, an on-demand subreport is shown as a hyperlink on the main report. The text is the name of the subreport.

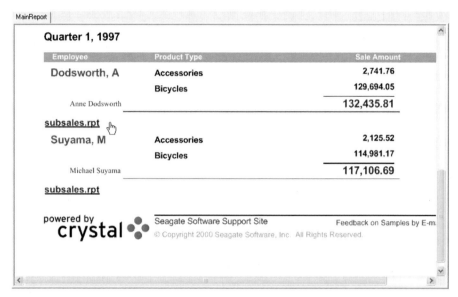

**Figure 9-9. On-demand subreports shown as a hyperlink.**

When you click on the hyperlink the subreport is processed and displayed on a new tab in the viewer. Each on-demand subreport is displayed on its own tab.

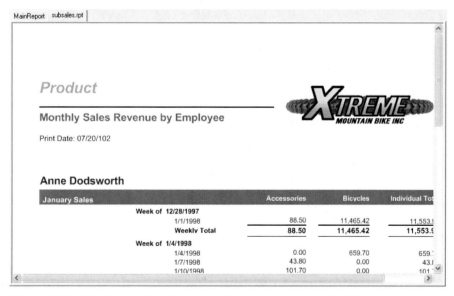

**Figure 9-10. On-demand subreports shown on a separate tab.**

If you feel that displaying a hyperlink isn't professional enough, you can display a customized placeholder instead. When you are in design mode, right-click on the subreport object and choose Format Subreport. Then go to the Subreport tab that is shown in Figure 9-11.

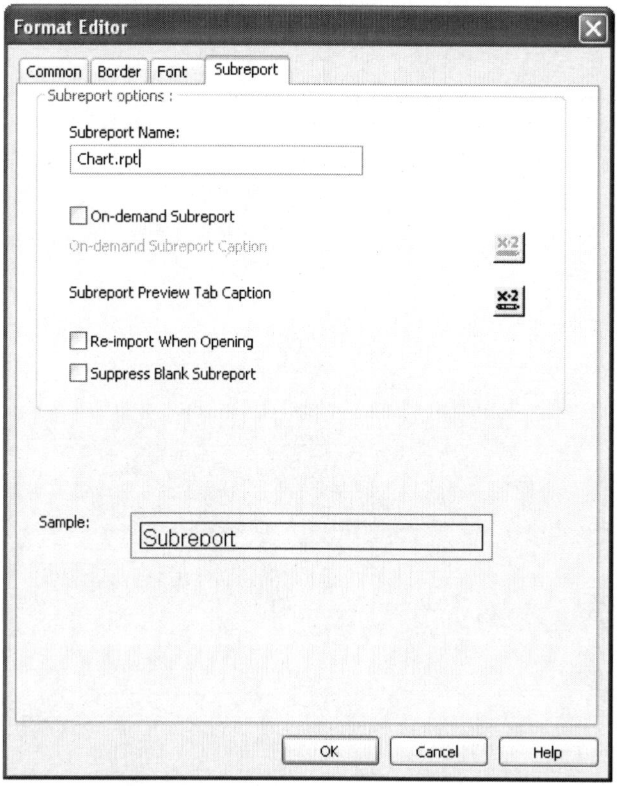

**Figure 9-11. Formatting the subreport placeholder.**

There is a formula button for modifying the caption that is displayed on the main report. You can enter a simple string in this formula or customize the string by concatenating data fields into it. The rest of the tabs on this dialog box can be used to format how the placeholder looks. For example, you can change the font, the background color and the border. Figure 9-12 shows the placeholder formatted with a border and a larger font size.

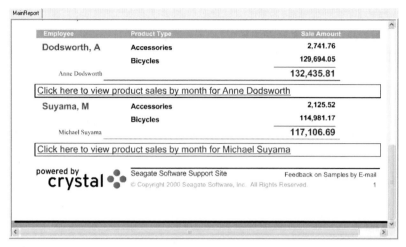

Figure 9-12. The subreport placeholder.

## Best Of The Forum

Questions are always being posted to the forum about subreports. Here are a few more that I frequently see and I thought would be beneficial for you.

**Question:** My main report uses a portrait page orientation and my subreport is formatted for landscape. But when I print the report, the subreport comes out in portrait mode as well. How can I get the subreport to print in landscape mode?

**Answer:** You can't. Crystal Reports uses the orientation of the main report for printing the subreport. You can't use different page orientations for subreports.

**Question:** I have a few separate reports and I want to export them all to a single PDF file. How can I do this?

**Answer:** There are third party utilities that let you merge PDF files into a single file. I haven't used them before, but you can use Google to search for them. Another alternative is to create an empty master report to hold the reports. Put each subreport in its own section on the master report so that they print one after the other. It can be exported to a single PDF file. The only limitation is that these subreports can't have subreports of their own. Crystal Reports doesn't allow nesting subreports more than one level deep.

**Question:** The data in my report is printed on a separate detail line for each record. But, I want to print a list of all the names on a single line going across the page. How do I do this?

**Answer:** Create a subreport that concatenates the fields together in one string as they are printed. The string should be a shared variable and the formula would look like this (assuming that X is the string variable):

X := X & {table.field} & " ";

Use a formula on the main report to print this shared variable after the subreport. If you want to hide the subreport, refer Tutorial 9-6.

# Connecting to Databases

Throughout this book we practiced creating many sample reports in the tutorials. Within each tutorial, we always based the report off the Xtreme.mdb database and left it at that. Although this was done to keep things simple and focus on the topic at hand, there is so much more to what Crystal Reports can do. We are way overdue for learning more about databases and how Crystal Reports can connect to them. In this chapter, we are going to move beyond using the simplistic MS Access sample database that comes with Crystal Reports and examine how to get more out of our data and learn about advanced data access.

The backbone of every report is the database that stores the data it prints. Companies of all sizes utilize different aspects of Crystal Reports to distribute information to their users. Large corporations merge data from different servers into reports that consolidate and chart information from a dozen or more tables. Small businesses optimize their report distribution and expand their client base by providing their data in an XML format and letting companies from around the world generate reports on it. Home offices often do simple tasks such as printing monthly sales reports and generating mailing labels from an Access database or an Excel spreadsheet.

Crystal Reports is designed to work with many types of data. Reports can be generated regardless of where the data is stored; SQL Server, MS Access or even the Outlook email repository. Crystal Reports affords many ways to connect to databases. Learning each method can be quite an undertaking. This chapter sorts out these options and presents them in an easy to understand format. You can determine which method best meets your needs and how to quickly implement it.

# Using the Database Expert

The Database Expert is where you do 90% of your work connecting to data sources. It lets you establish the connection to the data source, select the tables to print from, and make sure the tables are linked together properly. You get to see the Database Expert in two places. It is within the Report Expert when creating a new report and it is a standalone dialog box when you choose the menu options Database > Database Expert. It is shown in Figure 10-1.

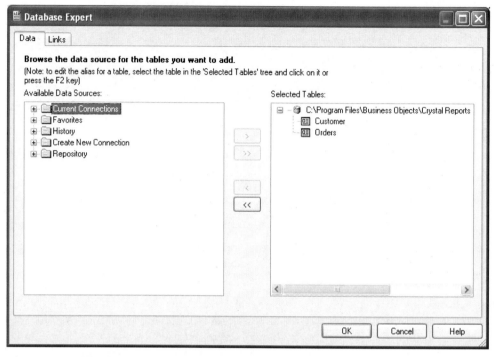

**Figure 10-1. The Database Expert dialog box.**

The left side of the dialog box gives you five options for adding a new data source. They are as follows:

Current Connections: List all data sources that are currently open.

Favorites: Just as you might have a list of favorite web pages within your internet browser, Crystal Reports lets you create a list of your 'favorite' data sources. If you regularly print from numerous data sources, this makes it easy to find the data sources that are the most important.

History: Shows a list of the last five recently used data sources. If you work with a small number of data sources on a regular basis, you'll find them listed here.

Create New Connection: Add a new data source by choosing from a list of all the types of data sources available. This list of data sources is quite extensive and we'll cover it in more detail next.

Repository: Shows the contents of your repository through the Business Objects Enterprise Explorer.[44]

---

[44] This book only covers the professional edition of Crystal Reports. Please consult your documentation for information about the enterprise edition.

To add a new data source, first determine which folder it would be listed in. If this is the first time you're using Crystal Reports, selecting Create New Connection would be your best choice because it lets you choose from the myriad of data sources available. If you've already created reports before, it will probably be easier to select one of the first three categories. If you are editing a current report and want to add a new table, you can click on the Current Connections folder. If you use a data source on a regular basis, you can add it to the Favorites list and choose it from there. If you have used the data source on another report recently, it will probably be listed in the History folder.

Creating a new connection is the most complex of all the categories because you have to determine what type of data source you want to connect to and know how to connect to it. This information is unique to each type of connection. Figure 10-2 shows a picture of the available data sources.

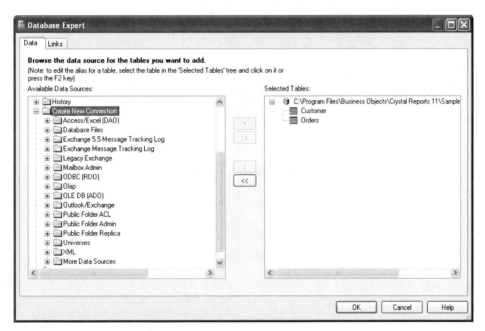

**Figure 10-2. List of available data sources.**

In addition to that, if you click on the More Data Sources folder, over a dozen more data sources are listed. There are too many types to cover in this chapter, but let's review some of the more common ones listed in Table 10-1.

**Table 10-1. Common Data Sources**

| Data Source | Description |
| --- | --- |
| Acccess/Excel/ Database Files | Select a PC database/Excel file using its file location. |

| ODBC (RDO) | Connect using an ODBC driver by selecting an existing System DSN[45]. |
| --- | --- |
| OLE DB (ADO) | Builds a connection string to access data sources using an OLE DB driver. It asks you for the data source to connect to and any relevant information regarding its location and logon information. |
| XML | XML is a generic file format for describing data. It continues to increase in popularity as more companies realize how easy it is to share information using XML. You can even report from data off of another company's web server if they have a public web services URL (Amazon.com does this for reporting their book's sales rankings). |
| Field Definitions Only | Found within the More Data Sources folder, it specifies a field definition file with a .ttx extension. This is only for backwards compatibility and isn't used for new development. |

To select the data source from the Database Expert dialog, click on the proper folder category to expand it. This triggers a dialog box which asks for information about the data source. The dialog is specific to the type of data source being opened because each data source has different requirements to open the data source. For example, opening an Excel file will prompt you for a file path and filename, but opening a SQL Server database will prompt you for the server name and authorization credentials. Upon entering the information, the dialog box closes and the data source name is shown in the Database Expert and listed under its folder. Under the data source name is the list of available tables, views and stored procedures.[46] Click on the plus signs next to the individual items to expand the list.

### Tip

There is one small quirk about the Available Data Sources window you should be aware of. It occurs when you click on the plus sign to expand a folder and a data source dialog box opens up. If you accidentally close the dialog box without adding a new data source, there is no option to open the dialog box again. You have to click on the minus sign to close the folder and then click on

---

[45] You should only use System DSN's. File DSN's and User DSN's are buggy and shouldn't be relied upon.
[46] If you don't see everything listed in the Database Expert that you expected (particularly stored procedures), right-click the data source and select Options. Look in the Data Explorer area to make sure that what you want isn't being excluded.

the plus sign to expand it again. This triggers the dialog box to open a second time. Once you've added a data source to that folder, this isn't an issue because there will now be an item listed as the first item and clicking on it lets you add another data source.

Add the tables you need by selecting them and clicking on the right arrow button. Double-clicking on the table adds it to the list as well. When all the necessary tables have been added, go to the Links tab to establish the relationship between the tables.

## Adding Common Data Sources

Let's look at the steps involved for connecting to common data sources and adding tables from each one. We'll see that although there are many similarities between them, each is unique in its own way.

## Connecting to MS Access

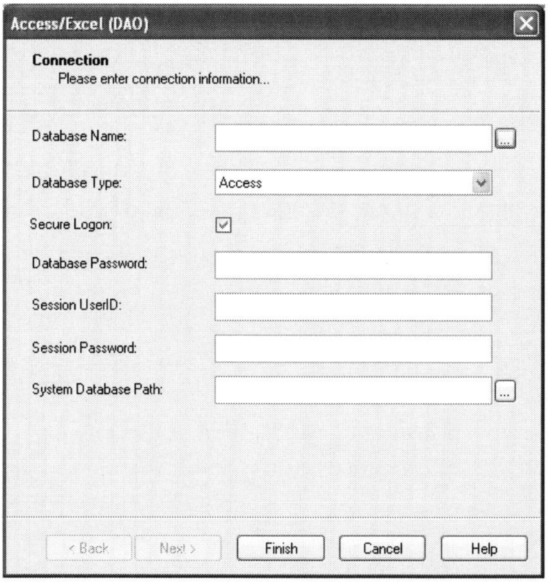

Figure 10-3. Microsoft Access connection dialog box.

Microsoft Access has a few different ways to connect to it. On the most simplistic level, you only need to enter a file path and filename for the Database Name property. It is easiest to click on the File Open button to the right and navigate to where the file is located on your computer or network.

In some cases, the Access database is secured and you have to enter a password to access it. You have to click on the Secure Logon checkbox so that you can enter the authentication credentials. If you have a file-level security password for the database, you can enter it in the Database Password property. If you have a specific User ID and Password for yourself, enter it for the properties Session User ID and Session Password. The last property, System Database Path, is where you would enter the location of the .mdw file (where the user credentials are stored).

When you click the Finish button, Crystal Reports examines the database and lists all the available tables in the database. Choose the appropriate tables and move them to the Selected Tables list.

## Connecting to MS Excel

Selecting a Microsoft Excel spreadsheet uses the same dialog box as Access, but it is easier to use. With Excel, all you have to do is set the Database Type property to be the version of Excel you are using and set the filename in the Database Name property.

The difference between Access and Excel is that Access is a database that stores information in tables and Excel stores data in spreadsheets. After selecting the correct spreadsheet file and clicking the Finish button, Crystal Reports displays the worksheet names instead of table names. You have to choose which worksheets to pull data from and move them to the Selected Tables list.

| Note |
| --- |

When you create a new Excel spreadsheet file, there are actually three worksheets created by default. Most likely, you will use the first spreadsheet and leave the other two unused. When Crystal Reports opens the Excel file, it will see each worksheet and list each one as its own table. Even though the other two worksheets don't have any data on them, they are still listed. Just ignore them and use the first worksheet as your table.

Crystal Reports interprets each column in a spreadsheet as a database field. Crystal Reports looks at the column headings to determine the field names.

## Connecting to SQL Server

SQL Server is a much more sophisticated and powerful database than MS Access. With its power comes more knowledge to work with it. So there are more variations on how to connect to the server and pass authorization credentials. SQL Server has two ways of connecting to it: ODBC DSN (Open Database Connectivity using a Data Source Name) and OLE DB (Object Linking and Embedding). The method that you use depends on your technical knowledge and how your computer is set up.

Using an ODBC connection requires that an administrator set up your computer in advance to be able to talk to the database Of course, if you have the technical skills and you know the security information, you could do this yourself. Once the connection has been created on your computer, any program (including Crystal Reports) can reference the ODBC connection name and retrieve the database records.

The benefit to having an ODBC connection is that the connection details are hidden from the user. All the user needs to know is the name of the ODBC connection and they can retrieve the data. This helps keep the database secure. The drawback to using an ODBC connection is that it must be set up on your computer in advance. If you work in a company with hundreds of computers, it literally takes a full tech support team to go to every computer and set this up manually. This isn't very efficient. So Microsoft later decided that they needed a better way of connecting to databases and they came up with the OLE DB connection type to simplify the process.

OLE DB connections let you save the SQL Server authentication information within the actual program. Unlike ODBC, the authentication information isn't in a hidden place on your computer. It is within the application and stays with the application. You can copy the program to any computer in the company and it can connect to the database. No tech support teams are needed to run around the company setting up each individual computer. The drawback to using OLE DB is that sometimes, depending upon how the database is set up, it requires the user to have knowledge of the database's authentication information, and giving out the User ID and Password to users can present a security risk.

The type of connection you use is often determined by corporate policy. If your computer is set up to connect to the database using an existing ODBC connection, then that is what you use. If you were given a User ID and Password to access the database directly (or your windows login is authenticated to do so), then you can use an OLE DB connection to retrieve the data. If you are uncertain about which applies to you (and this whole discussion has lost you), consult your company tech support for advice on how they wish you to proceed.

### ODBC Connections

To connect using ODBC, you need the name of an existing ODBC DSN.[47] When you installed Crystal Reports, it automatically created the ODBC DSN called "Xtreme Sample Database 11". To connect to it, on the Data tab of the Database Expert open the ODBC (RDO) folder. This immediately opens the ODBC dialog box shown in Figure 10-4.

---

[47] Another option is to use a connection string. A connection string contains database information specific to the database you are using. This will either be provided to you by your technical support or you can consult the database help file. However, this isn't used much any more due to its complexity.

388                                    Chapter 10

**Figure 10-4. Selecting the ODBC connection.**

There are three options on the ODBC dialog box, of which you will probably just use one. The first option lists the names of the available data sources stored on your computer. As you can see in the above figure, the Xtreme Sample Database 11 connection is listed there. Click on it to select it and then click the Next button.

The other two options are File DSNs and connection strings. As mentioned earlier, they aren't used much anymore and I'm not going to discuss them.

Clicking the Next button changes the dialog box so that you are prompted for your connection information. You need to enter the User ID and Password for accessing the database. If your Windows login also serves as the login to SQL Server, then you don't have to enter anything for the User ID and Password. The fact that you are logged into the computer is sufficient.

After entering the User ID and Password and clicking the Finish button, you are returned to the Data tab. It now displays your data source and the tables associated with it. At this point you can select the tables you want on your report and proceed to the Links tab (which is discussed later in the chapter).

# OLE DB Connections

Connecting to databases using an OLE DB connection is very common due to the overhead of maintaining ODBC connections. To create a new connection, go to the Data tab on the Database Expert and open the Create New Connection folder. Within it find the OLE DB (ADO) folder and open it. This opens the OLE DB dialog box shown in Figure 10-5.

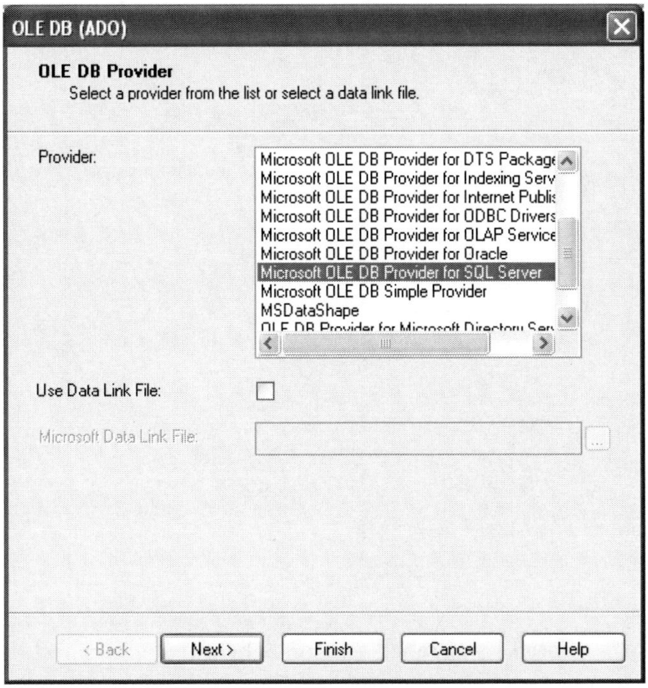

**Figure 10-5. Selecting an OLE DB connection.**

The Provider list shows you all the available OLE DB connection types. As you can see in the above figure, it is an extensive list. Scroll down to find the SQL Server provider (or whichever database type you are using) and select it. Then click the Finish button.

The OLE DB dialog box changes to prompt you for the server name, connection info, and database name. It is shown in Figure 10-6.

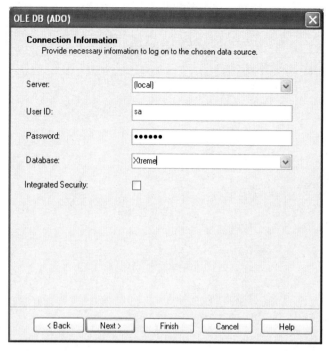

**Figure 10-6. OLE DB connection info.**

Entering all the information on this dialog box probably requires help from your tech support or the database administrator. You first need to enter the server name. If you weren't given one, you can click the dropdown list and it will show you a list of available servers that it sees on the network. If you are running a copy of SQL Server on your computer, you can enter a server name of "(local)". If you have a special User ID and Password for accessing SQL Server, enter that next. If your Windows login is used as your SQL Server login, then click the Integrated Security option in the middle. Lastly, enter the database name. Again, if you don't know the exact database name, you can click the dropdown list to see a list of available databases on the server and select the one you need.

## Tip

If you click the Database dropdown and don't see any databases listed, then it means that you haven't entered the proper connection information. To retrieve the list of databases, the dialog box tries to locate the database server you entered and send it your login credentials. If it succeeds, it retrieves the list of database names. If it fails, the database list stays empty and you have to double-check that you entered the correct information.

After clicking the Next button, you are presented with an Advanced Information page displaying technical details like encryption flag, service number, and other stuff that doesn't have any relevance to us. There is nothing required of you to do on this screen except click the Finish button to close the dialog box.[48]

Click the Finish button to save your changes and return to the data table. The new connection is now shown and the various tables are shown under it. Click on the Links tab to set relationships between the tables.

### Viewing the Available Tables

After selecting the data source to pull data from, you get to select the tables that have the data you want to print. Below the data source name is a list of the available tables, views and stored procedures to choose from. You might assume that this is a static list of tables. But Crystal Reports gives you the ability to customize what is shown in this list. By right-clicking on the data source and choosing Options, it opens the Database Options dialog box. You can also open this dialog box by choosing the menu options File > Options and clicking on the Database tab (shown in Figure 10-7).

---

[48] For the extremely technical readers, you can actually modify the OLE DB properties to customize the connection. With all the reports I've created over the years, I've never needed to do this.

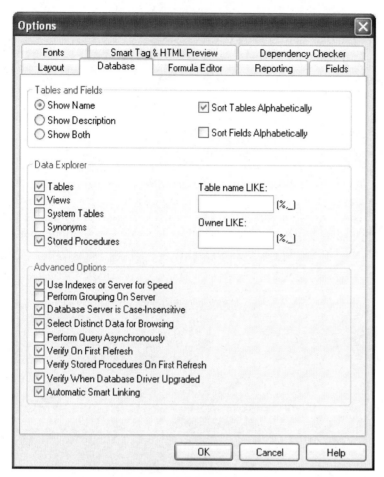

**Figure 10-7. Setting the database options.**

The middle portion of this dialog box, titled Data Explorer, determines what is listed below the data source. There is a checkbox next to each option. The checkboxes that are selected by default are Tables, Views and Stored Procedures. The options to show System Tables and Synonyms are disabled. You can check and uncheck any of these options if you want to show or hide them on the Database Expert dialog box.

On the right side are two filters for determining which tables should be displayed. In corporations that have specifications for how tables are named, there are usually naming conventions in place which assign standard prefixes to the table name based upon the data they store. For example, financial application tables could have a prefix of 'fn'. If you are working with a database with hundreds of tables, it can be difficult to find the table you need. By using the option to filter tables by name, you could tell Crystal Reports to only display the financial tables that start with 'fn'.

When specifying the table name filter Crystal Reports gives you two characters that serve as wildcards. The '_' represents any single character and the '%' represents any length of characters. To specify that you only want to see the financial tables, you would use the filter 'fn%'.

> **Caution**
>
> When you create a connection to the database server and look at the list of available tables and stored procedures, you might be confused to see a group of names that you don't recognize. This is because SQL Server uses internal system tables and stored procedures for managing each database. These are tables that you do not need to be familiar with because they are used internally to maintain the database. When the Data Explorer section has the System Tables option unchecked, Crystal Reports hides the system tables. Unfortunately, this option doesn't apply to stored procedures and there is no way to hide the system stored procedures. But once you get used to seeing them, it will be easy to ignore them and just locate the stored procedures you need.

The top portion of the Database Explorer determines how the tables and fields are shown throughout the report. This includes the Field Explorer window and anywhere you can pick from a list of fields. You can set the tables to either be shown by their table name, description or both. You can also set whether the tables and fields should be sorted alphabetically or shown in the natural order.

 Crystal Reports XI R2 gives you the ability to change the sort order within the Field Explorer window. By right-clicking on the table name in the Field Explorer, you have the option to sort the database fields alphabetically.

The bottom portion of the dialog box, Advanced Options, controls different aspects of the report which affect report performance and how Crystal Reports talks to the database server. We cover these options in the areas that apply to them.

### Creating a List of Favorite Data Sources

Before leaving the Data tab of the Database Expert dialog box, you have the choice of saving the data source in your list of favorites. Just like your browser has a list of your favorite websites, Crystal Reports lets you keep a list of favorite data sources. If this is going to be a data source that you will refer to frequently, right-click on it and select the menu option Add To Favorites. This adds all the connection details of the data source to the Favorites folder so that you can quickly find it the next time you need to print from it again.

## Linking Tables

After connecting to the data source and selecting the tables you want to print, you proceed to the second tab of the Database Expert dialog box. This is the Links tab. This tab is only available when you select two or more tables. You need to link the tables together so that Crystal Reports knows how they are related. For example, a pet store that wants to print a list of its products by animal needs to build a report using an animal table and a product table. To match the product to the appropriate type of animal, both tables will be linked by the field Animal ID. It would be impossible to determine which products are associated with which animal without this link. The Links tab, shown in Figure 10-8, is used for setting the fields that link the different tables together.

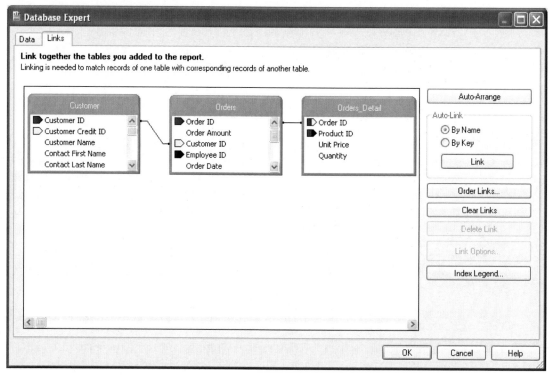

**Figure 10-8. The Links tab.**

When the Links tab is first displayed, it creates default links for you. In an effort to make it easier for you, Crystal Reports tries to figure out which fields in each table should be linked to each other. It does this based upon the field name, data types and indexes. This is the equivalent of Crystal's "best guess" for the relationships between the different tables.

**Tip**

To get the most benefit out of the auto-arranged links, design your tables with field names that use a consistent naming convention and have well thought out indexes. This will result in a higher probability that Crystal Reports will create the appropriate default links.

The default links that Crystal creates are not set in stone. You are free to delete them or add more according to your needs. To delete a link, simply click on it (to select it) and then click on the button labeled Delete Link. You can also just press the Delete key after selecting it. To add a new link, drag and drop the field from one table onto the matching field in the other table.

There are a couple of buttons that are helpful for managing links. The Auto-Arrange button rearranges the tables on the screen into an easier-to-read layout. This is useful when handling a report with many tables. A multitude of tables makes it difficult to visualize the relationship with one another and the overall structure. If the Auto-Arrange button doesn't help, you can reposition the tables yourself by dragging them around within the window.

The Auto-Link button rebuilds the links based on whether you want to link by field name or by index. This comes in handy for undoing any new links you added, should you want to start from scratch. The Clear Links button removes all the links between the tables so you can start with a blank slate do it yourself.

A primary way of improving report performance is to link on fields that have an index associated with them. Creating an index on a field tells the database server to build internal sorting tables so that the data can be read much faster. If an index isn't created for a field, then the database has to search through every record in the table to find the data. This is very inefficient. Crystal Reports tells you which fields have indexes by using the triangular icon to the left of the field name. When you see this icon, you know that the database table has been optimized for searching on these fields and your reports will run faster if you link on them. Each icon is colored so that you can see where the index is in the hierarchy of all the indexes in the table. By clicking on the Index Legend button, you see the dialog box in Figure 10-9 and see how the color schemes are laid out.

**Figure 10-9. Index Legend color schemes.**

Another button on the Links tab is the Link Options button. It lets you modify how the two tables are linked together. You make the changes in the Link Options dialog box, shown in Figure 12 -10.

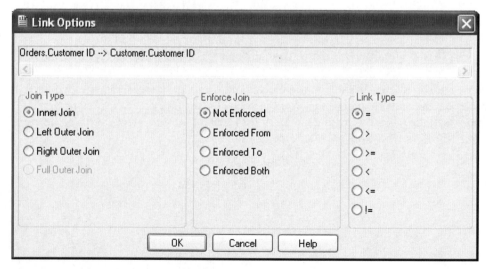

**Figure 10-10. The Link Options dialog box.**

The Link Options dialog box establishes the type of relationship between the two fields. It sets the type of join (Inner, Left Outer, Right Outer, or Full Outer) as well as how the fields are compared (equal to each other, less than, etc.). By default, fields are joined together when they are equal to each other. But you can modify this to give you greater flexibility with your report. You can link tables if one field is less than the other (<), greater than the other (>), or even when the fields are not equal to each other (!=). The link type options on the right side of the dialog box let you make this type of modification.

Let's look at the join options in more detail. Changing these options can result in totally different data being returned to the report and it is important to understand each one. Table 10-2 shows a list of the different linking options and how they affect the resulting data.

**Table 10-2. Join Options**

| Join Type | Result Set Description |
| --- | --- |
| Inner Join | Records from the left table are matched with records from the right table. Only records with an exact match are included. |
| Left Outer Join | All records from the left table are included. Records from the right table are only included if there is a matching record between the left and right tables. If the table on the left doesn't have a matching record with the right table, then the missing fields are filled with NULLs. |
| Right Outer Join | All records from the right table are included. Field values from the left table are included if there is a matching record in the left table. NULL values are stored in the missing fields if there is no matching record in the left table. |
| Full Outer Join | Every record from both tables is included. When records from both tables match, the fields in the new result set are filled in as normal. The other fields are set to NULL when there is no matching record for one of the tables. |

To see how each join type works, let's look at two simple tables and see what data is returned for each type of join. The two tables are Product and Product Type. We will only look at a few records in each table for illustration purposes. They are linked together by the field Product Type ID. Since both tables have a field called Product Type ID, I use the letter P to designate fields that come from the Product table and the letters PT to designate the Product Type table.

**Table 10-3. Product Table (P)**

| Product ID | Product Name | Product Type ID |
|---|---|---|
| 1 | Helmets | 10 |
| 2 | Tires | 12 |
| 3 | Grease | 13 |

**Table 10-4. Product Type Table (PT)**

| Product Type ID | Product Type Name |
|---|---|
| 10 | Accessories |
| 11 | Clothing |
| 12 | Parts |

An inner join displays the records from both tables when there is a matching record between the two tables. In this sample, only two records have a matching Product Type ID.

**Table 10-5. Inner Join**

| P.Product ID | P.Product Name | P.Product Type ID | PT.Product Type ID | PT.Product Type Name |
|---|---|---|---|---|
| 1 | Helmets | 10 | 10 | Accessories |
| 2 | Tires | 12 | 12 | Parts |

Both tables have one record missing from the result set. The Product table is missing the last record because the right table doesn't have a matching Product Type ID of 13. The Product Type table is missing the second record because the Product table doesn't have a record with a Product Type ID of 11.

The left outer join uses all tables from the left table, but only uses records from the right side when there is a match.

**Table 10-6. Left Outer Join**

| P.Product ID | P.Product Name | P.Product Type ID | PT.Product Type ID | PT.Product Type Name |
|---|---|---|---|---|
| 1 | Helmets | 10 | 10 | Accessories |
| 2 | Tires | 12 | 12 | Parts |
| 3 | Grease | 13 | NULL | NULL |

The three records are all from the Product table. The last record in this result set has NULL in the last two columns because the Product Type table doesn't have an ID of 13 in it.

The right outer join uses all tables from the right table, but the only records it uses from the left side are the ones with a match.

**Table 10-7. Right Outer Join**

| P.Product ID | P.Product Name | P.Product Type ID | PT.Product Type ID | PT.Product Type Name |
|---|---|---|---|---|
| 1 | Helmets | 10 | 10 | Accessories |
| NULL | NULL | NULL | 11 | Clothing |
| 2 | Tires | 12 | 12 | Parts |

The three records are all from the Product table. The second record in this result set has NULL columns from the Product table because it doesn't have an ID of 11 in it.

The full outer join selects all the records from both tables. If there isn't a matching record, it fills in NULL for the missing fields.

**Table 10-8. Full Outer Join**

| P.Product ID | P.Product Name | P.Product Type ID | PT.Product Type ID | PT.Product Type Name |
|---|---|---|---|---|
| 1 | Helmets | 10 | 10 | Accessories |
| NULL | NULL | NULL | 11 | Clothing |
| 2 | Tires | 12 | 12 | Parts |
| 3 | Grease | 13 | NULL | NULL |

If you compare this table to the two previous tables, it's as if the full outer join combines the results of left outer join with the results of the right outer join.

Now that you have an understanding of how different join types affect the result set that Crystal Reports uses to build a report, let's look at the last button on the Links tab. The Order Links button sets the order in which the links between the tables are created. This is used only when there is more than one link shown. The tables will be linked automatically, in the order that they are shown in the dialog box. The default linking order processes the links on the left before the links on the right. Changing the default linking order is useful when there is a hierarchy of tables joined together and the order to which they are joined is important. This can happen when you are using a link to return a subset of records from two tables, and these records are then linked to another table. Changing the order of the links changes the resulting data.

## *Using Multiple Data Sources*

Complex reports often require printing data of different origins. This can happen when you have tables in a SQL Server database and they need to be linked to tables in an Oracle database or a MySql database. Although Crystal Reports is capable of printing such reports, it doesn't always run flawlessly. What is happening internally is that Crystal Reports uses a different programming library for each type of database. Due to compatibility differences between data types and connection methods, Crystal Reports can occasionally experience problems providing the exact result set you expect.

Prior to processing a report, Crystal Reports takes the data connectivity information that is saved with a report and generates custom SQL statements for the database. These statements are then delivered to the database server. Although every major database vendor claims to be compliant with SQL standards, they each have their own subtle differences that can cause them to reject the SQL language of another database vendor. But Crystal Reports doesn't have the capability to, within a single report, generate SQL that is compatible with multiple variations of the SQL specification. It will inevitably create non-compatible SQL for one of the databases and you will have a compatibility issue.

That is not all. Different database servers manage their standard data types differently, chiefly in the way they store them internally. The way one database represents an Integer can be totally different from another database. When Crystal Reports tries to link these two fields together, it will have problems because the data looks like different data types.

While it is true that Crystal Reports is designed to work with the majority of database servers, it doesn't imply that the database servers themselves will work with one another. Since every database vendor tries to be better than the competition, companies are more concerned about performance than compatibility.

| Tip |
| --- |

If your database server has a way of connecting to another database natively, it is best to use that method rather than having Crystal Reports connect to the different databases. For example, you can have SQL Server connect to an Oracle database and SQL Server does the work of talking to the Oracle database. When Crystal Reports connects to the SQL Server database, it sees the Oracle data as being part of the SQL Server database. Crystal Reports doesn't realize that it is retrieving data from an Oracle database. This lets Crystal Reports only use the SQL Server libraries for accessing data and linking the tables and gives you much more reliable results. You also get better performance because the database server maintains the additional connection and links.

Fortunately, with version XI, the internal libraries have been optimized and problems that previous versions of Crystal Reports experienced are no longer an issue. Nonetheless, there are best practices to follow that help ensure you get the results you want.

When linking tables together, use fields that are of the String data type. String is the most consistent data type among different database servers and has the least likelihood of causing problems. This is no guarantee against all problems, however. For example, a string can be represented by variable and fixed length data type and this can create incompatibilities as well.

Rather than try to link tables from different data sources together, use subreports to print the data instead. The benefit of using subreports is that their data sources are treated separately from the main table. Also, it has only to worry about working with a single database driver. This independence eliminates a lot of potential problems. Using subreports also allows for more flexible linking options between a main report and subreport. You aren't limited to linking with strings and you can also use formulas to perform data type conversions when necessary.

There are certain types of reports where using a subreport isn't an option. An example is when all the detail fields need to be printed side by side. You can't use subreports because the fields will have to be printed underneath the other records.

# Connecting to Stored Procedures

As mentioned earlier in the chapter, stored procedures can be used as a data source just like a table. Crystal Reports can open a stored procedure, retrieve the data and print it. The benefit of using stored procedures is that they let you use the SQL language to process complex logic that isn't possible just by linking two tables together.

| Tip |
| --- |
| If your database has stored procedures but you don't see them listed in the Database Expert dialog box, it's probably because the option to view them has been disabled. To enable them, select the menu options File > Options and click on the Database tab. In the middle section, you'll see a Stored Procedures checkbox. Check it to tell Crystal Reports to list them. |

The one thing that can make retrieving data from a stored procedure unique is when it has input parameters. When a stored procedure uses input parameters, it has to be given a value for each parameter before it can run. Crystal Reports does this for you by automatically creating a new report parameter for every parameter in the stored procedure. It also gives the new report parameter the same name as the stored procedure parameter. So there is a one-to-one mapping of parameters between the stored procedure and the report and they have identical names and data types. When the report runs, the user is prompted to enter a value for each report parameter and Crystal Reports passes these parameter values to the stored procedure.

Let's look at a sample stored procedure. The following code is a stored procedure from the Northwind database.[49]

```
CREATE PROCEDURE CustOrderHist
@CustomerID nchar(5)
AS
SELECT ProductName, Total=SUM(Quantity)
FROM Products P, [Order Details] OD, Orders O, Customers C
WHERE C.CustomerID = @CustomerID
AND C.CustomerID = O.CustomerID
```

In this stored procedure, there is one input parameter called @CustomerID and it is a 5 character string. When this stored procedure is selected as the data source for a report, Crystal Reports automatically creates a report parameter called @CustomerID as a String data type. The report prompts the user to enter a Customer ID when it runs. The report passes this value to the stored procedure and the stored procedure only returns records with a matching ID.

## Stored Procedure Concerns

Since databases treat stored procedures differently from regular tables, there is an uncommon situations you should be aware of them in case you have a similar circumstance. It involves how you name stored procedure parameters.

If you are using two stored procedures and linking them together, make sure that the stored procedure parameters have different names. As I mentioned earlier, when Crystal Reports creates a new report parameter for a stored procedure, it gives it the same name as the stored procedure parameter name. The problem arises when you have two stored procedures that use the same parameter name. When Crystal Reports creates a new parameter for the second stored procedure, it sees that the report already has a parameter with that name and won't create a new one. You now have one parameter that is shared between two stored procedures. For a specific parameter such as InventoryNumber, then this is probably fine because you most likely want both stored procedures to filter on the same inventory number. But if you have a generic parameter name such as ID, then this will cause problems. It could represent Customer ID for one stored procedure and Order ID for another stored procedure. Having Crystal Reports pass the same value to both stored procedures would give you very wrong results.

The ironic part is that even though Crystal Reports doesn't create a new report parameter, when you are building the report Crystal Reports still prompts you to enter the second parameter value. So you think that you are entering two different parameters, but you are really just overwriting the first parameter value with the second value. You won't realize

---

[49] The Northwind database is an optional database that is installed when you install SQL Server.

there is a problem until you run the report. It can be difficult to track down this problem unless you are aware of this quirk. If you need to have a separate report parameter for each stored procedure, you will have to edit the stored procedures directly and rename one of the parameter names so that there is no conflict.

# Working with SQL Statements

Crystal Reports talks to databases using the computer language call Structured Query Language, commonly referred to as SQL. With SQL, Crystal Reports can specify the data that it wants to retrieve as well as how it should be filtered and sorted. As a user, you aren't required to understand SQL because Crystal Reports does all this for you behind the scenes. But even though you aren't required to know it, being able to use it can help you write more sophisticated reports and improve performance. Just as you aren't required to be an auto mechanic to drive a car, knowing how they work can help get you out of a jam when you're stuck on the side of the road. This section of the chapter gives you the basics of SQL so that you can get a better understanding of how Crystal Reports talks to databases. But this is by no means a complete tutorial. If you want to learn SQL so well that you become comfortable writing it all on your own, then you can find plenty of helpful books about it at the bookstore.

Although SQL can be quite complex, for our purposes we will focus on three distinct parts: table selection, filtering records, and sorting/grouping. Each of these parts is identified by a SQL keyword. They are listed in Table 10-9.

**Table 10-9. The three primary SQL keywords**

| SQL Keyword | Description |
| --- | --- |
| SELECT…FROM | Specifies the tables and fields to retrieve. |
| WHERE | Filters the data so that only specific records are returned. |
| ORDER BY / GROUP BY | Performs sorting and grouping |

The following sections explain these three parts of the SQL statement and show the options for customizing them.

## Selecting Tables and Fields

The SELECT ... FROM portion of the SQL statement is created in the Database Expert dialog box when selecting the tables and fields to print. For example, if you told the Database Expert that you wanted to use the tblCustomer table and print the fields CustomerID and CustomerName, then the SQL statement would look like this:

```
SELECT CustomerID, CustomerName FROM tblCustomer
```

The first portion of the statement is the SELECT keyword. It specifies the fields to display. The next keyword is FROM. It specifies which table to pull the data from.

A good way to understand how SQL works is to look at the SQL statements that Crystal Reports creates for your reports. You can get a "behind the scenes" look at what Crystal Reports is doing by selecting the menu items Database > Show SQL Query. This opens the Show SQL Query dialog box. Figure 10-11 shows the exact SQL statement that Crystal Reports uses for the customer example we just discussed.

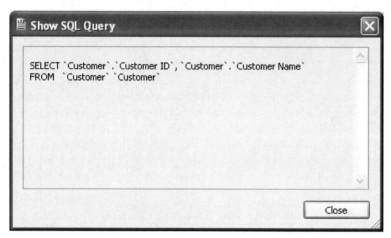

**Figure 10-11. The Show SQL Query dialog box.**

This dialog box displays the SELECT...FROM portion of the SQL statement, but it doesn't let you change it (it is read-only). Notice how it is a bit more verbose than my previous example. Crystal Reports always lists the table name in front of each field and puts a lot of quotes around everything. This is a very formal version of SQL that Crystal Reports uses. As you create more complex reports, you'll see how the corresponding SQL statement becomes more complex as well.

# Filtering Records

When printing records from one or more tables, you probably don't need to print every single record. It is common to print only a subset of the original records. For example, rather than print every customer in the database, the report only prints customers that have been added within the past thirty days. SQL statements use the WHERE clause to filter out records that you don't want.

The WHERE clause lists each condition that must be met before a record is selected. For example, if the sales figure must be greater than $100,000, then the WHERE clause would read like this:

WHERE TotalSales > 100000

If there is more than one condition, you need to use the Boolean operators AND or OR to specify which conditions need to be met. If you use the AND operator, both conditions must be met for the record to be selected. If you use the OR operator, only one of the two conditions must be met for the record to be selected. Let's add on to our previous example and say that in addition to the total sales being greater than $100,000, the region must be Rio De Janeiro. Since both conditions need to be met, we'll use the AND operator.

WHERE TotalSales > 10000 AND Region='Rio De Janeiro'

Crystal Reports uses the record selection formula for filtering records. In Chapter 4 we learned how selection formulas can be created using either the Select Expert or the Record Selection Formula Editor. We also saw how we can be in the Select Expert dialog box and click on the Show Formula button to see the actual formula that Crystal Report is creating behind the scenes. But now that we have a better understanding of SQL, we want to see the actual SQL statement passed to the database. By selecting the menu option Database > Show SQL Query we can see the SQL statement. Figure 10-12 shows how the previous example would look in Crystal Reports.

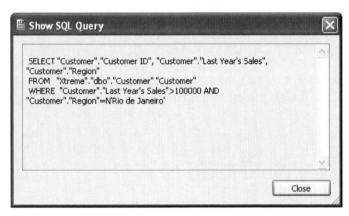

Figure 10-12. SQL query for a WHERE clause.

# Grouping and Sorting Records

The two SQL statements that control grouping and sorting are GROUP BY and ORDER BY. Grouping records with the GROUP BY statement is pretty easy. All you do is list the applicable fields after each keyword. For example, if you want to group by the Customer ID, then you would use:

GROUP BY CustomerId

Using the ORDER BY keyword works the same way. There is one minor addition in that you can also specify the sort order. By default, all fields are sorted in ascending order. To sort in ascending order, just list the field name without doing anything else. If you want to sort in descending order, you need to use the DESC keyword. The following example shows what the previous SQL statement looks like if we sort it by the region in descending order.

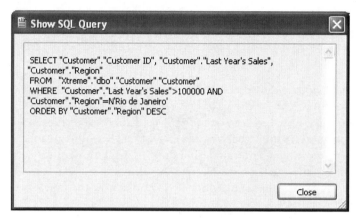

**Figure 10-13. SQL query for ordering by the Region field in descending order.**

# Saving Report Data

Crystal Reports lets you save the report data with the .RPT report file. This gives you two primary benefits. The first being that the user doesn't need to have a live connection to the data source. This lets you email the .RPT file to someone working off-site and they can view the report. The second benefit is that if a report takes a long time to pull its data from the database and process the report, then the report can be loaded in a fraction of the time when the data is saved with it. There is no need to request the data from the server and process it locally.

| Tip |
|---|
| Even though saving data with reports makes it much more efficient to view reports, you can do even more to improve performance. If a report has over 10,000 records, but those records are viewed in small sets, then you should create Saved Data Indexes. This creates indexes on the computer to process the records returned from the record selection formula more efficiently. To create Saved Data Indexes, select the menu items Report > Report Bursting Indexes. When it opens, select the fields that you would use in the record selection formula and save it. However, if the record selection formula returns the majority of the data in the report, then you won't see the performance gains due to the overhead required to create the indexes. So only do this if you think the record selection formula will return a much smaller number of records. |

In one respect, saving data with the report sounds similar to the benefits of just converting it to a PDF file and then emailing/viewing the PDF file. After all, both methods let the user view the report without accessing the live database. The benefit to saving the data in the report and keeping it in the native Crystal Reports format is that the reader is still able to work with the data. For example, they can drill-down into groups, enter new parameter values, change the sorting, etc. This isn't possible when viewing a static PDF file.

> **Note**
>
> To make sure that drill-down data is also saved with your report, disable the option Perform Grouping on the Server. This is found under the menu options File > Report Options.

You need to plan what data will be saved with your report. If you expect a user to massage the data once they get the report (e.g. changing parameters, use different sorting, etc), then you have to make sure that they have all the data they need. For example, let's say that you are working with the report and you set the record selection formula to be all Customer IDs less than 100. When you send the report to the user, then this is the only data that they will have. If they try to change the record selection formula to Customer IDs less then 500, then there won't be any additional data available for printing. The original records are still the only records in the report. The user would have to reconnect to the database server to read the Customer IDs less than 500.

The key to making sure that the report has the right data is to determine what data actually gets saved with the report. Crystal Reports doesn't have a feature to view the raw data associated with a report, so you have to figure it out yourself. A good rule of thumb is that anytime Crystal Reports has to communicate with the database server, then it is getting a new copy of the data. Some examples of this are when you log on to the server, add a new field to the table, or verify the database (when the structure has changed). In many cases, you'll know that new data is being retrieved when you are prompted with the question "Refresh Data?" and you answer Ok.

Re-querying the database commonly happens after you click the Refresh Report Data (F5) button, enter a new selection formula, enter new parameter values, etc. At this point you can save the report and all the data will be saved with it as well. If you decide to continue testing the report with new parameter values or selection formulas, then always tell the report to "Use Saved Data" so that it doesn't re-query the database. By telling it not to refresh the report data, then you always keep the last set of data stored with the report. Even though you might not be viewing it at that moment, whomever you send the report to will still have access to all the data.

Although Crystal Reports doesn't let you see the actual data saved with the report, it does give you some high-level information about it. The Performance Information dialog box gives you information such as how many records are saved, the record size, and how much space the data requires. Open the Performance Information dialog box by selecting the menu items Report > Performance Information. Then click on the Saved Data category. It is shown in Figure 10-14.

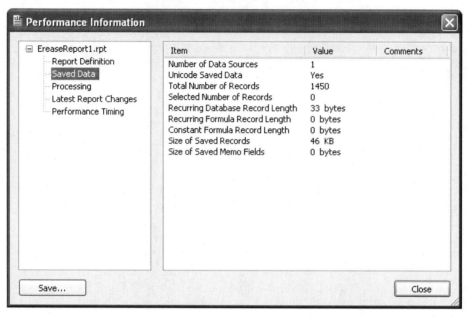

**Figure 10-14. Viewing saved data statistics with the Performance Information dialog box.**

# Changing the Data Source

Many reports are very straight forward and all the tables come from the same data source. The tables that are used when you designed the report are the same tables that will be used when the report is put into production. But this isn't always the case. It is common for the requirements to change and for a report to use a data source different from what it was originally designed for. Or, you may have a development server that is used for designing and testing reports and a production server that is used when the report is finished. Crystal Reports has a number of features that make it easier to change the location of the tables. It lets you set the location of a data source, change the name that a table is referenced by, and verify whether a database is valid.

## Using the Set Location Dialog Box

There are two ways of changing the data source. You can either switch to a different database or you can change out individual tables. If you switch to a new database, then the tables in the new database should be the same tables located on the old one. Prior to switching to the new database, you want to make sure that their names match exactly. If want to stay on the same database, but change individual tables, then the table structures should be similar to each other. If some of the field names have changed or there are missing fields, you will get the chance to map the old field names to new field names in the new table.

To change a report's data source, open the Set Datasource Location dialog box by selecting the menu options Database > Set Datasource Location. It is shown in Figure 10-15.

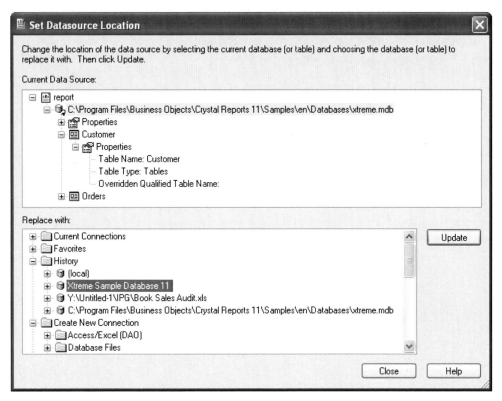

**Figure 10-15. The Set Location dialog box.**

The top of the dialog box shows the current data source. It lists the database server and the tables used. You can also click on each item to see its properties (name and type). The bottom window is labeled "Replace With". It shows the same data sources that you would see if you were looking at the Database Expert dialog box.

If you want to have the report change to a completely different database, select that database from the Current Data Source window at the top. Go to the Replace With window at the bottom and find the new database that you want to switch to. Select it and then click the Update button.

To replace an individual table, go to the top window and locate the existing table. In the bottom window, either open the Current Connections folder or the History folder and find the new table name. Select the new table and click the Update button.

**Caution**

When you open the Set Location dialog box and click on one of the database servers, a list of all the available tables in the database is created. If at a later point you go into the database server to make changes to the tables (e.g. adding or deleting tables), the Set Location dialog box won't recognize those changes. It will still show the original list of tables. It only queries the database server the first time it is opened. You can update the list by right-clicking on the Table category and selecting Refresh.

If you find that the Update button isn't enabled, you haven't selected data sources that are compatible with each other. For example, if you have a table selected as the Current Data Source, then you have to have a table selected in the Replace With window. You can't select a database in one window and a table in the other window.

## Changing PC-Style Databases

PC-style databases are unique from database servers like SQL Server because they reference a physical file. This file can be located on your hard drive or on a shared network drive. The physical location of the database file can cause you problems when you distribute the file because everyone might not have their database located in the same location. The Set Datasource Location dialog box gives you a few options for working with the file path of a PC-style database.

In the top portion of the dialog box, find the database name and right below it click on the Properties category. Find the Database Name property and right-click on it to get the pop-up menu shown in Figure 10-16.

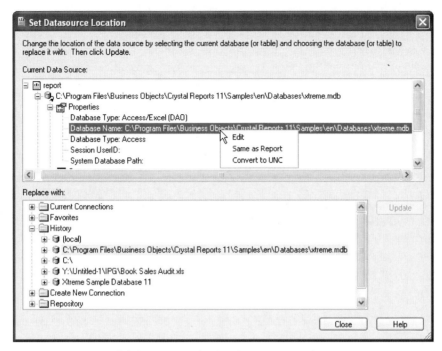

**Figure 10-16. Modifying PC-style database properties.**

Figure 10-16 shows three options for setting the database location:

- Edit lets you manually type in the physical file path location of the file. You have to make sure that everyone who gets a copy of this report has the database file at the exact same file path.

- Same As Report tells Crystal Reports to look for the database in the exact same folder that the report is located in. This means that you don't have to worry about where the database file is located on the user's computer as long as the report is in the same folder.

- Convert to UNC is used when the database file is located on a shared drive on the network. Although most users have similar drive letters for shared network drives, this usually isn't enforced throughout most companies. Thus, users can use different drive letters to connect to the same shared drive on the network. Using the Convert to UNC option converts the file path to the Universal Naming Convention for files on the network. It does this by using the server name and the share name that the network administrator created. How the user maps their drive letters becomes irrelevant because the file always points to the same location on the network.

By using one of these three options with PC-style databases, you can ensure that the file path maps to the correct location.

## Verifying the Current Data Source

Since a report is separate from the data source, it is very possible that someone can make changes to a database without you knowing it. For example, changing a field's name causes the report to lose its reference to that field. Modifying a field's data type can also affect how the report formats the data. If you are working on a large project, someone could modify a table and not realize that you are using it on an existing report. If a change is made to either the database location or the table structure since the last time you modified the report, this will impact the reports that use that data source. Either the report won't be able to find the tables, or some of the fields will be missing.

Crystal Reports has a Verify Database function that checks the data source to see if it has changed since the report was created. This should be done whenever you suspect that the tables have been modified since the last time the report was updated. Access this function by selecting the menu options Database > Verify Database. It will display a confirmation box if the database is up to date. If Crystal Reports determines that the fields in your report have changed in some way, it lets you re-map them to their equivalent fields in the new table structure. This is discussed in the next section.

| Tip |
| --- |

If you want Crystal Reports to verify your database each time you open the report, select the menu options Report > Options to open the Database Options dialog box. Then select the appropriate Verify properties.

## Re-mapping Fields

When replacing one table with another table, it is possible that one or more of the fields on the report won't have exact matches in the new table. If the fields in a table are renamed or deleted, this affects the existing fields on your report. When this happens, Crystal Reports gives you the option to remap the existing fields to the new fields in the database.

After using the Set Location dialog box or when using the Verify Database function, Crystal Reports checks if any changes have been made to the table. If it detects that a change has occurred that affects fields being used on the report, it opens the Map Fields dialog box shown in Figure 10-17. It shows the fields that don't have a matching field in the current table. It also shows you the new fields in the data source so that you can match the old fields to the new fields. Crystal replaces them accordingly.

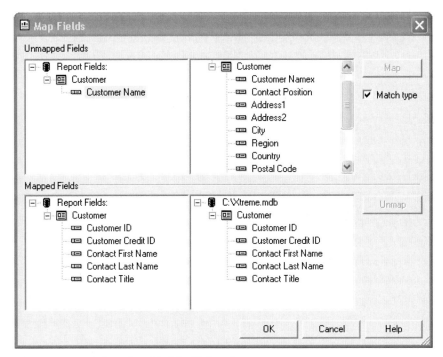

**Figure 10-17. The Map Fields dialog box.**

This dialog box is only displayed when necessary. If changes are made to fields that aren't being printed, then it isn't necessary to re-map these fields. Fields that only had their data types changed are not mapped either, but you should check their output when the report runs to make sure they are formatted properly.

The Map Fields dialog box is divided into two halves. The top half shows the unmapped fields. The left-most window shows the fields that are in the report but don't have a matching field in its assigned table. The right-most window shows all the fields from the currently selected tables. Select one of the unmapped fields in the left window and then select one of the available fields in the right window. Click on the Map button to replace the old field with the new field. You might notice that not all the fields are listed in the right-most window. This is because the checkbox to the right, labeled "Match type," is checked by default. This requires you to only match fields that have the same data type. It won't list the fields that don't have the same data type. If you uncheck this checkbox, all fields are displayed and you can replace a field with a field of a different data type. You should be cautious when mapping different data types and you should preview the report to make sure that the formatting and spacing of the fields are appropriate. The formatting of the old field may not have carried over properly.

If there are fields that are currently mapped, but you still want to replace them with a different field, use the window in the lower half of the dialog box. In the left-most window, click on the field to replace and then click the Unmap button. This moves the field to the Unmapped window in the top half and you can now follow the previous steps to re-map it with a new field.

 There are times when you decide to swap out one field for another. Unfortunately, this requires you to delete the original field and possibly lose a lot of formatting. You could try using the Map Fields dialog box to switch them because this won't lose your formatting, but there isn't a menu option to open the Map Fields dialog box. You're in a tough spot.

A new feature in Crystal Reports XI R2 is the ability to swap fields on a report. If you hold down the Shift key before dragging a field from the Field Explorer window, you can drop it onto an existing field on the report and the two fields get swapped with each other. The size, placement and formatting all stay the same. When doing this, a double-arrow will appear above the report to indicate that the fields are about to be swapped. This is shown in Figure 10-18.

**Figure 10-18. Swapping a field with an existing report object.**

After you accept the mapping changes, the report is automatically updated so that all report fields and formulas have the old field name replaced with the new field name. This saves you the trouble of going back through a report and modifying all formulas that referenced that field. This is the same effect as using a program like MS Word and using the Search and Replace function.

# Logging On and Off of Databases

When you create a new report and select the data sources in the Database Explorer dialog box, Crystal Reports automatically logs you onto the data source. This is so that it can find out what tables and stored procedures are there as well as getting a list of fields in each one. As you work on the report, you stay connected to the data source so that the report can load the records from the data source and process them. If you want to conserve resources, you can use the option to save the data with the report and disconnect from the data source. This frees up resources on the database server.

| Note |
| --- |

Crystal Reports keeps your database connections open until you specifically close them. Even if you close all your open reports, the database connection stays open.

To log off of the database server, select the menu options Database > Log On or Off Server. This opens the Data Explorer dialog box shown in Figure 10-19

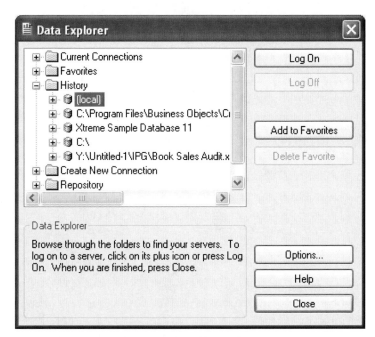

**Figure 10-19. Logging on and off databases.**

Click on the Log Off button to log off the database. If you are already logged off and wish to log back on, click the Log On button. If you want a particular data source to be added to your Favorites list, click the Add to Favorites button. And if you wish to remove it from the Favorites list, click the Delete Favorites button. Clicking the Options button brings up the data options dialog box that can also be found by selecting the menu options Report > Options.

# Using Unlinked Tables

In most reports, when you add multiple tables to a report it is assumed that you will link them together. But Crystal Reports gives you the ability to use standalone tables in a report that aren't linked to the other tables. At first this can cause problems because there is no synchronization between the two data sources. If you put fields from both data sources in the details section, Crystal Reports will print out the detail records for both tables accordingly. But since they aren't linked, the results can be a little chaotic. It could also create a Cartesian result set where each detail record in one data source is repeated for every detail record in the other data source. This results in a report where the page count quickly explodes into the thousands. In fact, when you add an unlinked table to the report, Crystal Reports gives you a warning message that doing this is generally not supported.

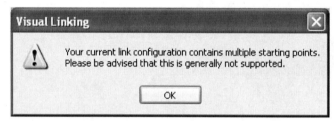

**Figure 10-20. Warning message for unlinked tables.**

As a general rule, if you want to print the detail records from multiple data sources, then you need to use subreports. This lets you group the detail records into separate reports to keep the data organized. With all these potential problems of unlinked tables, is there a time you would want to use them? Of course.[50]

Unlinked tables are helpful when you only want to print a single record from the table. This can either be a table with one record in it, or a table that uses a record selection formula to only return a single record. This makes it easy for Crystal Reports to extract the correct information from the table and since there is only one record, you don't have to worry about getting a Cartesian result set.

The primary use for unlinked tables is putting information in the report/page header or footer. If you remember back to the discussion of subreports, there was one example where we put the corporate contact information into the report header. We used an unlinked subreport to pull a single record from the table and display it in the page header. In this example, you could easily replace the subreport with an unlinked table. This makes the report easier to develop and maintain because all the data sources are contained in the main report and you don't have to use subreports. You could also use unlinked tables

---

[50] Otherwise I wouldn't have brought it up! ☺

when there is a utility table that stores property-value pairs that store regularly changing data (like tax rates) and using them in a formula.

## Setting a Table's Alias

When fields are added to a report, they are referenced by a combination of their table name and their field name. During the course of designing a report and making changes to it, the fields can have their tables renamed or the table can be replaced with a different table. If you created formulas based upon a field in a table that has changed, then these formulas could potentially become invalid. In this situation, you would expect to have to go back through the formulas and update the table names for each field. Fortunately, Crystal Reports has a way around this problem.

In the prior discussion about re-mapping old field names to new field names, you learned that Crystal Reports automatically performs a search-and-replace to overwrite the old field names with new field names. However, it handles changes to the name of a table differently. The report still uses the old table name in the formulas, but behind the scenes these table names now reference the new table name. This can be a bit confusing because on the surface it appears that the formula still references the old table because its name hasn't changed. However, you are really looking at the table's alias.

An alias is a name that is assigned to a database table that isn't the actual name of the table. You can think of an alias as a unique identifier that points to a table. You can change which table the unique identifier points to, but the name of this identifier never changes.

Every table in a report is referred to by an alias. When a table is first added to a report, an alias is created and its name matches the name of the table. Since the table and its alias have the same name you don't even realize that an alias was created. When you use the Set Location dialog box to change a data source's table to a new table, the alias name stays the same, but the table it refers to is now different.

As an example, consider a report that prints fields from a table called CustomerData. The table is later modified so that the name is now called Customer. You use the Set Location dialog box to change the CustomerData table to the Customer table. When you close the dialog box you will see that the formulas still reference the table using the CustomerData table name. You might get confused and wonder if you really changed the table name or not. Rest assured that you did change the table name, you are just looking at the alias.

You can also use aliases to make it easier to design a report. For example, if you are using a table name that is extremely long, you can use an alias to give it a shorter name. Some companies have large databases and use a very cryptic specification for naming tables. You can use an alias to give the table a more readable name. For example, rather than referring to a financial table as "AR2007EOY" you could refer to it as "Accts Receivable 2007 Year End". Everywhere in your report where this table is referenced, you will see the alias name that you assigned it rather than the actual name of the table used in the database.

To manually change the alias of a table, you have to go into the Database Expert dialog box. Select the menu options Database > Database Expert. This opens the Database Expert dialog box with the selected tables shown in the right-most window. Click on the table that you want to assign an alias to and press the F2 key. This puts the name in edit mode and you can change it.

If you are using multiple data sources, it's possible that you will add two tables with the same name to your report. Crystal Reports forces you to give one of the tables a new alias so that there isn't a naming conflict. Before it lets you add the table, it prompts you with the Database Warning dialog box in Figure 10-21. It tells you that there is already a table with that same alias and asks if you really want to add another alias for that table. If you click Yes, then it uses the table name with "_1" appended to the end of the filename. The table gets added to your current connections using the new alias name.

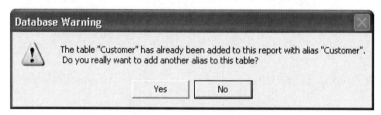

**Figure 10-21. The Database Warning dialog box.**

| Tip |
| :---: |

It isn't obvious when a table is using an alias that is different than the actual table name. If you are given a report that you didn't design, a table that uses an alias can make it difficult to determine what the actual table name really is. To find out which tables have aliases and what table is used, open the Set Location dialog box. The drop down box lists the table aliases that are associated with each data source. Directly beside the alias name is the actual table name shown in parentheses. You can also click on the Properties folder to see the actual table name. See Figure 10-22 for an example of using an alias with the Customer table.

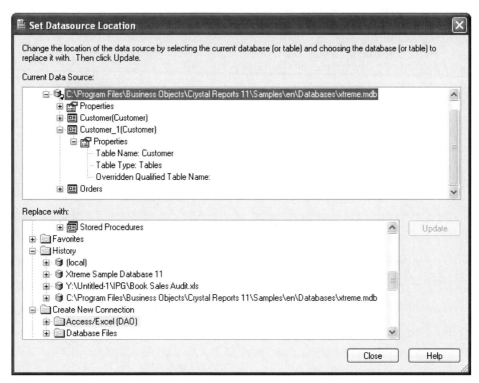

**Figure 10-22. Finding a table's alias.**

# Cancelling Long Running Reports

Some reports can take an exceptionally long time to process. This can be the result of querying the database for a large volume of data or the report having to process many records. If you run a report and find that it is taking too long to process you might want to cancel it. This lets you wait till later to run the report (when you have more time), or redesign the report to be more efficient. Crystal Reports can be set up so that you can cancel a report before it's finished printing. To use this functionality, open the Database Options dialog box by selecting Report > Options and clicking on the Database tab. Select the option Perform Query Asynchronously. When the report starts running, you can cancel the request by clicking the stop button (it has a red "X" on it) located next to the Refresh button on the Preview tab.

# Maximizing SQL Performance

No matter what your reporting requirements are, at some point you will probably print a report that takes longer to process than you would like. And you'll scratch your head and think to yourself, "There has to be a way to speed this up." And you are right. In most cases, there are various techniques you can use to make a report run faster. In this chapter we will look at the most common ways of improving performance. We also look at a few SQL tricks that make your reporting job easier by using the power of the SQL language.

When a report runs, there are three potential areas where bottlenecks can occur. First, the database server has to locate and process all the records prior to passing them across the network. At the same time, the database server is also doing work for other people on the network. You could have a report that is normally very efficient suddenly start running very slowly if someone else sent a large data request to the server at the same time. Fortunately, database servers are optimized to do this processing as efficiently as possible and this generally isn't the reason for most performance problems.

Second, the database server has to pass all the records to the client computer. The speed at which these records are transferred is constrained by the physical limitations of the network design as well as the traffic already on the network. At a smaller company, the infrastructure might not support transferring thousands of records very quickly. At a larger company, the network is certainly more powerful, but now you are competing with everyone else who is passing files back and forth along the same network pipes.

Lastly, once Crystal Reports receives all the records, the report engine has to process them to create the report. Depending on the complexity of the formulas, sorting/grouping and whether subreports are used, this can be a very time intensive process.

As the report designer, your goal is to analyze each aspect of the reporting process and see if you can make changes to reduce the impact that each of these three potential bottlenecks can have.

The solution for improving most report performance is to transfer the workload from the client machine to the database server. This is called "pushing down data" to the server. Pushing down data derives a big improvement in performance by having the server perform the majority of the data processing. As mentioned in the beginning, database servers are designed to provide the optimum performance when processing massive quantities of data. It can filter out records that don't meet a certain criteria in a fraction of the time that the report engine would take. Pushing down data has the secondary benefit of passing less data along the network back to the client. The report gets the data quicker and there is less data for the report to process. You have now reduced the impact of two out of the three possible bottlenecks and your report will run much faster.

| Tip |
| --- |

If you are requesting an extremely large volume of data from the database server and this is causing performance problems, you should look into scheduling the reports to run overnight. This lets the database server dedicate its resources to working specifically on your reports and it doesn't cause performance problems for other users who are running smaller reports during the day. You can upgrade to the enterprise edition of Crystal Reports or look at cheaper third-party solutions that perform report scheduling.

The key piece to the performance puzzle lies in the SQL statement. By understanding what is going on in the SQL statement, you can find areas for improving performance.

In the previous chapter, we discussed how the SQL statement is broken down into three primary parts (SELECT...FROM, WHERE, and ORDER BY/GROUP BY). We are going to break down each aspect of the SQL statement and see how we can change the report design to improve the SQL statement. Since the SQL statement is how Crystal Reports talks to the database server, making it more efficient results in faster performing reports.

### *Optimizing Field Selection*

The SELECT statement determines which fields are selected from the tables and sent to Crystal Reports. Only fields listed after the SELECT keyword can be printed on the report. There are two ways to improve performance here. The first is to only select the records that you will print on the report. Fortunately, Crystal Reports does this for us by specifically listing each field on the report individually after the SELECT keyword.

The second method for improving performance is to have the database server do the work of calculating your formulas on the server. For example, if you have a formula in your report that calculates sales tax, you could have the database server do this calculation for you instead of Crystal Reports doing it. The database server is more optimized to process calculations.

The way to make the database server calculate the formulas is by using SQL expression fields. These are formulas built using only SQL functions. By limiting yourself to just SQL functions, Crystal Reports can pass the entire formula to the database server for processing. Crystal Reports doesn't have to do any of the work.

The one caveat to this is that the SQL function library is limited in scope. Many Crystal Reports formulas can't be converted to SQL expression fields. If you've been creating formulas in Crystal Reports for very long, you've gotten spoiled by all the great functionality built into the software. In fact, there aren't many programs on the market that give you so many built in functions. For example, Crystal Reports has dozens of functions for performing financial calculations and handling fiscal dates. But in most programs, you have to create these functions yourself. The same goes for database servers. You are limited to how much you can really do here. We are going to talk about SQL expressions in much greater detail later in the chapter, so we will focus more on what they can and can't do there.

The one good thing to consider is that Crystal Reports is already very efficient at calculating formulas. Converting all your formulas to SQL expressions isn't a high priority for optimizing your reports. In most cases, there won't be a huge performance gain. The critical time you want to do this is when you are processing reports involving tens of thousands of records or more.

## Optimizing Record Selection

The WHERE clause of the SQL query specifies how records are filtered. It lists the fields to be filtered on and the criteria for specifying which records to select. This is what you do when using the Record Selection dialog box to specify which records you want displayed on the report.

When Crystal Reports builds the SQL query to pass to the database server, it looks at the record selection formula and tries to convert it to its SQL equivalent. When it is successful with the conversion, the database filters the records at the server prior to passing the result set back to Crystal Reports. This results in a significant performance improvement.

When the record selection formula can't be converted to a valid WHERE clause, it won't be included in the SQL query passed to the database server. Only the SELECT portion of the SQL statement is sent. This results in the database server passing all the records from the SELECT statement back to the client computer. More traffic is put on the network and Crystal Reports has to manually process all the records using the selection formula. The result is a much slower performance than what would have been, had all the filtering been done on the server.

Of course, your goal is to write record selection formulas that can be converted to SQL and processed on the database server. Let's look at how to make this happen as frequently as possible.

Before any formula can be converted to SQL, the report needs this feature turned on. The option "Use Indexes or Server for Speed" must be enabled for the report to push data down to the server. This option tells Crystal Reports to use indexes when selecting records from a database and it also tells it to use the server to improve performance whenever possible. You can set this option to be turned on by default for all reports or for just the current report. To make it the default setting for all reports, select the menu options File > Options. Click on the Database tab to select it there. If you want to set it for just the current report, select the menu options File > Report Options. The checkbox is near the middle of the dialog box.

---

**Note**

PC databases (e.g. MS Access) have an additional restriction for pushing down data. The fields in the record selection formula must be indexed.

After enabling this option for the report, you want to create a selection formula that would deliver the best performance for your report. The optimum selection formula is one that can be completely converted to SQL. However, you can't always write the formula so that it can be converted to SQL. As mentioned earlier, Crystal syntax has a lot more functionality than SQL. Since the purpose of a formula is to carry out the requirements of the report's design, you don't have a lot of choice about what will be in the formula. Converting the selection formula to SQL is a great benefit, but it is secondary the overall goal of generating the required data.

When determining whether a selection formula can be converted to SQL or not, Crystal Reports doesn't do any advanced analysis. If it sees a simple formula then it will usually try to convert it. But even something like including a calculation within the formula will throw it off and it won't convert it to SQL. The easiest way to write record selection formulas that are converted to SQL is to use the Select Expert dialog box. The Select Expert only creates very simple selection formulas and these can all be converted to SQL. Writing custom formulas is when you start running the risk of them not being converted.

Here are some rules to consider when creating your selection formulas:

- Use the following operators: =, <, >, <>, <=, >=, StartsWith and Like.

- The left side of the comparison operator must be a database field. It can not be a formula field or perform any calculations.

- On the right side of the comparison operator, you can do simple calculations

- The IsNull() function can be converted.

- Use the boolean operators And, Or.

- Use the In range operator for numbers and dates only. Do not use it for strings.

# Optimizing Boolean Operators

There are some special considerations when using a selection formula that has multiple conditions. By default, when you use the Select Expert dialog box, each condition is joined using a Boolean And. For a record to be selected for printing it must meet all the criteria specified in the selection formula. If it doesn't match any one of the criteria, then it doesn't get printed. When Crystal Reports tries to convert the record selection formula to SQL, it looks at each condition individually and it converts the ones that can be converted. If a condition can't be converted, then it leaves it out of the SQL WHERE clause and performs the logic itself while printing the report.

The tricky part comes into play when you click the Show Formula button on the Select Expert dialog box and make changes to the formula. At this point, you can modify the formula to use a combination of Boolean operators including the Or operator. When a selection formula uses the Or operator, the rules change. The conversion now becomes an "all or nothing" process. Either all the conditions are converted to SQL or none of them are. To understand this process, you have to understand how each Boolean operator works.

When two or more conditions are combined using the And operator, Crystal looks at each condition independently. If a condition can be converted to SQL, it is appended to the WHERE clause and passed down to the server. Any conditions that can't be converted are left for the report engine to process. Crystal will pass as many conditions down to the server as possible and leave the rest for the client to perform. The result is improved performance because, even though the client has to process some of the records, there will be fewer to process. Many records have already been filtered out by the server.

The Or operator works differently from the And operator. When using the Or operator, Crystal Reports looks at all the conditions as a whole. Like the And operator, it tries to convert each condition into SQL. But this time, if it finds that any of the conditions can't be converted, none of them will be converted. For example, assume a record selection formula has three conditions and they are joined using the OR operator. If the first two conditions can be converted to SQL, but the last one can't, then none of them will be passed down to the server. The entire record selection formula will be processed by the client and you will see slower performance.

The reason for this is that when using the Or operator, every record has to be tested for each of the stated conditions. Only passing some of the conditions doesn't reduce the number or records that need to be passed to the client. For example, assume that there are two conditions and one of the two conditions was passed to the server. After the server processes the SELECT statement, it is left with 100 records. Even if the server performs the first test and 70 records fail, there is still a chance that these 70 records will pass the second test. However, the second test is on the client, which means the 70 records have to get passed to the client for testing. In effect, the server ends up passing all the records to the client using the Or operator and it didn't help speed up the processing at all.

If you are using a PC database, then those rules don't apply. Using a PC database means you can't use the OR operator at all. Whether the individual conditions can be converted to SQL or not won't have any effect.

One way to ensure the selection formula gets converted into SQL is to write it using SQL expressions. As mentioned previously, a SQL expression field is a formula that is built using only valid SQL functions. Since it only has valid SQL functions, Crystal Reports will always be able to convert it to a valid WHERE clause. SQL Expressions are explained in greater detail in a later section.

# Optimizing Grouping and Sorting

The GROUP BY and ORDER BY keywords specify how to group and sort the records. Just like performing record selections, this is a time intensive process that is best done on the database server. This section elaborates on the how-to of enabling reports to optimize grouping and sorting and the restrictions of doing so.

Optimizing and modifying a report's grouping and sorting is very similar to working with the record selection formulas. You want to push down data to the server for processing. You learned in the last section, that for Crystal Reports to push data down to the server, you have to turn the feature on. The same goes for grouping records. Enable the option called "Perform Grouping on Server". This makes the server do as much of the grouping, summarizing and subtotaling as possible.

> ### Note
>
> You can't select the option to perform grouping on the server unless the option to use the server for performance is also turned on. If it isn't selected, the grouping option is disabled.

To turn it on by default for all reports, select the menu items File > Options. Go to the database tab and click on the Perform Grouping on Server option if it isn't already checked. If you want to set the options for just the current report, select the menu options File > Report Options.

## Restrictions on Grouping and Sorting

Having the server perform the grouping has certain restrictions associated with it. These restrictions are as follows:

- The goal of performing grouping and sorting on the server is to reduce the number of records passed back to the client and consequently reduce the amount of processing the client has to do. To make this possible, the report is restricted to printing only the group fields and summary fields. The Details section must be hidden and there can't be any detail fields in any of the header or footer sections.

- The report derives all its data from a single data source or stored procedure. You can't have two different data sources linked together.

- Grouping can't be performed on a formula, and formulas can't be used in summary fields. If either one of these is true, then all records will be passed back to the client for processing. This probably comes as a surprise since some formulas can be used in a record selection formula and can be passed to the server for processing. It is not the case with grouping.

- Sorting can't be done using specified order. It is impossible for Crystal Reports to convert the logic required to perform specified order sorting into valid SQL statements. This is always done on the client machine.

- Running total fields must be based on summary fields. If a running total is based on a detail field, all the detail fields will be passed to the client to perform the calculation.

- The report cannot use summaries based on Average or Distinct Count.

- The fields that are being grouped must either be the actual database fields or SQL expressions. SQL expressions can always be sent to the server because they are built using valid SQL functions. This is discussed in the next section.

If you want to see a summary of the settings that affect whether grouping and sorting is performed on the server and where record selection is performed, you can see this in the Performance Information dialog box. Open the Performance Information dialog box by selecting the menu items Report > Performance Information. Then click on the Saved Data category. It is shown in Figure 11-1.

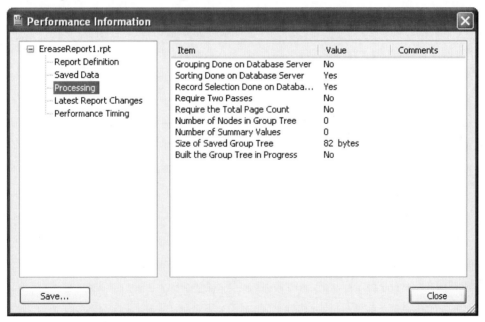

Figure 11-1. The Performance Information dialog box.

# Using SQL Expression Fields

Throughout this chapter we have been referring to SQL expression fields as the best way to improve report performance. Let's discuss them in more detail now. SQL expression fields are report formulas that only use SQL compatible functions. As mentioned in a previous section, using SQL expressions lets Crystal Reports pass much of the workload down to the database server so that reports run faster. The data returned to the client computer has already been processed and is ready to print.

Writing reports requires achieving a balance of functionality and performance. Many reports need to use custom formulas and functions to produce the proper output. But this can result in slower performance because it requires the report engine to do more work on the client computer using SQL expressions. The drawback to using SQL expressions is that they aren't as robust as formulas written with Crystal syntax or Basic syntax. Many formulas can't be rewritten using a SQL Expression. The functions found in the SQL language pale in comparison to Crystal Reports.

When deciding when to use SQL expressions instead of the standard formulas, you have to decide which gives you the best cost-benefit ratio. There are three places where formulas are used: as part of the report output, in the record selection formula, and as a sorting/grouping field. You should focus your attention on using SQL expressions in formulas that are used for either record selection or sorting/grouping. Formulas that are used as part of the report output don't have a major impact on report performance because the report engine can quickly calculate these as it processes each record.

To create a SQL expression field, look in the Field Explorer window for the SQL Expression Fields folder.[51] Right-click on the SQL Expression Fields folder and select New. A SQL Expression Name dialog box opens for you to enter a name for the expression. Once you enter a name and click the OK button the SQL Expression Editor window opens. You can see that the SQL Expression Editor is really just the Formula Editor with new functions and operators listed. These functions and operators are specific to the database server you are connected to.

---

[51] If you don't see SQL Expression Fields listed, then you are either using a PC Database or another non-compatible database. In general, you have to be using SQL Server or an ODBC database to create a SQL expression fields.

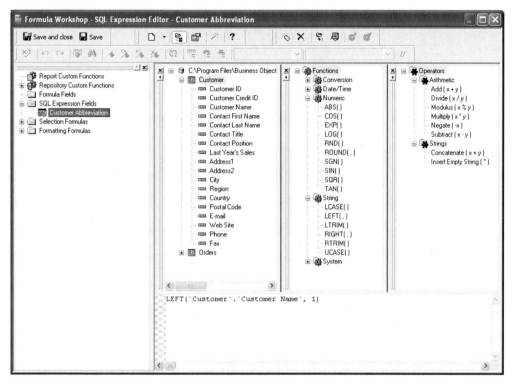

**Figure 11-2. The SQL Expression Editor dialog box.**

The process of creating a SQL expression is the same as creating other formulas. You select the functions to use and apply them to the listed database fields. The important difference between regular formulas and SQL Expressions is that SQL Expressions have limited functionality. The only fields that you can use in a SQL Expression are database fields. You can't use other formulas, parameters or special fields. The available functions are also limited to SQL specific functions.

Even though it is helpful to have the list of SQL functions listed within the Formula Workshop window, you still need to be familiar with proper SQL syntax for your database. This isn't always compatible with Crystal syntax. For example, in Crystal syntax you can concatenate two strings together using the & operator. But this will give you an error when used with SQL Server because it requires you to use the + operator.

| Caution |
|---|

The list of available functions is specific to the database server you are connected to. If you create a SQL Expression and later change database servers, the expression may not be valid if the new database doesn't support one of the functions used.

After adding a SQL Expression to the report, the SELECT statement passed to the database server is modified to include the SQL Expression. It becomes an additional field that is requested from the server. If you include the SQL expression in a record selection formula, or sorting/grouping formula, this is also added to the query. Figure 11-3 shows an example of how the SQL expression field is now included as part of the SELECT portion of the query as well as the WHERE clause. This increases the performance of your report because the database server is going to do the work of processing the formula and filtering the data.

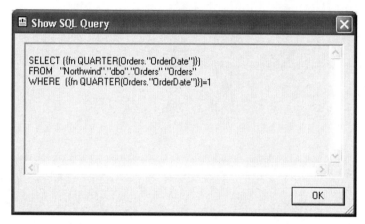

**Figure 11-3. The SQL Query using a SQL Expression.**

Using SQL expression fields whenever possible can give you a noticeable improvement in report performance.

| Tip |
| --- |

If your database allows nested sub-queries (a SELECT statement within a SELECT statement), you can use SQL Expressions to implement them. However, you have to use parentheses around the entire statement so that it recognizes it as a sub-query. Here is an example:

(Select "Employee"."First Name" + ' ' + "Employee"."Last Name")

## Writing Custom SQL Statements

The Database Expert, discussed in Chapter 10, gives you the ability to create sophisticated data sources by linking tables from different types of data sources (tables, views, stored procedures). Being able to customize how these tables are linked together can not only impact report performance, but it can create new ways of reporting on data that wasn't possible with the basic Crystal Reports functionality.

For example, the UNION keyword is a very powerful way to connect data from two tables together and make them appear as a single table. But the Crystal Reports Database Expert doesn't have a way to use the UNION statement. Linking tables using more advanced SQL statements requires creating custom SQL statements.

Building more advanced data sources with custom SQL statements requires adding a command object to your report. A command object is a custom SQL statement that you write yourself and it returns data to the report. In essence, you are creating a virtual table that Crystal Reports can build reports from. You can put any valid SQL statement in it that you want and it is passed directly to the database server. Of course, this requires more than just a cursory knowledge of SQL. Before you attempt adding command objects on your own, please make sure you have a solid knowledge of the SQL language or possibly ask someone who works on the database to assist you.

Not all databases let you create a new command object. If you are working with Sybase, DB2 or Informix, you have to use an ODBC connection. Connecting to these databases with native connections doesn't support command objects. To find out if this is possible for your database, look in the Database Explorer. If the database allows it, you'll see the Add Command option listed just below it. For example, in Figure 11-4 you can see how the SQL Server database and the MS Access database both have an Add Command option.

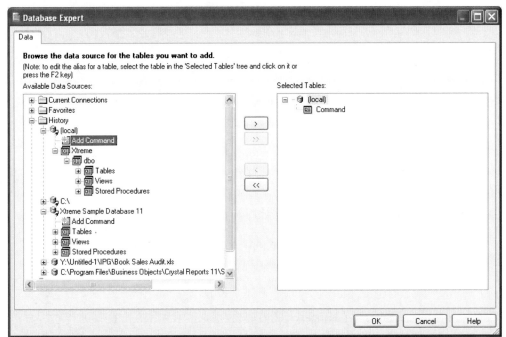

**Figure 11-4. Adding a Command object on the Database Expert dialog box.**

Before you can add the command, you first have to open the data source. This is the same way you would open any data source you need. Find the proper folder in Database Expert, specify its location, and set any user credentials necessary to login. Once you return to the Database Expert you'll see the Add Command option listed. Double click on it to open the Add Command dialog box shown in Figure 11-5.

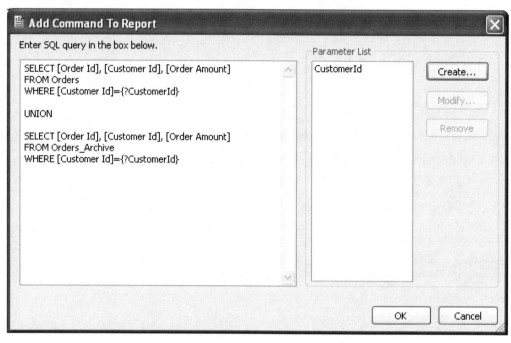

Figure 11-5. The Add Command dialog box.

The left side gives you a text editor to write the custom SQL statement. The SQL that is entered here is not modified by Crystal Reports at all. It is sent directly to the database server. Since each database server has a different set of syntax rules for its version of SQL, you have to make sure that what you enter is compliant with these rules.

When you click on the OK button to save the command, Crystal Reports sends the SQL statement to the database server to retrieve the records. Two things happen here. The first is that it checks whether you entered a valid SQL statement or not. If there is an error in your SQL statement, Crystal Reports alerts you to the exact error message returned by the database server and lets you go back and modify the SQL. If the SQL statement is error free, then Crystal reports retrieves the result set from the server and builds a field list that you can use to build the report.

Command objects can use parameters to filter out unwanted data on the server before it's returned to Crystal Reports. The right side of the dialog box gives you the ability to add new parameters. To create a new parameter, simply click on the Create button. It opens a dialog box which prompts you for the parameter name, prompting text, data type and default value. Enter this information and click the OK button to save your changes. If you need to edit it or delete it, click on the Modify or Remove buttons respectively. You can add more parameters by clicking on the Create button again.

Once a parameter has been added, it appears in the Parameter List window on the right. To use it in your SQL statement, either type it in directly, or put your cursor where you want the parameter to appear and then double-click on it in the list. Crystal Reports will enter it into the SQL statement for you.[52] Once you close this dialog box, you are prompted to enter the value for the parameter(s) used in the SQL statement. These values are passed to the database server with the rest of the SQL statement for processing.

If you have a lot of experience working with databases, then you might recognize the similarities between the command object and using stored procedures and wonder what the difference is between the two. To be honest, there really isn't much difference. Both let you write custom SQL statements that are very complex. Command objects are for people who either don't have permission to create stored procedures on the database server (database administrators are very protective of their servers), or you aren't familiar with the database server administrative tools. Crystal Reports makes it easy for anyone to create new commands without having to be a database administrator to learn how to use the software.

## Best Of The Forum

**Question:** I want to print the last sales record for each customer in my table. I can't figure out how to locate and print just the most recent records in a table.

**Answer:** I see this question posted to the forum every month or so and it is a problem I have on a regular basis because Crystal Reports can't do it natively. It requires adding a Command object to create custom SQL query. But when I try to use the SQL Max() function to find the most recent date, SQL forces me to group all my records together and I can't isolate the record that has that date. It's a tricky problem and I would have to re-work it each time. I finally wised up and wrote the SQL query on a post-it note and I keep it next to my computer. Now, I just look at the post-it note to refresh my memory.

```
Select * From Table AS T0
WHERE T0.DateField =
(SELECT Max(T1.DateField)
FROM Table as T1
WHERE T0.PrimaryKey=T1.PrimaryKey)
```

To make this query work for you, replace "Table" with your own table name. Next, replace "DateField" with the date that you are tracking and replace

---

[52] The benefit to double-clicking on the parameter name is that the curly brackets and question mark get added automatically. That way you don't have to remember the exact naming convention.

"PrimaryKey" with the field that is the unique identifier in the table. Of course, you should also replace the "*" with the specific fields you want to print.

This SQL query consists of a nested SELECT statement. The inner SQL statement is the key for making this work. It uses the Max() function to find the most recent date in the table for the current record. But rather than get into a problem with having to group the records together, it just finds the Max() date for the current record being processed by the outside SELECT statement. It does this by linking on the PrimaryKey field. Now, the outside SELECT statement can just select the single record that has the same date that was returned by the inner SELECT statement. In effect, the inner SELECT finds the last record for each customer and the outside SELECT gets the record that matches that date. This returns the most recent record for each customer.

## Joining Tables with UNION

Earlier I mentioned that you can use the UNION keyword to join tables in ways that standard linking doesn't allow, but I didn't go into the details of how to do it. Although this book isn't meant to teach you about writing SQL statements (there are already many books for that), I'm always surprised at how many people don't know about UNION and its benefits. As a reader of my book, I certainly don't want you to be one of those people "in the dark" about something so useful and yet so simple. It has certainly gotten me out of some tough reporting situations! So let's take a short break from pure Crystal Reports talk and see if I can enlighten you about the benefits of using the UNION keyword.

When you typically join two tables together, you do so using a field that is common between the two tables. Each record in the tables is analyzed and when the data in the fields match, those two records are joined together to make a new record. The new record has data from both tables in it. The UNION keyword is unique because it takes the data from one table and appends it to the end of the data from the other table. Unlike linking tables, which joins two records into one, UNION lists one record after the other. For example, if Table A has 25 records and Table B has 10 records, their UNION would create a new table with 35 records in it.

I find using UNION to be helpful in two situations. The first being when you have a table that archives past data on a periodic basis. The current table would have current year data and the archive table would have all the historical data in it. If you were to create a report to print the entire sales history for a particular customer, it would be tricky since the data is in two different tables. You could create a main report that prints the data from the current table and then create a subreport that pulls data from the archive table. Of course, the subreport would have to be formatted exactly the same as the main report so that the user doesn't notice that you are using two different reports for one list. This also makes it harder to maintain the report. A much better way is to use a UNION and it gives you just a single table that lists all the records in it. You can have one report without having to resort to using subreports.

The other situation I find UNION to be helpful in is when combining two similar tables into a single list. I frequently see databases that have tables with similar information in them but for whatever reason they are not in the same table and the field names are different. Sometimes this is due to poor database design and sometimes it's due to the way the application evolved and requirements changed over time. Like it or not, you have to make the best of it. Since the two tables have similar information, you frequently get requests to print reports that combine the two tables together.

Consider an example where a company buys out another company. You need to print a list of all the products that both companies have so you can look for a possible overlap. Rather than printing out two separate reports and comparing them side by side, you can use a UNION to combine the two tables and build one large report with all the products listed together.

Now that you know how the UNION keyword can help you, let's look at the three requirements for using it.

1. You need to have at least two tables (but more are acceptable as well).
2. The SELECT statements must have the same number of fields listed.
3. The fields must have matching data types and be in the same order.

Needing to have two or more tables is a given (otherwise there wouldn't be anything to combine). Getting the SELECT statements correct is critical. If the first SELECT statement lists three fields, for example a number, a string, and a date, then the second SELECT statement must also list three fields of the same data type. You can't have a different number of fields or change their order and expect the database to figure out what you want to do. It will return an error.

For an example, look at the previous Figure 11-5 that shows the Add Command dialog box. It uses a UNION to join two Orders tables together. Here is the code repeated for you.

```
SELECT [Order Id], [Customer Id], [Order Amount]
FROM Orders
WHERE [Customer Id]={?CustomerId}
UNION
SELECT [Order Id], [Customer Id], [Order Amount]
FROM Orders_Archive
WHERE [Customer Id]={?CustomerId}
```

The first SELECT statement pulls data from the current Orders table and the second SELECT statement pulls data from the historical ORDERS_ARCHIVE table. Notice that both SELECT statements use three fields and they are of the same data type. In this example, they also happen to be the exact same fields. But that isn't always the case and it certainly isn't a requirement. As long as the data types match, then you'll be fine. This SQL statement also uses a parameter to select the data for just one customer. In this example, the WHERE conditions just happen to be the same. But this isn't a requirement of the UNION. The WHERE clause for each SELECT statement can be completely different. As long as the SELECT statement follows rules #2 and #3 above, then that is all that is necessary.

As one more final example, let's look how the UNION statement can build a virtual table that could be used to link to other tables. If you have some temporary data you want to insert into your report and you don't want to create a physical table in the database to store it, you can use the UNION statement to create it virtually.

```
SELECT 1 As MonthNum, 'January' AS MonthName
UNION
SELECT 2, ' February'
UNION
SELECT 3, ' March '
UNION
SELECT 4, 'April'
UNION
SELECT 5, 'May'
UNION
SELECT 6, 'June'
UNION
SELECT 7, 'July'
UNION
SELECT 8, 'August'
UNION
SELECT 9, 'September'
UNION
SELECT 10,'October'
UNION
SELECT 11, 'November'
UNION
SELECT 12, 'December'
```

In this example, we are building a list of the months in the year. The first field is the month number and the second field is the month name. By using the UNION keyword we are joining all the individual SELECT statements into one big virtual table that contains one record for every month of the year.

It is also important to note that since we are creating raw data that doesn't come from an existing table, we need to define the field names manually. In the first SELECT statement, I use the AS keyword to define an alias for each field name. This tells the database server that the first column is called MonthNum and the second column is called MonthName.

Okay, you're probably tired of reading about the UNION keyword and ready to get back on topic. Let's look at more advanced uses of the command object and see how your report can modify live data on the database server as the report runs.

## Using Stored Procedures and Views

Hundreds of books have been written on how to use SQL and optimize it. Although I've been working with SQL for two decades, I'm still not an expert on it. But, I do know that if you have to use a complex command object for a report, you are most likely better off writing it as a stored procedure or creating a view. Not only are stored procedures faster, they have the benefit of letting you access the database using the full power of the SQL language. You can do such things as create multiple temporary tables, analyze data row by row, and almost write a small application within one stored procedure. Views are also more efficient than the command object, but they are a bit more limited than stored procedures. However, they do give you the ability to store the SQL for creating a complex join of many tables and saving it within the database server. Crystal Reports only needs to reference that view as if it were a table and it can easily pull data from it and your reports will run faster.

In addition to using stored procedures and views for performance improvements, another benefit is that all the database logic is consolidated in a central location on the server. If you create a stored procedure for your report, anyone writing reports can benefit from your work and use it in their reports as well (assuming they have proper access rights). You can create a database library of stored procedures/views that are specifically designed for reporting.

Depending upon your IT department's policies, you might not be able to create and save stored procedures/views. Some database administrators are very strict about who is allowed access to the database and many won't allow report designers to create additional objects on the server.[53] You need to find out what you are allowed to do on the server and what procedures must be followed.

There are times when a stored procedure can adversely affect report performance. Ideally, the purpose of a stored procedure is to process one or more complex SQL statements on the server and let Crystal Reports only work with the final result set. You are pushing the work down to the server so that the report runs much faster. This is all fine and good as long as you are only reporting off of a single stored procedure. The problem arises when you are joining data from a stored procedure to another table or another stored procedure.

In the previous chapter we discussed how using different join types makes your report run more efficiently because only matching records are retrieved from the database. Unfortunately, SQL Server doesn't let you use the JOIN keyword to link a stored procedure to another table. Because of this, Crystal Reports has to pull all the data into

---

[53] I'm certain that there has been the countless debates between report writers and DBAs about this.

separate result sets and join them manually on the client. To illustrate how this works, Figure 11-6 shows the SQL statement that Crystal Reports uses to join the CustomerDetail stored procedure with the Orders table.

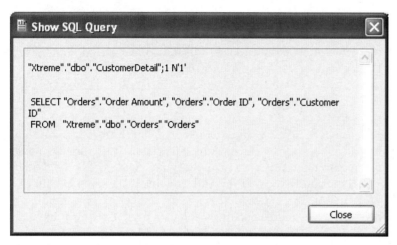

**Figure 11-6. Selecting data from the Orders table and Customer Detail stored procedure.**

To process this data, Crystal Reports has to make two separate requests to SQL Server. The first request pulls data from the CustomerDetail stored procedure and the second pulls data from the Orders table. Once it retrieves all the data from SQL Server and stores it in local memory, it manually processes each record to get the final result set. Clearly, this is extremely inefficient. If you are working with large data sets and one of the data sources is a stored procedure, this can seriously impact performance.

## Tip

If you are joining stored procedures on the client and performance needs to be improved, it's best to convert stored procedures to SQL views. SQL Server treats views the same as a standard table and lets you use them in JOIN statements. By using views, the work of processing all the data is performed by the SQL Server database and Crystal Reports only has to print the final result set. This can give you a huge performance boost depending upon how much data is involved. Unfortunately, a stored procedure that uses parameters can't be converted to a view because views don't support parameters. Also, stored procedures that use too much complex SQL can't be converted to a view and you will have to leave them as is.

One problem I encounter when sharing common logic among reports is testing the reports and keeping track of which report is using which stored procedure/view. At some point, the client will ask for a major change to a report and this requires changing the underlying stored procedure that provides data to the report. In many cases, changing the stored procedure has the potential to break compatibility with the other reports using it. Depending upon how drastic the change is, this can require a lot of testing across multiple reports to ensure that they still work. Sometimes, I have to save my changes as a new stored procedure/view to keep the other reports functioning. But, the worst part is when a report is using a stored procedure and I've forgotten about it (and consequently didn't test it). Just when I think everything is going great and I start to relax, I get a call about some arcane report that suddenly stopped working and I have to fix it immediately. This is why it is important to keep documentation on all stored procedures and views that your reports use.

## Inserting and Updating Data with Crystal Reports

A powerful feature of Crystal Reports is that it allows full access to the SQL language for manipulating databases. This means that not only can you pull information out of a database for printing, but you can also make changes to the live data in the database as the report prints. You can insert new records into the database as well as modify existing records. If you've always thought of reports as a passive viewer of data, then this changes that idea completely.

With this power comes the responsibility to use it correctly. Prior to using a report to modify data, you should always consult with your database administrator so that he/she knows what you plan on doing, as well as making sure you go about it the proper way.

| Caution |
|---|
| If this is used incorrectly, you could delete or overwrite critical data on the server. And you'll probably get invited to meetings with people at a much higher level than you whom you would have been happier never meeting. So please be careful with the following information. |

Giving your report the ability to modify the database involves a few different steps and has a few rules to it. Let's look at the rules involved in creating an updateable command object and then discuss each one in detail.

1. The database must support using two SQL statements in one command object.
2. The command object must return data.
3. Updateable command objects must placed be on a subreport.
4. Place the subreport in the appropriate section

***The database must support using two SQL statements in one command object.***

As we'll see later in the tutorial, updateable command objects require using two separate SQL statements in one command object. The first statement modifies the data and the second statement returns a dummy value. Databases like MS Access only allow one SQL statement per command object. Thus, it can't use updateable command objects. SQL Server does allow this.

***The Command object must return data.***

The nature of an updateable command object is that its job is to perform an action on the database server. This could be inserting or updating data. It isn't worried about returning data. Unfortunately, this causes a conflict with the way Crystal Reports processes data sources. When Crystal Reports generates a report, it tries to optimize the processing time by analyzing each table in the data source. If it finds that one of the tables doesn't return any data, it drops that data source. It only keeps tables that return data that gets printed on the report.

As an example, assume there is a table with only one of its fields being used on the report. You later delete that field and forget to remove the table from the data source. When you run the report, Crystal Reports realizes that the field has been deleted and that the table isn't needed anymore. It removes the table from the database request. This makes the report more efficient by not requesting unnecessary information.

The problem this creates for updateable commands is that since they don't return any data, Crystal Reports assumes that they aren't necessary and skips them. They don't get executed and your data never gets updated. The way to fix this is to put some type of SELECT statement in the command object to create a dummy field and print this field on your report. Since you are selecting a dummy value just to appease Crystal Reports, you can hide it on the report so that it isn't shown. What I like to do is use the SELECT statement to return the number 1.

SELECT 1 AS Dummy

This is fast because it doesn't have to query the database for any information. I also use the AS keyword to give the field an alias. This makes it easy for me to remember that this is just a dummy number that was created to make sure the command is executed.

***Updateable command objects must be placed on a subreport.***

If you create an updateable command object and put it on the main report, it will run fine, but Crystal Reports will run it twice. For reasons beyond my understanding, Crystal Reports always executes updateable command objects twice.[54] This results in your action being executed twice. So if you insert a record, it gets inserted twice. If you update data, it gets updated twice. Not only is this inefficient, but it can corrupt your data. The way

---

[54] It's very possible this is a bug because none of the other data sources are called twice.

around this problem is to create a subreport and call the command object from the subreport. The subreport will only get called once and there won't be any surprises.

### Place the subreport in the appropriate section

You have to be careful when deciding in which section to place the subreport that contains the command object. It gets called every time that section is displayed. If you just want the command to be executed once, then put the subreport in the Report Header or Report Footer. If you have a command that updates the data each time a new record is printed, you should put the subreport in the Details section. If you put the subreport in the wrong section, it is possible that it will either get called too many times or not enough.

| Caution |
|---|
| If your report has the option Save Data With Report turned on, then the SQL statements in the command object won't be called when you view the report. The command object is only called when the report queries the database for a new result set. Since the report is using saved data, it doesn't need to query the database for a new result set. To force the report to execute the SQL in the command object you either have to turn off the option to save data with the report, or manually refresh the report data. |

Let's put all these ideas together and try them out for ourselves with a tutorial. This tutorial creates a report history that tracks every report that was printed and when it was printed.

# Tutorial 11-1. Creating a Report History Table

As a report designer, a useful tool to have at your disposal is a list of each report that gets printed and when it was printed. You can review this list on a periodic basis to see how the reports are being used. The reports that are printed the most can be reviewed to make sure they are completely optimized and use as few resources as possible. The reports that are rarely printed can be reviewed to see why people aren't using them and if there are improvements that should be made to make them more useful.

In this tutorial, we are going to make it easy for you to track every report that gets printed and save this information to a database table. We are going to create a report which logs the report activity in a ReportHistory table in the database. You can then include this as a subreport in any report and you will be able to log every time someone prints that report. By including this subreport in all your reports, you will have a complete report history that tracks every report that gets printed within the company.

Before we create the report, you first need to create the ReportHistory table in your database. Since I don't know what type of database you are using, I can't exactly tell you the steps for doing this. But I can tell you the table structure so that you can create the table yourself.

The ReportHistory table has two fields: ReportName and ReportDate. The report name gets stored in the first field and the date that the report was printed is stored in the second field. The structure is shown below.

**Table 11-1. ReportHistory table structure**

| Field Name | Data Type |
|---|---|
| ReportName | Varchar(25) |
| ReportDate | DateTime |

Once you finish creating the ReportHistory table in your database, you are ready to start the tutorial to create the reports.

1.  Let's start by creating the report that uses a command object for logging the report activity to the database. Create a new report using the report wizard and after connecting to the data source, double-click the Add Command category to open the Add Command dialog box.

2.  Enter the following SQL into the Add Command dialog box.

```
INSERT INTO ReportHistory
(ReportName, ReportDate)
VALUES
('Report History Subreport', GetDate());
SELECT 1 AS Dummy
```

This command consists of two separate SQL statements. The first is an INSERT INTO statement that creates a new row in the ReportHistory table. It lists the two fields to be modified and the data to populate them with. The data is listed inside the pair of parentheses. The first data is a string that represents the report name and the second is the GetDate() function which returns the current date and time.

Even though this SQL statement uses the report name 'ReportHistorySubreport', this is only a temporary name. Once you add this subreport to the main report, you will change this report name string to match the name of the main report.

The second SQL statement selects the value 1 and puts it in the field Dummy. This is to comply with the rule that an updateable command must return a value or else Crystal Reports won't call it.

3.  Click the OK button to save the command and return to the report wizard.

If you have an administrator tool to look at database tables (e.g. SQL Enterprise Manager), you can check if you entered everything correctly. Look at the ReportHistory table and see that it already has data in it. If you recall from Chapter 10, when you save the command object Crystal Reports actually sends it to the database to check its validity. Thus, if the command executed successfully, it will have recorded its first entry in the table.

4.  Click the Next button on the report wizard to select the fields that should appear on the report.

5.  In this case, the only field to choose from is the Dummy field. Double-click on it so that it is put in the Fields to Display window.

6.  Click the Finish button to close the wizard and preview the report. All you should see is a simple report that shows the report date and the number 1.

7.  Since the only purpose of this report is to execute the SQL statement in the command object, we really don't want to see anything printed on the report. Delete the column header and the report date from the Page Header section, and delete the page number from the Page Footer section.

8.  Now that the unnecessary fields have been deleted, suppress all the sections except the Details section. We want this report to take up as little space as possible.

9.  All that is left on the report is the Dummy field. Right-click on it and select Format Field. Click on the Font tab and change the color to White. The Dummy field will print, but it won't be visible.

10. Save this report as **Report History Subreport.rpt**. You can re-use it in all your reports to track their activity.

Now that the subreport has been created, we need to add it into an existing report to see how well it works. The next set of steps walks you through adding it to any report you have. These steps can be repeated for your entire report library if you wish.

1.  Open up one of your reports and go into design mode.

2.  Select the menu options Insert > Subreport.

3.  On the Insert Subreport dialog box, select the option Choose an Existing Report and click the Browse button.

4.  Find the file 'Report History Subreport.rpt' that you created in the last set of steps and select it.

5.  When you return to the Insert Subreport dialog box, click the OK button to return to the main report.

6.  Place the subreport object in the Report Header of the main report.

    The report is almost finished. The only problem is that if we preview the report right now, it is going to update the ReportHistory table with the report name 'Report History Subreport'. We need to modify it so that is uses the main report's name instead.

7.  Double-click on the subreport object to open it in design mode.

8.  Select the menu options Database > Database Expert. This opens the Database Expert dialog box.

9. In the Selected Tables list on the right, you'll see the command object you created. Right-click on it and select Edit Command.

10. Change the report name string from Report History Subreport to the name of the main report that you are working with. This is the report name string that will be saved to the ReportHistory table.

11. Click the OK button twice to save all your changes and return to the subreport in design mode.

12. Click on the main report's design tab to bring it to the foreground. Then click the preview button to view the report. Since we hid everything on the subreport, the main report should look exactly the same as it did before you added the subreport. What you can't see is that in the background it was updating the ReportHistory table to log the current date and time that you viewed the report.

Remember, if you don't see the ReportHistory table being updated, it might be because you have the option to save the data with the report. Click the Refresh button to requery the database and force the command object to be executed.

As an additional challenge to this tutorial, let's add one twist. In the SQL statement, we returned the value 1 in a report field that was hidden on the subreport. But rather than returning a piece of dummy data, why don't we return something interesting that can be used on the report? For example, it could be useful to print at the top of the report the number of times the report was printed during the month. We can use SQL to count how many times the report was printed and filter on the records for the current month. The following code block does just that:

```
INSERT INTO ReportHistory
(ReportName, UserName, ReportDate)
VALUES
('Report History Subreport', User, GetDate());

SELECT Count(*) AS TimesPrinted
FROM ReportHistory
WHERE ReportName='Report History Subreport'
AND Month(GetDate())=Month(ReportDate)
AND Year(GetDate())=Year(ReportDate)
```

The first half is the same as before. It simply inserts a new record into the table. The second half uses the Count(*) function to count the number of records that would be returned using the filter. The filter selects the records matching the report name and only if they were added during the current month of the current year.

I leave it to you to replace the subreport's current command object with this new SQL statement. You will also have to modify the subreport to change the Dummy field's font color back to Black and put some descriptive text beside it so that the user knows that the value represents how many times the report was printed that month.

# Analyzing SQL Using the Microsoft SQL Profiler

There are two distinct stages when a report runs: generating the data and generating the report. Unfortunately, it isn't very clear about how much time is being spent on each stage. If you have a report that needs to be optimized, how do you know if you should optimize the data access part or the report generation part? You don't. It's a bit of guesswork and experimentation to try to get the best performance out of a report. But, if you are using Microsoft SQL Server, you can use the SQL Profiler to give you a more in-depth look at what is happening on the database side.[55] The SQL Profiler shows you every data request made on the server and it details how much time each process took. This information gives you the ability to determine exactly how much time is spent processing data and how much time is spent generating the report.

For example, earlier in the chapter I mentioned that stored procedures are treated differently from tables and are called separately. Consequently, I recommended converting stored procedures to views when possible. If you are curious how I knew that, it's because of the SQL Profiler. I had a report where I created multiple stored procedures because I 'knew' that this was best for performance. But, when I used the SQL Profiler to analyze the performance on the server, I saw that Crystal Reports was generating multiple calls to the database for the report and was therefore joining the result sets on the client side. Upon further experimentation and analysis I decided to change the stored procedures to views to see what would happen. Sure enough, the database calls were reduced and the report ran faster. I would never have known this just by using the Show SQL Query functionality in Crystal Reports.

As another example, a while back I overheard my client complaining that another programmer's reports were taking almost a full minute to run and they were only one line reports. At the end of the month, they had to run dozens of these reports and most of their day was wasted. I asked him about this and he said it was due to using the UNION clause to join multiple archive tables to the current data. This sounded reasonable, but I wanted to check it out for myself. I decided to use the SQL Profiler to do some research.

I found out that the unions were hammering the database and the performance was horrible. Upon examination of the actual SQL statements, I also saw that none of the filtering was being done on the server. Thus, after waiting for the database to process all the records, Crystal Reports then had to do its own filtering. Clearly, there were opportunities for optimization there. After some experimentation, I moved the WHERE clause to each SELECT statement prior to joining the tables with a UNION clause. My testing in the SQL Profiler showed that this reduced the amount of data the server had to join together and it greatly reduced the number of records passed back to Crystal Reports. After we put the changes into production, the report ran almost instantaneously and the client couldn't have been happier.

---

[55] I assume that Oracle and other database servers have similar tools. Please consult your documentation for more information.

To use the SQL Profiler, you can find it on the Windows Start menu. It is located within the SQL Server group and is simply called 'Profiler'. It's a pretty easy tool to get started with and not have to read any documentation. Start a new trace by selecting the menu options File > New Trace. This prompts you to login to the database. After logging in, click on the Events tab and browse through the myriad of events available for tracing. If it's your first time using the browser, just click the Run button to accept the default events and start the trace. You can always go back and create more detailed traces later.

If there is any activity on the database server it will immediately appear in the trace window. By watching the trace, you can see every database call made to the server and who requested it.[56] As you run your own report, you can see which calls are made to the database and see how long it takes to process each one. This gives you detailed metrics about how well your report optimized its SQL request. An example of the SQL Profiler is shown in Figure 11-7.

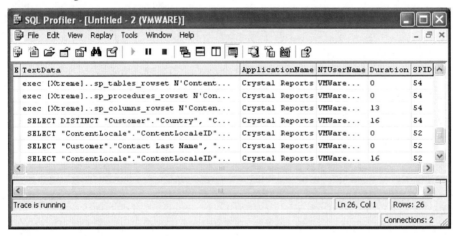

**Figure 11-7. SQL Profiler running a trace.**

You can see in this figure that the trace shows you every SQL statement that has been executed as well as who made the request and how long it took.

If you find that the profiler gives you too much information, when you start it you can deselect which fields and events to show. For example, you can have it only show the final SQL statements processed and ignore all the events leading up to processing the SQL statement. You can also have it filter just on your user name or application name so that you only see events that have to do with your testing.

Overall, the SQL Profiler is a very powerful tool that can be used by advanced users for digging into the details of what is happening behind the scenes of a database call. It helps you make an informed decision about which aspect of your report needs optimizing.

---

[56] You might find yourself just sitting and staring at the log as it scrolls past and you see how different people are using the database.

# SQL Expressions

Throughout this chapter we've discussed the different parts of a report that can be improved with SQL Expressions. The following table lists the different Crystal functions and their SQL Server equivalents. Although other databases are certain to have slight variations with their functions, they should be similar. You should consult your SQL documentation for the exact syntax of each function.

**Table 11-2. Converting Crystal functions to SQL functions.**

| Crystal Function | Sql Function |
|---|---|
| CStr(), CBool(), CDbl(), CDateTime(), ToNumber(), ToText(), etc. | Convert(,) |
| CurrentDate, CurrentTime(), PrintDate(), PrintTime() | CurDate(), CurTime(), Now() |
| WeekdayName() | DayName() |
| DatePart() | DayOfMonth() |
| DayOfWeek() | DayOfWeek() |
| DatePart() | DayOfYear() |
| Hour() | Hour() |
| Month() | Month() |
| MonthName() | MonthName() |
| DatePart() | Quarter() |
| DatePart() | Second() |
| DatePart() | Week() |
| DatePart() | Year() |
| Abs() | Abs() |
| Cos(), Sin() | ACos(), ASin() |
| Tan(), ATn() | ATan(), ATan2() |
| Ceiling() | Ceiling() |
| Cos() | Cos() |
|  | Cot() |

|  | Degrees() |
| --- | --- |
| Exp() | Exp() |
| Floor() | Floor() |
| Log() | Log() |
|  | Log10() |
| Mod | Mod() |
| Pi | PI() |
| ^ | Power() |
|  | Radians() |
| Rnd() | Rand() |
| Round() | Round() |
| Sgn() | Sign() |
| Sin() | Sin() |
| Sqrt() | Sqrt() |
| Tan() | Tan() |
| Truncate() | Truncate() |
| AscW() | Ascii() |
| ChrW() | Char() |
| x & y | Concat(), x + y |
|  | Insert() |
| LowerCase(), LCase() | LCase() |
| Left() | Left() |
| Length() | Length() |
| InStr() | Locate() |
| TrimLeft(), LTrim() | LTrim() |
| ReplicateString() | Repeat() |
| Replace() | Replace() |
| Right() | Right() |

| | |
|---|---|
| TrimRight(), RTrim() | RTrim() |
| | SoundEx() |
| Space() | Space() |
| Mid() | SubString() |
| UpperCase(), UCase() | UCase() |
| | IfNull() |

Being able to visualize data can have a tremendous impact on the reader. Compared to just printing raw numerical data, adding a chart to a report makes it possible for readers to quickly grasp the important relationships between data. Many times reports are used with proposals to sell a reader on an idea or plan. Adding a colorful chart can sell your idea more effectively than a dry report filled with endless numbers. This chapter shows you what types of charts are available as well as how to modify their appearance so that they can make your report more appealing and quickly get your message across.

## Choosing the Proper Chart

Charts are used to make it easy to compare sets of data. The visual aspect of a chart lets the reader immediately recognize things such as the differences in quantity, percentage of the whole or numerical trending. Crystal Reports gives you 16 different types of charts to choose from. Table 12-1 lists the types and shows a sample picture of each.

**Table 12-1. Example chart types.**

| Chart Type | Sample | Chart Type | Sample |
|---|---|---|---|
| Bar | | Radar | |
| Line | | Bubble | |
| Area | | Stock | |
| Pie | | Numeric Axis | |
| Doughnut | | Gauge | |

| | | | |
|---|---|---|---|
| 3D Riser | | Gantt | |
| 3DSurface | | Funnel | |
| XY Scatter | | Histogram | |

With the wide variety of charts available, it can be hard to decide which one to use. Of course, you want one that looks good, but more importantly is that it is appropriate for the data you are displaying. Certain chart styles are more effective at presenting certain types of data than others. Making this decision can be a bit tough at first. Table 12-2 lists each chart type and shows where it is effective. This table gets you started in the right direction for choosing the proper chart.

**Table 12-2. Effectiveness of different chart styles.**

| Chart Style | Effective at ... |
|---|---|
| Bar Chart | Comparing the differences between items and events. |
| | Comparing items and events against the same scale without relation to time. |
| | Showing relationships between sets of data using grouping. |
| | Note: The X-axis is generally non-numeric. When it is numeric, the interval isn't relevant. |
| Line Chart/Area Chart | Comparing continuous data over a period of time against a common scale. |
| | Tracking movement over time. |
| | Examining trends between two or more sets of data. |
| | Note: The X-axis represents a unit of time. |
| Pie/Doughnut Chart | Visualizing the percent of the whole. |

| | |
|---|---|
| | Examining relationships as part-to-whole. |
| | Note: There is only a single axis being represented. Thus, only one value is being charted. |
| 3D Riser/Surface Chart | Showing trends with relationship to time. |
| | Note: It uses a three dimensional surface to make it easy to analyze a large quantity of data. |
| X-Y Scatter Chart | Charting a large quantity of values without relation to time. |
| | Finding groups of data where there is a large percentage of similar data points. |
| Radar Chart | Comparing data sets in a star pattern. The importance/relationship of each data set is determined by having the target value start at either the center of the axis or the outside. |
| Bubble Chart | Comparing the significance of data points by looking at the size of each bubble compared to the other bubbles. Similar to the X-Y chart, but with a third data point. The third data point determines the bubble's diameter. Each bubble is proportional to the value compared to the other data points. |
| Stock Chart | Analyzing stock values. Shows the trading range for the day as well as first trade and last trade amounts. |
| Gauge | Plotting one or more data points using a dial format. |
| | Represents a number by its position on the dial. |
| Gantt | Plots activities in a business plan. Shows how long an activity took to complete as well as its relationship to the other activities. |
| | Each activity must have a start date and stop date associated with it. |
| Funnel | Shows stages in a sales process. |
| Histogram | Shows how data is distributed with relationship to the mean value. |
| | Makes it easy to visualize the pattern within a large number of data points. |

Table 12-2 has a lot of information in it, so let's try to make it easier to digest by looking at a table that highlights the important aspect of each chart. Table 12-3 lists different aspects you have to consider when using a chart and lists which one applies to which chart. The first columns, Time, tells you whether the chart plots data over a period of time (i.e. it plots dates). The second column, Show %, tells whether the chart visualizes what percent each data point has compared to the total chart. Bigger areas mean a larger percent. The third column, # of Data, tells you how many data points a chart is best used with. Some charts are best at showing a small number of data points and other charts are designed to plot many data points.

**Table 12-3. Common chart characteristics.**

| Chart | Time | Show % | # of Data |
| --- | --- | --- | --- |
| Bar | N | N | Small/Med |
| Line | Y | N | Small/Med |
| Area | Y | Y | Small/Med |
| Pie/Doughnut | N | Y | Small/Med |
| 3D Surface | Y | N | Small/Large |
| X-Y Scatter | N | N | Large |
| Radar | N | N | Small/Large |
| Bubble | N | N | Small/Large |
| Stock | Y | N | Small/Large |
| Gauge | N | N | Small |
| Gantt | Y | N | Small/Large |
| Funnel | Y | Y | Small/Med |
| Histogram | N | N | Large |

To use Table 12-2 and 12-3, think about why you are using a chart to present your data. Ask yourself what is the message you are trying to convey to the reader. Scan the list of reasons why one chart is more effective than the other charts. Once you see a description that best matches your purpose, select that type of chart.

For example, assume you have a report that prints the annual sales for each division in a corporation. The message you are conveying is which division had the largest sales volume as well as which division had the lowest sales. The charts that are good at comparing different data sets are the bar chart, the line chart and the X-Y chart. The bar chart immediately looks good because it is effective at comparing differences between items. The line chart also compares data, but it does so over a period of time. This doesn't apply here because the data is within the same time period (i.e. the same year). So the line chart is not a good choice. The X-Y chart compares data, but it is done with respect to two data points. In other words, both the X and Y axis must represent numerical data. The sales report is charted with the sales volume and the division name. Since the division name isn't numerical data, it can't be used with the X-Y chart. The best choice for the division annual sales report is the bar chart.

Let's build on this example by saying that you are given a new requirement where the report has to be modified so that it is now a drill-down report. It currently shows the annual sales per division and it needs to be modified so that you can drill-down on a division and see its monthly sales. This helps the reader determine if the division had a particular month that was exceptionally better than the other months or if the division was consistently improving. The purpose of this chart is very similar to the first chart. You want to tell the reader how the total sales compare to each other. But this example has a slight variation: you are now charting for a single division and the individual months are being compared to each other. You are working with data that changes over a period of time and looking for the trend. The only reason we didn't use a line chart in the first example was because the data didn't relate to time. This example does relate to time and it is also looking at the sales trend. So the line chart is an excellent choice for presenting the monthly sales figures.

# Adding a Chart

There are two ways to add a chart to a report: with the Report Expert and with the Add Chart Expert. If you are creating a report from scratch and you know in advance that it will use a chart, you can use the Report Expert to add the chart during the initial report creation. If you decide to add a chart later, right-click on the report and select Insert > Chart. This creates a floating rectangle that is attached to the mouse. As you move the mouse around, the rectangle moves with it. If a section doesn't allow a report to be placed there, then the cursor changes to a circle with a line through it to tell you that you can't place it there. When you move the mouse over a section that allows charts, the cursor changes back to the standard mouse cursor. Put the cursor in the section where you want to place the chart and click the mouse button to drop it there.

After placing the chart in the appropriate section, either the Chart Expert appears or a default chart is shown. If the Chart Expert doesn't appear automatically, then display it by right-clicking on the chart and select Chart Expert.

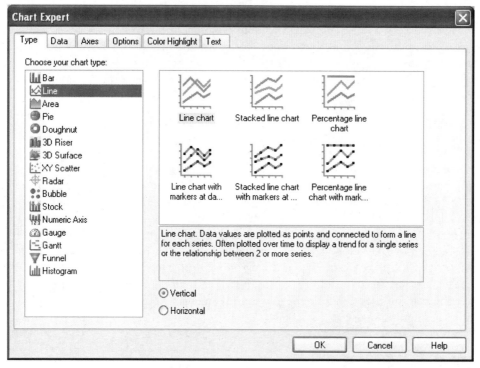

**Figure 12-1. Chart Expert dialog box.**

This dialog box has six tabs that are shown by default: Type, Data, Axes, Options, Color Highlight and Text. Each tab is discussed in detail in the following sections.

# Selecting a Chart with the Type Tab

The Type tab selects the type of chart to display. As we discussed in the previous sections, there are over a dozen different types of charts to choose from. As you click on each chart type in the list, examples are shown in the window to the right. Each example corresponds to a slight variation that you can choose from. The variation usually relates to how the values are plotted on the chart or their relationship to each other. For example each value could be plotted along the y-axis using its value, or it could be plotted as a percentage of the whole.

Charts that use an X-Y axis format have an option button that selects whether it is a vertical or horizontal chart. Vertical is chosen by default.

# Setting Data Points with the Data tab

The Data tab is the primary interface for configuring the chart and it is fairly complex. It sets the fields that determine the coordinates of each axis as well as maps the data points. It also has four buttons for setting the properties of specialized charts. The Advanced button shows the default layout and is available for every report. The Group button is enabled when your report has a grouping section and the Cross-Tab button is enabled when there is a cross-tab object on the report. The default selection, Advanced, is shown in Figure 12-2.

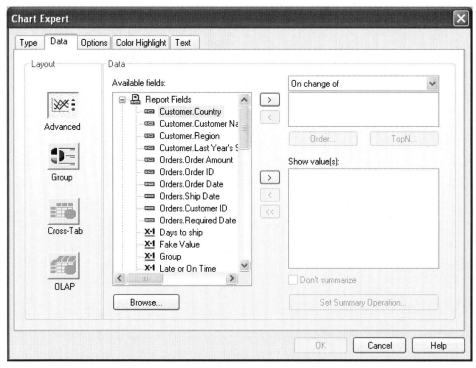

**Figure 12-2. The Data tab with the Advanced button selected.**

The Advanced button is always available for every report. The other three buttons are only enabled when data related to their chart type is in the report. The Group button is enabled when there is at least one group in the report. The Cross-Tab button must have a cross-tab object within the same section that the chart is placed in. The OLAP button is enabled when there are one or more OLAP grids within the same section as the chart.

> **Note**
>
> Each layout button on the Data tab creates a different type of chart. Although they are all on the same Data tab and appear to work together, they are completely independent. Only the last one selected is used to create the chart. For example, say that you set some properties on the Advanced tab. You then decide that you would rather use a Group chart instead. So you click on the

Group button and change the settings. When you run the report, the chart displayed on the report will be a group chart and reflect those settings. The settings you made with the Advanced button are ignored. In fact, when you close this dialog box and save your settings, only the settings for the current button are saved and any settings that were made with the other buttons are discarded.

The Advanced button on the data tab has three sections. The Available Fields list shows all the fields that the chart can use. To the right of the field list is the On Change Of list that sets which field(s) will have their data plotted. Below that is the Show Value(s) list. It sets the field(s) whose values are plotted on the chart. These sections are described next in more detail.

| Tip |
| --- |

People often ask why they can't find a particular formula field in the Available Fields list. This is because some formulas are classified as second-pass formulas and are calculated at the same time that the chart is being printed. Since all the data for that formula may not be available then the chart can't plot it. See Chapter 1 for more information about the two-pass report processing model and which formulas get calculated in each pass.

## The On Change Of List

The On Change Of list determines when a new element is shown on the chart. On a standard vertical chart, this would be the elements listed on the X-axis. For example, with a bar chart it determines when a new bar is drawn. If the selected field was Company Id, then a bar is plotted on the chart for each company. There are three options to choose from and they are listed in Table 12-4.

**Table 12-4. The Evaluate options.**

| Evaluate Option | Description |
| --- | --- |
| On Change Of | A new element is created when the value of the field changes. The value plotted on the other axis is the sum of all fields that are in each group. |
| For Each Record | A new element is created for each detail record in the table. Check the number of detail records because too many records will over-crowd the chart. |
| For All Records | Shows a single element on the chart. The value plotted on the other axis is the grand total of each field |

selected in the Show Value(s) list.

The On Change Of setting requires a little more explanation than the other two options, which are fairly straightforward. The On Change Of setting is used in conjunction with one or more report fields. It creates chart-only groups and summarizes the values within the group. The groups created by the chart have no affect on the rest of the report.

When selecting the On Change Of option, you add the grouping field(s) for the Show Value list below. The number of fields you add determines how many groups are in the report. If you only have one field, then each group name is listed as a single element on the chart. For example, Figure 12-3 shows a chart with an Evaluate field of Customer Name and the Show Value field (discussed later) is Order Amount. This creates an element for each customer and the y-axis charts the total amount of all the orders in the report.

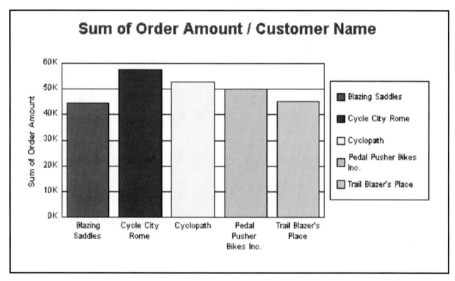

**Figure 12-3. A chart with one field in the Evaluate list.**

Having more than one field in the On Change Of list creates sets of data. Each set has the same number of elements in it and they are compared to each other as a group. The first element is the primary group and the second element is the sub-group. The primary group determines the sets that are charted. The sub-group charts each individual element within the primary group.

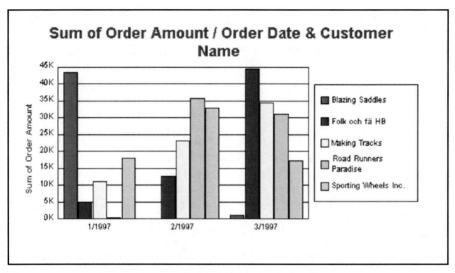

**Figure 12-4. A chart with two fields in the Evaluate list.**

The chart in Figure 12-4 also shows the total customer order amounts, but it does it based on the month the order was placed. Putting two fields in the Evaluate list does this: The Order Date by month, and the Customer Name. The Order Date is listed first so that the data sets are charted by month. The Customer Name is listed second so that it gets listed as a separate element on the chart.

For each field listed as an element, there are a few ways to customize it. Directly below the list are two buttons: TopN and Order. These are only enabled when you select one of the fields in the list. These two buttons bring up the same dialog boxes that are used with formatting groups. The TopN button lets you filter the groups according to their overall ranking. The Order button lets you select whether the groups are sorted by Ascending, Descending, or Natural Order. You can also tell it to sort in a specified order.

## Setting the Show Value Fields

The Show Value list determines the values that are plotted on the chart. On a standard vertical chart, this is where an element is plotted along the Y-axis. For example, in a bar chart it determines how high a bar is drawn on a bar chart. For each field listed, another element is drawn on the chart at each interval. If there is a line chart with three fields, then each field would have a separate line plotting its values.

The Show Value fields are charted using either their actual value or using a summary function. This is determined by what is selected in the On Change Of list. If this option is set to For Each Record, then each record gets charted according to its actual value and no summary calculation is performed. If the option selected is On Change Of or For All Records, then a summary calculation is performed to determine what value to plot. The On Change Of setting calculates a summary value for each group. The For All Records setting plots a single summary value for the entire report. This has the effect of plotting one element for each field listed.

The default summary calculation is the Sum() function. If you had selected a text field for the Show Value field, then the summary function would be Count(). You can change this by selecting the field and clicking on the Set Summary Operation button. This brings up the standard Change Summary dialog box where you click on the dropdown list to select a different summary function.

## Meeting the Minimum Field Requirements

The Evaluate setting and Show Value setting work together to determine the X, Y and Z axis on each chart. Due to the fact that each type of chart can be unique in how it uses the fields in these settings to create the chart, it is important to know how many fields to put in each setting.

Charts have different requirements for the number of data values it needs to plot each point. For example, a line chart needs two values. The first value marks the time interval and the second value marks where on the chart the point will appear. A slightly more complicated chart, the X-Y Scatter chart, has different requirements. It needs a single value to set the intervals along the X-axis of the chart and it needs two values to mark where the point should appear on the chart. Table 12-5 shows the minimum number of fields required by each chart type.

**Table 12-5. Required minimum number of fields for each type of chart.**

| Chart Type | # On Change Of | # Show Values |
| --- | --- | --- |
| Bar/Line/Area/Funnel | 1 | 1 |
| Pie/Doughnut | 1 | 1 |
| Pie/Doughnut multiple | 1 | Many |
| Gauge | 1 | Many |
| 3D Riser | 1 | 1 |
| 3D Surface | 2 | 1 |
| 3D Surface | 1 | Many |
| XY Scatter/Gantt | 1 | 2 |
| Bubble | 1 | 3 |
| Stock | 1 | 2 |
| Stock with open/close marks | 1 | 4 |

The middle column, # of On Change Of fields, tells you how many fields are required when you have selected the On Change Of option in the drop-down box. This doesn't apply if you selected either For Each Record or For All Records. This is because these selections automatically set the interval along the X-axis and you aren't allowed to add new fields. However, if a chart type has a requirement of two fields, then you won't be able to use the For Each Record or For All Records options.

The last column, # of Show Values, tells you how many fields are required in the Show Values list. Each chart type requires at least one field and some charts allow you to add an unlimited number of fields. The only restriction is that it is limited to how many can reasonably fit on the chart.

# Adding Group Charts

On the Data tab of the Chart Expert, below the Advanced button, is the Group button. It is used to create a chart that shows each group and one of its summary fields. It can only appear within the Report Header/Footer. When you click on the Group button, the interface changes to reflect the grouping specific options. This is shown in Figure 12-5.

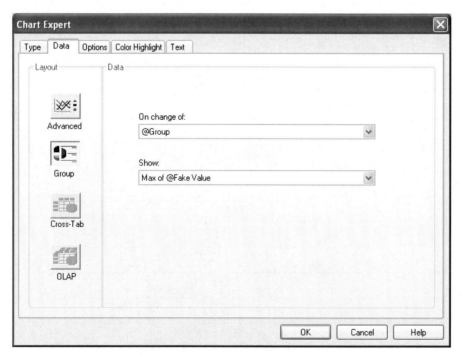

**Figure 12-5. The grouping options of the Data tab.**

There are two requirements for having the Group button enabled. The first requirement is that there is a group section. Of course, if your report doesn't have a group section then you certainly can't chart group values. The second requirement is that the group must have at least one summary field. This is because the group chart only plots summary fields. If you want to create a chart based on a group and your report doesn't meet these two requirements, then you can choose to place the chart within a Group Header/Footer and set the options using the Advanced button.

The Group button presents a very simple interface when compared to the Advanced button. This is because the Group button is used for creating a simple chart. Whereas the Advanced button allows you to have a lot of variations on how many fields are charted on each axis, the Group button only lets you select a single group and a single summary field to chart.

The top dropdown list shows the groups on your report. The groups that are listed here change depending upon where you place the chart. No matter how many groups are on your report, only two groups will be listed. These are the top two groups below the location where you are placing the chart. For example, if you place the chart in the Report Header/Footer section, then the first and second outermost groups are listed. However, if you place the chart in the first group's header/footer, then the next two groups directly below it will be shown in the dropdown list. If there is only one group below where the chart is located, then it will be the only one listed.

When you select the group, the lower dropdown list will show the summary fields for the group selected. From these summary fields, select which one to chart.

## Tutorial 12-1. Creating a Group Chart in the Page Header

Let's take a report that uses groups and print a bar chart in the page header that summarizes each group's value. This gives the user a high-level overview of how each group compares to the other groups. The Crystal Reports sample report, Summary Group.rpt, groups sales data by country and shows sub-totals of last year's sales. We will add a chart in the header that shows each country and chart's last year's sales.

1. Open the Crystal Reports sample report, Summary Group.rpt.

2. Select the menu options File > Save As and enter the filename, Summary Group Chart.rpt.

3. In Design mode, right-click on the chart and select the option Insert Chart. The chart's outline appears and it is attached to the mouse.

4. Position the chart outline in the Page Header section and click the mouse button to place the chart. This also changes the height of the Page Header so that the chart can fit on it.

5. Right-click on the chart and select the menu option Chart Expert. This opens the Chart Expert dialog box.

6. On the Type tab, it should have defaulted to the Bar Chart type. If not, select it now.

7. Click on the Data tab. The On Change Of option selects which data points are plotted on the chart. Crystal Reports has already selected Customer.Country by default. Leave it at this field.

8. The Show option selects which values are plotted within the chart. Crystal Reports selected the field Count Of Customer Name. We want to show last year's sales instead. Click on the drop-down list and select the field Sum of Customer.Last Year's Sales.

9. Click the Ok button to save the chart options.

10. Click on the Preview tab and you should see the chart displayed in the report header. It should look similar to this:

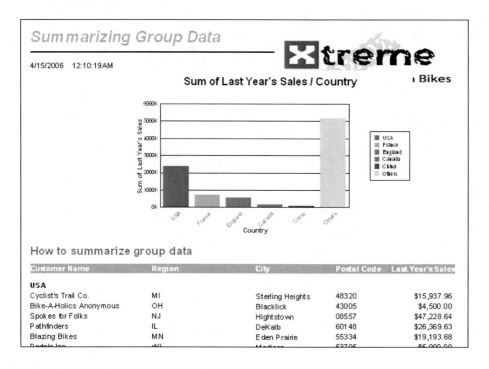

## Customizing Charts in a Group

Putting a chart in a group header implies that the chart will have the same look across all groups. In most cases, this is what you want because it creates consistency throughout the report. But there are times when you need to tweak the settings of one chart so that it is slightly different from the rest. As an example, assume a group chart plots between five and ten points for each group. The legend for each chart fits comfortably within the chart's border. However, one of the groups has fifty items and its legend uses a font so small that you can't read it. For this group, you would customize the chart so that it only shows the top ten items in the group and leave the remaining ones uncharted.

When making formatting changes to a chart, Crystal Reports gives you the option to apply the changes to all charts across the groups or just to the current chart. Before we look at how this works, let's review the different ways to modify a chart. The first way is the most obvious: you make changes to the chart while in Design mode. The second way is to make changes while in Preview mode. The benefit of Preview mode is that as you make the change you immediately see how it affects the report. The reason why this is important is that you can only customize individual group charts in Preview mode.

Preview mode works with chart objects in unique way. For all other report objects, when you make a change to one of the properties, this change is applied throughout the whole report for that object. For example, if you change a field to bold formatting, then every place in the report where that field is shown is now bold. But this is not the case with chart objects. In preview mode, Crystal Reports associates each chart with the group it's shown with. Any change made to a chart is only made to the chart for that individual group. It isn't applied to all the charts in the report. As you page through the report, you can right-click on an individual charts within each group and modify it.

You can't customize individual charts for each group in Design mode because no data is being displayed. All changes made to the chart are applied consistently throughout the report.

To format an individual chart, go to Preview mode and right-click the chart you want to change. Select the Chart Expert menu option and a submenu appears with the options, Applied To Group Template and Applied To This Instance. When you select the group template option, the changes you make are applied to chart for every group. By selecting the "This Instance" option, all changes you make only affect the single chart for that group. The other charts remain unchanged.

After making changes to an individual group instance, when you right-click the chart there are two new menu options: Apply Changes To All Charts and Discard Custom Changes. The first item, Apply Changes To All Charts, takes the changes you made to the current chart and applies them to chart template for the entire group. Thus, every chart in the group will now look like the currently selected one. The second item, Discard Custom Changes, cancels all changes you made to the custom chart and it reverts back to using the group template.

**Note**

Customizing a chart is only available for the Chart Expert menu option. The changes made using the other menu options are always applied to the group template and affect all charts the same.

# Tutorial 12-2. Customizing Group Charts

Let's look at how to customize an individual group chart by walking through a tutorial on it. In the last tutorial, we took the Crystal Reports sample report, Summary Group.rpt, and added a chart in the Page Header. In this tutorial, we will place a gauge chart in the Group Header and then modify an individual chart for only one of the groups. This demonstrates how one group can have formatting that is unique from the other charts.

1.  Open the Crystal Reports sample report, Running Totals Group.rpt.

2.  Select the menu options File > Save As and enter the filename, **Customize Group Chart.rpt**.

3.  In Design mode, right-click on the chart and select the option Insert Chart. The chart's outline appears and it is attached to the mouse.

4.  Position the chart outline in the Group Header section and click the mouse button to place the chart. This immediately opens the Chart Expert dialog box.

5.  The Data tab is selected by default so that you can pick the data points to plot.

6.  Click on the field Customer.Customer Name and click the arrow button to use it as the On Change Of field.

7.  Click on the field Group Running Total and click the arrow button to use it as the Show Value(s) field.

8.  Now that you've selected the data to chart, you want to select the type of chart to display. Click on the Type tab and choose the Gauge chart.

9.  Click the OK button to save your changes and have the chart placed on the report.

10. The default chart size is much larger than what we need. You can resize it to about half of its original size. If you preview the report, it might look something like this:

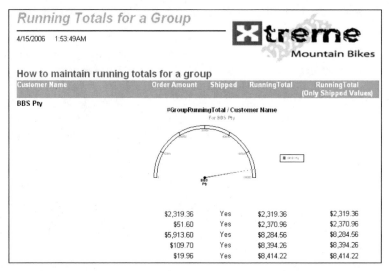

11. This is okay, but we can clean it up a bit. Go back into design mode and move the chart to the left side of the page.

12. We also want the chart to appear alongside the group data. Right-click on the gray area to the left of the Group Header and select Section Expert. Select the option

Underlay Following Sections. This lets the chart appear beside the data rather than above it.

13. To see how to customize an individual chart, let's make some obvious changes that will make the chart stand out from the rest. Go into Preview mode and make sure you are at the first page. Right-click on the chart and select Chart Expert > Applied to This Instance. This lets you only modify the chart for the first group.

14. Click on the Options tab and click on the Show Legend option to disable it.

15. Click on the Text tab and clear out the text from each option.

16. Click the OK button to save your changes. Look at the first page and you'll see that the chart on the first page doesn't have a legend or any chart titles. As you browse through the following pages you'll see that they haven't changed. The changes you made to the first chart don't affect the remaining charts.

# Adding Cross-Tab Charts

The Cross-Tab chart is similar to the Group chart because it takes one of the fields that the cross-tab object is grouped on and plots one of its summary fields. The related dialog box is shown in Figure 12-6.

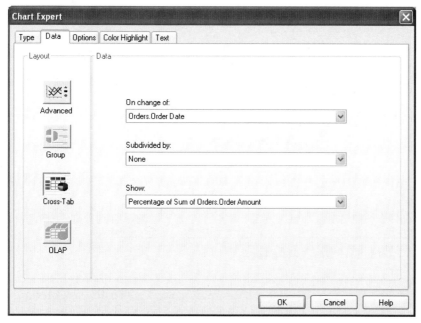

**Figure 12-6. The cross-tab options of the Data tab.**

The On Change Of dropdown list shows the two outer most group fields for the cross-tab object. If you have multiple fields listed for either the row or column setting, then the second and later fields are ignored and can't be used. The field selected in the dropdown list determines when a new element is drawn. Thus, the cross-tab chart can have either one element per row or per column.

The Show dropdown list, lets you select the summary field to plot. This serves the same purpose as the Show Value setting with the Advanced button. However, the Advanced setting lets you select multiple fields and the Cross-Tab settings only let you select one field.

The middle dropdown list, titled Subdivided By, lets you create a data set that is similar to having multiple fields in the Evaluate setting of the Advanced options.

# Setting Captions with the Text tab

Use the Text tab to set the captions that appear on the chart as well as their fonts. This tab is shown in Figure 12-7.

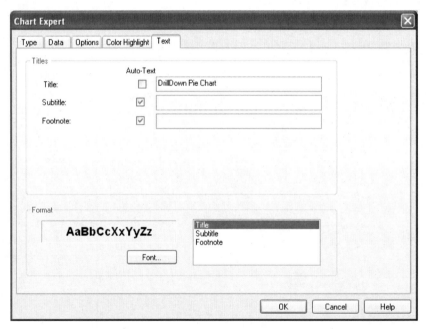

**Figure 12-7. The Text tab of the Chart Expert.**

The Text tab is very easy to understand and modify. It consists of two sections. The top section shows a checkbox for each title that appears on the chart. By default, each caption is set to Auto-Title. This means that the chart will set the caption when you print the report. It uses the chart's field names to determine what to print. For each caption, you can uncheck Auto-Title option and enter your own caption. What you enter overrides what the chart would have printed on its own. If you uncheck it and leave the text blank, then nothing is printed for that caption.

The lower half section sets the font for each caption. To change the font, select the caption name from the list on the right and then click on the Font button. This brings up the standard Font dialog box and you can set the properties as you wish. When you click OK, you are brought back to the Chart Expert. An example of how the new font settings look is shown above the Font button as well as within the section list on the right.

# Using the Options Tab

The Options tab, shown in Figure 12-8, has various miscellaneous properties for customizing the chart layout.

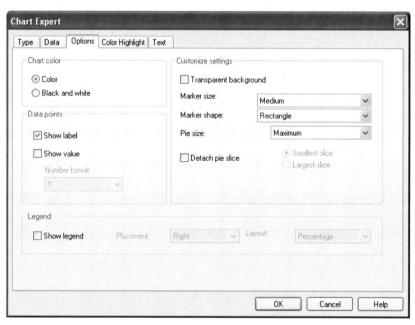

**Figure 12-8. The Options tab of the Chart Expert.**

There are four main areas on the Options tab. The Chart Color frame lets you set the chart to be in color or black and white. Black and white can be helpful when you are sending the report to the printer and you want set the shading of different areas. The Data Points frame is used to toggle displaying the data points on or off. A data point is an identifier on a chart's element telling what the element represents. This can be its text value or its coordinate on the chart. It's helpful to display the coordinates when precision is important and you can't determine exactly where the data points fall on the y-axis. Figure 12-9 shows a chart with the data points turned on.

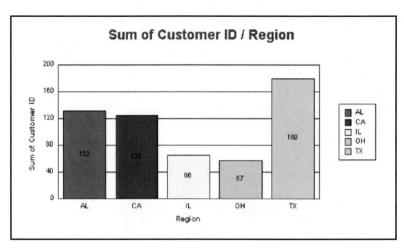

**Figure 12-9. Displaying the data points on a chart.**

The Customize Settings frame sets whether the chart background has a transparent background, how large the markers are and what shape the markers are. The Legend frame sets whether the legend is displayed, and where it is displayed. It can be displayed to the right or left of the chart or at the bottom.

## Setting the Color Highlighting

The colors that Crystal Reports applies to the chart objects may not be to your liking. You might want to set certain items to be a particular color, or apply colors depending upon the value that an item has. Crystal Reports lets you do this using the Color Highlighting tab.

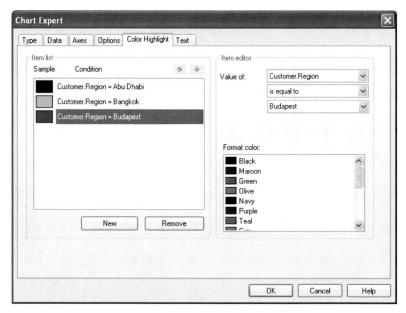

**Figure 12-10. Customizing chart colors with the Color Highlight tab.**

The Color Highlight tab works the same as the Highlighting Expert discussed in Chapter 5. You create rules based upon the values in the chart and apply a certain color for each rule. For example, in Figure 12-10, there are three rules for assigning chart colors. Each value for the Customer.Region field is assigned a different color.

Creating rules is quite simple. First click on the New button to create a default rule. On the right side are three drop down boxes. The first lets you choose the data point used to determine the color. This can be a data point along the X-axis or the Y-axis. The drop down box only lists data points used in the chart.

After selecting the data point, set the comparison field and the value to compare it to. Pick the color to apply from the list at the bottom. Any data point that matches these criteria is set to the chosen color.

Click the New button for each rule that needs to be applied and follow the same steps. When you are finished, preview the report and check that the colors follow the formatting you expected.

## Customizing the Chart Axes

In most cases, the default formatting of the X-axis and Y-axis will be fine. But there are times when you will want to customize the axes to fit your reporting requirements. You can do things like turn the gridlines on or off, set the minimum and maximum value ranges, and set the formatting of the data values. The Axes tab on the Chart Expert, shown in Figure 12-11, gives you many options for making these changes.

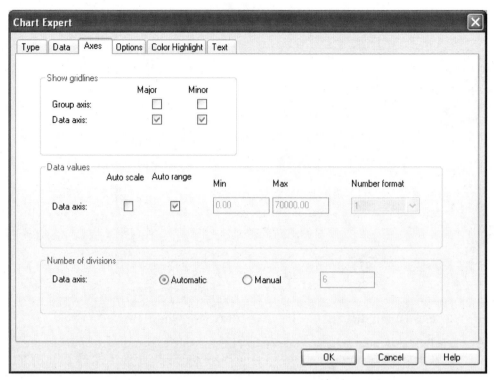

**Figure 12-11. Customizing a chart's axes.**

The Axes tab is broken into three sections. Each section controls a different part of the chart. The Show Gridlines section determines which axis the gridlines are shown at. They can be displayed along the major or minor axes. The type of chart you are displaying determines which gridlines are available.

The Data Values section sets the labels along the axis. The Auto Scale option is used when there are so many labels to display that they become hard to read. Turning this option on decreases the number of labels and this makes them easier to read. The Auto Range option sets a default range by evaluating all the possible values being charted. You can set the range by un-checking the Auto Range option and setting the minimum and maximum values manually. The Number Format drop down box lets you specify the number of decimals and whether the value should appear as a number, currency or percentage.

The Number of Divisions section sets the number of divisions along the data axis. You can set the Manual option to increase or decrease what Crystal Reports calculates to be the optimal number.

## Miscellaneous Formatting Options

The Chart Expert is the primary place where you create the type of chart to display and set the way it looks. However, Crystal Reports gives you additional ways to format charts at a more granular level. After inserting a chart onto a report, you can right-click it to see the options on the pop-up menu. The two menu options we are concerned with are Format Background and Chart Options.

The Format Background option opens the Format Background dialog box. This dialog box, shown in Figure 12-12, gives you a multitude of ways to change a chart's background. This ranges from changing the color, setting a pattern, or even using a picture in the background.

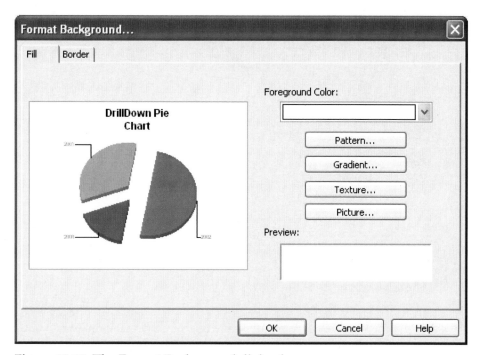

**Figure 12-12. The Format Background dialog box.**

The Format Background dialog box has two tabs. The first tab, Fill, sets how the background is filled. This can be solid color, a colored pattern or even a picture. By clicking on each of the options to the right of the dialog box, you are given a wide selection of choices. When clicking on the Foreground Color drop down box, a palette of colors appears and you pick the color you want. When clicking on the pattern button, it shows you a variety of patterns (e.g. cross-hatch, angles, bricks, etc.) to choose from. Again, pick the one you want to use on the chart. As you make your selections, the chart is updated to show a preview of the effects. Do this with the other options until the report has the look you want to stick with.

The second tab, Border, is more simplistic. It lets you set whether a border is shown around the chart's edges. If so, you can set the color, thickness and style.

Another dialog box is available for changing the details of how a chart is displayed. Right click on an existing chart and choose the Chart Options dialog box (shown in Figure 12-13).

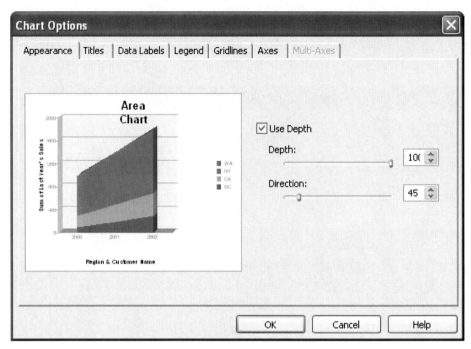

**Figure 12-13. The Chart Options dialog box.**

The Chart Options dialog box uses tabs running along the top to categorize the types of options to change. These tabs change based upon the type of chart being modified. Not only do the available tabs change, but the selections within each tab also change based on the chart type. For example, the Appearance tab for a pie chart has options to change the display angle, the gap between areas, and how far apart each area is from the center. But the Appearance tab for a bubble chart only sets the size of the bubbles and their shape.

Due to the wide number of tabs that can be displayed and the number of variations within each tab, I leave it up to you to fully explore each tab for the chart you are working with. After creating a chart, just open the Chart Options dialog box and click on each tab to see what is available. As you make changes, the preview reflects the new changes. If you just want to play around with the different choices, then remember to click the Cancel button when you are finished so that the changes don't get saved.

# Formatting Individual Chart Objects

The Chart Options dialog box you saw in the previous section applied to the chart as a whole. There are more Chart Options dialog boxes available for individual objects within the chart. For example, you can set the formatting for a certain group in a bar chart, change the fonts for individual axes, etc. This gives you another level of customization that goes even deeper than the previous Chart Options dialog box.

The way to access the Chart Options dialog box for individual report objects is to click on the chart object twice to give it the focus. The first time you click it, the outside edges of the chart are highlighted to show that you selected the chart. Now that the chart has focus, you have to click on the individual chart object to give it the focus. You can only select individual chart objects after selecting the chart object on the first click. It's almost like you are "drilling-down" into the chart to get to the individual objects. After one of the objects is selected, you can right-click on it to get the pop-up menu and select the Chart Options menu option.

Having so many ways to format a chart can be a blessing and a curse. Obviously, you want to have many options so that you can a lot of ways to customize a chart. Hence, this is a good thing. But the problem with having so many options is that it is tough to figure out everything you can do. There are too many places to look, and if you do find the property you want to change, you might not remember how you got there in the first place. For example, assume you have a chart where the values on the Y-Axis have a large span. You want to change the Y-Axis to a logarithmic scale so that the small values are easier to plot. If you open the Chart Expert dialog box and look at the Axes tab, you'll see options for changing the Min and Max properties and how many divisions there are, but nothing about using a logarithmic scale. You then go to the Chart Options dialog box and see that you can change the data type of the scale as well as setting dual axes. There are still no options for a logarithmic scale. At this point, you are getting frustrated and you search the help file. Unfortunately, the help file is no help because it doesn't mention logarithmic scales at all. You might come to the conclusion that although logarithmic scales are a popular charting option, it isn't possible with Crystal Reports. This would be a wrong conclusion because if you right-click on the y-axis chart object and select the menu option Data (Y) Axis Option, on the dialog box that opens there is a Scales tab that lets you display a logarithmic scale. Whew! It wasn't easy to find, but sure enough it is there.

All in all, you can do powerful customization of charts in your report, but finding where to do it can be the biggest challenge. If you are going to be doing a lot of advanced chart formatting, you would be better off by clicking on every individual chart object and becoming familiar with all the minute changes you can make to it. Crystal Reports gives you a powerful array of chart formatting options but you have to be familiar with them to take advantage of them.

# 13

## Creating Cross-Tab Reports

Cross-tabs are a powerful tool for creating summaries of data in a spreadsheet style format. They generate summary data in a grid where the rows and columns represent groups of data. This provides the user with a report format that is easy to read and uses a small footprint on the page.

Cross-tab reports are not for the faint of heart. Although they are easy to use once you get the hang of them, the act of taking data and reformatting it in a grid format can be a little intimidating at first. But after this chapter, you should have a good understanding of how to use cross-tab reports and you'll also get some practice with creating them.

## Understanding Cross-Tab Reports

Cross-tab reports format groups of data into an easy to read grid format. This grid format is very similar to the way a spreadsheet represents data. It lets the user visually analyze the data in a way that makes it easy to compare values in one group against the values in another group. Before we see what a cross-tab report looks like, let's look at a typical report that summarizes data within groups. After looking at Figure 13-1, we'll see it reformatted as a cross-tab report.

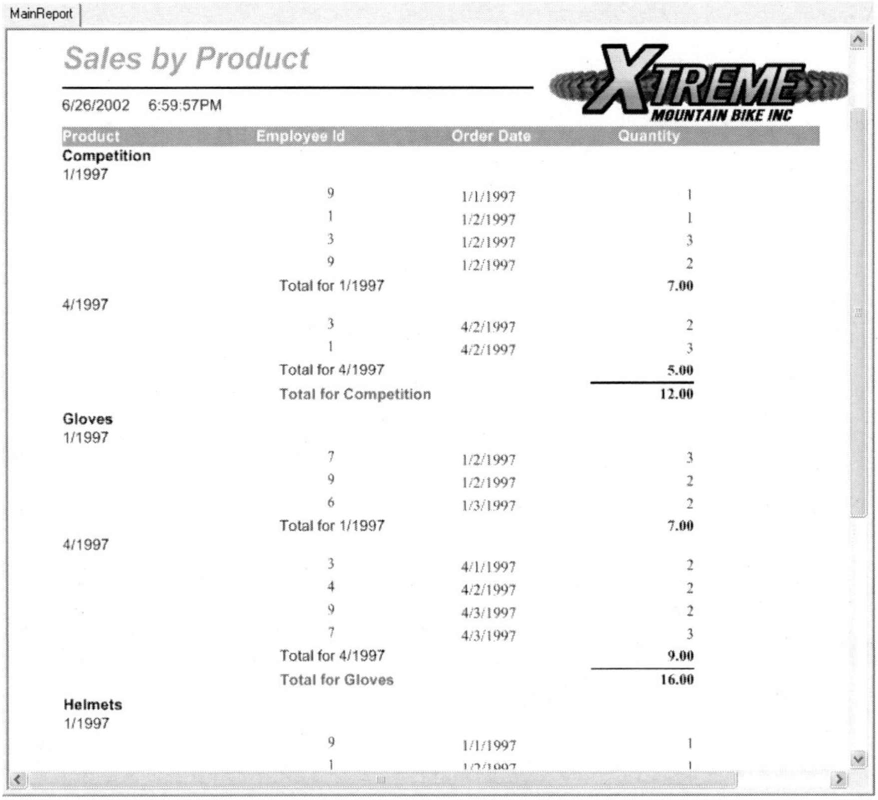
MainReport

Sales by Product

XTREME MOUNTAIN BIKE INC

6/26/2002 6:59:57PM

| Product | Employee Id | Order Date | Quantity |
|---|---|---|---|
| **Competition** | | | |
| 1/1997 | | | |
| | 9 | 1/1/1997 | 1 |
| | 1 | 1/2/1997 | 1 |
| | 3 | 1/2/1997 | 3 |
| | 9 | 1/2/1997 | 2 |
| | Total for 1/1997 | | **7.00** |
| 4/1997 | | | |
| | 3 | 4/2/1997 | 2 |
| | 1 | 4/2/1997 | 3 |
| | Total for 4/1997 | | **5.00** |
| | Total for Competition | | **12.00** |
| **Gloves** | | | |
| 1/1997 | | | |
| | 7 | 1/2/1997 | 3 |
| | 9 | 1/2/1997 | 2 |
| | 6 | 1/3/1997 | 2 |
| | Total for 1/1997 | | **7.00** |
| 4/1997 | | | |
| | 3 | 4/1/1997 | 2 |
| | 4 | 4/2/1997 | 2 |
| | 9 | 4/3/1997 | 2 |
| | 7 | 4/3/1997 | 3 |
| | Total for 4/1997 | | **9.00** |
| | Total for Gloves | | **16.00** |
| **Helmets** | | | |
| 1/1997 | | | |
| | 9 | 1/1/1997 | 1 |
| | 1 | 1/2/1997 | 1 |

**Figure 13-1. Grouping by Product and Quarter.**

This report has two grouping fields. The outermost group is by Product Type and the innermost group is the Order Date grouped quarterly. The group header for the Order Date is the first date in the period. The detail records show you the Employee ID, Order Date, and Quantity. There are two sub-totals of the quantity. The first occurs on the change of quarter and the next is on the change of product type.

This is a pretty standard grouping report and it shares a common problem with other grouping reports: the sub-total amounts are spread out across multiple pages. This makes it hard to compare numbers because they aren't consolidated into a single page. A user reading this report will find that they are continuously flipping pages to see how the sales of one product compare to the sales of another product.

Re-writing this report as a cross-tab report eliminates this problem. This cross-tab report takes two grouping fields and makes them the X-axis and Y-axis of the grid. Figure 13-2 shows the same report in cross-tab format.

*Quarterly Sales by Product*

6/26/2002   7:24:09PM

| | 1/1997 | 4/1997 | Total |
|---|---|---|---|
| Competition | 7.00 | 5.00 | 12.00 |
| Gloves | 7.00 | 9.00 | 16.00 |
| Helmets | 2.00 | 3.00 | 5.00 |
| Locks | 11.00 | 0.00 | 11.00 |
| Mountain | 5.00 | 2.00 | 7.00 |
| Saddles | 3.00 | 3.00 | 6.00 |
| Total | 35.00 | 22.00 | 57.00 |

**Figure 13-2. Cross-tab report by Product and Quarter.**

The cross-tab is much easier on the eyes. The outermost grouping field on the original report, Product Type, is represented on each row of the grid. The two columns represent the innermost group field, Order Date grouped by quarter. These columns span horizontally along the page. Notice that the cross-tab doesn't have any of the detail records listed. Detail records are used to calculate the summary data, but they are never shown. Only the summaries are listed.

The data inside the grid corresponds to the subtotals on the grouping report. The first row is for the Competition product type. It shows values of 7, 5 and a total of 12. When you look at the grouping report in Figure 13-1 you see that these match the subtotals for the Competition product type. Each row in the cross-tab report shows the same subtotals that are displayed in the grouping report for the product type groups. Thus, the cross-tab report took the sub-totals of a grouping report and formatted them as a grid. All the data is summarized into a very compact space and it doesn't span many pages like the grouping report would.

| Tip |
|---|

It helps to think of a cross-tab report as taking a multi-group report and just copying the group subtotals into a grid.

As powerful as the cross-tab report is for summarizing data, it has many limitations. These limitations are discussed throughout this chapter, but let's look at two obvious ones first.

The first limitation is that the original grouping report has a lot of data on it that isn't shown on the cross-tab. For example, the cross-tab report doesn't show the fields for Employee ID or the Shipping Date. In fact, it doesn't have any detail records shown. This is because cross-tabs can only show summary calculations.

The second limitation is that you can only print numbers in the summary fields. No text values are allowed. This is because each cell must calculate a summary function and summary functions can only return numbers. If you attempt to put a text field in the cell, the report defaults to printing a count of the text fields.

Given the benefits and drawbacks of cross-tab reports, you have to consider your alternatives before using the cross-tab report. The standard grouping report is easy to create and it is great for showing as much information as necessary. You also have complete control over the formatting. But the data could span many pages and this makes it harder to do analysis. The cross-tab report gives you the ability to quickly analyze summary data, but you have to give up looking at the detail records that make up the data.

### Tip

If you have a report that needs both detail records and summary data, a solution is to combine the two reports. First, create a grouping report that prints all the necessary detail information. Then add a cross-tab object to the report header. The first page shows the user a summary of the critical information and the remaining pages let them dive into the details.

## Planning the Rows and Columns of a Cross-Tab Object

Creating a cross-tab object can be a little intimidating the first time you create one. It can be confusing trying to figure out what to put in the rows and columns. A little planning prior to creating the cross-tab object can really help ease the process. When creating a cross-tab object, it helps to consider these tips.

The rows of a cross-tab object generally list the detail data. For example, it could show customers, employee names, or products. Since this data spans down the length of the page and continues onto the next page, you don't have to worry about how many rows are displayed.

The columns of a cross-tab object are usually used to collect the data into groups. For example, the columns frequently display data grouped by date (month, quarter, and year). Other common groups are department or region.

Later in this chapter, we'll see that after creating a cross-tab object, Crystal Reports has a property that lets you easily switch the data in the rows and columns back and forth. Since it is so easy to change their orientation, you might think that it is a trivial choice. From a purely technical standpoint, this is true. But from a practical standpoint, there are other factors to consider.

The primary goal of a cross-tab object is to summarize a large amount of data and present it to the user in an easy to use format. The best location for the fields is dependent upon the type of data you are summarizing and your user's preferences. For example, many cross-tab objects summarize dates by year and list them across the top of the page (in the column section). But, if your user prefers seeing the dates listed down the length of the page, then in this circumstance that is obviously the best way to do it because it meets the user's needs.

When I create cross-tab objects, the biggest factor for me is the inherent page size limitation. Not only can cross-tab objects span down the length of multiple pages, but they can also span horizontally across the page and overlap onto multiple pages. When possible, I try to avoid having the cross-tab span across multiple pages because most users are not comfortable with having to lay pages side-by-side to view the full cross-tab object. And, if a cross-tab object is part of a standard columnar report, then the formatting can get even more confusing.

When I see that the cross-tab columns span horizontally across multiple pages, the first thing I do is switch the paper orientation from Portrait to Landscape. This allows more data to appear in the columns and, in many cases, everything fits on a single page.

Before creating a cross-tab object, I determine the amount of data required for each field. If one of the fields has significantly less data to show, I use that as the column field. For example, consider an annual sales report that lists the customer name and summarizes by the year. Many companies have a lot of customers so I choose this as the row field and use the year as the column field. Thus, the customer names will span multiple pages and the cross-tab object can be displayed along the length of the report in landscape mode. But, consider a company that only wants to show the top five customers and break down sales by quarter. Using the date as the column would cause the cross-tab to stretch across multiple pages and be more difficult to read. In this case, I would choose the customer name as the column and the sales quarter as the row. That way, there are only a few customers listed along the top of the page and the dates can span down multiple pages and still be easy to read.

# Creating a Cross-Tab Object

The name "Cross-Tab Report" is a little misleading. It makes it sound like the whole report only shows the cross-tab grid and that no other data is printed. This isn't true. A cross-tab report refers to a report that has a cross-tab object in one of its sections. The rest of the report is just a typical report. This object is similar to the other report objects on a report. It has properties that let you modify its fields and how it's formatted.

There are two ways to add a cross-tab object to a report. On an existing report, right-click on the report and select Insert > Cross-Tab. This changes the mouse to the shape of a rectangle. Drag and drop the rectangle onto the report where you want the cross-tab object to be shown. An empty cross-tab object, shown in Figure 13-3, is displayed as a placeholder.

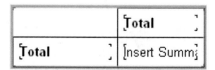

**Figure 13-3. The Cross-Tab placeholder.**

The second way to create a crosstab object is to choose the Cross-Tab Report Wizard from the Start Page. After selecting the data source and tables to pull data from, you are presented with the Cross-Tab Expert where you select the fields that are shown in the rows, columns, and summary fields. The Cross-Tab Expert is discussed next.

# Modifying the Cross-Tab Properties

After getting the empty cross-tab object on the report, you need to modify its properties so that it knows what data to display and how to display it. Right-click on the cross-tab object and select Cross-Tab Expert. This opens the Cross-Tab Expert shown in Figure 13-4.

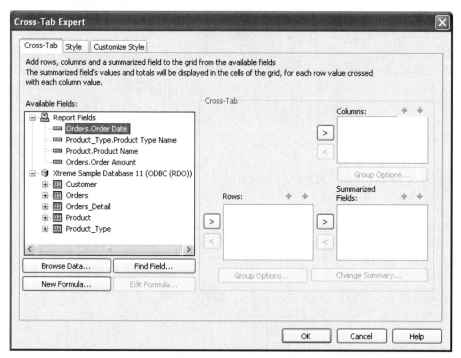

**Figure 13-4. The Cross-Tab Expert dialog box.**

| Caution |
| --- |

The Cross-Tab Expert shown in Figure 13-4 is what you'll see when you right-click on an existing cross-tab object and select Cross-Tab Expert. It is very similar, but not exact, to the Cross-Tab Expert dialog box you see when creating a new report using the Cross-Tab Report Wizard. The new report wizard dialog box is missing a few key buttons. The New Formula and Edit Formula buttons are not available. Secondly, the Group Options and Change Summary buttons are missing. The Change Summary button lets you show a percentage of the overall total in the summary field. The dialog box presented by the new report wizard box only lets you choose from the basic summary functions. The Group Options button lets you customize the sorting order of the groups. Thus, if you want to create new formulas, have advanced summaries, or customize the groups, you have to wait till the wizard is finished and go back and edit the cross-tab. I've found that when I need this type of functionality in the cross-tab object, it is easier to just create a new blank report and add the cross-tab object afterwards. By adding the cross-tab object later, I can first create whatever formulas I need as well as know that the Cross-Tab Expert will have its full functionality available.

The dialog box in Figure 13-4 has three tabs: Cross-Tab, Style, and Customize Style. The Cross-Tab tab, discussed next, sets the fields shown on the cross-tab object. The Style tab lets you apply a predefined style to the cross-tab. The last tab, Customize Style, lets you specify (in great detail) the formatting of each of the cross-tab elements.

The first tab, Cross-Tab, has an Available Fields area and three primary input areas: Rows, Columns, and Summarized Fields. The Available Fields area shows you all the fields that can be used within the cross-tab object. Add fields from this list into the appropriate sections to the right. Do this either by dragging and dropping the fields, or by selecting a field and clicking one of the arrow buttons. As we saw in other dialog boxes, you can preview the data in a field by selecting that field and clicking the Browse Data button.

All three input areas require you to add a minimum of one field before the cross-tab is functional. For example, you can't specify fields for the Rows and Summary Fields windows and not put a field in the Columns window. You can also add multiple fields to each window to make the sub-groups.

When you add a field to the Summarized Fields window, by default, it assigns one of two different summary functions to the field. If the field is numeric, then the Sum() function is used. If the field is text, then the Count() function is used. You can change the default summary function by clicking on the Change Summary button.

When changing the summary function for a numeric field, you can choose from all the summary functions in Crystal Reports. Summarizing on a text field is more restrictive because text fields aren't allowed to be printed in a cross-tab cell. Instead, you have to choose from a list of text compatible summary functions. Not every function works with a text field. For example, it isn't possible to calculate the average value of a text field.

However, you can determine the $5^{th}$ largest item of all available items and print that. The text compatible functions that you can choose from are in Table 13-1.

**Table 13-1. Summary functions available for text fields.**

| Function Name |
| --- |
| Count() |
| DistinctCount() |
| Nth Largest() |
| Nth Smallest() |
| Nth Most Frequent() |
| Minimum() |
| Maximum() |
| Mode() |

Summary functions are typically based on fields from a data source. But, there are times when you need to summarize a custom formula field. You can select a formula that already exists or you can create a new formula from the Cross-tab Expert dialog box. When you click the New Formula button, it brings up the Formula Editor dialog box. After you save and close this dialog box, the formula is added to the list of available fields at the bottom of the dialog box. You can then drag and drop the formula field into the Summary Fields window. Although this formula was created via the Cross-Tab Expert, it is added to the report just like any other formula and it can be placed anywhere on your report.

Once you are finished adding the fields, click the OK button. The cross-tab object is added to your report and you are put back at the report designer.

# Placing the Cross-Tab Object

If you look back at the cross-tab report example in Figure 13-2, you might notice that the cross-tab object as it appears in the report designer doesn't look like the cross-tab grid as it appears when printed on the report. This is because the report designer shows the cross-tab object as being a template for showing you what fields are used and how the cross-tab grid will be formatted. When the report is run, the cross-tab object expands vertically and horizontally so that it can print as many columns and rows as necessary to show each group. If you expect your report to have a lot of columns, it's best to place it close to the left side of the report to account for all the columns.

| Tip |
| --- |

Be careful when placing data fields (or any report object) after the cross-tab object. When a cross-tab object prints in a section, it grows as large as necessary to show all the data. If you place other report objects below the cross-tab component, in most cases the cross-tab will expand to overwrite those objects. To fix this, create a second section in that same area and place the data that comes after the cross-tab in the new section. Sections never overlap each other and this ensures that the data in the new section always prints after the cross-tab.

The cross-tab object can only be placed in certain sections: the Report Header/Footer and the Group Header/Footer. It can't be placed in the detail section because it can't print detail records. It also can't be placed in the Page Header because it would be duplicated on each page without any of its data changing. This would create redundant information that wastes space.

Be careful about where you put the cross-tab object. It prints out whatever information is available to it. Placing the cross-tab in the Report Header/Footer produces different results than putting it in the Group Header/Footer. When placed in the Report Header, it has access to every record in your report. It summarizes all the data in the report and could be quite large. When placed in the Group Header, it only has access to the data for that group. The cross-tab will be much smaller because it only prints a subset of all the report data.

## Tutorial 13-1. Creating a Cross-Tab Report

Let's create a simple cross-tab report to see the basic steps. We'll create an annual sales report for customers.

1.  The first task is to plan the cross-tab object by determining which fields belong in the rows and columns. The report summarizes data by customer and sales year. Since there are a lot of products and fewer years, we'll select the customer name as the row and the sales year as the column. Now let's build the report.
2.  Create a new report using the Cross-Tab Report Wizard.
3.  For the data source, choose the Xtreme.mdb database and select the tables Customer and Orders. Click the Next button.
4.  Check that two tables are linked by the Customer ID field. Click the Next button to confirm the table links.
5.  Find the field Customer.Customer Name in the Available Fields list and select it. Then drag it to the Rows list.

6. Find the field Orders.Order Date in the Available Fields list and select it. Then drag it to the Columns list.

We don't want the cross-tab to display the individual date for each order. That would be too much information and wouldn't give us the benefit of being able to summarize the sales data. So let's change the grouping function to group by year.

7. Click on the Orders.Order Date field in the Columns list and click the drop-down box to view the available summary functions. Select the function For Each Year to summarize annually.

8. For the summary field, click on the Orders.Order Amount field in the Available Fields list and drag it to the Summary Fields list. You can see that the default summary function is Sum, so we'll leave it like that.

9. Click the Finish button to save your changes.

10. Save the report as **Customer Annual Sales.rpt**.

11. Preview the report and it should look similar to the following figure.

|  | Total | 2003 | 2004 | 2005 |
|---|---|---|---|---|
| Total | $4,077,785.64 | $259,390.64 | $2,861,205.48 | $957,189.52 |
| 7 Bikes For 7 B | $53.90 | $0.00 | $53.90 | $0.00 |
| Against The Wi | $479.85 | $0.00 | $479.85 | $0.00 |
| AIC Childrens | $101.70 | $0.00 | $101.70 | $0.00 |
| Alley Cat Cycle: | $54,565.39 | $3,479.70 | $25,781.75 | $25,303.94 |
| Ankara Bicycle | $959.70 | $0.00 | $959.70 | $0.00 |
| Arsenault et Ma | $1,739.85 | $0.00 | $1,739.85 | $0.00 |
| Aruba Sport | $5,879.70 | $0.00 | $5,879.70 | $0.00 |
| Athens Bicycle | $8,819.55 | $0.00 | $8,819.55 | $0.00 |
| Auvergne Bicro | $41.90 | $0.00 | $41.90 | $0.00 |

# Grouping Data within a Cross-Tab

Just as reports can create groups and sub-groups on a report page, cross-tab objects can do the same. Cross-tab objects allow you to specify multiple data fields for the rows and columns. When you use multiple data fields, the cross-tab object shows multiple sets of data along a single row and/or column. This gives you the ability to group data in the cross-tab and create sub-totals for each group.

Crystal Reports organizes multiple fields on a top-down basis. This is based upon their order as listed on the Cross-Tab Expert dialog box. The top field is the outermost group. The second field is the next sub-group, and so on. For example, assume that the first field is Country and the second field is Customer Name. In this case, the outer most group is

Country and all the customers located within that country are shown. You also have the option of showing sub-totals for each Country value.

Placing more than one field in the Summary Fields section lets you show multiple values within each cross-tab cell. You also have the option of placing them side-by-side or stacking one on top of the other. Unlike placing multiple fields in the rows or columns, summary fields have no grouping relationship and one value doesn't affect the other. It simply lets you show more than one summary in each cell.

Let's walk through a tutorial to see how it works.

## Tutorial 13-2 Adding Groups to a Cross-Tab

In this tutorial, we are going to explore how groups work by modifying the report from the previous tutorial. We are going to add grouping to both the rows and columns. The customers are going to be grouped by country. The column is going to be modified so that the year is the outer-most group and the quarter is the inner-most group. A new summary function will be added so that the average sales amount is shown below the total sales amount.

1.  Open the "Customer Annual Sales.rpt" report that was created in Tutorial 13-1.
2.  Right-click on the top-left corner of the cross-tab object and select Cross-Tab Expert.
3.  The first modification we want to make is to group the customers by their country. Drag the Customer.Country field into the Rows list. This puts the field at the bottom of the list.
4.  We want the country to be the outermost group, but it was placed at the bottom of the list since we just added it. Click on the Country field and click the up arrow to move it to the top of the list.
5.  For the column, we want to add the Order Date field and group it by sales quarter. Drag the Order.Order Date field into the Columns list.
6.  Click on the new Order Date field and click the Group Options button. This opens the Cross-Tab Group Options dialog box.
7.  On the third drop-down box, select "For Each Quarter" as the way to print the column.
8.  Click the OK button to close the group options dialog box.
9.  For the summary section, we want to show the average of the order amounts. Drag the field Orders.Order Amount to the Summarized Fields list.
10. Click the Change Summary button to open the Edit Summary dialog box.
11. Change the summary function to Average. Click the OK button to close the summary dialog box.

    The Cross-Tab Expert dialog box should look like the following figure:

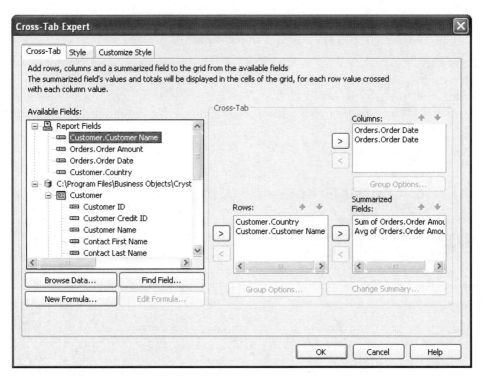

12. We are finished adding fields to the cross-tab object, so click the OK button to save your changes.

13. Save the report as **Customer Annual Sales Grouped.rpt**.

14. Preview the report and it should look similar to the following figure.

| | | | Total | 2003 | |
|---|---|---|---|---|---|
| | | | | Total | 1/2003 |
| Total | | Order Amount<br>Order Amount | $4,077,785.64<br>$1,861.15 | $259,390.64<br>$1,433.10 | $92,130.36<br>$1,880.21 |
| Argentina | Total | Order Amount<br>Order Amount | $1,664.70<br>$1,664.70 | $0.00<br>$0.00 | $0.00<br>$0.00 |
| | Bicicletas<br>Buenos Aires | Order Amount<br>Order Amount | $1,664.70<br>$1,664.70 | $0.00<br>$0.00 | $0.00<br>$0.00 |
| Aruba | Total | Order Amount<br>Order Amount | $5,879.70<br>$5,879.70 | $0.00<br>$0.00 | $0.00<br>$0.00 |
| | Aruba Sport | Order Amount<br>Order Amount | $5,879.70<br>$5,879.70 | $0.00<br>$0.00 | $0.00<br>$0.00 |
| Australia | Total | Order Amount<br>Order Amount | $9,899.99<br>$1,414.28 | $0.00<br>$0.00 | $0.00<br>$0.00 |
| | Bruce's Bikes | Order Amount<br>Order Amount | $17.50<br>$17.50 | $0.00<br>$0.00 | $0.00<br>$0.00 |
| | Canberra Bikes | Order Amount<br>Order Amount | $479.85<br>$479.85 | $0.00<br>$0.00 | $0.00<br>$0.00 |
| | Down Under<br>Bikes | Order Amount<br>Order Amount | $45.00<br>$45.00 | $0.00<br>$0.00 | $0.00<br>$0.00 |

Notice how the cross-tab object formats the groups. The country is listed to the far left and the customers that are in each country are located to the right of it. Along the top of the report is the year and just below that are the sales quarters. In each cell is the total order amount and the average order amount. Unfortunately, on this page of the report each customer only has one sale. Thus, the order total is the same amount as the average. However, you can see in the top Total row that the average calculation is different because the top row calculates the average order for the entire report.

There are a few things I don't like about this report. The first is that in the third column the phrase, "Order Amount" is repeated on each row. You can change that by right-clicking on the text and selecting "Edit Text". I also prefer having the summary fields listed side-by-side. To change this, go into the Cross-Tab Expert and on the Customize Style tab choose the Horizontal option for the summary fields. After making these changes, my report is shown in Figure 13-5.

| | | Total | | 2003 | |
|---|---|---|---|---|---|
| | | | | Total | |
| | | Total Order | Average Order | Total Order | Average Order |
| Total | | $4,077,785.64 | $1,861.15 | $259,390.64 | $1,433.10 |
| Argentina | Total | $1,664.70 | $1,664.70 | $0.00 | $0.00 |
| | Bicicletas Buen | $1,664.70 | $1,664.70 | $0.00 | $0.00 |
| Aruba | Total | $5,879.70 | $5,879.70 | $0.00 | $0.00 |
| | Aruba Sport | $5,879.70 | $5,879.70 | $0.00 | $0.00 |
| Australia | Total | $9,899.99 | $1,414.28 | $0.00 | $0.00 |
| | Bruce's Bikes | $17.50 | $17.50 | $0.00 | $0.00 |
| | Canberra Bikes | $479.85 | $479.85 | $0.00 | $0.00 |
| | Down Under Bi | $45.00 | $45.00 | $0.00 | $0.00 |
| | Kangeroo Trike | $107.80 | $107.80 | $0.00 | $0.00 |
| | Koala Road Bik | $64.42 | $64.42 | $0.00 | $0.00 |
| | Peddles of Pert | $5,879.70 | $5,879.70 | $0.00 | $0.00 |
| | Tasmanian Dev | $3,305.72 | $3,305.72 | $0.00 | $0.00 |
| Austria | Total | $28,813.41 | $1,440.67 | $16,180.28 | $5,393.43 |
| | Piccolo | $28,813.41 | $1,440.67 | $16,180.28 | $5,393.43 |

**Figure 13-5. Modified grouping report.**

In the next section, we'll see the different cross-tab properties and options that let us customize the look of cross-tab objects.

# Formatting the Cross-Tab Grid

As with every report object in Crystal Reports, the cross-tab object has many formatting options to make it look just the way you want. These changes can be categorized according to whether they affect the grid layout or whether they affect the individual fields within the grid.

Since the number of rows and columns of the cross-tab is dynamic, you can't control its final size on the report. But, you can control the individual row and column widths. This has a direct effect on the total size of the cross-tab grid when it prints. When you select a field in the cross-tab object and resize it, the entire row and column changes to reflect this change. Changing the width changes the width of the entire column. Changing the height changes the height of the entire row. Thus, a change to one field affects all the fields that are in the same column and row.

Set the formatting properties by right-clicking on the cross-tab object and selecting Format. Be careful when doing this because if your cursor is positioned above one of the fields in the cross-tab, you will get the format dialog boxes for that field. To set the formatting for the cross-tab object, position your cursor in the top left-hand corner of the cross-tab. This is where there are no other fields that could be selected by mistake.

Both the grid and the fields within the grid can be formatted using the standard formatting properties. Some examples of these properties are suppressing the object, setting the font properties, changing the border, etc. Most of these properties have a formula button so that their value can be the result of a formula that you program.

# Formatting the Style Properties

The grid has some unique formatting properties that don't appear with other objects. These are called the Style properties. Right-click on the cross-tab object and select Cross-Tab Expert.

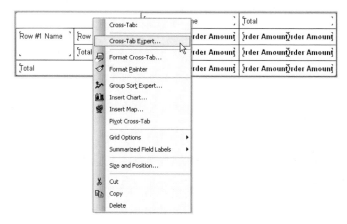

**Figure 13-6. Selecting the Cross-Tab Expert menu item.**

Click on the Style tab of the Cross-Tab Expert (the second tab) to choose from a list of more than a dozen predefined styles. As you click on each style, the right window shows a template of how your cross-tab object will be formatted. The Style tab makes formatting the cross-tab object easy.

Click on the Customize Style tab to make granular changes to the cross-tab's style. If you made any custom formatting changes previously, you are prompted about whether you want to save that style. If you choose Yes, the new style will be reflected on the Customize Style tab. If you choose No, the Customize Style tab will reflect the formatting of the cross-tab object before you opened the Cross-Tab Expert.

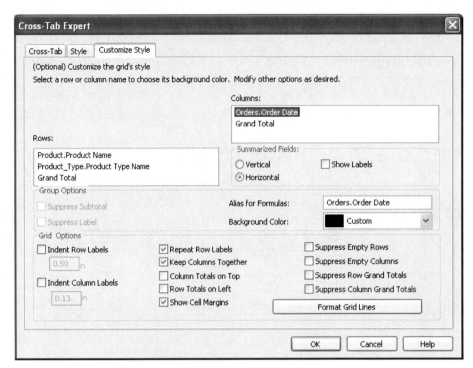

**Figure 13-7. The CustomizeStyle tab of the Format Cross-Tab expert.**

The Customize Style tab has numerous properties that you can use to format the cross-tab grid to look exactly like you want. There is a Rows window and a Columns window and within each window are the names of the grouping fields. Click on the field you want to format. The properties and their descriptions are listed in the Group Options frame directly below those windows. Each of these properties only affects the group field that is currently selected. These style properties are listed in Table 13-2.

**Table 13-2. Style formatting properties for cross-tab group options.**

| Style Property | Description |
| --- | --- |
| Suppress Subtotal | When you have multiple groups for a row or column, the cross-tab grid shows a subtotal for the top-most groups. This suppresses that subtotal from printing. |
| Suppress Label | Suppresses the label for a suppressed subtotal field. |
| Alias for Formulas | Changes the name that you use to reference the group in the conditional formatting formulas. |
| Background Color | Sets the background color for the cell. |

At the bottom of the dialog box is a frame titled Grid Options. The properties listed in this frame apply to the entire cross-tab. These grid options are listed in Table 13-3.

**Table 13-3. Grid options for the cross-tab object.**

| Grid Option | Description |
|---|---|
| Show Cell Margins | By default, each group field has a margin surrounding it. Turning this off makes the edge of the group field flush with the grid lines. |
| Indent Row Labels | The row labels can be indented so that they are offset from the Total row. This makes it easier to notice the Total row and it makes your report appear more professional. When this is checked, you can specify the indentation in inches. |
| Repeat Row Labels | When there are too many columns to fit on a single page, they will span across to the next page. Turning this option on causes the row labels to be printed on the additional pages. |
| Keep Columns Together | Select this option (it is selected by default) to force columns that span multiple pages to stay intact. Unselecting this option could cause a column to be split in half. |
| Row/Column Totals on Top | Forces row totals to be at the top-most row and column totals will be left-most column. Otherwise they appear at the bottom and to the right. |
| Suppress Empty Rows/Columns | Don't print rows/columns with no data. |
| Suppress Row/Column Grand Totals | Don't print the grand-totals for rows and/or columns. |

The Format Grid Lines button is used to set the line styles for the grid. Clicking on this button brings up the Format Grid Lines dialog box shown in Figure 13-8. For each grid line in the cross-tab object, you can set the color, style, and width properties. You can also suppress a line by un-checking both Draw options. If you don't want any grid lines to be shown then uncheck the Show Grid Lines option.

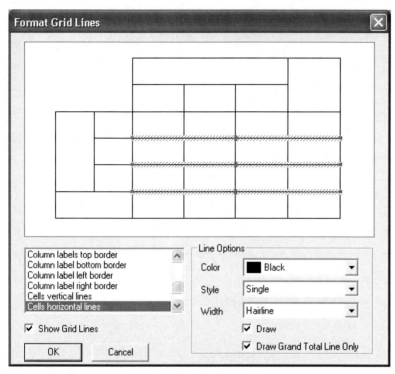

**Figure 13-8. The Format Grid Lines dialog box.**

One important point to be aware of when highlighting individual summary fields is that you can't modify them using the Cross-Tab Expert dialog box. This dialog box applies changes to the cross-tab report as a whole. It doesn't affect the data within the report. To do this, you have to move your cursor on top of the summary field and right-click. This opens the pop-up menu where you can select Format Field. See Figure 13-9 for an example.

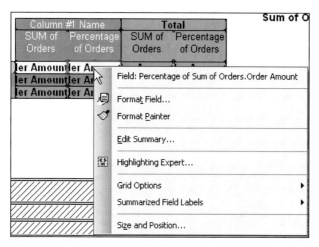

**Figure 13-9. Summary field pop-up menu.**

# Managing the Columns

One of the most interesting features of the cross-tab object is that it is dynamic. The number of columns changes according to the data being displayed. As an example, assume that you have a cross-tab report where the columns represent the historical sales figures per year. If a company has been in existence for five years, there will be five columns printed. Once a new year starts, a new column is automatically added to the cross-tab. Columns are created on an as needed basis without requiring any additional work on your part.

Dynamic columns are a blessing and a curse. The fact that you can even have dynamic columns is great. Being able to have the number of columns grow and shrink according to the data in a table is very powerful. You can't do this with standard reports objects. The drawback to this feature is that you can't control how many columns are created and you can't insert additional columns. You are at the mercy of the data.

Having columns dynamically added to your report is a problem when you get more columns than you expected. For example, assume that your company has twenty divisions world-wide and you formatted the cell's width so that there is just enough room on the page to represent each division. The report runs fine until six months later when your company acquires three new divisions. Now, your columns run off the edge and onto a new page. The number of pages printed has just increased and everyone is complaining to you about it. You have to watch out for this behavior and correct it, if necessary.

When a cross-tab object spans multiple pages, the only data printed on the "virtual" pages is what is generated by the cross-tab report. The other report objects on the report do not get printed. There is a setting on the Format Editor which lets you tell the report object to be printed on any additional pages generated by the cross-tab. Right-click on the object and select the Format Text (or Field, Graphic, etc.) to open the Format Editor. Click on the Common tab and check the setting Repeat on Horizontal Pages. You will have to do this individually for every report object that should appear on the additional cross-tab pages.

This setting doesn't work for the Page Number special field. Well, let me rephrase that. It will repeat the page number on each additional page, but it doesn't increment the counter. Thus, every page will have the same page number. To show a new page number on each page, replace the Page Number special field with the Horizontal Page Number special field instead. This special field automatically repeats on horizontal pages and increments the page number each time as well.

### Tip

For cross-tab objects that span across multiple pages, when they are used in subreports they present an interesting situation. You can limit a cross-tab object's size by placing it in a subreport. If you place a cross-tab object in a subreport, it will not print wider than the width of the subreport. By making the subreport object the width of a single page, the cross-tab object will only print on that page. This can be used to give the user a "preview" of the cross-tab report without spanning across multiple pages. If the user wants to see the entire cross-tab object, then they can double-click on it to open it in another tab.

On the other hand, there is a way to make a cross-tab object in the subreport span multiple pages in the main report. To do this, you have to add another cross-tab object to the main report and put it in the same section that holds the subreport. Make sure it spans the same number of pages as the cross-tab in the subreport. This makes the pages in the main report big enough to display the subreport cross-tab. Next, set the font color in the main report's cross-tab to be white or transparent. Lastly, hide the cross-tab gridlines. This makes the cross-tab object in the main report invisible, but still creates the pages necessary so that the subreport cross-tab object can be displayed.

Another problem with dynamic columns is that you can't insert empty columns in the grid. This is a common problem with reports that use the month of the year as the column. When the report is run at the end of the year, there are twelve columns and this is what you would expect. But when the report is run in February, only two columns are printed: January and February. Some people want their reports to show all twelve months even if they haven't occurred yet. Cross-tab reports won't do this. A similar problem is a report that uses the weeks of the year as the column heading. Assume a company is a production plant and they want to see the volume of units produced every week. Occasionally, the plant builds up too much inventory and is shut down for a week. The report should show a zero balance for the week that was shutdown. But since there wasn't any activity, no records exist for that week and a column won't be printed. The cross-tab report can't print a zero-filled column for that week because it doesn't have any data to even know that the week exists.

There really isn't an easy solution for this. The best advice is to create a second table with a record for each of the column headers in it and then write a SQL query that uses an Outer Join statement which will generate null data for the missing records. The way you handle each situation is unique and presents a new challenge.

# Advanced Tutorials

By now, you realize that cross-tab reports are a very powerful way of summarizing data and presenting it in an easy to read format. So far, we have been limited to basing cross-tabs on data fields, but there is so much more you can do with them. By using formulas and parameters as the summarized field, you can customize the formatting and data of the cross-tab. This increases the flexibility of cross-tab reports even more.

The next three tutorials demonstrate this by using the CrossTab.rpt sample report that is installed with Crystal Reports. Let's look at this report before continuing on with the tutorials.

| | 1/2003 | | 10/2003 | |
|---|---|---|---|---|
| | SUM of Orders | Percentage of Orders | SUM of Orders | Percentage of Orders |
| Descent | $23,612.06 | 21.30 % | $96,033.66 | 35.82 % |
| Endorphin | $3,651.08 | 3.29 % | $12,416.79 | 4.63 % |
| Mozzie | $28,861.68 | 26.03 % | $33,873.64 | 12.63 % |
| Competition | $56,124.82 | 50.63 % | 142,324.09 | 53.09 % |
| Active Outdoors Cr | $308.00 | 0.28 % | $9,762.67 | 3.64 % |
| Active Outdoors Ly | $1,266.15 | 1.14 % | $6,403.89 | 2.39 % |
| InFlux Crochet Glo | $0.00 | 0.00 % | $1,202.05 | 0.45 % |
| InFlux Lycra Glove | $8,531.10 | 7.70 % | $3,934.32 | 1.47 % |
| Gloves | $10,105.25 | 9.12 % | $21,302.93 | 7.95 % |
| Triumph Pro Helme | $5,557.82 | 5.01 % | $12,581.04 | 4.69 % |
| Triumph Vertigo He | $4,119.91 | 3.72 % | $5,686.48 | 2.12 % |
| Xtreme Adult Helme | $3,134.73 | 2.83 % | $11,722.02 | 4.37 % |
| Xtreme Youth Helm | $1,111.80 | 1.00 % | $564.92 | 0.21 % |
| Helmets | $13,924.26 | 12.56 % | $30,554.46 | 11.40 % |

**Figure 13-10. The CrossTab.rpt sample report.**

Figure 13-10 is a snapshot of the CrossTab.rpt sample report. The detail rows are Product Name and they are summarized by Product Type. Along the top of the report, the data is grouped by the quarters of the year and it shows the first month of the available data[57]. Within each quarter, the product sales are totaled and their percentage of the overall total is displayed.

## Tutorial 13-3. Customizing the Cross-Tab Layout.

The summary fields within most cross-tab reports show all the data as looking the same. This has the benefit of consistently producing a professional looking report each time. But in a large cross-tab report, it can sometimes be difficult to spot important information among the many pages of data. It helps to customize the look of the individual fields within the cross-tab. By associating a summary field with a formula, important cross-tab data is emphasized so it is easy to find.

In this tutorial, we will change the formatting of data that falls outside of a valid range. We will modify the total order amount for each product by highlighting products with less than $1,000 worth of sales. This alerts the manager that they need to either market the product better or discontinue it altogether.

1. Open the CrossTab.rpt sample report that was installed with Crystal Reports. Save it as CrossTab Highlight Sales.rpt.

2. Make sure you are on the Design tab and right-click on the Sum Of Orders.Order Amount field.

3. Select Format Field from the pop-up menu. This opens the Format Editor dialog box.

4. Click on the Font tab and you'll see that the Style property is set to Bold. We want to change this to Regular so that only the fields that are under $1,000 are emphasized. Click on the drop-down box and change Bold to Regular.

   Now we are going to create the formula which checks the summary field's value and if it is less than $1,000, we add highlighting to it.

5. For the Style property, click on the Formula Workshop button next to it to create a new formula. Enter the following formula:

```
If CurrentFieldValue < 1000 then
    crBold
Else
    DefaultAttribute
```

   This formula compares the current field's value to $1,000. If it is less, then the Style is set to Bold. If not, then the Style is left as its default attribute (regular).

6. Click the Save and Close button to close the Formula Workshop. Then click the OK button to close the Format Editor dialog box.

---

[57] Unfortunately, when grouping by fiscal quarters, there is no option to display the quarter as a number. You have to use a custom formula instead. We'll see how to do that in a later tutoriai.

The other summary field, Percentage of Others, has a default Style of Bold and we want to change it to Regular so that it matches the format of the order total summary field.

7. Right-click on the Percentage of Others summary field and select Format Field from the pop-up menu.
8. Click on the Font tab and change the Style property to Regular.
9. Click the OK button to save your change.
10. Preview the report to see what it looks like.

| | 1/2003 | | 10/2003 | |
|---|---|---|---|---|
| | SUM of Orders | Percentage of Orders | SUM of Orders | Percentage of Orders |
| Descent | $23,612.06 | 21.30 % | $96,033.66 | 35.82 % |
| Endorphin | $3,651.08 | 3.29 % | $12,416.79 | 4.63 % |
| Mozzie | $28,861.68 | 26.03 % | $33,873.64 | 12.63 % |
| Competition | $56,124.82 | 50.63 % | 142,324.09 | 53.09 % |
| Active Outdoors Cr | $308.00 | 0.28 % | $9,762.67 | 3.64 % |
| Active Outdoors Ly | $1,266.15 | 1.14 % | $6,403.89 | 2.39 % |
| InFlux Crochet Glo | $0.00 | 0.00 % | $1,202.05 | 0.45 % |
| InFlux Lycra Glove | $8,531.10 | 7.70 % | $3,934.32 | 1.47 % |
| Gloves | $10,105.25 | 9.12 % | $21,302.93 | 7.95 % |
| Triumph Pro Helme | $5,557.82 | 5.01 % | $12,581.04 | 4.69 % |
| Triumph Vertigo He | $4,119.91 | 3.72 % | $5,686.48 | 2.12 % |
| Xtreme Adult Helme | $3,134.73 | 2.83 % | $11,722.02 | 4.37 % |
| Xtreme Youth Helm | $1,111.80 | 1.00 % | $564.92 | 0.21 % |

The report shows three summary fields that are less than $1,000 and they are also bold. This lets the reader immediately notice which products should be reviewed for poor monthly sales.

## Tutorial 13-4. Customizing Data within the Cross-Tab

Formulas can also be used to customize the summary data that the cross-tab report is based on. For example, a formula can be used to dynamically change the value that gets summarized or it can change the text that is displayed within the cross-tab.

In this tutorial we are going to use formulas to change the data that the cross-tab is based on. If you look at the original report in Figure 13-10, you'll see that there are many similar products. For example, there are two Active Outdoors gloves, two Influx gloves, two Triumph helmets, etc. Let's assume that these products are similar enough to each other that we want the cross-tab report to merge each group into a single row. That way, we will only see a single row for Active gloves, a single row for Influx gloves, etc. To do this, we will base the row heading on a formula that uses the Product Name field.

1. Open the CrossTab.rpt sample report that was installed with Crystal Reports. Save it as **CrossTab Product Name Summarized.rpt**.

2. Make sure you are on the Design tab and right-click on the top left corner of the cross-tab object and select Cross-Tab Expert from the pop-up menu.

3. In the bottom left corner of the Cross-Tab Expert dialog box, click on the New Formula button.

4. Name the formula **Product Name Summary** and click the OK button. This opens the Formula Workshop dialog box. Enter the following formula:

```
if Left ({Product.Product Name}, 6) = "Active" then
    "Active Outdoors";
if Left ({Product.Product Name}, 6)= "InFlux" then
    "InFlux";
if Left ({Product.Product Name}, 7) = "Triumph" then
    "Triumph";
if Left ({Product.Product Name}, 6) = "Xtreme" then
    "Xtreme";
```

5. Click the Save and Close button to save your changes and check that there are no errors. If there are errors, make sure you entered the formula exactly as it is listed here. You also want to make sure that you have Crystal Syntax selected as the current programming language.

   After saving the formula, it will be listed in the Available Fields window. We want to put it into the Rows list and remove the Product Name field from that list. We are effectively swapping the Product Name field with the new Product Name Summary formula.

6. Click the Product Name Summary formula in the Available Fields window to select it. Click on the right arrow button for the Rows list. This inserts the summary formula at the bottom of the Rows list.

7. Click on the Product Name field in the Rows list and click the left arrow button to remove it from the Rows list.

   You have now swapped the data field for the summary formula. The Cross-Tab Expert should look like the following figure.

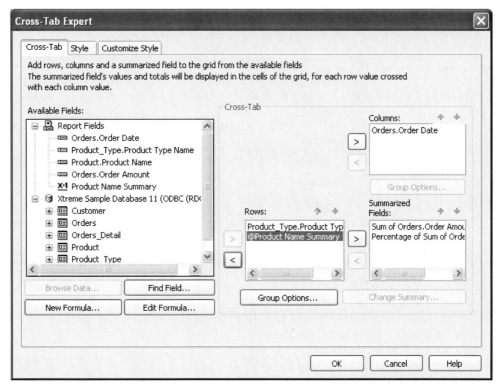

When the cross-tab report is run, it will use the summary formula to create the data rows. Since certain rows now have the same value for the Product Name, they will be merged into a single row.

8. Click on the Preview tab to see the report.

| | 1/2003 | | 10/2003 | |
|---|---|---|---|---|
| | SUM of Orders | Percentage of Orders | SUM of Orders | Percentage of Orders |
| **Descent** | $23,612.06 | 21.30 % | $96,033.66 | 35.82 % |
| **Endorphin** | $3,651.08 | 3.29 % | $12,416.79 | 4.63 % |
| **Mozzie** | $28,861.68 | 26.03 % | $33,873.64 | 12.63 % |
| Competition | $56,124.82 | 50.63 % | 142,324.09 | 53.09 % |
| **Active Outdoors** | $1,574.15 | 1.42 % | $16,166.56 | 6.03 % |
| **Influx** | $8,531.10 | 7.70 % | $5,136.37 | 1.92 % |
| Gloves | $10,105.25 | 9.12 % | $21,302.93 | 7.95 % |
| **Triumph** | $9,677.73 | 8.73 % | $18,267.52 | 6.81 % |
| **Xtreme** | $4,246.53 | 3.83 % | $12,286.94 | 4.58 % |
| Helmets | $13,924.26 | 12.56 % | $30,554.46 | 11.40 % |

You can see that the number of rows within the cross-tab has been reduced. The products that had similar names are now summarized into a single row for each product.

## Tutorial 13-5. Customizing the Column Grouping with Parameters

Rather than formatting the cross-tab object based upon the data within the report, you can use parameters to let the reader choose how to customize the cross-tab.

This tutorial customizes the cross-tab by modifying the grouping column. The report first asks the user whether they want to group by year or by quarter. The cross-tab changes the column data based upon the user's response.

1.  Open the CrossTab.rpt sample report that was installed with Crystal Reports. Save it as **CrossTab Using Parameters.rpt.**

2.  The first step is to create the parameter that prompts the user for how they want the cross-tab printed. Create a new parameter by going to the Field Explorer window, right-clicking on the Parameter Fields item and selecting New.

3.  For the parameter name, enter **Cross-Tab Grouping.**

4.  For the List of Values, leave it at the default value of Static.

5.  Use the Insert button to create two new parameters[58]: **Group by Quarter** and **Group by Year.**

6.  For the Options listed at the bottom, set Allow Custom Values to False.

    Now that the parameter is created, we need to create a formula that uses that parameter to set the date format and we'll use this formula in the cross-tab object.

7.  Make sure you are on the Design tab and right-click on the top left corner of the cross-tab object and select Cross-Tab Expert from the pop-up menu.

8.  Click the New Formula button and name the formula **Date Grouping.**

9.  Enter the following formula:

    ```
    if {?Cross-Tab Grouping} = "Group By Quarter" then
        CStr({Orders.Order Date}, "yyyy") & " - Q" & CStr(DatePart("q", {Orders.Order Date}),
    0)
    else
        CSTR({Orders.Order Date}, "yyyy")
    ```

    This formula checks what the user entered for the parameter value. If it is "Group By Quarter", the date is formatted to show the year and the quarter. If not, just the year is shown.

10. Click the Save and Close button to save the formula and check for errors.

---

[58] If you aren't familiar with creating parameters, please refer to Chapter 4.

11. Since the formula uses a parameter, you are prompted to set the parameter value. Choose the Group By Quarter option.

11. On the Cross-Tab Expert dialog box, select the Date Grouping formula in the Available Fields window and click on the right-arrow button for the Columns list.

12. Within the Columns list, we want to remove the Orders.Order Date field that was previously there. Select that field and click the left-arrow button to remove it from the list. The only field that should be left in the Columns list is the Date Grouping formula.

13. Click the OK button to close the Cross-Tab Expert dialog box.

14. Click on the Preview tab to look at the report. In an earlier step, you already selected Group by Quarter for the parameter value. The report should look similar to the following figure.

| | 2003 - Q1 | | 2003 - Q4 | | 2004 - Q1 | |
| | Order Amount | Order Amount | Order Amount | Order Amount | Order Amount | Order Amount |
|---|---|---|---|---|---|---|
| Descent | $23,612.06 | 21.30 % | $96,033.66 | 35.82 % | $370,455.42 | 37.56 % |
| Endorphin | $3,651.08 | 3.29 % | $12,416.79 | 4.63 % | $74,866.88 | 7.59 % |
| Mozzie | $28,861.68 | 26.03 % | $33,873.64 | 12.63 % | $115,256.55 | 11.69 % |
| Competition | $56,124.82 | 50.63 % | $142,324.09 | 53.09 % | $560,578.85 | 56.83 % |
| Active Outdoors Cr | $308.00 | 0.28 % | $9,762.67 | 3.64 % | $13,482.96 | 1.37 % |
| Active Outdoors Ly | $1,266.15 | 1.14 % | $6,403.89 | 2.39 % | $58,214.00 | 5.90 % |
| InFlux Crochet Glov | $0.00 | 0.00 % | $1,202.05 | 0.45 % | $11,608.25 | 1.18 % |
| InFlux Lycra Glove | $8,531.10 | 7.70 % | $3,934.32 | 1.47 % | $4,025.16 | 0.41 % |
| Gloves | $10,105.25 | 9.12 % | $21,302.93 | 7.95 % | $87,330.37 | 8.85 % |
| Triumph Pro Helme | $5,557.82 | 5.01 % | $12,581.04 | 4.69 % | $60,305.85 | 6.11 % |
| Triumph Vertigo He | $4,119.91 | 3.72 % | $5,686.48 | 2.12 % | $94,144.03 | 9.54 % |
| Xtreme Adult Helme | $3,134.73 | 2.83 % | $11,722.02 | 4.37 % | $26,252.68 | 2.66 % |
| Xtreme Youth Helm | $1,111.80 | 1.00 % | $564.92 | 0.21 % | $7,292.23 | 0.74 % |
| Helmets | $13,924.26 | 12.56 % | $30,554.46 | 11.40 % | $187,994.79 | 19.06 % |

15. If your report looks fine, then press the F5 key to refresh it and prompt for a new parameter value. Select Group By Year and your report should look similar to the following:

| | 2003 | | 2004 | | 2005 | |
|---|---|---|---|---|---|---|
| | Order Amount | Order Amount | Order Amount | Order Amount | Order Amount | Order Amount |
| Descent | $119,645.72 | 31.57 % | $1,579,798.63 | 35.20 % | $592,268.15 | 37.72 % |
| Endorphin | $16,067.87 | 4.24 % | $323,352.62 | 7.21 % | $110,829.89 | 7.06 % |
| Mozzie | $62,735.32 | 16.55 % | $579,824.81 | 12.92 % | $168,613.13 | 10.74 % |
| Competition | $198,448.91 | 52.37 % | $2,482,976.06 | 55.33 % | $871,711.17 | 55.52 % |
| Active Outdoors Cr | $10,070.67 | 2.66 % | $136,237.11 | 3.04 % | $40,676.43 | 2.59 % |
| Active Outdoors Ly | $7,670.04 | 2.02 % | $176,601.30 | 3.94 % | $59,708.77 | 3.80 % |
| InFlux Crochet Glo | $1,202.05 | 0.32 % | $49,787.15 | 1.11 % | $20,054.51 | 1.28 % |
| InFlux Lycra Glove | $12,465.42 | 3.29 % | $37,196.96 | 0.83 % | $24,874.19 | 1.58 % |
| Gloves | $31,408.18 | 8.29 % | $399,822.52 | 8.91 % | $145,313.90 | 9.26 % |
| Triumph Pro Helme | $18,138.86 | 4.79 % | $222,026.41 | 4.95 % | $73,899.28 | 4.71 % |
| Triumph Vertigo He | $9,806.39 | 2.59 % | $340,587.79 | 7.59 % | $92,481.51 | 5.89 % |
| Xtreme Adult Helm | $14,856.75 | 3.92 % | $183,258.19 | 4.08 % | $54,094.90 | 3.45 % |
| Xtreme Youth Helm | $1,676.72 | 0.44 % | $59,593.86 | 1.33 % | $21,015.24 | 1.34 % |
| Helmets | $44,478.72 | 11.74 % | $805,466.25 | 17.95 % | $241,490.93 | 15.38 % |

In this example, we used parameters to customize the cross-tab. This let the user decide how the Order Date field should be grouped. You can use parameters within formulas to let your users customize cross-tab reports in a variety of ways.

# Tutorial 13-6. Different Formulas for Each Row

As I was finishing this chapter, someone posted a question on the forum that is perfect for this chapter. Rather than explain it, I'll show the question here:

Hi, I was asked to display this data in a cross-tab and I'm wondering if this is possible: We have regions, services and clients. The clients are classified according to different services they take. Depending on this service, I have to create totals in a different way and show those totals in the crosstab. The crosstab should look like this:

| | Region1 | Region2 | Region3 |
|---|---|---|---|
| S1 | # orders | # orders | # orders |
| S2 | Total Sales | Total Sales | Total Sales |
| S3 | Total Date Diff | Total Date Diff | Total Date Diff |

For the S1 row, I have to count the number of order for service S1. For the S2 row I have to count the $ amount sold. For the S3 row I have to take 2 dates (d1 and d2) and show the difference.

> I know I'm showing different kinds of values in each row (and the general total will have no meaning) but I was asked to show them all together in the same table because they are related in some way and they need to see them together. Could I do something like this?

This is a great example of a very unique requirement for a cross-tab report. Let's build it ourselves and see how it's done. Of course, since we don't have her exact data available, we need to tweak the sample a bit. But, we'll worry about that when we come to it.

Before getting into building the report, let's look at the primary focus of how to create the report. The difficulty will be in creating a function that returns three different values within the cross-tab output.

The first requirement is that if the service is S1, the summary should count how many orders there were for that service. The cross-tab object's summary function is going to be Sum(). We want to increment the total by 1 for each order. Thus, for service S1, we are simply going to return the value 1 from the function and let the cross-tab total them. The formula would look like this:

```
If {Customer.Service} = "S1" Then
    1;
```

The second requirement is that if the service is S2, we want to get a total order amount. This is easy because all we have to do is return the order amount and the cross-tab will summarize it. The modification to the formula to account for this is:

```
If {Customer. Service } = "S1" Then
    1
Else If {Customer. Service } = "S2" Then
    {Orders.Order Amount};
```

The last requirement is that if the service is S3, we want to calculate the difference between two dates. The formula would be something like this:

```
If {Customer. Service } = "S1" Then
    1
Else If {Customer. Service } = "S2" Then
    {Orders.Order Amount}
Else
    {Orders.Ship Date}-{Orders.Order Date};
```

Let's take this function and create a report with it so that we can see it in action. We can't create the exact same report that was mentioned in the forum's post, but we can make something similar using the Xtreme.mdb database. Let's create the report based on the Customer table and the Orders table. This lets us group the customers by country, summarize the total order amounts, and do a simple date calculation.

1. Create a new report using the Standard Report wizard. Note: Don't use the Cross-Tab Wizard report type because we need to create a new function prior to creating the cross-tab object.

2. For the data source, choose the Xtreme.mdb database and select the tables Customer and Orders.

3. Link the two tables together using the Customer ID field.

4. Don't select any data fields to display on the report. Just click the Finish button to skip it and go to the report designer.

   This report doesn't have any data relating to customer services, so we will group customers by country instead. And since the example only needed three services, we will limit our report to just three countries.

4. Click the menu options Report > Select Expert.

5. Choose the field Country from the Customer table and click the OK button.

6. In the Select Expert, from the drop-down list choose "Is One Of".

7. For the field values, choose the countries Canada, England, and USA.

8. Click the OK button to save your changes.

9. Before building the cross-tab object, we first have to create the formula that will do our magic. Insert a new formula field and call it CrossTab Summary.

   Since we are going to group on Country, we will report the Service field in the previous formula with Country.

   ```
   Else If {Customer.Country} = "Canada" Then
       //Sum the difference in dates
       {Orders.Ship Date}-{Orders.Order Date}
   Else If {Customer.Country} = "England" Then
       //Sum the total order amount
       {Orders.Order Amount}
   Else If {Customer.Country} = "USA" Then
       //Sum the number of orders
       1;
   ```

10. Click the Save and Close button to check that you typed everything in correctly and save the changes.

11. Right-click on the report and select Insert Cross-Tab. Place the cross-tab object in the Report Header section.

12. Right-click on the cross-tab report and select Cross-Tab Expert.

13. When the dialog box opens, insert the following fields into the appropriate area. Move the Customer.Country field to the Rows category. Move the Orders.Order Date to the Columns category.

14. We need to use the function we created, so move the function CrossTab Summary to the Summarized Fields category.

Lastly, we want to modify how the Order Date is grouped. We don't want to have a separate column in the cross-tab for every order date. Instead, let's just have a column for each year.

15. Click on the Group Options button under the Columns category.

16. Change the selection "for each day" to "for each year". Click the OK button to close the Group Option dialog box.

    Before we close the Cross-Tab expert, let's turn off the row and column totals.

17. Click on the Customize Style tab. Click on the checkboxes Suppress Row Grand Totals and Suppress Column Grand Totals.

18. Click the OK button to save and close the Cross-Tab expert dialog box.

    Now that we are back in design mode, let's change the formatting of the summary function because the default is currency and we don't want to print dollar signs.

19. Right-click on the summary field in the bottom right-hand corner and select Format Field. Uncheck the option Display Currency Symbol.

20. Click the OK button to save the formatting changes.

21. Preview the report and your cross-tab should look similar to the following:

| | 2003 | 2004 | 2005 |
|---|---|---|---|
| Canada | 21.13 | 309.14 | 46.00 |
| England | 3,014.15 | 57,803.17 | 8,136.56 |
| USA | 122.00 | 1,051.00 | 351.00 |

The Canada row calculates the sum of date differences. The England subtotals calculate the sum of the order amounts. The USA subtotal calculates how many orders were placed. By basing the crosstab summary field on a formula, you can customize what is calculated within each cross-tab cell.

### Caution

Tutorial 13-6 shows how powerful the cross-tab object is for summarizing data. But, the caveat is that even though you can use formulas to customize cross-tab results, the summary function has to be the same for each cell. You can't use different summary functions for different results. For example, if you choose the Sum() function, then the results of the formula will be added together for each cell. If you select the Avg() summary function, then the cross-tab cells will show the average of all the formula results. It is not possible to have certain cells perform the Sum() function and others perform the Avg() function.

# Tutorial 13-7. Performing a SQL Distinct

Just to make sure that you have truly mastered the art of creating custom cross-tab functions, let's add one more level of difficulty to the previous tutorial. In the last tutorial, we counted the total number of orders for the country USA. The formula returned a '1' for each order so that each one would be added to the total. But, let's make this more challenging by saying that we only want to count the number of customers who placed orders and not the orders themselves. This presents a challenge because we want the cross-tab summary function to count a customer once, but then skip it afterwards. Since the cross-tab object calls the formula separately for each row in the database, how does it keep track of the first time a customer appears but not the other times? Pretty tricky stuff!

To do this, we keep the same basic formula, but we have to add additional logic to track which customers have been included in the summary and which ones haven't. If you are familiar with databases and the SQL language, this effectively emulates the SQL DISTINCT operator. If you like, stop here and think about how you would do it before continuing. Once you are ready, read on to see how I do it.

To trick the cross-tab object into only counting each customer one time, I build a string that lists each customer that has been counted. As each new customer gets counted, I add it to the end of the list. If a customer is already in the list, then I don't count it.

The general idea is that if the customer is not in the list, return a '1' so that it gets counted. If the customer is already in the list, return a '0'.

Unfortunately, this is a pretty simplistic interpretation of the problem and the first time I built this formula it didn't return the correct results. Let's look at the working version of the formula and I'll discuss the places where I went wrong and what I did to fix it.

```
Global StringVar CustomerList;
Local StringVar CustomerName;
If {Customer.Country} = "USA" Then
(
    CustomerName := "~" & Year({Orders.Order Date}) &
    {Customer.Customer Name} & "~";
    If InStr(CustomerList, CustomerName)=0 Then
        CustomerList := CustomerList & CustomerName;
        1
    Else
    (
        0
    )
)
```

Else If {Customer.Country} = "England" Then
   {Orders.Order Amount}
Else
   {Orders.Ship Date}-{Orders.Order Date};

The first step is to define the string variables used. The CustomerList is a global string. This is where we keep track of all the customers already counted. The key is declaring it as Global so that it doesn't lose its value between records. The CustomerName variable is where we store the current customer name.

Within the If statement, if the country is USA, we assign a value to the CustomerName variable. As you can see, we do more than just assign the customer name to the string. We add extra data that is associated with each customer. This is a bit complicated, so for a moment let's skip this detail so that we first understand the overall logic.

The next If statement checks to see if the CustomerName value is not included in the CustomerList string. The Instr() function tests to see if one string is already in another string. It returns zero if the new string is not already in the existing string. If the InStr() function says that CustomerName is not in the CustomerList string, then we return a 1 value. This tells the cross-tab to count it in the summary function. If the InStr() function says that CustomerName is already in the list, then return 0. This prevents it from being counted in the summary function more than once.

When the cross-tab sub-total is finished doing all its calculations, each customer will have only been included in the sub-total one time. Duplicates do not get counted.

Now that you see how the overall logic works, let's look at the CustomerName variable in more detail. The first time I built this formula, all I did was assign the Customer Name field to this variable. But this produced two problems, as we'll see next.

The first problem is that some customer names are subsets of another customer name. For example, there is a customer called "Spokes" and another customer called "Spokes For Folks". If the customer "Spokes For Folks" is already in the list, when we test to see if "Spokes" is in the list, the Instr() function will say that it is. This is because "Spokes" is the first part of "Spokes for Folks". The Instr() function isn't smart enough to realize that they are actually two different customers. To fix this problem you have to put delimiters around the customer name so that you know the exact beginning and end of the string. This formula puts a "~" at the beginning and end of the string to fix this problem.

The second problem is that when I ran the report, all the sub-totals were the same for every year. I doubted that the same number of customers placed orders in each year, so I researched further. I realized that as the cross-tab object builds the string of customer names, it is using the same string for each column (the Year) in the cross-tab object. There is no way to differentiate in which year the customer placed an order. Thus, each year has the same sub-total. To fix this, I used the Year() function to concatenate the order date's year value into the CustomerName string. This gives each customer a separate entry in the CustomerList string for each year. If you are going to use a similar formula in your report, you would replace the Year() function with a string that identifies the values in the cross-tab column.

By placing delimiters around the customer name and including the year, this lets the cross-tab object calculate correct results based on the full customer name and only include it for the years that orders were placed.

If you take the report that we built in Tutorial 13-6 and substitute this new formula and preview it, you'll see that the USA row shows the number of unique customers who had sales for each year.

| | 2003 | 2004 | 2005 |
|---|---|---|---|
| Canada | 21.13 | 309.14 | 46.00 |
| England | 3,014.15 | 57,803.17 | 8,136.56 |
| USA | 54.00 | 90.00 | 58.00 |

# Referencing Rows and Columns

Tutorial 13-3 looked at how to format individual cells with the CurrentValue function. You saw how to use conditional formatting to change the cell properties based upon what was being printed. The cross-tab object also has a function that lets you determine which row and column the current cell is located in. This lets you make changes across an entire section of the cross-tab object. Rather than focusing on individual cells, this gives you a higher level view of what is being printed.

The function GridRowColumnValue() returns the value of the row or column that the cell is in. Pass it the name of the group field (either the row's field name or the column's field name), and it returns the current value. For example, if the column groups by months of the year, passing the function the date field will result in the third column returning the month name "March". A formula can look at both the current row value and column value to determine the cell's exact location within the cross-tab. In most cases, you'll probably just use one field to apply a specific formatting to an entire row or column. The following line of code returns the Product Type Name of the current row being printed.

```
GridRowColumnValue("Product_Type.Product Type Name");
```

Notice that you need to pass both the table name and the field name to the function. You have to type it in exactly as it is shown in the cross-tab expert. It might be easier to create an alias to refer to the row or column field. This is done by going to the Cross-Tab Expert dialog box and selecting the Customize Style tab. Click on the row or column field you want to modify and enter a new name in the Alias for Formulas input box (located in the Group Options section). Now the GridRowColumnValue() function can reference the alias name instead of the field name. For example, if you assign an alias for the Product

Type Name field and called it Product Type, then you could change the previous line of code to the following:

GridRowColumnValue("Product Type");

Using an alias makes the field name a little shorter and you no longer have to reference the table name either.

# Using Arrays to Store Cross-Tab Data

Using the CurrentValue and GridRowColumnValue() functions gives you excellent control over formatting the cross-tab object. But you can get a lot more power by combining these two functions together. You can use them to store the entire cross-tab object in arrays. These arrays can be used to overwrite the cross-tab data with your own custom formulas or you can reference the arrays elsewhere in your report.

The GridRowColumnValue() function returns the current row or column being printed in the cross-tab object. You can use this to determine the X-Y coordinates of the current cell and store its value in the proper array. Use the CurrentValue function to determine what value should be stored in the array. As the cross-tab object is being created, you can use these functions to duplicate each value in an array.

To copy the cross-tab values into arrays, you need to know how the cross-tab object is built internally. The cross-tab object creates its values by going from top to bottom and then left to right. It starts at the first column of the first row and prints down the cross-tab object till it gets to the last row. Then it starts at the top of the next column and works its way down again (see Figure 13-11).

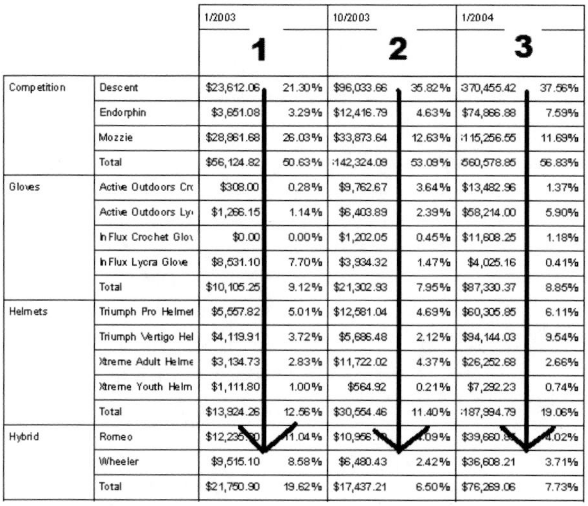

| | | 1/2003 | | 10/2003 | | 1/2004 | |
| | | **1** | | **2** | | **3** | |
|---|---|---|---|---|---|---|---|
| Competition | Descent | $23,612.06 | 21.30% | $96,033.66 | 35.82% | 370,455.42 | 37.56% |
| | Endorphin | $3,651.08 | 3.29% | $12,416.79 | 4.63% | $74,866.88 | 7.59% |
| | Mozzie | $28,861.68 | 26.03% | $33,873.64 | 12.63% | :115,256.55 | 11.69% |
| | Total | $56,124.82 | 50.63% | :142,324.09 | 53.09% | 560,578.85 | 56.83% |
| Gloves | Active Outdoors Cr | $308.00 | 0.28% | $9,762.67 | 3.64% | $13,482.96 | 1.37% |
| | Active Outdoors Ly | $1,266.15 | 1.14% | $6,403.89 | 2.39% | $58,214.00 | 5.90% |
| | In Flux Crochet Glo | $0.00 | 0.00% | $1,202.05 | 0.45% | $11,608.25 | 1.18% |
| | In Flux Lycra Glove | $8,531.10 | 7.70% | $3,934.32 | 1.47% | $4,025.16 | 0.41% |
| | Total | $10,105.25 | 9.12% | $21,302.93 | 7.95% | $87,330.37 | 8.85% |
| Helmets | Triumph Pro Helmet | $5,557.82 | 5.01% | $12,581.04 | 4.69% | $60,305.85 | 6.11% |
| | Triumph Vertigo Hel | $4,119.91 | 3.72% | $5,686.48 | 2.12% | $94,144.03 | 9.54% |
| | Xtreme Adult Helmet | $3,134.73 | 2.83% | $11,722.02 | 4.37% | $26,252.68 | 2.66% |
| | Xtreme Youth Helm | $1,111.80 | 1.00% | $564.92 | 0.21% | $7,292.23 | 0.74% |
| | Total | $13,924.26 | 12.56% | $30,554.46 | 11.40% | :187,994.79 | 19.06% |
| Hybrid | Romeo | $12,235 | 11.04% | $10,956 | 09% | $39,660 | 02% |
| | Wheeler | $9,515.10 | 8.58% | $6,480.43 | 2.42% | $36,608.21 | 3.71% |
| | Total | $21,750.90 | 19.62% | $17,437.21 | 6.50% | $76,269.06 | 7.73% |

**Figure 13-11. Print order of the cross-tab object.**

As the cross-tab object is created, you need to copy each value into the array. There are two challenges here. The first challenge being that Crystal syntax doesn't have a multi-dimensional array data type.[59] Instead, you have to use a single array for each column and pair them up. Matching columns with arrays can be difficult because you have to know your data well enough to know how many columns there are ahead of time. This allows you to plan the number of arrays you'll need and to think of a proper name for each one. This technique works best with reports that have a limited number of columns (e.g. the months of the year). For cross-tabs that have a dynamic number of columns, you will have to write a lot of code to account for each possible one.

The second challenge with using multiple arrays is knowing when to switch to the next array. Since each column is printed consecutively and there is one array for every column, you will completely fill each array one at a time. It's important to know the printing order because you need a way to determine when to quit populating one array and start on the next array. You can use the column header value to determine when to start a new array. By comparing the current column value to the previous column value (stored in a variable that you track), you know that when they are different, the new column is starting and you have to start populating the next array.

Since you are storing the entire cross-tab object in arrays, you get the benefit of letting the cross-tab cells reference each other. This lets you create your own summary functions that aren't allowed by Crystal Reports. For example, you could use the cross-tab object to sum the data in the detail columns as normal. But you can override the Total column to display the average of the three columns. As another example, you could calculate a running total across each row. Of course, this isn't a trivial matter because it is going to take a decent amount of code to create the arrays and perform the calculations. But, after going through the tutorials in this book you should have enough practice to do it without too much trouble.

If you want to populate the cross-tab with new data, Crystal Reports lets you override the current cell value using the Display String setting. It is found in the cross-tab's Format Editor dialog box on the Common tab. You can use the Formula button to display any string in the current cell of the cross-tab. This formula can take existing values from the cross-tab object (using the arrays you built) and create custom formulas for any column. Taken to the extreme, you could use the Display String setting to build your own cross-tab objects.

It's important to realize that each column can only reference the columns that come before it. Since columns print consecutively, you can't reference a future column. For example, when column three starts printing you know that the arrays for columns one and two have already been filled. You can use their values in a calculation. But since column four hasn't been printed yet, this array is still empty and those values can't be referenced yet.

---

[59] A multi-dimensional array uses two indexes to simulate X-Y coordinates.

A second use for copying the cross-tab object into arrays is that you can use these arrays elsewhere in your report. This lets you use the cross-tab object for calculating the summary functions at the beginning of the report and reference those totals in different calculations elsewhere in the report.

## Tutorial 13-8. Copying a Cross-Tab into Arrays

For this tutorial, we are just going to focus on how to copy the cross-tab object into arrays. Since there are so many things you can do with these arrays, I'll leave it up to you to customize it as your needs dictate.

If you need more examples, Tutorial A-4 in Appendix A demonstrates how to use the cross-tab functions for customizing output. Tutorial A-5 goes into great detail on how to copy the cross-tab into arrays and override the cross-tab data with custom formulas. Those tutorials should provide you with ample code samples so that you can learn how to implement these techniques in your own reports. Unfortunately, the tutorials in Appendix A discuss financial reporting and are very advanced. It might be easier to jump to the parts that discuss customizing the cross-tab object. If you don't want to read the entire tutorials in Appendix A, look up the GridRowColumnValue() function in the index and read the pages that demonstrate its usage.

When you're writing a complex piece of code for the first time, it's more than likely not going to work. There is going to be some small bug in the code that you didn't notice and will cause it to return the wrong results. That means you have to dig into your code and debug it to figure out what is wrong. The problem with writing code in the cross-tab object is that it is a black box – you have no idea what is going on inside it. If the results are wrong, debugging it can be very difficult.

The way to debug the cross-tab object is to print out the expected results using the Display String property. This lets you see how a variable changes as the cross-tab prints. What I like to do is to start writing the code in very small increments and print test values each step of the way. This lets me immediately find an error and fix it before I go any further. If I wait until the end to start debugging it, it could take much longer to find the problem. In essence, I'm accepting the fact that something will probably go wrong. I test early so that I can catch small bugs before they become bigger problems. In this tutorial, I'm going to walk you through the steps that I use to debug the code in a cross-tab object. This will make the tutorial a bit longer than necessary, but it will be good to demonstrate the process for debugging your own report.

1.  Open the CrossTab.rpt sample report that was installed with Crystal Reports. Save it as **CrossTab Arrays.rpt**.

    This cross-tab report uses the Order Date as the column field and groups by quarter. This creates a cross-tab object that has many columns and spans multiple pages. For this tutorial, we want to make the cross-tab easier to manage. We are going to have it group by year so that there are only three columns to work with.

2. In Design mode, right-click on the cross-tab object in the top left corner. Select Cross-Tab Expert.

3. In the Columns list to the right, click on the Order Date field to select it.

4. Click on the Group Options button to open the Cross-Tab Group Options dialog box.

5. Change the grouping from For Each Quarter to For Each Year.

6. Click the OK button twice to save your changes and return to the Design tab.

7. Preview the report to confirm that the column header shows the year and that there are three years listed (2003-2005).

| | 2003 | | 2004 | | 2005 | |
|---|---|---|---|---|---|---|
| | SUM of Orders | Percentage of Orders | SUM of Orders | Percentage of Orders | SUM of Orders | Percentage of Orders |
| Descent | $119,645.72 | 31.57 % | $1,579,798.63 | 35.20 % | $592,268.15 | 37.72 % |
| Endorphin | $16,067.87 | 4.24 % | $323,352.62 | 7.21 % | $110,829.89 | 7.06 % |
| Mozzie | $62,735.32 | 16.55 % | $579,824.81 | 12.92 % | $168,613.13 | 10.74 % |
| Competition | $198,448.91 | 52.37 % | 2,482,976.06 | 55.33 % | $871,711.17 | 55.52 % |
| Active Outdoors Cr | $10,070.67 | 2.66 % | $136,237.11 | 3.04 % | $40,676.43 | 2.59 % |
| Active Outdoors Ly | $7,670.04 | 2.02 % | $176,601.30 | 3.94 % | $59,708.77 | 3.80 % |
| InFlux Crochet Glo | $1,202.05 | 0.32 % | $49,787.15 | 1.11 % | $20,054.51 | 1.28 % |
| InFlux Lycra Glove | $12,465.42 | 3.29 % | $37,196.96 | 0.83 % | $24,874.19 | 1.58 % |
| Gloves | $31,408.18 | 8.29 % | $399,822.52 | 8.91 % | $145,313.90 | 9.26 % |
| Triumph Pro Helm | $18,138.86 | 4.79 % | $222,026.41 | 4.95 % | $73,899.28 | 4.71 % |
| Triumph Vertigo H | $9,806.39 | 2.59 % | $340,587.79 | 7.59 % | $92,481.51 | 5.89 % |
| Xtreme Adult Helm | $14,856.75 | 3.92 % | $183,258.19 | 4.08 % | $54,094.90 | 3.45 % |
| Xtreme Youth Heln | $1,676.72 | 0.44 % | $59,593.86 | 1.33 % | $21,015.24 | 1.34 % |
| Helmets | $44,478.72 | 11.74 % | $805,466.25 | 17.95 % | $241,490.93 | 15.38 % |
| Romeo | $23,192.58 | 6.12 % | $276,706.16 | 6.17 % | $120,656.37 | 7.68 % |
| Wheeler | $15,995.53 | 4.22 % | $163,199.97 | 3.64 % | $76,334.44 | 4.86 % |
| Hybrid | $39,188.11 | 10.34 % | $439,906.13 | 9.80 % | $196,990.81 | 12.55 % |
| Micro Nicros | $15,272.64 | 4.03 % | $40,337.31 | 0.90 % | $14,931.26 | 0.95 % |
| Mini Nicros | $37,137.87 | 9.80 % | $83,209.51 | 1.85 % | $10,265.55 | 0.65 % |
| Kids | $52,410.51 | 13.83 % | $123,546.82 | 2.75 % | $25,196.81 | 1.60 % |
| Guardian "U" Lock | $35.00 | 0.01 % | $18,028.29 | 0.40 % | $8,436.60 | 0.54 % |
| Guardian ATB Loc | $2,362.97 | 0.62 % | $34,409.55 | 0.77 % | $18,949.90 | 1.21 % |
| Guardian Chain Lo | $157.30 | 0.04 % | $19,708.85 | 0.44 % | $4,080.44 | 0.26 % |
| Guardian Mini Locl | $5,083.36 | 1.34 % | $20,225.99 | 0.45 % | $3,310.98 | 0.21 % |
| Guardian XL "U" L | $19.90 | 0.01 % | $33,226.65 | 0.74 % | $4,817.87 | 0.31 % |
| Xtreme Mtn Lock | $1,576.53 | 0.42 % | $41,125.60 | 0.92 % | $1,841.06 | 0.12 % |
| Xtreme Rhino Lock | $3,790.02 | 1.00 % | $52,246.15 | 1.16 % | $19,500.80 | 1.24 % |
| Xtreme Titan Lock | $0.00 | 0.00 % | $17,036.38 | 0.38 % | $28,446.70 | 1.81 % |
| Locks | $13,025.08 | 3.44 % | $236,007.46 | 5.26 % | $89,384.35 | 5.69 % |
| Total | $378,959.51 | 100.00 % | 4,487,725.24 | 100.00 % | 1,570,087.97 | 100.00 % |

8. Click on the Design tab to go back to editing the cross-tab object.

We are going to create the formula which creates three arrays (one for each year) and copies the cross-tab data into them. This is done by associating the formula with a conditional formatting property of the dialog box. We don't want to actually change the conditional formatting, we just want to use it to force the cross-tab object to run the formula for each cell. It's best to attach it to a formatting property that you never use and have it return a dummy value. Personally, I never use the CSS Class Name property so that is where I'm going to put it. You can use a different property if you like.

9. Right-click on the Sum Of Orders field on the cross-tab object (the field in the first column and on Row #2-Product Name) and select Format Field. This opens the Format Editor dialog box.

10. Select the Common tab and click on the Formula button for the CSS Class Name property.

11. Enter the following formula:

```
NumberVar CurrentRow;
NumberVar CurrentYear;
if CurrentYear <> Year(GridRowColumnValue("Orders.Order Date")) Then
(
    CurrentYear := Year(GridRowColumnValue("Orders.Order Date"));
    CurrentRow := 0;
);
CurrentRow := CurrentRow + 1;
"";
```

12. Click the Save and Close button to save the formula.

This formula uses the CurrentRow variable to track the row being printed by the cross-tab. Each time another cell prints, its value is incremented by one. It also uses the GridRowColumnValue() function to find out which column is being printed. If the column is different than the previous column printed (the CurrentYear variable), we know that we are at the top of a new column and at the first row. When this happens, the CurrentRow variable is reset back to zero.

The last line of the formula is important because it returns an empty string. You have to be careful when attaching a formula to a non-related field property so that you don't change the property. By returning an empty string, we make sure that the CSS Class Name property stays unchanged. If you are using a different property in your own report, make sure to return the appropriate value so that the formatting doesn't change it.

I mentioned earlier that we'll test the code periodically to make sure it is working as expected. To do so, let's print the CurrentRow value on each cell to see if it is really being incremented the way we expect it to.

13. The Format Editor dialog box should still be open. Click on the Formula button for the Display String property and enter the following code:

```
NumberVar CurrentRow;
Cstr(CurrentRow,"#");
```

This formula first declares the CurrenRow variable so that it can be shared with the previous formula. Next, it converts it to a string so that it can be displayed in the cell. It has to be converted to a string because the Display String property only accepts strings.

14. Click the Save and Close button to save the formula.

15. Click the OK button to close the Format Editor dialog box.

At this point, we've created a variable to track the current row and print it in the cross-tab cell so that we can confirm that it is working properly. If you preview the report, it should look like the following figure:

| | 2003 | | 2004 | | 2005 | | Total | |
|---|---|---|---|---|---|---|---|---|
| | SUM of Orders | Percentage of Orders | SUM of Orders | Percentage of Orders | SUM of Orders | Percentage of Orders | SUM of Orders | Percentage of Orders |
| Descent | 1 | 31.57 % | 1 | 35.20 % | 1 | 37.72 % | 291,712.50 | 35.60 % |
| Endorphin | 2 | 4.24 % | 2 | 7.21 % | 2 | 7.06 % | 150,250.38 | 6.99 % |
| Mozzie | 3 | 16.55 % | 3 | 12.92 % | 3 | 10.74 % | 311,173.26 | 12.60 % |
| Competition | 98,448.91 | 52.37 % | 182,976.06 | 55.33 % | 371,711.17 | 55.52 % | 553,136.14 | 55.20 % |
| Active Outdoors Cr | 4 | 2.66 % | 4 | 3.04 % | 4 | 2.59 % | 186,984.21 | 2.90 % |
| Active Outdoors Ly | 5 | 2.02 % | 5 | 3.94 % | 5 | 3.80 % | 243,980.11 | 3.79 % |
| InFlux Crochet Glo | 6 | 0.32 % | 6 | 1.11 % | 6 | 1.28 % | 71,043.71 | 1.10 % |
| InFlux Lycra Glove | 7 | 3.29 % | 7 | 0.83 % | 7 | 1.58 % | 74,536.57 | 1.16 % |
| Gloves | 31,408.18 | 8.29 % | 99,822.52 | 8.91 % | 145,313.90 | 9.26 % | 576,544.60 | 8.96 % |
| Triumph Pro Helm | 8 | 4.79 % | 8 | 4.95 % | 8 | 4.71 % | 314,064.55 | 4.88 % |
| Triumph Vertigo He | 9 | 2.59 % | 9 | 7.59 % | 9 | 5.89 % | 442,875.69 | 6.88 % |
| Xtreme Adult Helm | 10 | 3.92 % | 10 | 4.08 % | 10 | 3.45 % | 252,209.84 | 3.92 % |
| Xtreme Youth Helm | 11 | 0.44 % | 11 | 1.33 % | 11 | 1.34 % | 82,285.82 | 1.28 % |
| Helmets | 44,478.72 | 11.74 % | 305,466.25 | 17.95 % | 241,490.93 | 15.38 % | 091,435.90 | 16.96 % |
| Romeo | 12 | 6.12 % | 12 | 6.17 % | 12 | 7.68 % | 420,555.11 | 6.53 % |
| Wheeler | 13 | 4.22 % | 13 | 3.64 % | 13 | 4.86 % | 255,529.94 | 3.97 % |
| Hybrid | 39,188.11 | 10.34 % | 139,906.13 | 9.80 % | 196,990.81 | 12.55 % | 676,085.05 | 10.50 % |
| Micro Nicros | 14 | 4.03 % | 14 | 0.90 % | 14 | 0.95 % | 70,541.21 | 1.10 % |
| Mini Nicros | 15 | 9.80 % | 15 | 1.85 % | 15 | 0.65 % | 130,612.93 | 2.03 % |
| Kids | 52,410.51 | 13.83 % | 23,546.82 | 2.75 % | 25,196.81 | 1.60 % | 201,154.14 | 3.13 % |
| Guardian "U" Lock | 16 | 0.01 % | 16 | 0.40 % | 16 | 0.54 % | 26,499.89 | 0.41 % |
| Guardian ATB Loc | 17 | 0.62 % | 17 | 0.77 % | 17 | 1.21 % | 55,722.42 | 0.87 % |
| Guardian Chain Lo | 18 | 0.04 % | 18 | 0.44 % | 18 | 0.26 % | 23,946.59 | 0.37 % |
| Guardian Mini Lock | 19 | 1.34 % | 19 | 0.45 % | 19 | 0.21 % | 28,620.33 | 0.44 % |
| Guardian XL "U" Lc | 20 | 0.01 % | 20 | 0.74 % | 20 | 0.31 % | 38,064.42 | 0.59 % |
| Xtreme Mtn Lock | 21 | 0.42 % | 21 | 0.92 % | 21 | 0.12 % | 44,543.19 | 0.69 % |
| Xtreme Rhino Lock | 22 | 1.00 % | 22 | 1.16 % | 22 | 1.24 % | 75,536.97 | 1.17 % |
| Xtreme Titan Lock | 23 | 0.00 % | 23 | 0.38 % | 23 | 1.81 % | 45,483.08 | 0.71 % |
| Locks | 13,025.08 | 3.44 % | 236,007.46 | 5.26 % | 89,384.35 | 5.69 % | 38,416.89 | 5.26 % |
| Total | 78,959.51 | 100.00 % | 487,725.24 | 100.00 % | 570,087.97 | 100.00 % | 436,772.72 | 100.00 % |

This figure demonstrates two things. First, the row counter is working correctly because it increases by one for each row printed. At the top of each column, it resets the counter and starts counting from scratch. Second, it proves that the cross-tab really does generate data by going down each column before starting at the next column.

It's important to look at this figure and notice that the row number has only been printed in the detail cells for the Product Name field. The other fields and sub-totals have not been overwritten and still have their original values. This is because the cross-tab object treats each field separately. This can be good or bad. It is good because you have the option of deciding which data you want to capture. If you want to perform custom calculations on a certain field, then you want to capture only that field's detail data. If you want to use the totals in another part of the report (or referenced by a sub-report), you will capture the values in the sub-total cells. Breaking this out into two different fields can be bad if you want to apply formatting or calculations across every value in the column. You will have to duplicate your code in all the detail fields and sub-totals to apply it to the entire column.

16. Now that we know that the row counter is working correctly, let's modify the formula to create three arrays that store the cross-tab data. Open the Formula Editor for the Sum of Orders field again. Click the Formula button for the CSS Class Name property.

17. Update the existing formula to the following code. The first half is unchanged.

```
NumberVar CurrentRow;
NumberVar CurrentYear;
if CurrentYear <> Year(GridRowColumnValue("Orders.Order Date")) Then
(
    CurrentYear := Year(GridRowColumnValue("Orders.Order Date"));
    CurrentRow := 0;
);
CurrentRow := CurrentRow + 1;

//Store the data in arrays
CurrencyVar Array Col1;
CurrencyVar Array Col2;
CurrencyVar Array Col3;
ReDim Preserve Col1[50];
Redim Preserve Col2[50];
Redim Preserve Col3[50];
Select CurrentYear
    Case 2003:
        Col1[CurrentRow] := CurrentFieldValue
    Case 2004:
        Col2[CurrentRow] := CurrentFieldValue
    Case 2005:
        Col3[CurrentRow] := CurrentFieldValue;
"";
```

This formula creates three arrays and populates the correct one based upon the current year being printed in the column header. Notice that I dimensioned the arrays to have 50 elements so that the cross-tab has room to grow.

18. To test that the arrays were populated correctly, we'll print their values. Go back into the Format Editor and click on the Formula button for the Display String property.

19. Enter the following formula:

```
NumberVar CurrentRow;
```

```
CurrencyVar Array Col1;
CurrencyVar Array Col2;
CurrencyVar Array Col3;
Select Year(GridRowColumnValue("Orders.Order Date"))
    Case 2003:
        CStr(Col1[CurrentRow])
    Case 2004:
        Cstr(Col2[CurrentRow])
    Case 2005:
        Cstr(Col3[CurrentRow]);
```

This formula declares all the array variables so that it can share them with the other formula. Then it uses the GridRowColumnValue() function to determine the current column and print the array associated with that column. If you preview the report, the data in each cell should be the same data that was printed prior to us making any changes. Look back at the figure in Step 7 to see if your cross-tab object has the same values.

Since this data is coming from the array, we know that the array is truly an exact copy of the cross-tab data. The formula works perfectly and we can now use this data elsewhere in the report or use it with custom functions within the cross-tab.

20. We need to remove the formula from the Display String property so that we aren't overriding the cross-tab data anymore. Open the Formula Editor dialog box and click on the Formula button for the Display String property. Delete the formula and save your changes.

# 14
# Mapping Data

Using maps to display data gives your reports a powerful means of quickly communicating geographical information to the reader. This can consist of sales by region, population growth by state, or even green house gas emissions by country. Maps are familiar to everyone and make it easy to quickly visualize information without reading a lot of text.

Crystal Reports lets you display different map layouts, show data in different formats, and zoom in on details. Associating organizational data with maps lets you visualize your business today and plan for growth tomorrow.

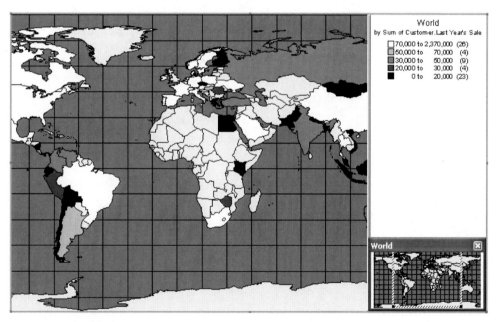

**Figure 14-1. A sample map showing sales by countries around the world.**

# Mapping Overview

When you include a map object on your report, there are three main areas involved: the map, the map legend, and the map navigator.

The primary area is the actual map. It shows the geographic area you've chosen and the data being presented. Although not shown in this figure, the map can also have a title displayed in the top center section. However, this can cover up essential mapping data, so you might be better off not using it.

Along the right side of the map is the map legend. It tells the reader how to interpret the data on the map. For example, this could consist of matching colors to the appropriate number range. There are also two title lines above the legend. You can use these to display a heading and a sub-heading for the map.

The bottom right-hand corner is the map navigator. This gives you a thumbnail image of the map and it shows a dotted box around the section of the map being shown on the report. Since the reader can zoom in and out of the map as well as move it left and right, the dotted box makes it easy to see where you are in relation to the whole map. The map navigator is only visible when the reader has clicked on the map object.

# Creating Maps

Adding a map to your report is a pretty simple process and it only involves three steps: setting the data fields, choosing the map type, and assigning the map title. Let's start out by examining the Map Expert and how to use it. To add a map to the report, choose the menu options Insert > Map. Alternatively, you can click the Insert Map button shown in Figure 14-2.

**Figure 14-2. Insert Map button.**

This opens the Map Expert dialog box, which has three tabs: Data, Type and Text. The Data tab lets you set where to place the map, choose the map layout, and select the data fields. The Data tab is shown in Figure 14-3.

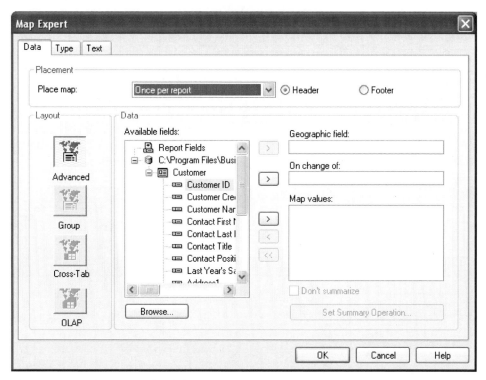

**Figure 14-3. The Data tab of the Map Expert.**

The top section, Placement, determines where to place the map on your report. You can either place it in the Report Header or the Report Footer. If your report has groups defined, then you can also choose to put it in either the header or footer of one of the groups. Maps are similar to charts in that they can't be placed in the Details section.[60]

The Data section of the dialog box is where you set the fields for mapping. There are three areas to enter fields. The Geographic Field is the field that has the location information in it. This can be a country, state or city. The On Change Of field determines at what point to plot the data. In most cases, this is the same as the Geographical Field. In fact, when you assign a field to the Geographic Field, Crystal Reports automatically assigns the same field to the On Change Of field (which you can override if necessary). The last section, Map Values, is where you place the summary field which gets plotted on the map. The default summary function is Sum() which you can change by clicking the Set Summary Operation button below it.

The buttons in the Layout section work the same as the layout buttons in the charting chapter. Each button is enabled depending upon the type of report being used. If it is a basic report, then the Advanced button is enabled. If the report has groups and at least one

---

[60] You can simulate placing a map in the Details section by setting the property Underlay Following Sections.

summary value, then the Group button is enabled. If it is a cross-tab object then the Cross-Tab button is enabled. The OLAP button is enabled when mapping on an OLAP grid.

# Setting the Map Type

The second tab of the Map Expert is the Type tab. It lets you choose between five different ways of plotting data. The five types of maps to choose from are Ranged, Dot Density, Graduated, Pie Chart, and Bar Chart. Each one has a different purpose and you have to set certain properties to control how it looks. The options are shown in Figure 14-4.

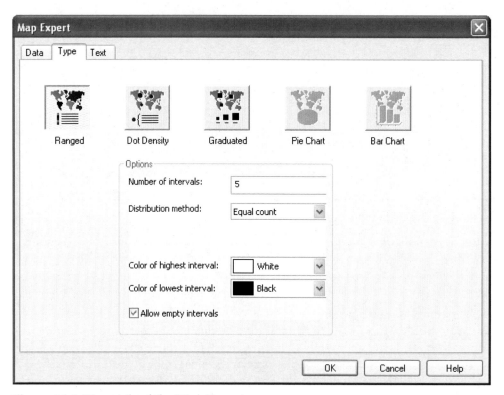

Figure 14-4. Type tab of the Map Expert.

## Caution

The available map types are shown in two groups. When looking at the Map Expert dialog box, you'll either be able to choose from the first three or the last two map types, but not all of them at the same time. This is because each has different requirements for the type of data it can display.

The first three types are Ranged, Dot Density, and Graduated. They simply plot a single value on each point on the map. Thus, they only need data for the map location and a summary value.

The second two types are Pie Chart and Bar Chart. They are a little more complex because they map multiple values on each point. They need three different data fields to work properly. In addition to needing the geographic area and the value to plot, they need a third data field that the value can be plotted against. This data field could be a group of products that will be compared against each other in a pie chart, or a date field to be used as the X-axis in a bar chart.

The way to determine which group of map types will be available is by looking at the On Change Of field. If the On Change Of field is the same data field for Geographic Area, then you can only use the types Ranged, Dot Density, and Graduated. However, if the Geographic Area field is different from the On Change Of field, then there is a third data field to work with and you will be able to use the Pie Chart or Bar Chart map types.

## Ranged Map Type

The Ranged map type splits the numerical data into groups of values. Each group has a beginning and ending value and is represented by a specific color. Figure 14-5 is an example of a Ranged map showing the sales by US city.

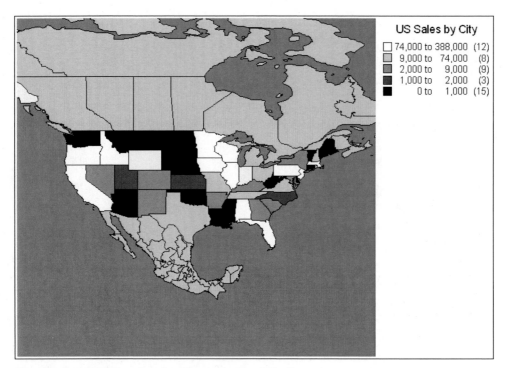

**Figure 14-5. Range map showing sales by US city.**

The legend in the top right hand corner shows the range of values displayed and which colors map to each range. In parentheses, it also tells you how many locations fall within that range. For example, there are twelve states that have sales between $74,000 and $388,000.

Ranged map types have different options for calculating the beginning and end point of each range. When you select the Ranged type in the Map Expert, the bottom section changes so that you can set these options. Figure 14-6 shows how this looks.

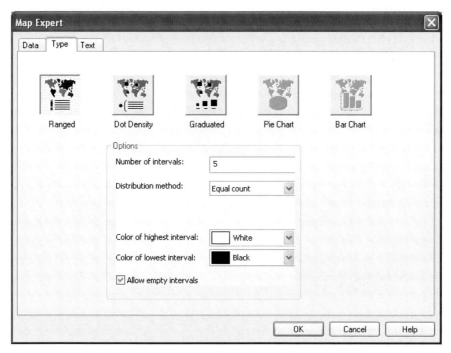

**Figure 14-6. Ranged map type options.**

The first and second options, Number of Intervals and Distribution Method, work together. The first option determines how many intervals to use. If you have a large number of areas getting mapped, increasing the number of intervals makes it easier to differentiate between the groups. The second option, Distribution Method, determines how the range of values is calculated. You can choose between Equal Count, Equal Range, Natural Break, and Standard Deviation.

The Equal Count option sets the range so that each group has an equal number of areas that it accounts for. The option Equal Ranges looks at the overall range of values to choose and breaks them up mathematically. Thus, each range spans the same number of data points. The option Natural Break calculates the average value for each range and tries to minimize the differences between them. The option Standard Deviation assigns intervals in such a way that the middle interval breaks at the mean (or average) of the data values. The intervals above and below the middle range are one standard deviation above or below the mean.

The remaining options let you choose the range of colors displayed on the map as well as whether to display intervals that don't have any data points to map.

## Dot Density Map Type

The Dot Density map type plots a dot on the map for every occurrence of a specified item. The areas of the map having more data points will have a larger number of dots displayed.

This can be useful for seeing trends based upon geographical characteristics such as proximity to a major city or coastal areas. Figure 14-7 shows an example of the dot density map. The legend in the top right corner tells you the quantity that each dot represents.

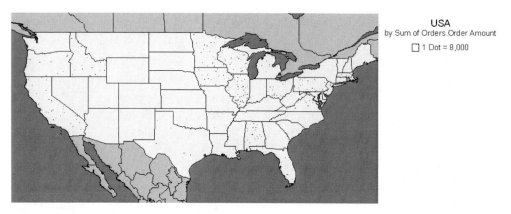

**Figure 14-7. Dot density map type.**

The only problem with the dot density report is that the dots are pretty small. The map in the above figure has the option to use the larger sized dots and they are still difficult to see.

## Graduated Map Type

The graduated map type is similar to the ranged map type in that each mapped area falls within a certain range and this range is plotted graphically at its location. The difference between the two is how they graphically represent that data point. The ranged type assigned a color to each range and fills each area with the appropriate color. The graduated type shows a single symbol on the map and changes the symbol's size based upon its value. The larger the value, the larger the symbol. Figure 14-8 shows an example of a graduated map type that uses circles to represent each range. You can see that this example only uses three dots to represent the ranges, and their sizes are quite different.

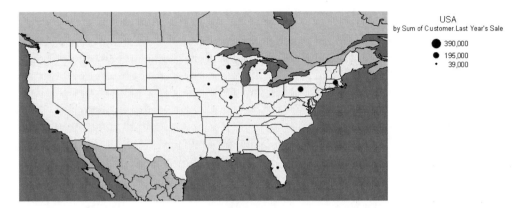

**Figure 14-8. Graduated map type showing US sales by state.**

Unlike the ranged map type, the graduated type doesn't give you the ability to specify ranges for the symbol size. You have to accept what Crystal Reports chooses. You only get to pick what the symbol looks like. By clicking on the Customize button in the Options section, you get the Symbol Style dialog box shown in Figure 14-9.

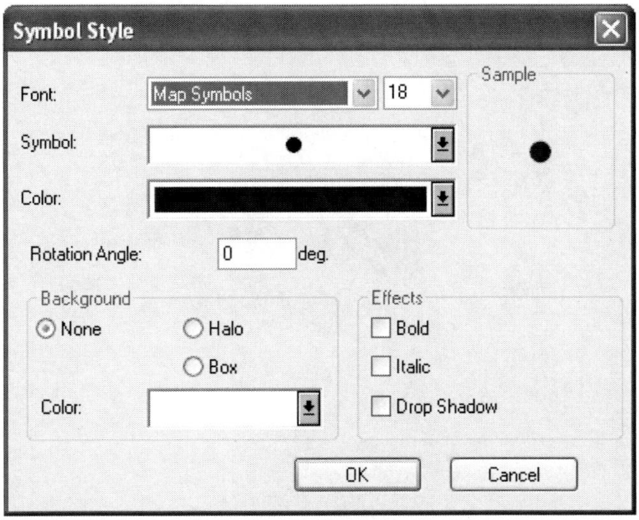

**Figure 14-9. Customize the graduated symbol.**

This dialog box lets you select the font, font size, symbol and color. You can also set different effects such as the symbol's rotation, if it has a halo or box around it, and whether it is bold, italic or has a drop shadow. This gives you the opportunity to customize the symbol to some degree.

## Pie Chart Map Type

The pie chart map type shows how each data item compares to all the other data items being mapped. In other words, each item mapped is given a different percentage of the pie's shape. The pie can display data in two different ways: by area or by category. If you map by area, then the pie chart assigns one segment of the pie to each location within that area. You can look at the pie chart and see which locations have the greatest allocation. You can also map the data by category within each area. For example, the categories could be based on product sales and the pie chart would assign one segment for each product. You can look at the map and see which products have the greatest percentage of sales in each area.

To tell the Map Expert which field to use for comparison (e.g. product type, location, etc.), use the On Change Of property on the Data tab. We'll look at that in more detail in Tutorial 14-2. Figure 14-10 is an example of a pie chart map type.

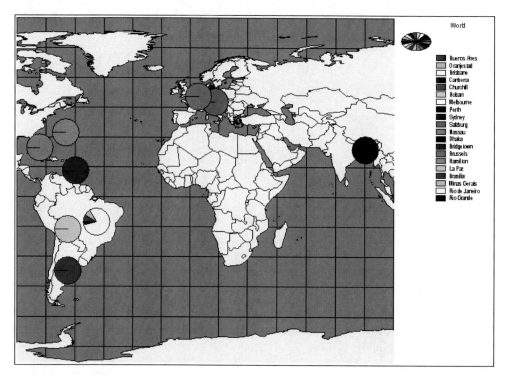

**Figure 14-10. Pie chart map type.**

## Bar Chart Map Type

The bar chart map type is similar to the pie chart map type in that a bar chart is displayed on top of each area. The difference between the two is that the bar chart doesn't show a percentage of the whole. Instead, each bar shows a scalar representation of each value. Just like a typical bar chart, taller bars represent larger values. Bar chart types are also useful for showing values as they change over time. For example, you could see whether the sales in an area have improved over the past decade.

Just like the pie chart, use the On Change Of property on the Data tab to specify which field to use for mapping the x-axis (e.g. product type, date, etc.).

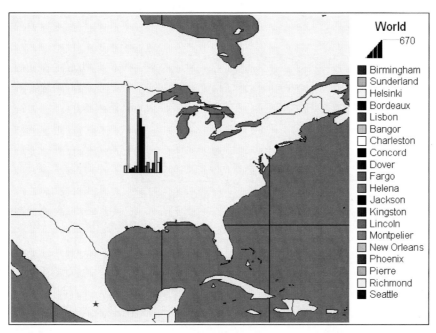

**Figure 14-11. A bar chart map with bars that represent different cities.**

# Setting the Map Text

The last step of creating a map is setting the text. You can set the map title and change the text above the map legend. The Text tab is the third tab of the Map Expert.

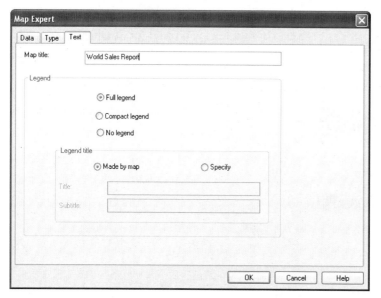

Figure 14-12. Setting the map text with the Text tab of the Map Expert.

This is a pretty simple tab without many options on it. The first option is the Map Title. This displays the title in the top center of the map. Below the Map Title is the Legend section. You can set the size of the legend as well as the text that is displayed. You are allowed two lines to display information.

Although putting the map title in the top center of the map is a perfectly good location for the title, it can sometimes get in the way as you zoom in on different countries and move the map around. For an example of how the map title initially looks, see Figure 14-13.

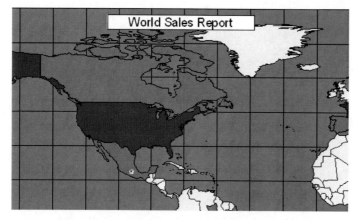

Figure 14-13. Example showing the title on the map.

Rather than putting the title on the Map Title, I prefer putting it with the map legend instead. This locates the title to the side of the map and doesn't run the risk of blocking any important geographical data as the user navigates around the map. Not only that, but you can show a title and sub-title.

# Tutorial 14-1. Adding a Map to your Report

Let's walk through two tutorials of how to add a map to a new report. You'll see that you can quickly create a map in just a few simple steps. We are going to create a map that shows Last Year Sales value for each country.

1.  From the Start Page, create a new blank report using the Xtreme.mdb database and select the Customer table. Click the OK button to close the Database Expert and you should now be looking at a blank report in design view.

2.  To add a map to the report, choose the menu options Insert > Map. Alternatively, you can click the Insert Map button.

3.  When the Map Expert opens, you are going to leave the default options of placing the map in the report header and using the Advanced tab.

4.  For the data fields, click on the field Customer.Country and move it to the section Geographic Field.

5.  Also move the field Customer.Country to the section On Change Of.

6.  For the summary value, move the field Customer.Last Years Sales to the section Map Values. This tells Crystal Reports to summarize last year's sales amounts for each country, and it completes all the data needed for your map.

7.  Click on the Type tab and make sure the Ranged type is selected. We're not concerned about how the groups of ranges are calculated, so we'll leave the default options alone and let Crystal Reports set the ranges.

8.  Click on the Text tab and leave the Map Title blank.

9.  For the Legend Title, click the Specify radio button and enter the text Last Year Sales by Country on the first line.

10. Click the OK button to close the Map Expert and preview the report. It should look similar to the following map.

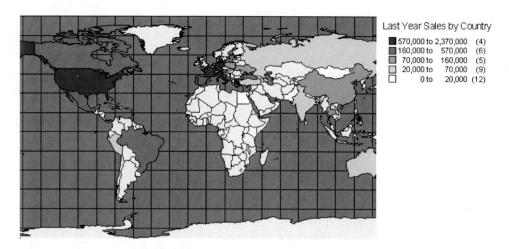

Now that you've made this initial report, you can go back and play with the other options. You can change how the ranges are calculated, see what a Graduated map looks like, etc.

### Caution

As you work with a map and tweak it to make it better, be aware that sometimes Crystal Reports will reset your settings. For example, you could be working with a Dot Density map of just US Cities and things are looking pretty good. Then you decide to change the value to summarize on. After making your change you preview the report and see that the map is now of the entire world. Not only that, but instead of Dot Density, it is now a Ranged map type. You have to go back and redo your settings. You should be aware of this quirk so that you don't think you did something wrong.

## Tutorial 14-2. Mapping with Pie Charts

For the second tutorial, let's get a little fancy and create a map type that plots multiple values: the pie chart. We learned earlier that the pie chart and bar chart types are only available when the Data tab has different fields for Geographic Area and On Change Of. By using a third data field, we can plot values against a category. Let's see how this works by mapping the total sales by city against multiple product types. We'll use a pie chart to see what percentage of sales each product has within a state. Since it is a pie chart, the percentages must add up to 100% for each state. In the second part of this tutorial, we will change the map type to a bar chart to see how it maps total sales dollars for each product rather than percent of total sales.

1.  Create a blank report using the Xtreme.mdb database.

2. We want to show sales based on product type and city. This information is spread out across many tables and requires them all to be linked together. Add the following tables to the report: Customer, Orders, Orders Detail, Product, and Product Type.

3. Check the Links to make sure all tables have been linked together by their primary IDs (if you selected all the correct tables in Step 2, then this should be done automatically). Click the OK button to save the table info.

   Before creating the map, we first need to create a formula that tracks sales by product. The table Orders Detail tracks how many products were ordered and what each one cost, but not the total amount. Let's create the formula to do that now.

4. Create a new formula and call it **Product Sales.**

5. In the Formula Workshop dialog box, use Crystal Syntax to enter the following formula:

   {Orders_Detail.Unit Price} * {Orders_Detail.Quantity}

6. Save and close the Formula Workshop.

7. Now let's create the map and we'll use the Product Sales formula in it. Select the menu items Insert > Map. This opens the Map Expert dialog box.

   On the Data tab, we want to map product sales by state. We also want to show how the sales compare to each other based on product type.

5. To map by state, select the field Customer.Region and assign it to the Geographic Area section.

6. To compare sales by product type, select the field Product_Type.Product Type Name and assign it to the On Change Of section.

7. To map the data on total sales, select the formula Product Sales that you created in step 4 and add it to the Map Values list. At this point, the Data tab of the Map Expert dialog box should look like the following:

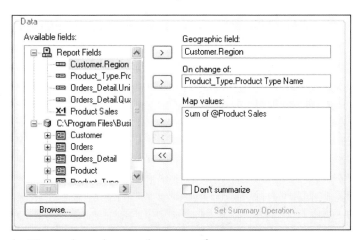

8. Click on the Type tab to choose what type of map to use.

Notice that the only map types available are the Pie Chart and Bar Chart. This is because we chose different fields for the Geographic Field and On Change Of fields.

9.  The default type is Pie Chart and we'll leave that as it is. Click the Ok button to save your changes and preview the map.

10. The default view is of the whole world and we only want to view the United States. Right-click on the report and select the menu option Resolve Mismatch. Choose the map USA.

11. Click the Ok button to save the current map and preview the report. It should look similar to the following figure.

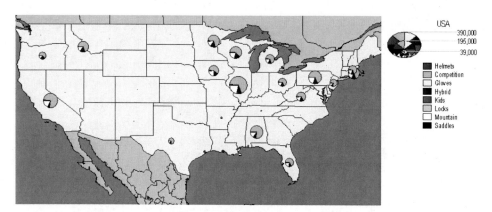

A couple of options you could play with are making the pie charts larger or turning off proportional sizing so that they are all the same size.

12. After you had a chance to review the pie chart map, and possibly modify it to see what happens, let's change the map type to bar chart. This lets you see how it differs from the pie chart. Right-click on the map and choose Map Expert.

13. Click on the type tab and choose Bar Chart. Preview the report and the pie charts have been replaced with bar charts. The length of each bar is indicative of the total sales for each product type.

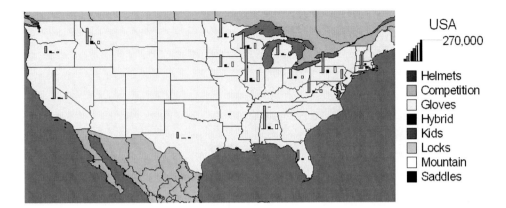

# Viewing the Map

When viewing the map on a computer, the reader has many options for changing the map and drilling down into more depth.[61] The first thing to notice is that when viewing the report, the two visible map related objects are the map itself and the legend. However, when you click on the map object, then the map navigator appears in the bottom right hand corner. The map navigator is only visible when the map object is selected.

If by chance, the map navigator doesn't appear, then you can enable it by right-clicking on the map and selecting Map Navigator from the pop-up menu. If you deliberately don't want the map navigator to be shown, then go back to the pop-up menu and unselect that option.

## Using the Map Navigator

The map navigator makes it easy to change the current view of the map. You can zoom in or out, and pan the view in different directions. The map navigator gives you a small-scale version of the map and shows a small box on top of it that designates the portion of the map you are currently viewing. An example of the map navigator is shown in Figure 14-14.

---

[61] Of course, when the map is printed on paper the only thing you can do is view the current image.

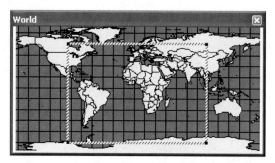

**Figure 14-14. A close-up view of the Map Navigator.**

As you can see in this figure, there is an outline of a box on top of the overall map. This outline defines the perimeter of the viewable area. By putting the mouse on the corners of the box, you can change the dimensions to be either smaller or larger. If you make the box smaller, you are zooming in on a particular region of the map. If you make the box larger, you are zooming out. Notice that you can only change the size of this box by dragging the corners - you can't use the top or side edges to do this. This limitation ensures that the box keeps the correct proportions.

The box outline is also used for panning to a different location on the map. If you move the mouse anywhere within the boundary of the box, then the mouse changes to a crosshairs icon. By holding down the mouse button, you can move the box around and it pans the larger map to the new location.

An interesting thing about the map navigator is that it isn't attached to the map. Even though it appears in the bottom right-hand corner by default, it can be placed anywhere on the map. You can move it higher so that it is closer to the report legend, or even move it on top of the map if that makes navigating it easier.

All the navigational tools provided by the map navigator are also available on the map's pop-up menu. By right-clicking on the map, the pop-up menu has the equivalent functionality for everything we've discussed. To zoom in or out, choose the appropriate menu option and the mouse cursor changes to a magnifying glass. Click anywhere on the map to zoom on that region. If you want to change the viewing area, select the Pan menu option and the cursor changes to a left-right arrow. Use this arrow by clicking on the map and holding down the mouse button to drag the map around.

## Changing the Geographical Area Displayed

The default view displayed on the map is of the entire world. In many circumstances, you need to see a much smaller and more specific geographical area. For example, if your company only sells products in North America, then that is the only portion of the map you want to see. Showing Europe on your report would be extraneous information and would clutter up the map. Crystal Reports gives you many options for setting the geographical area to display.

To set a new geographical area on the map, right-click on the map and select the menu option Resolve Mismatch.[62] This opens the Resolve Mismatch dialog box on the Change Map tab. In the lower left corner is a list of the maps to choose from. This list is pretty extensive and includes maps such as Asia, Australia, Australia Capitols, Europe, France, Germany, etc. You can scroll through this list to see all the options.

On the bottom right side of the dialog box is a preview of the map to be displayed. As you click on the different maps, you get to see what they look like in the preview window before saving it. This dialog box is shown in Figure 14-15.

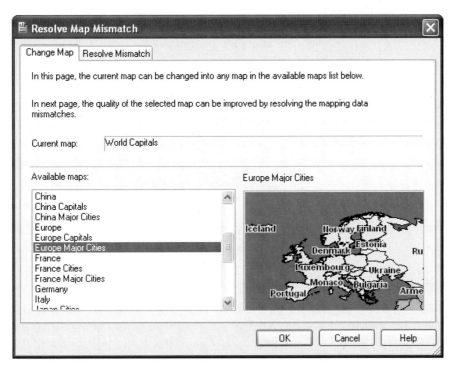

**Figure 14-15. The Change Map tab lets you preview available maps.**

Once you find the map that shows the geographical area you need, click the OK button to close the dialog box. The map is updated to show the new location.

# Resolving Unmatched Map Areas

When choosing the field to map to the Geographical Area section in the Map Expert, you have to make sure that the data in that field is going to be what Crystal Reports expects.

---

[62] Unfortunately, there isn't a separate menu option for setting the geographic area. It is part of the Resolve Mismatch dialog box functionality. Thus, you just have to memorize where it is.

The names of cities, states and countries have to be exact. If there is any incorrect data, or something isn't spelled right, then Crystal Reports has no idea where to map the data. To correct this, there is a dialog box that lets you specify which data belongs to which geographical areas. The Resolve Map Mismatch dialog box is shown in Figure 14-16.

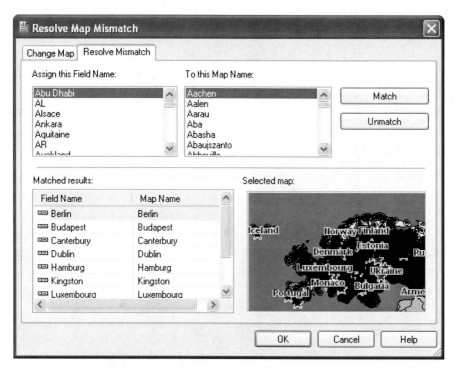

Figure 14-16. The Resolve Mismatch dialog box makes corrections.

To open this dialog box, right-click on the map and select the menu option Resolve Mismatch. When the dialog box opens, click on the second tab, Resolve Mismatch. The top portion of the dialog box is where you fix the problem names. The list on the left side is the existing data in your table that doesn't have a matching name for the current map view. The list on the right side is all the possible names that Crystal Reports has in its database for the current map view. The list at the bottom is all the names in the table that are correctly matched with a corresponding geographical area.

To match names on the map, scroll through the list on the left side and click on the item that needs matching. Then scroll through the list on the right and find the area that it should be matched with. Click the Match button to match them up and they are added to the list of matched items at the bottom. If you match up two items and later decide this isn't correct, then click on the appropriate row in the bottom list and click the Unmatch button. This removes them from the bottom list and puts them back at the top in the list of unmatched items.

# All Maps are not Created Equal

One thing that might cause you problems when you start changing the map view is that not all maps are created equal. What I mean by this is that not all maps have the same level of detail in them. Picking maps that are larger in scope (e.g. the whole world) gives you a macro view of the data. Picking smaller maps (e.g. just the U.S.) gives you detail on a smaller scale. For example, if you choose the World map, then you will only see your data displayed by country. If you try to display the data about the cities within each country, then Crystal Reports won't know how to map the information. In fact, if you go to the Resolve Map Mismatch dialog box, you'll see that all the cities are unmatched and Crystal Reports doesn't know what to do with them. Now, if you decide to change the map to the U.S., then all the cities will map fine. Since this covers a smaller geographic area than the world map, you get more finite mapping. You have to be cautious when choosing the map to display and test it out to make sure it is appropriate for what you want to show.

Since each map has a different scope, there are circumstances where you might see Crystal Reports displaying summary values based on country when you wanted to see it by city. Again, this is because the map scale is too large and it doesn't even have city information available to know how to map it.

If it seems like Crystal Reports is ignoring a lot of the data, or it is summarizing incorrectly, then go to the Resolve Map Mismatch dialog box and see if the data you want to map doesn't have a match. Assuming the geographic names are correct (and there aren't a bunch of typos), this tells you that you picked a map with the wrong scope. Look at what type of data it can't resolve (e.g. cities, states, etc.) and change your map accordingly and that should give you better results.

# Changing Map Layers

When you initially view a map you are looking at it from a very high level. If you use the Zoom In option to make the map larger, you are effectively getting closer to the map. As you get closer and closer you will keep seeing more information on the map. It's as if you are jumping out of a plane with a parachute and as you get closer to the ground you keep seeing more details. Crystal Reports shows you this detail information using layers. As you zoom in on the map, new layers get displayed.

Crystal Reports lets you choose which layers to show on a map as well as the order that they are shown in. The Layer Control dialog box gives you an interface for seeing which layers are available for each map and setting their properties. It is shown in Figure 14-17.

**Figure 14-17. The Layer Control dialog box lets you modify visible layers.**

To open the Layer Control dialog box, right-click on the map object in preview mode and select Layers. To change the order in which the layers appear, click on the layer you want to change and click the Up or Down buttons.

You can also add additional layers or remove existing ones. To add new layers, click the Add button and navigate to the installation folder:

C:\Program Files\Business Objects\MapInfo Mapx\Maps.

In this folder are all the available map layers. Select the one you want and click the OK button to add it to the list. If you don't want a particular layer anymore, select it and click the Remove button. You can also hide the layer, but not completely remove it, by unchecking the Visible property.

As the user zooms in on the map, the point at which a new layer becomes visible is controlled by its zoom range. You can set the zoom range by clicking on the layer you want to modify and then clicking on the Display button. This opens the Display Properties dialog box shown in Figure 14-18.

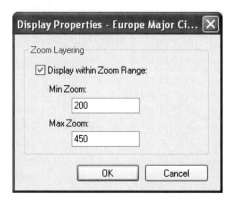

**Figure 14-18. Setting the display properties of a layer.**

The two numerical values set the min and max zoom ranges in which the layer appears. If you uncheck the option Display Within Zoom Range, then the layer will be visible at all times.

# Distributing Reports

Reports are written to communicate information to people. This could be as simple as a list of the CDs you have in your music collection or as complex as a set of financial statements for a multi-national corporation. While these reports can be for your own personal use, many reports are for others to read. They can be passed out to others in the office, displayed on the internet, or used to bill clients. It's important that you find the best way to get your reports to the people who want to read them.

How reports are distributed has been changing over the past two decades. In the past, reports were always printed out and distributed on paper. But in the days of the internet, this has become archaic. Even the most secure institutions now give you incentives for replacing paper based reports such as your monthly credit card statement and financial portfolios with an online-only version. In fact, many people have speculated that one day we will work in a 'paperless environment' where everything is done electronically. While we certainly aren't at that point yet, paper reports are quickly losing favor among companies and their customers.

Crystal Reports gives you many options for distributing your reports. While printing them out is the most obvious of the different methods, you can also send them via email, display them on the internet, and export them to file formats that can be used by other applications.

## Exporting Reports

You can export reports in a variety of formats that are displayed by common applications that most people already have on their computers (Adobe Acrobat PDF, MS Excel, MS Word, etc.). This lets people see and understand your data without owning a copy of Crystal Reports. For example, the PDF format is the most common way of presenting data via the web. In fact, it has become the de facto standard and most users already have the Adobe Acrobat viewer installed on their computer. If you want to deliver reports that let users have dynamic interaction with the data, you can export them to an Excel spreadsheet and give your users the ability to perform more advanced data analysis.

Crystal Reports gives you eleven types of export formats to choose from. Not only can you choose between which application to export to (Adobe Acrobat, Excel, etc.), but you can also choose whether the export should focus on keeping the layout intact or just exporting the raw data.

If users are primarily using the report for viewing, keeping the layout and format intact is of primary importance. You want to make sure the exported file looks as close to the original report as possible. Aspects such as font size, shading, graphics, and object placement should remain unchanged as much as possible.

If the user wants to perform analysis on the data or import it into another application, the report layout is no longer important and instead you want to export the raw data. You want each record in the report to have its own line in the export file. In fact, having formatting in the export actually hinders being able to use the data because it is extraneous information.

If you want the export to focus on keeping the report layout intact, this is referred to as page-based. If you want to export raw data for analysis, this is called record-based. Let's look at which export formats are page-based and which are record-based.

**Table 15-1. Export formats**

| Format | Page or Record | File Extension |
| --- | --- | --- |
| Adobe Acrobat PDF | Page | .PDF |
| Crystal Reports | Page | .RPT |
| HTML 3.2/4.0 | Page | .HTML |
| MS Excel | Page | .XLS |
| MS Excel – Data only | Record | .XLS |
| MS Word | Page | .RTF |
| MS Word – Editable/RTF | Page | .RTF |
| ODBC | Record | n/a |
| Record Style | Record | .REC |
| Separated Values – CSV | Record | .CSV |
| Tab Separated | Record | .TTX |
| Text | Record | .TXT |
| XML | Record | .XML |

Note: Cross-tabs are not supported in CSV

Exporting reports is fairly easy and it's a nearly identical process for each format type. To export a report, select the menu options File > Export > Export Report. This opens the dialog box in Figure 15-1.

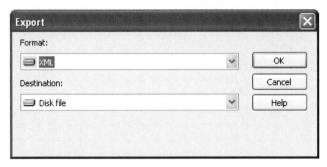

**Figure 15-1. Export dialog box.**

The first dropdown list lets you choose a format type. The different types are listed in table 15-1 and we'll talk about each in detail in the following sections. The second dropdown list lets you choose the destination. Most of the time you will probably export it to a disk file. However, you can also export it to an application or as an attachment to an email. If you export it to an application, it saves the report as a temporary file and then automatically opens the file with the chosen application. It uses the file extension to determine which application to open it with. For example, if you export to an .XLS file, then Excel is opened and the export file is automatically loaded. If you save it with a .TXT extension, then Notepad is opened and loads the export file.

Once the application is opened, you can work with it to make changes and do analysis. Just remember to save the file yourself when you are finished because Crystal Reports only saved it to a temporary file and that file is gone after you close the application.

If you choose to export the report as an email attachment, it creates the file and opens the Send Mail dialog box that prompts you for the recipient's email address and the subject and message information.

After selecting the export format type on the dialog box, click the OK button. A second dialog box appears that prompts you to enter export options. We'll learn about the export options in the next section. After entering the options, click the OK button to export the file.

If you find yourself entering the same options for a particular format type, you can set default values that will be used each time. By selecting the menu items File > Export > Report Export Options, you can open the export options dialog box and set the properties you use most often. The next time you export a report, these settings will already be made and you can simply click the OK button to export the file. Of course, you still have the option of making changes to the dialog box if you want to temporarily override the default values you set earlier.

Each export format type uses a different options dialog box because each has a different list of requirements. While there are similarities between all the dialog boxes (e.g. choosing the page range), each dialog box has unique features and needs to be explained independently.

The following is a list of the different format types that Crystal Reports supports.

- Adobe Acrobat PDF

- Crystal Reports

- HTML

- MS Excel 97-2000

- MS Excel 97-2000 Data Only

- MS Word / Editable RTF

- ODBC Databases

- Record Style

- Separated Values

- Tab Separated Text

- Text

- Report Definition

- XML

Let's look at the details of each format type and see how they affect the export output.

## Adobe Acrobat PDF

PDF files have become the de facto file format for electronic document distribution. It is the one format you can assume that everyone's computer can read.[63] Adobe's software lets you view PDF files stored on your hard drive or directly off the internet.

Crystal Reports has been exporting reports to the PDF format for many years and they can produce a replica of the original report. As such, this is a report-based export because the report layout and formatting are preserved exactly.

| Tip |
| --- |
| In version 10 and XI of Crystal Reports, when you export to a PDF file the font size is reduced by 5% from what is on the report. This helps avoid truncating fields in the final PDF file. If you wish to have Crystal Reports keep the font size at the original size specified in the report, you have to add a field to the |

---

[63] For those who don't have the Adobe Acrobat Reader installed on their computer, you can download it from the company's website at www.Adobe.com.

Windows Registry. Run the Regedit.exe program to create the following field and assign a value of 1 to it:

HKEY_CURRENT_USER\SOFTWARE\Business Objects\Suite 11.0\
Crystal Reports\Export\PDF \ForceLargerFonts.

The export options dialog box for PDF files is very simple. It is shown in Figure 15-2.

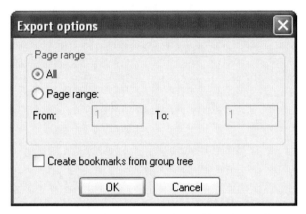

**Figure 15-2. PDF export options (for Crystal Reports XI R2).**

The only option you can set is the page range. You can either print the entire report or set the beginning and ending page range.

 Figure 15-2 is the Export Options dialog box from Crystal Reports XI R2. The new option that comes with the R2 edition is the ability to create bookmarks in the PDF file from the group tree. If you have not installed R2, you will not be able to create bookmarks in the PDF file.

## Crystal Reports

Exporting to the Crystal Reports format is the same as saving the report and using the Save Data with Report option. There are no export options to choose from because the entire report is exported.

## HTML

Exporting to HTML is inherently different from exporting to the other file formats. HTML files are meant to be viewed in a web browser and this can impose certain requirements on how you present the data to the user. The first requirement is that you have a web server that can host the files. Most companies today have an online presence so this usually isn't a problem. What could be a challenge is getting the web master to agree to host the files for you. You will most likely want a special area of the site designated for hosting all the corporate reports. Once you have decided that it is okay to put the reports online, you also need to consider whether they need to be located in a secure area of the website. Many reports have sensitive data that you don't want the general public to have access to. As you can see, exporting reports to HTML involves making a lot of decisions that go beyond just saving the file on your hard drive.

There is one aspect of exporting HTML files that make them unique from other file formats: the output looks differently depending upon which browser you are using. As the internet has evolved over the years, so have the browsers that are used to display web pages. Different browsers can display the exact same information but look completely different. This has been referred to as the "Browser Wars" because each company tries to establish their dominance in the browser marketplace and be the one to set what the standards should be. Of course, this has resulted in untold confusion for web designers trying to build web pages because it is almost impossible to create a web page that looks the same in different browsers. This also wreaks havoc for users trying to figure out how to best view different web pages.[64]

The common practice for creating websites is to break out users into two general groups and decide which group your users fall into. You can categorize users as either HTML 3.2 or HTML 4.0. If you expect that your users have older computers and haven't updated their browser in many years (e.g. prior to Netscape Navigator 4's release), then export to HTML 3.2. If your users have fairly recent computers and have updated their browsers, you can export to HTML 4.0.

Exporting the HTML 3.2 is the safest choice, but you lose formatting when doing so. Since you are using older technology, there aren't as many features available for displaying data. Browsers back then were even less compliant than they are today. HTML 4.0 uses DHTML (Dynamic HTML) to give you greater precision for placing individual report objects on the web page and better formatting. Your reports will look much better when exporting to HTML 4.0. Of course, no matter which format you choose to export to, you need to test the output using the browsers that you think your users will have.

Set the HTML version you want to export to by selecting the menu options File > Export > Export Report. After making your selection you are presented with the HTML export options dialog box shown in Figure 15-3.

---

[64] For me personally, I always use the latest version Firefox for surfing the internet. But just last night I was on a site that had garbage all over it and I had to copy the URL into Internet Explorer to view it properly. I doubt if we'll ever get to the point where the major browser vendors actually agree to be compliant with each other.

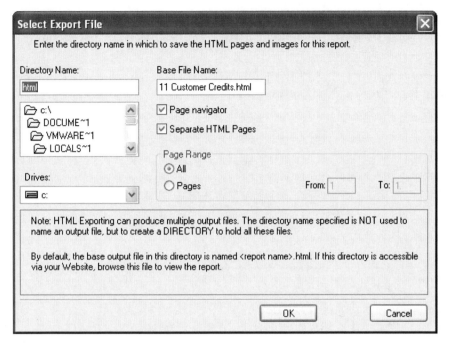

**Figure 15-3. HTML export options.**

The first option is to set where you would want to save the HTML file. This works a little differently than the typical Save As dialog box that you are familiar with. Rather than specifying an existing directory you want to save the file in, you specify a new directory you want created. When you click the OK button it creates the new directory and saves the files to it. If you enter a directory name that already exists, then it can potentially overwrite any existing files with the same file names.

The two input areas below the directory name let you choose the drive and location where the new directory should be created.

| Note |
| --- |

When setting where the file should be stored, if you have access to the web server via the network, you can have Crystal Reports export directly to the web server. This typically isn't the best idea because you always want to test report output prior to putting it on the production server. I suggest that you first save it to your local hard drive and testing it with different web browsers installed on your computer. Once you feel that the report is ready, you can copy it to the web server for public use.

On the right side of the dialog box is where you specify the file properties. The Base File Name input box is where you type in the name that you want the HTML file exported as.

Below that you can specify if you want to use page navigation links and whether you want the HTML page to be broken up into multiple pages. Let's look at these two options in more detail.

The Page Navigator option lets you have four navigational hyperlinks at the bottom of each page: First Page, Previous Page, Next Page and Last Page. This is shown in Figure 15-4.

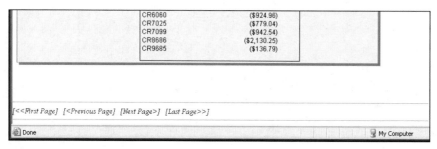

Figure 15-4. HTML page navigation.

The user clicks on the hyperlinks to navigate between the different pages. Notice that there isn't a way to jump to a specific page elsewhere in the report. You can only move between consecutive pages or jump to the beginning or end of the report. However, as we'll see in a minute, there is a trick to easily navigate to any page in the report. If you decide not to put navigational links at the bottom of each page, you will have to create your own method of allowing the user to navigate between pages in the report. One idea would be to create a Table of Contents page with each page listed as a hyperlink. When the user is finished reading the page they can click the browser's Back button to return to the main page.

The second option lets you choose between exporting the report to a single page or to multiple pages. If you export to multiple pages, Crystal Reports takes the file name you gave it and appends consecutive numbers to it for each report page. So, if you told it to name the file 'CustomerSales.HTML' then the first page would be 'CustomerSales1.HTML', the second page would be 'CustomerSales2.HTML', and so on. Since the page names correspond to the page number, this makes it possible to jump to a particular page number without using the navigational links at the bottom of the page. Just enter a new page number in the browser's address bar to jump to a specific page. Although this is easy to do, it certainly isn't obvious and not all users will be familiar with it. You might want to mention this trick somewhere on your report.

If you export the report as a single page, then there will just be one file called 'CustomerSales.HTML'. The benefit to the user is that all the data is on the same page and it doesn't require any navigational links. The drawback is that if this is a very large report, then the user has to scroll up and down to read the entire report. This can be inconvenient for lengthy reports.

Although you are exporting to a single web page, Crystal Reports will not reformat the report as if it were printed on one page. Instead, the individual report pages are printed on one large web page. Let's see how this is different from changing a report's paper size and sending it to the printer. Consider that you print a report using a paper size of 8 ½ x 11 and it prints 40 records on each page. You then change the paper size to be 8 ½ x 14 in landscape mode and now it prints 60 records on each page. By making the paper size longer, Crystal Reports reformatted the report to take advantage of the extra space. Exporting to HTML doesn't work this way.

When exporting to a single HTML page, Crystal Reports doesn't consider the HTML page to be one long page and format it so that all the records appear on a single continuous page. Instead, it effectively takes a snapshot of each of the pages in the report and shows them consecutively one after the other. You can almost think of them as 'virtual pages'. It even repeats the page header and page footer over and over. If you have the Page Navigator option turned on, hyperlinks will be shown after each page footer that jump to the next 'virtual page'. Of course, there are times when you want this (e.g. printing invoices) and there are times when you would rather have all the rows printed consecutively without showing page breaks. Regardless, this is the way it works and you should be aware of it so that you know what to expect.

After setting the file name and determining how to handle page navigation and multiple pages, the last option is setting the page range. Below that is an informational area where Crystal Reports gives you some notes to help clarify what the options do. Click the OK button to export the file and test it in your browser.

# MS Excel 97-2000

Excel is the most popular spreadsheet program for Windows. It makes it easy for the everyday user to take a large amount of data and perform all types of analysis on it as well as creating pivot tables and charting the results. Exporting Crystal Reports to Excel is very popular because it lets you, the report designer, do the work of aggregating a large amount of data into a user friendly format. This makes it easy for an end user to get the report data in an Excel spreadsheet and work with it. If the end user was responsible for taking all the raw data and processing it directly in Excel, it would probably be too difficult for many people. Exporting from Crystal Reports lets less technical users benefit from your Crystal Reports expertise.

The ideal way to export a report to Excel is to do some planning prior to creating the report. By making some design decisions prior to creating the report, the export process can go much easier and give you more accurate results. Of course, you can send any type of report to Excel, but some reports might not convert as well as others. The best thing for you to do is first read an excellent whitepaper written by Business Objects. The 16 page file "scr_ExportExcel.pdf" gives expert advice on report design, shows both good and bad examples, and gives you troubleshooting advice. The web address for the whitepaper is:[65]

http://support.businessobjects.com/communitycs/technicalpapers/scr_exportexcel.pdf

If you don't have time to read their whitepaper, here are a few highlights from it.

- Think of your report as a spreadsheet and place report objects accordingly. Objects should be placed on the report using a grid format and place them side by side without overlapping.

- Turn on rulers and have report objects snap to the guidelines. By simulating the appearance of a spreadsheet in design mode, it is easier to make the report fit the format of a spreadsheet and line up accordingly.

- Give objects in the same row the same height. By using objects with consistent heights, the Excel rows can appear next to each other without creating additional white space between rows.

When exporting to Excel, the export options dialog box lets you modify how to convert report objects into excel columns. It is shown in Figure 15-5.

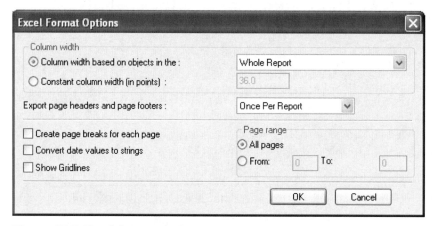

**Figure 15-5. Excel format options.**

The top portion sets the column widths. You can either have Crystal Reports analyze the report objects and best match the column widths for each cell, or you can simply set all the column widths to be a specific size. The option you choose is dependent upon your report layout. If the report prints out a series of similar numbers along each column, then you can use a fixed column width for the entire report. After the report is exported you can view it in Excel and it's very possible that you will only have to make minor changes for it to be

---

[65] Business Objects has been known to restructure their website and URLs will become extinct. If this address doesn't work, search their support site for the document "scr_exportexcel.pdf".

finalized. On the other hand, if the report prints a variety of data with different sized report objects, then you want Crystal Reports to format each column based upon the size of the report object.

When choosing the option to make the column widths based on the report objects, you can choose which report objects get priority for setting the column sizes. The default selection, whole report, evaluates the report objects in the report and sets the Excel columns to get the best match. If you choose a particular section (e.g. the Details section), then Crystal Reports gives a greater priority to those report objects when setting column width. In general, it's a good idea to use the Details section as the primary area for setting column widths since that is where the core data is located. But in many cases, Crystal Reports does a pretty good job of getting most report objects to fit onto the spreadsheet in a way that closely matches the original report.

The third option on the dialog box sets how often page headers and footers appear. You can either have them appear only at the top and bottom of the spreadsheet (i.e. just once for the entire file), or have them repeat throughout the report. The benefit of having them repeat is that the spreadsheet best mimics the look of the report. But if you are expecting to do data analysis in Excel, then don't repeat the header and footer because you want all the detail data to be together from the beginning to the end.

The lower portion of the dialog box gives you three more ways to format the report. The first option is to have Excel insert page breaks so that when you print the spreadsheet then the pages mimic the original report. The second option lets you convert dates to strings in their original format. Many times when Excel sees a date value in a field, it reformats it. If you find that Excel's reformatting is conflicting with how you want the dates to appear, enable this option. This forces Excel to show dates exactly how they are displayed on the report. The last option lets you enable or disable the display of gridlines in the spreadsheet. And of course, the dialog box also lets you set the page range to export.

## MS Excel 97-2000 Data Only

The reason most people want to export to Excel files is so that the end user can work with the data, create custom formulas, and perform their own analysis within the spreadsheet. In fact, many people find that all the additional formatting provided by Crystal Reports gets in the way of them doing this analysis. In these circumstances, it is ideal to just export the raw data to Excel and leave out all the extraneous information altogether. Crystal Reports lets you do this by giving you a data only option for exporting to Excel.

When choosing the data only export option of exporting to Excel, you are shown the export option dialog box shown in Figure 15-6.

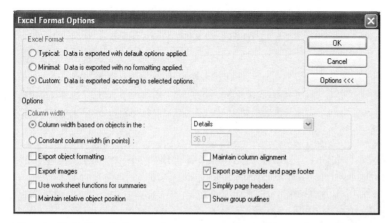

**Figure 15-6. Excel data only export options (from Crystal Reports XI R2).**

For pure data analysis you want to turn off all formatting possible. But depending upon the circumstance, some users might want some formatting included so that the data is easier to read and understand. It's your job to find the right balance of how much formatting should stay and how much should go. The export options in this dialog box are primarily concerned with how much formatting you want to exclude from being exported.

Let's start out by looking at the different formatting options at the bottom of the dialog box. This lists the details of what you can and can't include. Each of the options are listed below with a description of what they do.

The Export Object Formatting option lets you keep the formatting for each report object. This applies to the object's font, background color, etc.

The Export Images option includes images in your report.

The option Use Worksheet Functions For Summaries, tells Crystal Reports to attempt to convert the group summary formulas to their equivalent formulas in Excel. The benefit is that when the user changes the data in the Excel spreadsheet then the summaries get recalculated. If you disable this option, Crystal Reports stores the actual formula result in Excel. It is a static value and will not get updated when the user enters new numbers on the spreadsheet.

## Caution

Crystal Reports only converts summary formulas to worksheet functions when the summary is based on a database field. If the summary is based on a formula field, then this is too complicated for Crystal Reports to convert to an Excel formula and instead it just exports the summary result (the actual number). You also have to have the detail rows exported to the spreadsheet as well. If you suppress the detail section then there wouldn't be any data for the spreadsheet to calculate a summary formula on. Also note that grand total fields are never converted to Excel formulas.

The option Maintain Relative Object Position looks at how objects are positioned to each other. It will use blank columns to adjust the spacing to be as accurate as possible. This has the potential to insert empty values into certain columns so that the spreadsheet layout matches the report. Depending upon the report formulas you use, this could cause empty cells to generate incorrect results.

The option Maintain Column Alignment looks at columns and their related summary functions and keeps them in alignment on the spreadsheet.

The option Simplify Page Headers just exports a maximum of one line per header. If the header has more than one line, then only the bottom line is exported. If this option isn't selected, all the lines of the header are exported (but they are kept on a single row in the Excel spreadsheet).

> ## R2
> The last option on the Excel Format Options dialog box is Show Group Outlines. This is only available with the R2 edition. When the report is exported, it includes grouping information for use with Excel outline symbols to make navigating the spreadsheet data easier.

Now that you understand how the formatting options work, let's see how we go about selecting which ones we want. At the top of the dialog box are three options. They let you set how much customization of the formatting you want to apply. The first option exports with the default options enabled. These default options are Use Worksheet Functions for Summaries, Maintain Column Alignment, Export Page Header and Footer, and Simplify Page Headers.

The second choice, minimal exporting with no formatting only uses the option Use Worksheet Functions For Summaries. It is the bare-bones exporting of raw data.

The third choice, custom exporting according to selected options, lets you select the options at the bottom of the dialog box according to your own preferences. No pre-selected options are chosen and only the ones you click on are used.

# MS Word / Editable RTF

Exporting to MS Word gives you the ability to open your report in a Word document. You can make changes to the document and print out a new report. The one unique aspect of the export is that the file does not use a .DOC file extension. Instead, it uses the .RTF file format which is compatible with Word.

Similar to Excel, there are two export options when exporting to Word. The first export type, Word – RTF, creates an exact replica of the report in the Word document. It does this by placing report objects inside text frames. This gives it the ability to use precise placement of report objects. This is ideal for forms that are printed onto paper and given to the user for filling out by hand. They can use the blank spaces to fill in the information. Unfortunately, using text objects to format report objects isn't conducive to using the computer for making changes to the report document. It is too restrictive for data input.

Crystal Reports gives you a second export option, MS Word – Editable RTF, for making online changes. This export type puts the report object's values in the document as text lines. This makes it easier to make changes within the document because the values are put onto the report as if you had typed them yourself.

The drawback to the Editable RTF export is that the Word document isn't an exact match to the original report layout. By putting the report values on text lines, you lose some of the object formatting and the layout can be shifted a little. The document can still be similar to the original report, but not exact. The non-editable RTF option gives you much more accuracy. You can think of editable RTF making it easy to make changes on the computer whereas the original Word RTF export is good for printing forms to be filled out on paper.

The export options dialog box is very simplistic. For exporting to Word, you only get to set the page range to print. If you export to editable RTF, you also get the option of inserting hard page breaks at the end of each page.

## ODBC Databases

Crystal Reports lets you export your report data into any ODBC compliant database. It creates a new record in the database for every detail row in the report. When exporting the data, it not only creates a field for every column in the detail section, but a field is also created for each report object. This includes the report header and footer, page header and footer, and the group header and footer. It exports the column headers along with the data. Since the column headers are static text objects, the data doesn't change. The same data is repeated on every row. This gives you a lot of extra data that is probably worthless to you. After exporting the data, you will want to review the table design and clean it up where necessary. You'll probably delete a lot of extraneous columns before you have the raw data you need.

The export options dialog box for ODBC databases is very simplistic. The first dialog box lets you select which ODBC connection to export to. This lists all ODBC connections that you have installed on your computer. Choose the ODBC connection you want and then you are either prompted for the file name (if it is a file based database like MS Access) or the table name. The default table name is CREXPORT, but you can change it to something more descriptive of your report data.

## Record Style, Separated Values, Tab Separated Text, Text

Crystal Reports gives you a variety of ways to export reports to text files. The benefit to exporting to text files is that virtually any program that lets you import data can read text files. They are the least common denominator among software programs for sharing data.

The only drawback to using text files is figuring out the best way to format the data so that it can be imported by your program. The most common format that programs import is CSV (comma separated values). With the CSV format, commas are used to separate each field. Another popular format is tab separated. Let's look at each of the different types of text files that Crystal Reports exports to and find out how they differ.

---

### Caution

When Crystal Reports XI exports to CSV files, the page header is repeated at the beginning of each detail row in the report (it even happens when the Detail section is suppressed). To get around this problem, Business Objects recommends that you trick Crystal Reports by creating a false group header around the entire report and putting the report header fields in this new group header. Unfortunately, this is not always successful. If you want the detailed steps for doing this, go to the Business Objects support site (support.BusinessObjects.com) and search for the knowledge base article c2014451.[66] This has been fixed for Crystal Reports XI R2 and I suggest that you upgrade to it if you are exporting to CSV. The details of how to fix this are in the XI R2 note at the end of this section.

---

The Record Style format only exports fields from the group and detail sections. It does not export the other header and footer sections. It treats each field as a fixed length string and always uses that number of characters for the field. If the field doesn't need all the characters allocated to it, then it fills the remaining characters with spaces. For example, if a customer name can be up to 25 characters long but the name is only 11 characters long, then there will be 14 spaces saved with it.

When importing a record style text file into an external program, you usually tell the program how the record is structured. Since there are no separators between the fields, the program importing the file doesn't know when one field ends and the next field begins. Each record is just one long row of characters. You have to define the fields in the table by specifying the starting point and length of each field. Then the external program importing the data knows how to parse each field out of the record.

The Separated Values format exports fields from all sections of the report. This includes all the headers and footers (report, page, group) and the detail section. Each field is separated by a character that you specify. The most common character is the comma, but you could also use the Tab character or any other character you specify. The export options dialog box, shown in Figure 15-7, let's you set the separator as well as the character delimiter.

---

[66] Reading the user comments at the bottom of this page shows you how frustrated people have become with this problem

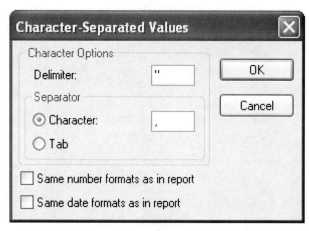

**Figure 15-7. Character-Separated Values export options dialog box.**

The top portion sets the delimiter used around strings. In most cases, you will surround a string value with two double quotes. However, if there is some other delimiter you wish to use, just enter it into the top input box. The second option is the separator between fields. It uses a comma by default, but you can specify any character or use the Tab character. The last two checkboxes let you set whether the number and date values are formatted exactly as they appear in the report.

The last two formats, Tab Separated Text and Text have a unique approach to exporting. They basically reprint the report as it appears within Crystal Reports. The output file mimics the layout of the report as it is designed. While the other formats we've discussed so far were more concerned with exporting raw data and all the data appears on a single row, these two formats create an output file that keeps that layout of the original report and is more visually appealing. The top of the file shows the report and page header and this is followed by the group headers and then the detail section. Lastly, all the footer sections are exported just like the regular report. Of course, even though the report layout is kept intact, the formatting is not exported because the file is just a basic text file.

There are two differences between the Tab Separated Text format and the Text format. The first separates each field with the tab character. So even though the report layout stays the same, all the fields are much closer together because they are only separated by the tab character. The Text format uses spaces to separate the fields from each other. Just like the record style format discussed earlier, each field has a fixed number of characters allocated to it and spaces are used to fill in the gaps. The text format is more visually appealing and "human friendly" because the extra spaces help position the fields with the same layout as the original report.

R2 Crystal Reports XI R2 has a new dialog box for exporting reports to the CSV format. It is shown in Figure 15-8 below.

The top portion of this dialog box has similar options as Figure 15-7. The bottom half has the new options. The Mode option gives you the option of

Standard Mode or Legacy Mode. The Mode option was created to resolve a common problem with previous versions of Crystal Reports. When exporting reports to CSV, the report header information is repeated at the beginning of each detail section. By choosing Standard Mode, this problem has been eliminated and the report header is no longer exported. If you choose Legacy Mode, the report header will be exported the same as it was in previous versions. In most cases, the new Standard Mode option will give you the best data exports.

The bottom half of the dialog box allows you to conditionally suppress sections from being exported to CSV. If you only want the detail data printed with no other section information, choose the Do Not Export option for all sections.

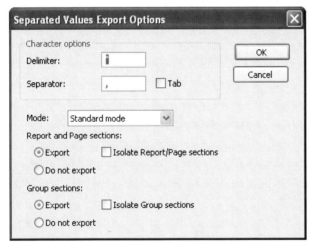

Figure 15-8. CSV export dialog box for Crystal Reports XI R2.

# Report Definition – Documenting Your Report

The Report Definition format documents your report structure. It lists every section of the report and details its structure. Every formula and field used within the report is documented within the report definition file. You can save this file in a common folder on the network so that anyone who needs to use the report can see the report's structure and how various formulas are built.

# XML

XML (eXtensible Markup Language) is quickly becoming the standard for data exchange between applications as well as sharing data among corporations. XML is popular because it is a self-defining file. It uses a hierarchy of elements and each element has tags and values to define them. You can export a report to XML and it builds a hierarchy of tags which match your report structure. For example, the following code is an excerpt from an XML export for the Details section.

```
- <FormattedAreaPair Level="2" Type="Details">
  - <FormattedArea Type="Details">
    - <FormattedSections>
      - <FormattedSection SectionNumber="0">
        - <FormattedReportObjects>
          - <FormattedReportObject xsi:type="CTFormattedField" Type="xsd:timeInstant" FieldName="{Orders.Order Date}">
              <ObjectName>TShipVia1</ObjectName>
              <FormattedValue>1/6/04</FormattedValue>
              <Value>2004-01-06T00:00:00</Value>
          </FormattedReportObject>
          - <FormattedReportObject xsi:type="CTFormattedField" Type="xsd:timeInstant" FieldName="{Orders.Ship Date}">
              <ObjectName>TOrderAmount1</ObjectName>
              <FormattedValue>08-January-2004</FormattedValue>
              <Value>2004-01-08T04:29:38</Value>
          </FormattedReportObject>
          - <FormattedReportObject xsi:type="CTFormattedField" Type="xsd:long" FieldName="{Orders.Order ID}">
              <ObjectName>TCity1</ObjectName>
              <FormattedValue>1143</FormattedValue>
              <Value>1143.00</Value>
          </FormattedReportObject>
          - <FormattedReportObject xsi:type="CTFormattedField" Type="xsd:decimal" FieldName="{Orders.Order Amount}">
              <ObjectName>TShipped1</ObjectName>
              <FormattedValue>$62.33</FormattedValue>
              <Value>62.33</Value>
          </FormattedReportObject>
        </FormattedReportObjects>
      </FormattedSection>
    </FormattedSections>
  </FormattedArea>
</FormattedAreaPair>
```

**Figure 15-9. XML excerpt defining the Details section.**

Notice how each line is indented as the levels get deeper. This shows the hierarchy of the elements. The first line defines a row in the Details section. Below that, it maps out the field names, their data type, and the value for that field. It does this for each field in that row of the detail section. This is repeated for every row on the report.

The biggest drawback to XML files is their size. As you might imagine, when even the smallest detail has to be written out within a complex hierarchy, the amount of information necessary to convey a report's information can grow dramatically. Don't be surprised if the XML file for a simple report is more than a megabyte in size.

Even though the file sizes can be huge, the benefit is that XML files are compatible with many programs. You can also use a CSS (Cascading Style Sheet) to define how each element is formatted. This lets you customize how the XML file is printed.

## Best Of The Forum

**Question:** I want my users to be able to export to PDF format, but not the MS Office formats. Since Word and Excel files can be modified, this lets them invalidate the data and it presents a security risk. Is it possible to keep the user from exporting to certain formats?

**Answer:** Yes, you can disable certain export features. When running the Crystal Reports installation on a computer, you can specify which export options are installed and which ones are not available.

# Internationalization

In today's world of global corporations, it is common for reports to be deployed to users in different countries. As a report designer, you want to create a single report and distribute it to all users without making any changes. Crystal Reports makes it possible for you to recognize the regional settings that the computer is running on and display report text with the appropriate language.

The function ContentLocale returns the current regional setting on the local computer. This can be found by going to the Windows Control Panel and selecting Date, Time, Language and Regional Options. The ContentLocale function returns an abbreviation of what was selected. For example, English in the United States is "En_US" and French in Belgium is "Fr_Be".[67] By using this abbreviation, you can determine which language the user is working with and display the appropriate text on the report.

There are two ways that a report can display text based upon the regional settings. The first method is to create a formula that examines the ContentLocale value and populates a series of shared variables for each text object on the report. Create a separate formula for each text object that returns the appropriate string. An example here is a formula called @SetLanguage:

```
Shared StringVar ReportHeading;
Shared StringVar OrderDate;
Select Left(ContentLocale,2)
   Case "en":
     (
     ReportHeading := "World Sales Report";
     OrderDate := "Order Date";
     )
   Case "fr":
     (
     ReportHeading := "Rapport Des Ventes Mondiales";
     OrderDate := "Date De Commande";
     );
"";
```

This formula creates two shared string variables, ReportHeading and OrderDate. It looks at the first two characters of the ContentLocale function and sets those variables to the

---

[67] You will have to perform testing to determine the abbreviations that apply to the regions you are working with.

appropriate text for the language. After this formula is called, the text in each shared variable will be in the proper language. The @SetLanguage formula should be placed in the report header section so that it is called first.

The next step is to create a variable for each text object on this report. In this example there are two text objects, so we would need two formulas. The formula simply returns the appropriate shared string variable that was populated with the @SetLanguage formula. For example, the ReportHeading formula would be as follows:

```
Shared StringVar ReportHeading;
ReportHeading;
```

Place this formula in the Page Header section so that it prints at the top of each page.[68] Repeat this step for all the text objects on a report.

The problem with the @SetLanguage formula is that it has to be created in every report. It is very likely that you want to use this same formula for multiple reports and you are going to have to duplicate it every time. Not only that, but if you need to make any changes, you will have to make them in every report and redistribute them to each user. This is quite a maintenance nightmare!

Rather than storing the language strings in a report formula, a second way to internationalize a report is to store the language strings in a database table. This makes maintaining reports much easier because all the reports can reference the same table. You can make changes in one place and you don't need to redistribute the reports.

A possible language table would have a field for every text object on the report. Within the table, there is a record for each language. A sample database table called Language is shown in Table 15-2.

**Table 15-2. Sample table structure for the Language table.**

| ContentLocaleID | ReportHeader | OrderDate |
|---|---|---|
| En | World Sales Report | Order Date |
| Fr | Rapport Des Ventes Mondiales | Date De Commande |

You can use the record selection formula to filter on the Language.ContentLocaleID field to select the proper language. Replace each text object on the report with the corresponding field from the table and the correct language will be shown on the report.

For companies with many international reports, using a database is the ideal solution. Unfortunately, this has its own set of problems to contend with. You can't use the ContentLocale formula in the record selection formula. It can only be evaluated in the

---

[68] If by chance you need to put this formula in the Page Header section along with the SetLocation formula, also add the function EvaluateAfter({@SetLanguage}); to ensure that it is called after the language text has been set.

second report pass after all the records have been read into the report. So you can't filter the data in the Language table based on regional settings. This creates quite a problem. There are various ways to handle this but none of them are perfect. You have to figure out which one you are comfortable implementing and which works best for your situation. Some possible solutions are as follows:

- Specify the language within the record selection formula. For example, you could use this record selection formula: {Language.ConentLocaleID}="en". Unfortunately, this means that each report can only be used for one language. You still get the benefit of sharing the database among multiple reports, but you need a separate copy of the report for each language and must modify the record selection formula accordingly.

- A trick I discuss in the chapter on parameters is to use the report as a subreport within a blank main report. The blank main report only has one formula which returns the ContentLocale function. Link this formula to a parameter in the subreport so that it can be used in the record selection formula.69 By having the main report pass the ContentLocale function to the subreport, the regional setting is available to the subreport when the records are being read from the database. This is a semi-acceptable solution except that treating the report as a subreport is a bit unusual and having to do it for many reports can be a hassle. Caution: since Crystal Reports doesn't let you nest subreports more than one level deep, this solution only works if the report doesn't have subreports.

- Depending upon your database, it could be possible to get around using the ContentLocale function by associating each report with a regional setting. One way to do this is to find a unique identifier in the report that can be used to differentiate where the report is being printed. For example, if the report header uses an address table to print the office's location, you can use that to determine which country the report is being printed from. You can add a locale field to the table that holds the office location. By linking the Language table to the corporate office table and joining on the locality field, each report can print in the correct language with modifying the record selection formula or calling the ContentLocale function.

- If you're building a reporting solution using Visual Studio .NET or Java, you can use a parameter within the record selection formula to set the locality. You set the parameter within your application prior to displaying the report. This is the best solution, but it only works if you know how to use one of these programming languages.70

---

[69] To see the actual steps for doing this, refer to Chapter 4 on parameters.

[70] I cover how to set parameters with a programming language in the second volume of this Encyclopedia series, "Programming .NET 2005".

| Tip |
| --- |

To test whether your report works with each of the possible regional settings, you can change the region through the Control Panel. However, Crystal Reports doesn't immediately recognize when a change is made. It continues to use the original setting. Crystal Reports only checks the regional settings one time and stores it internally for the duration of your login. Even closing and re-opening Crystal Reports doesn't update it. You need to log off and log back on to the computer to force Crystal Reports to recognize the new regional setting.

When printing date and time information in other countries, sometimes it is helpful to determine the local time zone of where the report is being printed and shift the time according to the regional settings. Crystal Reports gives you three date and time functions that reference regional settings. They are listed in Table 15-3.

**Table 15-3. Region specific data and time functions.**

| Function | Description |
| --- | --- |
| DataTimeZone | The time zone of the DataTime special field (when the report's data was last refreshed). |
| PrintTimeZone | The time zone of the PrintTime special field (when the report was printed). |
| ShiftDateTime(DateTime, OldTimeZone, NewTimeZone ) | Shifts the date and time zone to appear in a new time zone. You have to pass it the date and time to shift as well as the current and new time zones.[71] |

---

[71] The time zone string is very lengthy and has a complex format. Refer to the help file for more information of using the ShiftDateTime() function.

# APPENDIX A
## Financial Reporting

Of all the work I've done with reports and all the white papers I've read, I've never seen anyone discuss how to write financial reports. Yes, there are many examples of what financial reports look like and there are sample .RPT files you can download, but no one has actually documented the steps of how to create them. It seems like this must be a secret that is only given to those who are part of some underground group. Considering that Crystal Reports is the primary reporting tool in many financial departments, I think this is something that should be common knowledge. Even for someone like myself who has audited the financial statements of many corporations, using a reporting tool to create these reports from scratch is not an easy task and having a reference guide for doing so would be very helpful. This appendix hopes to rectify this problem once and for all and give you the steps for creating common financial reports.

In this chapter, we're going to learn the basics of how accounting works as well as how to create the primary financial reports associated with it. Not only that, but we'll also look at some other frequently used reports that people have problems with. We are going to create a Balance Sheet, Income Statement and a Multi-Year Income Statement using cross-tabs.

There are three potential problems encountered when creating financial reports:

1. Many times the person assigned to creating the financial reports isn't familiar with financial reporting concepts. The report designer is usually familiar with the database structure and some general business concepts, but is not an expert in accounting. Asking someone to quickly get up to speed on accounting principles and financial reporting is a lot to ask.

2. Financial reports are complex. Creating them with a reporting tool like Crystal Reports requires that you go about it very methodically and test frequently. It's not a simple matter of using the Report Expert to select the tables and fields to print and applying a Crystal Reports template.

3. Financial databases are all different. Each software program uses a different database structure for their accounting tables. Following a generic set of guidelines for creating reports requires you to focus on learning the concepts and then applying these concepts to the actual database you are working with. Even after you get a good understanding of the concepts involved, each accounting database can have its own set of quirks that require you to be creative when designing the reports.

This appendix addresses each of these three problems in the following ways:

- We learn basic accounting principles. This makes it possible for someone who only has basic business experience to learn how accounting transactions are recorded. Most importantly, you'll learn what it means when a number is either a debit or a credit.

- We look at how accounting information is stored in a database. Since each database is different, we establish some general guidelines about what to look for in a database and how to interpret the data.

- We use tutorials to design each financial report in detail. This shows you how financial reports are structured and the steps to build them in Crystal Reports.

As you can probably figure out, this is advanced stuff we're talking about. We're going to take it one step at a time so that by the end of the appendix you will have had the opportunity to create each of these financial reports and understand the decisions necessary to do them on your own.

Let's get started by learning the basic accounting principles that every company uses.

# Basic Accounting Principles

Considering that many of us cringe at the idea of having to balance our check book (myself included), it wouldn't be a surprise to if understanding debits and credits makes you want to run away screaming. But like it or not, learning what all those debits and credits do is very important for being able to write financial reports. In this section, I'm going to introduce you to the concepts of accounting and how financial databases are built. The information is going to be greatly simplified so that it is easier to understand. Once you are finished, you should be able to apply the knowledge at your company.

Writing financial statements isn't easy because each company has their own rules for how they want their financial information presented. Having to analyze the list of accounts in combination with all the journal entries and customizing the report can be a bit overwhelming. But, no matter how a company wants their information presented, the accounting rules that must be followed are well established. It's imperative that you understand the basic accounting principles that every company uses before learning how to create the different financial reports.

| Note |
| --- |

The purpose of this section is to help you understand how the accounting principles work, but it is not to teach you how to put these principles into practice for a company. Learning how to use the accounting principles on a daily basis requires a formal education in accounting. But having a basic knowledge of these rules will make it easier for you to look at the records in a financial database and get an understanding of what they are doing. You can create reports with this data because you will know whether it accurately portrays the underlying data.

When looking at the financial transactions in a database, there are basically two things you are concerned about: the account name and the dollar amount. The account name is pretty easy to understand. For example, if the account is called 'Cash' or 'Money Market Account,' then you know it is an asset dealing with money. If it is called 'Insurance Expense' or 'Parking Fees,' you know it is an expense to pay for something. The second part, the dollar amount, is where things get tricky. And to be honest, this is what is going to cause you all kinds of grief until you get a solid understanding of how money is accounted for.

From a financial standpoint, everything a business does results in monetary transactions. For example, if money is borrowed from the bank, cash is received and the company has a new loan that needs to be paid back. If equipment is purchased, there is an increase in the total value of fixed assets owned and either cash is reduced or a new loan is recorded. These transactions are recorded as a set of entries where each amount is either a debit or a credit. The way that each gets recorded is dependent upon how the transaction is classified and whether it is increasing or decreasing the item. Let's look at how this works.

# The Double-Entry Method of Accounting

Businesses record their financial transactions using the double-entry method of accounting. It classifies each dollar value as either a debit (DR) or a credit (CR) . The dollar amounts are listed in two columns with debits listed on the left and credits listed on the right. Debits are generally recorded as positive numbers and credits are recorded as negative numbers. Let's see this process in action with two example transactions. The first transaction shows how to record taking a loan out from the bank. Cash is increased by $1,000 and a new loan is payable to the bank for $1,000.

| Account | Debit (DR) | Credit (CR) |
|---|---|---|
| Cash | $1,000 | |
| Bank Loan | | $1,000 |

As a slightly more complex example, here is how you would record buying a car for $30,000. You put down a 10% deposit ($3,000) and get a $27,000 loan.

| Account | Debit (DR) | Credit (CR) |
|---|---|---|
| Car | $30,000 | |
| Cash | | $3,000 |
| Bank Loan | | $27,000 |

Let's look at how these two examples work. First, the amount for each entry is either recorded as a debit or a credit (we'll look at how that works next). Second, the total amounts in the Debit column equal the total amounts in the Credit column. Double-entry accounting requires that both sides add up to the same amount. If they don't, something is wrong and the transaction wasn't recorded properly. There is actually a report, called the Trial Balance, which looks at all the transactions in the system and checks to make sure that the total debits equals the total credits.

The first example records two entries and the second example records three entries. Each transaction, at a minimum, has to have at least two entries. Something has to go in the debit column and something has to go in the credit column. But it is very common for transactions to involve many entries. As long as the total amount of debits equals the total amount of credits, the number of transactions isn't important.

The last thing to notice is that all amounts are positive figures. If you look at the Cash account in the first example, it makes sense that the $1,000 is positive because you are receiving money from the bank. But in the second example, you are making a $3,000 down payment on the car and the amount is still recorded as a positive amount. Since you are giving money to the seller, you might think that it should be a negative number. In double-entry accounting, when you want to record a negative amount for an asset, you record it as a credit. The accounting software will know that this is a negative number and will subtract it from your total cash balance.

# Debits and Credits

There are five account types: Assets (what the company owns), Liabilities (what the company owes to someone else), Revenues (how the company makes money), Expenses (how the company spends money), and Shareholder Capital (company stock). Double-entry accounting establishes rules for each account type that determines when an amount should be recorded as a debit or a credit. It also tells you when the number should be treated as a positive number or negative number. Table A-1 lists what these rules are. Once you understand this table, everything else will start to fall into place.

**Table A-1. Double-entry accounting rules.**

| Account Type | Debit (DR) | Credit (CR) |
|---|---|---|
| Assets | + | - |
| Liabilities | - | + |
| Revenues | - | + |
| Expenses | + | - |
| Shareholder Capital | - | + |

Listed next to each account are the Debit and Credit columns. Each column either has a + or a – in it. If an entry increases the account value, it goes in the + column. If the entry decreases the account value, it goes in the – column.

Let's see how this chart is used with the two previous examples. In the first example, we received cash from the bank and now we have a new loan to pay back for $1,000. Cash is an asset and Table A-1 shows that when an asset increases then the amount goes in the debit column. Consequently, for the second line we got a loan and owed the bank money (a liability). If you look in Table A-1, you see that when a liability increases then the amount should go in the credit column.

The second example had us buying a car for $30,000. The value of the car, $30,000, was put in the debit column because it increases the value of the asset. We also had to pay a down payment of $3,000 and this was put in the credit column. This is because Table A-1 states that when an asset decreases value then the amount goes in the credit column. We also had a new loan that was payable to the bank (a liability), so $27,000 was put in the credit column because it increased the liability balance.

As you can see, by determining the account type that an entry relates to and if it increases that account or decreases it, we can look at Table A-1 and see whether the amount should be a debit or a credit. The beauty of this whole system is that once you understand how to use Table A-1, you can make the appropriate entries in the accounting system. The debits will always equal the credits and everything balances (this makes auditors very happy).[72]

So that you get a better idea of how to classify accounts in the proper account type, Table A-2 gives you examples of some accounts and how they are classified.

**Table A-2. Sample accounts for each account type.**

| ASSETS | LIABILITIES |
|---|---|
| Cash, Bank Accounts | Accounts Payable |
| Accounts Receivable | Bank Loans |
| Land, Buildings | Taxes Payable |
| Inventory | |

---

[72] Luca Pacioli, who became known as the "Father of Accounting" in 1494, wanted to emphasize how important it is to keep your books balanced. He is quoted as saying, "A person should not go to sleep at night until debits equal credits!"

**Table A-2 cont.**

| REVENUES | EXPENSES | SHAREHOLDER CAPITAL |
|---|---|---|
| Sales | Payroll Salaries | Capital Stock |
| Investment Income | Interest Expense | Retained Earnings |
| Disposal of Equipment | Utilities | |

This table isn't supposed to make you an overnight expert on classifying financial transactions. It's to help you look at someone's database records and get an idea of what is going on. If you see that there are a lot of credit entries relating to loans, when you look at your financial report you will probably see a large debt balance. If you don't see a lot of debt, either they are paying it off (e.g. credit entries for the cash accounts), or your report might be completely wrong and you need to go back and check that you didn't miss something.

Of course, if you're not an accountant, it's difficult to know how to classify every account. Fortunately, you don't have to do this. In most accounting systems, the different accounts are grouped together by the first digit in their account number. For example, all assets might start with a '1' and all liabilities might start with a '2'. So it's pretty easy to look at the chart of accounts and immediately know the classification system. The easiest thing to do is start at the top of the chart and look for the obvious accounts every company has. For assets, look for the cash accounts. If they start with a '1' then all the assets will start with a '1'. Next, look for are the liability accounts. If you see account names like 'Accounts Payable' and 'Long Term Loans' and they start with a '2', then all liabilities will start with a '2'. You can use Table A-1 to jot down notes listing the numerical pattern for each account type. After that you won't have to worry about it anymore.

## Do Banks Have this Backwards?

Now that you are an 'expert' on debits and credits, the next time you get your bank statement you might notice something that appears wrong. Sometimes you'll see a note that says something like, "This month your account has earned X dollars of interest. It has been credited to your account." After reading this appendix, you might be thinking, "Wait a minute. I know that cash is an asset and when I increase an asset I put it in the debit column. So why does the bank say they are crediting my account when they are putting money into it?"

Banks are in the business of holding your money for a period of time and giving it back to you in the future. They actually owe you this money and they think of you as a liability. We now know that to increase a liability you list the amount in the credit column. When a bank says that they are putting more money in your account, this is more money that they owe you (a liability) and in their accounting system this will be recorded as a credit for your account. So you should always be happy when a bank says that they are going to "credit your account".

Although it's great that debits and credits are used so that everything stays in balance, there is one aspect of them that will most likely cause you confusion. Look at Table A-1 and see how revenues are accounted for. When revenues increase they are recorded as credits. Since credits are negative numbers, when the company makes money the report will show negative numbers. This is going to cause a lot of problems when people think the company is losing money. Unfortunately, we know that we have to keep credits negative so that they offset the debits and everything balances. To get around this problem, we'll find out later how to switch the signs on certain balances, but behind the scenes we'll use the natural numbers for the calculations.

## Contra-Accounts

An account type that hasn't been mentioned yet is a contra-account. This is an account that offsets (or counteracts) the balance of another account. Contra-accounts have the opposite sign of the account they offset. For example, a contra-account for an asset will have a credit balance. This offsets the asset's debit balance.

Contra-accounts are usually associated with amounts that are charged on a periodic basis. One example of this is accumulated depreciation. When a company buys a large fixed asset, they are supposed to slowly decrease its balance over a certain number of years. This is called depreciation. If a company bought a large piece of machinery for $50,000, after the first year they might have to mark down the value to $45,000. After the second year, it might be marked down to $40,000 (and so on). No money is actually spent. These amounts are only recorded on paper so that the company can keep track of its current value. Over the years, all this depreciation eventually grows large enough where the asset's value on paper is recorded as having a zero balance. Keeping track of how much depreciation has accumulated over the years is stored in a contra-account called Accumulated Depreciation.

Contra-accounts are important to use for two reasons. The first reason is that they contradict something we learned earlier. I said earlier that accounts are grouped within the same numerical grouping and that they all follow the debit and credit rules listed in Table A-1. Even though contra-accounts use the opposite sign, they are always listed right after the account they offset. In the case of the machinery example, the machinery account might have an account number of 1600 and be a debit balance. Its contra-account, accumulated depreciation, will have a credit balance so that it offsets the machinery balance. We want to keep them listed together so it is given an account number of 1650.

When you see a contra-account listed on a financial report, remember that it uses the opposite sign of the accounts around it.

The second reason contra-accounts are important is that financial reports often format contra-accounts differently to make them standout. Most accounts are listed just by their account name. Contra-accounts are often listed with the word "Less:" preceding them. In addition to that, sometimes they are indented as a group and a sub-total is displayed. For example, here is how the machinery accounts might be shown on the report.

Fixed Assets
    Machinery                                           $50,000
      Less: Accumulated Depreciation          - $5,000
        Net Machinery                        $45,000

By changing the formatting of an account and its associated contra-account, the reader can scan the report and immediately notice which accounts use contra-accounts and see their current balance. When you design financial reports you'll have to be on the lookout for contra-accounts and put in special rules to format them appropriately. We'll practice this in a tutorial later in the appendix.

# The Chart of Accounts

The Chart of Accounts shows each account that a business uses in its financial transactions. It also lists the account number and generally a description. Although it is a simple list, it can be very lengthy because most companies have dozens, if not hundreds, of accounts.

An account's purpose is to give you a way of tracking financial data of the business. The larger the business, the more granular you want to track your financial information. For large corporations, accounts can even be duplicated across different business divisions and geographical locations. Thus, each account number can be quite lengthy and broken into segments. On the opposite end of the spectrum is my consulting business. Although my software package lists dozens of accounts for my business, I certainly don't need to track international divisions and I'm fine with an account number that is just four digits long.

Account numbers are listed in ascending order based on liquidity. Liquidity is defined as how fast something can be converted to cash. The faster you can receive cash for something, the more liquid it is. The most liquid accounts are listed first with the least liquid being last.

Let's look at the liquidity of two assets: checking accounts and inventory. Checking accounts are very liquid because you could drive to the bank and withdraw your money immediately. The account numbers for bank accounts could be in the range of 1100-

1200.[73] Inventory is not very liquid because you have to wait until someone buys it before you get cash for it. This could take weeks or even months. Inventory account numbers could be in the range of 1800 or 1900.

A benefit of having accounts numbers ordered by liquidity is that this makes it easy to write financial reports. Corporations like to see the most liquid accounts shown first and all you have to do is sort by account number.

## Making Journal Entries

When bookkeeping used to be done manually, there were separate books for recording each type of business transaction. These books were called journals. There could be a Cash Journal, Sales Journal, Accounts Payable Journal, etc. Thus, the entries within a transaction became know as journal entries. As we discussed earlier, the journal entries must balance the debits with the credits.

In addition to the specific journals, there was also a General Journal for recording infrequent transactions that couldn't be put into one of the journals. For example, you could record sales of stock here. After all entries were posted to each journal, they were summarized in the General Ledger.

In today's accounting systems, having different tables to mimic the journals isn't necessary. Depending upon the database model and the expected volume of transactions, it is reasonable to have a single table for tracking all journal entries.

Since journals were paper based, they weren't big enough to store entries for more than a single year in them. New journals were used and year-end journal entries were made to prepare them for the next year. Certain balances were carried forward into the new journals so that the accounts wouldn't lose their values. Other transactions were recorded to make adjustments to accounts with accrued balances.

Similar to the paper journals, most accounting systems archive data after one or two years. This keeps their performance optimal so you can access the data quickly. Year-end journal entries are still necessary to keep current balances accurate and to make year-end adjusting entries. When creating reports, you need to examine the tables to find out what date range the entries span. Knowing whether there is archived data and how account balances are carried forward is important for setting the correct date filters.

| Tip |
|---|

If you want more information about how accounting works, you can read a fun online tutorial at:

---

[73] These are just examples and actual account numbers are based upon the numbering system and how many other accounts must be identified.

http://www.dwmbeancounter.com/moodle/

# Identifying Key Accounting Tables

When given the task of creating a report, one of the first steps is identifying which tables will be used as the data source. The same applies to creating financial reports. There are three primary tables necessary for financial reporting:

- List of Account Types

- Chart of Accounts

- Journal Entries

If you aren't familiar with the database, it can sometimes take a bit of work to figure out which tables hold this information. You have to know what type of data to look for and make sure it is complete (sometimes the data is spread out across multiple tables).

Once you identify these three tables and determine how they are organized, you can start building your reports. Unfortunately, every accounting database is different and it isn't always easy to determine which tables you need. The next section focuses on helping you figure out how to identify each of the key tables. But first, let's look at the database tables we'll be working with.

## Sample Accounting Databases

To give you practice with learning how to identify the key tables within an accounting database, I'm going to use three different databases as examples. The first database is the sample installed with Crystal Reports XI R2. The other two databases come from software packages in use by businesses today. We'll be working with data from the Microsoft Small Business Financials package and Quickbooks Professional software. This gives you 'real world' experience by working with databases used with actual accounting systems. Of course, your own reports will probably be using a different accounting system, but this should give you enough practice that you can apply these guidelines to your own database.

The next sections discuss the databases we'll be working with and look at their relevancy to what we are doing. Additionally, each description is accompanied with a figure showing you a snapshot of all the tables in the database. This gives you an idea of how accounting tables are named and it lets you refer back to each figure throughout this appendix for reference.

### Crystal Reports XI R2

The version of Crystal Reports you are using with this book is probably the original version that was released in 2005. However, Business Objects actually updated this version of Crystal Reports and released a new edition called 'R2'. This update was to make Crystal

Reports compatible with the Microsoft development tools called Visual Studio 2005 and with Business Objects Enterprise XI R2.

In the R2 edition, Business Objects quietly hid inside the installation folders a new version of the Xtreme.mdb database. This update to the database includes new accounting tables that give you realistic accounting data to learn from. The sample financial reports were also updated to use these new accounting tables. The sample database and financial reports that came with previous versions of Crystal Reports were ridiculously simplistic and had no real value for training purposes. Business Objects recognized this problem and made the new Xtreme.mdb database much more realistic.

The R2 software download is available to anyone with a licensed version of Crystal Reports XI. You can get more information about this free update in this book's Prefix.

After downloading the files, install them to your computer. You will find the new financial database here:

C:\Program Files\Business Objects\Common\3.5\Samples\En\
Databases\Xtreme.mdb

Figure A-1 shows the tables in the Xreme.mdb database file.

| Create table in Design view | Employee | Journal Entry Type | Purchase Order |
| Create table by using wizard | Employee Addresses | Linked Inventory Accounts | Purchase Payment |
| Create table by entering data | Financials | List Totals | Purchases |
| Account | Inventory | Manager | Receipt |
| Account Class | Inventory Purchase | Monthly Account Budgets | Sales Return |
| Account Heading | Inventory Return | Orders | Sales Return Detail |
| Account Type | Inventory Sale | Orders Detail | Supplier |
| Bill | Inventory Transaction | Pay Cheque | Vendor |
| Bill Payment | Inventory Transaction Type | Product | Xtreme Info |
| Credit | Invoice | Product Type | |
| Customer | Journal Entries Run | Purchase | |
| Customer Payment | Journal Entry | Purchase Detail | |

**Figure A-1. Crystal Reports XI R2 Extreme.mdb database tables.**

### Microsoft Small Business Financials

Microsoft sells a financial software package tailored towards mid-sized businesses called Microsoft Small Business Financials. This is a robust accounting package used by many businesses. For the sake of this chapter, I'm just going to refer to it as MS Financials. You can find out more information at the following URL:

http://www.microsoft.com/businesssolutions/smallbusinessfinancials/
default.mspx

Figure A-2 shows the tables in the MS Financials database.

| | | |
|---|---|---|
| frl_acct_code | frl_entity | frl_seg_desc |
| frl_acct_seg | frl_per_bal_hist | frl_system_options |
| frl_batch_ctrl | frl_period_bal | frl_tbl_ctrl |
| frl_batch_ctrl_hist | frl_period_ctrl | frl_tran_detail |
| frl_book_ctrl | frl_proj_bal_hist | frl_tran_detail_hist |
| frl_curr_bal_hist | frl_proj_category | frl_user_fields |
| frl_currency_bal | frl_proj_code | frl_year_ctrl |
| frl_currency_ctrl | frl_project_bal | testtbl |
| frl_currency_exchg | frl_seg_ctrl | tmpBalanceSheet |

**Figure A-2. MS Financials database tables.**

### *Quickbooks Professional - QODBC*

Quickbooks is the most popular accounting software for small businesses. I currently use 'Quickbooks Pro 2006' for my own consulting practice and I'm pretty happy with it. Although QuickBooks comes with a complete set of financial statements built into the software, I thought it would be fun to see how the database is structured. Unfortunately, once I got into analyzing the database structure I found it a bit confusing. It wasn't very obvious how they stored their data and it took some time to figure it out. Nonetheless, some of you may also have to deal with difficult databases and this could provide you with good examples of what you might encounter.[74]

The only problem with writing reports with QuickBooks is that there isn't a freely available database driver for accessing the QuickBooks database. I found a third party database driver on the internet and they offer a 30 day free trial. I downloaded it and imported the entire QuickBooks database into an Access database. They call their software QODBC and you can find more information at this URL:

http://www.qodbc.com/qodbc.htm

Figure A-3 shows the tables in the QuickBooks database.

---

[74] Sometimes the best example is a bad example!

| | | |
|---|---|---|
| Create table in Design view | Deposit | JournalEntryLine |
| Create table by using wizard | DepositLine | ListDeleted |
| Create table by entering data | Employee | OtherName |
| Account | EmployeeEarning | PaymentMethod |
| ARRefundCreditCard | Entity | PayrollItemNonWage |
| ARRefundCreditCardRefundAppliedTo | Estimate | PayrollItemWage |
| Bill | EstimateLine | Preferences |
| BillExpenseLine | EstimateLinkedTxn | PriceLevel |
| BillItemLine | Host | PriceLevelPerItem |
| BillLinkedTxn | HostSupportedVersions | PurchaseOrder |
| BillPaymentCheck | InventoryAdjustment | PurchaseOrderLine |
| BillPaymentCheckLine | InventoryAdjustmentLine | PurchaseOrderLinkedTxn |
| BillPaymentCreditCard | Invoice | ReceivePayment |
| BillPaymentCreditCardLine | InvoiceLine | ReceivePaymentLine |
| BillToPay | InvoiceLinkedTxn | ReceivePaymentToDeposit |
| BuildAssembly | Item | Sales |
| BuildAssemblyComponentItemLine | ItemAssembliesCanBuild | SalesLine |
| Charge | ItemDiscount | SalesOrder |
| ChargeLinkedTxn | ItemFixedAsset | SalesOrderLine |
| Check | ItemGroup | SalesOrderLinkedTxn |
| CheckExpenseLine | ItemGroupLine | SalesReceipt |
| CheckItemLine | ItemInventory | SalesReceiptLine |
| Class | ItemInventoryAssembly | SalesRep |
| ClearedStatus | ItemInventoryAssemblyLine | SalesTaxCode |
| Company | ItemNonInventory | SalesTaxPaymentCheck |
| CompanyActivity | ItemOtherCharge | SalesTaxPaymentCheckLine |
| CreditCardCharge | ItemPayment | ShipMethod |
| CreditCardChargeExpenseLine | ItemReceipt | StandardTerms |
| CreditCardChargeItemLine | ItemReceiptExpenseLine | Template |
| CreditCardCredit | ItemReceiptItemLine | Terms |
| CreditCardCreditExpenseLine | ItemReceiptLinkedTxn | TimeTracking |
| CreditCardCreditItemLine | ItemSalesTax | ToDo |
| CreditMemo | ItemSalesTaxGroup | Transaction |
| CreditMemoLine | ItemSalesTaxGroupLine | TxnDeleted |
| CreditMemoLinkedTxn | ItemService | Vendor |
| Customer | ItemSubtotal | VendorCredit |
| CustomerMsg | JobType | VendorCreditExpenseLine |
| CustomerType | JournalEntry | VendorCreditItemLine |
| CustomField | JournalEntryCreditLine | VendorCreditLinkedTxn |
| DateDrivenTerms | JournalEntryDebitLine | VendorType |

Figure A-3. Quickbooks database tables.

# Account Types Table

This table lists the different account types that the accounts are grouped into. This is a pretty simple table. It has a primary key for identifying each record and it lists the account type. The actual names used are typically very similar to the account types listed in Table A-1: Assets, Liabilities, Revenues, Expenses and Shareholder Equity. To find the proper table, look for a table name with the word "Account" in it as well as some type of word relating to classifying data.

If you look at Xtreme tables listed in Figure A-1, you'll see three tables with the word "Account" in them and another descriptive word. It appears that accounts are broken down into three categories: Type, Heading and Class. Once I opened up the tables and looked at the data, I saw that the table "Account Type" had what I was looking for. There were five records with names matching Table A-1. However, I was curious about what was in the other tables. Upon inspection I saw that the table "Account Class" broke each account into more descriptive sub-types such as "Cash", "Operating Revenue", "NonOperating Revenue", etc. The table, "Account Heading" lists appropriate headings that should appear on financial reports. Some examples are: "Current Assets", "Inventory Assets", "Current Liabilities", "Long Term Liabilities", etc. All these tables will prove to be very useful when we build our own financial reports.

The MS Financials database, shown in Figure A-2, has two tables with the word "Account" in them. The first table, "frl_acct_code", is the list of the individual accounts. The second table, "frl_acct_seg", lists the account segments. When I opened up this table to see how they define segments, all I saw were references to another segment ID field. I closed the table and upon further review of the other table names in the database, I saw the tables "frl_seg_ctrl" and "frl_seg_desc". These two tables appear to be their method for breaking down an account number into individual segments (group of numbers). Each group defines the department/division that the account applies to as well as the account type. It's clear that prior to designing the financial reports, support documentation will have to be consulted to get a thorough understanding of how the account segments are used to structure the account number.

The QuickBooks database, shown in Figure A-3, has the most tables listed of all three databases that we discuss. Unfortunately, there is only one table relating to accounts and that is the "Accounts" table which lists the individual account codes. There doesn't appear to be a table we could use that specifies an account type. Nor is there anything related to helping us classify the accounts into groups. We'll have to make a mental note about that and continue looking for the other necessary tables.

So far in our search for a table that lists the account types, we see that the Xtreme.mdb table will be the easiest to report from.[75] It has ample tables for classifying accounts into groups. The MS Financials database uses a segment notation for classifying accounts and the QuickBooks database doesn't appear to have anything related to account types (let's hope we find out otherwise before we are done).

From what we've seen of the database structures, we can already make a logical assumption about which accounting software is tailored to which type of company. The MS Financials database uses a segment notation to break down accounts into different departments and

---

[75] This is logical, considering that it was created for the purpose of being used with the new financial report samples that come with Crystal Reports.

divisions. Clearly, this is designed for a large corporation which needs separate financial statements for each department/division and they are probably in different locations around the world. At the opposite end of the spectrum is the QuickBooks database which, as far as we can tell, doesn't even break down accounts into their type. This is geared for a small sized business which doesn't have sophisticated reporting requirements.

## Chart of Accounts Table

The chart of accounts lists all the accounts used in a company's financial transactions. In the Xtreme.mdb database, this table is called "Account". In addition to listing the account number and name, it also has fields that link to the other account related tables (type and class) and the balance to date. The MS Financial database uses the table "frl_account_code". It has fields for specifying whether its normal balance is a debit or credit, whether it is active, and the last date it was used.

The Quickbooks database stores its chart of accounts in a table called "Account". It has fields for storing the full account name, checking whether the account is currently active, its total balance, and tax information. Interestingly enough, it also has a field called "Account Type". This is the data that we couldn't locate in the previous section. It appears that rather than store this information in a separate table, the account type is listed with each record. From a database modeling standpoint, this is actually a poor design decision and not at all standard. It is much more efficient to have a small table that lists the account types and then link them to this table. But at least we now know where the account type information is and this will make reporting much easier.

Another interesting aspect of QuickBooks is that account numbers are not required. There is an option in the QuickBooks application that lets you enable or disable the use of account numbers. We learned earlier that a benefit of having account numbers is that it orders accounts on the basis of liquidity. QuickBooks' financial reports list accounts alphabetically. Liquidity has no relevance. Again, we see that QuickBooks is designed for small businesses because this would not be acceptable for a large corporation.

## Journal Entries Table

Finding which table stores the journal entries in the Xtreme.mdb database is pretty simple. It is called "Journal Entry". The table lists the account number, a balance, whether it is a debit or credit, and a description. The MS Financials database doesn't have any tables with the word "Journal" in them, but it does have a table name that abbreviates the word "transaction". Upon opening "frl_tran_detail", I find that this is the correct table because it does have the journal entries in it. In fact, this table is a bit different from what we've talked about because it doesn't list whether the amount is a debit or a credit. Instead, it lists each number as a positive or negative number. The entries we've looked at so far were always positive and we had to look at whether it was classified as a debit or credit. But with MS Financials, the sign tells us that. Positive numbers are debits and negative numbers are credits. We get the same information from either type of table, but as we'll see when we design the reports, we have to create a different type of formula to handle this type of data. Upon further inspection of the MS Financials database you will also see a table called "frl_tran_detail_history". This table archives the transactions prior to the current year. This is an important table to use when creating multi-year reports. You'll have to use the SQL UNION statement to combine the two tables into a single result set prior to reporting from it.[76]

The QuickBooks database is a little misleading at first. If you scan through the tables, you'll see one called "Journal Entry". My initial hunch is that this would be the table we want. Unfortunately, it doesn't list the journal entry transactions (and I actually can't figure out what it does). If you continue to scan the tables you'll see one called "Transaction". This is the one we want. Upon opening it, I see that it lists the account number, amount, transaction date and a memo field. This table, like MS Financials, doesn't specify whether the transaction is a debit or credit. Instead, it makes the amount positive or negative for debits and credits respectively.

## Specifying Date Ranges

When creating financial reports, it is important to understand how the date range affects an accounts final balance. When printing most reports, you usually specify a date range that has a beginning date and ending date. But this rule doesn't always apply when printing account balances on a balance sheet.

The date on a balance sheet is often worded "As Of" a certain date. For example, if it was for the end of the year, it would say, "As Of 12/31/2007". It won't say, "For the last twelve months of 2007". This is because the current value of assets and liabilities are calculated from the first day they were created. If an account has been in use for three years, then its current balance is the summation of every one of its transactions for the past three years. I call these "cumulative accounts" because their final balance is the accumulation of every transaction.[77] This is important because you might be tempted to use a date range to sum the transactions for just the current year. If you do that, then the final balance will be too small.

Revenue and expense accounts are accounted for using a date range. An income statement header is often worded, "For the Year Ended 200x". This tells the reader that the income was for the full twelve months of the year. When creating an income statement, you need to set a date range filter that specifies both the beginning date and ending date. Unlike the balance sheet, the income statement doesn't include transactions that occurred prior to its start date. If you include every transaction in the database, it would overstate the true amounts.

---

[76] See the Chapter 11, Database Connectivity, for more information about the UNION keyword.
[77] The term "cumulative account" is a term that I use because it describes how the account balance is calculated. You won't find it in an accounting text.

For an easy way to see how each type of account uses date ranges differently, let's look at an example of getting a new job. We'll compare how to report the cash balance in your checking account versus how to report how much money you made as an employee. Your cash balance is representative of the balance sheet and your income is representative of the income statement.

Let's assume you've been working on the job for three months and you started in December of 2006. Table A-3 shows the transactions within your checking account.

**Table A-3. Checking account transactions for new job.**

| Date | Description | Amount |
|------|-------------|--------|
| 12/31/2006 | I got my first paycheck! | $10,000 |
| 1/31/2007 | January paycheck | $10,000 |
| 2/28/2007 | February paycheck | $10,000 |

You can see that this job pays you $10,000 each month and you've deposited three paychecks so far. Let's look at how we would calculate the balances that would appear in the balance sheet and income statement reports for the years 2006 and 2007.

In 2006, the balance sheet is going to report how much cash you have in your bank account as of the end of the year. Since you were only paid once in 2006, the balance is $10,000. The income statement is going to report how much money you made in 2006. Again, you only worked one month so your income is reported as $10,000.

In 2007, things are a little trickier. For the balance sheet, you need to state what the checking account balance is as of 2/28/2007. If you just look at the transactions in the year 2007, you would report that your cash balance is $20,000. But that isn't correct because you know that if you called up the bank, they would tell you that there is $30,000 in your account. To calculate the cash balance, you need to add up every transaction since the checking account was opened. Thus, you would also include the 2006 transaction when you got your first paycheck. Now, your cash balance would be accurately reported as $30,000.

Reporting how much money you made in 2007 requires that you only look at the transactions during 2007. You were paid twice for a total of $20,000. You don't want to include all the transactions since you started working at the job (like you did with the checking account) because then you would overstate your 2007 income in 2007 by $10,000.

It's important to understand the differences between the ways these account balances are reported because you might have to use two different date ranges within the same report. If your report uses the same date range to report the cash balance and the income in 2007, one of the two balances would be wrong. If you don't specify the beginning date range, the cash balance will be accurate but the income balance will be too large. If you only specify the transactions in 2007, the income balance will be correct, but the cash balance will be too small.

If you find this a bit confusing, you will be glad to know that some databases take care of this problem for you. If you remember what we discussed earlier about archiving data, you learned that many databases will only keep a single year of data within the current table to save space. All account balances that are cumulative (like the checking account in the previous example) will have an entry on the first day of the year that states the account's previous balance. This entry summarizes all transactions prior to that date into a single entry. This makes it easy on you because if you use the same date range for all accounts, these cumulative accounts will still be accurate.

The date range for the revenues and expenses is always restricted to the period being reported. Revenue and expense accounts don't have transactions that carry balances forward from previous years. You must always state a beginning and ending date.

When creating a report, you need to determine whether you can use a single date range for your report or whether you need one date range for assets and liabilities and another date range for revenues and expenses. If the database carries forward the balances for assets and liabilities from the previous years, you can use one date range for the entire report. If the database spans multiple years and there aren't any transactions that carry the balance forward, the date range for assets and liabilities needs to include every transaction in the database. You need to review the database for these "balance forward" transactions to see if they exist or you can consult the documentation that came with the software.

# Balance Sheets

When we discussed debits and credits earlier in this appendix, we learned that debits and credits must equal each other so that the accounts stay in balance. There is also an official formula, the Accounting Equation, which is used to show that all accounts are in balance. The accounting equation is defined as: Assets = Liabilities + Owners Equity. This is commonly shortened to A = L + OE. In this formula, the total amount of assets (on the left) will equal the total amount of the liabilities plus the owner's equity. Now there are two ways for ensuring that a company's books are in balance.

The report which proves that a company's accounts follow the accounting equation is the Balance Sheet. It is one of the primary financial reports used by companies in their annual report presented to stockholders. It is also used by financial analysts, lenders, and investors for calculating financial ratios that evaluate a company's financial health.

Let's look at a balance sheet template so that we can understand the different aspects of it. We'll see how it is formatted so that the reader can see the balances of individual accounts and at the same time make sure that it follows the accounting equation. Figure A-4 shows a simplified balance sheet template.

### XYZ Company
### Balance Sheet
### As Of 12/31/200X

## ASSETS

| | |
|---|---|
| Current Assets | |
| Cash | XXX,XXX |
| Acounts Receivable | XXX,XXX |
| Less: Allowance for Bad Debts | -XXX,XXX |
| Inventory | XXX,XXX |
| Total Current Assets | XXX,XXX,XXX |
| Non-Current Assets | |
| Equipment | XXX,XXX |
| Less: Accumulated Depreciation | -XXX,XXX |
| Investments | XXX,XXX |
| Total Non-Current Assets | XXX,XXX,XXX |
| TOTAL ASSETS | XXX,XXX,XXX |

## LIABILITIES & OWNERS EQUITY

| | |
|---|---|
| Current Liabilities | |
| Accounts Payable | XXX,XXX |
| Notes Payable | XXX,XXX |
| Total Current Liabilities | XXX,XXX,XXX |
| Long-Term Liabilities | |
| Bank Notes | XXX,XXX |
| Debt Securities | XXX,XXX |
| Total Long-Term Liabilities | XXX,XXX,XXX |
| Owners Equity | |
| Capital Stock | XXX,XXX |
| Retained Earnings | XXX,XXX |
| Net Income | XXX,XXX |
| Total Owners Equity | XXX,XXX,XXX |
| TOTAL LIABILITIES & OWNERS EQUITY | XXX,XXX,XXX |

Figure A-4. A simplified balance sheet template.

The first thing you want to look at with a balance sheet is whether the balances match the accounting equation. In other words, do the assets equal the liabilities plus owner's equity? Assuming that the company has followed proper accounting practices, your balance sheet should be in balance.

We can see that the balance sheet is formatted to make it easy to check if it is in balance. The right-most column only shows two figures: Total Assets and the Total Liabilities & Stockholder's Equity. If these two numbers are the same, the accounting equation has been satisfied and you are in good shape. If not, either some accounts were missed or they were categorized in the wrong section.[78]

The second aspect of the balance sheet you want to be aware of is how the accounts are categorized. When you create a balance sheet, each category is going to be its own group. This lets Crystal Reports use indentation to separate each category and summarize the balances. We already saw that the two primary categories are Assets and Liabilities & Owner's Equity. Within each of these two categories are the sub-categories which provide a more detailed classification of each account. Each sub-category also has a sub-total associated with it. These sub-totals are one of the more important aspects of a balance sheet because readers use these values for calculating financial ratios.

It's important for you to recognize how the categories and sub-categories match up to your database tables. In the section that discussed the different accounting systems and their database structure, we saw that some databases had fields for classifying the accounts into sub-categories and some didn't. If your database has fields for the sub-categories, it becomes very easy to create a group for each sub-category and show sub-totals in the group footers. If your database doesn't give you this information, your balance sheet will either be limited in how it classifies accounts or you'll have to manually create the sub-categories using formulas. The more detailed information that your database has in it, the less work you have to do.

Earlier in the chapter, we learned that accounts are typically numbered in ascending order based on liquidity (from the most liquid to the least liquid).[79] The balance sheet follows this same ordering system. For example, in the assets section, cash is listed first and non-current assets such as machinery are listed last. Since accounts are already ordered by liquidity, you can sort your report on the account number and this aspect of the report is taken care of for you automatically.

One last thing to notice on the balance sheet is the contra-accounts. Contra-accounts decrease an account's balance and are typically formatted differently so that they stand out. In this balance sheet, there are two contra-accounts: Allowance For Bad Debts and Accumulated Depreciation (they are both in the Assets section). Each account is prefixed

---

[78] Since it's your job to just do the reporting, we have to assume that the balances in the database have been reviewed for accuracy and are correct. You certainly aren't responsible for determining if and how accounting mistakes were made.

[79] Again, liquidity is defined as how fast an account balance can be converted into cash.

with the word "Less:" in front of the name. In the actual database, the account isn't going to have the word "Less:" in its account name field. You are going to have to add this to the report yourself. This requires you to create a formula for the account name and when you see that an account is a contra-account, then you have to add the "Less:" prefix to the account name. We'll look at how this is done in the detailed tutorial steps.

### Handling Net Income

A company's net income is how much money they earned, less the expenses of running the company during that period. Near the bottom of the balance sheet, you can see that net income is shown as a single entry. This makes it appear to be a single account in the database, but that is not the case. It is a sub-total of many related accounts. Depending upon your database and at what point of the year you are in, there are different ways for you to arrive at the net income balance.

A company makes money and pays off expenses throughout the year. These transactions are tracked using revenue and expense accounts. At the end of the year, adjusting entries are made to summarize the net income balance and this is transferred into the Retained Earnings account. The income is reset to zero for the next year. Thus, all the net income for prior years is accumulated in the Retained Earnings account. If a balance sheet is printed after the year-end adjusting entries were made, the net income balance will be zero. The balance sheet will only need to show the retained earnings balance since there is no net income. You can filter out the revenues and expenses from the balance sheet so that they aren't displayed.

If the balance sheet is printed during the year, the adjusting entries haven't been made yet. Thus, the balance sheet needs to show the net income because it hasn't been closed out yet and still has a balance. To do this, you need to summarize the revenues and expenses together to get a final balance for the net income (or a net loss if the company didn't make a profit). The sub-total should be shown on the balance sheet as a single entry titled Net Income.

Depending upon how familiar you are with accounting, you might have to consult with an accountant to find out how your company handles net income. You could also review the journal entries at the end of the year to see if the year-end adjustments include posting the net income into retained earnings.

# Tutorial A-1.Designing a Balance Sheet

Now that you've learned the important aspects of the balance sheet, let's get started with creating one. This is going to be more involved than the other tutorials in the book. Each step will have more in-depth explanations listed after it before moving to the next step. Please make sure that you have plenty of time available so that you can go through each step slowly and fully comprehend it before moving to the next step.

1. Before creating the report, you need to fully understand the database you are reporting from. Identify the tables which hold account information, account classifications and the journal entries. This may require talking to the database administrator or someone in the accounting department.

   Earlier in the chapter, we looked at three examples of accounting databases and discussed their pros and cons. For this tutorial, we are going to use the updated version of the Xtreme.mdb database installed with Crystal Reports XI R2.[80] From the analysis we did previously, we can identify the following tables and fields which will be used on the balance sheet. They are listed in Table A-4.

**Table A-4. Balance sheet tables and fields.**

| Table | Field Name | Description |
|---|---|---|
| Account Type | Account Type ID | Primary key for table. |
| | Account Type | "Asset", "Liability", etc. Used as the main grouping field. |
| Account Heading | Account Heading Number | Primary key for table. |
| | Account Heading Name | The account sub-category. "Current Assets", "Sales Revenue", etc. |
| Account | Account Number | Primary key. Will also be used for sorting. |
| | Account Name | The account name. |
| Journal Entry | Date | Journal entry date. |
| | Amount | Transaction amount. |
| | Debit or Credit | Classifies the account as a debit or credit. |

The majority of these tables use their fields for creating the report groups. The Journal Entry table has the detailed information for creating the main content of the report. The Date field is used for filtering the records. The Amount field will be summed for the account balance.

2. Now that you're familiar with the database and which tables we'll be reporting from, let's create the report. Open Crystal Reports and choose Blank Report.

3. A new report opens and the Database Expert is displayed. Under the Create New Connection folder, locate the Access/Excel (DAO) option and click it. This opens the Access/Excel (DAO) dialog box.

4. For the Database Name, enter the path where you have the new Xtreme.mdb database file located. Click the Finish button to return to the Database Expert.

---

[80] If you need more information about the R2 release, please see the Prefix at the beginning of this book.

The majority of the balance sheet is going to be based on formulas and you can't create formulas until after the report wizard finishes. Right now we'll specify the tables used in the report, and wait till later to create the formulas.

5.  Select the following tables for the report: Account, Account Heading, Account Type, Account Class and Journal Entry.

6.  Click on the Links tab and the defaults links should be correct. Check yours against the next figure to see if they match. Correct them if necessary.

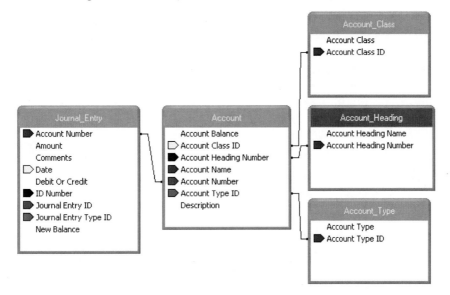

7.  Once the table links are correct, click the OK button to close the Database Expert. You are now in design mode with an empty report. The next step is to build the formulas used in the report.

The problem I've found with writing financial reports for companies is that when given the initial specifications (and I use that term loosely), the person requesting the report says something like, "For the account descriptions and classifications, just use what is stored in the database." I can tell you from experience that this is usually said by someone who hasn't taken the time to look at the database, and doesn't want to be bothered with it right now. Once you present them with a draft of the report to review, they are all too eager to rename the groups, change descriptions, and consolidate multiple accounts into a single account. This is to be expected because financial reports serve different purposes for different people. What is in the database can't fit the needs of everyone. Public reports generally follow a strict format while internal reports are tweaked to meet the needs of different managers. Since you are the report designer, you have to be flexible to account for change requests as the report is being designed. Depending upon how you designed the report, this can will either be no problem or cause you a lot of frustration.

I like to set up the report so that no actual database fields are used directly on the report. Instead, I create a formula for each database field and display that formula on the report. Initially, the formula simply returns the exact value of the database field. Since the formulas just repeat the data field, the report doesn't suffer a performance hit. This might seem a little wasteful, but as the report is reviewed and revised, the formulas can be easily tweaked to make custom changes where necessary. For example, the final formula for the account name will usually consist of a bunch of If-Then statements that modify the account name for specific account numbers.

What most report designers are tempted to do is drag and drop all the database fields onto the report designer. When it comes time to change account names or merge multiple accounts into a single group, they then have to create new formulas that make these changes and swap out the original fields with the new formulas. This creates a lot of extra work as you reposition the fields and fix the formatting. I suggest taking the extra two minutes in the beginning to create a few simple formulas that mimic the original fields. In the long run, you won't need to buy as much aspirin and you will have a much quicker turn-around time for change requests.

8. For each field that is displayed on the report, create a formula that returns its value. The formulas that you need to create are listed in Table A-5.

**Table A-5. Initial balance sheet formulas.**

| Formula Name | Formula |
| --- | --- |
| Account Type | {Account_Type.Account Type} |
| Account Heading Name | {Account.Account Heading Name} |
| Account Heading Number | {Account.Account Heading Number} |
| Account Number | {Account.Account Number} |
| Account Name | {Account.Account Name} |
| Amount | {Journal_Entry.Amount} |

Now that the basic formulas are built, let's place them on the report for the first draft of the balance sheet.

9. For group #1, click the Insert Group button (or select the menu options Insert > Group).

10. Select the formula {@Account Type} and click the OK button.

11. For group #2, click the Insert Group button. Choose the formula {@Account Heading Number}, but don't click the OK button yet.

12. For this group, we don't want to display the account heading number on the report. Instead, we want to display the heading's name. Click the Options tab and click the option Use Formula as Group Name. This opens the Formula Workshop dialog box.

13. For the formula, enter the following text:

{@Account Heading Name}

Notice that this formula references the Account Heading Name formula that was created from Table A-5. It does not reference the field directly. This is important because all changes to the heading name will be made in the formula. You never want to reference the actual data field anymore because then you would have to copy the field updates to this formula as well (and possibly forget to do it).

14. Click the Save and Close button to save the changes.

15. Click the OK button to save your changes for group #2.

16. Move the group #2 header field to the right a bit so that it is offset from group #1.

17. For group #3, click the Insert Group button. Choose the formula {@Account Number}.

18. Rather than display the account number on the report, we want to display the account name. Click the Options tab and choose the option Use Formula as Group Name. This opens the Formula Workshop dialog box.

19. For the formula, enter the following text:

{@Account Name}

20. Click the Save and Close button to save the changes.

21. Click the OK button to save your changes for group #3.

22. Suppress the Details section so that it is hidden for now.

    At this point, you've created three groups for showing the account categories and the account number. However, for the account number you don't want anything to be in the group header because you will show the summary data in the group footer. You need to move the group name field out of the header and put it in the footer.

23. Drag and drop the field Group #3 Name from the group header to the group footer. Move it to the right a bit so that it is offset from group #2.

24. Right-click on the grey area to the left of the Group Header #3 section and select Section Expert. Click the Suppress option so that it isn't shown.

    Preview the report and you will see the basic outline of the balance sheet. It should look similar to Figure A-5.

Asset
        Current Assets
                Chequing Bank Account
                Accounts Receivable

        Inventory Assets
                Gloves Inventory
                Helmets Inventory
                Locks Inventory
                Saddles Inventory
                Bikes (Competition) Inven
                Bikes (Hybrid) Inventory
                Bikes (Kids) Inventory
                Bikes (Mountain) Inventor

        Capital Assets
                Machinery
                Accumulated Amortization
                Buildings
                Accumulated Amortization
                Land

Equity
        Share Capital
                Common Shares
                Preferred Shares

        Retained Earnings
                Retained Earnings - Previ
                Current Earnings

Expense
        Cost of Goods Sold
                Gloves Cost
                Helmets Cost
                Locks Cost
                Saddles Cost
                Bikes (Competition) Cost
                Bikes (Hybrid) Cost
                Bikes (Kids) Cost
                Bikes (Mountain) Cost

        Payroll Expenses
                Wages & Salaries

        General & Administrative
                Accounting & Legal
                Advertising & Promotions
                Courier & Postage
                Amortization Expense (Bu
                Amortization Expense (Ma
                Insurance
                Bank Charges
                Interest Expense
                Office Supplies
                Property Taxes
                Miscellaneous

                Repair & Maintenance
                Telephone
                Internet
                Utilities

Liability
        Current Liabilities
                Accounts Payable
                Vacation Payable
                Federal Income Tax Payat
                Sales Tax Payable

        Long Term Liabilities
                Long Term Notes Payable

Revenue
        Sales Revenue
                Sales Gloves
                Sales Helmets
                Sales Locks
                Sales Saddles
                Bike Sales - Competition
                Bike Sales - Hybrid
                Bike Sales - Kids
                Bike Sales - Mountain
                Sales Returns

**Figure A-5. Pages 1 and 2 (side by side) of the balance sheet preview.**

You can see that the report is organized by the three group fields. The first group is the account type which lists the categories such as Asset, Liability, and Equity (group #1). The next group breaks down the accounts into categories such as Current Assets,

Inventory Assets, and Current Liabilities (group #2). Within each category group is listed the actual account names (group #3).

There is an initial problem with the current report layout. There are too many account types listed. If you look back at Figure A-4, you'll see that there are only two account types: Assets and Liabilities & Owners Equity. This corresponds to the Accounting Equation we discussed earlier. Another way to think about it is that the two account types are assets and 'everything else'. If it isn't an asset, it gets lumped into the Liabilities & Owners Equity section and we need to change the account type formula accordingly.

25. In the Field Explorer window, right click on the formula {@Account Type} and click the Edit option.

26. Change the existing formula to the following:

```
if {Account_Type.Account Type}="Asset" then
    "Assets"
else
    "Liabilities & Owners Equity"
```

This formula keeps the Asset type the same and changes all other types to Liabilities & Owners Equity.

The next step is the most important: displaying the account balances. After all, without numbers the report would mean nothing. However, if you just drag and drop the {@Amount} formula onto the report, all the balances will be wrong. You can't just display the account balance on the report because all numbers are stored in the database as positive numbers (even the negative numbers). You need to write a formula that determines whether an amount should be negated or left as a positive number.

There are two things that determine the sign of an amount. The first is its account type and the second is whether it is a debit or a credit. If you recall, you have to use the rules in Table A-1 to determine which numbers are positive and which are negative. In the next step, I give you the formula that does this.

27. In the Field Explorer window, right-click the formula {@Amount} and select Edit Formula.

28. Replace the existing formula with the following formula:

```
if {Account_Type.Account Type} = "Asset"  Then
    if {Journal_Entry.Debit Or Credit} = "Debit" Then
        {Journal_Entry.Amount}
    Else
        {Journal_Entry.Amount} * -1
Else
    if {Journal_Entry.Debit Or Credit} = "Credit" Then
        {Journal_Entry.Amount}
    Else
```

```
{Journal_Entry.Amount} * -1
```

This formula first looks at the account type and then it looks at whether the number is classified as a debit or credit. Using Table A-1, when the account type is Asset and the value is a debit, it increases the account value. Thus, the formula returns a positive number. When the account type is Asset and the value is a credit, it decreases the value. The number is negated by multiplying it by -1. The formula uses the opposite for the other accounts (as dictated by Table A-1).

You should note that the Expense account doesn't follow the rules in Table A-1. According to Table A-1, expenses are treated the same as the Asset accounts, but this formula doesn't do that. This is because expenses are included in the Net Income calculation and they must be combined with revenues. This is a special circumstance that we'll learn more about later in this tutorial.

29. After entering the new formula and saving it, drag and drop the formula to the Details section. Make sure that the Details section is suppressed because we don't want to show every journal entry on the report. We just want to show the sub-totals in the group footers.

The amount needs to display a sub-total in the group footers. This summarizes the data at each level. The next three steps walk you through adding each sub-total.

30. Right-click on the {@Amount} formula in the Details section and select Insert > Summary.

31. On the Insert Summary dialog box, change the Summary Location property to Group #3 - @Account Number. Click OK to create the summary field in the footer section of Group #3.

32. There needs to be a sub-total for the account heading. Right-click on the {@Amount} formula in the Details section and select Insert > Summary. On the Insert Summary dialog box, change the Summary Location property to Group #2 - @Account Heading Number. Click OK to create the summary field in the footer section of Group #2.

33. We need another sub-total for the account type. Right-click on the {@Amount} formula in the Details section and select Insert > Summary. On the Insert Summary dialog box, change the Summary Location property to Group #1 - @Account Type. Click OK to create the summary field in the footer section of Group #1. This is what lets the user check that Assets are equal to Liabilities & Owner's Equity.

34. Modify the formatting of the account type sub-total so that it is more prominent. Drag it to the right a couple inches and make it bold.

35. The sub-totals in group #1 and #2 each need descriptions so that the user knows what data they are associated with. For each section add a new text object. Type in the word Total.

36. In the Field Explorer, find the folder Group Name Fields and click the plus sign to expand it. Drag each group name into the text box that is in that group's footer section. This concatenates the group name field immediately after the word "Total" so

that they appear side-by-side. Lastly, check how they are formatted so that they look the same as the sub-total field.

Let's look at the report to see where we are so far. If you preview it, you should see something similar to the next two figures. I split the report into two separate figures so that it is easier to read. Figure A-6 is the Assets section and Figure A-7 is the Liabilites & Owners Equity section.

| Assets | | | |
|---|---|---|---|
| Current Assets | | | |
| Chequing Bank Account | $893,260.52 | | |
| Accounts Receivable | $513,702.31 | | |
| Total Current Assets | $1,406,962.83 | | |
| Inventory Assets | | | |
| Gloves Inventory | $49,078.35 | | |
| Helmets Inventory | $70,036.97 | | |
| Locks Inventory | $6,653.65 | | |
| Saddles Inventory | $9,703.35 | | |
| Bikes (Competition) Inventory | $2,475,428.11 | | |
| Bikes (Hybrid) Inventory | $316,590.39 | | |
| Bikes (Kids) Inventory | $67,194.43 | | |
| Bikes (Mountain) Inventory | $661,500.14 | | |
| Total Inventory Assets | $3,656,185.37 | | |
| Capital Assets | | | |
| Machinery | $389,366.53 | | |
| Accumulated Amortization (M | ($58,689.08) | | |
| Buildings | $818,269.00 | | |
| Accumulated Amortization (B | ($56,249.34) | | |
| Land | $223,541.00 | | |
| Total Capital Assets | $1,316,238.11 | | |
| Total Assets | | $6,379,386.30 | |

Figure A-6. Balance Sheet preview showing the Assets section.

| Liabilities & Owners Equity | |
|---|---|
| **Current Liabilities** | |
| Accounts Payable | $3,127,663.26 |
| Vacation Payable | $61,661.54 |
| Federal Income Tax Payable | $64,230.77 |
| Sales Tax Payable | $67,003.27 |
| Total Current Liabilities | $3,320,558.83 |
| **Long Term Liabilities** | |
| Long Term Notes Payable | $559,467.00 |
| Total Long Term Liabilities | $559,467.00 |
| **Share Capital** | |
| Common Shares | $2,000,000.00 |
| Preferred Shares | $200,000.00 |
| Total Share Capital | $2,200,000.00 |
| **Retained Earnings** | |
| Retained Earnings - Previous | $102,455.97 |
| Total Retained Earnings | $102,455.97 |
| **Sales Revenue** | |
| Sales Gloves | $3,622.02 |
| Sales Helmets | $14,110.09 |
| Sales Locks | $2,189.96 |
| Sales Saddles | $2,723.95 |
| Bike Sales - Competition | $677,750.33 |
| Bike Sales - Hybrid | $87,612.96 |
| Bike Sales - Kids | $14,862.44 |
| Bike Sales - Mountain | $154,317.77 |
| Sales Returns | ($17,757.85) |
| Total Sales Revenue | $939,431.67 |
| **Cost of Goods Sold** | |
| Gloves Cost | ($1,653.08) |
| Helmets Cost | ($6,415.29) |
| Locks Cost | ($994.41) |
| Saddles Cost | ($1,238.18) |
| Bikes (Competition) Cost | ($308,940.14) |
| Bikes (Hybrid) Cost | ($39,914.24) |
| Bikes (Kids) Cost | ($6,744.33) |
| Bikes (Mountain) Cost | ($70,110.97) |
| Total Cost of Goods Sold | ($436,010.63) |
| **Payroll Expenses** | |
| Wages & Salaries | ($256,923.07) |

**Figure A-7. Balance sheet showing the Liabilities & Owners Equity section.**

The balance sheet is looking pretty good at this point, but there is one glaring problem: the Liabilities & Owners Equity section lists accounts for revenues and expenses. As discussed earlier, this has to do with the company's net income and we need to handle it appropriately. To summarize the earlier section, if a company transfers the net income into retained earnings with a year-end adjusting entry, there is no need to show net income. If it doesn't do this, you should summarize the net income as a single line item.

In the sample financial database provided with the Crystal Reports software, there are no year-end adjusting entries. Thus, we have to summarize the net income as a single amount on the balance sheet and display it within the Liabilities & Owners Equity section.

| **Note** |
| --- |

If your accounting system does close-out the net income balance into retained earnings, you should exclude all revenue and expense accounts from your report. This can be done in the record selection formula by only selecting records from the appropriate account types. For example, the records selection formula for this database would be:

{Account_Type.Account Type} IN ["Asset", "Equity", "Liability"]

If you recall from the discussion of the {@Amount} formula modification, the expense accounts didn't have their amounts switched according to the rules in Table A-1. This is because we are going to add the expenses together with the revenues so that they are summarized into a single Net Income sub-total. This lets the balances for the two account types offset each other.

To create the Net Income balance on the report, we are going to list it as if it were an individual account with its own sub-total. I'm going to include it within the Retained Earnings heading since they are related. This requires modifying the account heading values so that they all say Retained Earnings (thus including them in that group). For the account number and account name fields, we want them to return a single number and name so that they get consolidated into one line on the balance sheet. This requires modifying four formulas.

37. Right-click on the formula {@Account Heading Number} and select Edit Formula. Change the formula to the following:

```
if {Account_Heading.Account Heading Number}>="4000" Then
    "3500"
else
    {Account_Heading.Account Heading Number}
```

The account heading numbers 4000 and greater all represent revenue and expense accounts. The same applies for the account numbers. This formula takes those accounts and gives them the number 3500. This reclassifies them as retained earnings. We also need to do the same for the account heading names since the names are displayed on the report.

38. Right-click on the formula {@Account Heading Name} and select Edit Formula. Change the formula to the following:

```
if {Account_Heading.Account Heading Number}>="4000" then
    "Retained Earnings"
else
    {Account_Heading.Account Heading Name}
```

39. Let's modify the account details so that all the accounts are consolidated into a single account called Net Income. Right-click on the formula {@Account Number} and select Edit Formula. Change the formula to the following:

    ```
    if {Account.Account Number}>="4000" then
      "4000"
    else
      {Account.Account Number}
    ```

    This changes all revenue and expense accounts to have the same account number of 4000.

40. Right-click on the formula {@Account Name} and select Edit Formula. Change the formula to the following:

    ```
    if {Account.Account Number}>="4000" then
      "Net Income"
    else
      {Account.Account Name}
    ```

    This changes the account names of all revenue and expense accounts to be Net Income. Now that the account number and account names are all the same, the total net income balance will appear as a single line item within the Retained Earnings section.

    At this point, the balance sheet is pretty much finished. The report balances, the accounts are in the correct categories, and net income appears as a single line within retained earnings. There are just a few additional changes we should make. We need to clean up the formatting a bit to make it look more professional and we'll add some features that you will likely need with your own reports.

    The first feature to add is giving the user the ability to specify which year to print. This requires adding a report date parameter. We also have to create a record selection formula that filters the records based on this date.

41. In the Field Explorer window, right-click on the Parameter Fields category and select New. This opens the Create New Parameter dialog box.

42. Enter the parameter name **Date Range**. Make it of type Date, and click the OK button to save your changes and create the parameter.

43. Choose the menu items Report > Record Selection Formulas > Record. This opens the Formula Workshop dialog box.

44. Enter the following formula into the code window:

    ```
    {Journal_Entry.Date} <= {?Date Range}
    ```

45. Click the Save and Close button to save your changes and close the dialog box.

| **Note** |
| --- |

Earlier in this appendix, you learned that you have to careful when setting the date range. It is dependent upon whether the accounting system uses year-end closing entries for revenues and expenses, as well as, what point in the fiscal year the report is being printed. For example, even if the company closes out its net income balance to retained earnings, you would still need to include revenues and expenses if the balance sheet is printed mid-year. This is because you have to account for all the transactions that took place in the months after the end of the year. To modify this formula for your particular circumstance, you need a different date range formula for revenues and expenses than you do for the other accounts. For example, if this were printed in mid-year, we only want transactions from the first day of this year thru the report date. An example record selection formula would be the following code. You can modify it according to your circumstances.

```
({Account_Type.Account Type} in ["Asset", "Equity", "Liability"] and
{Journal_Entry.Date} <= {?ReportDate})
OR
({Account_Type.Account Type} in ["Revenue", "Expense"] and
{Journal_Entry.Date} IN Date(Year({?ReportDate}), 1, 1) To {?ReportDate})
```

46. Let's add company information in the report header. Make the Report Header larger so that it is about a half inch tall. Right-click on it and select Insert Text Object. Place the text object near the top and center it.

47. Enter the text **Xtreme, Inc.** in the text object.

48. Right-click on the report header and insert another text object below the previous one. Enter the text **Balance Sheet**.

49. Drag and drop the parameter {?Date Range} onto the report header and place it below the previous text object.

50. Click on all three text objects and center them as well as make them bold.

51. Click on the Group #1 Name object and change its font size to 12.

52. Click on the Group #3 Name object (the account name) and turn off the bold formatting property. Do the same for the subtotal object directly to the right of it in the same section. By making the objects in this section a normal font, the other groups will stand out more.

Many financial reports use borders around important sub-totals to highlight them on the report. The balance sheet is no exception.

53. Right-click on the amount sub-total in the Group Footer #2 section and select Format Field.

54. Click on the Border tab. In the Line Style area, add a single line to the top and bottom areas.

55. Right-click on the amount sub-total in the Group Footer #1 section and select Format Field.

56. Click on the Border tab. In the Line Style area, add a single line to the top area and for the bottom area add a double line.

What we haven't worked on yet are the contra-accounts. If you recall, contra-accounts are used to offset the balance of another account. They are listed after the main account and have special formatting so that it is obvious to the reader that it is a contra-account. In this database, we have two contra-accounts: Accumulated Depreciation (Machinery) and Accumulated Depreciation (Building). For these two accounts, let's insert the text "Less:" in front of the account name so that the reader knows that it's a contra-account.

57. In the Field Explorer window, right-click on the {@Account Name} formula and select Edit.

58. Modify the existing formula to be the following:

```
//Consolidate Revenue and Expense accounts into Net Income
if {Account.Account Number}>="4000" then
    "Net Income"
//Modify the contra-account names
else if {Account.Account Number} in ["1845", "1865"] then
    "Less: " & {Account.Account Name}
//For all other accounts, return the name as expected
else
    {Account.Account Name}
```

In addition to consolidating the revenue and expense accounts into net income, this formula changes the names of the two contra-accounts (account numbers 1845 and 1865).

As a last exercise, let's look at consolidating multiple accounts into a single account. Public companies often don't want to show every minor account in their financial reports. They want to take the accounts with small balances (referred to as 'non-material' accounts) and merge them into one account that has a more material balance. In another circumstance, you could be writing a financial report for a business manager and he or she doesn't want to see the accounts that don't apply to their area. While you can't delete the accounts from the report (then it wouldn't balance anymore), you can merge them into a single "Miscellaneous" account.

For this database, the Xtreme mountain biking company sells bicycles and various cycling accessories (gloves, helmets, etc.). The accessories are not the primary source of revenue for the company and their total balance isn't very much. Let's modify the report so that the accounts that track sales for the accessories are consolidated into a single account. The account numbers for the accessories are 1510, 1520, 1530, and 1540.

59. In the Field Explorer window, right-click on the {@Account Number} formula and select Edit.

60. Overwrite the existing formula with this new formula:

```
//Consolidate revenues and expenses into one account
if {Account.Account Number}>="4000" then
    "4000"
//Merge the bike accessories into one account
else if {Account.Account Number} in ["1510", "1520", "1530", "1540"] then
    "1510"
else
    //All other accounts return the natural account number
    {Account.Account Number}
```

Lastly, you need to change the account name for these accounts to be the same. We'll call them, "Other Bike Accessories".

61. In the Field Explorer window, right-click on the {@Account Name} formula and select Edit.

62. Overwrite the existing formula with this new formula:

```
//Consolidate Revenue and Expense accounts into Net Income
if {Account.Account Number}>="4000" then
    "Net Income"
//Modify the contra-account names
else if {Account.Account Number} in ["1845", "1865"] then
    "Less: " + {Account.Account Name}
//Merge the bike accessories into one account
else if {Account.Account Number} in ["1510", "1520", "1530", "1540"] then
    "Other Bike Accessories"
//For all other accounts, return the name as expected
else
    {Account.Account Name}
```

After making all these changes, your report should look similar to Figure A-8.

XYZ Company
Balance Sheet
April 30, 2007

**Assets**

| | | |
|---|---|---|
| **Current Assets** | | |
| Chequing Bank Account | $893,260.52 | |
| Accounts Receivable | $513,702.31 | |
| Total Current Assets | $1,406,962.83 | |
| **Inventory Assets** | | |
| Other Bike Accessories | $135,472.31 | |
| Bikes (Competition) Inventory | $2,475,428.11 | |
| Bikes (Hybrid) Inventory | $316,590.39 | |
| Bikes (Kids) Inventory | $67,194.43 | |
| Bikes (Mountain) Inventory | $661,500.14 | |
| Total Inventory Assets | $3,656,185.37 | |
| **Capital Assets** | | |
| Machinery | $389,366.53 | |
| Less: Accumulated Amortization (Machinery) | ($58,689.08) | |
| Buildings | $818,269.00 | |
| Less: Accumulated Amortization (Building) | ($56,249.34) | |
| Land | $223,541.00 | |
| Total Capital Assets | $1,316,238.11 | |
| Total Assets | | $6,379,386.30 |

**Liabilities & Owners Equity**

| | | |
|---|---|---|
| **Current Liabilities** | | |
| Accounts Payable | $3,127,663.26 | |
| Vacation Payable | $61,661.54 | |
| Federal Income Tax Payable | $64,230.77 | |
| Sales Tax Payable | $67,003.27 | |
| Total Current Liabilities | $3,320,558.83 | |
| **Long Term Liabilities** | | |
| Long Term Notes Payable | $559,467.00 | |
| Total Long Term Liabilities | $559,467.00 | |
| **Share Capital** | | |
| Common Shares | $2,000,000.00 | |
| Preferred Shares | $200,000.00 | |
| Total Share Capital | $2,200,000.00 | |
| **Retained Earnings** | | |
| Retained Earnings - Previous Year | $102,455.97 | |
| Net Income | $196,904.50 | |
| Total Retained Earnings | $299,360.47 | |
| Total Liabilities & Owners Equity | | $6,379,386.30 |

Figure A-8. Balance sheet final preview.

# Income Statements

The Income Statement, also known as the Profit and Loss Statement, tells you whether or not a company made money over a certain period of time. In its simplest form, it lists revenues and expenses and at the end it shows the net income (or net loss if the company doesn't make money). Within each category it breaks down the revenues and expenses into sub-categories. For example, expenses can be broken down into salaries, advertising, rent, etc.

Income statements come in all shapes and sizes. They can be compact or they can be detailed to show more information. Different industries have different types of income statements to focus on different aspects of their business. For example, a retail company that has a large amount of inventory on hand will show a detailed accounting of their inventory and the cost of goods sold. But a service company, which typically doesn't sell products, won't have any inventory listed.

Income statements used for internal purposes will often be very different than external reports. I recently built an income statement for a financial manager at a large university. She wanted every account category summarized except for expenses. She wanted the expenses grouped by department and listed in extreme detail so that she could analyze how each department manager was allocating their funds. This would not be the type of income statement I would write if it was to be viewed by people outside of her department.

When you design the income statement, you have to research the best format so that it meets the needs of your intended audience. A sample income statement is shown in Figure A-9.

| XYZ Company Income Statement 12/31/200X | |
| --- | --- |
| Net Revenue | 300,000 |
| Cost of Goods Sold | 100,000 |
| **Gross Margin** | **200,000** |
| Selling Expenses | 50,000 |
| General & Administrative Expenses | 25,000 |
| **Operating Income** | **125,000** |
| Interest Expense | 10,000 |
| Other Expense | 15,000 |
| **Net Income Before Taxes** | **100,000** |
| Taxes | 10,000 |
| **Net Income** | **90,000** |

**Figure A-9. Income Statement Template.**

The income statement looks very different compared to the balance sheet that we created in the previous tutorial. The important aspects of the income statement are as follows.

- Only income related accounts are used on the report. In contrast to the balance sheet which encompasses every account in the chart of accounts, the income statement filters out everything except revenues and expenses.

- Individual accounts are not listed. The income statement is very small because only account categories are shown. The sub-total for each category is the summation of all accounts that belong to that category.

- Indentation is not used to separate one category from the other. All category names are left-justified and lined up with each other. While it is certainly acceptable to use indentation, many times this is not done.

- No negative numbers are shown. On the income statement, the only category that has a positive balance is the Net Revenue category. Every category after that gets subtracted from the Net Revenue balance because it is an expense. Even though the expenses are subtracted, they are still shown on the report as positive numbers. The exception is when the company loses money during the period. Then the balance is shown as a negative number and is usually called Net Loss.

- When you look at most reports, the balance for a section is usually a summary of the categories that came before it. Take the balance sheet as an example. The balance for the Current Assets section is the sub-total of all the accounts that are classified as current assets. But this is not the case with the income statement. The balance shown for each section is a summation of all the account balances that were shown prior to it. For example, if you look at the Gross Margin balance you will see that it is 200,000. This is the result of taking the Net Revenue balance of 300,000 and subtracting Cost of Goods Sold for 100,000. The next section, Operating Income, has a balance of 125,000. It is calculated by taking the previous section's balance (Gross Margin at 200,000) and subtracting the Selling Expenses and General & Administrative Expenses balances. This effectively creates a running total balance down the report with each section summarizing the current balance as of that point in the report.

Now that you see the differences between the income statement and the balance sheet, you might be surprised to find out that they have very similar report designs. If you went through the previous tutorial and understood how to create the balance sheet report, then the income statement tutorial will be very easy for you. The biggest difference between the two reports is that the account balance needs to be a new formula so that it creates a running total of the section balances as the report is printed. Other than that, the grouping process and the method of handling debits and credits is almost the same.

# Multi-Column Income Statements

Although the income statement frequently reports on the current year data only, it is also common to have the income statement show multiple years or even break down a single year into individual months or quarters. Having the income statement show multiple columns adds another level of difficulty to the report design.

When you want a report to summarize data across multiple columns, you need to use the cross-tab object. In most circumstances, cross-tabs are fairly easy to create and add to a report. But income statements have rules that need to be followed and adhering to these rules is more difficult within the confines of the cross-tab object. A basic cross-tab object simply can't be used to create an income statement. Fortunately, if you recall from Chapter 13 on cross-tabs, we covered advanced techniques for analyzing and manipulating the data that is printed within each cross-tab cell. These advanced techniques make it possible for us to use the cross-tab object to build a multi-column income statement.

While cross-tab objects make it possible to create a multi-column income statement, they do have three specific limitations:

- The formatting is limited when compared to being able to place objects anywhere within the report designer. It's much easier to place objects wherever you want within the report designer than formatting individual cells in the cross-tab object.

- A standard report lets you drill-down on the report data for more detailed information. Cross-tab objects don't have drill-down capabilities.

- Using the advanced formatting techniques of the cross-tab object requires being very comfortable with building cross-tab objects. Although this appendix will give you all the steps necessary for building the income statement, a certain skill level is still required to be able to apply the steps to your own report.

The next few tutorials walk you through the steps of creating a single year income statement as well as a multi-year income statement using the cross-tab object. Since both of these reports display the same information, they will be using the same formulas. Rather than repeat these steps in each tutorial, I'm going to have you create a base report which has all the necessary formulas in it and save it as "Income Statement Template.rpt". It won't display any data on it, but you can use it as the starting point for creating both types of income statements which will actually display the data.

The difference between the income statement in this chapter and the one that you will write for your company is in the sections and categories used. You will either have more categories or they might be named differently. Fortunately, this is controlled through a single formula and is easy to modify. So that aspect shouldn't present you with any problems and most of what you do in this tutorial should be directly applicable to your own reports.

### Note

Since the design of the income statement is very similar to the design of the balance sheet, many of the steps in the next tutorial are identical to the balance sheet tutorial. Although for many of you this information will be redundant, there are many people who will have jumped directly to this tutorial without working through the balance sheet tutorial. Because of this, I'm going to keep the same commentary in both tutorials for the benefit of those who only read one of them. If you've already been through the balance sheet tutorial, feel free to skip over some of the notes if you recognize them. Just be sure not to skip any of the detail steps so that your income statement will work correctly.

## Tutorial A-2. Designing the Income Statement Template

This tutorial walks you through the initial steps of creating an income statement. This includes selecting the database tables and writing the formulas. It is used as the foundation for the next two income statement tutorials.

The first step in designing an income statement is to define the sections and categories on the income statement. Ideally, you were given report specifications of what the income statement should look like and you can use this to define the sections and categories. In the sample income statement in Figure A-9, the sections are shown as the rows in bold (Gross Margin, Operating Income, Net Income Before Taxes, and Net Income). The categories are Net Revenue, Cost Of Goods Sold, Selling Expenses, etc. If you weren't given any specs for what the income statement should look like, you should interview the person who will be reading it.

Since income statements have so much variation between them, it's unlikely that the accounting database you are using will have a table defining the sections of the income statement. You will need to create a formula that defines each section and return the appropriate one based upon the account number.

For the categories, it's possible that there is a table that lists the account categories that you can use in the income statement. If not, you'll also need to create a formula that defines each category and returns the correct one based upon the account number. Fortunately, the Xtreme.mdb database that we are using in this tutorial has a table that can be used to define the categories. The Account Class table breaks down each account into specific categories that are perfect for displaying on the income statement.

Before creating the report, you need to fully understand the database you are reporting from. Identify the tables which hold account information, account classifications and the journal entries. This may even require talking to the database administrator or someone in the accounting department.

Earlier in the chapter, we looked at three accounting databases and discussed their pros and cons. For this tutorial, we are going to use the updated version of the Xtreme.mdb database installed with Crystal Reports XI R2.[81] From the analysis we did previously, we can identify the following tables and fields which will be used on the balance sheet. They are listed in Table A-6.

**Table A-6. Necessary tables and fields for the income statement.**

| Table | Field Name | Description |
|---|---|---|
| Account Class | Account Class ID | Primary key for table. |
| | Account Class Name | The account category. "Operating Revenue", "Cost Of Goods Sold", etc. |
| Account Type | Account Type | Whether an account is an asset, liability, revenue, or expense. |
| Account | Account Number | Primary key. Will also be used for sorting. |
| | Account Name | The account name. |
| Journal Entry | Date | Journal entry date. |
| | Amount | Transaction amount. |
| | Debit or Credit | Classifies the account as a debit or credit. |
| | Journal Entry Type ID | Classifies the type of transaction made. Will be used to filter out year-end transactions. |

The Account Class table is used for grouping the records. The Journal Entry table has the detailed information for creating the main content of the report. The Date field is used for filtering the records. The Amount field will be summed for the account balance.

1. Now that you're familiar with the database and which tables we'll be reporting from, let's create the report. Open Crystal Reports and choose Blank Report.

2. A new report opens and the Database Expert is displayed. Under the Create New Connection folder locate the Access/Excel (DAO) option and click it. This opens the Access/Excel (DAO) dialog box.

3. For the Database Name, enter the path where you have the new Xtreme.mdb database file located. After entering the file path, click the Finish button to return to the Database Expert.

   The majority of the income statement is going to be based on formulas and you can't create formulas until after the report wizard finishes. So you initially want to specify the tables to print from, but not the fields.

4. Select the following tables for the report: Account, Account Class, Account Type and Journal Entry.

---

[81] For more information about the R2 download, please refer to the Prefix at the beginning of the book.

5.  Click on the Links tab and the default links should be correct. Check yours against the next figure to see if they match and correct them if necessary.

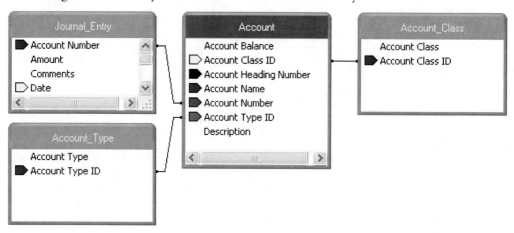

6.  Once the table links are correct, click the OK button to close the Database Expert. You are now in design mode with an empty report.

    Before working on the report, let's set the record selection formula so that only the necessary records are displayed. There are three conditions that need to be accounted for:

    -   Only display the revenue and expense accounts. Since this is an income statement, we don't want any of the balance sheet related accounts used. The Xtreme.mdb database has Revenue accounts with an Account Type ID of 4 and Expense Accounts have an Account Type ID of 5.

    -   Filter on a parameter that prompts the user for which year they want to print the income statement.

    -   Only the transactions that occur during the normal course of the business year should be used. Year-end closing statements should be excluded. In the Xtreme.mdb database, closing statements are defined by a Journal Entry Type ID of 9.

    We're going to build the record selection formula that handles these conditions. But first, we need to create the parameter that prompts the user for which year they want to print.

7.  In the Field Explorer window, right-click on the Parameter Fields category and select New. This opens the Create New Parameter dialog box.

8.  Enter the parameter name **Year To Print**. Change the Type to Number. Click the OK button to save your changes.

9. Create the record selection formula by selecting the menu options Report > Select Expert. This opens the Choose Field dialog box.

10. Select the field Account.Account Type ID. This opens the Select Expert dialog box.

11. For the Account Type ID selection criteria, select Is Any One Of.

12. In the drop-down box to the right, choose the numbers 4 and 5. This selects revenue and expense accounts.

13. Create a new criteria by clicking the New tab and choose the field Journal_Entry.Journal Entry Type ID.

14. For the selection criteria choose Is Not Equal To. In the drop-down box to the right select the number 9. This excludes year-end closing entries.

15. Click the New tab and choose the field Journal_Entry.Date.

16. For the selection criteria choose Formula. Enter the following formula in the input area to the right.

    Year({Journal_Entry.Date}) = {?Year To Print}

17. These are the three formulas you need to filter the report data. To confirm that you entered them all correctly, click on the Show Formula button and you should see the following formula listed:

    {Account.Account Type ID} in [5, 4] and
    {Journal_Entry.Journal Entry Type ID} <> 9 and
    Year({Journal_Entry.Date}) = {?Year To Print}

    Check your formula against this one and make sure everything matches. Once it is correct, click the OK button to save your changes.

    The next step is to build the formulas that the report is based on.[82] The problem I've found with writing financial reports for companies is that when given the initial specifications (and I use that term loosely), the person requesting the report says something like, "For the account descriptions and classifications, just use what is stored in the database." I can tell you from experience that this is usually said by someone who hasn't taken the time to look at the database, and doesn't want to be bothered with it right now. Once you present them with a draft of the report to review, they are all too eager to rename the groups, change descriptions, and consolidate multiple accounts into a single account. This is to be expected because financial reports serve different purposes for different people. What is in the database can't fit the needs of everyone. Public reports generally follow a strict format while internal reports are tweaked to meet the needs of different managers. Since you are the report designer, you have to be flexible to account for change requests as the report is

---

[82] As stated in the introduction, the next three paragraphs are a repeat of what was discussed in the balance sheet tutorial. If you've already worked through that tutorial you can skip to the following step.

being designed. Depending upon how you designed the report, this can will either be no problem or cause you a lot of frustration.

I like to set up the report so that no actual database fields are used directly on the report. Instead, I create a formula for each database field and display that formula on the report. Initially, the formula simply returns the exact value of the database field. Since the formulas just repeat the data field, the report doesn't suffer a performance hit. This might seem a little wasteful, but as the report is reviewed and revised, the formulas can be easily tweaked to make custom changes where necessary. For example, the final formula for the account name will usually consist of a bunch of If-Then statements that modify the account name for specific account numbers.

What most report designers are tempted to do is drag and drop all the database fields onto the report designer. When it comes time to change account names or merge multiple accounts into a single group, they then have to create new formulas that make these changes and swap out the original fields with the new formulas. This creates a lot of extra work as you reposition the fields and fix the formatting. I suggest taking the extra two minutes in the beginning to create a few simple formulas that mimic the original fields. In the long run, you won't need to buy as much aspirin and you will have a much quicker turn-around time for change requests.

18. For each field that is displayed on the report, create a formula that returns its value. The formulas that you need to create are listed in Table A-7.

**Table A-7. Initial balance sheet formulas.**

| Formula Name | Formula |
| --- | --- |
| Account Class | {Account_Class.Account Class} |
| Account Class ID | {Account.Account Class ID} |
| Amount | {Journal_Entry.Amount} |

These formulas are the easy ones because they are a direct copy of an original data field. But, we still need to define the sections of the income statement. There are three sections and each section has certain account classes associated with it. The Account Class ID field will define the sub-group within each section. Table A-8 lists each section and the account classes that belong to it.

**Table A-8. Income statement sections and the related account classes.**

| Section Name | Account Class ID | Account Class |
| --- | --- | --- |
| Gross Margin | 17 | Operating Revenue |
|  | 19 | Cost Of Goods Sold |
| Operating Income | 20 | Payroll Expense |

| | 21 | General & Administrative Expense |
|---|---|---|
| Net Income | 22 | Interest Expense |
| | 23 | Amortization/Depreciation Expense |
| | 26 | Bank Service Charges |

19. When writing your own income statement report, I recommend creating a similar table. Make a list of all the sections to be shown on the income statement and identify which account classes belong to each section. If your accounting database doesn't have a table that lists the accounting classes, you need to map out which account numbers belong to each section. Since there will be a lot of accounts that need this information, it can be helpful to write down the account ranges instead. This will make it easier to write the section formula.

   We'll create a formula that uses a Select Case statement to return the appropriate Section Name and Section ID. This is determined by the current Account Class ID value listed in Table A-8. Let's create that formula now.

20. In the Field Explorer window, right click on the Formula Fields category and select New. Enter the formula name **Section ID** and click the OK button.

. In the Formula Workshop dialog box, enter the following formula:

```
Select {Account_Class.Account Class ID}
    Case 17, 19:
       1
    Case 20, 21:
       2
    Case 22 to 26:
       3;
```

21. Click the Save and Close button to save your changes.

22. Create another formula for the section name. In the Field Explorer window, right click on the Formula Fields category and select New. Enter the formula name **Section Name** and click the OK button.

23. In the Formula Workshop dialog box, enter the following formula:

```
Select {Account_Class.Account Class ID}
    Case 17, 19:
       "Gross Margin"
    Case 20, 21:
       "Operating Income"
    Case 22 to 26:
       "Net Income";
```

24. Click the Save and Close button to save your changes.

At this point, you've set the record selection formula and created the necessary formulas. Let's add the report header information before finishing the template.

25. Make the Report Header section larger so that it is about a half inch tall. Right-click on it and select Insert Text Object. Place the text object near the top and center it.

26. Enter the text **Xtreme, Inc.** in the text object.

27. Right-click on the report header and insert another text object below the previous one. Enter the text **Income Statement.**

28. Drag and drop the {?Year to Print} parameter onto the report header and place it below the previous text object.

29. Right-click on the parameter field and select Format Field.

30. Click on the Number tab and choose the format -1123.

31. Click on all three text objects and center them as well as make them bold.

32. Save the report as **Income Statement Template.rpt.**

You are now finished creating the income statement template and it is ready to be used with the next two tutorials. Unfortunately, since we haven't placed any of the formulas on the report yet, there isn't anything to preview. But that's okay because that is the next order of business.

# Tutorial A-3. Single Year Income Statement

This tutorial walks you through the steps of creating an income statement that only displays a single year. It places all the report objects within the report designer so that you can format them however you wish. Since an income statement only shows summary data for each account class, we will give it drill-down capabilities where the user can get the balance of individual accounts within each class.

1. Open the "Income Statement Template.rpt" report that you created in Tutorial A-3.

2. Save it as **Income Statement Single Year.rpt** so you don't accidentally overwrite the template report.

3. Since the template report has all the formulas already created, let's place them on the report for the first draft of the income statement. Even though the income statement only shows two groups, we are going to add a third group and hide it. This allows the user to drill down into the details of each account class.

4. For group #1, click the Insert Group button (or select the menu option Insert > Group). Select the formula {@Section ID}, but don't click the OK button yet.

5. We don't want to display the section number on the report. Instead, we want to display the section name. Click the Options tab and click the option Use Formula as Group Name. This opens the Formula Workshop dialog box. For the formula, enter the following text:

{@Section Name}

6. Click the Save and Close button to save the changes.

7. Click the OK button to save your changes for group #1.

8. For group #2, click the Insert Group button. Choose the formula {@Account Class ID}, but don't click the OK button yet.

9. For this group, we don't want to display the account class number on the report. Instead, we want to display the class name. Click the Options tab and click the option Use Formula as Group Name. This opens the Formula Workshop dialog box. For the formula, enter the following text:

{@Account Class}

10. Click the Save and Close button to save the changes.

11. Click the OK button to save your changes for group #2.

12. For group #3 (the drill-down group), click the Insert Group button. Choose the field {Account.Account Number}, but don't click the OK button yet.

13. For this group, we don't want to display the account number on the report. Instead, we want to display the account name. Click the Options tab and click the option Customize Group Name Field. In the drop-down box choose the field {Account.Account Name}.

14. Click the OK button to save your changes for froup #3.

    When you create a new group, Crystal Reports automatically puts the group name in the header section. However, we want all groups to show the total balance and this can only be done in the footer section. We need to move the group names out of the header sections and put them in the corresponding footer sections.

15. Move the group #1 name field to the group #1 footer section.

16. Suppress the group #1 header section so that it doesn't use any space.

17. Move the group #2 name field to the group #2 footer section.

18. Click on the group #2 name and click on the Bold button to turn off the bold formatting.

19. Suppress the group #2 header section so that it doesn't use any space.

20. Move the group #3 name field to the group #3 footer section.

21. Click on the group #3 name and click on the Bold button to turn off the bold formatting.

22. Suppress the group #3 header section so that it doesn't use any space.

23. Hide the group #3 footer section. This keeps the individual accounts from being displayed.

24. Suppress the Details section so that it isn't visible.

25. Preview the report and it should look similar to Figure A-10.

```
                                    Xtreme, Inc.
                                 Income Statement
                                        2004

Operating Revenue
Cost of Goods Sold
     Gross Margin
Payroll Expense
General & Administrative Expense
     Operating Income
Interest Expense
Amortization/Depreciation Expense
Bank Service Charges
     Net Income
```

**Figure A-10. Income statement preview with groups.**

With the exception of not having any balances listed, the report preview looks really good. The proper account categories are within each section and the section names are listed after the categories. Now, let's show the balances on the report.

In the balance sheet report, we created a formula called Amount that was used in calculating the sub-total for each account. This formula used Table A-1 to determine whether a balance should be positive or negative based upon the account type and whether it was a debit or credit. The same rules that apply for a balance sheet apply for the income statement. We are just going to copy that same formula to this report.

26. In the Field Explorer window, right-click the Formula Fields category and select New.

27. For the formula name, enter **Amount**.

28. In the Formula Workshop window, enter the following formula:

```
if {Account_Type.Account Type} = "Asset"  Then
   if {Journal_Entry.Debit Or Credit} = "Debit" Then
      {Journal_Entry.Amount}
   Else
      {Journal_Entry.Amount} * -1
Else
   if {Journal_Entry.Debit Or Credit} = "Credit" Then
      {Journal_Entry.Amount}
   Else
      {Journal_Entry.Amount} * -1
```

29. Click the Save and Close button to check for errors and save your changes.

30. The bottom half of this formula is really the only portion necessary for the income statement because it handles the revenue and expense accounts. The first half of the formula handles assets which only appear on the balance sheet. I'm using the same formula on both reports for consistency purposes, as well as, making sure that it stays compliant with the rules in Table A-1.

31. Drag and drop the {@Amount} formula onto the Details section of the report. Even though the Details section is suppressed and the {@Amount} balance won't be displayed, this makes it easy for us to add sub-totals to the group footers.

32. Delete the Amount column header that Crystal Reports added to the report automatically when you dropped the formula onto the report.

33. Right-click on the {@Amount} formula in the Details section and select Insert > Summary.

34. On the Insert Summary dialog box, click the Summary Location drop down box and choose Group #3.

35. Click the OK button to save your changes and insert the summary field into group #3.

36. Click on the summary field and turn off the bold formatting so that the font matches the group #3 field.

37. Right-click on the {@Amount} formula in the Details section and select Insert > Summary.

38. On the Insert Summary dialog box, click the Summary Location drop down box and choose Group #2.

39. Click the OK button to save your changes and insert the summary field into group #2.

40. Click on the summary field and turn off the bold formatting so that the font matches the group #2 field.

41. For the report sections (e.g. Gross Margin, Operating Income, etc.), we can't add a summary field to the group footer because the balances are not sub-totals of the accounts within that section. Instead, each section balance is a running total of all the balances that came before it. We need to add a running total field and put it in the group footer for the section group.

42. Right-click on the {@Amount} field in the Details section and select Insert > Running Total. This opens the Create Running Total Field dialog box.

43. For the running total name, enter Section Balance.

44. Click the OK button to save your changes and insert the running total onto the report.

45. Crystal Reports automatically put the running total field in the Details section. Drag it into the group #1 footer and line it up with the summary field in group #2.

46. Set the format of the running total field to bold.

47. Delete the running total's column header field that was automatically placed on the Page Header section by Crystal Reports.

At this point, we are almost finished. If you look at the report, you'll see that each group has a balance associated with it. The account class groups show the sub-totals of the account balances within each category and the sections print the running total balances. This is shown in Figure A-11.

**Xtreme, Inc.**
**Income Statement**
**2004**

| | |
|---|---:|
| Operating Revenue | $2,785,136.67 |
| Cost of Goods Sold | ($1,303,591.84) |
| **Gross Margin** | **$1,481,544.83** |
| Payroll Expense | ($667,999.98) |
| General & Administrative Expense | ($46,187.33) |
| **Operating Income** | **$767,357.52** |
| Interest Expense | ($24,612.36) |
| Amortization/Depreciation Expense | ($50,167.44) |
| Bank Service Charges | ($259.71) |
| **Net Income** | **$692,318.01** |

**Figure A-11. Income statement preview with balances.**

There is one last change that needs to be made to the report. If you recall, one of the rules of the income statement is that all balances must be shown as positive. Even though the expenses reduce the revenue balance and have negative values, the standard format of the income statement requires that they be shown as positive numbers. However, if we modify the {@Amount} formula to reverse the sign of the balances, this will make them positive numbers and the running total field will be incorrect. Luckily, Crystal Reports gives us a way to change the sign of a number without affecting how it is used in calculations. This is done with the Format Editor dialog box. The option called Reverse Sign For Display lets you flip the sign of a number without changing the underlying value used in calculations. This option was added primarily for use in financial reports such as this.

48. Right-click on the summary field in the group #2 footer and select Format Field. This opens the Format Editor dialog box.

49. Click on the Number tab and click the Customize button. This opens the Custom Style dialog box.

    Near the bottom of the dialog box is the Reverse Sign For Display option. If you click this button, will reverse the signs for the sub-totals of all the classes. But, we don't want to select this because it would reverse the sign for the revenue accounts as well. That would make it look like the company lost money, when in fact, it made money. We have to use conditional formatting to reverse the sign only for the expense accounts.

50. Click on the Formula button to open the Formula Workshop dialog box.

51. Enter the following formula:

    {Account_Type.Account Type} = "Expense"

52. Click the Save and Close button to save your changes.

    We need to do the same for balance in group #3 so that if the user drills-down on the data then the signs match.

53. Right-click on the summary field in the group #3 footer and select Format Field. This opens the Format Editor dialog box.

54. Click on the Number tab and click the Customize button. This opens the Custom Style dialog box.

55. Click on the Formula button to open the Formula Workshop dialog box.

56. Enter the following formula:

    {Account_Type.Account Type} = "Expense"

56. Click the Save and Close button to save your changes.

You are now finished with the income statement (congratulations!). Preview the report and it should look similar to Figure A-12.

```
                          Xtreme, Inc.
                       Income Statement
                            2004


    Operating Revenue                      $2,785,136.67
    Cost of Goods Sold                     $1,303,591.84
       Gross Margin                        $1,481,544.83

    Payroll Expense                          $667,999.98
    General & Administrative Expense          $46,187.33
       Operating Income                      $767,357.52

    Interest Expense                          $24,612.36
    Amortization/Depreciation Expense         $50,167.44
    Bank Service Charges                         $259.71
       Net Income                           $692,318.01
```

**Figure A-12. Income statement final version.**

# Tutorial A-4. Multi-Year Income Statement

This tutorial walks you through the steps of creating a multi-year income statement. It uses the cross-tab object to display multiple columns which summarize the account balances for each year. Using a cross-tab object for the income statement is fairly complex and is going to require advanced formatting techniques. You should be very comfortable with all the concepts covered in the cross-tab chapter to make sure you get the most out of this tutorial.

1. Open the "Income Statement Template.rpt" report that you created in Tutorial A-2.

2. Save it as Income Statement MultiYear.rpt so that you don't accidentally overwrite the template report.

3. Resize the Report Header section so that it is a couple of inches tall.

4. Click on the cross-tab object in the menu bar and place it in the report header to the far left.

5. Right-click on the top left corner of the cross-tab object and select Cross-Tab Expert.

   The first step is to add the two formulas that will be the rows in the cross-tab object. Each one has to group on the numeric ID field, but display the text field in the cross-tab.

6. In the Available Fields list, click on the formula @Section ID and move it to the Rows list.

7. Click on the @Section ID formula in the Rows list and then click the Group Options button.

8. Select the Options tab and select the option Use a Formula As Group Name.

9. Click the Formula button to open the Formula Workshop dialog box.

10. Enter the following formula:

    {@Section Name}

11. Click the Save and Close button to save your changes.

12. Click the OK button to return to the Cross-Tab Expert.

13. In the Available Fields list, click on the formula @Account Class ID and move it to the Rows list. It should now be directly below the @Section ID formula.

14. Click on the @Account Class ID formula in the Rows list and then click the Group Options button.

15. Select the Options tab and select the option Use a Formula As Group Name.

16. Click the Formula button to open the Formula Workshop dialog box.

17. Enter the following formula:

    {@Account Class}

18. Click the Save and Close button to save your changes.

19. Click the OK button to return to the Cross-Tab Expert.

    The next step is to select the date field that will be summarized in the columns.

20. In the Available Fields list, click on the field Journal_Entry.Date and move it to the Columns list.

21. Click on the Journal_Entry.Date field in the Columns list and then click on the Group Options button.

22. At the bottom of the dialog box, click on the drop-down box for The Column Will Be Printed and choose For Each Year. This will summarize the date column for each year.

    Lastly, we need to add the field that will be summarized in the cross-tab.

23. In the Available Fields list, click on the @Amount formula and move it to the Summarized Fields list.

To make sure that you have added the fields correctly, Figure A-13 shows what your Cross-Tab Expert dialog box should look like.

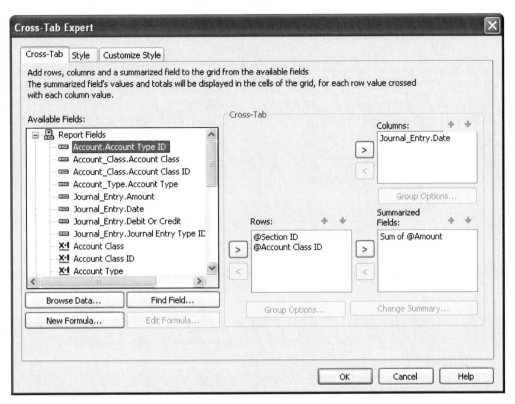

**Figure A-13. Cross-Tab Expert field selections.**

24. If everything looks good, click the OK button to save your changes for the Cross-Tab Expert.

A preview of your report should look like Figure A-14.

|  |  | Total | 2004 |
|---|---|---|---|
| Total |  | $692,318.01 | $692,318.01 |
| Gross Margin | Total | $1,481,544.83 | $1,481,544.83 |
|  | Operating Reve | $2,785,136.67 | $2,785,136.67 |
|  | Cost of Goods : | ($1,303,591.84) | ($1,303,591.84) |
| Operating Income | Total | ($714,187.31) | ($714,187.31) |
|  | Payroll Expens( | ($667,999.98) | ($667,999.98) |
|  | General & Admi | ($46,187.33) | ($46,187.33) |
| Net Income | Total | ($75,039.51) | ($75,039.51) |
|  | Interest Expens | ($24,612.36) | ($24,612.36) |
|  | Amortization/D( | ($50,167.44) | ($50,167.44) |
|  | Bank Service Cl | ($259.71) | ($259.71) |

Xtreme, Inc.
Income Statement
2004

**Figure A-14. Income Statement first draft.**

This report has the basic structure of the income statement, but it still needs a lot of work before we are finished with it.

The first problem with the cross-tab is that it only shows one year. This is because the record selection formula that was written in Tutorial A-2 is only allowing journal entries that have the same year as the report parameter. The formula should allow the past two years to be included in the output. We can fix that by changing the record selection formula.

25. Select the menu options Report > Selection Formulas > Record. This opens the Formula Workshop.

26. The part of the formula that filters on the journal entry date needs to be modified to allow the previous year to be displayed. Modify the formula to the following:

{Account.Account Type ID} in [5, 4] and
{Journal_Entry.Journal Entry Type ID} <> 9 and
Year({Journal_Entry.Date}) in {?Year To Print}-1 to {?Year To Print}

27. Click the Save and Close button to save your changes.

28. Click the report preview button to refresh the report. If you are prompted about refreshing the report data, click Yes so that the prior year data is read into the report. The report preview should now show both years in the cross-tab.

The next step is to hide the grand totals for the rows and columns. These are unnecessary and use up too much report space.

29. Right-click the top left corner of the cross-tab object and select Cross-Tab Expert.

30. Click the Customize Style tab at the top of the dialog box.

31. At the bottom of the dialog box, in the Grid Options section, check both of the options Suppress Row Grand Total and Suppress Column Grand Total. This disables the grand totals for the entire cross-tab.

    When the cross-tab object displays multiple groups, it makes two columns and displays each group name in its own column. For the income statement, we want the section names (e.g. Gross Margin, Operating Income, etc.) to be listed below the categories. This is done by turning on the option to indent the group names.

32. Right-click the Row #1 Name field (the Section ID) and select Row Options > Indent Labels. This reformats the cross-tab rows so that the section names appear under the account class summaries.

    Let's change the formatting of the categories that are bold. We only want the sections to be bold.

33. Select the Row #2 Name field and click the Bold button to turn off bold formatting.

34. Select the Row #2 summary field (in the last column) and click the Bold button to turn off bold formatting.

If you preview your report at this point, it should be looking really good now. The rows are indented properly so that you can see the difference between the sections and the categories. There are also two years listed in the columns so that this is truly a multi-year income statement.

There are two big problems left with the report and they both deal with the summary balances listed on each row. The first problem is that the expenses are listed as negative numbers. While this is certainly accurate, one of the rules of the income statement is that only positive numbers are to be shown. Negative numbers need to have their sign flipped so that they look like positive numbers. Even though they are still treated as negative numbers within the calculations, the display of them should be positive.

The second problem is that the section balances are not correct. As we discussed in the previous tutorial, section balances are a running total of all the account class balances that came before it. Unfortunately, the cross-tab object is showing a sub-total of the account class balances within each section. We can't tell it to show the running total balance because Crystal Reports doesn't allow multiple summary functions for the same field. We have to use the same summary function for every row.

To get around these problems, we have to use formulas within the cross-tab object to manually flip the signs of the expense balances and to create manual running total balances for the sections. In addition to that, we have to overwrite the cross-tab summary balance with our own running total calculations. Sound complicated? It is. This is where it helps to have a solid understanding of the advanced cross-tab techniques.

Before getting into the details of creating the formulas, let's first review the cross-tab specific functionality we need. This will help refresh your memory and it makes a good reference to look back on. Table A-9 lists the cross-tab formulas we'll be using and gives a short description of how to use each one.

**Table A-9. Cross-tab formulas used in the income statement.**

| Formula | Description |
| --- | --- |
| GridRowColumnValue() | Returns the current value of either the row or column summary field. The fieldname parameter is a string that must match one of the summary fields for the rows or columns. If you get an error that the field is not valid, you probably didn't type in the full name exactly (including the symbol). Open the Cross-Tab Expert and click on the Customize Style tab. The acceptable fields are shown in the Rows and Columns lists. Make sure you enter the field name exactly as it is shown in the list. |
| Display String | An option on the Format Editor dialog box that lets you use a formula to override the numeric value in the cross-tab cell. The formula has to return a string. |
| CurrentFieldValue | Returns the value of the cross-tab cell currently being printed. We will use this to keep a manual running total of all the balances in the cross-tab report. Note: it needs to be converted to a number using the ToNumber() function. |

The first step of fixing how the balances are displayed is making the expense accounts display their balances as positive numbers. To do this you have to determine how to identify which accounts are expense accounts. By looking at the Account table in the Xtreme.mdb database, we can see that the revenue accounts have an Account Class ID value of 17 and expense accounts have multiple Account Class IDs. So it's easier to test for an account being "not a revenue" since it only includes one number. We will flip the sign for any account that has a class ID not equal to 17. For your own database, if you aren't lucky enough to have a single field that identifies this, you will have to use the account range to identify expense accounts.

35. Right-click on the summary field for the Row #2 summary field (located in the last column) and select Format Field. This opens the Format Editor dialog box for the Account Class sub-total field.

36. Click on the Number tab and click the Customize button. This opens the Custom Style dialog box.

37. Find the option Reverse Sign For Display and click on the Formula button next to it. This opens the Formula Workshop dialog box.

38. Enter the following formula:

GridRowColumnValue("@Account Class ID") <> 17;

37. Click the Save and Close button to save your changes.

38. Click the OK button to close the Format Field dialog box.

The expense accounts will now be displayed as positive numbers on the report.

The next step is to fix the section balances. They are currently displaying the sub-total of their related account classes and we need them to display a running total that runs from the top to the bottom of the cross-tab. This requires creating a formula which calculates a manual running total. The difficulty is that within the cross-tab object the running total needs to calculate the total for a column of the cross-tab object and then reset to zero when a new column starts. Since each column represents a different year, we want each year to have its own running total calculation. If the running total doesn't get reset for each column, then the balance from one year would carry over into the following year and the results would be incorrect.

The final section of Chapter 13 showed how cross-tabs are calculated by starting at the top of the first column and moving down. After the last row is printed in the first column, then it moves to the top of the second column. For the running total to be reset for each column, there needs to be a way to identify when a new column is being printed. You can test for the end of a column by checking if it is printing the last row. Or if you want to check when a new column is starting, you can do it by checking if it is on the first row. A final way to do it is to keep track of the previous column printed and see if it is different than the current column being printed. If so, you know that the cross-tab is starting a new column.

For this report, since the account section label in the row never changes, the easiest way to test for a new column is to look at the first printed account section and see what data is being displayed. By testing to see if the current section is equal to the first section printed, you know that the cross-tab is at the top of a new column. For this tutorial, I know that the first section is called Gross Margin and it has a Section ID of 1. I will use this in the running total formula as the criteria for resetting the running total balance for each year.

39. Right-click on the summary field for the Row #1 summary field (located in the last column) and select Format Field. This opens the Format Editor dialog box for the Section ID sub-total field.

40. Click on the Common tab.

41. Find the Display String option and click the Formula button beside it. This opens the Formula Workshop dialog box.

42. Enter the following formula:

Global NumberVar RunningTotal;

```
//Reset the running total balance for the first section in each column
IF GridRowColumnValue("@Section ID")=1 THEN RunningTotal := 0;
RunningTotal := RunningTotal + ToNumber(CurrentFieldValue);
//Display the running total in the current cross-tab cell
ToText(RunningTotal) & " ";
```

This formula uses the function GridRowColumnValue() to get the current Section ID value. If it is 1, we know that we are at the first row and the running total is reset to zero. If not, the running total balance is unchanged. The next line uses the CurrentFieldValue function to get the current value being printed (the section's sub-total) and adds it to the running total balance. Finally, the running total is printed in the cross-tab using the ToText() function. Thus, we used the Display String option to overwrite the section's sub-total balance with the manual running total balance.

Notice that the formula also appends a space after the ToText() function. This is so that the section balance lines up with the sub-total balance that is shown above it. Since the Display String option requires you to return a string value and not a number, you are responsible for the formatting. If a field has special formatting in the cross-tab object, you have to format the string to replicate it.

43. Click the Save and Close button to save the formula and close the Formula Workshop.

44. Click the OK button to close the Format Field dialog box.

45. We also want to make the section balances appear bold so that the font matches the section name. Select the Row #1 summary field and click the Bold button.

If you've made it this far, then the hardest part it over. We just need to clean up the formatting so that it looks more professional. We want to remove the grid lines from the cross-tab object. Grid lines are not part of the standard formatting for an income statement.

46. Right-click in the top left corner of the cross-tab object and select Cross-Tab Expert.

47. Click on the Customize Style tab.

48. At the bottom right corner of the dialog box, click on the Format Grid Lines button.

49. At the bottom left corner of the Format Grid Lines dialog box, uncheck the option Show Grid Lines.

50. Click the OK button two times to return to the report designer. The grid lines should no longer be visible.

51. Select the Column #1 Name header field and click the Align Center button so that the year is centered in the column.

52. Save the report so that you don't lose any of your hard work.

Preview the report and it should look similar to Figure A-15.

```
                              Xtreme, Inc.
                            Income Statement
                                 2004

                                           2003          2004

        Operating Revenue                254,805.00    2,785,136.67

        Cost of Goods Sold               117,976.17    1,303,591.84

    Gross Margin                         136,828.83    1,481,544.83

        Payroll Expense                  616,615.37      667,999.98

        General & Administrative Expense  39,224.86       46,187.33

    Operating Income                    -519,011.40      767,357.52

        Interest Expense                  22,561.33       24,612.36

        Amortization/Depreciation Expense 48,048.50       50,167.44

        Bank Service Charges                 240.81          259.71

    Net Income                          -589,862.04      692,318.01
```

**Figure A-15. Multi-year income statement.**

# Tutorial A-5. Comparative Multi-Year Income Statement

Anytime you create a report that shows two consecutive years side by side, someone always comes along and says, "Hey - can you add a third column that shows the difference between the two years?". Income statements are no exception. In fact, having a third column to show the changes between the two years is more of the rule than the exception. Let's modify the previous tutorial so that we add a third column which shows the change from the previous year to the current year.

The cross-tab object has built-in totals for both the rows and columns. It can summarize all the values printed in the entire cross-tab. For this tutorial, what we need the cross-tab to do is subtract the first column (the prior year) from the second column (the current year) and print the difference in the third column. Unfortunately, there is no way to set an option on the cross-tab to make it automatically calculate the difference between two columns. It can only add them together. We have to create formulas that do it manually instead. The good news is that we can use what we learned from the previous tutorial to make this work. The bad news is that, once again, this is going to get very tricky, very quickly.

We need to figure out how to make the cross-tab object subtract the first column from the second column. The first time I built a report like this, I created an array for each column in the cross-tab and used a formula to populate it as the cross-tab was built. This allowed me to put another formula in the total column which subtracted each row and printed the difference. Although this worked really well, the coding is incredibly complex.[83]

Since the cross-tab is designed to add numbers together and not subtract them, a second idea is to make the balances in the first column negative numbers so that when the cross-tab adds them to the second column, it is really subtracting them. This sounds like a good idea except that negating the amounts in the first column is also going to make them show up on the report as negative numbers. To get around this, we will have to flip the signs so that they appear as they did originally.

Negating numbers and flipping signs can get pretty confusing. In addition to that, if you recall from the previous tutorial, we already flipped the signs for the expense accounts so that they show up as positive numbers on the report. This means that, in some cases, an amount will get its sign flipped twice. If we aren't careful, it will be very easy to lose track of which amounts get flipped and which ones don't. The key to making this work is to make as few changes as possible to the original formulas. The changes that are made have to be the same for every formula. By staying consistent with each formula, it will be easier to apply the changes and reduce the risk for making mistakes.

1.  Open the report "Income Statement MultiYear.rpt" from the previous tutorial.

2.  Save the report as **Income Statement Comparative.rpt** so that you are working on a new copy.

    The first step is to have the cross-tab display the Total column. Since the Total column will be updated after every change we make, this allows us to double-check our work at each step throughout this tutorial.

3.  Right-click on the top left corner of the cross-tab object and select Cross-Tab Expert.

4.  Click on the Customize Style tab. Un-check the option Row Totals On Left and the option Suppress Row Grand Totals. This enables the display of the grand total column and puts it in the right-most column.

5.  Click the OK button to save your changes and close the Cross-Tab Expert dialog box.

    If you preview the report, you'll see that the Total column on the right adds both years together. While this is accurate, it is not what we want. We need to negate all values for the previous year so that they are effectively subtracted in the Total column. We will modify the @Amount formula so that the amounts for the previous year have their sign switched.

6.  In the Field Explorer window, right-click on the Amount formula and select Edit. This opens the Formula Workshop.

7.  Update the existing formula to the following code.

    //Determine if the amount should be negated or not

---

[83] You can also use this idea of populating arrays in a cross-tab for calculating any type of formula in the total column.

```
NumberVar FlipSign := 1;
if Year({Journal_Entry.Date}) < {?Year To Print} then
    FlipSign := -1;

if {Account_Type.Account Type} = "Asset"  Then
    if {Journal_Entry.Debit Or Credit} = "Debit" Then
        {Journal_Entry.Amount} * FlipSign
    Else
        {Journal_Entry.Amount} * -1 * FlipSign
Else
    if {Journal_Entry.Debit Or Credit} = "Credit" Then
        {Journal_Entry.Amount} * FlipSign
    Else
        {Journal_Entry.Amount} * -1 * FlipSign
```

This formula creates a variable called FlipSign and stores a 1 in it. It uses the {?Year To Print} parameter to find out if the journal entry date is for the current year or the previous year. If it is the previous year, the FlipSign variable becomes -1. The FlipSign variable is how we will negate the prior year balance.

The second portion of the formula is the same formula that we used for the other income statement. But this time, each amount is multiplied by the FlipSign variable. If the date is for the current year, the FlipSign is 1 and this has no affect on the amount field. But, if it is for the previous year, multiplying the value by FlipSign will negate the amount.

8. Click the Save and Close button and click the OK button to save your changes and return to the report designer.

If you preview the report, you'll see that the balances in the prior year had all their balances negated. You will also notice that the Total column for the account classes is now accurate (this doesn't apply to the sections yet). The Total column is showing the difference between the category columns. So far, so good.

Getting the Total column to calculate the difference between the two columns seems to have messed up how the amounts in the prior year column are displayed. They are all negative now and we want them to be positive. In the previous tutorial, we used the option Reverse Sign for Display to reverse the signs for the expense accounts. Now, we need to modify that formula so that it flips the sign for all balances of the prior year. We don't want to change what it is doing for the current year because that is fine. We need to add additional logic to account for the prior year.

9. Right-click on the Row #2 summary field and select Format Field. This opens the Format Field dialog box.

10. On the Number tab, click the Customize button.

11. For the Reverse Sign on Display option, click the Formula button directly beside it.

12. Enter the following formula:

```
//Flip the sign for current year expenses
```

```
Year(GridRowColumnValue("Journal_Entry.Date")) = {?Year To Print}
AND GridRowColumnValue("@Account Class ID") <> 17
    OR
//Flip the sign for prior year revenues
Year(GridRowColumnValue("Journal_Entry.Date")) < {?Year To Print}
AND GridRowColumnValue("@Account Class ID") = 17;
```

This formula is a bit more complicated because it has to perform the opposite logic depending upon which year is being printed. For the current year, it will continue to reverse the sign for expenses. But for the prior year, it reverses the sign for revenues.

13. Click the Save and Close button and then click the OK button to save your changes and return to the report designer.

    If you preview the report, you should see that the balances for the account class sub-totals are shown as positive for both years. This is looking closer to the original income statement now. We need to make the same changes for the section balances because those amounts are still shown as negative. The difference is that the sections use a running total formula to calculate their balance. We need to modify the running-total calculation so that it will flip the sign for the prior year amounts.

14. Right-click the Row #1 summary field and select Format Field. This opens the Format Field dialog box.

15. Click the Common tab and then click on the Formula button next to the Display String option.

16. Enter the following formula:

```
//Reverse the sign for prior year balances
numbervar FlipSign := 1;
if Year(GridRowColumnValue("Journal_Entry.Date")) < {?Year To Print} then
    FlipSign := -1;
global numbervar RunningTotal;
//Reset the running total balance for the first section in each column
if GridRowColumnValue("@Section ID")=1 then RunningTotal := 0;
RunningTotal := RunningTotal + ToNumber(CurrentFieldValue);
//Display the running total in the current cross-tab cell
ToText(RunningTotal * FlipSign) & " ";
```

The first part of this formula uses the same logic as the @Amount formula from earlier. It creates a variable called FlipSign and stores a -1 value for the prior year amounts. The remaining portion of the formula is almost identical to the original formula. The difference is that on the last line the RunningTotal variable is multiplied by the FlipSign variable. This negates the balance for the prior year.

17. Click the Save and Close button and then click the OK button to save your changes and return to the report designer.

If you preview the report, you'll see that the section balances show the correct amounts and they are no longer negative. The two columns that list current and prior years should be identical to the income statement from the previous tutorial.

Even though we turned on the Total column at the beginning of this tutorial, we haven't done anything with it yet and it isn't accurate. It needs to have the sign for its expense accounts flipped and the section sub-totals need to be changed to running totals.

The Total column has separate formatting from the rest of the cross-tab object fields and it needs to have its own formulas built. We are effectively going to copy the formulas from the original income statement and apply them to the fields in the Total column. Since the Total column is not specifically related to a particular year, we don't have to add the additional logic that tests for the prior year and flips the sign.

18. Right-click on the Row #2 total field (located in the last column) and select Format Field. This opens the Format Editor dialog box.

19. Click on the Number tab and click the Customize button. This opens the Custom Style dialog box.

20. Find the option Reverse Sign For Display and click on the Formula button next to it. This opens the Formula Workshop dialog box.

21. Enter the following formula:

GridRowColumnValue("@Account Class ID") <> 17;

22. Click the Save and Close button and click the OK button to save your changes and return to the report designer.

If you preview the report, you'll see that the signs for the amounts in the account class total column are correct. Next, we have to modify the section sub-total so that it is a manual running-total formula.

23. Right-click on the Row #1 total field (located in the last column) and select Format Field. This opens the Format Editor dialog box for the Section ID sub-total field.

24. Click on the Common tab.

25. Find the Display String option and click the Formula button beside it. This opens the Formula Workshop dialog box.

26. Enter the following formula:

```
Global Numbervar GrandRunningTotal;
GrandRunningTotal := GrandRunningTotal + ToNumber(CurrentFieldValue);
//Display the running total in the current cross-tab cell
ToText(GrandRunningTotal) & " ";
```

This formula creates a variable called GrandRunningTotal and for every section it adds the CurrentFieldValue amount to it. It displays the running total balance on the cross-tab using the ToText() function.

27. Click the Save and Close button. Then click the OK button to save your changes and return to the report designer.

    If you preview the report now, you should see that the report is almost finished. All the balances in the Total column correctly subtract the prior year balance from the current year balance and display the result. The signs on all the numbers are correct as well. There are just a few minor formatting issues that need to be fixed before you are finished.

28. Right-click on the Total column header field and select Edit Text.

29. Enter the text "Change". This tells the user that the last column represents the difference between the two years and not the total balance.

30. Click on the Row #1 total field and then click the Bold button. This makes the field bold so that its format matches the other section fields.

31. Click on the Row #2 total field and then click on the Currency button. This turns off the currency formatting for that field. None of the other fields in the cross-tab are formatted as currency so this one shouldn't either.

    Save your report and preview it. It should look similar to Figure A-16.

|  |  | 2003 | 2004 | Change |
|---|---|---|---|---|
| **Xtreme, Inc.** |  |  |  |  |
| **Income Statement** |  |  |  |  |
| **2004** |  |  |  |  |
|  | Operating Revenue | 254,805.00 | 2,785,136.67 | $2,530,331.67 |
|  | Cost of Goods Sold | 117,976.17 | 1,303,591.84 | $1,185,615.67 |
| **Gross Margin** |  | **136,828.83** | **1,481,544.83** | **1,344,716.00** |
|  | Payroll Expense | 616,615.37 | 667,999.98 | $51,384.61 |
|  | General & Administrative Expense | 39,224.86 | 46,187.33 | $6,962.46 |
| **Operating Income** |  | **-519,011.40** | **767,357.52** | **1,286,368.93** |
|  | Interest Expense | 22,561.33 | 24,612.36 | $2,051.03 |
|  | Amortization/Depreciation Expense | 48,048.50 | 50,167.44 | $2,118.94 |
|  | Bank Service Charges | 240.81 | 259.71 | $18.91 |
| **Net Income** |  | **-589,862.04** | **692,318.01** | **1,282,180.05** |

Figure A-16. Multi-year comparative income statement.

# APPENDIX B
## Basic Syntax Reference

Chapter 7 taught you how to program using Crystal syntax. This appendix builds on that chapter by showing you details of the Basic syntax. It was written as a companion tutorial with Chapter 7 that shows what is unique about Basic syntax compared to Crystal syntax. It doesn't try to teach you programming all over again. The best way to use this appendix is to read through Chapter 7 first and become familiar with the programming concepts. When you are comfortable, come back to this appendix as a reference for what the differences are with Crystal syntax.

The end of this appendix has conversion tables from Crystal syntax to Basic syntax. The tables list the function names only and you'll notice that most of them have identical names. There are only a few differences. If you need more information about how the functions work, look at the table headings and flip back to Chapter 6 to see the details.

Basic syntax is very similar (and in many ways identical) to the Basic programming language found on many computers, as well as the Microsoft macro language VBA. If you are already familiar with programming with VBA, then it would be easier for you to learn Basic syntax instead of Crystal syntax.

When creating formulas, if you want to program in Basic syntax you need to be aware that Crystal Reports defaults to using Crystal syntax. To change this, look at the top of the Formula Workshop to find a drop-down box that says Crystal Syntax. Click on it to change it to Basic Syntax (see Figure B-1). After you switch to Basic syntax, you'll notice that the syntax trees are refreshed so that the functions and operators are specific to the Basic syntax.

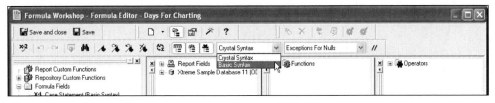

**Figure B-1. Language Selection**

It is very tedious to specify Basic syntax every time you create a new formula. To change the default language to Basic syntax, select the menu options File > Options Formula Editor and select Basic syntax as the default programming language.

## Writing Comments

Basic syntax comments are designated with a single apostrophe. All text after the apostrophe is ignored. You can also use the familiar REM keyword.

```
'This is a comment
REM This is also a comment
```

## Line Terminators

Basic syntax assumes that each programming statement only takes a single line of text. Hitting the Enter key marks the end of the line. If a statement needs more than one line, the line continuation character _ is used.

```
X = 5 'This is a single line
Y = "This takes " _
& "two lines"
```

## Returning a Value

Formulas return a value by assigning it to the Formula variable. Formulas must always return a value. The following code returns the value True.

```
Formula = True
```

If a formula has multiple statements that return a value, all the assignments must be of the same data type. Although there is no way to specifically tell Crystal Reports the data type to return, the compiler will compare all the assignments and check them for consistency. As an example of what not to do, see the following code:

```
'The following IS NOT VALID due to the different data types returned and produces an error
If Age > 65 Then
  Formula = "Retired"
Else
  Formula = Age
End If
```

## Simple Data Types

Basic syntax uses the same data types as Crystal syntax. However, the naming convention varies slightly. In Crystal syntax all data type have "Var" at the end (e.g. NumberVar, StringVar, etc.) Basic syntax doesn't use the "Var" suffix after each data type. It simple uses the data type name by itself: Boolean, Number, Currency, String, DateTime, Date, and Time.

# Declaring Variables

To use a variable in a formula, you first have to declare it. This consists of giving it a name and specifying its data type. Declaring a variable follows the format of declaring the variable using the Dim keyword followed by the variable name. Use the As keyword to specify the data type.

```
Dim var As dataype
```

Just like Crystal syntax, there are three keywords for setting a variable's scope (whether other formulas can reference it): Dim, Global, and Shared.

Dim: The variable can only be seen within the current formula. The variable is private to that formula and can't be used anywhere else in the report. This is the default scope if you don't specify it.

Global: The variable can be seen within any formula inside the same report. Sub-reports do not have access to the variable.

Shared: Similar to Global, but the variable can also be seen within sub-reports.

```
Dim HireDate As Date
Shared AffiliateCities() As String
```

# Variable Assignment

In Basic syntax, to assign a value constant to a variable use the equal sign.

```
X = 5
Y = "Mr. " & {Customer.Last Name}
```

# Array Data Types

To declare an array variable in Basic syntax, use a set of parentheses in the variable declaration.

```
Dim X() As String
```

To reference an element of the array, use parentheses with the index number.

```
X(1) = 5
Formula = X(3)
```

The ReDim statement changes the number of elements in the array and resets their values. If you want to keep the existing values intact, then also use the Preserve keyword.

```
Redim var(number)              'Redimension array and reset all values
Redim Preserve var(number)     'Preserve existing values
```

Assigning values to an array is done in different ways. If you know what the values of an array are during the development process, you can initialize the array with these values using the Array() function. Pass the Array() function all the elements as a comma delimited list and it returns an array that is fully populated with these elements. When using the Array() function you don't have to specify the array size. Crystal Reports figures that out for you.

As expected, if you want to simply assign a value to an individual element in the array, then the index must be within the array's bounds. But if you are assigning an entire array to another array variable and they are different sizes, you do not have to redimension the target array. The target array gets overwritten and it will have the size of the existing array.

```
'Demonstrate initializing an array and then overwriting it
Dim MonthsInSeason() As String
MonthsInSeason = Array("May", "June", "July")
If LongSummer = True Then
    MonthsInSeason = Array("May", "June", "July", "August")
End If
```

## Range Data Types

To declare a variable as a Range data type, declare it as one of the standard data types and put the Range keyword at the end of the declaration. The data types that are allowed to have a related Range data type are Number, Currency, String, DateTime, Date, and Time.

```
Dim var As datatype Range
```

```
Dim X As Number Range
```

# Conditional Structures

The If statement uses the standard syntax of testing a condition and performing one action if the condition is true and another action if it's false. The code in the Else block is executed if the test returns false. Basic syntax also supports the ElseIf statement. An If block must always be finished with and End If.

Basic syntax for a nested If statement:

```
If condition1 Then
    ...code...
ElseIf condition2 Then
    ...code...
Else
    ...code...
End If
```

In Basic syntax, the Select Case statement is built by first typing the keywords Select Case followed by the variable name you want to test. After that, list the test conditions and the related code blocks using Case statements. You can list multiple conditions for a single Case statement by separating the conditions with a comma. If none of the Case statements return true, then the code in the Case Else block is executed. Finish a Case block with End Select. The following code is a template for how to fill in a Case statement.

```
Select Case var
    Case condition1
        ...code...
    Case condition1, condition2
        ...code...
    Case Else
        ...code...
End Select
```

# Looping Structures

Looping structures let you execute a block of code multiple times. The number of times this code block is executed depends upon the type of loop used and what happens within the code block. The looping structures covered are: For Next, While, and a variety of Do loops.

## For Next Loop

The For Next loop has the syntax of using the For statement followed by a variable and the start and ending range. You have to decide in advance how many times the code block gets executed.

The default loop increment is 1. Use the Step keyword to define a new increment. Terminate the For block using the Next statement. Putting the variable name after the Next statement is optional. You can prematurely exit the loop by using the Exit For statement.

```
For var = start To end Step increment
    ...code...
    If condition Then
        'exit the loop for special circumstances
        Exit For
    End If
Next
```

## While and Do Loops

Basic syntax has more variations of the looping structures than Crystal syntax. The While and Do loops all have the standard syntax. The While keyword is used to continue looping as long as the condition evaluates to True. The While block is terminated with a Wend statement.

The Do loops are terminated with a Loop statement. The Until keyword is used to continue looping when a condition evaluates to False. You can exit a Do loop with an Exit Do statement.

Code template for While ... Wend:

```
While true_condition
    ...code...
Wend
```

Code template for Do While ... Loop:

```
Do While true_condition
    ...code...
Loop
```

Code template for Do Until ... Loop:

```
Do Until false_condition
    ...code...
Loop
```

Code template for Do ... Loop While:

```
Do
    ...code...
Loop While true_condition
```

Code template for Do ... Loop Until:

```
Do
    ...code...
Loop Until false_condition
```

# Function Conversion Charts

The following charts show the equivalent functions between Basic syntax and Crystal syntax. Though many are the same, each table does have a few variations listed. The tables use the same table numbers so that you know where they are in the book and you can reference the sections if you need more information.

**Table 6-1. String Analysis Functions**

| Basic Syntax | Crystal Syntax |
| --- | --- |
| AscW(str) | AscW(str) |
| ChrW(val) | ChrW(val) |
| Len(str) | Length(str) |
| IsNumeric(str) | IsNumeric |
| InStr(start, str1, str2, compare) | InStr(start, str1, str2, compare) |
| InStrRev(start, str1, str2, compare) | InStrRev(start, str1, str2, compare) |
| StrCmp(str1, str2, compare) | StrCmp(str1, str2, compare) |
| Val(str) | Val(str) |

**Table 6-3. String Parsing Functions**

| Basic Syntax | Crystal Syntax |
| --- | --- |
| Trim(str) | Trim(str) |
| LTrim(str) | TrimLeft(str) |
| RTrim(str) | TrimRight(str) |
| Mid(str, start, length) | Mid(str, start, length) |
| Left(str, length) | Left(str, length) |
| Right(str, length) | Right(str, length) |

**Table 6-4. String Manipulation Functions**

| Basic Syntax | Crystal Syntax |
| --- | --- |
| Filter(str, find, include, compare) | Filter(str, find, include, compare) |
| Replace(str, find, replace, start, count, compare) | Replace(str, find, replace, start, count, compare) |
| StrReverse(str) | StrReverse(str) |
| ReplicateString(str, copies) | ReplicateString(str, copies) |

| | |
|---|---|
| Space(val) | Space(val) |
| Join(list, delimiter) | Join(list, delimiter) |
| Split(str, delimiter, count, compare) | Split(str, delimiter, count, compare) |
| Picture(str, template) | Picture(str, template) |

**Table 6-5. Conversion Functions**

| Basic Syntax | Crystal Syntax |
|---|---|
| CBool(number), CBool(currency) | CBool(number), CBool(currency) |
| CCur(number), CCur(string) | CCur(number), CCur(string) |
| CDbl(currency), CDbl(string), CDbl(boolean) | CDbl(currency), CDbl(string), CDbl(boolean) |
| CStr() | CStr() |
| CDate(string), CDate(year, month, day), CDate(DateTime) | CDate(string), CDate(year, month, day), CDate(DateTime) |
| CTime(string), CTime(hour, min, sec), CDate(DateTime) | CTime(string), CTime(hour, min, sec), CDate(DateTime) |
| CDateTime(string), CDateTime(date), CDateTime(date, time), CDateTime(year, month, day) | CDateTime(string), CDateTime(date), CDateTime(date, time), CDateTime(year, month, day) |
| CDateTime(year, month, day, hour, min, sec) | CDateTime(year, month, day, hour, min, sec) |
| ToNumber(string), ToNumber(boolean) | ToNumber(string), ToNumber(boolean) |
| ToText() | ToText() |
| IsDate(string), IsTIme(), IsDateTime() | IsDate(string), IsTIme(), IsDateTime() |
| IsNumeric(string) | IsNumeric(string) |
| ToWords(number), | ToWords(number), |

| ToWords(number, decimals) | ToWords(number, decimals) |
|---|---|

**Table 6-8. Math Functions**

| Basic Syntax | Crystal Syntax |
|---|---|
| Abs(number) | Abs(number) |
| Ceiling(number, multiple) | Ceiling(number, multiple) |
| Fix(number, decimals) | Truncate(number, decimals) |
| Int(number), numerator \ denominator | Int(number), numerator \ denominator |
| Pi | Pi |
| Remainder(numerator, denominator), | Remainder(numerator, denominator), |
| numerator Mod denominator | numerator Mod denominator |
| Round(number, decimals), RoundUp(number, decimals) | Round(number, decimals), RoundUp(number, decimals) |
| Sgn(number) | Sgn(number) |
| Sqr(number), Exp(number), Log(number) | Sqr(number), Exp(number), Log(number) |
| Cos(number), Sin(number), Tan(number), Atn(number) | Cos(number), Sin(number), Tan(number), Atn(number) |

**Table 6-12. Date and Time Functions**

| Basic Syntax | Crystal Syntax |
| --- | --- |
| CurrentDate, CurrentTime, CurrentDateTime | CurrentDate, CurrentTime, CurrentDateTime |
| DateSerial(year, month, day), DateTime(hour, minute, second) | DateSerial(year, month, day), DateTime(hour, minute, second) |
| DateAdd(interval, number, date) | DateAdd(interval, number, date) |
| DateDiff(interval, startdate, enddate, firstdayofweek) | DateDiff(interval, startdate, enddate, firstdayofweek) |
| DatePart(interval, date, firstdayofweek, firstweekofyear) | DatePart(interval, date, firstdayofweek, firstweekofyear) |
| MonthName(date, abbreviate) | MonthName(date, abbreviate) |
| Timer | Timer |
| WeekDay(date, firstdayofweek) | DayOfWeek(date, firstdayofweek) |
| WeekdayName(weekday, abbreviate, firstdayofweek) | WeekdayName(weekday, abbreviate, firstdayofweek) |

# Books by Brian Bischof

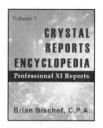

### Crystal Reports Encyclopedia, Volume 1: Professional XI Reports

Make your reporting projects a success with this comprehensive, tutorial based guide. If you're just learning or are a seasoned expert, there is something here for you.

### Crystal Reports Encyclopedia, Volume 2: Programming .NET 2005

Written for Visual Studio .NET developers, this book provides in-depth information for integrating Crystal Reports into windows and web applications alike.

### Crystal Reports .NET Programming

Visual Studio .NET 2003 programmers can build first-class reports with this comprehensive guide that walks you through each step of the process. This is the missing manual that should have been included with Visual Studio .NET.

### The .NET Languages: A Quick Translation Guide

This is the only book that shows you the programming code for VB6, VB.NET and C# side by side. Syntax translation tables make it easy to convert code between all languages.

### Pro Visual Studio .NET

Co-authored by Brian Bischof, reveals and demystifies Visual Studio .NET to enable programmers to do their job more quickly and with fewer errors.